Students' Online Risk Behaviors:

Psychoeducational Predictors, Outcomes, and Prevention

Thanos Touloupis
University of the Aegean, Greece

Alivisos (Loisos) Sofos
University of the Aegean, Greece

Aikaterini Vasiou
University of Crete, Greece

IGI Global
Scientific Publishing
Publishing Tomorrow's Research Today

Vice President of Editorial	Melissa Wagner
Managing Editor of Acquisitions	Mikaela Felty
Managing Editor of Book Development	Jocelynn Hessler
Production Manager	Mike Brehm
Cover Design	Phillip Shickler

Published in the United States of America by
IGI Global Scientific Publishing
701 East Chocolate Avenue
Hershey, PA, 17033, USA
Tel: 717-533-8845
Fax: 717-533-8661
Website: https://www.igi-global.com E-mail: cust@igi-global.com

Library of Congress Cataloging-in-Publication Data

Names: Touloupis, Thanos, 1986- editor. | Sofos, Alivisos Loisos, 1966- editor. | Vasiou, Aikaterini, 1968- editor.
Title: Students' online risk behaviors : psychoeducational predictors, outcomes, and prevention / Edited by Thanos Touloupis, Alivisos Sofos, Aikaterini Vasiou.
Description: Hershey, PA : IGI Global Scientific Publishing, [2025] | Includes bibliographical references and index. | Summary: "This book aims to motivate professionals who can contribute to the international understanding about multidimensional contributors and outcomes of online risk behaviors among school and university students. The book focuses on prevention actions aimed to promote a safe online culture both in the school and university community"-- Provided by publisher.
Identifiers: LCCN 2024053579 (print) | LCCN 2024053580 (ebook) | ISBN 9798369341919 (hardcover) | ISBN 9798369352106 (paperback) | ISBN 9798369341926 (ebook)
Subjects: LCSH: Education--Effect of technological innovations on. | Internet and children--Safety measures. | Internet and teenagers--Safety measures. | Students--Psychology.
Classification: LCC LB1028.3 .S777 2025 (print) | LCC LB1028.3 (ebook) | DDC 371.33--dc23/eng/20241213
LC record available at https://lccn.loc.gov/2024053579
LC ebook record available at https://lccn.loc.gov/2024053580

British Cataloguing in Publication Data
A Cataloguing in Publication record for this book is available from the British Library.

Table of Contents

Detailed Table of Contents

School-aged students are an especially vulnerable group to internet threats such as inappropriate content, potentially harmful interactions, addictive behaviors, and age-inappropriate marketing. Internet threats have negative implications on students' social, emotional, psychological, and academic lives. However, there is scant research seeking students' voices regarding these issues and a lack of neurodivergent student representation. Current initiatives in research and education that focus on internet safety, inclusive education, and neurodiversity emphasize the importance of enabling students to share their perspectives in meaningful ways. Amplifying the inclusion of neurodivergent student voices is significant, because without understanding their perspectives, adults may not effectively communicate strategies to manage internet threats to those who most need it. This topic requires further investigation to ensure a nuanced approach to internet safety messages that responds to the needs of the students who adults are hoping to reach.

The investigation of non-consensual sexting and its contributors in adolescence are significantly under-investigated. The present study investigated non-consensual sexting among adolescents, examining via a mediation model the contributing role of perceived parental love and support, peer pressure and sexual self-concept. Overall, 204 Greek junior high school students (53% boys) of third grade from randomly selected schools filled out a self-report questionnaire that included scales related to the variables involved. Based on the results, adolescents and mainly boys exhibited above average non-consensual sexting behaviors. Sexual self-concept proved to be a full mediator between perceived parental love and support and non-consensual sexting and a partial mediator between perceived peer pressure and non-consensual sexting. The findings imply the necessity of intensifying related school prevention actions, strengthening at the same time adolescents' interpersonal relationships with peers and parents, as well as their sexual self-concept as protective factors against non-consensual sexting.

The study aimed to investigate the complex ways in which adolescents engage in sexting behaviors and the role of gender, relationship status, and self-esteem in this behavior. One hundred and eighty-six Greek adolescents (93 boys and 93 girls) participated in this study and completed a self-reported questionnaire

The following chapter explores technology facilitated sexual violence (TFSV) among adolescents with a particular focus on its conceptualization, prevalence, impact, and coping strategies. Various forms of TFSV are discussed, including online sexual harassment (OSH), image-based sexual abuse (IBSA), sexual aggression and coercion (SAC), and harassment based on gender and sexuality (HBGS). The gendered nature of TFSV is highlighted, with girls being more vulnerable to victimization and boys more likely to perpetrate. It also analyzes the detrimental effects of TFSV on adolescents' mental health, well-being, social and academic functioning. Additionally, the chapter draws attention to the challenges of identifying and researching TFSV due to underreporting and the evolving nature of technology. It concludes by emphasizing the need for comprehensive prevention and intervention strategies to address this pervasive and serious social phenomenon.

This study explores the relationships between internet addiction, academic achievement, and empathy levels among 179 eighth-grade students. Using regression analyses, the research investigates how internet addiction impacts academic performance and empathy, and whether gender plays a role in internet addiction. Results indicate no statistically significant correlation between internet addiction and either academic achievement or empathy levels. However, a moderate positive correlation is found between empathy and academic performance. These findings suggest that internet addiction may not be a strong predictor of academic or empathic outcomes in adolescents. The study underscores the importance of promoting empathy to enhance academic success and highlights the need for balanced internet use. Future research should consider longitudinal designs and diverse samples to further explore these complex relationships. Implications for educational practices include integrating social-emotional learning programs to foster empathy and support students' overall well-being.

Technological advances have brought a revolution in communication, which in turn has influenced many aspects of personal relationships. According to the literature, young adults utilize the newest technological means in their communications and sexting has become a frequent means of sexual communication in romantic relationships. On the one hand, sexting is captured as a tremendous concern due to its possible negative effects on individual and relational level, but on the other, it is seen as part of normal sexual development which could also promote partners' sexuality and satisfaction. The aim of this chapter is

The following chapter explores technology facilitated sexual violence (TFSV) among adolescents with a particular focus on its conceptualization, prevalence, impact, and coping strategies. Various forms of TFSV are discussed, including online sexual harassment (OSH), image-based sexual abuse (IBSA), sexual aggression and coercion (SAC), and harassment based on gender and sexuality (HBGS). The gendered nature of TFSV is highlighted, with girls being more vulnerable to victimization and boys more likely to perpetrate. It also analyzes the detrimental effects of TFSV on adolescents' mental health, well-being, social and academic functioning. Additionally, the chapter draws attention to the challenges of identifying and researching TFSV due to underreporting and the evolving nature of technology. It concludes by emphasizing the need for comprehensive prevention and intervention strategies to address this pervasive and serious social phenomenon.

This study explores the relationships between internet addiction, academic achievement, and empathy levels among 179 eighth-grade students. Using regression analyses, the research investigates how internet addiction impacts academic performance and empathy, and whether gender plays a role in internet addiction. Results indicate no statistically significant correlation between internet addiction and either academic achievement or empathy levels. However, a moderate positive correlation is found between empathy and academic performance. These findings suggest that internet addiction may not be a strong predictor of academic or empathic outcomes in adolescents. The study underscores the importance of promoting empathy to enhance academic success and highlights the need for balanced internet use. Future research should consider longitudinal designs and diverse samples to further explore these complex relationships. Implications for educational practices include integrating social-emotional learning programs to foster empathy and support students' overall well-being.

Technological advances have brought a revolution in communication, which in turn has influenced many aspects of personal relationships. According to the literature, young adults utilize the newest technological means in their communications and sexting has become a frequent means of sexual communication in romantic relationships. On the one hand, sexting is captured as a tremendous concern due to its possible negative effects on individual and relational level, but on the other, it is seen as part of normal sexual development which could also promote partners' sexuality and satisfaction. The aim of this chapter is to build on the existing literature to explore the determinants of sexting, as well as the effects of sexting on romantic relationships, by focusing on young university adults. The chapter will conclude with implications for education, clinical practice, and policy, which could facilitate practitioners' work, as well as others who directly and indirectly relate to young university students.

The lives of present-day young learners are more influenced by relationships built in the digital world than ever before. Although it is undeniable that a proper use of these resources may return relevant learning and developmental benefits, their misuse can build up new forms of personal attack and harassment that tend to be unknown to a victim's immediate context. Throughout this chapter, some of the most prominent forms of online risk behaviors involving privacy invasion, mainly cyberbullying and sexting, will be conceptualized alongside their main effects on the academic life of potential victims. Furthermore, the immediate need and relevant characteristics of prevention and response protocols will be discussed, as well as the role played by educational personnel and relatives in relation to both preventing and dealing with these phenomena. This chapter, therefore, highlights the urgency of these situations, as well as the relevance and contemporaneity of the matter.

This chapter is an in-depth overview of the critical role that psychoeducational programs play in training students to negotiate the complexity of the digital age. In response to the growing issues provided by online hazards, this chapter examines the design, implementation, and impact of programs designed to provide students with the necessary information. Based on educational psychology concepts, the chapter gives practical recommendations for educators and facilitators looking to develop programs that not only inform but also actively involve students in critical discussions about responsible online behavior. The chapter underlines the importance of interactive techniques in addressing the psychoeducational components of online behavior via the perspective of experiential learning. As schools aspire to create a digitally empowered generation, this chapter is a great resource for educators, providing concrete insights for designing meaningful programs that prepare students with the resilience and knowledge needed to navigate the ever-changing digital landscape responsibly.

This chapter synthesizes findings from 17 systematic reviews examining 178 cyberbullying intervention programs, categorized by target audience, core components, and effectiveness. The majority of the included interventions predominantly target school-aged children, while common components of effective programs include skill training, cognitive and affective strategies, and behavioral change methods. There is considerable variability in effectiveness, influenced by factors such as delivery methods, participant demographics, and the integration of technology. It becomes apparent that there is a need to create standardized instruments and tailored approaches aiming enhance the consistency and long-term impact of cyberbullying interventions. Future research should focus on creating and implementing said tools in methodically rigorous studies, identifying critical components that can enhance interventions' positive outcomes, optimizing digital tools for delivery, and conducting longitudinal and follow-up studies to ensure the long-term sustainability of intervention outcomes.

The authors designed pedagogical agents with dual roles to be integrated into the Geo-Histor learning environment: preventing risky behavior and promoting reading strategies aimed at improving adolescent students' metacognitive awareness. In order to reduce risky behaviors, they have incorporated the use of pedagogical agents that are deemed to be appropriate for the learning environment. To inform their design, they considered the latest research on agent anthropomorphism and voices. The preferences of 53 10th graders who participated in the preliminary study were considered in the initial design phase. During the main research project, comparisons were made between the experimental group using the interactive learning environment and the control group. The use of pedagogical agents during the interactive intervention resulted in the students' focus on the academic material and not on useless internet wandering. There was an increase in comprehensive knowledge of history, distance from parroting, deeper understanding, and consolidation of the material, followed by an increase in performance.

The study investigates the effectiveness of psychodrama as an intervention method for preventing cyberbullying in schools. Its aim is to highlight the need for new approaches that address the social and emotional needs of students, as traditional prevention methods often fail to fully address the complexity of cyberbullying. Psychodrama, a therapeutic approach that uses drama and role-playing, is identified as an effective tool for promoting empathy, self-awareness, and emotional expression among students. Through a series of semi-structured interviews with school psychologists, the chapter examines their views on psychodrama, the techniques they consider most effective, and the obstacles they experience in implementing it for cyberbullying prevention. The findings reveal that psychodrama helps make schools safer and more supportive and that psychologists need regular training and support to use it well.

Preface

The digital age has transformed the way students interact, learn, and socialize, creating unprecedented opportunities and challenges. Among these challenges are the risks associated with online behaviors, which can have profound implications for students' emotional, social and academic well-being. Recognizing the critical need for a comprehensive examination of these issues, *Students' Online Risk Behaviors: Psychoeducational Predictors, Outcomes, and Prevention* brings together an interdisciplinary collection of research and insights. This volume reflects the shared commitment of scholars, educators, and practitioners to better understand, mitigate, and prevent the negative effects of online risks while promoting a safer digital environment for students.

The chapters in this book address diverse aspects of online risk behaviors, ranging from addiction and cyberbullying to sexting and technology-facilitated violence. Through empirical studies, theoretical discussions, and reviews, contributors examine the complex interplay of individual, social, and environmental factors that influence students' online behaviors. Notably, the chapters highlight the voices of neurodivergent students, the unique vulnerabilities of children with autism, and the nuanced dynamics of peer and parental influences. By integrating these perspectives, the book provides a holistic view of the psychoeducational predictors and outcomes of online risk behaviors.

Our goal as editors is to provide readers with a resource that not only identifies the problems but also offers actionable solutions. From prevention strategies and intervention programs to educational policies and practical recommendations, this book equips educators, parents, and policymakers with the tools needed to address these pressing issues. It is our hope that this volume will inspire continued research and collaboration across disciplines to create safer and more supportive online spaces for all students.

CHAPTER OVERVIEWS

Psychoeducational Predictors

Chapter 1: Peer Influence on Students' Online Addiction Behaviors: Implications for Prevention Strategies Through Multidimensional Addiction Behavior Scale

This chapter investigates how peer influence shapes students' online addiction behaviors, highlighting factors such as peer pressure, social norms, and modeling. It introduces the Multidimensional Addiction Behavior Scale (MABS) as a pivotal tool for assessing and addressing digital addiction. The authors propose prevention strategies that leverage peer-led initiatives, educational programs, and institutional efforts to foster healthier online habits.

Chapter 2: Are Children With Autism Safe Online? Risks, Parental Mediation, and Wellbeing

Focusing on children with autism spectrum disorder (ASD), this chapter explores their unique vulnerabilities to online risks. It underscores the critical role of parental mediation in ensuring their safety and discusses effective strategies for raising awareness and creating inclusive online spaces. The chapter synthesizes relevant literature to inform stakeholders about the challenges and opportunities in supporting autistic children in the digital era.

Chapter 3: Neurodivergent Students' Views on Internet Threats: A Call for Research

This chapter emphasizes the importance of amplifying neurodivergent students' voices regarding online threats. It critiques the lack of representation in existing research and advocates for a nuanced approach to internet safety that considers their perspectives. By doing so, the chapter aims to enhance the effectiveness of strategies designed to address online risks for neurodivergent students.

Chapter 4: Non-Consensual Sexting Among Adolescents: The Role of Parents, Peers, and Sexual Self-Concept

Examining non-consensual sexting among adolescents, this chapter identifies key contributing factors such as parental support, peer pressure, and sexual self-concept. Through a mediation model, it highlights the interplay between these variables and offers insights into prevention strategies that strengthen interpersonal relationships and foster positive self-concepts among adolescents.

Chapter 5: Sexting Profiles Among Adolescents: The Role of Gender, Relationship Status, and Self-Esteem

This chapter delves into the diverse sexting behaviors exhibited by adolescents, analyzing the influence of gender, relationship status, and self-esteem. It categorizes sexting profiles into safe, risky, and passive behaviors, providing actionable insights for developing psychoeducational interventions that promote healthy digital communication.

Psychoeducational Outcomes

Chapter 6: Digital Play Addiction Tendency Behaviors in Early Children: Reflections in Social Environments

Using teacher interviews, this chapter examines how digital play addiction impacts early childhood development and classroom dynamics. It discusses the negative effects on attention, empathy, and social participation, emphasizing the need for guided technology use and proactive strategies to mitigate the risks associated with digital play.

Chapter 7: Online Gaming Addiction (OGA): Influence on Learning and Socialization of Students With Disabilities

This chapter explores the effects of online gaming addiction on students with disabilities, addressing its impact on learning and socialization. It evaluates various intervention strategies, including cognitive-behavioral therapy and time management techniques, to mitigate the adverse effects of gaming addiction and promote balanced usage.

Chapter 8: Technology-Facilitated Sexual Violence in Adolescence: Forms, Contributors, and Effects

This chapter examines the prevalence and impact of technology-facilitated sexual violence (TFSV) among adolescents, focusing on forms such as online harassment and image-based abuse. It highlights the gendered nature of TFSV and calls for comprehensive prevention and intervention measures to address its profound social and psychological effects.

Chapter 9: Decoding Adolescents' Internet Addiction, Academic Achievement, and Empathy Levels

Investigating the complex relationships between internet addiction, academic performance, and empathy levels, this chapter finds no significant correlation between addiction and academic outcomes. However, it identifies a positive link between empathy and academic success, advocating for social-emotional learning programs to enhance students' overall well-being.

Chapter 10: Unfolding the Association Between the Multiple Determinants of Sexting Behaviors and Relationship Satisfaction in University Students: Theoretical and Clinical Implications

This chapter builds on the existing literature to explore the determinants of sexting, as well as the effects of sexting on romantic relationships, by focusing on young university adults.

Chapter 11: Impact of Sexting, Inappropriate Content Sharing, and Cyberbullying on Youth Education

This chapter discusses the educational consequences of sexting, inappropriate content sharing, and cyberbullying. It highlights the need for prevention protocols and the involvement of educators and parents in addressing these issues to create supportive and safe learning environments.

Psychoeducational Prevention

Chapter 12: Empowering Students in the Digital Age Through Psychoeducational Programs

This chapter underscores the importance of psychoeducational programs in equipping students with the skills to navigate online risks. Drawing on concepts from educational psychology, it provides practical recommendations for designing programs that foster responsible digital behavior and resilience.

Chapter 13: Interventions on Cyberbullying: An Overview of Systematic Reviews

Synthesizing findings from multiple systematic reviews, this chapter categorizes cyberbullying interventions by effectiveness and target audience. It identifies critical components of successful programs and advocates for standardized approaches to enhance the long-term impact of these interventions.

Chapter 14: Alice and the Risky Wonderland: Pedagogical Agents in Dual Roles

This chapter presents the design and implementation of pedagogical agents in an interactive learning environment to prevent risky behaviors and promote academic engagement. It highlights the positive outcomes of using these agents, including improved focus, deeper understanding, and enhanced performance.

Chapter 15: The Role of Psychodrama in the Prevention of Cyberbullying: School Psychologists' Perspective

This chapter explores psychodrama as an innovative approach to preventing cyberbullying, emphasizing its ability to promote empathy and emotional expression. Based on interviews with school psychologists, it highlights the benefits and challenges of implementing psychodrama in educational settings.

CONCLUSION

The process of assembling this book has been deeply rewarding and a testament to the power of collective effort. We are profoundly grateful to the contributors who shared their expertise and insights, enriching this volume with their diverse perspectives. Their dedication to advancing knowledge in this critical field is evident in the depth and rigor of their work. We also extend our gratitude to our respective institutions, whose support has made this project possible. The University of the Aegean and the University of Crete have provided us with invaluable resources and encouragement throughout this journey.

Special thanks go to the peer reviewers, whose thoughtful feedback and constructive critiques have elevated the quality of this book. Their meticulous attention to detail ensured the clarity, coherence, and relevance of each chapter. Finally, we would like to acknowledge the publishers, whose collaboration and guidance have been instrumental in bringing this volume to life. Their commitment to disseminating scholarly work is deeply appreciated.

We invite readers to engage with the chapters that follow, to reflect on the findings, and to consider the implications for their own work and communities. The digital world is a dynamic and ever-changing landscape, and addressing the risks associated with students' online behaviors requires continuous commitment to learning and adaptation. By fostering awareness, empathy, and proactive interventions, we can create a digital environment that empowers students to thrive.

As editors, we are honored to contribute to this important conversation. We hope that this book serves as a valuable resource and catalyst for meaningful change. May it inspire educators, researchers, and policymakers to take decisive action in ensuring the safety and well-being of students in the digital age. Together, we can build a future where technology is a tool for growth and connection, rather than a source of harm.

Thanos Touloupis
University of the Aegean, Greece

Alivisos (Loisos) Sofos
University of the Aegean, Greece

Aikaterini Vasiou
University of Crete, Greece

Chapter 1
Peer Influence on Students' Online Addiction Behaviors:
Implications for Prevention Strategies Through Multidimensional Addiction Behavior Scale

Ranjit Singha
https://orcid.org/0000-0002-3541-8752
Christ University, India

Yogesh Kanna S.
Christ University, India

ABSTRACT

This chapter explores how peer influence affects students' online addiction behaviours, emphasizing peer pressure, social norms, and modelling. It outlines the risks and protective factors in peer interactions, supported by empirical evidence, and considers moderating factors such as peer group dynamics and individual traits. The chapter proposes prevention strategies, including educational programs, peer-led initiatives, and institution-based efforts. It also highlights the Multidimensional Addiction Behaviour Scale (MABS) as a critical tool for assessing addiction across five dimensions—Psychological, Biological, Social and Environmental, Cognitive and Behavioral, Motivation and Readiness for change. MABS is invaluable for detecting, preventing, and intervening in digital addiction by offering comprehensive insights into how peer dynamics influence online behaviours and supporting the development of targeted strategies for healthier digital habits.

INTRODUCTION

The digital age has significantly increased the number of students participating in online activities in recent years. Unfortunately, this increase in internet usage has led to a variety of online addiction behaviours among students. The prevalence of online addiction among students is on the rise, as evidenced by their excessive use of social media, online gaming, and other internet-based activities. Many students

DOI: 10.4018/979-8-3693-4191-9.ch001

engage in excessive online activity, negatively impacting their academic performance, physical health, and social relationships (Cao et al., 2023; Khan, 2023; Zhang et al., 2024; Zhao, 2021). It is impossible to overstate the importance of resolving this matter, given the impact of online addiction behaviours on students' immediate well-being and the long-term implications for their future development and success.

Peers significantly influence students' behaviours, including their online activities. Individuals are particularly susceptible to peer pressure during adolescence, which can substantially impact their decisions and behaviours. In order to formulate effective prevention strategies, it is imperative to understand the extent to which peers influence online addiction behaviours. Peers can influence students' online behaviours in both positive and negative ways. Although some peers may promote healthy internet usage, others may intentionally or inadvertently encourage excessive and addictive behaviours (Wang et al., 2022). Educators, parents, and policymakers can more effectively address the underlying causes of online addiction and implement targeted interventions to mitigate its effects by conducting a comprehensive examination of the dynamics of peer influence.

The purpose of this chapter is to explore the intricate relationship between online addiction and peer influence among students. It investigates how peers can shape students' online activities, highlighting both the risks associated with online addiction and potential protective factors. The chapter examines the characteristics, symptoms, and consequences of online addiction, as well as the mechanisms through which peers impact online behaviours, such as social norms, peer pressure, and modelling. By reviewing empirical studies and research findings, the chapter illustrates peers' significant role in online addiction behaviours and emphasizes the multifaceted nature of this influence.

The discussion extends to practical strategies and recommendations for educators, parents, and policymakers aimed at preventing and mitigating online addiction. These strategies include fostering positive peer influence, implementing educational programs, and developing supportive environments that address individual and social factors. The chapter also highlights the importance of using evidence-based approaches to enhance the effectiveness of prevention efforts.

The chapter concludes with a summary of critical insights and outlines future research directions to deepen our understanding of online addiction and peer influence. This includes exploring longitudinal studies, diverse populations, and the impact of family dynamics. The chapter aims to establish a comprehensive framework for creating and implementing effective prevention strategies that promote students' well-being in the digital era, recognizing the critical role of peer influence in shaping online behaviours and addiction patterns.

BACKGROUND

Excessive use of the internet, social media, gaming, and other online activities has become a growing concern among students in the digital age, typifying online addiction. This behaviour frequently results in academic decline, social isolation, and mental health issues like anxiety and depression. It is imperative to understand the numerous factors that contribute to online addiction due to the ubiquitous presence of technology in the lives of students. Peers are among the most influential factors in shaping students' online conduct. In this context, it is imperative to investigate the dynamics of peer influence, as peer interactions can both exacerbate and mitigate the risk of developing addictive online behaviours (Watts et al., 2023; Wang & Zeng, 2024).

The purpose of this chapter is to examine the complex relationship between online addiction and peer influence in students. This chapter endeavours to identify the risks and protective factors associated with peer interactions by analyzing how peers influence online activities. The goal is to inform the development of effective prevention strategies and provide a comprehensive understanding of how peer influence operates in online behaviour. Ultimately, this chapter aims to enhance the corpus of knowledge that can assist educators, parents, and policymakers in developing environments that promote healthy online behaviours among students.

In order to investigate the correlation between peer influence and the online addiction behaviours of students, this chapter examines several critical areas. Initially, it offers a comprehensive analysis of the characteristics, symptoms, and repercussions of online addiction. Subsequently, it investigates how peers influence online behaviours, including peer pressure, social norms, and modelling. The following is a review of empirical studies and research findings that illustrate the influence of peers on online addiction behaviours. We then present practical strategies and recommendations for educators, parents, and policymakers, focusing on preventing and reducing online addiction among students through positive peer influence and mitigating negative impacts. The chapter also explores the factors that moderate the intensity and direction of peer influence on online addiction behaviours, such as individual characteristics, peer group dynamics, and situational factors. The chapter identifies future directions, explores potential areas for future investigation, and highlights gaps in current research to enhance our understanding of peer influence on online addiction behaviours and refine prevention efforts.

This chapter has explored the complex interplay between peer influence and online addiction among students, revealing the significant role peers play in shaping online behaviours. Key findings include a robust correlation between online addiction and peer influence, highlighting how peer dynamics are central to the development and reinforcement of such behaviours. Additionally, the chapter identifies various moderating factors, such as individual personality traits, self-esteem, peer group cohesion, and cultural attitudes, which affect susceptibility to online addiction. The Multidimensional Addiction Behaviour Scale (MABS) is a valuable tool for comprehensive assessment, integrating psychological, biological, social, cognitive, and motivational factors. Effective prevention strategies must address these factors by focusing on peer group dynamics, individual resilience, and supportive environments through initiatives like peer-led programs, educational workshops, school policies, and parental guidance. Future research should prioritize longitudinal studies, explore diverse populations, and examine specific mechanisms of peer influence while integrating technological and familial aspects. A collaborative approach among educators, parents, mental health professionals, and policymakers is crucial for developing a supportive framework that tackles online addiction's multifaceted nature. Proactive prevention strategies are essential for promoting healthy online behaviours and safeguarding students' well-being. In summary, this chapter provides a thorough analysis of peer influence on online addiction. It outlines a framework for effective prevention and intervention, advancing our efforts to reduce online addiction among students and encourage balanced digital engagement.

THEORETICAL FRAMEWORK

Peer influence is a well-documented phenomenon in psychological and sociological research, with numerous theories offering insight into its mechanisms and effects. Social Learning Theory and Social Identity Theory are two of the most prominent theories that are relevant to the study of peer influence (Wang & Zeng, 2024). According to social learning theory, individuals acquire behaviours, attitudes, and emotional responses by observing others. Albert Bandura developed this theory, emphasizing the role of reinforcement, imitation, and modelling in the learning process (Rumjaun & Narod, 2020). According to social learning theory, individuals acquire behaviours by observing the actions of others (models) and the outcomes of those actions. Rewarding the observed behaviours increases their likelihood of imitation. Students frequently emulate their peer's online behaviours in the context of peer influence, mainly when they observe their peers receiving social approval or other favourable outcomes (Shi et al., 2023).

Henri Tajfel and John Turner developed Social Identity Theory, primarily focusing on self-identity and group membership. This theory posits that the social groups individuals adhere to provide them with a sense of identity and self-esteem. Social Identity Theory underscores the significance of group norms and in-group favouritism in shaping behaviour. In order to preserve their social identity and acceptability, students may adhere to the norms and behaviours prevalent within their peer groups. This theory highlights how a peer group's specific online behaviours can significantly influence an individual's online activities (Harwood, 2020). We establish a framework for understanding the extent and rationale of peer influence by applying these theories to the context of online addiction behaviours among students.

According to social learning theory, students are inclined to emulate and observe their peers' online behaviour. For instance, a student may be more likely to adopt similar behaviours if they witness their peers spending a significant amount of time on social media or engaging in online gaming, and they perceive these activities as rewarding through social interaction or status (Kerman et al., 2023). In this context, the reinforcement mechanism plays a crucial role; perceived rewards such as social approval and popularity significantly influence the perpetuation of online addiction behaviours.

Social Identity Theory adds an extra layer of understanding by emphasizing the importance of group dynamics and identity. In order to cultivate a sense of identity and belonging, students frequently endeavour to align their conduct with the norms and values of their peer groups. Individual students may feel pressure to conform to these behaviours to preserve their social identity and group membership if the peer group frequently engages in online activities and values them. This conformity can increase online usage, leading to addictive behaviours as students prioritize group norms over individual well-being (Mukhopadhyay & Bhattacharjee, 2023).

Both theories emphasize the significance of the social environment in forming online behaviours. By comprehending these theoretical frameworks, educators, parents, and policymakers can more effectively develop prevention strategies and better understand the mechanisms of peer influence. For instance, interventions could emphasize promoting positive role models, establishing peer-led initiatives promoting healthy online behaviours, and cultivating group norms prioritizing balanced internet use. By acknowledging the dual functions of group identity and observation in peer influence, it is possible to develop more sophisticated and effective strategies for reducing online addiction among students.

PEER INFLUENCE DYNAMICS

Students' online addiction behaviours are influenced by a variety of peer influences, each of which plays a unique role. Peer pressure, social norms, and modelling are among the most significant forms of peer influence. Peer pressure refers to the direct or indirect pressure that peers apply on the individual to conform to specific behaviours, attitudes, or activities. Peer pressure can induce students to engage in excessive use of social media, online gaming, or other internet activities in order to conform to their peers in the context of online addiction (Kim & Lim, 2020). This pressure can be explicit, such as when friends explicitly encourage one to participate in online activities, or implicit, such as when the desire to be accepted motivates the individual to emulate the online habits of their peers. The unwritten laws and expectations within a peer group regarding acceptable behaviour are social norms. Social norms significantly influence online addiction behaviours, as students frequently align their internet usage with what is considered normal or prevalent within their peer group. In order to preserve the group's cohesion and acceptability, individual members will probably likely emulate the collective's spending of a substantial amount of time on specific online platforms (Kuss & Griffiths, 2011).

Modelling is the process of acquiring behaviours through observing and imitating others. Students frequently regard their classmates as role models in the context of online activities. Other students are inclined to emulate the behaviours of influential peers or famous members of a group who frequently engage in online activities, such as playing online games for extended periods or continuously checking social media (Kaval & Siyez, 2023). The modelling effect is incredibly potent when the peer group perceives the observed behaviour as rewarding or admired. Peer influence dynamics are subject to variation across various online platforms and activities, each of which offers distinct opportunities to reinforce online addiction behaviours. Peer influence is ubiquitous on social media platforms such as Snapchat, TikTok, and Instagram. Students are exposed to their classmates' posts, stories, and activities, which can result in a fear of missing out (FOMO) and a sense of competition. The desire to remain informed about the lives of one's peers and to maintain an active online presence can result in excessive use. Addictive behaviours are further reinforced by peer approbation in the form of likes, comments, and followers as students seek social capital and validation (Mallick et al., 2023).

Fortnite, Minecraft, and World of Warcraft are multiplayer online games that foster a social atmosphere significantly influenced by peers. Students frequently establish factions or teams in these gaming communities, fostering a sense of shared identity and belonging. Prolonged gaming sessions may result from peer pressure to participate, enhance abilities, and accomplish group objectives. Students may be compelled to match the commitment and time investment of their classmates in order to avoid disappointing the team due to the collaborative nature of these games (Lu & Wang, 2008). Discord, Messenger, and WhatsApp facilitate continuous communication among peers. Compulsive monitoring and continuous engagement may result from the expectation to respond promptly and be available online. Group conversations can foster an environment in which frequent online activity is normalized and encouraged, which can result in addictive usage patterns (Chatterjee, 2021).In addition to enabling students to consume content, platforms such as Twitch, TikTok, and YouTube enable them to generate and distribute their own. The peer influence is dual: students are motivated to produce content that will be well-received by their peers, and they are also influenced by the content their peers consume and share. Pursuing views, likes, and subscriptions can lead students to spend an inordinate amount of time online, consuming and producing content (Chang & Lee, 2024). As these forms of peer influence and their manifestation across various online platforms and activities are examined, it becomes evident how intricately connected peer dynamics are to the online addiction behaviours of students. Understanding these dynamics is essential for the development of targeted interventions that address the specific ways in which peers influence online behaviours, thereby reducing the risks of online addiction.

EMPIRICAL EVIDENCE

Research consistently demonstrates a robust correlation between students' online addiction behaviours and peer influence. Research suggests that peer dynamics play a substantial role in developing and reinforcing these behaviours among adolescents and young adults. Numerous empirical findings underscore the diverse manifestations of peer influence and its influence on online addiction. Students with high levels of online activity among their classmates are likelier to exhibit similar behaviours. Peer groups frequently normalize excessive internet use, with their collective practices significantly influencing what is considered acceptable or typical behaviour. Additionally, participation in online activities may result in an increase in screen time and a greater probability of developing addictive behaviours due to peer pressure (Zhou & Fang, 2015).

Peer group norms significantly impact the usage of social media by secondary school students. The researchers discovered that students were more likely to spend excessive time on social media platforms if their classmates also engaged in high levels of social media use. The research underscored the substantial impact of peer group norms on individual behaviours as students adapted their online activities to conform to the perceived norms of their peer group. Conformity to group norms significantly predicted social media addiction as students strived to gain acceptance and meet their peers' expectations (Dennen et al., 2020). Peer pressure to engage in online gaming made students more susceptible to developing a gaming addiction. Peer pressure was identified as criticResearchers identified peer pressure as a critical factor in the duration and intensity of students' online gaming activities (Huang et al., 2023). behaviours of their peers, mainly when they believed they were influential or famous. The results suggested that students were more inclined to participate in comparable online activities, such as online gaming, social media use, and video streaming if they observed their classmates engaging in these activities. The modelling effect was more pronounced when the observed behaviours were linked to social rewards, such as increased social status or peer approval (Kerman et al., 2023).

The study examined the influence of social identity on the involvement of middle school students in online activities. The study discovered that students who strongly identified with their peer group were more likely to participate in the prevalent online activities within that group. Students demonstrated a greater propensity for online addiction when their peer group's identity was closely associated with frequent internet use, which encompassed both positive and negative behaviours. The study underscored the significance of group identity in the development of individual online behaviours and the potential for social identity-based interventions to address online addiction (Vincent-Ruz & Schunn, 2018). These studies collectively underscore the substantial influence of peers on the online addiction behaviours of students. They emphasize the necessity of comprehensive strategies that consider peer dynamics when addressing online addiction. The risks associated with online addiction among students can be significantly mitigated by interventions that target peer group norms, reduce peer pressure, and provide positive role models.

MODERATING FACTORS

A variety of moderating factors influence peer influence, leading to a variable effect on online addiction behaviours. These factors can amplify or mitigate the impact of peer influence on individual behaviours. The most significant moderators are situational factors, peer group dynamics, and individual characteristics. Specific personality characteristics can influence an individual's susceptibility to peer influence. For example, individuals who exhibit high levels of extraversion may be more susceptible to peer influence due to their innate desire for social interaction and approval.

In contrast, individuals with higher conscientiousness levels may demonstrate greater self-control and be less susceptible to peer pressure (Franzen & Mader, 2023). Peer influence is frequently more prevalent among individuals with low self-esteem, as they may seek validation and acceptance from their peers by adhering to group behaviours, such as participating in online activities. Individuals with higher levels of self-esteem may be more adept at managing their online behaviours and less susceptible to peer pressure (Hagen et al., 2020).

Younger adolescents are generally more susceptible to peer influence than older adolescents or young adults. Early adolescence is characterized by an extreme need for social validation and identity formation, increasing peer influence's impact (Meehan et al., 2022). The level of cohesion within a peer group can moderate the intensity of peer influence. Small, closely bonded groups may elevate the likelihood of engaging in addictive online behaviours due to the increased pressure to adhere to group norms. In contrast, individuals may feel less compelled to align their behaviours with those of the group in less cohesive groups (Jahan & Kim, 2020). The norms and values a peer group uphold significantly influence how peer influence shapes online behaviour. The likelihood of online addiction among members of organizations that prioritize and condone excessive internet usage may rise. In contrast, organizations prioritizing balanced internet usage and offline activities may mitigate addiction (Henneberger et al., 2020).

High-status or famous colleagues may exert a more significant influence. If influential colleagues within a group engage in or endorse specific online behaviours, others are more likely to emulate them. These critical members' conduct can set a precedent for the rest of the organization (Shi et al., 2023). The availability and accessibility of internet-enabled devices can moderate the influence of colleagues. Students with unrestricted access to technology are more susceptible to peer pressure to participate in online activities. However, limited access can impede the development of addictive behaviours, regardless of peer influence (Zhou & Fang, 2015). The presence of parental and educational monitoring and restrictions can substantially mitigate peer influence. School policies that restrict online activities and stringent parental supervision can mitigate the likelihood of students developing online addiction, even in the presence of peer pressure (Shek et al., 2018).

Cultural attitudes toward internet usage and social conduct may also serve as moderators. In cultures that normalize and even encourage high internet usage, peer influence toward online addiction may be more potent. In contrast, peer influence on online addiction may be less pronounced in cultures that prioritize offline interactions and restrict screen time (Kuss & Griffiths, 2011). When these moderating factors are considered, the relationship between peer influence and online addiction behaviours becomes complex and multifaceted. Individual characteristics, peer group dynamics, and situational factors influence the manifestation of peer influence and its ultimate impact on students' online behaviours. Understanding these factors is critical in order to create effective and nuanced strategies that can reduce the dangers of online addiction among students.

MULTIDIMENSIONAL ADDICTION BEHAVIOUR SCALE

The Multidimensional Addiction Behaviour Scale (MABS) is a newly developed instrument designed to comprehensively assess addiction by examining a broad spectrum of influencing factors. Created by Ranjit Singha, a PhD scholar at Christ (Deemed to be University), MABS evaluates five key dimensions: Psychological Factors, Biological Factors, Social and Environmental Factors, Cognitive and Behavioral Patterns, and Motivation and Readiness for Change. By integrating these diverse aspects, MABS provides a holistic perspective on addiction, making it valuable for clinical assessments and research purposes. This tool aids in the development of targeted interventions and treatment strategies through a nuanced analysis of an individual's addiction profile. The dimensions were meticulously selected based on an extensive literature review to ensure content validity during the scale's development.

Psychological factors assess the mental health aspects and emotional triggers contributing to addiction (Ferrer-Pérez et al., 2024; NIDA, 2014; Smith & Borden, 2020). Biological factors evaluate physiological predispositions affecting addiction (Ferrer-Pérez et al., 2024; Hayes et al., 2020; NIDA, 2014; Sinha, 2011). Social and environmental factors consider the influence of social interactions and environmental contexts on addictive behaviours (NIDA, 2014; Paul et al., 2024). Cognitive and behavioural patterns analyze thought processes and habitual actions related to addiction (Fordham et al., 2021; Heinz et al., 2019; NIDA, 2014). Motivation and readiness for change assess an individual's willingness and preparedness to overcome addiction (Crane et al., 2024; DiClemente et al., 2004; NIDA, 2014; Opsal et al., 2019).

The theoretical foundation of the Multidimensional Addiction Behaviour Scale (MABS) draws from the Biopsychosocial model of addiction, which emphasizes that addiction is a complex interaction of biological, psychological, and social factors. According to this model, addiction encompasses not only physiological dependence but also psychological cravings and social influences (Levounis, 2015). MABS reflects these dimensions by evaluating psychological distress, physical symptoms, and behavioural patterns associated with addiction. Behavioural theories like the Theory of Planned Behavior (Ajzen, 1991) suggest that attitudes, subjective norms, and perceived behavioural control shape behaviour. In the context of addiction, these theories shed light on how personal attitudes towards addictive behaviours, social pressures, and perceived control over such behaviours can influence the likelihood of addiction. MABS incorporates behavioural assessments to measure these factors and their impact on workplace performance.

Furthermore, the MABS underwent rigorous expert validation, including I-CVI and CVR values analysis and face validation. With solid content validity and reliability, as demonstrated by high I-CVI and CVR values, the MABS effectively captures the complex nature of addiction behaviour. The Multidimensional Addiction Behaviour Scale (MABS) proves to be a valuable tool for shaping prevention strategies and understanding peer influence on students' online addiction behaviours. By providing a comprehensive assessment of addiction through its multidimensional approach, MABS offers critical insights into how peer dynamics contribute to online addiction. Its ability to evaluate psychological, biological, social, cognitive, and motivational factors enables a nuanced understanding of how peer influence affects online behaviours. This holistic perspective helps in designing targeted interventions and preventive measures that address both the individual and social aspects of addiction. Consequently, MABS is instrumental in developing effective strategies to mitigate the impact of peer influence on students and foster healthier online behaviours.

CASE STUDY

The XYZ Institute, located in Bangalore, is a renowned educational institution known for its commitment to academic excellence and holistic student development. However, like many modern educational institutions, XYZ Institute faced challenges with students' online addiction behaviours, particularly concerning excessive social media use, gaming, and other online activities. Recognizing the need for early detection and prevention of addiction among its students, the institution sought a reliable and comprehensive tool to assess and address these issues.

In collaboration with Ranjit Singha, a PhD scholar at Christ (Deemed to be University), the XYZ Institute administered its students the Multidimensional Addiction Behaviour Scale (MABS). The MABS is designed to assess addiction comprehensively by considering a range of Psychological Factors, Biological Factors, Social and Environmental Factors, Cognitive and Behavioral Patterns, and Motivation and Readiness for Change.

Administration and Process

With the support of the institution's counselling and student wellness teams, Ranjit Singha conducted the MABS assessments among the student population. The process involved several steps:

- **Initial Screening:** The MABS was administered to a representative sample of students across various departments. This initial screening aimed to identify early signs of online addiction and to understand the underlying factors contributing to such behaviours.
- **Development of Individual Risk Profiles:** Based on the MABS results, individual risk profiles were developed for each student. These profiles highlighted the specific factors contributing to their online addiction, including peer influence, psychological distress, and social-environmental factors.
- **Intervention and Prevention Strategies:** The self-awareness that students developed through the administration of MABS was instrumental in helping them recognize and understand their behaviours. This newfound awareness became the foundation for their healing process. Additionally, the XYZ Institute gained valuable insights into planning future preventive strategies, which can be implemented over time to support student well-being further.

Outcomes and Impact

The administration of MABS at XYZ Institute yielded significant positive outcomes:

- **Early Detection:** The MABS facilitated the early detection of students at risk of developing online addiction. This allowed for timely interventions, preventing the escalation of problematic behaviours.
- **Individualized Support:** Developing individual risk profiles enabled the institution to offer personalized support to students, addressing their specific needs and challenges.
- **Increased Self-Awareness:** Through the MABS assessments and subsequent counselling, students gained greater self-awareness regarding their online behaviours and the factors influenc-

ing them. This awareness empowered them to make informed choices and adopt healthier online habits.

- **Strengthened Prevention Strategies:** The insights gained from the MABS helped the institution refine its prevention strategies. By understanding the role of peer influence and other factors in online addiction, the XYZ Institute implemented more effective educational programs and peer-led initiatives.

The case of XYZ Institute in Bangalore demonstrates the value of the Multidimensional Addiction Behaviour Scale (MABS) in addressing online addiction behaviours among students. By facilitating early detection, providing individualized support, and fostering self-awareness, the MABS played a crucial role in promoting digital wellness and preventing addiction within the student community. This case underscores the importance of comprehensive assessment tools like the MABS in tackling the multifaceted issue of online addiction in educational settings.

IMPLICATIONS FOR PREVENTION STRATEGIES

A multifaceted approach involving various stakeholders is crucial to mitigating the detrimental effects of peer influence on students' online addiction behaviours. Prevention strategies should prioritize creating supportive environments, enhancing individual resilience, and modifying peer group dynamics (Cham et al., 2019). Peer influence can be a powerful tool for promoting healthy online behaviours(De Oliveira Collet et al., 2024). Training influential students to serve as role models and advocates for balanced internet use can shape group norms, encouraging healthier online habits among their peers. Comprehensive educational programs that address the dangers of online addiction and the impact of peer pressure can foster critical thinking and self-awareness. These programs should include interactive elements like peer testimonials, role-playing, and discussions to enhance engagement and retention. Schools play a vital role in shaping students' attitudes and behaviours. Implementing school-wide policies that promote digital literacy and responsible internet use, such as cyber wellness workshops, "digital detox" days, and digital citizenship education, can create an environment that fosters healthy online behaviours. Schools can also offer resources like counselling services, peer support groups, and mentorship programs to support students struggling with online addiction (Feher et al., 2023). These programs, where older students guide younger peers on healthy internet use, can establish a supportive community and provide positive role models. Schools can also harness the power of social media by encouraging students to create and spread positive messages about balanced online behaviours. Regular workshops involving students, parents, and educators can provide a unified approach to addressing online addiction, equipping participants with the knowledge and strategies needed to recognize early signs of addiction, manage screen time, and maintain a healthy online-offline balance.

Schools are instrumental in promoting a balanced approach to online behaviours by enforcing policies that limit non-essential internet use during school hours and incorporating physical activities into the school day. Providing mental health support services and peer support groups within the school setting can also help students address online addiction or related mental health issues. Parents play a crucial role in guiding their children's online behaviours (Yu & Liu, 2023). By modeling healthy online habits, maintaining open communication, and staying informed about their children's online activities, parents can effectively reduce the negative influence of peers and promote responsible internet use. Educators also have a significant impact on students' online behaviours. By incorporating discussions about digital wellness into their teaching and serving as role models, educators can instill a sense of responsibility and awareness in students. Training educators to recognize signs of online addiction and peer pressure ensures that they can intervene early and provide necessary support (Liu et al., 2023). Mental health professionals contribute by offering personalized counselling and working with schools to develop evidence-based prevention programs. This collaborative approach, involving educators, parents, mental health professionals, and students, ensures a comprehensive strategy for fostering healthier and more balanced online behaviours among the student population.

FUTURE DIRECTIONS:

As we advance in understanding and addressing online addiction among students, several critical areas warrant further exploration to enhance prevention strategies and intervention effectiveness. These future directions will help address existing research gaps and improve our approach to managing online addiction.

- **Longitudinal Studies:** Current research predominantly relies on cross-sectional data, limiting our ability to conclude causality and long-term impacts. Longitudinal studies are essential to track the evolution of online addiction behaviours over time and understand how peer influence develops and changes. These studies will provide insights into the persistence of addiction patterns and the effectiveness of various interventions across different developmental stages.
- **Diverse Populations:** Most studies focus on specific demographics, often neglecting the diversity of socio-economic, cultural, and age groups. Future research should include a broader range of populations to provide a more comprehensive understanding of how peer influence affects online addiction across different contexts. This inclusivity will help develop culturally and contextually relevant interventions, enhancing their applicability and effectiveness.
- **Mechanisms of Peer Influence:** Further investigation into the specific mechanisms of peer influence—such as peer pressure, social norms, and modelling—is crucial for designing targeted interventions. Understanding how these mechanisms operate will allow for the creation of more nuanced prevention strategies that address the root causes of online addiction rather than merely its symptoms.
- **Comparative Studies of Interventions:** Research comparing the effectiveness of various prevention and intervention programs is needed to identify the most successful strategies for different populations and environments. Comparative studies can help determine which approaches are most effective in reducing online addiction and provide evidence-based recommendations for implementing effective programs.
- **Integration of Technology:** Exploring the use of technology to monitor and influence online behaviours presents a promising area for research. Investigating the effectiveness of AI-based tools, digital wellness apps, and other technological innovations in detecting early signs of addiction and promoting healthy online behaviours can provide new avenues for intervention and prevention.
- **Family Dynamics and Parental Influence:** Understanding the role of family dynamics and parental influence in online addiction is critical. Research should explore how parental attitudes and behaviours interact with peer influence to affect online addiction. Developing strategies that

involve families in prevention efforts can strengthen support systems and enhance the overall effectiveness of interventions.

- **Evaluation of School-Based Programs:** Further research is needed to assess the effectiveness of school-based prevention programs, such as peer-led initiatives, digital literacy curricula, and counselling services. Evaluating these programs' impact on reducing online addiction will help refine and improve school-based approaches, ensuring they address students' needs effectively.
- **Policy Implications:** Examining the policy implications of research findings can inform the development of guidelines and regulations at the school, community, and governmental levels. Research should focus on how policies can promote healthy online use and mitigate the risk of online addiction among students.
- **Cross-Cultural Studies:** Cross-cultural research can reveal universal patterns and culturally specific factors affecting online addiction and peer influence. Understanding these variations will help tailor prevention programs to different cultural contexts, enhancing their global applicability and effectiveness.
- **Interdisciplinary Approaches:** Integrating methods and insights from psychology, sociology, education, and technology studies can provide a comprehensive understanding of online addiction. Interdisciplinary research can lead to more holistic intervention programs that address the multifaceted nature of addiction and peer influence.

By pursuing these future directions, researchers and practitioners can develop more effective and nuanced strategies to combat online addiction among students. This comprehensive approach will ultimately contribute to healthier online behaviours and improved well-being in diverse student populations.

CONCLUSION

This chapter has underscored the significant role of peer interactions in shaping students' online addiction behaviours, particularly through peer pressure, social norms, and modelling. By identifying both protective and risk factors within peer dynamics and examining how individual traits interact with peer influences, the chapter provides a nuanced understanding of the complex relationship between peer influence and online addiction. The prevention strategies recommended, including educational programs, peer-led interventions, and school-based initiatives, offer practical approaches to mitigating the adverse effects of peer influence on online behaviours.

Moreover, the chapter highlights the importance of the Multidimensional Addiction Behaviour Scale (MABS) as a comprehensive tool for assessing addiction across psychological, biological, social, cognitive, and motivational dimensions. MABS not only facilitates the detection and prevention of addictive behaviours but also supports targeted interventions, particularly in the context of digital addiction. By integrating these insights and tools, institutions can more effectively address the challenges posed by online addiction and promote students' overall well-being.

In conclusion, the Multidimensional Addiction Behaviour Scale (MABS) emerges as a pivotal tool in the realm of prevention and intervention strategies for online addiction among students. Its multidimensional approach offers critical insights into how peer dynamics influence online behaviours, enabling the design of targeted interventions that address both individual and social dimensions of addiction. MABS is

REFERENCES

Ajzen, I. (1991). The theory of planned behaviour. *Organizational Behavior and Human Decision Processes*, 50(2), 179–211. DOI: 10.1016/0749-5978(91)90020-T

Cao, X., Wu, Y., Cheng, B., & Ali, A. (2024). An investigation of the social media overload and academic performance. *Education and Information Technologies*, 29(5), 10303–10328. DOI: 10.1007/s10639-023-12213-6

Cham, S., Cheng, G., & Lee, R. (2019). Digital addiction: Negative life experiences and potential for technology-assisted solutions. In Rocha, Á., Adeli, H., Reis, L., & Costanzo, S. (Eds.), *New knowledge in information systems and technologies* (Vol. 931, pp. 921–931). Springer., DOI: 10.1007/978-3-030-16184-2_87

Chang, M. L. Y., & Lee, I. O. (2024). Functional connectivity changes in the brain of adolescents with internet addiction: A systematic literature review of imaging studies. *PLOS Mental Health*, 1(1), e0000022. DOI: 10.1371/journal.pmen.0000022

Chatterjee, S. (2021). Impact of addiction to online platforms on quality of life. *AJIS. Australasian Journal of Information Systems*, 25(1), 1–25. DOI: 10.3127/ajis.v25i0.2761

Crane, C., Hotton, M., Shelemy, L., & Knowles-Bevis, R. (2024). The association between individual differences in motivational readiness at entry to treatment and treatment attendance and outcome in cognitive behaviour therapy: A systematic review. *Cognitive Therapy and Research*, 48(4), 10504. DOI: 10.1007/s10608-024-10504-x

De Oliveira Collet, G., De Morais Ferreira, F., Ceron, D. F., De Lourdes Calvo Fracasso, M., & Santin, G. C. (2024). Influence of digital health literacy on online health-related behaviors influenced by internet advertising. *BMC Public Health*, 24(1), 1949. DOI: 10.1186/s12889-024-19506-6 PMID: 39033160

Dennen, V. P., Choi, H., & Word, K. (2020). Social media, teenagers, and the school context: A scoping review of research in education and related fields. *Educational Technology Research and Development*, 68(4), 1635–1658. DOI: 10.1007/s11423-020-09796-z

DiClemente, C. C., Schlundt, D., & Gemmell, L. (2004). Readiness and stages of change in addiction treatment. *The American Journal on Addictions*, 13(2), 103–119. DOI: 10.1080/10550490490435777 PMID: 15204662

Feher, G., Tibold, A., & Esgalhado, G. (2023). Editorial: New addictions in the era of digitalization. *Frontiers in Human Neuroscience*, 17, 1302635. DOI: 10.3389/fnhum.2023.1302635 PMID: 37905242

Ferrer-Pérez, C., Montagud-Romero, S., & Blanco-Gandía, M. C. (2024). Neurobiological Theories of Addiction: A Comprehensive Review. *Psychoactives*, 3(1), 35–47. DOI: 10.3390/psychoactives3010003

Fischer-Grote, L., Fössing, V., Aigner, M., Fehrmann, E., & Boeckle, M. (2024). Effectiveness of online and remote interventions for mental health in children, adolescents, and young adults after the onset of the COVID-19 pandemic: Systematic Review and Meta-Analysis. *JMIR Mental Health*, 11, e46637. DOI: 10.2196/46637 PMID: 38315524

Fordham, B., Sugavanam, T., Edwards, K., Stallard, P., Howard, R., Nair, R. D., Copsey, B., Lee, H., Howick, J., Hemming, K., & Lamb, S. E. (2021). The evidence for cognitive behavioural therapy in any condition, population or context: A meta-review of systematic reviews and panoramic meta-analysis. *Psychological Medicine*, 51(1), 21–29. DOI: 10.1017/S0033291720005292 PMID: 33455594

Franzen, A., & Mader, S. (2023). The power of social influence: A replication and extension of the Asch experiment. *PLoS One*, 18(11), e0294325. DOI: 10.1371/journal.pone.0294325 PMID: 38019779

Hagen, R., Havnen, A., Hjemdal, O., Kennair, L. E. O., Ryum, T., & Solem, S. (2020). Protective and vulnerability factors in self-esteem: The role of metacognitions, brooding, and resilience. *Frontiers in Psychology*, 11, 01447. DOI: 10.3389/fpsyg.2020.01447 PMID: 32719640

Harwood, J. (2020). Social identity theory. In Bulck, J. (Ed.), *The International Encyclopedia of Media Psychology* (pp. 1–7). John Wiley & Sons., DOI: 10.1002/9781119011071.iemp0153

Hayes, A., Herlinger, K., Paterson, L., & Lingford-Hughes, A. (2020c). The neurobiology of substance use and addiction: Evidence from neuroimaging and relevance to treatment. *BJPsych Advances*, 26(6), 367–378. DOI: 10.1192/bja.2020.68

Heinz, A., Beck, A., Halil, M. G., Pilhatsch, M., Smolka, M. N., & Liu, S. (2019). Addiction as learned Behavior patterns. *Journal of Clinical Medicine*, 8(8), 1086. DOI: 10.3390/jcm8081086 PMID: 31344831

Henneberger, A. K., Mushonga, D. R., & Preston, A. M. (2020). Peer Influence and Adolescent Substance Use: A Systematic Review of Dynamic Social Network Research. *Adolescent Research Review*, 6(1), 57–73. DOI: 10.1007/s40894-019-00130-0

Huang, L., Cao, Y., Liu, Y., Zhu, W., & Zhou, M. (2024). Peer effects on rural children's depression: Do online games matter? *European Child & Adolescent Psychiatry*, 33(6), 1707–1720. DOI: 10.1007/s00787-023-02271-z PMID: 37553541

Jahan, N., & Kim, S. W. (2020). Understanding online community participation behaviour and perceived benefits: A social exchange theory perspective. *PSU Research Review*, 5(2), 85–100. DOI: 10.1108/PRR-12-2019-0036

Kaval, A., & Siyez, D. M. (2024). An internet addiction model based on cognitive-behavioral approach among adolescents: Maladaptive cognitions, psychopathology, and situational cues. *Journal of Rational-Emotive & Cognitive-Behavior Therapy*, 42(2), 194–213. DOI: 10.1007/s10942-023-00502-5

Kerman, N. T., Banihashem, S. K., Karami, M., Er, E., Van Ginkel, S., & Noroozi, O. (2023). Online peer feedback in higher education: A synthesis of the literature. *Education and Information Technologies*, 29(1), 763–813. DOI: 10.1007/s10639-023-12273-8

Kerman, N. T., Banihashem, S. K., Karami, M., Er, E., Van Ginkel, S., & Noroozi, O. (2023). Online peer feedback in higher education: A synthesis of the literature. *Education and Information Technologies*, 29(1), 763–813. DOI: 10.1007/s10639-023-12273-8

Khan, A. N. (2023). Are students at risk? Elucidating the impact of health risks of COVID-19 on emotional exhaustion and academic performance: Role of mindfulness and online interaction quality. *Current Psychology (New Brunswick, N.J.)*, 43(13), 12285–12298. DOI: 10.1007/s12144-023-04355-0 PMID: 36820197

Kim, S., & Lim, Y. (2020). Peer Pressure and SNS Addiction in Adolescents: The Mediating Role of SNS-Use Motives. *Canadian Journal of School Psychology*, 36(1), 23–33. DOI: 10.1177/0829573520963277

Kuss, D. J., & Griffiths, M. D. (2011). Online Social Networking and Addiction—A review of the Psychological literature. *International Journal of Environmental Research and Public Health. International Journal of Environmental Research and Public Health*, 8(9), 3528–3552. DOI: 10.3390/ijerph8093528 PMID: 22016701

Levounis, P. (2015). Bench to Bedside: From the science to the practice of addiction medicine. *Journal of Medical Toxicology; Official Journal of the American College of Medical Toxicology*, 12(1), 50–53. DOI: 10.1007/s13181-015-0515-7 PMID: 26553278

Li, S., Hong, Y., & Craig, S. D. (2023). A Systematic Literature review of social learning Theory in Online Learning Environments. *Educational Psychology Review*, 35(4), 108. Advance online publication. DOI: 10.1007/s10648-023-09827-0

Liu, J., Wu, L., Sun, X., Bai, X., & Duan, C. (2023). Active parental mediation and adolescent problematic internet use: The mediating role of Parent–Child relationships and hiding online behavior. *Behavioral Sciences (Basel, Switzerland)*, 13(8), 679. DOI: 10.3390/bs13080679 PMID: 37622819

Lu, H., & Wang, S. (2008). The role of Internet addiction in online game loyalty: An exploratory study. *Internet Research*, 18(5), 499–519. DOI: 10.1108/10662240810912756

Mallick, D., Chakraborty, P., & Ghosh, S. (2023). Visual representation for patterned proliferation of social media addiction: Quantitative model and network analysis. *SN Computer Science*, 4(6), 712. DOI: 10.1007/s42979-023-02164-7

Marco-Fondevila, M., Rueda-Tomás, M., & Latorre-Martínez, M. P. (2022). Active participation and interaction are key performance factors of Face-to-Face learning. *Education Sciences*, 12(7), 429. DOI: 10.3390/educsci12070429

McAloon, J., & Armstrong, S. M. (2024). The effects of online behavioral parenting interventions on child outcomes, parenting ability, and parent outcomes: A systematic review and meta-analysis. *Clinical Child and Family Psychology Review*, 27(2), 523–549. DOI: 10.1007/s10567-024-00477-4 PMID: 38613631

Meehan, Z. M., Hubbard, J. A., Moore, C. C., & Mlawer, F. (2022). Susceptibility to peer influence in adolescents: Associations between psychophysiology and behaviour. *Development and Psychopathology*, 36(1), 69–81. DOI: 10.1017/S0954579422000967 PMID: 36148857

Mukhopadhyay, J., & Bhattacharjee, A. (2023). A comprehensive analysis of affective health and sex differences in adolescents as a function of peer pressure and internet addiction. *Journal of Psychosexual Health*, 5(3), 159–166. DOI: 10.1177/26318318231206711

National Institute on Drug Abuse. (2014). *Drugs, brains, and behavior: The science of addiction*. National Institute on Drug Abuse. https://nida.nih.gov/sites/default/files/soa_2014.pdf

Niu, G., Chai, H., Li, Z., Wu, L., Sun, X., & Zhou, Z. (2019). Online Parent-Child Communication and Left-Behind Children's Subjective Well-Being: The Effects of Parent-Child Relationship and Gratitude. *Child Indicators Research*, 13(3), 967–980. DOI: 10.1007/s12187-019-09657-z

Opsal, A., Kristensen, Ø., & Clausen, T. (2019). Readiness to change among involuntarily and voluntarily admitted patients with substance use disorders. *Substance Abuse Treatment, Prevention, and Policy*, 14(1), 47. DOI: 10.1186/s13011-019-0237-y PMID: 31694664

Paul, F. A., Dangroo, A. A., Saikia, P., Ganie, A. U. R., Zaid, M., Das, M., & Gogoi, R. (2024). Societal and individual impacts of substance abuse. In R. Baikady, S. M., Sajid, J. Przeperski, V. Nadesan, M., Rezaul Islam, & J. Gao (Eds.), *The Palgrave Handbook of Global Social Problems* (Vol. 1, pp. 1–24). Palgrave Macmillan. DOI: 10.1007/978-3-030-68127-2_430-1

Rumjaun, A., & Narod, F. (2020). Social learning theory—Albert Bandura. In B. Akpan, & T. J. Kennedy (Eds.), *Science Education in Theory and practice* (Vol. 1, pp. 85–99). Springer Texts in Education. Springer, Cham. DOI: 10.1007/978-3-030-43620-9_7

Shek, D. T. L., Zhu, X., & Ma, C. M. S. (2018). The influence of parental control and parent-child relational qualities on adolescent internet addiction: A 3-year longitudinal study in Hong Kong. *Frontiers in Psychology*, 9, 642. DOI: 10.3389/fpsyg.2018.00642 PMID: 29765349

Shi, C., Hu, P., Fan, W., & Qiu, L. (2023). Competitive peer influence on knowledge contribution behaviors in online Q&A communities: A social comparison perspective. *Internet Research*, Vol. ahead-of-print No. ahead-of-print. DOI: 10.1108/INTR-07-2022-0510

Sinha, R. (2011). New findings on biological factors predicting addiction relapse vulnerability. *Current Psychiatry Reports*, 13(5), 398–405. DOI: 10.1007/s11920-011-0224-0 PMID: 21792580

Smith, C. H., & Borden, K. A. (2020). Introduction to the special issue on substance use disorders and addictions. *Professional Psychology, Research and Practice*, 51(1), 1–4. DOI: 10.1037/pro0000299

Vincent-Ruz, P., & Schunn, C. D. (2018). The nature of science identity and its role as the driver of student choices. *International Journal of STEM Education*, 5(1), 48. DOI: 10.1186/s40594-018-0140-5 PMID: 30631738

Wang, W., Liu, J., Liu, Y., Wang, P., Guo, Z., Hong, D., & Jiang, S. (2022). Peer relationship and adolescents' smartphone addiction: The mediating role of alienation and the moderating role of sex. *Current Psychology (New Brunswick, N.J.)*, 42(26), 22976–22988. DOI: 10.1007/s12144-022-03309-2

Wang, Y., & Zeng, Y. (2024). Relationship between loneliness and internet addiction: A meta-analysis. *BMC Public Health*, 24(1), 858. DOI: 10.1186/s12889-024-18366-4 PMID: 38504216

Wardrip, P. S. (2020). Educators enacting online learning support roles in remote educational experiences. *Educational Technology Research and Development*, 69(1), 213–216. DOI: 10.1007/s11423-020-09883-1 PMID: 33250611

Watts, L. L., Hamza, E. A., Bedewy, D. A., & Moustafa, A. A. (2023). A meta-analysis study on peer influence and adolescent substance use. *Current Psychology (New Brunswick, N.J.)*, 43(5), 3866–3881. DOI: 10.1007/s12144-023-04944-z

Weinstein, E., & James, C. (2022). School-based initiatives promoting digital citizenship and healthy digital media use. In Nesi, J., Telzer, E. H., & Prinstein, M. J. (Eds.), *Handbook of adolescent digital media use and mental health* (Vol. 1, pp. 365–388). Cambridge University Press., DOI: 10.1017/9781108976237.020

Yu, S., & Liu, H. (2023). Longitudinal detection of directed motivational currents in L2 learning: Motivated behaviours and emotional responses. *Current Psychology (New Brunswick, N.J.)*, 43(8), 7497–7510. DOI: 10.1007/s12144-023-04945-y

Zhang, J., & Zeng, Y. (2024). Effect of college students' smartphone addiction on academic achievement: The mediating role of academic anxiety and moderating role of sense of academic control. *Psychology Research and Behavior Management*, 17, 933–944. DOI: 10.2147/PRBM.S442924 PMID: 38464809

Zhang, X., Abbas, J., Shahzad, M. F., Shankar, A., Ercisli, S., & Dobhal, D. C. (2024). Association between social media use and students' academic performance through family bonding and collective learning: The moderating role of mental well-being. *Education and Information Technologies*, 29(11), 14059–14089. DOI: 10.1007/s10639-023-12407-y

Zhao, L. (2021). Social media addiction and its impact on college student's academic performance: The Mediating role of stress. *The Asia-Pacific Education Researcher*, 32(1), 81–90. DOI: 10.1007/s40299-021-00635-0

Zhou, N., & Fang, X.-Y. (2015). Beyond peer contagion: Unique and interactive effects of multiple peer influences on internet addiction among Chinese adolescents. *Computers in Human Behavior*, 50, 231–238. DOI: 10.1016/j.chb.2015.03.083

ADDITIONAL READING

Andreassen, C. S. (2015). Online social network site Addiction: A Comprehensive Review. *Current Addiction Reports*, 2(2), 175–184. DOI: 10.1007/s40429-015-0056-9

Lee, S., Kim, M. S., & Lee, H. K. (2019). Prevention Strategies and interventions for Internet use disorders due to addictive behaviours based on an integrative conceptual model. *Current Addiction Reports*, 6(3), 303–312. DOI: 10.1007/s40429-019-00265-z

Lim, G. P., Appalasamy, J. R., Ahmad, B., Quek, K. F., & Ramadas, A. (2024). Peer-led lifestyle interventions for the primary prevention of cardiovascular disease in the community: A systematic review of randomized controlled trials. *BMC Public Health*, 24(1), 812. DOI: 10.1186/s12889-024-18328-w PMID: 38486215

Touloupis, T. (2021). A Literature Review on Cyberbullying among Students: Do Gender and School Achievement Matter? *Proceedings of 14th annual International Conference of Education, Research and Innovation (ICERI)* (pp. 4613-4620). Seville, Spain. ISBN: 978-84-09-34549-6 https://dx.doi.org/DOI: 10.21125/iceri.2021.1064

Touloupis, T. (2021). *Use of Facebook and Cyberbullying during the Period of Covid-19 among Students with Learning Difficulties: The Role of Loneliness.* Virtual presentation in 15th annual International Technology, Education and Development Conference (INTED 2021). Valencia (Spain), March 8-10. DOI: 10.21125/inted.2021.1543

Touloupis, T. (2022). Facebook Use and Cyberbullying by Students with Learning Disabilities: The Role of Self-Esteem and Loneliness. *Psychological Reports*, 127(3), 1237–1270. DOI: 10.1177/00332941221138471 PMID: 36367133

Touloupis, T. (2022). Investigating the Relationship Among School Connectedness, Intensity of Facebook Use and School Adaptation in Ukrainian Refugee Junior High School Students. *ICERI Proceedings.* DOI: 10.21125/iceri.2022.2225

Touloupis, T., & Athanasiades, C. (2020). A comparison between primary school principals' and teachers' perceptions of students' online risk behaviours: The role of perceived self-efficacy. *Cambridge Journal of Education*, 50(4), 1–18. DOI: 10.1080/0305764X.2020.1740170

Touloupis, T., & Athanasiades, C. (2022). Cyberbullying and empathy among elementary school students: Do special educational needs make a difference? *Scandinavian Journal of Psychology*, 63(6), 609–623. DOI: 10.1111/sjop.12838 PMID: 35698831

Touloupis, T., & Athanasiades, C. (2022). Internet Addiction among Students of Psychology: The Role of Resilience and Perceived Economic Hardship. *Psychology: The Journal of the Hellenic Psychological Society*, 27(1), 175–193. DOI: 10.12681/psyhps.30840

Touloupis, T., & Athanasiades, C. (2023). *Does Self-esteem Enhancement Matter in the Prevention of Cyberbullying in Elementary Schools? The Case of the TABBY Program.* Virtual presentation in 16th annual International Conference of Education, Research and Innovation (ICERI), Seville (Spain), November 13-15. DOI: 10.21125/iceri.2023.2530

Touloupis, T., & Athanasiades, C. (2023). *Investigating Cyberbullying and Empathy Among Elementary School Students With and Without Special Educational Needs.* Virtual presentation in 16th annual International Conference of Education, Research and Innovation (ICERI), Seville (Spain), November 13-15. DOI: 10.21125/iceri.2023.2529

Touloupis, T., Sofologi, M., & Tachmatzidis, D. (2023). Pattern of Facebook use by university students during the COVID-19 pandemic: Relations with loneliness and resilience. *Social Network Analysis and Mining*, 13(1), 1–16. DOI: 10.1007/s13278-023-01073-0 PMID: 37033471

Touloupis, T., & Teli, A. (2021). Internet Addiction among Adolescents: The Role of Social Self-Efficacy and General Locus of Control. In Jaworski, J. J. (Ed.), *Advances in Sociology Research* (Vol. 36, pp. 81–112). Nova Science Publishers., DOI: 10.52305/GPAQ8046

Treasure, A. M., Hall, S. M., Lesko, I., Moore, D., Sharan, M., Van Zaanen, M., Yehudi, Y., & Van Der Walt, A. (2022). Ten simple rules for establishing a mentorship programme. *PLOS Computational Biology. PLoS Computational Biology*, 18(5), e1010015. DOI: 10.1371/journal.pcbi.1010015 PMID: 35551516

Vodă, A. I., Cauti anu, C., Grădinaru, C., Tănăsescu, C., & de Moraes, G. H. S. M. (2022). Exploring digital literacy skills in social sciences and humanities students. *Sustainability (Basel)*, 14(5), 2483. DOI: 10.3390/su14052483

Xiao, X., Cai, J., & Yang, Q. (2024). The relationship between internet addiction and adolescent learning engagement: The role of future orientation and cognitive reappraisal. *Current Psychology (New Brunswick, N.J.)*, 43(27), 23103–23114. DOI: 10.1007/s12144-024-05982-x

KEY TERMS AND DEFINITIONS

Addiction Behaviors: Patterns of excessive use or engagement that lead to negative consequences and dependence.

Biological: Physiological and genetic factors influencing susceptibility to addiction and its development.

Cognitive and Behavioral: Thought processes and habitual actions that sustain and exacerbate addictive behaviours.

Motivation and Readiness for Change: An individual's willingness and preparedness to alter addictive behaviours and seek recovery.

Peer Influence: The impact of friends and social groups on shaping and reinforcing online addiction behaviours.

Prevention Strategies: Methods and interventions designed to reduce the risk and occurrence of addiction behaviours.

Psychological: Mental health factors, such as stress and emotional triggers, that contribute to addiction.

Social and Environmental: External factors like social interactions, peer pressure, and environment affect addiction behaviours.

Chapter 2
Are Children With Autism Safe Online?
Risks, Parental Mediation, and Wellbeing

Layan Zuheir Abdulla
United Arab Emirates University, UAE

Maria Efstratopoulou
https://orcid.org/0000-0002-5162-2104
United Arab Emirates University, UAE

ABSTRACT

The chapter examines the online experiences of children with autism spectrum disorder (ASD), focusing on their unique vulnerabilities to internet-related risks. It explores common online threats faced by autistic children and investigates the crucial role of parental mediation in ensuring the online safety of children with ASD, discussing mediation strategies and their effectiveness. Finally, the chapter addresses the importance of raising awareness about online safety for autistic children and promoting inclusive online communities. Throughout, the chapter synthesizes relevant literature to provide a comprehensive understanding of the challenges and opportunities in supporting safe and positive online experiences for children with ASD. The chapter aims to inform parents, educators, and policymakers about the specific needs of autistic children in the digital age and highlight effective strategies for support and intervention.

THE DIGITAL INCLUSION: SETTING THE CONTEXT FOR AUTISTIC CHILDREN

In a digitally connected world, the numerous opportunities for learning, socializing, and entertainment that the internet offers are undeniable. This integration of technology in the life of every single person is increasingly viewed as a basic human right, yet a significant digital divide exists between typically developing individuals and those with disabilities, including autistic children (Chadwick et al., 2019). This divide is a complex multi-level phenomenon as individual cognitive differences interact with family-level support systems and broader societal barriers. While digital exclusion may appear protective, it creates a paradoxical effect. Attempts to protect autistic children from online risks through restricted access may prevent them from developing needed digital literacy skills and online resilience. From here

DOI: 10.4018/979-8-3693-4191-9.ch002

emerges the need to balance protection with opportunity for digital skill development. As more young people engage with online platforms, concerns about their safety in the digital space grows, particularly for those with special needs or neurodevelopmental conditions such as autism spectrum disorder (ASD).

The online world presents a two-edged weapon for all children, yet due to the unique profiles of children with autism, they may face additional vulnerabilities in navigating the digital world. Although the online world offers a wide range of benefits, it exposes them to various risks that need careful consideration (Chadwick et al., 2019). These risks can be broadly categorized into exposure to harmful content, experiencing negative online interactions, and engaging in risky online behaviors (Livingstone & Haddon, 2009, as cited in Chadwick et al., 2019).

For children with ASD, the online benefits are of added value; in the digital world, they can find the information that aligns with their interests in a relatively comfortable environment. The internet, however, does present potential risks for this vulnerable population. Despite the fact that autistic teenagers have proven a high level of awareness of privacy and online safety as revealed by the Rocheleau and Chiasson study (2022), there is a common perception that autistic children and those with intellectual disabilities may be more vulnerable online. This perception can lead to restricting their digital access, potentially impeding their autonomy and participation in the digital world (Chadwick et al., 2019) failing to recognize that these same digital platforms can provide valuable opportunities for social interaction, self-expression, and learning in a controlled environment. The apparent contradiction, however, between Rocheleau and Chiasson's (2022) findings of high privacy awareness among autistic teenagers and the common perception of their heightened vulnerability deserves attention. While previous studies like MacMillan et al. (2020) characterized autistic users as "naive" to online risks based on parent reports, Rocheleau and Chiasson's direct engagement revealed sophisticated privacy awareness and risk mitigation strategies among autistic teens. This would suggest the need to investigate whether the very caution demonstrated by this age group can be misinterpreted by observers as vulnerability rather than what it might actually represent - informed and deliberate privacy choices.

The Declaration of Rome, issued at the World Congress on Child Dignity in the Digital World in 2017, addressed a global crisis: "global society is failing its children" in the digital age (Declaration of Rome, 2017). This failure is particularly true for autistic children, who are at risk every time they navigate the online world. Difficulties in social interaction and communication in addition to behavioral and other cognitive traits of children with ASD can potentially lead to misunderstandings, social isolation, excessive time spent on specific websites or online activities, difficulty with impulse control and inability to recognize deception which all contribute to the increased vulnerability to cyberbullying and online harassment. Here comes the role of parental mediation to ensure that their children with autism can benefit from digital inclusion by maintaining the right balance between protection and autonomy.

This chapter explores the risks faced by children with ASD, particularly those aged 6-12, in the digital landscape, the factors that contribute to their vulnerability online, the importance of understanding these risks to develop targeted interventions and the effective strategies for parental mediation towards creating a safer and more supportive online environment for children with autism. It is important to note that research in this field often spans various age groups. In some cases, studies involving adolescents or young adults with ASD may be referenced when they provide valuable insights that could be relevant to understanding younger children's experiences or when research specific to the 6-12 age group is limited.

COGNITIVE AND BEHAVIORAL CHALLENGES

Even among higher-functioning individuals with ASD, cognitive challenges may exist and add to the complexity of the cases (Helverschou et al., 2011). Common cognitive difficulties manifest in problems with attention, concentration, distractibility, and short-term memory impairment. Together with the other prevalent challenges of concrete thinking and difficulties with abstract concepts, individuals with ASD show uneven cognitive profiles with some demonstrating strengths in some areas and weaknesses in others; these weaknesses may extend to social cognition, with difficulties in understanding social situations. A study by Lampri et al., (2024) points to the broad heterogeneity in cognitive development within the autism spectrum reflected in a significant variability in figurative language processing abilities among individuals with ASD. Nuske et al. (2020) found that children with ASD, particularly those who are minimally verbal, demonstrate more frequent self-regulation difficulties compared to typically verbal children with ASD. These difficulties are demonstrated in a range of ways such as being easily distractible, showing impulsive behaviors, needing prompting and reminders for compliance, difficulties with transitions between activities, low frustration tolerance, and rigid or inflexible behaviors. These cognitive and behavioral characteristics associated with ASD contribute to the increase of online vulnerability of autistic children. Impulsivity and a lack of inhibition control are typical behaviors of ASD children and adolescents and are likely to lead to hasty decision-making and a reduced ability to discern online risks (Rocheleau & Chiasson, 2022). Autistic children may also have restrictive interests and engage in repetitive behaviors, which could lead to excessive time spent on specific websites or online activities (Kuo et al., 2014; Rocheleau & Chiasson, 2022). They tend to focus on a narrow range of topics online and spend prolonged periods visiting websites containing information relevant to their restricted interests, such as video games and anime rather than engaging in general social interaction. The repetitive nature of these games, which mostly involve shooting or killing may appeal to autistic individuals' tendency toward repetitive behaviors (Kuo et al., 2014).

Another relevant area of concern is the autistic children's tendency to respond to online scams and phishing attempts due to difficulties in recognizing deception (Neupane et al., 2018; Rocheleau & Chiasson, 2022). Although there appears to be a lack of published research examining the ability of autistic young people to detect phishing attempts, there are speculative considerations regarding how autism-related characteristics might influence vulnerability or resilience to online deception among the autistic population. The diverse nature of ASD suggests that susceptibility to phishing attempts may vary among autistic individuals and depends on the individual's ability to practice inhibitory control; this is defined as the ability to stop or prevent actions or reactions that are triggered by stimuli (Tiego et al., 2018). When a potential online reward is in line with an autistic individual's specific interests, he/she is likely to perform poorly in the inhibitory condition or notice the content risks (Christ et al., 2007). The lack of inhibition control leads to impulsivity, hasty decision-making and a reduced ability to discern online risks and manipulation (Rocheleau & Chiasson, 2022). This makes autistic individuals more susceptible to falling for online scams and phishing attempts. On the contrary, in cases when the phishing attempts do not resonate with the interests of the autistic individual, the autism-associated characteristics can potentially serve as a protective factor. It is worth noting, however, that the gap in the literature requires empirical research to examine the first-hand experiences of autistic individuals with online phishing attempts and explore how autism-related characteristics might influence vulnerability or resilience to online deception among the autistic population.

SOCIAL AND COMMUNICATION CHALLENGES

The nature and severity of social communication and interaction challenges that children and adults with ASD face vary widely (Helverschou et al., 2011). These often include: difficulties in understanding and using non-verbal communication, such as eye contact, facial expressions, and gestures; challenges in developing, maintaining, and understanding relationships; problems with social-emotional reciprocity, such as sharing interests and/or emotions with others; literal interpretation of language leading to difficulties understanding sarcasm, jokes, or figurative speech; and challenges in adapting communication style to different social contexts (Lampri et al., 2024). The presentation and impact of these challenges can vary significantly among individuals with ASD. The autistic traits together with other factors like co-occurring conditions, environment, social circle, ability to cope, and ability to navigate daily demands influence the diverse needs of autistic people. Consequently, the translation of the social-communication challenges to digital spaces may present a complex and sometimes paradoxical picture. While online environments eliminate some traditional social communication barriers such as the need to interpret immediate non-verbal cues, they may introduce challenges of a different type. The asynchronous nature of online communication, for example, may create additional cognitive load in interpreting time-delayed interactions or maintaining multiple conversation threads. These types of complexities challenge the assumptions that digital communication eases social interaction for autistic individuals, suggesting instead that it transforms rather than eliminates social-communicative demands.

The social interaction and communication challenges that autistic children often experience are likely to extend and manifest in digital spaces potentially posing risks for individuals with ASD. As Romano and Porto (2016) point out, language and cognition are intrinsically linked, with discourse emerging as a dynamic, complex, and interactive process in real communicative contexts. For individuals with ASD, this interaction between cognition and communication may pose a core challenge. Children with ASD may experience social-cognitive challenges that affect their ability to interpret social cues, understand sarcasm or figurative language, and navigate the complexities of online social interactions (Rocheleau & Chiasson, 2022). These impairments in pragmatics, particularly in figurative language processing, are a defining feature of ASD (Lampri et al., 2024).

These social cognitive difficulties can persist as children with ASD get older and interact online which can manifest in misunderstandings, social isolation, and an increased risk of cyberbullying and online harassment (Kowalski & Fedina, 2011; MacMillan et al., 2020; Rocheleau & Chiasson, 2022). Lampri et al. (2024) note that "Even autistic individuals with high verbal or/and IQ skills appear to have difficulty in social use and understanding of language in context" (p. 675) suggesting that social cognitive difficulties persist even as individuals with ASD develop in other areas and Chadwick (2019) mentions that "risk may increase contingent upon higher levels of sociability, loneliness, anxiety and depression, poorer insight, judgement, discrimination and ability to detect deception online" (p. 180). While Mazurek and Wenstrup (2013) focused on adolescents with ASD, their findings suggest that individuals on the autism spectrum may use the internet to engage with their limited interests from an early age. This tendency could potentially start at a younger age facilitating the social connections of children with peers who share similar passions and compensating for offline social difficulties (Mazurek & Wenstrup, 2013; Rocheleau & Chiasson, 2022). The online environment provides a more accessible platform for communication and social connection compared to face-to-face interactions (Benford & Standen, 2009). Because online communications are often anonymous and asynchronous, they alleviate some of the primary stressors autistic individuals encounter in offline social settings. These stressors typically include the challenges of interpreting body language and the pressure to respond promptly in conversations (Benford & Standen, 2009). The digital landscape provides autistic users greater control over how they present themselves to others. This increased control often results in reduced anxiety and social pressure compared to real-world interactions (Benford & Standen, 2009; Burke et al., 2010; Schultz et al., 2013). As a result, many autistic individuals find online social platforms to be more comfortable and manageable spaces for social engagement; this comfort with digital environments extends to various screen-based activities. While many of the leisure activities that autistic transition-age youth engage in are solitary screen-based activities, they still help them learn, gain a sense of achievement, increase autonomy, and cope with stress, rather than lead to isolation (Folta et al., 2022).

The work of Lei et al. (2023) has investigated how the social and communication challenges faced by autistic children in offline settings can extend to online environments. They explored the relationship between social camouflaging in autism and safety behaviors in social anxiety among autistic adolescents. As masking autism traits and impression management were significantly associated with social anxiety symptoms, the need to camouflage autism traits and the masking behaviors to cope with social anxiety practiced by autistic children in attempting to fulfil their desire to fit in could indirectly reinforce autistic children's anxious thoughts and aggravate existing social anxiety symptoms.

RISK TYPES

As the internet and digital technologies have become integral parts of all children's lives, offering numerous opportunities for learning, communication, and entertainment, navigating the online world continues to present more unique challenges and risks to all navigators particularly for children and neurodiverse users. As Mai et al. (2022) remark, children's understanding of the internet and its associated risks develops gradually, with significant shifts occurring between ages five and eight. During this period, children's perception of the internet evolves from a vague, mysterious entity to a more concrete understanding of it as a network or information source. Older children (7-8 years) demonstrate a clearer online-offline distinction, greater risk awareness, and increased sense of personal agency in managing online risks compared to younger children (5-6 years). For autistic children, this developmental process may be more complicated due to specific ASD characteristics. One such characteristic is the potential difficulty with theory of mind, which refers to "the ability to attribute mental states, such as desire, knowledge, and belief, to oneself and other people as a means of explaining behavior" (Gernsbacher et al., 2005, p. 326). Challenges with theory of mind may impact the ability of children with ASD to recognize potential online risks involving social manipulation. The tendency for literal interpretation is another challenge that might make it difficult for children with ASD to distinguish between the real and virtual worlds or understand online social subtleties; this includes difficulties that may influence how autistic children interpret and respond to online social cues. In other words, executive functioning difficulties may affect the ability of children with ASD to navigate online environments safely and, while they give their attention to their selected interests by focusing on certain online activities, they potentially overlook associated risks. As Strohmeier and Gradinger (2022) emphasize, the rapidly evolving nature of digital technologies necessitates ongoing research and adaptation of prevention and intervention efforts.

Understanding these potential differences is the ground for developing appropriate strategies to support autistic children in safely navigating the online world and fostering their digital literacy skills. Rice (2024) highlights the importance of parental involvement in inclusive online, distance, and digital education as even before the COVID-19 pandemic, parents were expected to take on instructional responsibilities in online educational programs for their children with disabilities. This necessitates parents' digital literacy to effectively navigate digital platforms while ensuring their children's safety and educational needs are met. Understanding that autistic children may struggle with interpreting social cues in online interactions (Macmillan et al., 2022), for example, allows parents to focus on teaching explicit strategies for recognizing potential threats or deception. Likewise, by recognizing that autistic individuals may have difficulty generalizing safety rules across different online contexts (Chadwick, 2019), researchers can develop interventions that specifically address this challenge. This could involve creating adaptive learning tools that present safety scenarios across various online platforms which can help autistic children build more online safety skills. That is how awareness of individual factors, including cognitive levels, motor and sensory functions, and behavioral phenotypic characteristics when developing support strategies allows parents and specialists to tailor support to the specific needs and strengths of each autistic child and can significantly impact how we approach online safety and digital inclusion for autistic youth.

The remaining part of this section will examine each of these risk areas in more depth, considering the unique vulnerabilities of autistic children as well as potential protective factors and intervention strategies. Online risks for autistic children can be broadly categorized into contact risks, content risks, and conduct risks (Livingstone & Haddon, 2009):

- Contact risks involve harmful interactions with others online and may include sexual exploitation and cyberbullying.
- Content risks and these refer to exposure to inappropriate or harmful online material. Such as exposure to age-inappropriate content and misinformation.
- Conduct risks through problematic behavior by the child such as oversharing personal information and difficulties understanding privacy norms and posting.

Contact Risks: Social Interactions and Online Exploitation

The most concerning contact risk is the potential for sexual exploitation on SNSs (Chadwick et al., 2017; MacMillan et al., 2020; Normand & Sallafranque-St-Louis, 2016; as cited in Rocheleau & Chiasson, 2022). Online sexual solicitation is typically defined in research as the actions of an online predator who attempts to manipulate a young person into discussing sexual topics, sharing private sexual information, or participating in sexual activities via the internet (Mitchell et al. 2001, 2007b; Ybarra & Mitchell 2004). In other words, it is any behavior that involves the deliberate targeting of minors for sexual purposes in digital environments. The social naivety of autistic children, their desire for friendship, and the difficulty they face in understanding inappropriate behavior may make them targets for online predators and challenges with understanding privacy norms may lead to oversharing of personal information online (Mai et al., 2022). Although autistic teenagers exhibit diverse patterns of social engagement on social SNSs, with some actively using SNS to connect with others, many engage more passively, primarily using these platforms to stay informed about their interests and maintain existing friendships. As Rocheleau and Chiasson (2022) note, "autistic teenagers also vary widely in their level of social engagement on SNS, which may impact their privacy and safety online" (p.5). This variability in social engagement reflects the spectrum of social skills and desires for social connection among autistic youth and justifies the fact that some individuals with intellectual or developmental disabilities, including some with ASD, may be particularly vulnerable to sexual exploitation online. Rocheleau and Chiasson (2022) state that "Those with intellectual disability may be particularly vulnerable to financial and sexual exploitation online, especially without education, training, and experiential learning opportunities to cultivate their knowledge on how to recognize and respond to threats on SNS" (p. 4). Among the several specific forms of sexual exploitation that autistic individuals may encounter online are unwanted sexual messages or inappropriate comments from strangers, nude photographs and the exploitation of shared interests to build trust with autistic individuals, potentially as a form of grooming. These few examples of the range of online sexual risks that autistic individuals may face necessitates tailored education and support to help them navigate these challenges safely.

The lack of proper education will make these individuals not only struggle to recognize inappropriate sexual content or interactions online, but also have difficulty reporting abuse if it occurs. Children with intellectual disabilities often lack access to proper sex education. In their article on cybervictimization of young people with intellectual or developmental disabilities, Normand and Sallafranque-St-Louis (2016) discuss the limited sexual knowledge of individuals with intellectual disabilities or ASD compared to their typically developing peers. They cite a study by Murphy and O'Callaghan (2004) that demonstrated this disparity in sexual knowledge between adults with intellectual disabilities and typically developing youth.

The authors note that this knowledge gap extends to various aspects of sexuality, including pregnancy, contraception, sexually transmitted diseases, and legal matters related to sexuality (Murphy & O'Callaghan, 2004; Cheng & Udry, 2005). This limitation is attributed to a number of factors that include:

- Lack of formal sex education for this population (Murphy & O'Callaghan, 2004)
- Limited access to informal sex education due to stigmatization and social isolation (Murphy & O'Callaghan, 2004; Isler et al., 2009)
- Parents' tendency to provide less sexual information to children with intellectual or developmental disabilities
- Fewer opportunities for romantic relationships and sexual experiences (Murphy & O'Callaghan, 2004; Cheng & Udry, 2005; Isler et al., 2009)

For autistic children, this may mean they are less equipped to identify and report inappropriate online sexual content or interactions. Due to difficulty in communication skills, autistic children, especially those with limited verbal abilities, may have trouble disclosing or describing online abuse experiences if they occur.

Cyberbullying represents another contact risk for autistic children. Consistent with previous research, Rocheleau and Chiasson found evidence that cyberbullying was more of an issue for autistic teenagers in their sample than the non-autistic teenagers, even though most of the autistic teenagers were more concerned and cautious about their privacy and safety on SNS. While cyberbullying shares some characteristics with traditional bullying, such as intentionality, repetition, and power imbalance (Kowalski et al., 2014), research suggests it is a distinct phenomenon (Dempsey et al., 2009; Wang et al., 2009). Although cyberbullying is less prevalent than traditional bullying (Modecki et al., 2014), its potential for anonymity, wide audience reach, and constant accessibility may make it more distressing for victims (Holfeld & Mishna, 2018).

Research suggests that autistic children may be more vulnerable to online bullying and harassment due to differences in social communication and interaction skills compared to their non-autistic peers (Rocheleau & Chiasson, 2022). Holfeld et al. (2019) found that rates of cyber victimization (73.9%)

exceeded rates of cyber bullying (17.4%) among youth with ASD, suggesting that children with ASD are disproportionately targeted in online environments. The authors mention that autistic users may be more vulnerable to cyberbullying and social exclusion online, often due to misunderstandings between autistic and non-autistic users rather than inherent deficits. This has also been confirmed in a study by Efstratopoulou et al. (2021) who reveal that social interaction, a key area of development for autistic children, was negatively impacted during online learning. The study shares parents' concern that interaction between ASD students and their peers was almost nonexistent during online class sessions. This suggests that online environments may deprive autistic children of social learning opportunities, potentially increasing their vulnerability to social manipulation or isolation online.

This connects to Pope Francis's statement that "A society can be judged by the way it treats its children" (Declaration of Rome, 2017) which takes on added significance when considering autistic children online and poses a challenge to ensure that our digital society is safe for all children, including those with different cognitive profiles and communication styles. Rocheleau and Chiasson's (2022) discussion of SNS design, however, does not yet show any remarkable progress in the field as SNS design still caters to non-autistic social norms, potentially aggravating bias-based cyber victimization for autistic users. This refers to harmful online behaviors targeting individuals or groups due to their personal characteristics or identities. This includes discriminatory, demeaning, or aggressive actions based on factors such as nationality, faith, ethnicity, gender identity, sexual orientation, or disability. Such victimization can occur through the different digital means, including social media posts, online comments, text messages, and shared videos or images (Blaya, 2019; Wachs & Wright, 2019). The challenges that autistic children face in interpreting social cues and understanding others' intentions make it harder for them to identify when they are being cyberbullied or to respond appropriately. That is, with the high prevalence of cyberbullying among autistic children as reported by Carrington et al. (2017) who shared that 90% of the autistic students in their study had experienced some form of bullying during their school life, including cyberbullying, the need for targeted interventions and support for this population in online environments becomes a necessity.

Content Risks: Exposure to Inappropriate Material

Content risks are another type of hazard for autistic children who may be more vulnerable to inappropriate or explicit online content (Rocheleau & Chiasson, 2022). These risk types involve children and young people encountering or being exposed to potentially harmful digital content. Autistic children may accidentally or intentionally encounter inappropriate or disturbing online content (Mai et al., 2022) and may have difficulty avoiding it. This may include age-inappropriate material that may promote violence, self-harm or suicide through images or videos, sometimes disguised as child-friendly material; in other cases, the inappropriacy is in the form of mature themes that are not meant to be processed by children. Harmful digital content includes hate speech that may discriminate based on personal traits or identities. Dangerous behaviors or ideologies such extreme dieting and radicalization are other forms of harmful content. Other types of content promoting pornography and inaccurate information may be harder for autistic children to identify as false or misleading. Children with ASD may also be susceptible to misinformation due to difficulties in critical thinking and discerning reliable sources (Rice et al., 2023). The concern is that such content may not only be upsetting and confusing but may also have negative impacts on a child's development, mental health, or behavior. Martins et al. (2020) found that many children with ASD preferred content aimed at younger audiences, often due to its slower pace and easier-to-understand narratives. This preference for simpler content could potentially leave them less prepared for more complex or mature online content they may encounter as they grow older. The study also found that children with ASD often enjoyed repetitive viewing of content, which might increase exposure to any problematic messages or themes present in that content. YouTube, for example, is particularly popular among children with ASD. While this platform offers a wealth of content, it presents risks in terms of exposure to inappropriate material or misinformation. Some parents, reported that their children believed YouTube creators were speaking directly to them or were their friends, highlighting a potential misunderstanding of the nature of online content that could increase vulnerability to manipulation or exploitation. These findings highlight another type of online risks in which parents of children with ASD require targeted support and education.

Conduct Risks: Online Behavior and Safety

Autistic children's online conduct hazards emerge through problematic online behaviors that can put autistic children at risk in particularly three key areas. Autistic children may overshare personal information, post inappropriate content, or engage in unauthorized online purchases due to impulsivity and a lack of understanding of online safety practices (Just & Berg, 2017; Rocheleau & Chiasson, 2022).

Autistic children may engage in oversharing personal information due to difficulties understanding privacy norms and potential consequences. Just and Berg (2017) uncovered the fact that parents described their autistic children as both "clever" and "naive"; although they are able to technically navigate online spaces, they are unable to recognize dangers in sharing personal details. Rice and Carter (2015) found that many autistic children struggled to understand what content was appropriate to post or share online. This included difficulties with understanding what photos are appropriate to share of themselves and others, recognizing when sharing details about family members could be problematic and determining what personal information should remain private. Some children, for example, would share their passwords, personal photos, or location information without recognizing the risks. Parents reported their children being "devious" in creating multiple accounts even when forbidden, while being "oblivious" to the dangers of sharing personal information on those accounts.

Online purchasing by autistic children is another problematic behavior. Just and Berg (2017) documented cases where children engaged in significant unauthorized spending, such as one child spending £2,500 within 24 hours on game points using their parent's cards. The compulsive and persistent nature of some autistic children's behavior may manifest in cases where they memorize credit card details and PINs from watching parents, continue attempting failed transactions just to collect gaming points and make repeated purchase attempts despite cards being cancelled.

Challenges with impulse control and the lack of education and experiential learning opportunities about online safety leave autistic children less equipped to safely survive complex social situations online, potentially leading to unintentional engagement in problematic behaviors.

Time spent online by autistic children and their increased social engagement may typically expose them to a greater variety of online risks (Alareeki et al., 2022; MacMillan et al., 2020) including the range of contact, content and conduct risks discussed earlier. The autistic children's social anxiety coupled with a strong desire for online interaction, can lead to risky behaviors in terms of contact risks which in turn may lead to other conduct risks; the lack of education and experiential learning opportunities about online safety may leave autistic children potentially vulnerable to unintentional and unsafe engagements.

Parents, educators and the digital world developers' understanding of the challenges and vulnerabilities faced by this population and the risk categories with the kinds of threats they may cause is key for developing targeted interventions, educational programs, and support systems for a more a more inclusive and secure online environment.

THE ROLE OF PARENTAL MEDIATION IN SUPPORTING AUTISTIC CHILDREN'S SAFE AND POSITIVE INTERNET USE

This section examines parental mediation strategies for supporting autistic children's safe and beneficial internet use. It will include a review of research on different types of mediation, discuss their effectiveness and limitations, and provide evidence-based recommendations for parents.

Parents of autistic children have become increasingly aware of the potential risks in their children's online experiences. Just and Berg (2017) explored the online safety concerns of parents and caregivers of children with ASD through a focus group study. Their research highlighted the significance of parents' observation of their children's use of the online space and their preferred platforms and revealed their key worries with the primary concern of their children's potential vulnerability to online predators. Parents expressed apprehension about the increased risk of cyberbullying, their children's social media connections and the content they share online, particularly the types of photos their children might post. Parents reported their children primarily engaged with social aspects of platforms like YouTube and online games, rather than traditional social networking sites.

Bottema-Beutel et al. (2020) found that 69% of autistic participants viewed their family's contributions to their high school experience positively, highlighting the importance of parental support in various aspects of their lives, including online activities. In the context of online safety, Sasson and Mesch (2014) concluded that family cohesion and open communication between parents and autistic youth are associated with reduced online risks. This, however, does not diminish the importance of balance between protection and fostering autonomy. While safeguarding autistic children from online dangers is essential, it is equally important to provide opportunities for growth, socialization, and independence in digital spaces.

Finding the right equilibrium between protection and autonomy is a complex but necessary task. By doing so, parents can help maximize the benefits of online experiences for their autistic children while effectively mitigating potential risks. This approach allows autistic children to explore and engage with the digital world safely, promoting their development and well-being in an increasingly connected world.

Types of Parental Mediation for Online Safety

Research has identified four distinct types of parental mediation strategies that parents employ to protect their children online and these are: active mediation, restrictive mediation, technical mediation and monitoring (Livingstone & Helsper, 2008; Livingstone et al., 2017; Steinfeld, 2021)

The first approach, active mediation, as the name indicates, involves parents engaging in discussions and shared activities with their children around internet use. This strategy includes explaining online content, talking about potential risks and benefits, and actively participating in children's online experiences. Livingstone and Helsper (2008) note that active mediation combines conversational and interpretive elements, with parents helping children understand their digital experiences.

Restrictive mediation, the second type, is about setting rules and limitations on internet use. Parents employing this strategy establish clear boundaries around screen time, restrict access to certain types of content or platforms, and set specific conditions for online activities. According to Steinfeld (2021), these restrictions often focus particularly on peer-to-peer interactions, such as social media use, online gaming, and messaging platforms, as these are perceived as carrying higher risks.

The third approach, technical mediation, utilizes software tools and technological solutions to manage children's internet access. This includes installing filtering software, using parental control applications, and implementing technical restrictions on specific websites or applications. Livingstone et al. (2017) found that parents often employ these tools alongside other strategies, and that their effectiveness in isolation has been questioned.

Monitoring, as the fourth strategy, is when parents track or check their children's online activities, typically after use. This includes reviewing browsing histories, examining social media activities, and keeping track of online communications. While monitoring can help parents stay informed about their children's online behaviors, research suggests it may impact parent-child trust and communication if not implemented thoughtfully (Livingstone & Helsper, 2008).

Evidence on Mediation Effectiveness

Studies on parental mediation strategies have yielded mixed results regarding their effectiveness. Active mediation has been associated with increased online opportunities but does not necessarily reduce risks. As Livingstone et al. (2017) note, "enabling mediation is positively related to online opportunities, and restrictive mediation is negatively related to online opportunities" (p. 97). Likewise, Steinfeld (2021) found that active mediation was positively associated with increased internet activity of any sort, which enables experimentation and autonomy in using the digital space, and did not correlate with increased risk.

While restrictive mediation is potentially effective in reducing online risks, it can also limit children's opportunities and skills development. Livingstone and Helsper (2008) found that "a significant reduction in online risks was associated with the parental restriction of user-user interaction" (p. 596); caution, however, comes at the cost of limiting beneficial online activities. Steinfeld (2021) found that restrictive mediation correlated with decreased internet activity and increased risks, possibly due to lack of adolescent experience and autonomy in navigating online risks.

Technical mediation and monitoring have shown limited effectiveness in reducing risks. Livingstone et al. (2017) report that technical restrictions were not necessarily effective in reducing risk. Steinfeld's (2021) study also did not find a significant relationship between monitoring and children's positive use of the internet, aligning with previous findings.

Steinfeld (2021) mixed-method study conducted to examine the various aspects of children and adolescent internet use, parental mediation strategies, and online risks found that parents often combine different mediation strategies, including active mediation and restrictive mediation. The effectiveness of mediation strategies appeared to be age-dependent, with parents using less mediation as adolescents grow older. Research on autistic children in particular is limited but suggests that parental mediation may be particularly important due to autistic traits. Helsper et al. (2024) emphasize that children with special educational needs and disabilities (SEND) might need different or more intense forms of mediation highlighting the need for consciously tailored approaches to respond to their specific needs and abilities.

Research suggests that parents of autistic children often employ more restrictive mediation strategies compared to parents of neurotypical children. Macmillan et al. (2020) found that parents of autistic children were more likely to use prohibitive measures like confiscating devices or strictly monitoring online activities. While these approaches stem from valid safety concerns, they may inadvertently limit autistic children's opportunities to develop important digital literacy skills and learn from first-hand experiences online. Overly restrictive parental mediation, however, can have unintended negative consequences. As Rocheleau and Chiasson (2022) note, autistic teenagers report feelings of distress when their parents take control of their devices to adjust privacy settings, as their phones serve as important tools for managing autism-related challenges. This is a call for parents to be mindful of their child's autonomy and comfort when implementing safety measures. In a study analyzing reviews of parental control apps, Ghosh et al. (2018) found that children, including those with autism, strongly disliked apps they perceived as restrictive or invasive of their privacy. Mediating media usage for older children and adolescents can be particularly challenging, as they are in a phase where they seek more independence from their parents while still needing parental support (Priya & Maheswari, 2024). This tension may be even more evident for autistic adolescents who may require additional support but also benefit from opportunities to develop autonomy. Many felt such apps negatively impacted their relationship with their parents and their sense of autonomy. Instead, the authors recommend taking a more "teen-centric" approach with autistic teens to give them more agency in managing their online behaviors and prevent the backfire of an overly restrictive approaches to online safety.

Implementing Mediation Strategies for Autistic Children

Because many autistic children are drawn to technology and may benefit from its use for learning, communication, and social connection (Cardy et al., 2023), complete restriction of access is not the wisest solution. Macmillan et al. (2022), for example, found that some autistic young people reported benefits of online communication, such as removing the pressure of direct eye contact and allowing more time to process information. This is a simple example on why parents need to leverage technology in ways that align with their child's interests and needs. This can be done by guiding children towards high-quality educational content, assistive technologies, or monitored social platforms designed for children with special needs. Parents can support their child in finding safe online communities related to their interests, which can provide social connection and motivation for developing digital skills (Grove et al., 2018).

Among the four identified parental mediation strategies for internet use, research suggests that a balanced approach may be most effective for autistic children,. Macmillan et al. (2020) found that while some technical restrictions were helpful, autistic young people also desired more support to independently manage their online interactions and expressed a need for more practical support in learning how to block unwanted contact independently. Parents can take an active co-use approach by explaining online safety concepts, helping children navigate social media platforms safely, and discussing strategies for identifying trustworthy information online. At the same time, using some technical restrictions like content filters or time limits may help reduce risks while still allowing beneficial technology use. In other words, while some technical restrictions can be helpful, there is a need to build skills for independent online risk management keeping in mind the child's age, developmental level, and individual characteristics. The authors suggest that future interventions should focus on empowering autistic young people with practical strategies to navigate online interactions safely on their own, rather than relying solely on parental restrictions.

Shin and Ismail (2014) investigated parental and peer mediation in young adolescents' engagement in risk-taking on social networking sites (SNSs). Although this study did not specifically involve autistic participants, its findings can inform approaches for autistic children, with appropriate modifications. The study revealed that control-based parental mediation can potentially cause rebound effects, while discussion-based mediation showed some effectiveness in reducing certain online risks. For autistic children, ongoing conversations about online experiences can be structured and supported using visual aids or social stories to help them process and communicate about their internet use effectively. This approach, inspired by Wisniewski et al.'s (2017) framework balancing parental control with self-regulation, can be adapted to suit the communication needs of autistic children. Having these conversations can help autistic children develop critical thinking skills about internet use and create a safe space for them to discuss online interactions without fear of judgment or device removal. Parents can ensure teaching specific digital literacy and online safety skills, tailored to their child's age and comprehension level. This might include simplified strategies for recognizing potential threats, understanding privacy settings, and knowing when to seek help (Bahiss et al., 2010). It is worth mentioning here that involving autistic children in establishing online safety rules and using clear and concrete language can always enhance their understanding and cooperation.

It is important to note that these strategies should be introduced gradually, using age-appropriate language and examples. What works for an autistic teenager may need significant modification for a younger child. Rocheleau and Chiasson (2022) found that some autistic teenagers were motivated to follow online safety guidelines because they took their parents' and teachers' advice seriously. For younger children, this might translate into creating simple, clear rules with visual supports while being always conscious to balance protection with the development of independent skills

Other strategies that emerge from the literature highlight the benefits of a multidisciplinary approach in ASD research (Hemdan et al., 2023). This is because ensuring online safety for children with ASD requires collaboration between parents, educators, technology developers, and mental health professionals for the development of inclusive online platforms and content that are accommodating to neurodiverse users. Just and Berg (2017) proposed developing collaborative tools to facilitate communication between autistic users and their parents regarding online privacy protection. These tools could include visual schedules or social stories about online privacy and apps that allow autistic children to easily communicate their online experiences to parents without feeling overwhelmed. Such tools may help balance autonomy and safety by keeping parents informed while respecting the child's privacy.

Wasserman (2019) argues that people with intellectual disabilities, including some autistic individuals, can benefit from opportunities for positive risk-taking online. This involves the parents' collaboration to create controlled environments for their children to practice navigating potential online challenges. Examples of controlled environments may include supervised social media accounts where children can practice appropriate posting and interaction, moderated online forums where autistic children can engage in discussions about their interests with peers and simulated online shopping experiences to teach about financial safety and decision-making.

Recommendations

To develop online safety strategies for autistic children, parents need to follow a carefully staged approach that evolves with the child's growing digital literacy and self-regulation skills. As Livingstone et al. (2017) highlight, the key is to gradually increase online autonomy while maintaining appropriate safeguards. This process requires careful consideration of each child's individual needs, abilities, and pace of learning.

This approach starts by establishing closely supervised internet sessions focused on specific tasks that align with their child's interests and abilities. This initial stage allows parents to observe how their child interacts with digital content, identify potential challenges, and provide immediate support when needed. Parents might sit with their child while exploring educational websites related to the child's special interests, using this time to both support learning and model safe browsing behaviors.

As children demonstrate basic digital literacy skills, parents can begin expanding their online independence progressively and in a structured manner. This means allowing independent browsing on pre-approved websites while maintaining active monitoring. During this phase, parents should focus on teaching specific safety skills, such as:

- Recognizing inappropriate content and learning how to exit uncomfortable situations
- Understanding basic privacy concepts in concrete, practical terms
- Learning to distinguish between safe and unsafe online interactions
- Developing strategies to manage online communication challenges

The transition to more independent internet use should be accompanied by ongoing discussion and skill-building while actively engaging in teaching safe search techniques and responsible social media use. This might involve creating practice scenarios where children can apply safety skills in a controlled environment before encountering real-world situations.

Simultaneous collaboration between parents and other stakeholders is recommended to create comprehensive support systems for autistic children's online safety. Parents need to actively engage with their child's educators, participate in parent support networks, and whenever possible, work with technology developers. This respectively ensures consistency between home and school approaches to online safety, provides opportunities to share experiences and strategies with others facing similar challenges, and helps parents learn from collective wisdom, avoid common pitfalls, and identify needs to implement appropriate safety tools that work for their autistic children's specific requirements.

Parents' own ongoing education about digital safety is equally important for effective mediation. This means staying consistently informed about emerging platforms and potential risks in the rapidly evolving digital landscape. Parents need to develop a deep understanding of how autistic children might experience online environments differently from their neurotypical peers, as this knowledge helps in crafting more effective and empathetic safety strategies. Learning about new safety features and tools specifically designed for special needs users ensures parents can implement the most appropriate technological supports. Perhaps most importantly, parents must develop skills to effectively communicate about online safety in ways that resonate with their autistic child, using language and examples that align with their child's understanding and processing style.(Synthesized from Livingstone et al., 2017; Helsper et al., 2024; Daud et al., 2014)

To conclude, effective parental mediation for autistic children online requires a subtle approach that protects against genuine risks while fostering independence and skill development. Implementing strategies that respect autonomy, encourage open communication, and focus on building digital literacy skills is the way to help parents ensure the online safety and well-being of their autistic children while supporting their growth and self-determination in digital spaces.

RAISING AWARENESS AND PROMOTING INCLUSIVE ONLINE COMMUNITIES

ASD is a complex neurodevelopmental condition that affects individuals in numerous ways. Despite the increasing awareness of the disorder, misconceptions and stigma surrounding autism persist, often leading to social isolation and exclusion for those on the spectrum. With the prevalence of electronic screen media use among children with ASD compared to their typically developing peers (Mazurek et al., 2012), parents', educators', and healthcare professionals' concern about autistic children and adolescents' screen time and its significant implications for their social development, communication skills, and overall well-being grows. On the other hand, in the survey by Bottema-Beutel et al. (2020), however, 15% of autistic respondents felt their family members, who play the biggest role in supporting them and mediating their online experiences, needed more autism awareness and knowledge. This suggests that even involved parents may lack full understanding of their autistic child's specific experiences and support needs, including in digital contexts. That is why improving the education of parents and the other influencers on autism and digital media use could enhance their ability to effectively mediate and support the autistic youth online activities. Raising awareness and promoting inclusive online communities have become necessary for addressing these issues and developing a more supportive environment for individuals with ASD. A better understanding of the roles and needs of the influencers in the lives of the autistic youth can help in developing more comprehensive and effective approaches to support their wellbeing and safety as they navigate digital environments.

Addressing stigma and misconceptions about autism is a critical first step in promoting inclusivity. As Ennis-Cole (2019) notes, media portrayals of autism can significantly influence public perception, often presenting a limited or stereotypical view of ASD. According to some parents, many people still associate autism primarily with the character from the movie "Rain Man," failing to recognize the spectrum's diversity (Ennis-Cole, 2019). To combat these misconceptions, it is necessary to provide accurate, evidence-based information about ASD in online communities.

The first step in raising awareness can be by sharing personal stories and experiences from individuals with ASD and their families. Ennis-Cole (2019) includes numerous parent perspectives that highlight both the challenges and joys of raising a child with autism. One parent, for example, said, "I wish others could see how brilliant my son is, despite his inability to talk" (Ennis-Cole, 2019, p. 53). By making these voices heard in online spaces, others can understand the diverse realities of living with autism and challenge stereotypes.

Alongside this, creating inclusive online communities that accommodate the needs of individuals with ASD is as effective for promoting their social engagement, learning opportunities, and overall well-being. Promoting empathy, understanding, and support from peers is an effective strategy for creating truly inclusive online communities. Ennis-Cole (2019) mentions the value of "mentor parents" who provide support and guidance to other parents of children with ASD. The same concept can be extended to peer support among individuals with ASD and between neurotypical and neurodiverse individuals. Online forums, social media groups, and virtual meetups can provide spaces for interaction, shared experiences, mutual support, and learning. Another effective approach is using visual tools like sketchnotes, which combine drawings, text, and visual elements, to help neurotypical individuals better understand how those with ASD might process information differently (Ennis-Cole, 2019). These visual representations can make complex concepts more accessible and foster empathy by illustrating the unique perspectives of individuals with ASD.

Speaking about inclusive online spaces, no one can ignore the vital role that technology can play to better achieve more accessible and inclusive digital environments. Ennis-Cole (2019) discusses various technologies that can support individuals with ASD in communication and social interaction. An example is incorporating specific tools into online platforms such as providing options for alternative text-based communication alongside video chats and educating users about their purpose to create more accessible and inclusive digital environments. This can make online interactions more comfortable for individuals with ASD who may struggle with traditional social cues. Wong et al. (2014, as cited in Ennis-Cole, 2019) identified several evidence-based practices for supporting individuals with ASD, some of which can be adapted to online environments. For instance, using clear, concrete language and providing visual support can make online interactions more accessible and comfortable for individuals with ASD.

Based on Steinfeld (2021) research findings, a balanced approach is the most ideal to promote online safety and digital citizenship among neurotypical adolescents which ideally applies to autistic children and adolescents. Implementing active mediation strategies that foster open discussions about online experiences, risks, and responsible behavior, encouraging supervised peer-to-peer learning and mentoring programs where older, more experienced Internet users can guide younger ones in navigating online spaces safely and respectfully is an approach that acknowledges both the challenges and the strengths associated with ASD. Additionally, developing educational programs that simulate real-world online scenarios, allowing adolescents to practice empathy, problem-solving, and supportive behaviors in a controlled environment are ways to create more inclusive online communities that nurture empathy, understanding, and peer support among adolescents with and without ASD with conscious consideration of individual differences among autistic children.

By addressing stigma and misconceptions through accurate information and personal stories, encouraging empathy and understanding through education and visual tools, leveraging technology to support communication and interaction, fostering peer support, and implementing evidence-based practices in online community design and moderation, we contribute to the creation of more inclusive online spaces and to the understanding and support of individuals across the autism spectrum.

CONCLUSION

The digital landscape presents both unique opportunities and significant challenges for autistic children. As this chapter has demonstrated, the distinct cognitive and behavioral characteristics of this population including difficulties with social interaction, communication challenges, and potential issues with impulse control create specific vulnerabilities in online environments. However, these same digital spaces can offer valuable opportunities for learning, social connection, and self-expression if properly supported.

Research reveals that thorough understanding of how autism-related characteristics interact with online risks and how difficulties with theory of mind and literal interpretation of language may impact autistic children's ability to recognize potential online risks is required for establishing effective online safety measures against the different types of online risks. Parental mediation emerges as a critical factor in supporting autistic children's safe and beneficial internet use. While no single mediation strategy offers complete protection, the evidence suggests that combining different approaches - active, restrictive, technical, and monitoring - with careful consideration of the child's individual needs can be most effective.

The research also emphasizes the importance of moving beyond simple protection toward building resilience and digital literacy skills in ways that accommodate autistic children's unique learning styles and communication needs. This includes developing structured learning environments that allow children to gradually build online safety skills while receiving appropriate support. This also requires parents to play the role of active guides in their children's digital experiences not just as protectors, with their effectiveness depending largely on their ability to adapt mediation strategies to their child's specific communication style, interests, and processing patterns.

The future of online safety for autistic children lies in developing approaches that protect while empowering, recognizing both the challenges and the opportunities that digital technologies present for this population. Success requires ongoing collaboration between all stakeholders to ensure that autistic children can safely access the benefits of the digital world while developing the skills needed for independent online navigation.

REFERENCES

Alareeki, A., Shipton, L., & Lashewicz, B. (2022). "They're either afraid or ignorant": Experiences of stigma and blame among fathers raising autistic children. *Research in Autism Spectrum Disorders*, 96, 101999. Advance online publication. DOI: 10.1016/j.rasd.2022.101999

Bahiss, K., Cunningham, S. J., & Smith, T. (2010). Investigating the usability of social networking sites for teenagers with autism. In *Proceedings of the 11th International Conference of the NZ Chapter of the ACM Special Interest Group on Human-Computer Interaction* (pp. 5-8). ACM. DOI: 10.1145/1832838.1832840

Benford, P., & Standen, P. (2009). The Internet: A comfortable communication medium for people with Asperger syndrome (AS) and high functioning autism (HFA)? *Journal of Assistive Technologies*, 3(2), 44–53. DOI: 10.1108/17549450200900015

Blaya, C. (2019). Cyberhate: A review and content analysis of intervention strategies. *Aggression and Violent Behavior*, 45, 163–172. DOI: 10.1016/j.avb.2018.05.006

Bottema-Beutel, K., Cuda, J., Kim, S. Y., Crowley, S., & Scanlon, D. (2020). High school experiences and support recommendations of autistic youth. *Journal of Autism and Developmental Disorders*, 50(9), 3397–3412. DOI: 10.1007/s10803-019-04261-0 PMID: 31630296

Buijs, P. C. M., Boot, E., Shugar, A., Fung, W. L. A., & Bassett, A. S. (2017). Internet safety issues for adolescents and adults with intellectual disabilities. *Journal of Applied Research in Intellectual Disabilities*, 30(2), 416–418. DOI: 10.1111/jar.12250 PMID: 26914835

Burke, M., Kraut, R., & Williams, D. (2010). Social use of computer-mediated communication by adults on the autism spectrum. In *Proceedings of the 2010 ACM Conference on Computer Supported Cooperative Work* (pp. 425-434). ACM. DOI: 10.1145/1718918.1718991

Cardy, R., Smith, C., Suganthan, H., Jiang, Z., Wang, B., Malihi, M., Anagnostou, E., & Kushki, A. (2023). Patterns and impact of technology use in autistic children. *Research in Autism Spectrum Disorders*, 108, 102253. Advance online publication. DOI: 10.1016/j.rasd.2023.102253

Carrington, S., Campbell, M., Saggers, B., Ashburner, J., Vicig, F., Dillon-Wallace, J., & Hwang, Y. S. (2017). Recommendations of school students with autism spectrum disorder and their parents in regard to bullying and cyberbullying prevention and intervention. *International Journal of Inclusive Education*, 21(10), 1045–1064. DOI: 10.1080/13603116.2017.1331381

Chadwick, D. D. (2019). Online risk for people with intellectual disabilities. *Tizard Learning Disability Review*, 24(4), 180–187. DOI: 10.1108/TLDR-03-2019-0008

Chadwick, D. D., Chapman, M., & Caton, S. (2019). Digital inclusion for people with an intellectual disability. In Attrill-Smith, A., Fullwood, C., Keep, M., & Kuss, D. J. (Eds.), *The Oxford handbook of cyberpsychology*. Oxford University Press., DOI: 10.1093/oxfordhb/9780198812746.013.17

Chadwick, D. D., Quinn, S., & Fullwood, C. (2017). Perceptions of the risks and benefits of Internet access and use by people with intellectual disabilities. *British Journal of Learning Disabilities*, 45(1), 21–31. DOI: 10.1111/bld.12170

Cheng, M. M., & Udry, R. (2005). Sexual experience of adolescents with low cognitive abilities in the U.S. *Journal of Developmental and Physical Disabilities*, 17(2), 155–172. DOI: 10.1007/s10882-005-3686-3

Christ, S. E., Holt, D. D., White, D. A., & Green, L. (2007). Inhibitory control in children with autism spectrum disorder. *Journal of Autism and Developmental Disorders*, 37(6), 1155–1165. DOI: 10.1007/s10803-006-0259-y PMID: 17066307

Daud, A., Omar, S. Z., Hassan, M. D. S., Bolong, J., & Teimouri, M. (2014). Parental mediation of children's positive use of the Internet. *Life Science Journal*, 11(8), 360–369.

Dempsey, A. G., Sulkowski, M. L., Nichols, R., & Storch, E. A. (2009). Differences between peer victimization in cyber and physical settings and associated psychosocial adjustment in early adolescence. *Psychology in the Schools*, 46(10), 962–972. DOI: 10.1002/pits.20437

Efstratopoulou, M., Delligianidou, S., & Sofologi, M. (2021). Exploring parents' experience on distance learning for students with ASD. *European Journal of Special Education Research*, 7(1), 14–23. DOI: 10.46827/ejse.v7i1.3525

Ennis-Cole, D. (2019). *Seeing autism through parents' feedback, sketchnotes, technology, and evidence-based practices*. Springer., DOI: 10.1007/978-3-030-15374-8

Folta, S. C., Bandini, L. G., Must, A., Pelletier, J., Ryan, K., & Curtin, C. (2022). Exploring leisure time use and impact on well-being among transition-age autistic youth. *Research in Autism Spectrum Disorders*, 96, 101996. Advance online publication. DOI: 10.1016/j.rasd.2022.101996

Gernsbacher, M. A., Geye, H. M., & Ellis Weismer, S. (2005). The role of language and communication impairments within autism. In Fletcher, P., & Miller, J. F. (Eds.), *Language disorders and developmental theory* (pp. 73–93). John Benjamins Publishing Company. DOI: 10.1075/tilar.4.06ger

Ghosh, A. K., Badillo-Urquiola, K., Guha, S., LaViola, J. J.Jr, & Wisniewski, P. J. (2018). Safety vs. surveillance: What children have to say about mobile apps for parental control. In *Proceedings of the 2018 CHI Conference on Human Factors in Computing Systems* (pp. 1-14). ACM. https://doi.org/DOI: 10.1145/3173574.3173698

Grove, R., Hoekstra, R. A., Wierda, M., & Begeer, S. (2018). Special interests and subjective wellbeing in autistic adults. *Autism Research*, 11(5), 766–775. DOI: 10.1002/aur.1931 PMID: 29427546

Helsper, E. J., Veltri, G. A., & Livingstone, S. (2024). Parental mediation of children's online risks: The role of parental risk perception, digital skills and risk experiences. *New Media & Society*, 26(1), 1–20. DOI: 10.1177/14614448241261945

Helverschou, S. B., Bakken, T. L., & Martinsen, H. (2011). Psychiatric disorders in people with autism spectrum disorders: Phenomenology and recognition. In Matson, J. L., & Sturmey, P. (Eds.), *International handbook of autism and pervasive developmental disorders* (pp. 53–74). Springer. DOI: 10.1007/978-1-4419-8065-6_5

Hemdan, A., Khalil, G., Amin, K., & Elwahab, M. A. (2023). A comprehensive review of autism spectrum disorder detection using the Internet of Things. *Sensors (Basel)*, 23(3), 1649. Advance online publication. DOI: 10.3390/s23031649 PMID: 36772688

Holfeld, B., & Mishna, F. (2018). Longitudinal associations in youth involvement as victimized, bullying, or witnessing cyberbullying. *Cyberpsychology, Behavior, and Social Networking*, 21(4), 234–239. DOI: 10.1089/cyber.2017.0369 PMID: 29624446

Holfeld, B., Stoesz, B., & Montgomery, J. (2019). Traditional and cyber bullying and victimization among youth with autism spectrum disorder: An investigation of the frequency, characteristics, and psychosocial correlates. *Journal on Developmental Disabilities*, 24(2), 61–76.

Isler, A., Beytut, D., Tas, F., & Conk, Z. (2009). A study on sexuality with the parents of adolescents with intellectual disability. *Sexuality and Disability*, 27(4), 229–237. DOI: 10.1007/s11195-009-9130-3

Just, M., & Berg, T. (2017). Keeping children safe online: Understanding the concerns of carers of children with autism. In Bernhaupt, R., Dalvi, G., Joshi, A., Balkrishan, D. K., O'Neill, J., & Winckler, M. (Eds.), *Human-Computer Interaction – INTERACT 2017* (pp. 34–53). Springer., DOI: 10.1007/978-3-319-67687-6_3

Kowalski, R. M., & Fedina, C. (2011). Cyber bullying in ADHD and Asperger Syndrome populations. *Research in Autism Spectrum Disorders*, 5(3), 1201–1208. DOI: 10.1016/j.rasd.2011.01.007

Kowalski, R. M., Giumetti, G. W., Schroeder, A. N., & Lattanner, M. R. (2014). Bullying in the digital age: A critical review and meta-analysis of cyberbullying research among youth. *Psychological Bulletin*, 140(4), 1073–1137. DOI: 10.1037/a0035618 PMID: 24512111

Kuo, M. H., Orsmond, G. I., Coster, W. J., & Cohn, E. S. (2014). Media use among adolescents with autism spectrum disorder. *Autism*, 18(8), 914–923. DOI: 10.1177/1362361313497832 PMID: 24142797

Lampri, S., Peristeri, E., Marinis, T., & Andreou, M. (2024). Figurative language processing in autism spectrum disorders: A review. *Autism Research*, 17(4), 674–689. DOI: 10.1002/aur.3069 PMID: 38071498

Lei, J., Leigh, E., Charman, T., Russell, A., & Hollocks, M. J. (2024). Understanding the relationship between social camouflaging in autism and safety behaviours in social anxiety in autistic and non-autistic adolescents. *Journal of Child Psychology and Psychiatry, and Allied Disciplines*, 65(3), 285–297. DOI: 10.1111/jcpp.13884 PMID: 37632264

Livingstone, S., & Helsper, E. (2008). Parental mediation of children's internet use. *Journal of Broadcasting & Electronic Media*, 52(4), 581–599. DOI: 10.1080/08838150802437396

Livingstone, S., Ólafsson, K., Helsper, E. J., Lupiáñez-Villanueva, F., Veltri, G. A., & Folkvord, F. (2017). Maximizing opportunities and minimizing risks for children online: The role of digital skills in emerging strategies of parental mediation. *Journal of Communication*, 67(1), 82–105. DOI: 10.1111/jcom.12277

Macmillan, K., Berg, T., Just, M., & Stewart, M. E. (2020). Are autistic children more vulnerable online? Relating autism to online safety, child wellbeing and parental risk management. In *Proceedings of the 11th Nordic Conference on Human-Computer Interaction: Shaping Experiences,* Shaping Society (pp. 1-11). ACM. https://doi.org/DOI: 10.1145/3419249.3420160

Macmillan, K., Berg, T., Just, M., & Stewart, M. E. (2022). Online safety experiences of autistic young people: An interpretative phenomenological analysis. *Research in Autism Spectrum Disorders*, 96, 101995. Advance online publication. DOI: 10.1016/j.rasd.2022.101995

Mai, A., Guelmino, L., Pfeffer, K., Weippl, E., & Krombholz, K. (2022). Mental models of the Internet and its online risks: Children and their parent(s). In Moallem, A. (Ed.), Lecture Notes in Computer Science: Vol. 13333. *HCI for Cybersecurity, Privacy and Trust. HCII 2022* (pp. 42–61). Springer., DOI: 10.1007/978-3-031-05563-8_4

Martins, N., King, A., & Beights, R. (2020). Audiovisual media content preferences of children with autism spectrum disorders: Insights from parental interviews. *Journal of Autism and Developmental Disorders*, 50(9), 3092–3100. DOI: 10.1007/s10803-019-03987-1 PMID: 30905049

Mazurek, M. O., Shattuck, P. T., Wagner, M., & Cooper, B. P. (2012). Prevalence and correlates of screen-based media use among youths with autism spectrum disorders. *Journal of Autism and Developmental Disorders*, 42(8), 1757–1767. DOI: 10.1007/s10803-011-1413-8 PMID: 22160370

Mazurek, M. O., Shattuck, P. T., Wagner, M., & Cooper, B. P. (2012). Prevalence and correlates of screen-based media use among youths with autism spectrum disorders. *Journal of Autism and Developmental Disorders*, 42(8), 1757–1767. DOI: 10.1007/s10803-011-1413-8 PMID: 22160370

Mazurek, M. O., & Wenstrup, C. (2013). Television, video game and social media use among children with ASD and typically developing siblings. *Journal of Autism and Developmental Disorders*, 43(6), 1258–1271. DOI: 10.1007/s10803-012-1659-9 PMID: 23001767

Mitchell, K. J., Finkelhor, D., & Wolak, J. (2001). Risk factors for and impact of online sexual solicitation of youth. *Journal of the American Medical Association*, 285(23), 3011–3014. DOI: 10.1001/jama.285.23.3011 PMID: 11410100

Modecki, K. L., Minchin, J., Harbaugh, A. G., Guerra, N. G., & Runions, K. C. (2014). Bullying prevalence across contexts: A meta-analysis measuring cyber and traditional bullying. *The Journal of Adolescent Health*, 55(5), 602–611. DOI: 10.1016/j.jadohealth.2014.06.007 PMID: 25168105

Murphy, G. H., & O'Callaghan, A. (2004). Capacity of adults with intellectual disabilities to consent to sexual relationships. *Psychological Medicine*, 34(7), 1347–1357. DOI: 10.1017/S0033291704001941 PMID: 15697061

Murphy, G. H., & O'Callaghan, A. C. (2004). Capacity of adults with intellectual disabilities to consent to sexual relationships. *Psychological Medicine*, 34(7), 1347–1357. DOI: 10.1017/S0033291704001941 PMID: 15697061

Neupane, A., Satvat, K., Saxena, N., Stavrinos, D., & Bishop, H. J. (2018). Do social disorders facilitate social engineering?: A case study of autism and phishing attacks. In *Proceedings of the 34th Annual Computer Security Applications Conference* (pp. 467-477). Association for Computing Machinery. https://doi.org/DOI: 10.1145/3274694.3274730

Normand, C. L., & Sallafranque-St-Louis, F. (2016). Cybervictimization of young people with an intellectual or developmental disability: Risks specific to sexual solicitation. *Journal of Applied Research in Intellectual Disabilities*, 29(2), 99–110. DOI: 10.1111/jar.12163 PMID: 25871891

Nuske, H. J., Pellecchia, M., Kane, C., Seidman, M., Maddox, B. B., Freeman, L. M., Rump, K., Reisinger, E. M., Xie, M., & Mandell, D. S. (2020). Self-regulation is bi-directionally associated with cognitive development in children with autism. *Journal of Applied Developmental Psychology*, 68, 101139. Advance online publication. DOI: 10.1016/j.appdev.2020.101139 PMID: 34177028

Priya, N., & Maheswari, P. U. (2024). Influence of different parental mediation strategies on adolescents' hedonistic smartphone use: Parent-adolescent reports. *Mobile Media & Communication*, 12(1), 1–22. DOI: 10.1177/20501579241260649

Rice, M. F. (2024). Diffractive perspectives on parents' role in inclusive online, distance, and digital education. *Computers in the Schools*, 41(2), 145–163. DOI: 10.1080/07380569.2024.2325433

Rice, M. F., Cantergiani, K., & Macias, D. (2023). A research-based conceptual framework for inclusive K-12 online, distance, and digital education. *Journal of Research on Technology in Education*, 1–17. Advance online publication. DOI: 10.1080/15391523.2023.2264982

Rocheleau, J. N., & Chiasson, S. (2022). Privacy and safety on social networking sites: Autistic and non-autistic teenagers' attitudes and behaviors. *ACM Transactions on Computer-Human Interaction*, 29(1), 1–39. DOI: 10.1145/3469859

Romano, M., & Porto, M. D. (2016). Discourse, cognition and society. In Romano, M., & Porto, M. D. (Eds.), *Exploring discourse strategies in social and cognitive interaction* (Vol. 4, pp. 1–20). John Benjamins Publishing Company. DOI: 10.1075/pbns.262.01rom

Sasson, H., & Mesch, G. (2014). Parental mediation, peer norms and risky online behavior among adolescents. *Computers in Human Behavior*, 33, 32–38. DOI: 10.1016/j.chb.2013.12.025

Schultz, S. M., Jacobs, G., & Schultz, J. (2013). A promising practice: Using Facebook as a communication and social networking tool. *Rural Special Education Quarterly*, 32(4), 38–44. DOI: 10.1177/875687051303200405

Shin, W., & Ismail, N. (2014). Exploring the role of parents and peers in young adolescents' risk taking on social networking sites. *Cyberpsychology, Behavior, and Social Networking*, 17(9), 578–583. DOI: 10.1089/cyber.2014.0095 PMID: 25126969

Shin, W., & Lwin, M. O. (2017). How does "talking about the internet with others" affect teenagers' experience of online risks? The role of active mediation by parents, peers, and school teachers. *New Media & Society*, 19(7), 1109–1126. DOI: 10.1177/1461444815626612

Steinfeld, N. (2021). Parental mediation of adolescent Internet use: Combining strategies to promote awareness, autonomy and self-regulation in preparing youth for life on the web. *Education and Information Technologies*, 26(2), 1897–1920. DOI: 10.1007/s10639-020-10342-w

Strohmeier, D., & Gradinger, P. (2022). Cyberbullying and cyber victimization as online risks for children and adolescents. *European Psychologist*, 27(2), 141–150. DOI: 10.1027/1016-9040/a000479

Tiego, J., Testa, R., Bellgrove, M. A., Pantelis, C., & Whittle, S. (2018). A hierarchical model of inhibitory control. *Frontiers in Psychology*, 9, 1339. Advance online publication. DOI: 10.3389/fpsyg.2018.01339 PMID: 30123154

Wachs, S., & Wright, M. F. (2019). The moderation of online disinhibition and sex on the relationship between online hate victimization and perpetration. *Cyberpsychology, Behavior, and Social Networking*, 22(5), 300–306. DOI: 10.1089/cyber.2018.0551 PMID: 30945942

Wang, J., Iannotti, R. J., & Nansel, T. R. (2009). School bullying among adolescents in the United States: Physical, verbal, relational, and cyber. *The Journal of Adolescent Health*, 45(4), 368–375. DOI: 10.1016/j.jadohealth.2009.03.021 PMID: 19766941

Wasserman, D. (2019). A case for greater risk tolerance in Internet use by adults with intellectual disabilities: A comment on Chalghoumi et al. *Ethics & Behavior*, 29(3), 223–226. DOI: 10.1080/10508422.2018.1522256

Wisniewski, P., Ghosh, A. K., Rosson, M. B., Xu, H., & Carroll, J. M. (2017). Parental control vs. teen self-regulation: Is there a middle ground for mobile online safety? In *Proceedings of the 2017 ACM Conference on Computer Supported Cooperative Work and Social Computing* (pp. 51-69). ACM. https://doi.org/DOI: 10.1145/2998181.2998352

Wisniewski, P., Xu, H., Rosson, M. B., & Carroll, J. M. (2017). Parents just don't understand: Why teens don't talk to parents about their online risk experiences. In *Proceedings of the 2017 ACM Conference on Computer Supported Cooperative Work and Social Computing* (pp. 523-540). ACM. https://doi.org/DOI: 10.1145/2998181.2998236

World Congress: Child Dignity in the Digital World. (2017, October 6). *The Declaration of Rome*. Retrieved from https://www.childdignity.com/declaration-of-rome

Ybarra, M. L., & Mitchell, K. J. (2004). Online aggressor/targets, aggressors, and targets: A comparison of associated youth characteristics. *Journal of Child Psychology and Psychiatry, and Allied Disciplines*, 45(7), 1308–1316. DOI: 10.1111/j.1469-7610.2004.00328.x PMID: 15335350

Chapter 3
Neurodivergent Students' Views on Internet Threats: A Call for Research

Bessie Stone
Queensland University of Technology, Australia

Beth Saggers
Queensland University of Technology, Australia

Marilyn Campbell
https://orcid.org/0000-0002-4477-2366
Queensland University of Technology, Australia

Christine Yates
Queensland University of Technology, Australia

ABSTRACT

School-aged students are an especially vulnerable group to internet threats such as inappropriate content, potentially harmful interactions, addictive behaviors, and age-inappropriate marketing. Internet threats have negative implications on students' social, emotional, psychological, and academic lives. However, there is scant research seeking students' voices regarding these issues and a lack of neurodivergent student representation. Current initiatives in research and education that focus on internet safety, inclusive education, and neurodiversity emphasize the importance of enabling students to share their perspectives in meaningful ways. Amplifying the inclusion of neurodivergent student voices is significant, because without understanding their perspectives, adults may not effectively communicate strategies to manage internet threats to those who most need it. This topic requires further investigation to ensure a nuanced approach to internet safety messages that responds to the needs of the students who adults are hoping to reach.

DOI: 10.4018/979-8-3693-4191-9.ch003

INTRODUCTION

As adults we are aware of the many threats the Internet can pose to students. In this chapter, we will review relevant literature related to these threats and discuss the implications of these threats for students from neurodivergent backgrounds. We will then report on considerations when conducting future research into neurodivergent students' perceptions of Internet threats. Neurodivergent students' perspectives can be beneficial to better inform policy and implement targeted and supportive strategies for safe and supportive online engagement on the Internet.

The concept of neurodiversity highlights that diversity in thoughts, communication, and interactions; uniqueness in cognitive traits; and variations in learning styles are important and valued (den Houting; 2019; Dwyer, 2022; Santhanam, 2023). Neurodivergent students are defined as learners who experience diversity in their cognitive processing and whose neurological development differ from what is considered as typical patterns of brain function or considered neurotypical (Fung et al., 2022; Leadbitter et al., 2021). Autistic students are a key student cohort who identify as neurodivergent as autistic students' brains often exhibit distinct differences in structure, function, and connectivity when compared to the brain of neurotypical students (Pellicano & Houting, 2022). Therefore, there may be differences in how neurodivergent students perceive, process, and respond to Internet threats (Banerjee, 2023). It is important for us to consider the perspectives of neurodivergent students about threats to safe Internet engagement because this could inform our understanding about Internet safety education into diverse education settings with more nuanced and responsive messages (Lau et al., 2023; Lebenhagen, 2020; Macmillan et al., 2022). Amplifying student voices and different student cohorts can help support our educative endeavors and ensure they are responsive to the needs of neurodivergent student groups.

There is scant research on Internet threats which includes student voice. Therefore, this chapter, linked to an early career researcher funded project, presents a call for research that asks neurodivergent students for their perspectives regarding what they consider to be threats to themselves and others on the Internet, reports on methodological processes that have been used in our preliminary work, and proposes an innovative framework, called Inclusive New Literacies (Stone, 2018; Stone & Saggers, 2023) which could be used to conduct this kind of research in the future. The framework is aimed at promoting inclusivity of all students to inform new Internet safety initiatives, educational policies, and research into Internet safety with more nuanced messages based on a student voice approach. In addition, the chapter proposes using d/Discourse theoretical framework (Gee, 2004, 2015; Gee & Handford, 2012), and presents some methodological suggestions to support amplifying neurodivergent students' views on the threats of the Internet that can inform preventative Internet safety education for this student cohort.

Students' Use of the Internet

Over the past few decades, across the world, students have embraced the use of the Internet (Dolly & Samantaray, 2024; Third, 2016). The range of activities that students engage in individually or as a member of a group and the length of time they engage online varies. While there has been a shift in the different social media sites that students use, social media applications such as Facebook, YouTube, Instagram, WhatsApp, and Snapchat are some of the more recent online technologies that students engage with for communication and entertainment (Alhujaili et al., 2022; Anderson & Jiang, 2018; Chapin, 2021; Torrijos-Fincias et al., 2021). Similarly, students use Internet websites such as roblox.

com and twitch.tv as resources for live streaming, communication, and video gaming (Anderson, 2018; Hernández et al., 2022).

Internationally, the benefits of Internet engagement for students and opportunities for students to promote numerous daily online access and engagement activities through ubiquitous and mobile technologies are well documented (Anderson & Jiang, 2018; Gaspard, 2020; Kopecký et al., 2021; Third, 2016). The prevalence of these forms of digital interactions has notably surged over the past five years. Within the Australian context, the Internet holds a pivotal role in the lives of Australian students aged 8–17 years old, as most Australian students use it to learn, play, socially interact, and be entertained (eSafety Commissioner, 2022). Students can also benefit from Internet content by using it to acquire and disseminate knowledge, and to access formal and informal educational resources (Gaspard, 2020). In addition, students use the Internet as a resource for finding creative outlets, informal learning about topics such as languages, fashion, fitness, and learning to play instruments (Cernikova et al., 2018; Gaspard, 2020). Moreover, many students search for mental, physical, and sexual health information while a minority of students engage online to participate in creative or civic activities. For example, studies conducted in the US, UK, Canada, Australia, Spain, Denmark, and Ireland revealed that students used the Internet to acquire medical information, explore health information, and to access legal and civil information (Denvir, 2016; Freeman et al., 2018; Vejmelka & Matković, 2021). The Internet also provides opportunities for students to engage with communities; build and sustain relationships; and stay connected with their peers, friends, families, and social circles (Gaspard, 2020). As engagement with the Internet continues to increase significantly there is no doubt that the Internet will continue to play an important role in the lives of students for learning, socialization, playing, and entertainment (eSafety Commissioner, 2022; Hamid et al., 2015; Pouwels et al., 2021; Torrijos-Fincias et al., 2021).

Although some students perceive the benefits of the Internet and have reported positive views about it, they are also cautious and have reported negative online experiences and engagement and that the Internet can be harmful (Cernikova et al., 2018; eSafety Commissioner, 2022; Guerra et al., 2019; Savoia et al., 2021). Similarly, there are long-standing concerns from adults that as students engage in a wider variety of online activities, they become more vulnerable to Internet threats (Anderson & Jiang, 2018; eSafety Commissioner, 2022; Gaspard, 2020; Global Kids Online, 2016).

What are Internet Threats?

As adults we are aware of the potentially dangerous, harmful, risky, negative, or bothersome experiences that exposure and encounters in online digital environments can have on students (Beyens et al., 2015; Choo et al., 2015). For example, the prevalence of exposure and access to Internet threats such as drug use, gory and violent material, self-harm and suicidal behaviors, sexual images, and sexual messages when using the Internet is reportedly high among Australian students who are 14–17 years old (eSafety Commissioner, 2022). Researchers have classified experiences which students could encounter into four key areas: i) content, ii) contact, iii) conduct, and iv) contract (Livingstone & Stoilova, 2021). Please see Figure 1.

Figure 1. The CO:RE Classification of Online Risk to Children

CO RE	Content Child engages with or is exposed to potentially harmful content	Contact Child experiences or is targeted by potentially harmful *adult* contact	Conduct Child witnesses, participates in or is a victim of potentially harmful *peer* conduct	Contract Child is party to or exploited by potentially harmful contract
Aggressive	Violent, gory, graphic, racist, hateful or extremist information and communication	Harassment, stalking, hateful behaviour, unwanted or excessive surveillance	Bullying, hateful or hostile communication or peer activity e.g. trolling, exclusion, shaming	Identity theft, fraud, phishing, scams, hacking, blackmail, security risks
Sexual	Pornography (harmful or illegal), sexualization of culture, oppressive body image norms	Sexual harassment, sexual grooming, sextortion, the generation and sharing of child sexual abuse material	Sexual harassment, non-consensual sexual messaging, adverse sexual pressures	Trafficking for purposes of sexual exploitation, streaming (paid-for) child sexual abuse
Values	Mis/disinformation, age-inappropriate marketing or user-generated content	Ideological persuasion or manipulation, radicalisation and extremist recruitment	Potentially harmful user communities e.g. self-harm, anti-vaccine, adverse peer pressures	Gambling, filter bubbles, micro-targeting, dark patterns shaping persuasion or purchase
Cross-cutting	**Privacy violations** (interpersonal, institutional, commercial) **Physical and mental health risks** (e.g., sedentary lifestyle, excessive screen use, isolation, anxiety) **Inequalities and discrimination** (in/exclusion, exploiting vulnerability, algorithmic bias/predictive analytics)			

From The 4Cs: Classifying online risk to children (CO:RE Short Report Series on Key Topics). By S. Livingstone and M. Stoilova. 2021. Leibniz-Institut für Medienforschung| Hans-Bredow-Institut (https://doi.org/10.21241/ssoar.71817). Copyright 2021 by Leibniz-Institut für Medienforschung| Hans-Bredow-Institut. Reprinted with permission.

Categorizing Internet threats into these four dimensions provides a framework to understand the different kinds of threats that students may face and to inform initiatives to create safer and more positive and beneficial online environments for all students. In addition, this categorization also makes it possible to understand Internet threats and their implications from students' perspectives (El Asam & Katz, 2018; Jang & Ko, 2023).

INTERNET THREATS AND IMPLICATIONS FOR STUDENTS

Exposure to inappropriate content (e.g, sexual images and messages), potentially harmful interactions (e.g., cyberbullying, behaviors, stalking, and harassment) and age-inappropriate marketing (e.g., advertising alcohol and drug use) can have severe and long-lasting implications for students (Tao et al., 2022). For example, these threats lead to emotional and psychological implications such as emotional distress, lowered self-esteem, sadness, and anger which negatively impact on students' mental health and wellbeing (Hunehäll Berndtsson & Odenbring, 2021; Vejmelka & Matković, 2021; Weeks & Subrahmanyam, 2019). Additionally, the pervasive nature of exposure to these Internet threats erodes students' safety and trust in online environments by leaving students isolated from peers and trusted adults and compromising their wellbeing and ability to report risks. This is concerning because students often assess the trustworthiness of online people by observing other people's profiles, activities, and behaviors (Jozsa et al., 2021). Therefore, Internet threats can remain unchecked and normalized, leaving students increasingly vulnerable to potential exploitation, manipulation, coercion, and weakened ability to safeguard themselves from these risks (Ahmadu & Kontagora, 2021; Cernikova et al., 2018; van der Hof,

2020). There are also significant negative impacts of exposure to these threats on students' academic performance and social relationships, as students may experience challenges with focusing and engaging meaningfully in their studies and interactions. It is important to explore the implications of Internet threats in terms of risky sexual behaviors, misconduct, and drug and alcohol use as these threats often occur together (Kwak et al., 2022).

The implications of exposure to Internet threats can be even more serious for neurodivergent students, such as autistic students and students with ADHD, because of unique cognitive, behavioral, and social communication. The combination of these challenges means that they may experience greater degrees of consequences than their neurotypical peers with experiences such as sexting and sexualized behaviors, cyberbullying, addictive behaviors, and alcohol and drug marketing, which may lead to increased vulnerability to manipulation and exploitation (Chou et al., 2017; Curry et al., 2021; van der Hof, 2020). We need to know if neurodivergent students experience differences in either severity or different implications because of their neurodivergence. We now present literature that explore the same Internet threats discussed above including sexting and sexualized content, cyberbullying, addictive behaviors, and alcohol and drug marketing in terms of what research has found for students including neurodivergent students.

Sexting and Sexualized Content

While the Internet and digital technologies offer important opportunities for communication and connections, students are increasingly dependent on social media sites, instant messaging, cyber technology, and online platforms for friendships, new patterns of sexual relations, and romantic partner-seeking despite perceived threats (Brandell & Brown, 2015; Jozsa et al., 2021). Students' motivation to use the Internet to find same-age sexual peers or strangers for sexual relationships has added developmental complexity to their transition to young adulthood (Lloyd, 2020). In a study conducted by Jozsa and colleague (2021) the findings indicate that student participants engaged with adults who they described as risky or untrustworthy. Participants in the study also revealed that adults demonstrated overly sexual behaviors in online interactions and other people's misrepresentation of their online identities made them feel unsafe. Despite this concern, the participants seldom mentioned sexual health risks and the legal risks of sexual interaction with adults (Jozsa et al., 2021). The study suggested that although some students' sexual needs are met through social media interactions, some students may not be equipped with the knowledge and skills to engage safely in sexualized online adult spaces. These findings suggest that Internet safety education should address students' online sexual safety (Jozsa et al., 2021).

Sexting, the practice of using social media and the Internet to exchange and view sexualized content is prevalent among students (Hunehäll Berndtsson & Odenbring, 2021; Scholes-Balog et al., 2016; Strassberg et al., 2017). Research by Weeks and Subrahmanyam (2019) indicates that Snapchat and WhatsApp are preferred social media for sexting by some students because they perceive that messages sent through these platforms are safe and temporarily stored, without permanent implications. Internet threats including inappropriate exposure to sexual images and messages, are highly prevalent among Australian students aged 14–17 years (eSafety Commissioner, 2022), and parents of students in this age group are also often unaware that their children have been exposed to sexual online material despite most parents having conversations with their children about inappropriate content online (Ahern, 2016; Corcoran et al., 2022).

Risky sexual behavior has been linked with increased daily Internet usage (Kwak et al., 2022). Research by Hunehäll Berndtsson and Odenbring (2021) and Strassberg et al., (2017) indicates that the sharing and consumption of online sexualized content is widespread among students, especially girls. In addition, Weeks and Subrahmanyam (2019) found a correlation between students' accidental exposure or intentional viewing and posting of sexualized and sexually explicit content and pornography on social media and an increased likelihood of engaging in non-relational, recreational, or casual sex. Implications of students engaging with or being exposed to sexual Internet content threats include being coerced and blackmailed, being victims of revenge pornography, and the unsolicited sharing of students' private images (Bates, 2017; Lloyd, 2020). These implications can impact on students' emotional wellbeing, mental health, friendships, academic success, and privacy, which highlight the importance of hearing students' voices about the potential sexual risks that they face and how safe and responsible online behaviors can be encouraged (Bates, 2017).

Neurodivergent Students: Sexualized Content and Diverse Sexual Orientations

As a growing proportion of neurodivergent students use the Internet, there has been the development of user-friendly sites to support students who experience communication challenges and lower levels of literacy (Normand & Sallafranque-St-Louis, 2016). Many of the risk factors associated with sexting and sexualized content found in the literature are applicable to neurodivergent students. However, there is a consensus among researchers that for neurodivergent students there is a greater prevalence of sexual and physical abuse; seeking companionship from strangers online; a lack of sexual knowledge and the legal aspects of sexuality; and greater likelihood of social isolation because of the perception of few opportunities to have romantic or sexual partners, when compared with their neurotypical peers (Normand & Sallafranque-St-Louis, 2016; Smusz et al., 2024).

In a study by Smusz et al., (2024) some neurodivergent students reported challenges with recognizing appropriate versus inappropriate sexual behaviors. This is concerning because over the recent years, there has been an increased research interest concerning the possession of extreme sexual material by neurodivergent individuals and the risk of users of child sexual exploitation material for neurodivergent individuals (Allely et al., 2019; Brown, 2024; Fortin et al., 2019). There are further concerns because of the rapid growth in technological advances, the potential sexual and sexualized threats for neurodivergent students in using the Internet, and the possible limitations associated with detecting these risks (Higham et al., 2021). The literature reviewed indicate that neurodivergent students may be vulnerable to this threat because of challenges with mental health issues such as anxiety, social and emotional abilities, theory of mind, decoding social cues and gestures, and preoccupation with things (Allely & Creaby-Attwood, 2016; Smusz et al., 2024). Neurodivergent students may also have limited sexuality education which may push them toward alternative means of learning about sexuality such as pornography (Smusz et al., 2024). Studies have highlighted the importance of prioritizing sexual health screening, repetitive and individualized sexual education and early intervention strategies that affirm sexual orientations and address support in the following areas: the development of sexual knowledge; modelling of socially desirable behaviors and; social-skills training relating to interpersonal skills, gender and sexual identity, masturbation, and contraceptives (Allely & Creaby-Attwood, 2016; Beddows & Brooks, 2015; Smusz et al., 2024; Weir et al., 2021a).

There appears to be a higher rate of neurodivergent students who also identify with diverse genders and sexualities (Warrier et al., 2020; Walsh et al., 2018). This is important because sexual and gender diverse neurodivergent students use the Internet more prolifically than their peers and are a vulnerable population in this age group (Jozsa et al., 2021; Kuo et al., 2014). The prevalence of students who identify as neurodivergent with diverse sexual orientations and gender identities is on the increase (Weir et al., 2021a). Additionally, neurodivergent students are overrepresented in the LGBTQIA+ group (Hillier et al., 2020; Kallitsounaki et al., 2023). Research indicates that gender diverse individuals are more likely to be autistic and report autistic traits compared to cisgender individuals (Walsh, et al., 2018; Warrier et al., 2020). Similarly, neurodivergent individuals have a higher tendency to be gender-diverse than neurotypical individuals (Strang et al., 2018; Warrier et al., 2020). Likewise, the existing research that focuses on the intersectionality between students in neurodivergent and LGBTQIA+ communities is growing (Al-Faham, et al., 2019; Hillier et al., 2020; Skagerberg et al., 2015). Awareness of the intersectional crossover between the LGBTQIA+ diversity and neurodivergence has been highlighted by organizations such as Autism Spectrum Australia which marched at Mardi Gras and has an LGBTIQA+ committee (Autism Spectrum Australia, 2023). Most research that focuses on the perceived threats of social media, social networking, and online video gaming are from the perspectives of neurotypical students and less on the perceived threats for a more diverse range of youth such as neurodivergent students and students with diverse sexual orientations and gender identities (Alhujaili et al., 2022; eSafety Commissioner, 2022; Jozsa et al., 2021).

It is important to consider the intersectional crossover between the LGBTQIA+ diversity and neurodivergence within the context of Internet threats because of negative social, emotional, virtual, physical, psychological, and academic implications for neurodivergent students. Students with diverse sexual orientations and gender identities are at higher risk of encountering predatory behavior, homophobia, gender-based discrimination, cyberbullying, online hate speech, online harassment, and unsolicited exposure of personal information through online communities, messaging applications, social media platforms, and online forums (Abreu & Kenny, 2018; Dias et al., 2021; Wagaman, 2020). Research also highlights the prevalence of online discrimination and harassment based on gender, sexuality, and disability (eSafety Commissioner, 2023; Evelyn et al., 2022; Parliament UK, 2019).

The amount of screen time students spend on digital devices and parental supervision are the two main predictors of their involvement in and exposure to Internet threats such as online grooming and harassment (Khurana et al., 2015; Tintori et al., 2023). These kinds of threats may be generated and created by users, including by students, and shared extensively or remain confined within a small circle of people (Livingstone & Haddon, 2009; Livingstone & Stoilova, 2021). The mobility and private use of students' digital devices such as smartphones, laptops, and tablets reduce capacity for adult supervision and awareness of Internet content threats and make students more vulnerable to harmful and inappropriate online content (Kopecký et al., 2021). These findings are significant because they highlight that being both neurodivergent and sexual and gender diverse can intensify the negative implications of Internet threats. Initial findings have prompted an urgent call for further research to understand the inequalities and challenges that sexual and gender diverse and neurodivergent students may face (Bennett & Goodall, 2016; Dewinter et al., 2017; Øien et al., 2018; Shumer et al., 2016).

Cyberbullying

In findings from current global research, students reported the Internet as a platform for perpetrating and experiencing cyberbullying (Alotaibi, 2019; Baldry et al., 2018; Lee & Shin, 2017; Tao et al., 2022; Vejmelka & Matković, 2021). A study by Tao and colleagues (2022) revealed a correlation between the amount of time that students spent using digital devices for both educational or recreational reasons, and a higher likelihood of experiencing cyberbullying (either as perpetrators or targets). Social network sites such as Facebook have become dominant platforms which expose students to newer and higher levels of Internet conduct threats such as cyberbullying and exposure to unsolicited sexual messages that were not possible in the physical and analogue world (Chapin, 2021). Students who experience cyberbullying are more likely to commit self-harming behaviors and attempt suicide (Yang, et al., 2021). Forms of cyberbullying such as verbal harassment and social exclusion lead to significant emotional distress such as lowered self-esteem, sadness, and anger, reduced task engagement, increased stress levels and negatively impact on students' well-being (Alhujailli et al., 2020; Tao et al., 2022).

In a study with Australian students, Black and colleagues (2022) used a story writing method within a focus group discussion. The participants used stories to describe situations such as meeting strangers online and incidents where people were hurt in online contexts, acts and consequences of cyberbullying, and the hurtful exchange of words online. They revealed that some threats to safe online engagement included rumors being spread, personal accounts being hacked, unconsented sharing of photos, unauthorized appropriation of online identities and data, catfishing, breakdown of peer support, and exclusion from peer groups (Black et al., 2022).

In comparison, a study by Chapin (2021) found that 30% of students reported that they were affected by cyberbullying, however only 12.5% stopped using Facebook and 18% informed authority figures such as a parent or school official. The findings also suggested that students who experience cyberbullying may experience sleep disturbances, low self-esteem, self-harming behaviors, and headaches, and that students who are cyberbullied may perpetrate violence as adults. The study also revealed that despite frequent use of and exposure to Facebook, some students exhibited increased third-person perception, believing that other people were more likely to experience negative effects of using Facebook such as cyberbullying than themselves. However, other students exhibited decreased third-person perception which is associated with self-protective and precautionary strategies such as deleting friends, blocking abusive users, and reactionary behaviors such as quitting Facebook.

In contrast, a study by Alotaibi (2019) revealed a high prevalence of cyberbullying among students, with 74.5% of the surveyed respondents reporting being both victims and perpetrators. Attitude, perceived behavioral control, social media use, lack of parental controls, and insufficient regulations significantly influenced the students' behavioral intention to engage in cyberbullying. Findings from this study also showed that the incidence of cyberbullying, whether students were perpetrators or victims, reduced their academic performance and engagement in academic tasks, and led to overall lowered academic achievement (Alotaibi, 2019). Toa and colleagues (2022) argue that students need to acquire digital literacy skills to mitigate cyberbullying rather than parent restrictive control because strict parental restrictions on Internet engagement may prevent students from acquiring digital literacy skills that are necessary to navigate safely online. Internet contact threats such as cyberbullying can be hurtful with lasting emotional and academic consequences on students (Tao et al., 2022). More research that draws on students' voices about these threats is needed to support students with effective coping and literacy skills to mitigate the effects of these consequences (Alhujailli et al., 2020; Yang et al., 2021).

Neurodivergent Students and Cyberbullying

The prevalence and implications of cyberbullying among students vary according to factors such as disability, neurodiversity, obesity, gender, and sexual orientation (Baldry et al., 2018; Lee & Shin, 2017; Yang et al., 2021). This is significant because some neurodivergent students frequent the Internet more than their neurotypical peers and consequently may be more susceptible to higher levels of Internet threats (Alhujaili et al., 2022; Kuo et al., 2014). Some neurodivergent students spend more than five hours per day on social media sites such as YouTube primarily for social interactions and entertainment purposes (Alhujaili et al., 2022).

There has been increased attention to cyberbullying incidents among neurodivergent students because of its impact on their social, emotional, and academic wellbeing (Carrington et al., 2017). For example, autistic students experience higher levels of depression, anxiety, and social difficulties resulting from cyberbullying compared with their neurotypical peers. Although Internet threats such as cyberbullying occur outside of formal educational contexts, the serious implications on neurodivergent students extend to school and have enormous impact on students' academic and social success (Carrington et al., 2017). The negative effect of cyberbullying on students' psychological outcomes and students' neurodivergence needs to be considered in developing strategies to better understand, prevent, and address cyberbullying.

Addictive Behaviors

Research indicates that students are increasingly becoming drawn and addicted to screens, feeling a compulsion to maintain relationships through digital platforms, stay constantly connected and entertained online, and to remain updated with information through technology (Gonzalez et al., 2023; Torrijos-Fincias et al., 2021). Addictive behaviors may be characterized by components such as diminished inhibitory control, salience, craving, mood modification, withdrawal, and relapse (Brand et al., 2019; Hirota et al., 2020). Students may become preoccupied with the Internet when offline and may fantasize about being online. Addictive behaviors may be presented in the form of excessive Internet use, online gambling, excessive smartphone use, and gaming disorders such as being hooked on online video games (Bányai et al., 2019; Derevensky et al., 2019; Savolainen et al., 2018; Torrijos-Fincias et al., 2021). There is a correlation between extended time spent online and the prevalence of greater vulnerability to Internet addiction, online gambling, and gaming disorder (Derevensky et al., 2019; Gaspard, 2020).

Research findings point to the seamless integration of interactive online gambling into students' lives and a concerning increase in gambling among students (Derevensky et al., 2019; Savolainen et al., 2018). A study by Gonzalez and colleagues (2023) indicates that students who were at significant risk of participation in problematic online gambling were students who i) had a male gender identity, ii) were from higher years of schooling, iii) presented with problematic Internet use, and iv) came from an immigrant background. Online gambling is also associated with other Internet threats such as sexting, cyberbullying, and engaging and meeting up with strangers (Gonzalez et al., 2023). Students have revealed factors that drive their gambling range from entertainment, thrill seeking, curiosity, social interaction, financial incentives, and skill development (Gonzalez et al., 2023).

Research reveals that many students have demonstrated a limited understanding of gambling, its implications, consequences, and the importance of quitting and exercising restraint while ahead (Derevensky et al., 2019; Savolainen et al., 2018). Students may underestimate, disregard, or be uninformed about potential risks and dangers associated with Internet gambling such as financial loss, pleasure seeking, potential addiction, negative impact on schoolwork, and relationship and social implications (Derevensky et al., 2019; Gonzalez et al., 2023). Strict rules, and restrictive bans and regulations set by parents may not be effective to reduce Internet addictions such as extreme gaming and problematic Internet gambling or their implications (Alqahtani, 2016; Choo et al., 2015; Gonzalez et al., 2023). Students have reported that parent-child bond and parent-child relationship are important to reduce and prevent Internet addictions such as pathological gaming therefore it is important for school counsellors and practitioners to collaborate with parents to strengthen the bonds rather than set restrictions (Choo et al., 2015). These concerns and access to and consumption of high-speed Internet technology for online gambling emphasize the need for further research to better understand students' perspectives of this trend and implement successful preventative and intervention strategies such as regulations on online gambling.

In a study by Torrijos-Fincias and colleagues (2021) student participants reported that they perceive risks related to Internet addictive behaviors based on their personal experiences or the experiences of others. However, they downplayed and overlooked their own excessive use of screen time and technology use despite being aware of the risks. Studies have shown Internet addictive behaviors such as excessive Internet use are associated with challenges in consumption of time, interpersonal relationships, decreased well-being, poor academic performance, decreased academic productivity, physical health issues, and mental health problems like anxiety and depression (Anderson & Jiang, 2018; Gonzalez et al., 2023; Hirota et al., 2020). It is important to address addictive behaviors as an Internet threat because students frequently rely on their personal judgment and trial-and-error methods, and may not have access to appropriate educational interventions, instructions, and tools to responsibly use screen time and mitigate and efficiently manage the risk of online addictive behaviors (Gonzalez et al., 2023; Torrijos-Fincias et al., 2021). Furthermore, findings from a study by Tao and colleagues indicate that digital literacy is a protective factor against Internet addictive behaviors. Therefore, students should have the opportunity to share their perspectives about addictive Internet behaviors and learn about the occurrence, implications, consequences, and intervention strategies for this Internet threat.

Neurodivergent Students and Addictive Behaviors

As Internet gaming continues to escalate in popularity as a recreational activity, research is growing to measure the prevalence of Internet gaming disorder and addiction among neurodivergent populations of video game players such as those with autism and attention-deficit hyperactivity disorder (ADHD) (Concerto et al., 2021). Moreover, online environments add complexity to social understanding and social interaction challenges that neurodivergent students may experience (Carrington et al., 2017). Some neurodivergent students also tend to present with more severe symptoms of Internet addictive behaviors such as preoccupation symptoms than their peers (Hirota et al., 2020). The Internet is used by some neurodivergent students because they may prefer the excitement that it generates for future activities rather than to spend time offline with others and it provides an alternative for boredom (Hirota et al., 2020). Although the Internet may offer social interaction opportunities for neurodivergent students, excessive preoccupation with the Internet negatively impacts their social and academic functioning.

For example, Chou et al., (2017) conducted a study with students with ADHD and found that there was an association between social skill challenges and an increased risk of Internet gaming addiction. Internet addiction may limit the opportunity for students to experience meaningful face-to-face interactions, to develop and practice social skills and modify their behavior. As a result, some neurodivergent students may potentially be lured to ill-designed or insecure digital services that leave them vulnerable to fraud, scams, and identity theft. The authors concluded that social skills challenges should be targeted in prevention and intervention programs aimed at supporting neurodivergent students who have challenges with Internet addiction (Chou et al., 2017). Similarly, Hirota and colleagues (2020) suggest social skills training, psychoeducation, and cognitive behavioral therapy as potential interventions to address Internet addictive behaviors of neurodivergent students.

Alcohol and Drug Marketing

Research shows that vaping, smoking, and alcohol consumption are factors that are linked with increase daily Internet usage among students (Chu et al., 2017; Kwak et al., 2022). Internet alcohol marketing and advertising practices are targeted to generate sales of these products to students and there are often limited regulation or enforcement of marketing policies concerning minors by government authorities (Williams & Schmidt, 2014). Drug and alcohol advertisements on social media may purposely and inadvertently market unwanted and age-inappropriate behaviors to students (Auger et al., 2015). Students' excessive Internet usage and drug and alcohol consumption decrease their learning habits, and their academic achievement when their overall learning habits, and social, physical, psychological, and cognitive functions deteriorate because of frequent exposure to drug and alcohol online marketing (Kwak et al., 2022). Another risk factor of high levels of alcohol consumption and alcohol misuse is premature death and disability (Griswold et al., 2018).

In their study, Weeks and Subrahmanyam (2019) investigated how online contexts can be used for risky networking and communication, how students create and consume risky online content, and the correlation of such content with their behaviors and beliefs. Weeks and Subrahmanyam (2019) highlighted the prominent role of social media platforms, such as Facebook, Instagram, Twitter, and Snapchat, in exposing students to substance-related content, particularly alcohol advertising material and alcohol marketing. Their findings confirmed that exposure to alcohol marketing on social media platforms is linked to increased alcohol consumption and binge drinking behaviors among students (Weeks & Subrahmanyam, 2019). Weeks and Subrahmanyam also concluded that repeated exposure to Internet content threats can result in students becoming desensitized to the impact of these threats. Students from various racial, ethnic, and marginalized groups may experience perceive targeted exposure to drug and alcohol marketing, which is linked to negative health behaviors with vape, e-cigarette, tobacco, alcohol, and marijuana use (Cho et al., 2019; Rose et al., 2019). Since many students are increasingly being exposed to and engaged in contract risks such as age-inappropriate marketing of drug and alcohol marketing, it is important to understand students' views about various types of safety and health education implications related to online drug and alcohol marketing.

Over the past decade there has been an extraordinary growth and marketing of vapes and e-cigarette (Huang et al., 2018). Many students are exposed to vaping products and e-cigarette advertising, which may promote product use because they perceived online advertisements as appealing and harmlessly targeting non-smokers (Cho et al., 2019; Douglass et al., 2020). Instagram is used to expose students to vaping and e-cigarette marketing through images of vaping activities and behaviors, display of vaping products, advertisement, and text (Cho et al., 2019). Student participants have confirmed the prevalence of vaping among students at school (Chu et al., 2017). Although students may perceive vaping and e-cigarettes as harmless, research has shown evidence of a strong association between using e-cigarettes and vaping nicotine and implications such as for students' mood disorder, attention-deficit disorders, major depression, suicidal behavior, permanent reduction of impulse control, and pulmonary effects (Boudi et al., 2019; Douglass et al., 2020; Hammond et al., 2019; Obisesan et al., 2019). Adults such as school counselors have reported lack of formalized training related to vaping to improve their knowledge and skills in these areas (Cole et al., 2022; Giordano et al., 2023). Future research is needed to incorporate data from students' perspectives to mitigate the risk of drug marketing to students, and to improve educational campaigns and initiatives, and public health surveillance of drug marketing to students (Chu et al., 2017).

It is apparent that while the Internet has become essential to the lives of students, it poses real threats to students with very serious implications. Students are often aware that there are Internet threats; however, they do not always have the knowledge, capacity, and skills to identify these threats or take the necessary precautionary or reactionary measures when engaging online (Annansingh & Veli, 2016). Although adults may be guided on how to protect students by providing information on Internet-control software and activities such as setting restrictions on students' Internet use in a non-coercive manner (Kwak et al., 2022), it is necessary to continuously engage with and amplify student voices on topics such as privacy rights, data security, parental or guardian consent, and rules, regulations, and guidelines of service agreements (Abilock & Abilock, 2016; Martin et al., 2023). The intent of this is to increase awareness of the implications of Internet threats and develop educational systems and protective strategies that can be applied to, and promote healthy sexual behaviors, foster positive interactions, and prevent drug and alcohol consumption. Therefore, gaining students' perspectives about their awareness and identification of Internet threats is a major issue that needs further research as students will continue to develop their online presence and frequently engage with the Internet (Annansingh & Veli, 2016).

Neurodivergent Students and Alcohol and Drug Marketing

Neurodivergent students, such as autistic students, may choose to consume drugs and alcohol in an attempt to reduce social anxiety, get rid of an irritable mood or boredom, cope with challenges that they face, help them feel accepted by their peers, and socially integrate with others (Adhia et al., 2020; Higgins, 2019; Levy, 2022; Weir et al., 2021b). Neurodivergent students may engage in vaping if they see their peers and parents engaging in this behavior (Higgins, 2019). While the literature has indicated some benefits of drug and alcohol use for some neurodivergent people, hazardous and underaged consumption of alcohol and drugs have negative implications for the social, emotional, psychological, and academic lives of students from neurodivergent backgrounds. Implications of alcohol consumption include concerns about becoming addicted, medication interactions, health problems such as experiencing hangover, and concerns about acting unsociable when drunk (Rothman et al., 2023). Underage alcohol consumption can i) lead to vehicle crashes and injuries because it impairs students' judgment about risks that are associated with drinking and driving; ii) significantly increase unsafe sexual and aggressive behaviors; and iii) interference with brain development and cognitive processes which may impact academic performance (National Institute on Alcohol Abuse and Alcoholism, 2021). This is concerning for neurodivergent students because they may be at a higher risk for: i) causing or experiencing motor vehicle accidents; ii) experiencing challenges with regulating emotions and cognitive processes such as theory of mind, executive functioning, and sensory processing (Curry et al., 2021); iii) engaging in inappropriate sexual behaviors and experiencing aggression (Allely et al., 2019; Brown, 2024; Fortin et al., 2019; Roberts et al., 2015; Smusz et al., 2024); and iv) using substances to cope with social anxiety and manage behaviors and mental health symptoms (Levy, 2022; Weir et al., 2021b).

Currently, there is limited empirical evidence suggesting that neurodivergent students use and misuse alcohol more than their neurotypical peers or that they are more vulnerable to alcohol and drug marketing risks compared to their neurotypical peers (Butwicka et al., 2017; Haasbroek & Morojele, 2022; Huang et al., 2021; Sturm & Kasari, 2019; van der Hof, 2020). Similarly, there is a dearth of literature about neurodivergent students' vaping status and its association with the Internet (Higgins, 2019). Nevertheless, the implications of Internet alcohol marketing may be a significant threat for neurodivergent students. Moreover, as the number of students diagnosed with neurodivergent conditions increases (World Health Organization, 2024) and students engage more with the Internet, reducing the risk of online exposure to drug and alcohol use for neurodivergent students has the potential to save their lives and protect them against a wide range of implications (Griswold et al., 2018; Stamates et al., 2016). To attain this goal, further research is needed to investigate if neurodivergent students perceive that they are at risk for drug and alcohol marketing and to develop targeted prevention efforts and effective health promotion strategies (Adhia et al., 2020).

While the engagement of neurodivergent students with the Internet has increase at a rapid pace and neurodivergent students are adapting to these changes, the development of and implementation of Internet safety research from the perspective of neurodivergent students have not kept abreast (Annansingh & Veli, 2016). Similarly, digital safety guidelines, educational initiatives, policies, practices, and protocols have fallen behind this pace (Annansingh & Veli, 2016). Consequently, neurodivergent students are exposed to Internet threats because of limited knowledge of Internet threats that they face and the support that adults can provide for neurodivergent students. Neurodivergent students such as autistic students are at increased risk of vulnerability to Internet threats and their views on Internet safety are currently under researched. We need to educate students to mitigate the risk of these threats.

Mitigating Internet Threats: Adults' Endeavors

As awareness of Internet threats grows, adults endeavor to minimize threats and the impact of these threats to protect young people in a variety of ways. There is contradictory and limited evidence of widespread means to identify and prevent Internet threats and to support and develop healthy Internet habits including bans on use of mobile phones and talks from experts in education and curriculum programs that are conducted by government ministries, schools, and community organizations (eSafety Commissioner, 2022; Kopecký et al., 2021). Many of these programs are designed to support parents and educators to understand students' Internet activities and to guide their use of the Internet, technologies, and consider time restrictions (Choo et al., 2015). Students may repeat advice they have learned from safety programs even if they do not personally connect with or relate the advice to their own experiences (Alqahtani, 2016).

The research of Black and colleagues (2022) reinforces the relational nature of students' online experiences and variations in students' perception of adults to support them against Internet threats. Students' stories about their perspectives about Internet threats depict parents as sources of comfort and positive agents who can intervene online to remove or ameliorate threats, punish perpetrators, take bullying seriously, and ask a parent to remove harmful photos from social media (Black et al., 2022).

Students may have a good understanding of parental controls and good antivirus programs but strict rules, and restrictive bans and regulations set by parents may not be effective to reduce Internet addictions such as extreme gaming (Alqahtani, 2016; Choo et al., 2015). The imposition of restrictions on access to digital technologies for Internet access may result in more passive coping strategies by students (Kopecký et al., 2021). Students use passive reactions including strategies such as ignoring messages and delaying a response to messages whereas their active reactions include reporting to parents and friends, refusal to engage with the stranger, and reporting and blocking the stranger (Cernikova, et al., 2018). Students have reported that parent-child bonds and parent-child relationships are important to reduce and prevent Internet addictions such as pathological gaming. Parental involvement and parent–child closeness, bond, and relationship have a greater impact on reducing and preventing Internet threats such as bullying and pathological symptoms of video gaming over time rather than setting restrictions (Carrington et al., 2017; Choo et al., 2015). Stakeholders such as students, their parents, schools, and local authorities should have updated information on Internet threats trends and work in close collaboration to ensure that there is a clear understanding of Internet threats and how to implement effective Internet safety measures for students (Annansingh & Veli, 2016).

Conversely, some students may feel isolated, ashamed, and despaired because they perceive adult authorities such as parents and school staff to be unapproachable or unhelpful (Black et al., 2022). Although students may be reluctant to approach their teachers, they may acknowledge the support and intervention from school counsellors, principals, and police (Black et al., 2022). These findings highlight the need for adults to be better informed about students' perspectives of Internet threats such as contact with strangers and conduct such as cyberbullying and gambling.

However, are our educative endeavors working and for whom? In recent years, eSafety educational initiatives focusing on protection from Internet threats such as sexting and sexualized behaviors, cyberbullying, addictive behaviors, and alcohol and drug marketing have been developed (eSafety Commissioner, 2022). To develop students' understanding of Internet privacy, adults often give them advice about not revealing personal details or meeting up offline with strangers, and adults teach about security measures when using technologies such as not accessing or downloading from websites that are suspicious when using technologies (Alqahtani, 2016; Chapin, 2021). Moreover, research to date shows that there have been initiatives to develop students' digital literacy skills to support their use of coping strategies such as blocking and changing privacy settings when they experience Internet threats such as unwelcomed messages and cyberbullying (Tao et al., 2022). However, despite extensive Internet safety messages to students, there has been little research assessing the extent to which safety messages are being taken seriously by them. Anecdotal evidence suggests that students may perceive that they will not personally be adversely affected by Internet threats, and this is concerning as only a small number of students report negative Internet experiences to adults for fear of being denied access to devices as a consequence (Buglass et al., 2021; Moody et al., 2021). There is a lack of priority in research that promotes representation of student voices regarding their perspectives and experiences of Internet safety.

The Need for Neurodivergent Student Voice

Adult perspectives regarding Internet threats and Internet safety are presented in literature in the context of students' Internet use and the risks that are involved (Black et al., 2022). The literature depicts students as being in need of adult perspectives and support to ensuring their safety in online environments.

Buglass and colleagues (2021) highlight how parents and regulators have a set pattern of perceiving that students are at high risks of Internet threats. Their findings show that although adults may be more vigilant about students' online safety and have concerns about their own online safety, they believe that the Internet has more apparent risks for students than for themselves.

Vulnerability of exposure to Internet threats is similar for students and adults (Buglass et al., 2021). Therefore, the link between Internet threats and age may not be straightforward and students may not be at higher risk because of their age. Additionally, research suggests that students may have a higher and more practical and realistic sense of vulnerabilities and potential personal risks of Internet threats than adults because they may be more familiar with digital platforms and technologies (Buglass et al., 2021). Studies which have considered the perspectives of students on the threats they can encounter online have postulated that there is a difference between adult and student conceptions of Internet threats (Vandoninck et al., 2014). Given that adults may be optimistically biased to perceive that students are more susceptible to Internet threats, it is important to gain students' perspectives of Internet threats and exposure to these threats to ensure there is promotion of safe and positive online engagement for students that is responsive to their needs and perspectives (Buglass et al., 2021).

Although there are some studies which purport to hear young people's voices on Internet safety, such as Todd and Medina (2019), most do not ask young people to share their own views and perspectives but ask about threats as viewed and perceived by adults. While there is no clear consensus among students about the negative and harmful effects the Internet has on their lives, research to date about Internet threats highlights the significance of acquiring a deeper understanding of threats that students perceive are associated with their own personal use of Internet content (Anderson & Jiang, 2018). Understanding Internet content threats from students' perspectives is crucial to addressing its impact on their safety and how we educate them.

The findings from a study by Cernikova and colleagues (2018) revealed that students engage in different levels of interactions with unknown people on the Internet. Students in the study reported negative experiences and reactions regarding non-verbal interaction, initiation of contact, communication, and face-to-face meetings (Cernikova et al., 2018). The authors concluded that the participants were capable of actively making decisions about initiation, continuing, or stopping interactions while using the Internet and digital technology. To maintain positive dialogue when communicating with unknown persons, students used positive strategies such as establishing conditions, selected appropriate and safe topics for conversations, avoided inappropriate topics, and were cautious about sharing their private information including their telephone number, home address, and full name. This study highlights the importance of gaining neurodivergent students' perspectives to accurately understand their negative online experiences and safety strategies that they used in online context (Cernikova et al., 2018).

As the patterns and practices of engagement shift from physical contexts to online and digital contexts, adults, including school leaders, teachers, parents/guardians, and researchers have shared that the Internet can be a platform for threatening, risky, and illegal activities (Kocturk & Yuksel, 2018; Velki & Ivanković, 2020). Internet threats are contextual to the user and the potential risks which the user is exposed to (Gasper, 2020; Vandoninck et al., 2014). Therefore, adults and students may have different concerns and perceptions about Internet threats. A student's reaction to Internet threats is contingent upon how they perceive the threats and their exposure to Internet threats does not always result in negative outcomes (Hamid et al., 2015; Jozsa et al 2021; Torrijos-Fincias et al., 2021; Weeks & Subrahmanyam, 2019).

What do Students Think are the Threats? Do They Apply These Threats to Themselves?

Students may be aware of various Internet threats but may not always perceive that they are vulnerable to these Internet threats. In a 2020 study, Gaspard investigated 676 Australian secondary school students' perceptions of their negative and problematic experiences about the Internet. Although the majority of students maintained that the Internet led to positive experiences, approximately 40% of boys and 45% of girls identified it as a platform of concern. Online safety was students' first concern and being careful how they behave online was the second concern. When applying Livingstone and Haddon's (2009) Internet threat categories to the study only four boys and four girls thought content was a problem, while 32 boys and 22 girls were concerned about conduct, which was mainly fears about sharing personal information. However, only 31% of responses could be recorded using these two categories. The results reflect that although students may often be aware of what to do to keep themselves safe, students may not identify different types of threats seen or perceive that they need to be personally acted upon in different ways. This disparity between students' awareness of Internet threats and their ability to categorize and apply appropriate safety strategies highlights a crucial gap in online digital literacies and Internet safety education (Tao et al., 2022).

Some research has highlighted that students have acknowledged their awareness of online threats. In addition, students have shared that they have the knowledge and skills that are needed to protect themselves from Internet threats. For example, in a study conducted by Alqahtani (2016) some students shared that they felt unsafe connecting to and using the Internet in public places such as an Internet café despite using their own devices, and some also felt unsafe using the Internet in their own homes. However, it has been reported that despite students' skills and knowledge and recognition of various threats, they may underestimate the severity and real-life concerns and risk to their safety.

Importantly, peer and friendship support plays a crucial role in enhancing students' proactive coping, especially in situations where direct contact is a risk (Gaspard, 2020). For example, it was revealed in a study conducted by Walsh and Tener (2022), that a common opinion among survivors of sextual Internet threats such as sexting and sextortion was that their peers and parents were the most suitable sources of support and assistance if they faced negative outcomes. Students' friendships provided support and forgiveness, a moral compass against harmful online behaviors, and mitigated the effects of negative online experiences (Black et al., 2022). However, students' perspectives on inclusive and safe Internet use where they can connect with their peers without the risks of negative consequences such as exposure to sexual content, unwanted solicitation, being teased, cruel and insulting comments, cyberbullying, and privacy violations are currently underrepresented (Ahmadu & Kontagora, 2021; Moody et al., 2021).

One study that has included student voice conducted by Ahmadu and Kontagora (2021) explored what Nigerian students aged 11–17 years old say about what threats they consider to be in their online activities. Twenty percent had mistakenly found themselves on violent sites with horrific pictures, 10% corroborated being hurt by insulting comments on social media sites, and 20% intentionally visited sites with violent or gruesome pictures. Findings from this study are aligned with Gaspard's (2020) study which highlighted that boys and girls shared common apprehensions, including fears about the Dark Web and the rapid circulation of online content.

The current limited body of Internet safety research indicates that students wish to provide more input into research and online safety education to illuminate and address the Internet threats and concerns they face (eSafety Commissioner, 2022; Moody et al., 2021). Student input is more critical now than ever before because advancements in online platforms for multiplayer gaming, social networking, and social media as well as restrictions to physical interactions brought about by the recent global pandemic have given rise to even more students engaging with the Internet for longer periods of time (Bleszynski et al., 2022; Magis-Weinberg, 2021). We now present a review of literature on neurodivergent students' perspectives about Internet threats and reinforce that because their differences in thoughts, communication, and interactions; uniqueness in cognitive traits; and variations in learning styles, their voice needs to be heard (den Houting; 2019; Dwyer, 2022; Santhanam, 2023).

What do Neurodivergent Students Think About Internet Threats?

Previous research on threats students experience have mostly utilized adult voice or the perspective of typically developing students, that have excluded neurodivergent student perspectives about their online experiences and threats to online safety (Macmillan et al., 2022). We are therefore interested to know whether neurodivergent students see Internet threats as adults perceive and explain them. Do they identify digital spaces as having the potential to be dangerous in general or do they differentiate and act differently toward different kinds of Internet threats? This is an important issue given the current international Internet safety focus and requires further investigation.

Neurodivergent students' insights and involvement in research increase the accuracy of the findings and provide data about the threats they face, their needs, and how we can keep them safe. It is important therefore that research with neurodivergent students consider a co-constructed model. A co-constructed model when undertaking research with neurodivergent students enables more accurate interpretations of the perspectives of students who are active Internet participants (Cernikova et al., 2018). A study by Bertilsdotter and colleagues (2019) for example argues that it is important to include neurodivergent people as researchers, participants, and collaborators in all stages of research to achieve higher quality research and to amplify the voices, perspectives, and experiences of neurodivergent people. An earlier study by Saggers (2015) highlighted the importance of attending to and reflecting on the perspectives of neurodivergent students as crucial for developing inclusive educational approaches and practices. Although this is frequently discussed in scholarly articles and research findings, it is uncommon for neurodivergent students to be asked to share their perspectives about Internet threats.

Vulnerability to Internet threats increases for neurodivergent students when they leave school because there are more opportunities for them to pursue special interests and fewer opportunities for structured online support and supervision from support networks such as parents/guardians, caregivers, educators, and schools (Flower et al., 2021; Kostin, 2022; Mills et al., 2022). By listening to the voices of neurodivergent students, specific threats to promoting safe and positive Internet experiences can be identified, and recommendations put forward to better support online experiences for all students that reflect their views. We see that there has been scarce research from the perspective of neurodivergent students and suggest using an innovative framework to investigate their views on the threats of the Internet so we can provide nuanced education for them.

Call for Research on Neurodivergent Student's Perspectives of Internet Threats

This chapter underscores the importance of prioritizing research that is aimed at understanding diverse students' perspectives to see what messages are influencing their knowledge and actions about Internet threats. This approach produces new perspectives about Internet threats and contributes to new ways of thinking about Internet safety rather than relying on the voice of adults or one group of students. We call for further mapping of recent definitions and understandings of students' perspectives of Internet safety. The dynamics of Internet threats need to be explored in nuanced ways such as through the perspectives of diverse groups of students, with strategies to reduce and prevent online threats to safe outcomes for students (Black et al., 2022). Nuanced ways such as through diverse students' voices subvert the deficit lens of students as being passive and vulnerable consumers of the Internet to persons with agency to use personal and relational resources such as peers, friends, parents, or teachers to keep them safe (Black et al., 2022). Capturing the voices and experiences of diverse students in research through methods such as interviews, stories, questionnaires, and surveys contribute to research of a higher quality and encourages agency to speak about their perspectives about Internet threats (Bertilsdotter et al., 2019; Black et al., 2022; Bone, 2017; Chown, 2017; Gaspard, 2020).

Three Considerations for Conducting Research into Neurodivergent Students' Perceptions of Internet Threats

This chapter reports on some possible considerations when conducting research into neurodivergent students' perceptions of Internet threats and ways to reduce the threats. The chapter is informed by a funded early career research exploratory pilot study. The pilot permitted the exploration of the following research objectives:

1. Explore student and neurodivergent student perspectives of Internet threats and their implications through a review of the literature.
2. Explore and identify formal qualitative data collection methods that may inform future research.
3. Ascertain neurodivergent students' perceptions of Internet threats and which threats they perceive apply to themselves.

An exploratory pilot study was appropriate for exploring threats that need to be understood (Hirota et al., 2020), and to support the investigation of the second research objective that was not adequately answered in the literature. Drawing on the conceptual frameworks used in our previous research, we suggest an innovative framework called Inclusive New Literacies (Stone & Saggers, 2023) and a theoretical framework of d/Discourse (Gee, 2004) to be used in future research into neurodivergent students' perception of Internet threats, whether they believe these threats apply to them, and their suggestions for reducing the harm Internet threats may cause. In addition, we mention some methodological considerations for conducting research on this matter.

1. Consideration for an Innovative Framework: Inclusive New Literacies

Stone (2018) innovatively developed and used an Inclusive New Literacies framework to gain primary school autistic students' perspectives about the potentials and constraints of online multiplayer games for their social interactions. The framework has been expanded upon and applied in the current exploratory study (see Figure 2).

Figure 2. Inclusive New Literacies Framework

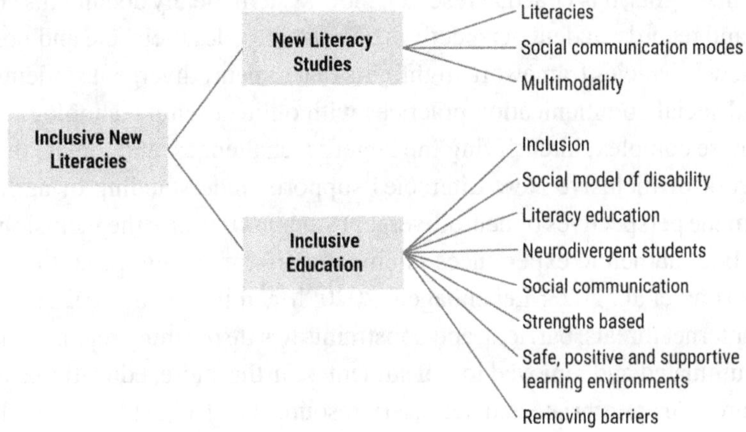

Note. From Stone and Saggers (2023). Reproduced and adapted with permission.

Inclusive New Literacies is about recognizing and embracing the skills, capabilities, and knowledges that diverse students require for meaning making through semiotic resources such as digital, multimodal, and multimedia technologies in online and offline contexts (Stone & Saggers, 2023). This framework emphasizes the notion that new literacies provide, facilitate, or enable multimodal and differentiated support for all students within physical, virtual, online, and offline spaces, whether or not they have a medical diagnosis or disability. Furthermore, the notion of Inclusive New Literacies emphasizes the importance of meaning making in online contexts for neurodivergent students such as autistic students rather than focusing only on the literacy practices of neurotypical students and the physical and face-to-face uses of spoken and written language.

The framework is also embedded within the field of inclusive education, and contributes recent understandings of neurodiversity, neurodivergence, autism, inclusion, literacy education, and social communication (Stone & Saggers, 2023). The new understandings that this framework provides are pivotal to the pursuit of knowledge from students within underrepresented groups and to amplify youth voices about how Internet threats pertain to them. This conceptual framework supports understanding of authentic meanings of Internet threats from the perspectives of neurodivergent students. The framework provides expanded understandings of literacies which embrace an integration of a broad and flexible group of multimodal resources, skills, abilities, strategies, and competencies that neurodivergent students use to share their insights with others about the online spaces that they navigate (Stone & Saggers, 2018; Stone et al., 2019).

Inclusive New Literacies is recognized as an innovative concept that has been developed with links to Global Kids Online and eSafety initiatives to include youth voice to identify and remove threats to their meaning making and safe and positive engagement in online, offline, digital, physical, virtual, and face-to-face platforms (Moody et al., 2021; Stone & Saggers, 2018; Stone et al., 2019; Stone & Saggers, 2023; Third, 2016). This is important because experiences of Internet threats such as cyberbullying are more common among students with low levels of digital literacy (Tao et al., 2022). Other than the current study, no other research internationally has used this approach that has high-impact strategies for developing social understanding and designing and monitoring Internet use in and beyond educational contexts. If governments, educators, and adults are to illuminate the threats to safe and positive Internet use to support students' rights, it is vital that research more systematically documents consultation with all groups of students and records student perspectives of what impedes their safe and positive engagement.

The Inclusive New Literacies framework highlights that as neurodivergent students engage in diverse situated literacy and social communication practices with online digital technologies and people, these practices become more complex, intensifying the benefits, challenges, and threats they experience. The conceptual framework of Inclusive New Literacies supports understanding of authentic meanings of Internet threats from the perspectives of neurodivergent students because the inclusion of neurodivergent voices and views about authentic experiences is empowering, meaningful, and beneficial to neurodivergent individuals (Lau et al., 2023; Lebenhagen, 2020; Macmillan et al., 2022). Inclusion within the framework means Internet threats, barriers, and constraints to safe meaning making and social communication should be illuminated and removed for all students. Furthermore, educational and policy changes should be made to provide appropriate and necessary resources and adjustments for all students to safely participate in social communication and quality literacy experiences in online contexts regardless of their medical diagnosis and backgrounds. This framework can be used with a renewed focus on the safe online and digital literacies and social communication practices of all students (Stone, 2018; Stone et al., 2019; Stone & Saggers, 2023). Students with higher levels of digital literacies experience fewer Internet threats than those with lower levels of literacies (Tao et al., 2022).

2. A Suggested Theoretical Framework for Future Research – d/Discourse

The current exploratory study with neurodivergent students required a theoretical approach that supports the combination of language in use with social practices, social groups, interactions, meaning making, and technologies. Therefore, descriptions of Internet threats extend deeper than words to include aspects of online literacy practices, such as through the semiotic resources offered through online multiplayer games and social media (Gee, 2004, 2015; Gee & Handford, 2012). Gee (2004) distinguishes "discourses" from "Discourses" and holds that "discourse" denoted by a lower-case 'd' refers to spoken and written language, which includes talk and printed text. Gee (2015) argues that there are other systems of meaning making other than spoken and written language. Gee (2014) adds that, within big 'D' "Discourses", language represents situated meanings, social practices, experiences, and perspectives within particular groups and enables people to enact various identities. Therefore, the theoretical framework of this study consists of perspectives of d/Discourse (Gee & Handford, 2012) within the contexts of Internet safety and the perspectives of autistic students as a neurodivergent group. The d/Discourse theory provides a framework for analyzing neurodivergent students' perspectives of Internet content, contact, conduct, and contract threats related to structures of knowledge, online activities, social actions, and insights into truths about social groups, and interactions and relationships with others within and from their online worlds (Gee, 2004; Livingstone & Stoilova, 2021). The Discourses of the Internet are fitted with semiotic resources, such as other people, virtual characters, tools, actions, symbols, strategies, perspectives, and values, that may cause risks to meaning making and safe engagement during online activities (Gee, 2004; 2015; Gee & Handford, 2012).

Drawing on Gee (2004) and Gee and Handford (2012), online Discourse is the unique combination of ways that spoken and written language are combined with other semiotic resources such as interactions, perspectives, values, beliefs, images, actions, and objects that can shape social identities. The d/Discourse theory (Gee, 2014) evokes the notion that students can be identified as members of various Discourses because of situated contexts, situated uses of language, and integrated, shared, and common affinities. Neurodivergent students may be members of more than one online Discourse community. The perceived threats of each online Discourse community may be different because of their situated context and the relationship between the semiotic resources. The notion of a "Big 'D' Discourse" will enable descriptive interpretations of neurodivergent student perspectives of Internet threats within the situated contexts and shared affinity spaces of the Internet (Gee, 2004, 2015; Gee & Handford, 2012). More specifically, the theoretical lens of d/Discourse can be drawn on to guide thematic data analysis and to support descriptions of student perspectives of which content, contact, conduct, or contract threats they perceive apply to themselves (Braun & Clarke, 2021; Livingstone & Haddon, 2009). This theoretical framework represents an integrated stance that is fused with ideas, concepts, and theoretical assumptions from contemporary literacies research (Street et al., 2017) as well as from inclusive education research about neurodiversity, learning, online technology, and digital engagement (Brosnan et al., 2017; Luchs, 2021). Elements of d/Discourse have implications for conceptually framing this research through an Inclusive New Literacies lens (Stone & Saggers, 2023).

3. Consideration of Methodological Factors

This section draws on methodological considerations used in the current early career research that investigates autistic students' views of perceived online threats and which apply to them. If you are thinking about doing research in this space, here are some key considerations to bear in mind. We discuss hints for recruiting participants, a rationale for conducting Zoom semi-structured interviews, and considerations for conducting semi-structured interviews with autistic participants.

Considerations for Recruiting Participants. Following Global Kids Online guidelines for piloting qualitative studies, up to 15 autistic students were invited to participate in the current exploratory pilot study (Global Kids Online, 2016). Participants aged 12–18 years old were invited to participate in an audio and video recorded/audio recorded semi-structured individual interview at a time and in a mode convenient to them. All participants needed to meet the criterion of having a medical diagnosis of autism that has been confirmed by an experienced clinician such as a psychiatrist, pediatrician, or neurologist using the Diagnostic and Statistical Manual of Mental Disorders, Fifth Edition (American Psychiatric Association, 2013). Participants were sought if they frequently engaged in Internet activities or had a high interest in online activities such as online gaming and use of social media. Frequent engagement in Internet activities or a high interest in online activities refers to the pattern of usage, behavior, and activities of autistic students who spend a significant amount of time online daily or weekly and show a high enthusiasm and repeated interest in one or more Internet related activities (Jiujias, et al., 2017; Nowell et al., 2021; Stone, 2018). These activities may have included regular and considerable daily or weekly engagements with social media, online entertainment, online communities and forums, online gaming, online communication, web browsing, and online content creation (Torrijos-Fincias et al., 2021).

Recruitment was done at arm's length via collaborating organizations and the university webpage to reduce the risk of exerting undue pressure from students to participate. No student or their family members were approached specifically or singled out (Bergen & Labonté, 2020). Recruitment processes and materials included a formal recruitment email invitation, recruitment flyer, postings to online bulletin boards and social media sites, and informal personal conversations. The participants were not known to the researchers which further minimized the potential for coercion. No offering of undue inducement was made (Global Kids Online, 2016).

It is important that information about the research is adapted to accommodate the needs of participants with autism (Harrington & Foster, 2014; Scott-Barrett et al., 2019). Therefore, consent forms were written to be clearly understood by the research participants and to cover all the necessary consent information as provided in the recruitment material. To maximize participant understanding of the research the child participant information sheet was developed in two different formats. The first version had clear and concrete language to explain the research purpose, potential risks of participation such as discomfort, inconvenience, and distress, the data collection procedure, and what is expected of the participants. The second version incorporated a combination of images and simplified language with basic wording. As some participants were under 18 years of age, the informed, written, and voluntary consents of the parents/caregivers needed to be sought for their children's voluntary participation in the research.

The parent/caregiver-child consent forms templates and instructions needed to address the requirements for informed consent and assent, participant-initiated withdrawal, and requirements to inform participants of anticipated conditions under which termination of participation may occur. The participants needed to be reminded of their rights to decline to comment, answer particular questions, and withdraw during the interviews. The usefulness of nonverbal signals by autistic students to indicate the desire to end an interview needed to be acknowledged (Harrington & Foster, 2014).

Rationale for Using Zoom. Zoom was considered suitable for the current study. It is suggested that qualitative research with autistic students use Zoom or another similar platform such as Teams (Gray et al., 2020; Saavedra, 2022). The Zoom audio and video recorded semi-structured individual interviews can be similar to the face-to-face individual structure, with the basic pattern of interaction being a question-answer talk sequence (DeJonckheere & Vaughn, 2019). As technologies advance, more qualitative researchers are creating alternatives to traditional face-to-face interviews to collect qualitative data. Researchers have found that online video conferencing can yield the same quality of data as face-to-face interviews and in some cases foster participant openness and expressiveness to the researcher (Archibald et al., 2019; Meherali & Louie-Poon, 2021). For example, video conferencing software such as Zoom is becoming increasingly popular and accessible.

Participants in previous research have reported several benefits of using Zoom for interviews, including its convenience and ease of use, its ability to enhance personal interface to discuss personal topics, and that it facilitates accessibility through the use of ubiquitous technologies such as cellular phones, tablets, and personal computers (Gray et al., 2020; Saavedra, 2022). Furthermore, researchers who utilized Zoom and similar video conferencing tools have reported that participants appreciated reduced travel time, being able to use personal devices, noted the ease of logging in, and appreciated being able to see their interviewer while having conversations about sensitive topics (Archibald et al., 2019; Meherali & Louie-Poon, 2021).

Zoom is viewed as an affinity space and a virtual platform within which students socially interacted with their peers and engaged in learning during restrictions because of the COVID-19 pandemic (Zaeske et al., 2022). For participants, Zoom semi-structured interviews enable advantages such as allowing participants to choose a familiar environment and convenient space where they want to be during the interview thereby reducing their discomfort. There are also added benefits for the participants such as using familiar technologies, time saving conveniences, and personal safety. The format of the Zoom semi-structured interviews enables autistic students to use their own voice and give fresh empirical accounts about their perspectives of threats associated with the Internet.

The electronic meeting invitation generated by Zoom, has a live link to the meeting that only requires a click of the link and a password to join the online interview. Zoom does not require participants to have an account or download a program. Therefore, participants do not need to have Zoom as an existing videoconferencing tool they have used in the past and that is already downloaded on their home devices or wherever they are doing the interview. If the research participants would like to download Zoom, the Zoom trials are free for a basic program and the research participants will be able to download the program (Archibald et al., 2019).

Zoom's prolifically available tools offer additional opportunities and advantages for synchronous qualitative data collection (Gray et al., 2020). Furthermore, given that the participants are often across various geographical settings, face-to-face interviews sometimes are not feasible. The specific attributes of Zoom will facilitate long-distance communication, semi-structured interview data collection across multiple sites, and reduce travel time (Wahl-Jorgensen, 2021). Zoom is considered suitable as the cost-effective software can economically support research aimed at diverse and geographically dispersed populations.

Furthermore, the use of Zoom-recorded interviews is encouraged to digitally capture verbal, audio, and visual data, and to facilitate ease of transcription (Archibald et al., 2019; Gray et al., 2020; Saavedra, 2022; Wahl-Jorgensen, 2021). Therefore, the recordings can provide a more accurate and higher level of permanency of capturing the participants' speech, than nonrecording methods such as handwritten notes. Using Zoom allows capture of the audio and video recorded semi-structured interviews in real time to discuss the participants' perspectives. This feature also supports participants' choices about being recorded with audio and video, or audio only. Participants who do not want their faces video-recorded can select an audio only option for the interview. The audio-only recording of the participants respects their request for privacy or for personal reasons. Zoom's password protection feature enables confidentiality. The recording capacity facilitates saving the interviews. Zoom benefits the research budget, user ease, administrative options, and level of comfort with the platform (Archibald et al., 2019; Gray et al., 2020; Saavedra, 2022; Wahl-Jorgensen, 2021).

Semi-structured Interview Schedule. Interviewees may have the tendency to dominate the interview, and thus, may stray from giving the relevant information that is needed to answer the research questions (Scott-Barrett et al., 2019). These limitations can be avoided by clearly and succinctly restating the research's focus and purpose of the interviews at the time of the interviews. Before the interviews start, the estimated time for completion needs to be communicated to the participants.

Previous research has suggested that repetitiveness in Internet interests, behavior, and activities for autistic students may occur with a high frequency (Chen et al., 2015; Craig et al., 2021). Research has also shown that autistic students can share their perspectives of Internet activities and recall many of their previous experiences and information about past events (Harrington & Foster, 2014). Autistic students may be members of more than one online Discourse community. The perceived threats of each of these Discourses may be different because of their situated contexts.

Considerations for Autistic Participants. Given the diverse ways that students make meanings and the social communication difficulties that autistic students are believed to face (American Psychiatric Association, 2013; Kelly et al., 2018), there was no single effective way to phrase the interview questions. Theory of mind suggests that some individuals with autism may have difficulties with the ability to understand the perspectives, thoughts, and feelings of others (Pelligra et al., 2015) and to understand that these perspectives, thoughts, and feelings may be different from their own (Baron-Cohen et al., 2013). Similarly, challenges with executive function suggest that some autistic students may find it difficult to process complex information during the interview sessions (Craig et al., 2016). Therefore, the Zoom semi-structured interviews needed to be paced appropriately for the researchers and the participants to interact comfortably through conversations for sharing perspectives, understandings, experiences, thoughts, and feelings.

During the interview sessions, consideration needed to be given for the uniqueness of each participant, and for their cognitive ability and age (Harrington & Foster, 2014). The researchers needed to avoid figurative and ambiguous language. If there were ambiguous or unfamiliar terms identified in the interview topics, the questions needed to be rephrased using prompts with simple language and explicitly explained for the participants (Jiménez & Orozco, 2021; Seidman, 2019). When necessary, the questions needed to be augmented with visual support following the suggestion that autistic students may often require strategies, for example visual cues, prompting, and contextual support, that show when they could contribute to conversations (Harrington & Foster, 2014). With these considerations, the interview questions needed to be kept concise, simple, and short.

During interviews, social desirability bias or confirmation bias may occur when research participants give responses that they think that the interviewer wishes to hear (Bergen & Labonté, 2020; Brinkmann, 2013). Therefore, the use of open-ended questions within the semi-structured interviews provided the opportunity for the participants to share information without being constrained by the researchers' perspectives. Likewise, to promote conversations, open-ended questions needed to be asked as a guide and questions needed to be asked in multiple ways so that participants could share their perspectives. In addition, the use of open-ended questions also provided a safeguard against leading the interviewees to a desired response. Research indicates that closed questions may be more appropriate for autistic students because some autistic students may share limited information when they are asked open-ended questions (Harrington & Foster, 2014). Therefore, the interview schedule needed to be designed to include closed questions and yes/no questions as well.

Some autistic students often have special interests and could be guided by their passion to talk at the listener and share facts about their own interests (Grove et al., 2016; Harrington & Foster, 2014; Nowell et al., 2021). To address the concern that participants may digress from the interview topics and talk unremittingly about their special interests, researchers should allow participants time to talk briefly about their interest, without encouragement through questions and comments, and then redirect their attention back to the relevant interview topic (Harrington & Foster, 2014). Giving autistic participants a voice during interviews and avoiding undue disturbance is good ethical practice and encourages participation (Lau et al., 2023; Lebenhagen, 2020; Macmillan et al., 2022). Consequently, the researchers needed to refrain from interrupting the participants during the interviews and withheld judgements about the participants' perspectives.

Although identity first language is preferred by the autistic community, the research context and the language preference of the individual research participants in the current research needed to be considered for the interviews. It is important that researchers consider the language preferences of the individuals they are engaging with when conducting this type of research (Benham, 2015; Graf et al., 2017; Shakes & Cashin, 2019).

Researchers need to consider possible technical difficulties and potential challenges such as an unreliable Internet connection, soundless video, temporary freezing, discordant audio-visual feeds, and difficulties uploading or using the interview recording (Archibald et al., 2019; Irani, 2019). Minor, moderate, and severe technological disruptions and difficulties can disrupt the flow of the interview and result in the loss of data. Therefore, these issues needed to be addressed as appropriate to the research design and aims (Saavedra, 2022). We troubleshooted issues using the following strategies for handling technological disruptions in case they arose before or during the interviews to maintain the integrity of data generation. We considered the importance of providing participants with the interview topics prior to the interview, limiting the interviews to 30 minutes, and emailing the participants to reschedule another Zoom individual interview in the event that Zoom's collaborative tools malfunction and other unforeseen technical difficulties or related disturbances were experienced during the first interview (Gray et al., 2020; Mirick & Wladkowski, 2019). Additionally, the semi-structured interviews needed to be more informal in nature than fully structured face-to-face interviews, and sensitive to the characteristics and needs of participants diagnosed with autism (American Psychiatric Association, 2013; Brinkmann, 2013; Lau et al., 2023; Lebenhagen, 2020; Macmillan et al., 2022). Drawing on the works by Archibald et al., (2019), Gray et al., (2020), Saavedra (2022), and Wahl-Jorgensen (2021), the structure of the Zoom semi-structured individual interviews enabled deepened understandings of the research focus from autistic students' points of view, uncovered meaning about Internet threats, and elicited their perspectives that are not directly accessible through currently published research.

A distress protocol was used to assess and accommodate the needs of participants who may have increased susceptibility to discomfort or distress during the Zoom audio and video recorded or audio recorded semi-structured individual interviews. The distress protocol was used with the aim to ensure the greatest benefits to the research participants through a balance of autonomy, beneficence, nonmaleficence, and justice while minimizing harm (Draucker et al., 2009). With guidance from Draucker et al., (2009), for example, the researchers observed for signs such as quietness, crying, and anger. The distress protocol also provided participants with sufficient information regarding the benefits and risks of the research so that they felt free to withdraw from the study. The participants' objections to take part in or withdraw from the study or any potential distress that they may experience was taken into account to minimize the harm of overriding their preference.

CONCLUSION

As neurodivergent students continue to expand their online activities, Internet threats and their implications range across social, emotional, virtual, physical, psychological, and academic contexts. Some risks of Internet use include display of sexting and sexualized content, cyberbullying, facilitation of addictive behaviors, and exposure to alcohol and drug marketing. Students have described situations such as meeting strangers online and incidents where people were hurt in online contexts, acts and implications of cyberbullying, and the hurtful exchange of words online (Black et al., 2022). Students have also revealed that some threats to safe online engagement include rumors being spread, personal accounts being hacked, unconsented sharing of photos, unauthorized appropriation of online identities and data, catfishing, breakdown of peer support, and exclusion from peer groups (Black et al., 2022).

Experiences and encounters with Internet threats evoke emotional reactions in students such as decreased self-esteem, sadness, and anger (eSafety Commissioner, 2022). The connection between Internet threats and gaining students' perspectives about these threats is important because although students may be able to articulate ways to keep safe online, they may not fully understand the threats of online usage and their behavior do not always correspond with their responses (Alqahtani, 2016). Some activities which may be labelled as Internet threats may be viewed by students as normal behavior, real-life challenges, and opportunities to develop friendships, to share information, and access pornography and sexual content. This highlights the necessity for adults to better acknowledge these instances, empowering them to offer appropriate support to students in situations where there are Internet threats. The task of effectively managing, controlling, and mediating these threats has become more complex as students' online activities occur within the privacy and confines of their bedrooms (Gasper, 2020).

Understanding neurodivergent students' perspectives, especially autistic students, about potential threats to safe and positive engagement with the Internet is an important preventative first step to keeping them safe from Internet threats. We need to know how applicable the Internet safety messages are for neurodivergent students as they tend to spend a lot of time on the Internet (Gallup et al., 2016; Kuo et al., 2014, Kwak et al., 2022). Research needs to provide new insights about what neurodivergent students believe the threats are when going online and which ones they particularly think apply to themselves. This information will be useful to students, parents/caregivers, schools, Internet safety programs, and researchers suggesting a student voice approach to Internet safety. This information can have implications for professional learning topics such as the importance of safe and ethical use of digital technologies in innovative approaches to teaching and learning. Knowing more about what threats students believe apply to them and how to enhance digital learning environments and invest in safe online learning will extend access to real-world education about how to support a diverse range of learners with their Internet use.

Additional outcomes include that new research will include feedback to Internet safety providers. Future work will provide recommendations for innovative and technological pedagogy for safe and positive online student engagement in the dimensions of Internet content, contact, conduct, and contract (Livingstone & Stoilova, 2021). Drawing on the Inclusive New Literacy Framework (Stone & Saggers, 2023), d/Discourse theory framework (Gee, 2004), and the work of Livingstone and Stoilva (2021), it is recommended that future research explores neurodivergent students' perspectives of Internet threats relating to the types of information, media, and online material that students encounter, are in receipt of, engage with, or are exposed to. There is also potential to investigate neurodivergent students' perspectives of their online interactions and connections with peers, relatives, educators, and strangers. Further research is needed to investigate this student cohort's perspectives on Internet threats that are associated with the actions and behaviors exhibited by students themselves and other online users. New research into neurodivergent students' perspectives about harmful contracts or commercial interests such as gambling and exploitative or age-inappropriate marketing and their rights, responsibilities, and agreements regarding Internet activities need to be conducted. Research needs to inform high-impact strategies for developing social understanding and designing and monitoring safe Internet use in education and technology innovations to support neurodivergent students' rights to online safety.

REFERENCES

Abilock, R., & Abilock, D. (2016). I agree, but do I know? Privacy and student data. *Knowledge Quest*, 44(4), 10–21.

Abreu, R. L., & Kenny, M. C. (2018). Cyberbullying and LGBTQ youth: A systematic literature review and recommendations for prevention and intervention. *Journal of Child & Adolescent Trauma*, 11(1), 81–97. DOI: 10.1007/s40653-017-0175-7 PMID: 32318140

Adhia, A., Bair-Merritt, M., Broder-Fingert, S., Pepen, R. A. N., Suarez-Rocha, A. C., & Rothman, E. F. (2020). The critical lack of data on alcohol and marijuana use by adolescents on the autism spectrum. *Autism in Adulthood: Challenges and Management*, 2(4), 282–288. DOI: 10.1089/aut.2019.0051 PMID: 36600961

Ahlström, B. H., & Wentz, E. (2014). Difficulties in everyday life: Young persons with attention-deficit/ hyperactivity disorder and autism spectrum disorders perspectives. A chat-log analysis. *International Journal of Qualitative Studies on Health and Well-being*, 9(1), 23376. Advance online publication. DOI: 10.3402/qhw.v9.23376 PMID: 24875238

Ahmadu, T. S., & Kontagora, H. L. (2021). How Nigerian junior secondary school students perceive internet child exploitation. In Elshenraki, H. (Ed.), *Combating the exploitation of children in cyberspace: Emerging research and opportunities* (pp. 95–116). IGI Global. DOI: 10.4018/978-1-7998-2360-5.ch005

Al-Faham, H., Davis, A. M., & Ernst, R. (2019). Intersectionality: From theory to practice. *Annual Review of Law and Social Science*, 15(1), 247–265. DOI: 10.1146/annurev-lawsocsci-101518-042942

Alhujaili, N., Platt, E., Khalid-Khan, S., & Groll, D. (2022). Comparison of social media use among adolescents with autism spectrum disorder and non-ASD adolescents. *Adolescent Health, Medicine and Therapeutics*, 13, 15–21. DOI: 10.2147/AHMT.S344591 PMID: 35136359

Alhujailli, A., Karwowski, W., Wan, T. T. H., & Hancock, P. (2020). Affective and stress consequences of cyberbullying. *Symmetry*, 12(9), 1536. Advance online publication. DOI: 10.3390/sym12091536

Allely, C. S., & Creaby-Attwood, A. (2016). Sexual offending and autism spectrum disorders. *Journal of Intellectual Disabilities and Offending Behaviour*, 7(1), 35–51. DOI: 10.1108/JIDOB-09-2015-0029

Allely, C. S., Kennedy, S., & Warren, I. (2019). A legal analysis of Australian criminal cases involving defendants with autism spectrum disorder charged with online sexual offending. *International Journal of Law and Psychiatry*, 66, 101456. Advance online publication. DOI: 10.1016/j.ijlp.2019.101456 PMID: 31706389

Alotaibi, N. (2019). Cyber bullying and the expected consequences on the students' academic achievement. *IEEE Access : Practical Innovations, Open Solutions*, 7, 153417–153431. DOI: 10.1109/ACCESS.2019.2947163

Alqahtani, A. M. (2016). Keeping safe online: Perceptions of Gulf adolescents. *Journal of Education and e-learning Research*, 3(4), 150–155. DOI: 10.20448/journal.509/2016.3.4/509.4.150.155

American Psychiatric Association, DSM-5 Task Force. (2013). *Diagnostic and statistical manual of mental disorders: DSM-5* (5th ed.). American Psychiatric Publishing, Inc., DOI: 10.1176/appi.books.9780890425596

Anderson, K. E. (2018). Getting acquainted with social networks and apps: Streaming video games on Twitch.tv. *Library Hi Tech News*, 35(9), 7–10. DOI: 10.1108/LHTN-08-2018-0054

Anderson, M., & Jiang, J. (2018). *Teens, social media and technology 2018*. Pew Research Center. https://www.pewresearch.org/internet/2018/05/31/teens-social-media-technology-2018/

Annansingh, F., & Veli, T. (2016). An investigation into risks awareness and e-safety needs of children on the internet: A study of Devon, UK. *Interactive Technology and Smart Education*, 13(2), 147–165. DOI: 10.1108/ITSE-09-2015-0029

Archibald, M. M., Ambagtsheer, R. C., Casey, M. G., & Lawless, M. (2019). Using Zoom videoconferencing for qualitative data collection: Perceptions and experiences of researchers and participants. *International Journal of Qualitative Methods*, 18, 1609406919874596. Advance online publication. DOI: 10.1177/1609406919874596

Auger, N., Daniel, M., Knäuper, B., Dourian, T., & Raynault, M.-F. (2015). Unintended messages in online advertising to youth: Illicit drug imagery in a Canadian sports marketing campaign. *The Journal of Adolescent Health*, 56(4), 429–432. DOI: 10.1016/j.jadohealth.2014.12.006 PMID: 25650109

Autism Spectrum Australia. (2023). *Learn more about Aspect's participation in Mardi Gras over the years*. https://www.autismspectrum.org.au/about-aspect/diversity-inclusion/lgbtqia/aspect-at-mardi-gras

Baldry, A. C., Blaya, C., & Farrington, D. P. (Eds.). (2018). *International perspectives on cyberbullying prevalence, risk factors and interventions* (1st ed.). Springer International., DOI: 10.1007/978-3-319-73263-3

Banerjee, A. (2023). Internet use and autism spectrum disorders. *Journal of Autism and Developmental Disorders*, 53(8), 3307–3308. DOI: 10.1007/s10803-023-05904-z PMID: 36710297

Bányai, F., Griffiths, M. D., Demetrovics, D., & Király, O. (2019). The mediating effect of motivations between psychiatric distress and gaming disorder among esport gamers and recreational gamers. *Comprehensive Psychiatry*, 94, 152117. Advance online publication. DOI: 10.1016/j.comppsych.2019.152117 PMID: 31422185

Baron-Cohen, S., Tager-Flusberg, H., & Lombardo, M. (2013). *Understanding other minds: Perspectives from developmental social neuroscience* (3rd ed.). Oxford University Press. DOI: 10.1093/acprof:oso/9780199692972.001.0001

Bates, S. (2017). Revenge Porn and Mental Health: A Qualitative Analysis of the Mental Health Effects of Revenge Porn on Female Survivors. *Feminist Criminology*, 12(1), 22–42. DOI: 10.1177/1557085116654565

Beddows, N., & Brooks, R. (2015). Inappropriate sexual behaviour in adolescents with autism spectrum disorder: What education is recommended and why. *Early Intervention in Psychiatry*, 10(4), 282–289. DOI: 10.1111/eip.12265 PMID: 26265030

Benham, J. (2015). *Proud to be autistic metaphorical construction and salience of cultural and personal identity in #StopCombatingMe* [Unpublished master's thesis]. Minnesota State University. https://cornerstone.lib.mnsu.edu/etds/420/

Bennett, M., & Goodall, E. (2016). A meta-analysis of DSM-5 autism diagnoses in relation to DSM-IV and DSM-IV-TR. *Review Journal of Autism and Developmental Disorders*, 3(2), 119–124. DOI: 10.1007/s40489-016-0070-4

Bergen, N., & Labonté, R. (2020). "Everything is perfect, and we have no problems": Detecting and limiting social desirability bias in qualitative research. *Qualitative Health Research*, 30(5), 783–792. DOI: 10.1177/1049732319889354 PMID: 31830860

Bertilsdotter Rosqvist, H., Kourti, H., Jackson-Perry, D., Brownlow, C., Fletcher, K., Bendelman, D., & O'Dell, L. (2019). Doing it differently: Emancipatory autism studies within a neurodiverse academic space. *Disability & Society*, 34(7-8), 1082–1101. DOI: 10.1080/09687599.2019.1603102

Beyens, I., Vandenbosch, L., & Eggermont, S. (2015). Early adolescent boys' exposure to internet pornography: Relationships to pubertal timing, sensation seeking, and academic performance. *The Journal of Early Adolescence*, 35(8), 1045–1068. DOI: 10.1177/0272431614548069

Black, R., Walsh, L., Waite, C., Collin, P., Third, A., & Idriss, S. (2022). In their own words: 41 stories of young people's digital citizenship. *Learning, Media and Technology*, 47(4), 524–536. DOI: 10.1080/17439884.2022.2044848

Bleszynski, J., Rumińska, A., Hamerlińska, A., Stefańska-Klar, R., & Warszawa, A. (2022). The experience of the COVID-19 pandemic by persons with ASD: Social aspects. *PLoS One*, 17(6), e0267123. Advance online publication. DOI: 10.1371/journal.pone.0267123 PMID: 35709250

Bone, K. M. (2017). Trapped behind the glass: Crip theory and disability identity. *Disability & Society*, 32(9), 1297–1314. DOI: 10.1080/09687599.2017.1313722

Boudi, F. B., Patel, S., Boudi, A., & Chan, C. (2019). Vitamin E acetate as a plausible cause of acute vaping-related illness. *Cureus*, 11(12), e6350. Advance online publication. DOI: 10.7759/cureus.6350 PMID: 31938636

Brand, M., Wegmann, E., Stark, R., Müller, A., Wölfling, K., Robbins, T. W., & Potenza, M. N. (2019). The interaction of person-affect-cognition-execution (I-PACE) model for addictive behaviors: Update, generalization to addictive behaviors beyond internet-use disorders, and specification of the process character of addictive behaviors. *Neuroscience and Biobehavioral Reviews*, 104, 1–10. DOI: 10.1016/j.neubiorev.2019.06.032 PMID: 31247240

Braun, V., & Clarke, V. (2021). Thematic analysis: A practical guide to understanding and doing. *Sage (Atlanta, Ga.).*

Brinkmann, S. (2013). *Qualitative interviewing*. Oxford University Press., DOI: 10.1093/acprof:osobl/9780199861392.001.0001

Brosnan, M., Holt, S., Yuill, N., Good, J., & Parsons, S. (2017). Beyond autism and technology: Lessons from neurodiverse populations. *Journal of Enabling Technologies*, 11(2), 43–48. DOI: 10.1108/JET-02-2017-0007

Brown, S. J. (2024). Assessing the risk of users of child sexual exploitation material committing further offences: A scoping review. *Journal of Sexual Aggression*, 30(1), 1–24. DOI: 10.1080/13552600.2022.2104394

Buglass, S., Binder, J., Betts, L., & Underwood, J. (2021). Asymmetrical third-person effects on the perceptions of online risk and harm among adolescents and adults. *Behaviour & Information Technology*, 40(11), 1090–1100. DOI: 10.1080/0144929X.2020.1742380

Butwicka, A., Långström, N., Larsson, H., Lundström, S., Serlachius, E., Almqvist, C., Frisén, L., & Lichtenstein, P. (2017). Increased risk for substance use-related problems in autism spectrum disorders: A population-based cohort study. *Journal of Autism and Developmental Disorders*, 47(1), 80–89. DOI: 10.1007/s10803-016-2914-2 PMID: 27734228

Carrington, S., Campbell, M., Saggers, B., Ashburner, J., Vicig, F., Dillon-Wallace, J., & Hwang, Y. (2017). Recommendations of school students with autism spectrum disorder and their parents in regard to bullying and cyberbullying prevention and intervention. *International Journal of Inclusive Education*, 21(10), 1045–1064. DOI: 10.1080/13603116.2017.1331381

Cernikova, M., Dedkova, L., & Smahel, D. (2018). Youth interaction with online strangers: Experiences and reactions to unknown people on the Internet. *Information Communication and Society*, 21(1), 94–110. DOI: 10.1080/1369118X.2016.1261169

Chapin, J. (2021). Adolescents, third-person perception, and Facebook. In Elshenraki, H. (Ed.), *Combating the exploitation of children in cyberspace: Emerging research and opportunities* (pp. 95–116). IGI Global., DOI: 10.4018/978-1-7998-2360-5.ch005

Chen, Y.-L., Chen, S.-H., & Shur-Fen Gau, S. (2015). ADHD and autistic traits, family function, parenting style, and social adjustment for Internet addiction among children and adolescents in Taiwan: A longitudinal study. *Research in Developmental Disabilities*, 39, 20–31. DOI: 10.1016/j.ridd.2014.12.025 PMID: 25617844

Cho, Y. J., Thrasher, J. F., Reid, J. L., Hitchman, S., & Hammond, D. (2019). Youth self-reported exposure to and perceptions of vaping advertisements: Findings from the 2017 International Tobacco Control Youth Tobacco and Vaping Survey. *Preventive Medicine*, 126, 105775. Advance online publication. DOI: 10.1016/j.ypmed.2019.105775 PMID: 31323286

Choo, H., Sim, T., Liau, A. K. F., Gentile, D. A., & Khoo, A. (2015). Parental influences on pathological symptoms of video-gaming among children and adolescents: A prospective study. *Journal of Child and Family Studies*, 24(5), 1429–1441. DOI: 10.1007/s10826-014-9949-9

Chou, W.-J., Huang, M.-F., Chang, Y.-P., Chen, Y.-M., Hu, H.-F., & Yen, C.-F. (2017). Social skills deficits and their association with Internet addiction and activities in adolescents with attention-deficit/hyperactivity disorder. *Journal of Behavioral Addictions*, 6(1), 42–50. DOI: 10.1556/2006.6.2017.005 PMID: 28245666

Chown, N., Robinson, J., Beardon, L., Downing, J., Hughes, L., Leatherland, J., Fox, K., Hickman, L., & MacGregor, D. (2017). Improving research about us, with us: A draft framework for inclusive autism research. *Disability & Society*, 32(5), 720–734. DOI: 10.1080/09687599.2017.1320273

Chu, K.-H., Allem, J.-P., Cruz, T. B., & Unger, J. B. (2017). Vaping on Instagram: Cloud chasing, hand checks and product placement. *Tobacco Control*, 26(5), 575–578. DOI: 10.1136/tobaccocontrol-2016-053052 PMID: 27660111

Cole, A. G., Lienemann, B. A., Sun, J., Chang, J., & Zhu, S.-H. (2022). California school staff reports of seeing students vaping at school and disciplinary actions. *The Journal of School Nursing: the Official Publication of the National Association of School Nurses*. Advance online publication. DOI: 10.1177/10598405221127694 PMID: 36168212

Concerto, C., Rodolico, A., Avanzato, C., Fusar-Poli, L., Signorelli, M. S., Battaglia, F., & Aguglia, E. (2021). Autistic traits and attention-deficit hyperactivity disorder symptoms predict the severity of internet gaming disorder in an Italian adult population. *Brain Sciences*, 11(6), 774. Advance online publication. DOI: 10.3390/brainsci11060774 PMID: 34207989

Craig, F., Margari, F., Legrottaglie, A. R., Palumbi, R., de Giambattista, C., & Margari, L. (2016). A review of executive function deficits in autism spectrum disorder and attention-deficit/hyperactivity disorder. *Neuropsychiatric Disease and Treatment*, 12, 1191–1202. DOI: 10.2147/NDT.S104620 PMID: 27274255

Craig, F., Tenuta, F., De Giacomo, A., Trabacca, A., & Costabile, A. (2021). A systematic review of problematic video-game use in people with autism spectrum disorders. *Research in Autism Spectrum Disorders*, 82, 101726. Advance online publication. DOI: 10.1016/j.rasd.2021.101726

Cricenti, C., Pizzo, A., Quaglieri, A., Mari, E., Cordellieri, P., Bonucchi, C., Torretta, P., Giannini, A. M., & Lausi, G. (2022). Did they deserve it? Adolescents' perception of online harassment in a real-case scenario. *International Journal of Environmental Research and Public Health*, 19(24), 17040. Advance online publication. DOI: 10.3390/ijerph192417040 PMID: 36554921

Curry, A. E., Metzger, K. B., Carey, M. E., Sartin, E. B., Huang, P., & Yerys, B. E. (2021). Comparison of motor vehicle crashes, traffic violations, and license suspensions between autistic and non-autistic adolescent and young adult drivers. *Journal of the American Academy of Child and Adolescent Psychiatry*, 60(7), 913–923. DOI: 10.1016/j.jaac.2021.01.001 PMID: 33453361

DeJonckheere, M., & Vaughn, L. M. (2019). Semistructured interviewing in primary care research: A balance of relationship and rigour. *Family Medicine and Community Health*, 7(2), e000057. Advance online publication. DOI: 10.1136/fmch-2018-000057 PMID: 32148704

den Houting, J. (2019). Neurodiversity: An insider's perspective. *Autism*, 23(2), 271–273. DOI: 10.1177/1362361318820762 PMID: 30556743

Denvir, C. (2016). Online and in the know? Public legal education, young people and the Internet. *Computers & Education*, 92–93, 204–220. DOI: 10.1016/j.compedu.2015.10.003

Derevensky, J. L., Hayman, V., & Lynette Gilbeau, . (2019). Behavioral addictions: Excessive gambling, gaming, internet, and smartphone use among children and adolescents. *Pediatric Clinics of North America*, 66(6), 1163–1182. DOI: 10.1016/j.pcl.2019.08.008 PMID: 31679605

Dewinter, J., De Graaf, H., & Begeer, S. (2017). Sexual orientation, gender identity, and romantic relationships in adolescents and adults with autism spectrum disorder. *Journal of Autism and Developmental Disorders*, 47(9), 2927–2934. DOI: 10.1007/s10803-017-3199-9 PMID: 28597143

Dias, C. C. V., da Silva, J. V. C., & Maciel, S. C. (2021). Construction and validity evidence of the Autistic Person's Socialization Beliefs Scale (APSBS). *Trends in Psychology*, 29(4), 581–594. DOI: 10.1007/s43076-021-00071-5

Dolly, S. K., & Samantaray, N. N. (2024). Navigating the digital landscape: Relationship between type of internet use and well-being among students—A mediation and moderation analysis. *Indian Journal of Psychiatry*, 66(3), 263–271. DOI: 10.4103/indianjpsychiatry.indianjpsychiatry_718_23 PMID: 39100120

Douglass, B., Solecki, S., & Fay-Hillier, T. (2020). The harmful consequences of vaping: A public health threat. *Journal of Addictions Nursing*, 31(2), 79–84. DOI: 10.1097/JAN.0000000000000332 PMID: 32487933

Draucker, C. B., Martsolf, D. S., & Poole, C. (2009). Developing distress protocols for research on sensitive topics. *Archives of Psychiatric Nursing*, 23(5), 343–350. DOI: 10.1016/j.apnu.2008.10.008 PMID: 19766925

Dwyer, P. (2022). The neurodiversity approach(es): What are they and what do they mean for researchers? *Human Development*, 66(2), 73–92. DOI: 10.1159/000523723 PMID: 36158596

El Asam, A., & Katz, A. (2018). Vulnerable young people and their experience of online risks. *Human-Computer Interaction*, 33(4), 281–304. DOI: 10.1080/07370024.2018.1437544

eSafety Commissioner (2022). *Mind the gap: Parental awareness of children's exposure to risks online.* Aussie Kids Online, Melbourne; eSafety Commissioner. https://www.esafety.gov.au/research/mind-gap

eSafety Commissioner (2023). *Online hate and discrimination.* https://www.esafety.gov.au/lgbtiq/learning-lounge/dealing-with-online-abuse/online-hate-discrimination

Evelyn, S., Clancy, E. M., Klettke, B., & Tatnell, R. (2022). A phenomenological investigation into cyberbullying as experienced by people identifying as transgender or gender diverse. *International Journal of Environmental Research and Public Health*, 19(11), 6560. Advance online publication. DOI: 10.3390/ijerph19116560 PMID: 35682144

Flower, R. L., Richdale, A. L., & Lawson, L. P. (2021). Brief report: What happens after school? Exploring post-school outcomes for a group of autistic and non-autistic Australian youth. *Journal of Autism and Developmental Disorders*, 51(4), 1385–1391. DOI: 10.1007/s10803-020-04600-6 PMID: 32662053

Fortin, F., Paquette, S., & Leclerc, C. (2019). The effect of child sexual exploitation images collection size on offender sentencing. *International Review of Law Computers & Technology*, 33(3), 330–348. DOI: 10.1080/13600869.2018.1560553

Freeman, J. L., Caldwell, P. H. Y., Bennett, P. A., & Scott, K. M. (2018). How adolescents search for and appraise online health information: A systematic review. *The Journal of Pediatrics*, 195, 244–255. DOI: 10.1016/j.jpeds.2017.11.031 PMID: 29398062

Fung, L. K., Ulrich, T. L., Fujimoto, K. T., & Taheri, M. (2022). Neurodiversity: An invisible strength? *Journal of the Minerals Metals & Materials Society*, 74(9), 3200–3202. DOI: 10.1007/s11837-022-05454-2

Gaspard, L. (2020). Australian high school students and their internet use: Perceptions of opportunities versus 'problematic situations.'. *Children Australia*, 45(1), 54–63. DOI: 10.1017/cha.2020.2

Gee, J. P. (2004). *Situated language and learning: A critique of traditional schooling*. Routledge.

Gee, J. P. (2015). *Unified discourse analysis: Language, reality, virtual worlds, and video games*. Routledge.

Gee, J. P., & Handford, M. (2012). *The Routledge handbook of discourse analysis*. Routledge.

Giordano, A. L., Morey, A. W., Kim, I. K., Song, J., & Kim, O. (2023). School counselors' experiences with student vaping and internet gaming: A report from the field. *International Journal for the Advancement of Counseling*, 45(3), 441–457. DOI: 10.1007/s10447-023-09518-z

Global Kids Online. (2016). *Global kids online research toolkit: Qualitative guide*. http://globalkidsonline.net/wp-content/uploads/2016/04/Qualitative-toolkit-guide-final-26-Oct-16.pdf

Gonzalez, R. M., Quinn, P., Gardiner, J., & Sutcliffe, A. (2023). 47 Problematic online gambling and predictors of participation in adolescents. *Archives of Disease in Childhood, 108*, Article A101–A101. https://doi.org/DOI: 10.1136/archdischild-2023-rcpch.170

Graf, W. D., Miller, G., Epstein, L. G., & Rapin, I. (2017). The autism "epidemic": Ethical, legal, and social issues in a developmental spectrum disorder. *Neurology*, 88(14), 1371–1380. DOI: 10.1212/WNL.0000000000003791 PMID: 28275086

Gray, L. M., Wong-Wylie, G., Rempel, G. R., & Cook, K. (2020). Expanding qualitative research interviewing strategies: Zoom video communications. *The Qualitative Report*, 25(5), 1292–1301. DOI: 10.46743/2160-3715/2020.4212

Griffin, K. A., Cunningham, E. L., & George Mwangi, C. A. (2016). Defining diversity: Ethnic differences in black students' perceptions of racial climate. *Journal of Diversity in Higher Education*, 9(1), 34–49. DOI: 10.1037/a0039255

Griswold, M. G., Fullman, N., Hawley, C., Arian, N., Zimsen, S. R. M., Tymeson, H. D., Venkateswaran, V., Tapp, A. D., Forouzanfar, M. H., Salama, J. S., Abate, K. H., Abate, D., Abay, S. M., Abbafati, C., Abdulkader, R. S., Abebe, Z., Aboyans, V., Abrar, M. M., Acharya, P., & Gakidou, E. (2018). Alcohol use and burden for 195 countries and territories, 1990–2016: A systematic analysis for the Global Burden of Disease Study 2016. *Lancet*, 392(10152), 1015–1035. DOI: 10.1016/S0140-6736(18)31310-2 PMID: 30146330

Grove, R., Roth, I., & Hoekstra, R. A. (2016). The motivation for special interests in individuals with autism and controls: Development and validation of the special interest motivation scale. *Autism Research*, 9(6), 677–688. DOI: 10.1002/aur.1560 PMID: 26496939

Guerra, C., Montiel, I., Molina, N., Escalona, Y., Riquelme, J., & Rojas, L. (2019). Analysis of a brief scale of Internet risk behaviors in Chilean youth. *Anuario de psicología (Barcelona, Spain)*, 49(1), 32–39. DOI: 10.1344/ANPSIC2019.49.4

Haasbroek, H., & Morojele, N. (2022). A systematic literature review on the relationship between autism spectrum disorder and substance use among adults and adolescents. *Review Journal of Autism and Developmental Disorders*, 9(1), 1–20. DOI: 10.1007/s40489-021-00242-1

Hamid, S., Waycott, J., Kurnia, S., & Chang, S. (2015). Understanding students' perceptions of the benefits of online social networking use for teaching and learning. *The Internet and Higher Education*, 26, 1–9. DOI: 10.1016/j.iheduc.2015.02.004

Hammond, C. J., Allick, A., Rahman, N., & Nanavati, J. (2019). Structural and functional neural targets of addiction treatment in adolescents and young adults: A systematic review and meta-analysis. *Journal of Child and Adolescent Psychopharmacology*, 29(7), 498–507. DOI: 10.1089/cap.2019.0007 PMID: 31313938

Harrington, C., Foster, M., Rodger, S., & Ashburner, J. (2014). Engaging young people with autism spectrum disorder in research interviews. *British Journal of Learning Disabilities*, 42(2), 153–161. DOI: 10.1111/bld.12037

Hernández, L., Hernández, V., Neyra, F., & Carrillo, J. (2022). The use of massive online games in game-based learning activities. *Revista Innova Educación, 4*(3), 7–30. https://dialnet.unirioja.es/descarga/articulo/8510469.pdf

Higgins, N. R. (2019). *Tobacco and E-cigarette use in youth with autism spectrum disorders.* [Doctoral Dissertation, Florida Institute of Technology]. Florida Tech Scholarship Repository. https://repository.fit.edu/etd/285

Higham, L., Girardi, A., & Edwards, H. V. (2021). Clinical and criminal profile of internet offenders with ASD. *Journal of Intellectual Disabilities and Offending Behaviour*, 12(2), 61–74. DOI: 10.1108/JIDOB-09-2020-0016

Hillier, A., Gallop, N., Mendes, E., Tellez, D., Buckingham, A., Nizami, A., & OToole, D. (2020). LGBTQ + and autism spectrum disorder: Experiences and challenges. *International Journal of Transgender Health*, 21(1), 98–110. DOI: 10.1080/15532739.2019.1594484 PMID: 33005905

Hirota, T., McElroy, E., & So, R. (2020). Network analysis of internet addiction symptoms among a clinical sample of Japanese adolescents with autism spectrum disorder. *Journal of Autism and Developmental Disorders*, 51(8), 2764–2772. DOI: 10.1007/s10803-020-04714-x PMID: 33040268

Huang, J., Duan, Z., Kwok, J., Binns, S., Vera, L. E., Kim, Y., Szczypka, G., & Emery, S. L. (2018). Vaping versus JUULing: How the extraordinary growth and marketing of JUUL transformed the US retail e-cigarette market. *Tobacco Control*, 28(2), 146–151. DOI: 10.1136/tobaccocontrol-2018-054382 PMID: 29853561

Huang, J.-S., Yang, F.-C., Chien, W.-C., Yeh, T.-C., Chung, C.-H., Tsai, C.-K., Tsai, S.-J., Yang, S.-S., Tzeng, N.-S., Chen, M.-H., & Liang, C.-S. (2021). Risk of substance use disorder and its associations with comorbidities and psychotropic agents in patients with autism. *JAMA Pediatrics*, 175(2), e205371. Advance online publication. DOI: 10.1001/jamapediatrics.2020.5371 PMID: 33394019

Hunehäll Berndtsson, K., & Odenbring, Y. (2021). They don't even think about what the girl might think about it': Students' views on sexting, gender inequalities and power relations in school. *Journal of Gender Studies*, 30(1), 91–101. DOI: 10.1080/09589236.2020.1825217

Irani, E. (2019). The use of videoconferencing for qualitative interviewing: Opportunities, challenges, and considerations. *Clinical Nursing Research*, 28(1), 3–8. DOI: 10.1177/1054773818803170 PMID: 30470151

Jang, Y., & Ko, B. (2023). Online safety for children and youth under the 4Cs framework—A focus on digital policies in Australia, Canada, and the UK. *Children (Basel, Switzerland)*, 10(8), 1415. Advance online publication. DOI: 10.3390/children10081415 PMID: 37628414

Jiménez, T. R., & Orozco, M. (2021). Prompts, not questions: Four techniques for crafting better interview protocols. *Qualitative Sociology*, 44(4), 507–528. DOI: 10.1007/s11133-021-09483-2

Jiujias, M., Kelley, E., & Hall, L. (2017). Restricted, repetitive behaviors in autism spectrum disorder and obsessive–compulsive disorder: A comparative review. *Child Psychiatry and Human Development*, 48(6), 944–959. DOI: 10.1007/s10578-017-0717-0 PMID: 28281020

Jozsa, K., Kraus, A., Korpak, A. K., Birnholtz, J., Moskowitz, D. A., & Macapagal, K. (2021). 'Safe behind my screen': Adolescent sexual minority males' perceptions of safety and trustworthiness on geosocial and social networking apps. *Archives of Sexual Behavior*, 50(7), 2965–2980. DOI: 10.1007/s10508-021-01962-5 PMID: 34581948

Kallitsounaki, A., & Williams, D. M. (2023). Autism spectrum disorder and gender dysphoria/incongruence. A systematic literature review and meta-analysis. *Journal of Autism and Developmental Disorders*, 53(8), 3103–3117. DOI: 10.1007/s10803-022-05517-y PMID: 35596023

Kelly, R., O'Malley, M.-P., & Antonijevic, S. (2018). "Just trying to talk to people … It's the hardest": Perspectives of adolescents with high-functioning autism spectrum disorder on their social communication skills. *Child Language Teaching and Therapy*, 34(3), 319–334. DOI: 10.1177/0265659018806754

Khurana, A., Bleakley, A., Jordan, A. B., & Romer, D. (2015). The protective effects of parental monitoring and internet restriction on adolescents' risk of online harassment. *Journal of Youth and Adolescence*, 44(5), 1039–1047. DOI: 10.1007/s10964-014-0242-4 PMID: 25504217

Kocturk, N., & Yuksel, F. (2018). A modern danger for adolescents: From online flirtation to sexual abuse. *Dusunen Adam : Bakirkoy Ruh Ve Sinir Hastaliklari Hastanesi Yayin Organi*, 31(3), 294–300. DOI: 10.5350/DAJPN2018310307

Kopecký, K., Fernández-Martín, F. D., Szotkowski, R., Gómez-García, G., & Mikulcová, K. (2021). Behaviour of children and adolescents and the use of mobile phones in primary schools in the Czech Republic. *International Journal of Environmental Research and Public Health*, 18(16), 8352. Advance online publication. DOI: 10.3390/ijerph18168352 PMID: 34444102

Kostin, I. A. (2022). Internet safety for schoolchildren and adults with autism spectrum disorders: Vulnerability and areas of assistance. In Arinushkina, A. A., & Korobeynikov, I. A. (Eds.), *Education of Children with Special Needs* (pp. 11–18). Springer., DOI: 10.1007/978-3-031-13646-7_2

Kuo, M. H., Orsmond, G. I., Coster, W. J., & Cohn, E. S. (2014). Media use among adolescents with autism spectrum disorder. *Autism*, 18(8), 914–923. DOI: 10.1177/1362361313497832 PMID: 24142797

Kwak, Y., Kim, H., & Ahn, J.-W. (2022). Impact of internet usage time on mental health in adolescents: Using the 14th Korea Youth Risk Behavior Web-Based Survey 2018. *PLoS One*, 17(3), e0264948. DOI: 10.1371/journal.pone.0264948 PMID: 35320295

Lacina, J., & Griffith, R. (2018). Diverse learners, diverse backgrounds. *The Reading Teacher*, 72(2), 141–142. DOI: 10.1002/trtr.1738

Lau-Zhu, A., Anderson, C., & Lister, M. (2023). Assessment of digital risks in child and adolescent mental health services: A mixed-method, theory-driven study of clinicians' experiences and perspectives. *Clinical Child Psychology and Psychiatry*, 28(1), 255–269. DOI: 10.1177/13591045221098896 PMID: 35522928

Leadbitter, K., Buckle, K., Ellis, C., & Dekker, M. (2021). Autistic self-advocacy and the neurodiversity movement: Implications for autism early intervention research and practice. *Frontiers in Psychology*, 12, 635690. DOI: 10.3389/fpsyg.2021.635690 PMID: 33912110

Lebenhagen, C. (2020). Including speaking and nonspeaking autistic voice in research. *Autism in Adulthood: Challenges and Management*, 2(2), 128–131. DOI: 10.1089/aut.2019.0002 PMID: 36601567

Lee, C., & Shin, N. (2017). Prevalence of cyberbullying and predictors of cyberbullying perpetration among Korean adolescents. *Computers in Human Behavior*, 68, 352–358. DOI: 10.1016/j.chb.2016.11.047

Levy, S. (2022). *Autistic traits, substance use, and social anxiety* (Publication No. 29062026) [Master's thesis, The University of Alabama]. ProQuest Dissertations and Theses.

Livingstone, S., & Haddon, L. (Eds.). (2009). *Kids online: Opportunities and risks for children* (1st ed.). Bristol University Press., DOI: 10.2307/j.ctt9qgvdsig

Livingstone, S., & Stoilova, M. (2021). *The 4Cs: classifying online risk to children* (CO:RE Short Report Series on Key Topics). Hamburg: Leibniz-Institut für Medienforschung | Hans-Bredow-Institut (HBI). https://doi.org/DOI: 10.21241/ssoar.71817

Lloyd, J. (2020). Abuse through sexual image sharing in schools: Response and responsibility. *Gender and Education*, 32(6), 784–802. DOI: 10.1080/09540253.2018.1513456

Luchs, C. (2021). Considering neurodiversity in learning design and technology. *TechTrends*, 65(6), 923–924. DOI: 10.1007/s11528-021-00667-9

Macmillan, M., Berg, T., Just, M., & Stewart, M. E. (2022). Online safety experiences of autistic adolescents: An interpretative phenomenological analysis. *Research in Autism Spectrum Disorders*, 96, 101995. Advance online publication. DOI: 10.1016/j.rasd.2022.101995

Magis-Weinberg, L., Gys, C., Berger, E., Domoff, S., & Dahl, R. (2021). Positive and negative online experiences and loneliness in Peruvian adolescents during the COVID-19 lockdown. *Journal of Research on Adolescence*, 31(3), 717–733. DOI: 10.1111/jora.12666 PMID: 34448303

Martin, F., Bacak, J., Polly, D., Wang, W., & Ahlgrim-Delzell, L. (2023). Teacher and school concerns and actions on elementary school children digital safety. *TechTrends*, 67(3), 561–571. DOI: 10.1007/s11528-022-00803-z PMID: 36249671

Meherali, S., & Louie-Poon, S. (2021). Challenges in conducting online videoconferencing qualitative interviews with adolescents on sensitive topics. *The Qualitative Report*, 26(9), 2851–2856. DOI: 10.46743/2160-3715/2021.4906

Mills, C., Sharp, N. L., Triandafilidis, Z., & Tracey, D. K. (2022). *'Thrown out into the world': Transition to post schooling for autistic young people*. Western Sydney University. https://doi.org/DOI: 10.26183/3gsv-mv41

Mirick, R. G., & Wladkowski, S. P. (2019). Skype in qualitative interviews: Participant and researcher perspectives. *The Qualitative Report*, 24(12), 3061–3072. DOI: 10.46743/2160-3715/2019.3632

Moody, L., Marsden, L., Nguyen, B., & Third, A. (2021). *Consultations with young people to inform the eSafety Commissioner's engagement strategy for young people*. Young and Resilient Research Centre, Western Sydney University.

National Institute on Alcohol Abuse and Alcoholism. (2021). *Underage drinking*. https://www.niaaa.nih.gov/publications/brochures-and-fact-sheets/underage-drinking

Normand, C. L., & Sallafranque-St-Louis, F. (2016). Cybervictimization of young people with an intellectual or developmental disability: Risks specific to sexual solicitation. *Journal of Applied Research in Intellectual Disabilities*, 29(2), 99–110. DOI: 10.1111/jar.12163 PMID: 25871891

Nowell, K. P., Bernardin, C. J., Brown, C., & Kanne, S. (2021). Characterization of special interests in autism spectrum disorder: A brief review and pilot study using the special interests survey. *Journal of Autism and Developmental Disorders*, 51(8), 2711–2724. DOI: 10.1007/s10803-020-04743-6 PMID: 33034785

O'Brien, J. E., & Li, W. (2020). The role of the internet in the grooming, exploitation, and exit of United States domestic minor sex trafficking victims. *Journal of Children and Media*, 14(2), 187–203. DOI: 10.1080/17482798.2019.1688668

Obisesan, O. H., Mirbolouk, M., Osei, A. D., Orimoloye, S. M., Uddin, I., Dzaye, O., El Shahawy, O., Al Rifai, M., Bhatnagar, A., Stokes, A., Benjamin, E. J., DeFilippis, A. P., & Blaha, M. J. (2019). Association between e-cigarette use and depression in the behavioral risk factor surveillance system, 2016–2017. *JAMA Network Open*, 2(12), e1916800. Advance online publication. DOI: 10.1001/jamanetworkopen.2019.16800 PMID: 31800073

Øien, R. A., Nordahl-Hansen, A., & Schjølberg, S. (2018). Mental health and ASD. In Volkmar, F. R. (Ed.), *Encyclopedia of Autism Spectrum Disorders* (2nd ed., pp. 2868–2872). Springer., DOI: 10.1007/978-3-319-91280-6_102050

Parliament, U. K. (2019). *Being disabled online*. https://publications.parliament.uk/pa/cm201719/cmselect/cmpetitions/759/75905.htm

Pellicano, E., & Houting, J. (2022). Annual research review: Shifting from 'normal science' to neurodiversity in autism science. *Journal of Child Psychology and Psychiatry, and Allied Disciplines*, 63(4), 381–396. DOI: 10.1111/jcpp.13534 PMID: 34730840

Pelligra, V., Isoni, A., Fadda, R., & Doneddu, G. (2015). Theory of mind, perceived intentions and reciprocal behaviour: Evidence from individuals with autism spectrum disorder. *Journal of Economic Psychology*, 49(8), 95–107. DOI: 10.1016/j.joep.2015.05.001

Pouwels, J. L., Valkenburg, P. M., Beyens, I., van Driel, I. I., & Keijsers, L. (2021). Social media use and friendship closeness in adolescents' daily Llves: An experience sampling study. *Developmental Psychology*, 57(2), 309–323. DOI: 10.1037/dev0001148 PMID: 33539132

Roberts, A. L., Koenen, K. C., Lyall, K., Robinson, E. B., & Weisskopf, M. G. (2015). Association of autistic traits in adulthood with childhood abuse, interpersonal victimization, and posttraumatic stress. *Child Abuse & Neglect*, 45, 135–142. DOI: 10.1016/j.chiabu.2015.04.010 PMID: 25957197

Rose, S. W., Mayo, A., Ganz, O., Perreras, L., D'Silva, J., & Cohn, A. (2019). Perceived racial/ethnic discrimination, marketing, and substance use among young adults. *Journal of Ethnicity in Substance Abuse*, 18(4), 558–577. DOI: 10.1080/15332640.2018.1425949 PMID: 29424638

Rothman, E. F., Graham Holmes, L., Brooks, D., Krauss, S., & Caplan, R. (2023). Reasons for alcohol use and non-use by underage U.S. autistic youth: A qualitative study. *Autism*, 27(1), 213–225. DOI: 10.1177/13623613221091319 PMID: 35499489

Saavedra, D. (2022). Responding to technological disruptions during online video interviews conducted via Zoom. *The Qualitative Report*, 27(6), 1479–1484. DOI: 10.46743/2160-3715/2022.5524

Saggers, B. (2015). Student perceptions: Improving the educational experiences of high school students on the autism spectrum. *Improving Schools*, 18(1), 35–45. DOI: 10.1177/1365480214566213

Santhanam, S. (2023). An interactive and neurodiversity-affirming approach to communication supports for autistic students through videogaming. *Language, Speech, and Hearing Services in Schools*, 54(1), 120–139. DOI: 10.1044/2022_LSHSS-22-00027 PMID: 36626352

Savoia, E., Harriman, N. W., Su, M., Cote, T., & Shortland, N. (2021). Adolescents' exposure to online risks: Gender disparities and vulnerabilities related to online behaviors. *International Journal of Environmental Research and Public Health*, 18(11), 5786. Advance online publication. DOI: 10.3390/ijerph18115786 PMID: 34072253

Savolainen, I., Kaakinen, M., Sirola, A., & Oksanen, A. (2018). Addictive behaviors and psychological distress among adolescents and emerging adults: A mediating role of peer group identification. *Addictive Behaviors Reports*, 7, 75–81. DOI: 10.1016/j.abrep.2018.03.002 PMID: 29892700

Scholes-Balog, K., Francke, N., & Hemphill, S. (2016). Relationships between sexting, self-esteem, and sensation seeking among Australian young adults. *Sexualization. Medicine and Society*, 2(2), 2374623815627790. Advance online publication. DOI: 10.1177/2374623815627790

Scott-Barrett, J., Cebula, K., & Florian, L. (2018). Listening to young people with autism: Learning from researcher experiences. *International Journal of Research & Method in Education*, 42(2), 163–184. DOI: 10.1080/1743727X.2018.1462791

Seidman, I. (2019). *Interviewing as qualitative research: A guide for researchers in education and the social sciences*. Teachers College Press.

Shakes, P., & Cashin, A. (2019). Identifying language for people on the autism spectrum: A scoping review. *Issues in Mental Health Nursing*, 40(4), 317–325. DOI: 10.1080/01612840.2018.1522400 PMID: 30633618

Shumer, D. E., Reisner, S. L., Edwards-Leeper, L., & Tishelman, A. (2016). Evaluation of asperger syndrome in youth presenting to a gender dysphoria clinic. *LGBT Health*, 3(5), 387–390. DOI: 10.1089/lgbt.2015.0070 PMID: 26651183

Skagerberg, E., Di Ceglie, D., & Carmichael, P. (2015). Brief report: Autistic features in children and adolescents with gender dysphoria. *Journal of Autism and Developmental Disorders*, 45(8), 2628–2632. DOI: 10.1007/s10803-015-2413-x PMID: 25772537

Smusz, M., Birkbeck, C., Bidgood, A., & Allely, C. S. (2024). Exploring the experience of romantic relationships and sexuality education in neurodivergent and neurotypical young individuals. *Sexuality and Disability*, 42(3), 735–764. Advance online publication. DOI: 10.1007/s11195-024-09857-8

Stamates, A. L., Lau-Barraco, C., & Linden-Carmichael, A. N. (2016). Alcohol expectancies mediate the relationship between age of first intoxication and drinking outcomes in college binge drinkers. *Substance Use & Misuse*, 51(5), 598–607. DOI: 10.3109/10826084.2015.1126745 PMID: 27007814

Stone, B. (2018). *The affordances of online multiplayer games for the social interactions of middle-primary school-aged students with ASD* [Doctoral dissertation, Australian Catholic University]. ACU Research Bank. https://acuresearchbank.acu.edu.au/download/f4cd5a0358eeade34196f4ed94bfdb85f780eb4108a9034804b99186e2536199/3529400/STONE_2018_The_affordances_of_online_mulitplayer_games.pdf

Stone, B., Mills, K. A., & Saggers, B. (2018). Online multiplayer games for the social interactions of children with autism spectrum disorder: A resource for inclusive education. *International Journal of Inclusive Education*, 23(2), 209–228. https://doi.org/10.1080/13603116.2018.1426051

Stone, B., Mills, K. A., & Saggers, B. (2019). Multiplayer games: Multimodal features that support friendships of students with autism spectrum disorder. *Australasian Journal of Special and Inclusive Education*, 43(2), 69–82. https://doi.org/10.1017/jsi.2019.6

Stone, B., & Saggers, B. (2023). Autism, literacies, and social communication: A framework of inclusive new literacies. In Tierney, R. J., Rizvi, F., & Ercikan, K. (Eds.), *International encyclopedia of education* (4th ed., pp. 434–447). Elsevier.

Strang, J. F., Janssen, A., Tishelman, A., Leibowitz, S. F., Kenworthy, L., McGuire, J. K., Edwards-Leeper, L., Mazefsky, C. A., Rofey, D., Bascom, J., Caplan, R., Gomez-Lobo, V., Berg, D., Zaks, Z., Wallace, G. L., Wimms, H., Pine-Twaddell, E., Shumer, D., Register-Brown, K., & Anthony, L. G. (2018). Revisiting the link: Evidence of the rates of autism in studies of gender diverse individuals. *Journal of the American Academy of Child and Adolescent Psychiatry*, 57(11), 885–887. DOI: 10.1016/j.jaac.2018.04.023 PMID: 30392631

Strassberg, D. S., Cann, D., & Velarde, V. (2017). Sexting by high school students. *Archives of Sexual Behavior*, 46(6), 1667–1672. DOI: 10.1007/s10508-016-0926-9 PMID: 28050742

Street, B., Phal, K., & Rowsell, J. (2017). Multimodality and New Literacy Studies. In Jewitt, C. (Ed.), *The Routledge handbook of multimodal analysis* (pp. 227–237). Routledge.

Sturm, A., & Kasari, C. (2019). Academic and psychosocial characteristics of incoming college freshmen with autism spectrum disorder: The role of comorbidity and gender. *Autism Research*, 12(6), 931–940. DOI: 10.1002/aur.2099 PMID: 30969478

Tao, S., Reichert, F., Law, N., & Rao, N. (2022). Digital technology use and cyberbullying among primary school children: Digital literacy and parental mediation as moderators. *Cyberpsychology, Behavior, and Social Networking*, 25(9), 571–579. DOI: 10.1089/cyber.2022.0012 PMID: 35877811

Third, A. (2016). *Method guide 6: Researching the benefits and opportunities for children online*. Global Kids Online. http://globalkidsonline.net/wp-content/uploads/2016/06/Guide-6-Global-opportunities-for-children-Third.pdf

Tintori, A., Ciancimino, G., Bombelli, I., De Rocchi, D., & Cerbara, L. (2023). Children's online safety: Predictive factors of cyberbullying and online grooming involvement. *Societies (Basel, Switzerland)*, 13(2), 47. Advance online publication. DOI: 10.3390/soc13020047

Todd, R. J., & Medina, V. G. (2019). Young people's conceptions and practices of safety in online environments: An examination of challenges, theoretical perspectives, current research, findings, and potential instructional interventions. *Proceedings of the 48th Annual Conference of the International Association of School Librarianship and the 23rd International Forum on Research in School Librarianship,* 1–22. https://journals.library.ualberta.ca/slw/index.php/iasl/article/view/7377/4289

Torrijos-Fincias, P., Serrate-González, S., Martín-Lucas, J., & Muñoz-Rodríguez, J. M. (2021). Perception of risk in the use of technologies and social media. Implications for identity building during adolescence. *Education Sciences*, 11(9), 523. Advance online publication. DOI: 10.3390/educsci11090523

van der Hof, S., Lievens, E., Milkaite, I., Verdoodt, V., Hannema, T., & Liefaard, T. (2020). The child's right to protection against economic exploitation in the digital world. *International Journal of Children's Rights*, 28(4), 833–859. DOI: 10.1163/15718182-28040003

Vandoninck, S., d'Haenens, L., & Smahel, D. (2014). *Preventive measures: How youngsters avoid online risks*. EU Kids Online. https://eprints.lse.ac.uk/55797/1/EU_Kids_Online_Report_Preventivemeasures.pdf

Vejmelka, L., & Matković, R. (2021). Online interactions and problematic internet use of Croatian students during the COVID-19 pandemic. *Information (Basel)*, 12(10), 399. Advance online publication. DOI: 10.3390/info12100399

Velki, T. & Ivanković, M. (2020). Benefits and dangers of the internet from the perspective of parents of primary school students. *Život i škola. 66*(1), 43–53. https://doi.org/DOI: 10.32903/zs.66.1.4

Wagaman, M. A., Watts, K. J., Lamneck, V., D'Souza, S. A., McInroy, L. B., Eaton, A. D., & Craig, S. (2020). Managing stressors online and offline: LGBTQ+ Youth in the Southern United States. *Children and Youth Services Review*, 110, 104799. Advance online publication. DOI: 10.1016/j.childyouth.2020.104799

Wahl-Jorgensen, K. (2021). The affordances of interview research on Zoom: New intimacies and active listening. *Communication, Culture & Critique*, 14(2), 373–376. DOI: 10.1093/ccc/tcab015

Walsh, R. J., Krabbendam, L., Dewinter, J., & Begeer, S. (2018). Brief report: Gender identity differences in autistic adults: Associations with perceptual and socio-cognitive profiles. *Journal of Autism and Developmental Disorders*, 48(12), 4070–4078. DOI: 10.1007/s10803-018-3702-y PMID: 30062396

Walsh, W. A., & Tener, D. (2022). "If you don't send me five other pictures I am going to post the photo online": A qualitative analysis of experiences of survivors of sextortion. *Journal of Child Sexual Abuse*, 31(4), 447–465. DOI: 10.1080/10538712.2022.2067093 PMID: 35445638

Warrier, V., Greenberg, D. M., Weir, E., Buckingham, C., Smith, P., Lai, M.-C., Allison, C., & Baron-Cohen, S. (2020). Elevated rates of autism, other neurodevelopmental and psychiatric diagnoses, and autistic traits in transgender and gender-diverse individuals. *Nature Communications*, 11(1), 3959–3959. DOI: 10.1038/s41467-020-17794-1 PMID: 32770077

Weeks, C. D., & Subrahmanyam, K. (2019). Adolescent and emerging adult perception and participation in problematic and risky online behavior. In Attrill-Smith, A., Fullwood, C., Keep, M., & Kuss, D. J. (Eds.), *The Oxford handbook of cyberpsychology* (pp. 77–97). Oxford University Press., DOI: 10.1093/oxfordhb/9780198812746.013.6

Weir, E., Allison, C., & Baron-Cohen, S. (2021a). The sexual health, orientation, and activity of autistic adolescents and adults. *Autism Research*, 14(11), 2342–2354. DOI: 10.1002/aur.2604 PMID: 34536071

Weir, E., Allison, C., & Baron-Cohen, S. (2021b). Understanding the substance use of autistic adolescents and adults: A mixed-methods approach. *The Lancet. Psychiatry*, 8(8), 673–685. DOI: 10.1016/S2215-0366(21)00160-7 PMID: 34217427

Williams, R. S., & Schmidt, A. (2014). The sales and marketing practices of English-language internet alcohol vendors. *Addiction (Abingdon, England)*, 109(3), 432–439. DOI: 10.1111/add.12411 PMID: 24219065

World Health Organization. (2024, May 13). *Autism*. https://www.who.int/news-room/fact-sheets/detail/autism-spectrum-disorders

Yang, B., Wang, B., Sun, N., Xu, F., Wang, L., Chen, J., Yu, S., Zhang, Y., Zhu, Y., Dai, T., Zhang, Q., & Sun, C. (2021). The consequences of cyberbullying and traditional bullying victimization among adolescents: Gender differences in psychological symptoms, self-harm and suicidality. *Psychiatry Research*, 306, 114219. Advance online publication. DOI: 10.1016/j.psychres.2021.114219 PMID: 34614443

Zaeske, L. M., Harris, T. P., Williams, A., Long, H., Kerr, B. A., & Birdnow, M. (2022). Adolescent technology-use and creative activities during COVID-19: A qualitative study. *Thinking Skills and Creativity*, 46, e101190. Advance online publication. DOI: 10.1016/j.tsc.2022.101190 PMID: 36405976

KEY TERMS AND DEFINITIONS

d/Discourse: Drawing on d/Discourse theory (Gee, 2014), "discourse" denoted by a lower-case 'd' refers to spoken and written language, which includes talk and printed text. Within big 'D' "Discourses", language represents situated meanings, social practices, experiences, and perspectives within specific groups and enables people to enact various identities and unique ways of perceiving, behaving, speaking, reading, writing, and valuing that are unique and acceptable to specific groups.

Digital Literacy: Digital literacy refers to the ability to make meaning in multimodal ways effectively, critically, and safely through the navigation of digital and online environments and responsible engagement with digital content and digital technologies.

Inclusive New Literacies: Inclusive New Literacies is about recognizing and embracing the skills, capabilities, and knowledges that diverse students require for meaning making through semiotic resources such as digital, multimodal, and multimedia technologies in online and offline contexts. The notion of Inclusive New Literacies emphasizes the importance of meaning making in online and digital contexts for neurodivergent students rather than focusing only on the literacy practices of neurotypical students and the physical and face-to-face uses of spoken and written language.

Internet: The Internet is a vast global system of interconnected networks that allows users to communicate, socialize, disseminate knowledge, access formal and informal educational resources, participate in creative and civic activities, build and sustain relationships, be entertained, and stay connected with their peers, friends, families, social circles, and communities through services and resources such as social media, email, and websites.

Internet Threats: Internet threats are potentially dangerous, harmful, risky, negative, or bothersome experiences that students are exposed to in online digital environments.

Neurodivergent Students: Neurodivergent students are defined as learners who experience diversity in their cognitive processing and whose neurological development differs from what is considered as typical patterns of brain function or considered neurotypical.

Safety in Online Environments: Safety in online environments refers to the knowledge, skills, resources, and practices used to protect against Internet content, contact, conduct, and contract threats to ensure secure, positive, and respectful online digital experiences.

Student Voice: Student voice refers to the active involvement of students to share their perspectives, ideas, and experiences in multimodal ways regarding issues that impact on their social, emotional, virtual, physical, psychological, and academic lives, empowering them to be heard and participate in decision-making processes.

Chapter 4
Non-Consensual Sexting Among Adolescents: The Role of Parents, Peers, and Sexual Self-Concept

Dimitrios Chasapis
University of the Aegean, Greece

Thanos Touloupis
https://orcid.org/0009-0008-8310-306X
University of the Aegean, Greece

Alivisos (Loisos) Sofos
University of the Aegean, Greece

Asimina Tsibidaki
University of the Aegean, Greece

Eleni Lipourli
https://orcid.org/0000-0002-8459-5253
University of the Aegean, Greece

ABSTRACT

The investigation of non-consensual sexting and its contributors in adolescence are significantly under-investigated. The present study investigated non-consensual sexting among adolescents, examining via a mediation model the contributing role of perceived parental love and support, peer pressure and sexual self-concept. Overall, 204 Greek junior high school students (53% boys) of third grade from randomly selected schools filled out a self-report questionnaire that included scales related to the variables involved. Based on the results, adolescents and mainly boys exhibited above average non-consensual sexting behaviors. Sexual self-concept proved to be a full mediator between perceived parental love and support and non-consensual sexting and a partial mediator between perceived peer pressure and non-consensual sexting. The findings imply the necessity of intensifying related school prevention actions, strengthening at the same time adolescents' interpersonal relationships with peers and parents, as well

DOI: 10.4018/979-8-3693-4191-9.ch004

as their sexual self-concept as protective factors against non-consensual sexting.

INTRODUCTION

The present study investigated non-consensual sexting (sending, receiving, forwarding messages or pictures/videos of sexual content) among adolescents, examining at the same time via a mediation model the contributing role of perceived parental love and support, perceived peer pressure and sexual self-concept.

Although cyberbullying has been widely investigated among adolescents (Rostam-Abadi et al., 2024; Şahin & Ayaz-Alkaya, 2023; Zhu et al., 2021), in recent years sexting has concerned the research community as a more specific sexual risky online behavior. Sexting has been defined as the exchange (sending, receiving, forwarding) of sexual messages and photographs or images (sexts) (Lenhart, 2009; Livingstone & Gorzig, 2011) via mobile phones and/or internet (Bianchi et al., 2019). In this context, three distinct roles are identified, regarding those who send, those who receive and those who forward the sexual material to third parties (Bianchi et al., 2019).

In many cases, sexting could be perceived as a consensual behavior. This lies in the fact that sexting can be experienced as a safer form of communication, compared to real romantic relationships, or that the exchange of such messages is considered to be expected between two people who are in some form of a romantic relationship (Lenhart, 2009). In this context, sexting happens between people with mutual respect and consent, without pressure and intention to cause harm to others, although there is always the risk of such material being leaked. However, there is always the risk of such sexual material being used, leaked and trafficked in an unfair/irresponsible way involving elements of harassment and/or violence (Ringrose et al., 2012). In such cases, sexting is considered a non-consensual behavior with negative mental health consequences (Dodaj et al., 2024; Parti et al., 2023). Therefore, it is important that related studies focus, not only on consensual, but also on non-consensual sexting. Investigating its non-consensual dimensions among young people it could be addressed if and to what extent related prevention actions are necessary.

The above is of greater importance for adolescents, since the formation of sex identity constitutes one of the most important developmental challenges during adolescence (Lightfoot et al., 2022). Nevertheless, the available international studies, which show that adolescents are involved in sending, receiving and forwarding sexts, are considered limited and tend to examine sexting as a unified phenomenon, without always emphasizing its distinct non-consensual dimensions (e.g., Gassó et al., 2019; Maheux et al., 2020; Touloupis, 2024; Van Ouytsel et al., 2017). Therefore, it is implied that the examination of non-consensual sexting in the under-investigated risk group of adolescents is imperative. Related findings could inform about the necessity of intensifying/planning prevention actions within the school community of secondary education.

As far as the role of gender in non-consensual sexting, the available studies reveal somehow inconsistent findings. For example, while an important part of the literature has shown boys' over-involvement in the phenomenon (Barroso et al., 2023; Casas et al., 2019; Hunehäll Berndtsson, 2022) other studies have concluded that this phenomenon concerns girls to a greater extent than boys (Burén & Lunde, 2018; Ghorashi, 2019). It is, therefore, implied that future related studies should make clearer the gender-based profile of adolescents who tend to get involved in sexting behaviors. In this way, it could be clarified if prevention of non-consensual sexting should be possibly intensified for boys or girls.

However, apart from the further investigation of the extent of non-consensual sexting among male and female adolescents, more contributors to this phenomenon should be identified. Highlighting these contributors could mean that the prevention actions should emphasize specific parameters. In this light, social learning theory (SLT; Bandura, 1985) proposes that a human behavior, such as non-consensual sexting, could be triggered and explained by the interaction between context-related and intrapersonal factors. At this point, it is worth mentioning that individuals' perceived sense of context-related and intrapersonal factors may influence their behavioral outcomes to a greater extent compared to the objective reality (Fraser et al., 1986; Winston et al., 1994).

As far as the context-related factors, the family and peers could be considered the two most representative levels in adolescents' daily life (Durwin & Reese-Weber, 2024), which could significantly influence adolescents' behaviors outside the school, such as non-consensual sexting. Regarding the family level, parents' role and specifically perceived parental love and support has been recently highlighted as a negative predictive factor of adolescents' sexting behaviors (Hunter et al., 2021; Vanwesenbeeck et al., 2018). In other words, adolescents who feel loved and supported by their parents seem to be less prone to engage with deviant behaviors, such as non-consensual sexting (Hunter et al., 2021; Vanwesenbeeck et al., 2018). Regarding the peer level, in international literature peers are considered an important influential factor for adolescents' choices and behaviors (Dunn & Graig. 2021; Lightfoot et al., 2022). This is why recent studies emphasize perceived peer pressure highlighting its positive predictive value for sexting among adolescents. In other words, the higher the adolescents' perceived peer pressure the more likely their involvement in sexting behaviors (Gregg et al., 2018; Hartikainen et al., 2021; Lee et al., 2016). In contrast, Hunter et al. (2018) conclude that perceived peer pressure is not associated with sexting, implying that this research field is somehow inconsistent and needs further investigation. Based on the above studies, it is deduced that the negative and positive contributing value of perceived parental love and support and perceived peer pressure, respectively, for adolescents' sexting is based on significantly limited and sometimes inconsistent findings, which do not always emphasize the non-consensual dimensions of sexting. It is, therefore, imperative that future studies further examine and clarify the contributing role of these perceived context-related variables (perceived parental support / peer acceptance) to non-consensual sexting. The latter is of greater importance considering that feeling loved and supported by parents and having constructive and not intrusive relationships with peers are critical for adolescents' positive psychological development and their behavior (Lightfoot et al., 2022; Lippman & Campbell, 2014).

As far as the intrapersonal predictors of non-consensual sexting, due to the sexual nature of this behavior, it would be expected that variables related to adolescents' sexuality may play a decisive role. For example, sexual preoccupation, namely individuals' increased interest in sexual fantasies, thoughts, or activities (Clancy et al., 2021), has been shown to be a positive predictive factor of adolescents' non-consensual sexting, as adolescents who are sexually pre-occupied seem to be vulnerable to get involved in non-consensual sexting (Touloupis, 2024). In this context, another sex-related variable, which could contribute to adolescents' non-consensual sexting, could be sexual self-concept, namely individuals' positive (sexual esteem) and negative perceptions and feelings (sexual anxiety) about themselves as a sexual beings (Snell, 1998). This speculation is based on the fact that individuals with general self-esteem and less anxiety about life seem to be less prone to sexting (Fannin, 2020; Scholes-Balog et al., 2016; Sesar et al., 2021). Accordingly, it could be stated that the positive and negative side of sexual self-concept (sexual esteem and sexual anxiety, respectively), could also make adolescents less prone to non-consensual sexting behaviors. However, to date, according to the authors' knowledge no related study has been identified.

Except for the contribution of perceived context-related and intrapersonal factors to non-consensual sexting, it has been also found that perceived parental responsiveness (similar to perceived parental love and support) positively contributes to adolescents' self-concept (Chen et al., 2020). Additionally, perceived peer pressure seemed to negatively influence adolescents' self-esteem (similar to the dimension of sexual esteem) (Uslu, 2013). Consequently, it could be supposed that both perceived parental love and support and perceived peer pressure could contribute to individuals' sexual self-concept, which in turn may contribute to their engagement with non-consensual sexting. Considering the above, as well as the previously mentioned framework of SLT (Bandura, 1985), it could be proposed a mediation model explanatory of non-consensual sexting. According to this model, perceived context-related factors (perceived parental love and support / peer pressure) may contribute to non-consensual sexting, not only directly, but also indirectly through the mediating role of sexual self-concept.

Therefore, based on the above literature review and gaps, the present study aimed to investigate non-consensual sexting among adolescents, examining at the same time via a mediation model the contributing role of perceived parental love and support, perceived peer pressure and sexual self-concept.

Specifically, the specific research goals were to investigate:

(a) The extent of non-consensual sexting (sending, receiving, forwarding messages or pictures/videos of sexual content to third parties).
(b) Gender-based differences in the extent of non-consensual sexting (sending, receiving, forwarding messages or pictures/videos of sexual content).
(c) The pattern of the relationships among the variables involved (perceived parental love and support / peer pressure, sexual self-concept) which contributes to non-consensual sexting.

According to the available literature, the hypothesized connection model of the variables involved is reflected in Figure 1.

Figure 1. Hypothetical structural model of the relationships among the variables

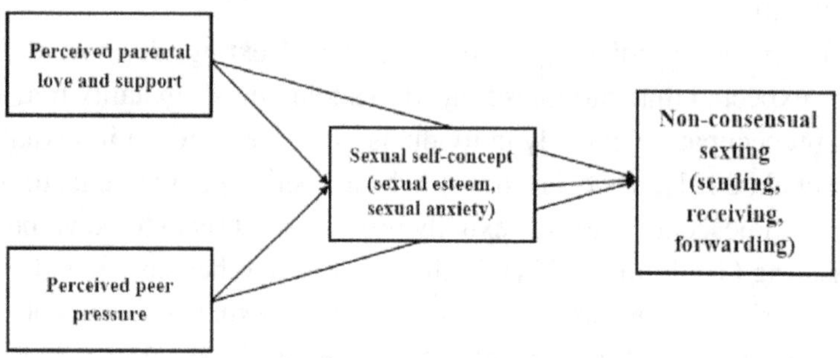

The corresponding research hypotheses were the following:

Hypothesis 1: Adolescents are involved in non-consensual sexting via sending, receiving and/or forwarding messages or pictures/videos of sexual content to third parties (Gassó et al., 2019; Maheux et al., 2020; Touloupis, 2024).

Hypothesis 2: Boys are involved to non-consensual sexting to a greater extent compared to girls (Barroso et al., 2023; Casas et al., 2019; Hunehäll Berndtsson, 2022).

Hypothesis 3: Perceived parental love and support and perceived peer pressure contribute to non-consensual sexting, not only directly (Hypothesis 3a; Hartikainen et al., 2021; Hunter et al., 2021), but also indirectly through the mediating role of sexual self-concept (Hypothesis 3b; Chen et al., 2020; Sesar et al., 2021; Uslu, 2013).

METHOD

Sample

Based on the results of the G*Power analysis (see Data Analysis Plan), the sample included 204 junior high school[1] students (53% boys) of randomly selected schools in the Prefectures of Thessaloniki and Pieria (Greece). Their mean age was 14.9 ($SD = .93$). All students made use of digital devices (e.g., mobile phones) and/or social media platforms (e.g., Facebook, Instagram, Twitter, TikTok) through their own or others' digital devices. The pilot sample was 31 students (60% boys) with a mean age of 15.1 years ($SD = .82$), which was not included in the total sample. The choice of the sample of students from the 3rd grade of junior high schools lies in the fact that this grade coincides developmentally with mid-adolescence, during which risky online behaviors, such as sexting, are widely identified among adolescents (Van Ouytsel et al., 2017).

Measures

The self-report questionnaire, except for the demographic questions (gender, age), included the following main parts:

Non-consensual sexting: Non-consensual sexting was investigated via the Sex & Tech Scale (The National Campaign to Prevent Teen and Unplanned Pregnancy, 2008), which has been previously used in a Greek adolescent population with good psychometric properties (Kamariotis, 2021). However, for the needs of the present study the scale was shortened including 4 questions about sending, 4 questions about receiving and 4 questions about forwarding material of sexual content. Questions are answered on 5-point Likert-type scale (from 1 = *Never* to 5 = *Very often*), reflecting the following three factors: *Sending* (e.g., "In the last year, have you sent to a/an known/unknown person a text message (e.g. via e-mail, Messenger, mobile phone) of sexual content to make him/her feel bad or offensive?"), *Receiving* (e.g., "In the last year, has someone you know or not posted a photo or video of sexual content on your profile (e.g., Facebook, Twitter) that made you feel bad or offended?"), *Forwarding* (e.g., "In the last year, have you forwarded to a/an known/unknown person a text message (e.g., via e-mail, Messenger, mobile phone, etc.) of sexual content about someone else?"). Testing the scale's factorial validity, a principal component analysis was applied using the Varimax-type rotation (KMO = .921, Bartlett Chi-square = 2034.093, $p < .001$). Three factors emerged with eigenvalue > 1.0 and significant interpretive value: Factor 1 = *Sending*, explaining 31.09% of the total variance with loading from .539 to .682,

Factor 2 = *Receiving*, explaining 27.14% of the total variance with loading from .499 to .603, Factor 3 = *Forwarding*, explaining 23.02% of the total variance with loading from .411 to .654. The internal consistency indexes were the following: Factor 1 (α = .883), Factor 2 (α = .855), Factor 3 (α = .822).

Parental love and support: Perceived parental love and support was investigated via the Greek version (using the forward and backward translation method) of Parental Love and Support Scale (Merrin et al., 2015). The scale includes 6 statements regarding students' feeling that they receive love and support from their parents and are answered on a 4-point Likert-type scale (0 = *Never* to 3 = *Always*). The statements reflect the unified factor *Parental love and support* (e.g., "My parents/guardians…encourage me to do well"). Testing the scale's factorial validity, a principal component analysis was applied using the Varimax-type rotation (KMO = .908, Bartlett Chi-square = 2831.118, $p < .001$). One factor emerged with eigenvalue > 1.0 and significant interpretive value: Factor 1 = *Parental love and support*, explaining 70.11% of the total variance with loading from .541 to .634. The internal consistency index of the factor was α = .891.

Peer pressure: Perceived peer pressure was investigated via the Greek version (using the forward and backward translation method) of the related subscale of the Peer Group Acceptance Scale (Williams & Anthony, 2015). The subscale includes 4 statements regarding students' psychological sense of peer pressure and are answered on a 3-point Likert-type scale (1 = *Not like me* to 3 = *A lot like me*). The statements reflect the unified factor *Peer pressure* (e.g., "I let my friends talk me into doing things I don't really want to do"). Testing the scale's factorial validity, a principal component analysis was applied using the Varimax-type rotation (KMO = .889, Bartlett Chi-square = 1781.209, $p < .001$). One factor emerged with eigenvalue > 1.0 and significant interpretive value: Factor 1 = *Peer pressure*, explaining 69.23% of the total variance with loading from .489 to .509. The internal consistency index of the factor was α = .842.

Sexual self-concept: Sexual self-concept was investigated via the Greek version (using the forward and backward translation method) of the Multidimensional Sexual Self-Concept Questionnaire (MSSCQ; Snell, 1998). The questionnaire includes 20 statements regarding positive and negative dimensions of sexual self-concept and are answered on a 5-point Likert-type scale (1 = *Not at all characteristic of me* to 5 = *Very characteristic of me*). The statements reflect two factors: *Sexual esteem* (10 items such as "I am pleased with how I handle my own sexual tendencies and behaviors.") and *Sexual anxiety* (10 items such as "I'm concerned about how the sexual aspects of my life appear to others."). Testing the scale's factorial validity, a principal component analysis was applied using the Varimax-type rotation (KMO = .852, Bartlett Chi-square = 3821.872, $p < .001$). Two factors emerged with eigenvalue > 1.0 and significant interpretive value: Factor 1 = *Sexual esteem*, explaining 34.29% of the total variance with loading from .448 to .539, Factor 2 = *Sexual anxiety*, explaining 29.83% of the total variance with loading from .401 to .508. The internal consistency indexes are the following: Factor 1 (α = .897), Factor 2 (α = .839).

Procedure

Upon obtaining approval for the study by the Research Committee of the Department of Primary Education of the University of the Aegean, the researchers emailed the randomly selected junior high schools describing all the necessary information about the nature of the study and attaching the research approval. In case of a positive response on behalf of school principals (response rate: 71%), the researchers forwarded the consent form via email, asking the school principals to deliver it to parents/guardians of students who attended the third grade. After the return of the signed consent forms (response rate:

64%), and upon consultation with the teachers of the participating schools, the researchers were invited to administer face to face the questionnaire to students whose parents/guardians had consented (January 2024 - March 2024). Before completing the questionnaire, students were asked if they make use of digital devices (e.g., mobile phones) and/or social media platforms (e.g., Facebook, Instagram, Twitter, TikTok) through their own or others' digital devices. Only 11 students replied negatively and they were excluded from the sample. Students' filled in the questionnaire in the classroom in about 15-20 minutes in the presence of the researchers in case of questions. The above procedure was also applied to the pilot study. Undoubtedly, all the ethical rules about anonymity and confidentiality were met in the study.

Data Analysis Plan

Without any missing cases different statistical tests were applied to the study. For each analysis an a priori power analysis of sample size was performed, using G*Power 3.1 (Faul et al., 2007), with power (1-β) of 85%, medium effect ($f = .05$), and an alpha error of probability $\alpha = .05$. The extent of adolescents' involvement in non-consensual sexting (Hypothesis 1) was investigated via descriptive statistics (Noncentrality parameter $\delta = 2.81$, Critical $t = 1.59$, $df = 82$, Actual power: .84, required sample per group: $N = 201$). Gender-based differences in the extent of adolescents' involvement in non-consensual sexting (Hypothesis 2) was tested through a MANOVA (Noncentrality parameter $\delta = 3.15$, Critical $t = 1.92$, $df = 81$, Actual power: .85, required sample per group: $N = 91$). To examine the bivariate relationships among the variables involved Pearson (Pearson *r*) correlations were performed (Noncentrality parameter $\delta = 2.98$, Critical $t = 2.32$, $df = 59$, Actual power: .84, required sample: $N = 201$). Furthermore, to explore the pattern of the relationships among the variables under study (Hypotheses 3), a path model was tested (based on the Mplus program with the Maximum Likelihood method). Firstly, preliminary multiple regressions were performed to investigate the predictive relationships per two variables at a time (Noncentrality parameter $\delta = 2.69$, Critical $t = 2.99$, $df = 55$, Actual power: .84, required sample: $N = 202$). Secondarily, the mediating role of sexual self-concept was checked for the path model (Noncentrality parameter $\delta = 3.22$, Critical $t = 2.15$, $df = 58$, Actual power: .85, required sample: $N = 202$). The assumptions of normality were met, since the skewness and kurtosis values of the variables were lower than $|3|$ and lower than $|10|$, respectively (Kline 2004).

RESULTS

Involvement in Non-Consensual Sexting

Based on the 5-point answering system of the non-consensual sexting scale, adolescents seemed to be involved in non-consensual sexting above average via sending ($M = 2.91$, $SD = .92$) and receiving messages or pictures/videos of sexual content ($M = 2.72$, $SD = 1.01$) and slightly above average via forwarding corresponding sexual material to third parties ($M = 2.58$, $SD = .81$).

Gender and Non-Consensual Sexting

According to MANOVA's results, non-consensual sexting seemed to be differentiated statistically significantly based on adolescents' gender, Pillai's Trace = .343, $F(4, 200) = 4.239$, $p < .01$, partial $\eta^2 = .42$. Based on the univariate analyses of variance, the above differentiation seemed to concern sending, $F(2, 202) = 3.442$, $p < .01$, partial $\eta^2 = .39$, sending, $F(2, 202) = 3.055$, $p < .01$, partial $\eta^2 = .34$, and forwarding messages or pictures/videos of sexual content $F(2, 202) = 2.128$, $p < .01$, partial $\eta^2 = .29$. Specifically, it was found that boys send ($M = 2.91$, $SD = .57$), receive ($M = 2.72$, $SD = 1.19$) και forward corresponding sexual material to third parties ($M = 2.58$, $SD = 1.12$) to a greater extent than girls ($M = 2.51$, $SD = .94$, $M = 2.31$, $SD = .82$ and $M = 2.15$, $SD = .43$, respectively).

Correlations Among the Variables

Based on Table 1, the following statistically significant correlations were observed: positive correlations among the non-consensual sexting behaviors (sending, receiving, forwarding), negative correlation between the two dimensions of sexual self-concept (sexual esteem, sexual anxiety), negative correlation between perceived parental love and support and perceived peer pressure, negative correlations between perceived parental love and support, on the one hand, and non-consensual sexting behaviors, on the other hand, positive correlations between perceived peer pressure, on the one hand, and non-consensual sexting behaviors, on the other hand, positive correlation between perceived parental love and support and sexual esteem (dimension of sexual self-concept), negative correlation between perceived parental love and support and sexual anxiety (dimension of sexual self-concept), negative correlation between perceived peer pressure and sexual esteem (dimension of sexual self-concept), positive correlation between perceived peer pressure and sexual anxiety (dimension of sexual self-concept), negative correlations between sexual esteem (dimension of sexual self-concept) and non-consensual sexting behaviors, and positive correlations between sexual anxiety (dimension of sexual self-concept) and non-consensual sexting behaviors.

Table 1. Correlations among the variables

	1	2	3	4	5	6	7
1. Sending	-						
2. Receiving	.648**	-					
3. Forwarding	.552**	.591**	-				
4. Perceived parental love and support	-109*	-.111*	-.115*	-			
5. Perceived peer pressure	.501**	.488**	.438**	-.109*	-		
6. Sexual self-esteem	-.415**	-.420**	-.401**	.402**	-.411**	-	
7. Sexual anxiety	.433**	.412**	.384**	-.392**	.309**	-.583**	-

Note: * $p < .05$, ** $p < .01$

The Structure of the Relationships Among the Variables

The results showed good fit indexes for the path model, $\chi^2(53, N = 204) = 15.848$, $p < .01$ (CFI = .989, TLI = .931, RMSEA = .054, SRMR = .051) explaining 63% of the variance of non-consensual sexting (Figure 2). To test the validity of this mediation model, the bootstrapping method was used. This non-parametric method was chosen for its ability to produce accurate confidence intervals (CI) for the indirect effect, without the need for assumptions about the normality of the data distribution.

Based on the bootstrapping analysis for the mediation model reflected in Figure 2, the indirect effects were statistically significant, with a 95% confidence interval that did not include zero (CI: .29, .51). This suggests that the mediating variable of sexual self-concept (sexual self-esteem, sexual anxiety) plays an important role in the relationship between perceived context-related variables (perceived parental love and support / peer pressure) and non-consensual sexting behaviors. Specifically, when sexual self-concept entered the relationship between perceived parental love and support and non-consensual sexting behaviors, the negative direct contribution of perceived parental love and support to sending ($\beta = -.09$, $p > .05$), receiving ($\beta = -.12$, $p > .05$) and forwarding messages or pictures/videos of sexual content to third parties ($\beta = -.10$, $p > .05$) were non-significant. This suggests that sexual self-concept proved a full mediator between perceived parental love and support and non-consensual sexting behaviors. The estimated size of all the indirect effects of sexual self-concept based on the mean of 5,000 bootstrap re-samples, ranged between .33 and .47, which supports that the full mediation process is statistically significant. Therefore, based on Figure 2, it seemed that perceived parental love and support contributed to sending, receiving and forwarding messages or pictures/videos of sexual content to third parties only indirectly, through the negative mediating role of sexual esteem, as a dimension of sexual self-concept (sending: $Z^2 = -3.48$, $p < .01$, receiving: $Z = -3.22$, $p < .01$, forwarding: $Z = -2.98$, $p < .01$), as well as through the positive mediating role of sexual anxiety, as a dimension of sexual self-concept (sending: $Z = 2.83$, $p < .01$, receiving: $Z = 2.55$, $p < .01$, forwarding: $Z = 2.11$, $p < .01$).

In contrast, when sexual self-concept entered the relationship between perceived peer pressure and non-consensual sexting behaviors, the positive direct contribution of perceived peer pressure to sending ($\beta = .38$, $p < .01$), receiving ($\beta = .44$, $p < .01$) and forwarding messages or pictures/videos of sexual content to third parties ($\beta = .35$, $p < .01$) were still significant. This suggests that sexual self-concept proved a partial mediator between the perceived peer pressure and the non-consensual sexting behaviors. The estimated size of all the indirect effects of sexual self-concept based on the mean of 5,000 bootstrap re-samples, ranged between .31 and .45, which supports that the partial mediation process is statistically significant. Therefore, based on Figure 2, it seemed that perceived peer pressure contributed to sending, receiving and forwarding messages or pictures/videos of sexual content to third parties, not only directly, but also indirectly through the negative mediating role of sexual esteem, as a dimension of sexual self-concept (sending: $Z = -2.37$, $p < .01$, receiving: $Z = -2.28$, $p < .01$, forwarding: $Z = -2.01$, $p < .01$), as well as through the positive mediating role of sexual anxiety, as a dimension of self-concept (sending: $Z = 2.87$, $p < .01$, receiving: $Z = 2.41$, $p < .01$, forwarding: $Z = 2.19$, $p < .01$).

Figure 2. Schematic representation of the path model for non-consensual sexting (N = 204)

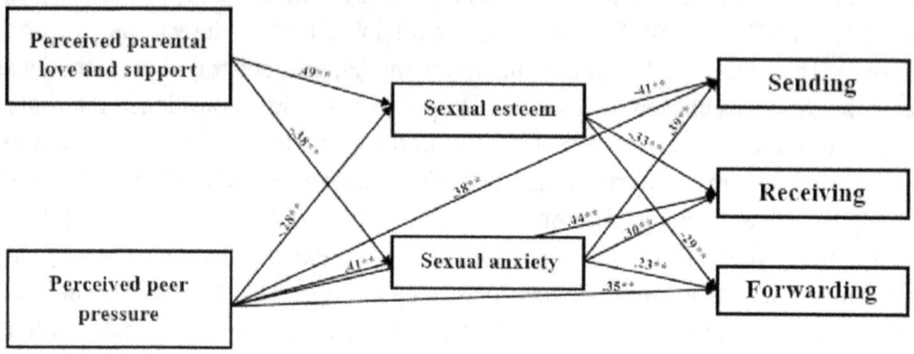

Note 1: The values on the arrows are standardized coefficients of the model. The following correlations were included in the model but not depicted in the Figure for clarity reasons:

Perceived parental love and support - Perceived peer pressure = -.22**, Sexual esteem - Sexual anxiety = -.59**, Sending - Receiving = .61**, Sending - Forwarding = .42**, Receiving - Forwarding = .44**

Note 2: ** $p < .01$.

DISCUSSION

The present study aimed to investigate non-consensual sexting among adolescents, examining at the same time via a mediation model the contributing role of perceived parental love and support, perceived peer pressure and sexual self-concept.

Firstly, based on the 5-point answering system of the related scale, it was found that adolescents are involved in non-consensual sexting above average via sending and receiving messages or pictures/videos of sexual content and slightly above average via forwarding corresponding sexual material to third parties. This finding confirms Hypothesis 1 and it is in line with studies which conclude adolescents' involvement in the phenomenon under study (Gassó et al., 2019; Maheux et al., 2020; Van Ouytsel et al., 2017). In contrast with the previous studies that examine sexting as a unified phenomenon, without clear distinction between its consensual and non-consensual dimensions, the present findings reflect the unsafe pattern (non-consensual) of sexting among today's adolescents (Touloupis, 2024). The latter raises concerns regarding the future online and sexual behavior of the participants as emerging adults.

Furthermore, boys were found to be involved in non-consensual sexting to a greater extent than girls. This finding confirms Hypothesis 2 and it is consistent with previous corresponding findings (Barroso et al., 2023; Casas et al., 2019; Hunehäll Berndtsson, 2022). The present finding could be somehow explained by the socially stereotyped image, according to which male adolescents are considered prone to engage in socially deviant and unacceptable behaviors to a greater extent than girls (Durwin & Reese-Weber, 2024). This stereotype could have influenced male adolescents' behavior not only in a physical but also in an electronic context, making them more susceptible to non-consensual sexting behaviors than girls. However, considering that recent studies highlight that both boys and girls are almost equally involved in similar risky online behaviors, such as cyberbullying (Touloupis & Athanasiades, 2022), it is implied the necessity to further investigate possible gender-based differences in non-consensual sexting.

Additionally, the path analyses results regarding the pattern of the relationships among the variables involved revealed that adolescents' sexual self-concept (sexual esteem, sexual anxiety) fully mediated between their perceived parental love and support and their non-consensual sexting behaviors. In contrast, students' sexual self-concept (sexual esteem, sexual anxiety) proved a partial mediator between their perceived peer pressure and non-consensual sexting. It is interesting that only perceived peer pressure (and not perceived parental love and support) seemed to contribute to non-consensual sexting, not only indirectly via the partial mediating role of sexual self-concept, but also directly. This finding partially confirms Hypothesis 3a, since it was expected that both perceived context-related factors (perceived parental love and support / peer pressure) would directly contribute to non-consensual sexting. Accordingly, this finding is in line with studies which mention the negative contributing role of perceived parental love and support to sexting behaviors (Hunter et al., 2021; Vanwesenbeeck et al., 2018) but it is in contrast with studies which conclude the positive contributing role of perceived peer pressure to sexting (Gregg et al., 2018; Hartikainen et al., 2021). Considering the significant influence of peers and the de-idealization of parental figures during adolescence (Burén et al., 2022; Hartikainen et al., 2021; Lightfoot et al., 2022; Maheux et al., 2020) it could be explained to some extent why only perceived peer pressure (and not perceived parental love and support) was found to have the potential to directly contribute to adolescents' involvement in non-consensual sexting. Nevertheless, future examination of the proposed mediation model could confirm or not the pattern of the relationships among the variables and the corresponding interpretations.

Also, the findings of the path analysis confirm Hypothesis 3b regarding the mediating role (partial or full) of sexual self-concept in the relationship between perceived context-related factors (perceived parental love and support / peer pressure) and non-consensual sexting. The present finding reflects similar studies which, although have not examined the mediating role of sexual self-concept in the above relationship, however have highlighted bivariate relationships between perceived context-related variables (parental responsiveness, peer pressure) and self-related variables (self-concept, self-esteem) (Chen et al., 2020; Uslu, 2013), as well as between self-related variables (self-esteem) and sexting (Sesar et al., 2021). It is, therefore, implied that individuals' positive (sexual esteem) and negative aspect (sexual anxiety) of sexual self-concept could act as an underlying psychological mechanism, which better explains the way perceived context-related factors contribute to non-consensual sexting. In other words, perceived parental love and support and perceived peer pressure may contribute to adolescents' sexual esteem and sexual anxiety (dimensions of sexual self-concept) and, subsequently, sexual self-concept influences their engagement with non-consensual sexting. In general, this pattern of relationships reflects the framework of SLT (Bandura, 1985), as there seems to be an interaction between perceived context-related factors (perceived parental love and support / peer pressure) and individual characteristics (sexual self-concept), which contributes to adolescents' involvement in non-consensual sexting.

The above findings should be interpreted cautiously due to specific limitations, such as the possibly socially acceptable responses, the numerically and geographically restricted sample, the restriction to the quantitative methodology, as well as the cross-sectional research design of the study. Despite the above limitations, the present study contributes to both a theoretical and an applied level. Theoretically, the findings offer research evidence about the extent of non-consensual sexting among the under-investigated age group of adolescents. Additionally, the findings propose an explanatory mediation model, which via the SLT framework could better capture the contributors of non-consensual sexting in adolescence. At an applied level, the findings have practical applications. In particular, they highlight the necessity of implementing school prevention actions, starting from preadolescence, with a focus on the prevention of risky sexual online behaviors among students. The effectiveness of these actions could be strengthened by the integration of experiential activities, aimed at strengthening adolescents' interpersonal relationships with peers and parents, as well as their sexual self-concept, as protective factors against non-consensual sexting.

FUTURE RESEARCH DIRECTIONS

Within the general scope of the book "Students' Online Risk Behaviors: Psychoeducational Predictors, Outcomes, and Prevention" and the more specific framework of the present chapter, future research directions emerge in this research field. For example, future related studies, conducted on a geographically and numerically more representative sample of adolescents, could follow a longitudinal research design to allow safer conclusions regarding the pattern of the relationships among the variables involved and, therefore, more generalizable results. Furthermore, supplementary qualitative data, via semi-structured interviews with adolescents, may highlight unexplored aspects of the issue. Finally, future studies could enrich the proposed mediation model by co-examining more variables related to the family and the school context, as well as other intrapersonal variables to offer a more multidimensional explanation of contributors to adolescents' non-consensual sexting.

CONCLUSION

Summing up, the present chapter concludes that non-consensual sexting concerns adolescents, and mainly boys. Furthermore, adopting the framework of the SLT, a mediation model was proposed which explains adolescents' engagement with non-consensual sexting. Based on this model, it seems that both perceived context-related variables, such as perceived parental love and support and perceived peer acceptance, and intrapersonal characteristics, such as sexual self-concept (sexual esteem, sexual anxiety), interact with each other and contribute in a more multifaceted way to adolescents' non-consensual sexting behaviors. Specifically, it was found that adolescents' sexual self-concept fully mediated between their perceived parental love and support and their non-consensual sexting behaviors. In contrast, students' sexual self-concept proved a partial mediator between their perceived peer pressure and non-consensual sexting.

REFERENCES

Bandura, A. (1985). Model of causality in social learning theory. In *Cognition and psychotherapy* (pp. 81–99). Springer US. DOI: 10.1007/978-1-4684-7562-3_3

Barroso, R., Marinho, A. R., Figueiredo, P., Ramião, E., & Silva, A. S. (2023). Consensual and non-consensual sexting behaviors in adolescence: A systematic review. *Adolescent Research Review*, 8(1), 1–20. DOI: 10.1007/s40894-022-00199-0

Bianchi, D., Morelli, M., Baiocco, R., Cattelino, E., Laghi, F., & Chirumbolo, A. (2019). Family functioning patterns predict teenage girls' sexting. *International Journal of Behavioral Development*, 43(6), 507–514. DOI: 10.1177/0165025419873037

Burén, J., & Lunde, C. (2018). Sexting among adolescents: A nuanced and gendered online challenge for young people. *Computers in Human Behavior*, 85, 210–217. DOI: 10.1016/j.chb.2018.02.003

Casas, J. A., Ojeda, M., Elipe, P., & Del Rey, R. (2019). Exploring which factors contribute to teens' participation in sexting. *Computers in Human Behavior*, 100, 60–69. DOI: 10.1016/j.chb.2019.06.010

Chen, W. W., Yuan, H., Yang, X., & Lai, S. K. (2020). Parenting, self-concept, and attitudes about romantic relationships. *Journal of Adolescence*, 82(1), 41–49. DOI: 10.1016/j.adolescence.2020.06.003 PMID: 32593052

Clancy, E. M., Howard, D., Chong, S., & Klettke, B. (2021). Dream it, do it? Associations between pornography use, risky sexual behaviour, sexual preoccupation and sexting behaviours among young Australian adults. *Sexes*, 2(4), 433–444. DOI: 10.3390/sexes2040034

Dodaj, A., Prijatelj, K., & Kuterovac Jagodić, G. (2024). Sexting Behavior Among Youths: Nature, Determinants, and Consequences. *Psihologijske Teme*, 33(1), 171–189. DOI: 10.31820/pt.33.1.9

Dunn, L. W., & Graig, J. G. (2021). *Understanding Human Development* [in Greek]. Papazisi.

Durwin, C. C., & Reese-Weber, M. (2024). *Educational Psychology: Theory and Practice* [in Greek]. Tziola.

Fannin, H. (2020). Sexting among adolescents: examining the association between sexting and self-esteem. *Physician Assistant Studies | Student Articles,* 11. https://doi.org/DOI: 10.33015/dominican.edu/2020.PAS.11

Fraser, B. J., Treagust, D. F., & Dennis, N. C. (1986). Development of an instrument for assessing classroom psychosocial environment at universities and colleges. *Studies in Higher Education*, 11(1), 43–54. DOI: 10.1080/03075078612331378451

Gassó, A. M., Klettke, B., Agustina, J. R., & Montiel, I. (2019). Sexting, mental health, and victimization among adolescents: A literature review. *International Journal of Environmental Research and Public Health*, 16(13), 2364. DOI: 10.3390/ijerph16132364 PMID: 31277335

Ghorashi, Z. (2019). Teenage sexting and sexual behaviors in an Iranian setting. *Sexuality & Culture*, 23(4), 1274–1282. DOI: 10.1007/s12119-019-09622-6

Gregg, D., Somers, C. L., Pernice, F. M., Hillman, S. B., & Kernsmith, P. (2018). Sexting rates and predictors from an urban midwest high school. *The Journal of School Health*, 88(6), 423–433. DOI: 10.1111/josh.12628 PMID: 29749003

Hartikainen, H., Razi, A., & Wisniewski, P. (2021, October). 'If You Care About Me, You'll Send Me a Pic'-Examining the Role of Peer Pressure in Adolescent Sexting. In *Companion Publication of the 2021 Conference on Computer Supported Cooperative Work and Social Computing* (pp. 67-71). DOI: 10.1145/3462204.3481739

Hunehäll Berndtsson, K. (2022). "Something you just don't talk about": An analysis of teenage boys' experiences of non-consensual sexting in lower secondary school. *Journal of Men's Studies*, 30(2), 155–173. DOI: 10.1177/10608265211042794

Hunter, S. C., Russell, K., & Knifton, L. (2018).*Individual, family, and school factors relating to sexting and bullying*. University of Strathclyde. DOI: 10.17605/OSF.IO/2EVG4

Hunter, S. C., Russell, K., Pagani, S., Munro, L., Pimenta, S. M., Marín-López, I., Hong, J. S., & Knifton, L. (2021). A social-ecological approach to understanding adolescent sexting behavior. *Archives of Sexual Behavior*, 50(6), 2347–2357. DOI: 10.1007/s10508-021-01988-9 PMID: 33982213

Kamariotis, T. (2021). *The phenomenon of sexting among adolescents and young adults: protective and risk factors [in Greek]*. Unpublished Doctoral thesis, Department of Psychology, Aristotle University of Thessaloniki.

Kline, R. B. (2004). *Principles and practice of structural equation modeling*. The Guilford Press.

Lee, C. H., Moak, S., & Walker, J. T. (2016). Effects of self-control, social control, and social learning on sexting behavior among South Korean youths. *Youth & Society*, 48(2), 242–264. DOI: 10.1177/0044118X13490762

Lenhart, A. (2009). *Teens and sexting* (Vol. 15). Pew Internet & American Life Project.

Lightfoot, C., Cole, M., & Cole, S. R. (2022). *Children's Development* [in Greek]. Gutenberg.

Lippman, J. R., & Campbell, S. W. (2014). Damned if you do, damned if you don't… if you're a girl: Relational and normative contexts of adolescent sexting in the United States. *Journal of Children and Media*, 8(4), 371–386. DOI: 10.1080/17482798.2014.923009

Livingstone, S., & Gorzig, A. (2011). Sexting. In S., Livingstone, L., Haddon, & A., Gorzig (Eds.), *Children, Risk and Safety on the Internet: Kids online in comparative perspective* (pp. 1-10). The Policy Press.

Maheux, A. J., Evans, R., Widman, L., Nesi, J., Prinstein, M. J., & Choukas-Bradley, S. (2020). Popular peer norms and adolescent sexting behavior. *Journal of Adolescence*, 78(1), 62–66. DOI: 10.1016/j.adolescence.2019.12.002 PMID: 31841872

Merrin, G. J., Hong, J. S., & Espelage, D. L. (2015). Are the risk and protective factors similar for gang-involved, pressured-to-join, and non-gang-involved youth? A social-ecological analysis. *The American Journal of Orthopsychiatry*, 85(6), 522–535. DOI: 10.1037/ort0000094 PMID: 26594921

Ministry of Education. (n.d.). *Junior High School* [in Greek]. Retrieved from https://www.minedu.gov.gr/gymnasio-m-2/to-thema-gumnasio

Parti, K., Sanders, C. E., & Englander, E. K. (2023). Sexting at an Early Age: Patterns and Poor Health-Related Consequences of Pressured Sexting in Middle and High School. *The Journal of School Health*, 93(1), 73–81. DOI: 10.1111/josh.13258 PMID: 36251455

Ringrose, J., Gill, R., Livingstone, S., & Harvey, L. (2012). *A qualitative study of children, young people and 'sexting': a report prepared for the NSPCC*. National Society for the Prevention of Cruelty to Children.

Rostam-Abadi, Y., Stefanovics, E. A., & Potenza, M. N. (2024). An exploratory study of the prevalence and adverse associations of in-school traditional bullying and cyberbullying among adolescents in Connecticut. *Journal of Psychiatric Research*, 173, 372–380. DOI: 10.1016/j.jpsychires.2024.03.033 PMID: 38593696

Şahin, S. S., & Ayaz-Alkaya, S. (2023). Prevalence and predisposing factors of peer bullying and cyberbullying among adolescents: A cross-sectional study. *Children and Youth Services Review*, 155, 107216. DOI: 10.1016/j.childyouth.2023.107216

Scholes-Balog, K., Francke, N., & Hemphill, S. (2016). Relationships between sexting, self-esteem, and sensation seeking among Australian young adults. *Sexualization, Media, &. Society*, 2(2), 1–8. DOI: 10.1177/2374623815627790

Sesar, K., Dodaj, A., & Jandrić, T. (2021). Young People Who Sext: The Role of Self-Esteem and Body-Esteem. *Central European Journal of Paediatrics*, 17(1), 52–65. DOI: 10.5457/p2005-114.288

Snell, W. E.Jr. (1998). The multidimensional sexual self-concept questionnaire. In Davis, C. M., Yarber, W. L., Bausenman, R., Schreer, G., & Davis, S. L. (Eds.), *Handbook of sexuality-related measures* (pp. 521–524). Sage.

The National Campaign to Prevent Teen and Unplanned Pregnancy. (2008). *Sex and Tech: Results from a Survey of Teens and Young Adults*. Author.

Touloupis, T. (2024). School Prevention of Non-consensual Sexting among Middle Adolescents: Does Sexual Preoccupation Awareness Matter? *Frontiers in Psychology (section: Media Psychology), 15,* 1384620. DOI: 10.3389/fpsyg.2024.1384620

Touloupis, T., & Athanasiades, C. (2022). Cyberbullying and Empathy among Elementary School Students: Do Special Educational Needs Make a Difference? *Scandinavian Journal of Psychology*, 63(6), 609–623. DOI: 10.1111/sjop.12838 PMID: 35698831

Uslu, M. (2013). Relationship between degrees of self-esteem and peer pressure in high school adolescents. *International Journal of Academic Research*, 5(3), 117–122. DOI: 10.7813/2075-4124.2013/5-3/B.19

Van Ouytsel, J., Van Gool, E., Walrave, M., Ponnet, K., & Peeters, E. (2017). Sexting: Adolescents' perceptions of the applications used for, motives for, and consequences of sexting. *Journal of Youth Studies*, 20(4), 446–470. DOI: 10.1080/13676261.2016.1241865

Vanwesenbeeck, I., Ponnet, K., Walrave, M., & Van Ouytsel, J. (2018). Parents' Role in Adolescents' Sexting Behaviour. In Walrave, M., Van Ouytsel, J., Ponnet, K., & Temple, J. (Eds.), *Sexting. Palgrave Studies in Cyberpsychology*. Palgrave Macmillan. DOI: 10.1007/978-3-319-71882-8_5

Williams, L. R., & Anthony, E. K. (2015). A model of positive family and peer relationships on adolescent functioning. *Journal of Child and Family Studies*, 24(3), 658–667. DOI: 10.1007/s10826-013-9876-1

Winston, R. B., Vahala, M. E., Nichols, E. C., & Gillis, M. E. (1994). A measure of college classroom climate: The College Classroom Environment Scales. *Journal of College Student Development*, 35(1), 11–18.

Zhu, C., Huang, S., Evans, R., & Zhang, W. (2021). Cyberbullying among adolescents and children: A comprehensive review of the global situation, risk factors, and preventive measures. *Frontiers in Public Health*, 9, 634909. DOI: 10.3389/fpubh.2021.634909 PMID: 33791270

ADDITIONAL READING

Barrense-Dias, Y., Akre, C., Auderset, D., Leeners, B., Morselli, D., & Surís, J. C. (2020). Non-consensual sexting: Characteristics and motives of youths who share received-intimate content without consent. *Sexual Health*, 17(3), 270–278. DOI: 10.1071/SH19201 PMID: 32594970

Confalonieri, E., Cuccì, G., Olivari, M. G., Parise, M., Borroni, E., & Villani, D. (2020). What are you sexting? Parental practices, sexting attitudes and behaviors among Italian adolescents. *BMC Psychology*, 8(1), 1–11. DOI: 10.1186/s40359-020-00425-1 PMID: 32539837

Dolev-Cohen, M., & Ricon, T. (2020). Demystifying sexting: Adolescent sexting and its associations with parenting styles and sense of parental social control in Israel. *Cyberpsychology (Brno)*, 14(1), 6. Advance online publication. DOI: 10.5817/CP2020-1-6

Holfeld, B., Mishna, F., Craig, W., & Zuberi, S. (2024). A latent profile analysis of the consensual and non-consensual sexting experiences among Canadian adolescents. *Youth & Society*, 56(4), 713–733. DOI: 10.1177/0044118X231202814 PMID: 38586084

Marengo, D., Settanni, M., & Longobardi, C. (2019). The associations between sex drive, sexual self-concept, sexual orientation, and exposure to online victimization in Italian adolescents: Investigating the mediating role of verbal and visual sexting behaviors. *Children and Youth Services Review*, 102, 18–26. DOI: 10.1016/j.childyouth.2019.04.023

Naezer, M., & van Oosterhout, L. (2021). Only sluts love sexting: Youth, sexual norms and non-consensual sharing of digital sexual images. *Journal of Gender Studies*, 30(1), 79–90. DOI: 10.1080/09589236.2020.1799767

Schokkenbroek, J. M., Ponnet, K., Van Ouytsel, J., Walrave, M., & Hardyns, W. (2023). Receive, forward, repeat: The link between sexting intention, sexting attitudes, and non-consensual sexting behaviours. *Telematics and Informatics*, 84, 102036. DOI: 10.1016/j.tele.2023.102036

Symons, K., Ponnet, K., Walrave, M., & Heirman, W. (2018). Sexting scripts in adolescent relationships: Is sexting becoming the norm? *New Media & Society*, 20(10), 3836–3857. DOI: 10.1177/1461444818761869

Valido, A., Espelage, D. L., Hong, J. S., Rivas-Koehl, M., & Robinson, L. E. (2020). Social-ecological examination of non-consensual sexting perpetration among US adolescents. *International Journal of Environmental Research and Public Health*, 17(24), 9477. DOI: 10.3390/ijerph17249477 PMID: 33348870

Verrastro, V., Saladino, V., Eleuteri, S., Barberis, N., & Cuzzocrea, N. B. F. (2023). Sexting, Self-esteem, and Social Media: A Comparison among Frequent, Occasional, and Non-sexting Italian Adolescent Girls. *Psychology in Russia : State of the Art*, 16(4), 3–20. DOI: 10.11621/PIR.2023.0401 PMID: 38162809

KEY TERMS AND DEFINITIONS

Middle adolescence: It is the middle stage (14-17 years) of the developmental period of adolescence.

Parental Love and Support: Parental love and support has to do with the affection, care, comfort, concern, nurture, and acceptance that a child can feel from their parents.

Peer Pressure: Peer pressure is the process by which members of the same social group influence other members to do things that they may be resistant to, or might not otherwise choose to do.

Sexting: Sexting is sending, receiving, or forwarding sexually explicit messages, photographs, or videos, primarily between mobile phones.

Sexual Self-Concept: A person's feelings about oneself as a sexual creature.

ENDNOTES

1 In Greece, Junior High School includes the first three grades (middle adolescence; 12-15 years old) of the six-year secondary education (Ministry of Education, n.d.).

2 Z = standardized normal distribution value

Chapter 5
Sexting Profiles Among Adolescents:
The Role of Gender, Relationship Status, and Self-Esteem

Theocharis Kamariotis
Aristotle University of Thessaloniki, Greece

Christina Athanasiades
Aristotle University of Thessaloniki, Greece

ABSTRACT

The study aimed to investigate the complex ways in which adolescents engage in sexting behaviors and the role of gender, relationship status, and self-esteem in this behavior. One hundred and eighty-six Greek adolescents (93 boys and 93 girls) participated in this study and completed a self-reported questionnaire regarding sexting as well as the Rosenberg self-esteem scale. Demographic information about gender and relationship status were also acquired. According to the results, adolescents showed a variety of sexting profiles, which, on the whole, were characterized by interpersonal interaction and risky involvement with the phenomenon. Female identity was related to safe sexting, having a relationship was related to risky sexting, while low self-esteem was related to passive sexting. Findings are discussed in light of their use in preventive psycho-educational interventions and in the counseling process.

INTRODUCTION

Sexting has been defined as the exchange of sexually explicit messages, pictures and videos through electronic devices (Livingstone & Gorzig, 2011). It refers to a set of electronic sexual behaviors, such as sending and receiving private sexual material, as well as to risky behaviors, such as posting sexual material online and sharing or forwarding nude or seminude photos and sexual messages without the consent of the initial sender (Katzman, 2010; Livingstone & Gorzig, 2011; Ringrose et al., 2012).

Sexting is also a way for someone to choose a sexual partner, to exchange information about his/her sexual history, about safe sex or sexual satisfaction and to negotiate the boundaries of a sexual relationship (Boyle & O'Sullivan, 2010). The benefits of this type of sexual communication are the reported feelings

DOI: 10.4018/979-8-3693-4191-9.ch005

of intimacy between sexual partners who exchange sexual messages (Le, 2016) and the improvement of sexual communication and sexual satisfaction (Bianchi et al., 2019; Hawkes & Hanipraja, 2020; Hudson & Marshall, 2018). Moreover, it is a way of exploring new sexual experiences or sexual orientation (Watson et al., 2018), a way of becoming more assertive regarding sexual relationships (Crimmins & Seigfried-Spellar, 2014) and a way of becoming more confident about body image (Jorgensen, 2019). Lastly, sexting offer adolescents, in particular, new ways to develop and maintain interpersonal relationships but also give them more opportunities to explore their relationships and define themselves (Simpson, 2013).

However, sexually explicit messages may not depict the true intentions and feelings, due to lack of face-to-face communication, resulting to misunderstanding between the sender and the receiver about the content of the conversation and the intention of those messages (Woolard, 2011). Adolescents have a need to conform to the trends they experience around them, so they either accept peer pressure to send such messages or photos, or seek to engage in the exchange of such messages in order not to be excluded from the social group (Rice et al., 2012; Walrave et al., 2014). As their reputation is very important in this developmental period, it has been found that adolescents who are popular with their peers or seek acceptance and popularity have a higher chance of engaging in sexting behaviors (Vanden Abeele et al., 2014). Moreover, adolescents do not seem to fully understand the consequences of their actions, as the frontal lobe which is the part of the brain responsible for logic and decision making is not fully developed before the age of 20 (Doring, 2014; Ostrager, 2010). Thus, the risky behaviors that teenagers often adopt are not the result of a lack of knowledge, but the result of impulsivity or emotional loading (Muscari, 2009).

The most prominent risk related to sexting is that sexually explicit material (either a message or picture/video) exchanged between two people is often shared or forwarded to others as well, without the consent of the initial sender, as mentioned above. This occurs either as an act of revenge of a sexual partner after a break-up, or to brag to peers about the sexual material one has received (VanOuytsel et al., 2017). Researchers outline the danger that adolescents face by engagement in these risky behaviors, caused by the public exposure of this electronic material (Ricciardelli & Adorjan, 2019).

Sharing sexual messages with others is a form of verbal or social bullying (such as being called offensive nicknames) and has been linked to sexting (Lippman & Campbell, 2014; VanOuytsel et al., 2017; Walrave et al., 2015). Furthermore, a significant relationship has been found between the publication of nude or semi-nude photos of girls on the Internet and their verbal victimization, originating from other girls (Phippen & Kennedy, 2018). Also, young people who view sexual material of themselves online are more likely to be involved as either victims or perpetrators in cyberbullying incidents (Jonsson et al., 2014). Youth may experience threats and blackmail as a result of engaging in posted sexting (Wolak & Finkelhor, 2011) and subsequently report effects such as anger, distress, and symptoms of anxiety and depression (Bilic, 2013; Siegle, 2010).

Although there is research that studies the individual forms, few studies have examined the ways in which individuals engage in various aspects of the phenomenon and adopt more than one such behavior in combination. Various categorizations based on involvement in sexting have been proposed in the literature. These are: the distinction between aggravated sexting (refers to cases where it is illegal or harmful) and experimental sexting (refers to cases where these individuals. seeking their sexual identity) (Wolak & Finkelhor, 2011), the distinction between active sexting (referring to the creation, display, publication or sending of sexual material) and passive sexting (referring to the acceptance of such material) (Temple & Choi, 2014), or segregation based on sharing such material, sending, receiving, or not engaging in the phenomenon (Gordon-Messer et al., 2013). The last two categorizations have often been used by research to study the phenomenon. However, none of them account for all forms of sexting. These are sending and receiving personal sexual material, exchanging text messages and photos/videos, sharing sexual material without the original sender's consent and posting it online.

Studies determine the prevalence of sexting between 2,5% and 27% regarding adolescents (Ricketts et al., 2015; Ringrose, et al, 2012; Ybarra & Mitchell, 2014), while another group of studies define it between 54% and 65,5% (McLaughlin, 2012; Strohmaier et al., 2014; Yoder et al, 2018). This wide range is explained due to methodological differences that are noticed in the studies. For example, in some cases the definition includes more behaviors and forms, while in others the definition is stricter or limited (e.g., studying cases that constitute illegal material, including only sexual images or only the use of mobile phones, etc) (Barrense-Dias et al., 2017). Apart from prevalence, research has studied various factors related to sexting, in order to investigate the way in which adolescents are involved in this behavior and the risk related to the exchange of sexually explicit messages of pictures/videos. Among these factors are gender, relationship status and self-esteem.

Sexual objectification and gender stereotypes influence involvement in sexting (Manago et al., 2012; VanOuytsel et al., 2014). During adolescence, girls usually are judged about their sexual expression (Dobson, 2019), such as sending a sexual picture (Hasinoff, 2013; Ringrose et al., 2013). This may lead to their calumniation, by calling them with names, such as "slut" (Ringrose et al., 2013; Walker et al., 2013), thus damaging their reputation, whereas this is not expected to happen to boys (Lenhart, 2009c). As a result, girls' attitudes towards sexting are more negative than boys' (Walrave et al., 2014), while they report that they have experienced more negative outcomes regarding sexting (Buren, 2018). On the other hand, boys tend to face less severe risks in relation to sexting (Ricciardelli & Adorjan, 2019), due to the fact that it is expected of them to adopt those sexual behaviors (Setty, 2019), for which they are applauded and admired. However, boys also face the consequences of gender stereotypes, because they are socially pressured to display their sexual activity (Ringrose, 2010).

Studies about *gender differences* reach to diversified conclusions, showing either more frequent involvement of girls (Hunter et al., 2018; Livingstone & Gorzig, 2014; Ybarra & Mitchell, 2014) or more frequent involvement of boys (Englander, 2015; Gregg et al., 2018; Hudson et al., 2014). At the same time, there are studies supporting that there are no gender differences about involvement in sexting (Gamez-Guadix & deSantisteban, 2018; Lee et al., 2016; Silva et al., 2016; Villacampa, 2017). On the other hand, it has been supported that there is a different set of sexting behaviors in which girls and boys are more involved (Patchin & Hinduja, 2019). For example, in some studies it is more likely for girls to receive sexual messages or share sexual pictures or videos of themselves with others (Houck et al., 2014; Martinez-Prather & Vandiver, 2014; Mitchell et al., 2012; Reyns et al., 2014), while other studies support that boys are more likely to send sexually explicit messages (Marume et al., 2018; The National Campaign, 2008) or forward pictures of others without their consent (Hilinski-Rosick & Freiburger, 2012).

Relationship status between sexters is a factor related to engagement in sexting. In particular, it was found that youngsters who are in a relationship, either casual or serious, are more likely to exchange sexually explicit messages or photos/videos (Baiden et al., 2020; Ghorasi, 2019; Hilinski-Rosick, & Freiburger, 2012). Sexting between two partners in any form of relationship is associated to emotions of affection, proximity, trust, amusement and sexual arousement, in anticipation to face to face contact (Hasinoff, 2013; Renfrow & Rollo, 2014). A relevant study among adolescents showed a significant association between sexting and higher perception of passion within their relationship (VanOuytsel et al. 2019). Thus, individuals who exchange sexually explicit messages with their partner, report high perceived satisfaction of their relationship (Parker et al., 2013).

Positive outcomes of sexting are related to the type of the relationship status. Adolescents sexters in a casual/dating relationship were more likely to share sexting material without consent of their partner, as compared to peer individuals who responded that they were in a serious relationship (Drouin et al., 2013). On the other hand, it was found that among adolescents, it was more likely for someone to send nudes or semi-nudes pictures of themselves or share pictures of others without their consent, when they were in a serious relationship (Hilinski-Rosick, & Ybarra, 2012).

The relationship between *self-esteem* and sexting among adolescents has also been studied. Global self-esteem refers to the sum of positive and negative feelings about self (Rosenberg, 1965) and it plays a key role to the formation of personality, while it is related to orderly sexual functionality and sexual communication (Hally & Pollack, 1993; Larson et al., 1998). Research findings are contradictory about the association between self-esteem and sexual behaviors, showing positive, negative or no relation between them (Ethier et al., 2006). However, it was found that global and sexual self-esteem were predictive factors of positive sexual communication, which in turn tended to enhance global and sexual self-esteem (Oattes & Offman, 2007). Moreover, it was found a positive association between sexting and low body image self-esteem in adolescents (Milton et al., 2019). In another study, a similar association was found only for girls in adolescence (Sorbring et al., 2014).

Research also showed a direct link between sexting and low self-esteem among adolescents (Baiden et al., 2020; Scholes-Balog et al., 2016). Another study concluded that adolescents who send or post sexually explicit images of themselves showed low level of self-esteem (Ybarra & Mitchell, 2014). Conversely, studies found no statistically significant relationship between sexting and self-esteem in adolescents (Burić et al., 2020; Gamez-Guadix & deSantisteban, 2018; Gregg et al., 2018; Temple et al. 2014).

The present study

Previous findings about the impact of gender and self-esteem to sexting, are limited or contradictory, while findings about relationship status are more concrete about its relationship to sexting, however it is not clear if it is related to safe or risky behaviors of the phenomenon. Lastly, most studies seem to measure the phenomenon of sexting as a whole, without making any distinction among the different manifestations of this behavior, such as sending and receiving interpersonal sexual messages or images/videos, posting sexual material online and sharing or forwarding nude or seminude photos and sexual messages without consent of the initial sender. The exchange of interpersonal sexual messages or images/videos is assumed to be a safer behavior, as it is private material between two consenting users, while posting online this material of forwarding it to others without consent is assumed to be a riskier behaviour, as it may lead to negative outcomes, such as cybervictimization or offline victimization. Studying sexting as a single construct (and with a single question about engagement in it) leads to different conclusions among studies when it is examined with other factors (Gasso, et al. 2019; Rice et al., 2014). Therefore, it is recommended that individual behaviors of sexting should be studied in their relationship to the factors examined (Barrense-Dias et al., 2017).

Despite the fact that there are studies that examine the individual behaviors of sexting, there are not any that investigate the different ways in which individuals are engaged in more than one sexting behaviors, in combination. Thus, this study aimed at investigating the different ways adolescents engage in sexting -based on the different types of sexting - in relation to gender, relationship status and self-esteem.

These data are important in order to conclude about potential risky and safe manifestations of sexting among adolescents and also to raise awareness about the potential danger related to use of exchanging electronic sexual material among this age group in particular.

Regarding involvement in sexting, it is hypothesized that adolescents are involved through different profiles, showing that sexting is not a single behavior (Hypothesis 1). According to literature review, there is not a priori hypothesis regarding gender, as the previous findings were contradictory. Regarding relationship status, it is hypothesized that those who are in a type of relationship are more likely to be involved in sexting (Hypothesis 2). Regarding self-esteem, it is hypothesized that it is negatively associated to sexting (Hypothesis 3).

METHOD

Participants

Data were collected from 186 adolescents aged 15-18, 93 of which were boys and 93 were girls, from economically diverse districts of Thessaloniki (second largest Greek city). Eighty percent lived in urban centers, 18.3% in suburban areas and 1.7% in rural areas or villages. The vast majority of adolescents (89.8%) answered that they own a "smart" mobile phone, 98.4% that they have a profile on some social media, such as Facebook, Twitter, etc., 78% that they publish photos on the internet and the 91% that they see other people's social media profiles/photos. Regarding their relationship status, 71% answered that they were not in a relationship, 20.4% that they were in a casual/dating relationship and 7% that they were in a serious relationship.

Measures

A self-reported questionnaire was used for the collection of research data consisted of a questionnaire about sexting behaviors, demographic questions regarding gender and relationship status and a scale examining self-esteem. Particularly:

Sex and Tech, The National Campaign to Prevent Teen and Unplanned Pregnancy (2008). The exchange of sexually explicit messages, images or videos.

The questionnaire investigates engagement in sexting using 7 statements about the exchange of sexually explicit messages (*"Sent a sexually suggestive message to someone, through email, IM, text, etc."*) and 7 statements about the exchange of sexually explicit pictures/videos (*"Received a nude or semi-nude picture/video from someone of himself/herself"*). From those statements, participants mark all that apply to them. Demographic information concerned gender (*"Are you a male or female"*) and relationship status (*"Which describes best your current relationship status, not in a relationship, casual or serious relationship?"*). Permission for adaptation and use of this questionnaire in the Greek context was given from the manufacturers. Initially, it was translated in Greek from the first author of this study and then a back translation occurred by a bilingual translator. Minimum differences were found between two translations and the necessary corrections took place.

Rosenberg Self-Esteem Scale, Rosenberg (1965).

The 10-item self-esteem scale of Rosenberg measures the global self-esteem (e.g., *"On the whole, I am satisfied with myself"*). Response options for each item range from 1 (*"Strongly disagree"*) to 4 (*"Strongly agree"*) and the sum of 10 questions is the total score. The higher score (maximum 40) indicate higher self-esteem. The score range in the present study was between 17 and 36 with a mean of 25,5. Reliability for the Rosenberg scale in the present study was α=.82

Procedure

Conduct of research occurred from March to June 2017 and it was approved by the Committee of Research Ethics of Department of Psychology of Aristotle University of Thessaloniki (Protocol No: 002/-26-01-2017). Sample was collected by high school students attending private coaching middle schools. Firstly, parents of adolescents were informed by the researcher about the survey and of those interested a written consent was acquired. Then, students were informed about the survey and they completed a hard copy of the questionnaire. The participation was voluntarily and anonymous. Students filled in the questionnaire in group in their coaching classroom, with the presence of the researcher. Completion lasted about 25 minutes. Consent of adolescents was confirmed at the beginning of the questionnaire ensuring them that they can withdraw at any time they want, without any effects.

RESULTS

Engagement in Exchange of Sexually Explicit Messages and Photos/Videos

Responding in the questions about sexting behaviors, 25,5% of the adolescents that participated in the study stated that they have sent sexual messages and 51,6% have received such messages. Moreover, 12,4% responded that they have sent and 33,3% have received nude or semi-nude photo/video of themselves. Lastly, roughly 8% shared sexual message or photos/videos without consent of the initial sender and roughly 25% received such material, originally meant to be private (Table 1).

Table 1. Frequencies and percentages of engagement in sexting behaviors (N=186)

	f	%
Sent a sexually suggestive message to someone (email, IM, text, etc.)	48	25,5
Posted a sexually suggestive message to someone's online profile (like on MySpace, Facebook, etc.)	0	0
NET sent/posted sexually suggestive messages.	25	13,4
Received a sexually suggestive message from someone (email, IM, text, etc.)	96	51,6
Shared a sexually suggestive message with someone other than the one(s) it was originally meant for	15	8,1
Had a sexually suggestive message (originally meant to be private) **shared with me**	40	21,5
None of these	75	40,3
Sent a nude or semi-nude picture/video (of yourself) to someone (via email, cellphone, etc.)	23	12,4

continued on following page

Table 1. Continued

	f	%
Posted a nude or semi-nude picture/video (of yourself) online (like on MySpace, Facebook, in a blog, etc.)	10	5,4
NET sent/posted a nude or semi-nude picture/video of yourself	9	4,8
Received a nude or semi-nude picture/video from someone (of himself/herself)	62	33,3
Shared a nude or semi-nude picture/video with someone other than the one(s) it was originally meant for	14	7,5
Had a nude or semi-nude picture/video (originally meant to be private) **shared with me**	48	25,8
None of these	93	50

Profiles of Engagement of Adolescents in Sexting

In order to examine the way in which adolescents engage in different types of sexting, the method of hierarchical cluster analysis was applied. Analysis aimed to categorize adolescents in profiles based on their responses in 6 questions about sexual messages and another 6 questions about sexual photos/videos, all regarding sending, receiving, posting and forwarding to others without consent of the initial sender.

Cluster Analysis was applied to the sample of participants based on a standard of similarity. This standard is calculated based on a group of variables evaluated for the total of participants, so as to group them in the same cluster when they show similar characteristics. In the present study, variables were binary, so the similarity standard chosen was "simple matching coefficient" by Sokal and Michener (Finch, 2005). Hierarchical agglomerative method and "Within groups average linkage" was used for cluster formation and merging. The sequence of merging clusters is represented in a tree diagram, with which the selection of the appropriate number of clusters was made. Elbow method was used to define the best interpreted number of clusters.

In the present study, a test with a predefined number of clusters was made. Using data from Graph 1 ("Elbow method") and Table 3, a model of 4 clusters was chosen for interpretation. Table 3 presents the last, in the hierarchy, stages of merging the clusters in hierarchical analysis carried out and the corresponding values of the coefficient for these stages. Studying the differences in values of this coefficient (as presented in the last column of Table 2) shows that the "elbow" is at the value .026 which is the first high value located and not corresponding to a large number of clusters. These values correspond on 3 clusters. However, it was chosen a 4-cluster solution as it was more suitable for interpretation. This is due to the fact that in a 4-cluster solution, there are 2 clusters (Cluster 3 and Cluster 4) with very similar means, but with significant quality differences (see Table 3).

Figure 1. Change in the values of the similarity coefficient in relation to the higher stages of clusters merging.

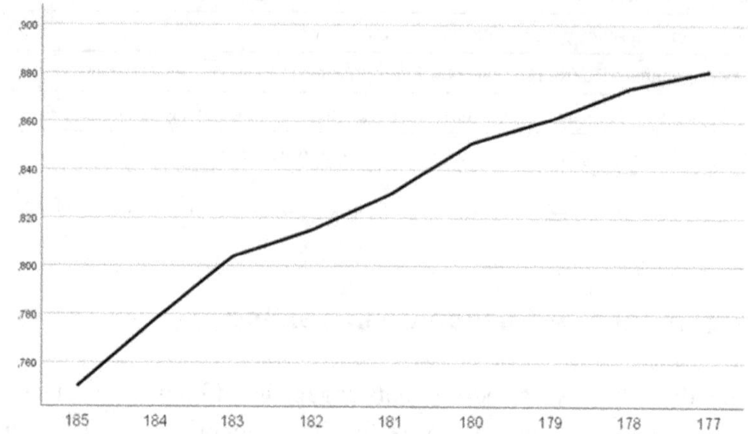

Table 2. Values of the similarity coefficient for the higher stages of merging the cluster of the hierarchy

Stage	Coefficient (C)	D(C)
177	.881	.007
178	.874	.013
179	.861	.010
180	.851	.021
181	.830	.015
182	.815	.011
183	.804	.026
184	.778	.028
185	.750	

Note. D(C) = value differences of the similarity coefficient corresponding to consecutive stages.

In Figure 2 a tree diagram is presented describing the way in which clusters were formed.

Figure 2. Formation of clusters at the higher part of hierarchy

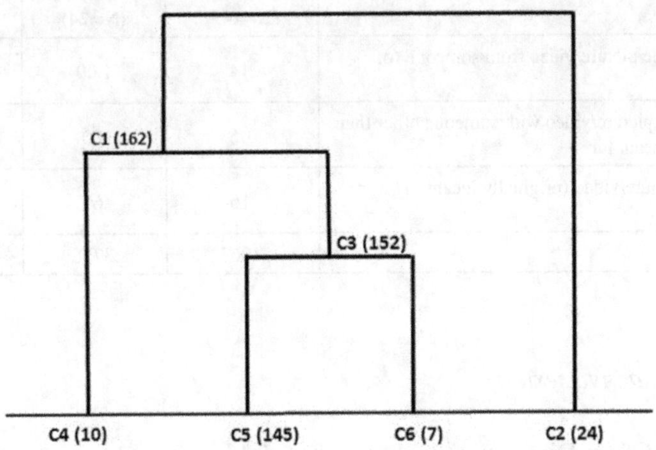

Each cluster was formed by interpreting the means of the variables, that is the frequency of involvement in all types of sexting behaviors. Two dimensions characterized each cluster, (a) interpersonal involvement in sexting, referring to sending or receiving private sexual material to/from someone and (b) risky involvement in sexting, referring to posting sexual material of self, online and forwarding it to others without the consent of the initial sender. Clusters are described analytically below, in combination with Table 4, where means of variables are presented for each of the clusters.

Table 3. Means of the four clusters over the variables examined

	Cluster 1 (N=145)	Cluster 2 (N=24)	Cluster 3 (N=10)	Cluster 4 (N=7)
Sent a sexually suggestive message to someone (email, IM, text, etc.)	.15	.38	1.00	1.00
Posted a sexually suggestive message to someone's online profile (like on MySpace, Facebook, etc.)	.00	.00	.00	.00
NET sent/posted sexually suggestive messages.	.06	.25	.30	1.00
Received a sexually suggestive message from someone (email, IM, text, etc.)	.40	1.00	1.00	.57
Shared a sexually suggestive message with someone other than the one(s) it was originally meant for	.10	.00	.00	.14
Had a sexually suggestive message (originally meant to be private) **shared with me**	.13	.87	.00	.00
Sent a nude or semi-nude picture/video (of yourself) to someone (via email, cellphone, etc.)	.04	.13	.70	1.00
Posted a nude or semi-nude picture/video (of yourself) online (like on MySpace, Facebook, in a blog, etc.)	.03	.25	.00	.00
NET sent/posted a nude or semi-nude picture/video of yourself	.01	.00	.10	1.00

continued on following page

Table 3. Continued

	Cluster 1 (N=145)	Cluster 2 (N=24)	Cluster 3 (N=10)	Cluster 4 (N=7)
Received a nude or semi-nude picture/video from someone (of himself/herself)	.14	1.00	1.00	1.00
Shared a nude or semi-nude picture/video with someone other than the one(s) it was originally meant for	.06	.00	.60	.00
Had a nude or semi-nude picture/video (originally meant to be private) **shared with me**	.16	.63	1.00	.00
Mean	.1067	.3758	.4750	.4758

Cluster 1 – *The inactive sexters*

Cluster 1 (N=145, C5 an Diagram 1) included the adolescents, who reported low score both at the questions about sending and receiving sexual messages and at the questions about posting material online or forwarding it to others without consent. Consequently, adolescents in this cluster were characterized by low interpersonal and low risky involvement in sexting.

Cluster 2 - *The passive sexters*

Cluster 2 (N=24, C2 at Diagram 1) included the adolescents, who reported high score at the questions regarding receiving interpersonal and risky electronic material with sexual content and low score at the questions regarding sending interpersonal sexual messages and forwarding such material without consent. Therefore, adolescents in this cluster were characterized by medium interpersonal involvement and low risky involvement in sexting.

Cluster 3 – *The risky sexters*

Cluster 3 (N=10, C4 at Diagram 1) included the adolescents, who reported high score at the questions regarding sending or receiving interpersonal sexual material and forwarding it to others without consent. Therefore, adolescents in this cluster were characterized by high interpersonal and high risky involvement in sexting.

Cluster 4 – *The safe sexters*

Cluster 4 (N=7, C6 at Diagram 1) included the adolescents, who reported high score at the questions regarding sending and receiving interpersonal sexual material and zero score at the questions about risky sexting behaviors. Therefore, adolescents in this cluster were characterized by high interpersonal and low risky involvement in sexting.

Effect of Gender, Relationship Status, and Self-Esteem on Sexting Profiles

The relationship between gender and the sexting profiles was studied by the x^2 independence test. In cases where the results from the independence tests were statistically significant, cells with positive adjusted standardized residuals z values greater than 1.96 were interpreted. Results showed statistically significant association between gender and the clusters ($x^2(3) = 10.16, p = .016$) regarding girls, who were significantly more in Cluster 4 ($z = 2.7$) of the "safe sexters".

Analysis of x^2 independence test was also used to examine the relationship between engagement profiles and relationship status. Results showed statistically significant association between relationship status and the clusters ($x^2(6) = 53.49, p < .001$). In particular, significantly more adolescents responding they are in a serious relationship were observed in Cluster 3 ($z = 4.2$) of the "risky sexters", significantly more adolescents being in a casual/dating relationship in Cluster 2 ($z = 5.4$) of the "passive sexters" and significantly more adolescents responding they are not in a relationship in Cluster 1($z = 5.4$) of the "inactive sexters". Findings showed that adolescents who were in a serious relationship were more likely to belong in the cluster characterized by high interpersonal and risky involvement in sexting.

The association between self-esteem and the engagement profiles was examined by One-way ANOVA. Results showed statistically significant effect of self-esteem at the clusters $F(2,180) = 5.740$, $p = .001$, $\eta^2 = .105$. Tukey multiple comparison test indicated that self-esteem was significantly low among adolescents who were included in Cluster 2 of the "passive sexters", compared to those who were included in Clusters 1 ($p = .001$), 3 ($p = .011$) and 4 ($p = .049$). Adolescents who were included in Cluster 2 of the "passive sexters" seem to be more likely to characterized by low self-esteem.

It is concluded that (a) girls exchange more frequently personal sexts, rather than engaging in risky behaviors of sexting, (b) adolescents sext more frequently when they are in a relationship, and (c) they receive rather than sending sexts more frequently, when they report low self-esteem.

DISCUSSION

The present study aimed to investigate the different profiles in which adolescents engage in sexting in relation to the factors of gender, relationship status and self-esteem.

Results showed that adolescents were involved in sexting through different profiles, showing that sexting is not a single behavior (Hypothesis 1). Profiles were characterized by two dimensions, the a) interpersonal involvement, referring to sending or receiving private sexual material to/from someone and the b) risky involvement in sexting, referring to posting sexual material online of self and forwarding to others without consent of the initial sender.

In particular, four profiles came up in which adolescents involved in several types of sexting. In two of them, adolescents engage significantly in sexting, however in one of them (the "safe sexters") they only exchanged interpersonal messages or photos/videos, while in the other one (the "risky sexters") they were also involved in risky sexting behaviors. Moreover, a profile came up (the "passive sexters"), in which adolescents received interpersonal or risky sexts, but they do not send any. Lastly, the majority of adolescents were grouped in the profile of "inactive sexters", which was characterized by low or non-engagement in sexting.

These profiles show that there is one group of adolescents who engage significantly in sexting, without putting themselves or others in risk, while there is also another group that they are involved in various sexting behaviors, some of which put themselves or others in danger. "Passive sexters" may came up as a distinct profile because of the fact that many risks resulting from sexting are reported for this age group, therefore adolescents avoid sending this kind of sexts, in order to protect themselves from danger. However, these adolescents still face important risks by receiving sexts without permission of the initial sender. Lastly, considering the profile of "inactive sexters", it can be concluded that most of the adolescents of the present study responded that they do not engage in sexting. It can also be concluded by these findings that as the frequency of engagement of adolescents in sexting behaviors increases, the number of people categorized in the respective profiles reduces. In other words, there is a small number of adolescents that they are involved extensively and in a risky way in sexting.

Regarding gender, results of the present study showed that significantly more adolescent girls were categorized as "safe sexters". This finding implies that girls exchanged in interpersonal messages or photos/videos with sexual implication more frequently than boys – in accordance with previous research findings (Hunter et al., 2018; Kopecky, 2012; 2015; Livingstone & Gorzig, 2014; Ybarra & Mitchell, 2014). Moreover, the significant association between girls and the "safe sexters" profile implies that girls do not usually engage in sexting behaviors that put themselves or others in risk, such as posting sexual messages or photos/videos online or forwarding sexual material to others without consent of the initial sender, in contrast to previous findings (Houck et al., 2014; Martinez-Prather & Vandiver, 2014; Reyns et al.,2014).

Gender stereotypes seem to influence engagement in sexting. Girls are involved in sexting, but they are not engaged in risky sexting behaviors and this may be due to the fact that girls are expected not to be expressive regarding their sexuality (Dobson, 2019), so they avoid stating that they involve in risky sexting in order not to be criticized and thus damage their reputation (Ringrose et al., 2013; Walker et al., 2013). Moreover, girls may indeed be not involved in risky sexting behaviors because they have experienced negative outcomes (Buren, 2018), as a result of stereotypic social criticism. Girls may also not engage in risky sexting because they have experienced more severe risks compared to boys, which results to more negative attitudes towards sexting (Walrave et al., 2014). It was found that a woman is more likely to be verbally victimized for posting a nude or half-naked photo of herself online than a man (Phippen & Kennedy, 2018). Therefore, they avoid adopting the sexting behaviors that include disclosure of personal material, in order to prevent the high probability of threat that they run.

On the other hand, no significant differences were found for boys. This may be due to the fact that boys are expected to adopt sexting behaviors (Setty, 2019) of every kind, for which they are applauded and admired and also they tend to face less severe risks in relation to sexting (Ricciardelli & Adorjan, 2019). This finding underscores the gender dynamics of sexting to the detriment of girls.

Regarding relationship status, hypothesis 2 was confirmed. Findings showed that adolescents who are in a serious relationship were more likely to be included in the profile of "risky sexters". Moreover, it was found that engagement in sexting was lower when they were in a casual/dating relationship and that it was more likely not to engage in sexting when they were in a non-relationship status.

These findings agree with a previous study, according to which it was more likely for adolescents to send nude or semi-nude pictures of themselves or share pictures of others without their consent, when they were in a serious relationship (Hilinski-Rosick & Freiburger, 2012). It seems that the thrill caused by their relationship drives them to exchange sexts more frequently, but also to post this material online or forward it without consent (Hilinski-Rosick, & Freiburger, 2012; VanOuytsel et al., 2019). Apart from thrill, the notion that the social status of an adolescent improves when he/she is in a relationship may lead them to show their love affairs in public. However, the finding that risky sexting is more likely to occur in a serious relationship is not in line with previous findings according to which, forwarding sexual material without consent is more common among adolescents who are in a casual/dating relationship (Drouin et al., 2013). This difference may be due to the content of the definition regarding relationship among adolescents of the present study. This means that the definition of relationship may be influenced by the cultural context in which research is held. Thus, despite the fact that adolescents claim that they are in a serious relationship, they treat it superficially. This may be caused by egocentrism and impulsiveness of adolescence (Muscari, 2009).

Regarding self-esteem, findings showed that adolescents with low self-esteem were less likely to engage in sexting, in line with previous findings (Barrense-Dias et al., 2017; Ybarra & Mitchell, 2014). Therefore, hypothesis 3 was confirmed. Moreover, self-esteem was significantly low among adolescents included in the profile of "passive sexters" characterized by high frequency of receiving sexts but not sending (either personal messages/photos or posting/forwarding without consent). This may be due to the fact that low self-esteem drives them to be less assertive, hesitating to ask others not to send them sexts. Moreover, regarding forwarding sexual material without consent, they may not prevent others from sending them sexts, because in that way they feel accepted by their peer group or in order not to be excluded by this group (Vanden Abeele et al., 2014; Walrave et al., 2014). However, whether they receive such material because they want to or because they cannot set boundaries, the conclusion of the present study is that this does not put them at risk, as these individuals belonged to an engagement profile characterized by low risk. According to the above findings, (a) sexting is a gendered phenomenon, (b) relationship status is related to risky sexting among adolescents and (c) female identity and low self-esteem are related to safe sexting. These findings contribute to the better knowledge of the phenomenon and give useful conclusions that can be used in the context of various preventive (psycho-educational) actions and the counseling process. First, these findings emphasize the importance of educating young people about gender roles. The goal of such prevention actions would be for young people to understand how social pressure is exerted on individuals to adopt sexting behaviors. Still, the goal would be to understand how gender stereotypes influence young people's views on how boys and girls are involved in the phenomenon. This stereotypical view often results in individuals being judged on the basis of their gender rather than their individualized behavior, leading to criticism of women (Lippman & Campbell, 2014; Walker et al., 2013). It is therefore important to be informed and raise awareness about the way in which stereotypical gendered perceptions affect electronic sexual communication in particular, but also the sexual life of people in general.

In addition, these findings indicate the need to raise awareness and educate young people on sexuality issues. This could include training in sexual communication and respect for sexual partner, so that sexting is a healthy expression of sexuality and a form of communication that contributes positively to a romantic or sexual relationship (Buren, 2018).

Furthermore, the need for preventive actions that promote self-esteem for oneself as a whole, but also in particular about sexual life, is emphasized. Although low self-esteem was related to safe sexting in this study, the fact that these adolescents received risky messages possibly without wanting to or without being assertive towards those who sent them, emphasizes the need to promote self-esteem. The goal would be to cultivate the skills of assertiveness and expression of personal desires, in order to minimize the influence that the opinions of others have and the factor of luck in the decision of someone to adopt or not to adopt a sexual behavior, either "real" or electronic. These actions are considered important in order to address the culture of sexual violence in secondary schools, to which sexting is claimed to contribute (VanOuytsel et al., 2017).

Finally, the findings of the present study underline the importance of informing young people about the sexting phenomenon itself. This training is important to describe the potential risks, but also to include the positive side of the phenomenon. Therefore, the aim of this training should be to give young people the appropriate information to highlight this positive side and to be able to make responsible decisions on how to use communication through sexting (Jørgensen et al., 2019). After all, it has been shown that sex education, which emphasizes abstinence as a means of protection, rather than information on the safe adoption of these behaviors, has the opposite effect from what it aims at (Patchin & Hinduja, 2020). In conclusion, the findings of the present study can serve as an objective information about sexting, which aims to deconstruct the negative or phobic attitude towards the phenomenon, which may be due to lack of information.

An important limitation of the above findings is that data were collected using self-reports of the participants. Therefore, socially accepted responses may affect the internal validity of the findings. Moreover, a limitation of the study is that there was a non-representative sample from a numerical and geographical point of view. The present study can be a springboard for further research about the factors related to sexting. Those may be the relationship of the phenomenon with sexual activity, perceived quality of relationship of sexters, other online risks (such as stalking) and gendered violence. Lastly, it is highlighted the need for further qualitative research in order to deepen our knowledge about instances in which sexting becomes harmful and to investigate the circumstances in which sexting is beneficial to sexters.

REFERENCES

Baiden, F., Amankwah, J., & Owusu, A. (2020). Sexting among high school students in a metropolis in Ghana: An exploratory and descriptive study. *Journal of Children and Media*, 14(3), 1–15. DOI: 10.1080/17482798.2020.1719854

Barrense-Dias, Y., Berchtold, A., Surís, J. C., & Akre, C. (2017). Sexting and the definition issue. *The Journal of Adolescent Health*, 61(5), 544–554. DOI: 10.1016/j.jadohealth.2017.05.009 PMID: 28734631

Bianchi, D., Morelli, M., Nappa, M. R., Baiocco, R., & Chirumbolo, A. (2018). A bad romance: Sexting motivations and teen dating violence. *Journal of Interpersonal Violence*, 1–21. DOI: 10.1177/0886260518817037 PMID: 30537886

Boyle, A., & O'Sullivan, L. (2010). General and sexual communication in established relationships: An exploration of possible links to condom use among young adults. *The Canadian Journal of Human Sexuality*, 19, 53–64. https://link.gale.com/apps/doc/A229542650/AONE?u=anon~627c2c01&sid=googleScholar&xid=ee5becb0

Burén, J. (2018). *Sexting among adolescents*. Department of Psychology, University of Gothenburg. DOI: 10.1016/j.chb.2018.02.003

Burić, J., Garcia, J. R., & Štulhofer, A. (2020). Is sexting bad for adolescent girls' psychological well-being? A longitudinal assessment in middle to late adolescence. *New Media & Society*, 1–20. DOI: 10.1177/1461444820931091

Crimmins, D. M., & Seigfried-Spellar, K. C. (2014). Peer attachment, sexual experiences, and risky online behaviors as predictors of sexting behaviors among undergraduate students. *Computers in Human Behavior*, 32, 268–275. DOI: 10.1016/j.chb.2013.12.012

Dir, A. L., Cyders, M. A., & Coskunpinar, A. (2013). From the bar to the bed via mobile phone: A first test of the role of problematic alcohol use, sexting, and impulsivity-related traits in sexual hookups. *Computers in Human Behavior*, 29(4), 1664–1670. DOI: 10.1016/j.chb.2013.01.039

Dobson, A. S. (2019). 'The Things You Didn't Do': Gender, Slut-Shaming, and the Need to Address Sexual Harassment in Narrative Resources Responding to Sexting and Cyberbullying. In Vandebosch, H., & Green, L. (Eds.), *Narratives in Research and Interventions on Cyberbullying among Young People* (pp. 147–160). Springer. DOI: 10.1007/978-3-030-04960-7_10

Döring, N. (2014). Consensual sexting among adolescents: Risk prevention through abstinence education or safer sexting? *Cyberpsychology (Brno)*, 8(1), 1–18. DOI: 10.5817/CP2014-1-9

Drouin, M., Vogel, K. N., Surbey, A., & Stills, J. R. (2013). Let's talk about sexting, baby: Computer-mediated sexual behaviors among young adults. *Computers in Human Behavior*, 29(5), 25–30. DOI: 10.1016/j.chb.2012.12.030

Englander, E. (2015). Coerced sexting and revenge porn among teens. *Bullying. Teen Aggression & Social Media*, 1(2), 19–21.

Ethier, K. A., Kershaw, T. S., Lewis, J. B., Milan, S., Niccolai, L. M., & Ickovics, J. R. (2006). Self-esteem, emotional distress and sexual behaviour among adolescent females: Inter-relationships and temporal effects. *The Journal of Adolescent Health*, 38(3), 268–274. DOI: 10.1016/j.jadohealth.2004.12.010 PMID: 16488825

Finch, H. (2005). Comparison of Distance Measures in Cluster Analysis with Dichotomous Data. *Journal of Data Science : JDS*, 3(1), 85–100. DOI: 10.6339/JDS.2005.03(1).192

Gamez-Guadix, M., & de Santisteban, P. (2018). "Sex Pics?": Longitudinal Predictors of Sexting Among Adolescents. *The Journal of Adolescent Health*, 63(5), 608–614. DOI: 10.1016/j.jadohealth.2018.05.032 PMID: 30170939

Gassó, A. M., Klettke, B., Agustina, J. R., & Montiel, I. (2019). Sexting, mental health, and victimization among adolescents: A literature review. *International Journal of Environmental Research and Public Health*, 16(13), 1–14. DOI: 10.3390/ijerph16132364 PMID: 31277335

Ghorashi, Z. (2019). Teenage Sexting and Sexual Behaviors in an Iranian Setting. *Sexuality & Culture*, 23(4), 1–9. DOI: 10.1007/s12119-019-09622-6

Ghorashi, Z., Loripoor, M., & Lotfipur-Rafsanjani, S. M. (2019). Mobile Access and Sexting Prevalence in High School Students in Rafsanjan City, Iran in 2015. *Majallah-i Ravanpizishki va Ravanshinasi-i Balini-i Iran*, 24(4), 416–425. DOI: 10.32598/ijpcp.24.4.416

Gordon-Messer, D., Bauermeister, J. A., Grodzinski, A., & Zimmerman, M. (2013). Sexting among young adults. *The Journal of Adolescent Health*, 52(3), 301–306. DOI: 10.1016/j.jadohealth.2012.05.013 PMID: 23299018

Gregg, D., Somers, C. L., Pernice, F. M., Hillman, S. B., & Kernsmith, P. (2018). Sexting rates and predictors from an urban Midwest high school. *The Journal of School Health*, 88(6), 423–433. DOI: 10.1111/josh.12628 PMID: 29749003

Hally, C., & Pollack, R. (1993). The effects of self-esteem, variety of sexual experience, and erotophilia on sexual satisfaction in sexually active heterosexuals. *Journal of Sex Education and Therapy*, 19(3), 183–192. DOI: 10.1080/01614576.1993.11074081

Hasinoff, A. A. (2013). Sexting as media production: Rethinking social media and sexuality. *New Media & Society*, 15(4), 449–465. DOI: 10.1177/1461444812459171

Hawkes, G., & Dune, T. (2013). Introduction: Narratives of the sexual child: Shared themes and shared challenges. *Sexualities*, 16(5-6), 622–634. DOI: 10.1177/1363460713497459

Hilinski-Rosick, C. M., & Freiburger, T. L. (2012). An Exploratory Analysis of the Prevalence of Teen Sexting. *Journal of Social Deviance*, 4, 120–149. DOI: 10.1080/10511253.2014.922593

Houck, C. D., Barker, D., Rizzo, C., Hancock, E., Norton, A., & Brown, L. K. (2014). Sexting and sexual behavior in at-risk adolescents. *Pediatrics*, 133(2), 276–282. DOI: 10.1542/peds.2013-1157 PMID: 24394678

Hudson, H. K., Fetro, J. V., & Ogletree, R. (2014). Behavioral indicators and behaviors related to sexting among undergraduate students. *American Journal of Health Education*, 45(3), 183–195. DOI: 10.1080/19325037.2014.901113

Hudson, H. K., & Marshall, S. A. (2018). Consequences and Predictors of Sexting Among Selected Southern Undergraduates. *International Journal of Sexual Health : Official Journal of the World Association for Sexual Health*, 30(1), 20–27. DOI: 10.1080/19317611.2017.1404540

Hunter, S. C., Russell, K., & Knifton, L. (2018). *Individual, Family, and School Factors Relating to Sexting and Bullying*. Retrieved July 15, 2019, from https://strathprints.strath.ac.uk/65064/

Jonsson, L. S., Priebe, G., Bladh, M., & Svedin, C. G. (2014). Voluntary sexual exposure online among Swedish youth–social background, Internet behavior and psychosocial health. *Computers in Human Behavior*, 30, 181–190. DOI: 10.1016/j.chb.2013.08.005

Jørgensen, C. R., Weckesser, A., Turner, J., & Wade, A. (2019). Young people's views on sexting education and support needs: Findings and recommendations from a UK-based study. *Sex Education*, 19(1), 25–40. DOI: 10.1080/14681811.2018.1475283

Katzman, D. K. (2010). Sexting: Keeping teens safe and responsible in a technologically savvy world. *Paediatrics & Child Health*, 15(1), 41–42. DOI: 10.1093/pch/15.1.41 PMID: 21197169

Kopecký, K. (2012). Sexting among Czech preadolescents and adolescents. *The New Educational Review*, 28(2), 39–48. DOI: 10.1016/j.sbspro.2015.08.289

Kopecký, K. (2015). Sexting among Slovak pubescents and adolescent children. *Procedia: Social and Behavioral Sciences*, 203, 244–250. DOI: 10.1016/j.sbspro.2015.08.289

Larson, J., Anderson, S., Holman, T., & Niemann, B. (1998). A longitudinal study of the effects of premarital communication, relationship stability, and self-esteem on sexual satisfaction in the first year of marriage. *Journal of Sex & Marital Therapy*, 24(3), 193–206. DOI: 10.1080/00926239808404933 PMID: 9670124

Le, L. (2016). *What's your sext drive: Examining female emerging adults' experiences of sharing visual sexual content through communication technologies*. Unpublished Master's thesis, University of Alberta, Alberta Canada. DOI: 10.7939/R3R785X28

Lee, C. H., Moak, S., & Walker, J. T. (2016). Effects of self-control, social control, and social learning on sexting behavior among South Korean youths. *Youth & Society*, 48(2), 242–264. DOI: 10.1177/0044118X13490762

Lenhart, A. (2009c). *Overview: Teens and sexting: How and why minor teens are sending sexually suggestive nude or nearly nude images via text messaging. Pew Internet and American Life Project.* Retrieved July 15, 2013, from https://img.ksl.com/slc/1897/189789/18978984.pdf

Lippman, J. R., & Campbell, S. W. (2014). Damned if you do, damned if you don't… if you're a girl: Relational and normative contexts of adolescent sexting in the United States. *Journal of Children and Media*, 8(4), 371–386. DOI: 10.1080/17482798.2014.923009

Livingstone, S., & Görzig, A. (2011) Sexting. In S., Livingstone, L., Haddon, & A., Gorzig (Eds.), *Children, Risk and Safety on the Internet: Kids online in comparative perspective* (pp.1-10), The Policy Press. DOI: 10.1332/policypress/9781847428837.003.0012

Livingstone, S., & Görzig, A. (2014). When adolescents receive sexual messages on the internet: Explaining experiences of risk and harm. *Computers in Human Behavior*, 33, 8–15. DOI: 10.1016/j.chb.2013.12.021

Manago, A. M., Taylor, T., & Greenfield, P. M. (2012). Me and my 400 friends: The anatomy of college students' Facebook networks, their communication patterns, and well-being. *Developmental Psychology*, 48(2), 369–380. DOI: 10.1037/a0026338 PMID: 22288367

Martinez-Prather, K., & Vandiver, D. M. (2014). Sexting among Teenagers in the United States: A Retrospective Analysis of Identifying Motivating Factors, Potential Targets, and the Role of a Capable Guardian. *International Journal of Cyber Criminology*, 8(1), 21–35.

Marume, A., Maradzika, J., & January, J. (2018). Adolescent Sexting and Risky Sexual Behaviours in Zimbabwe: A Cross-Sectional Study. *Sexuality & Culture*, 22(3), 931–941. DOI: 10.1007/s12119-018-9508-4

McLaughlin, J. H. (2012). Exploring the first amendment rights of teens in relationship to sexting and censorship. *University of Michigan Journal of Law Reform. University of Michigan. Law School*, 45(2), 315–350. DOI: 10.36646/mjlr.45.2.exploring

Milton, A. C., Gill, B. A., Davenport, T. A., Dowling, M., Burns, J. M., & Hickie, I. B. (2019). Sexting, Web-Based Risks, and Safety in Two Representative National Samples of Young Australians: Prevalence, Perspectives, and Predictors. *JMIR Mental Health*, 6(6), 1–16. DOI: 10.2196/13338 PMID: 31210139

Mitchell, K. J., Finkelhor, D., Jones, L. M., & Wolak, J. (2012). Prevalence and characteristics of youth sexting: A national study. *Pediatrics*, 129(1), 13–20. DOI: 10.1542/peds.2011-1730 PMID: 22144706

Muscari, M. E. (2009). *Sexting: New technology, old problem? Medscape Public Health and Prevention.* Retrieved December 7, 2012 https://www.episcopalcollegiate.org/uploaded/Academics/documents/Middle_School/Sexting_article_from_Medscape.pdf

Oattes, M., & Offman, A. (2007). Global self-esteem and sexual self-esteem as predictors of sexual communication in intimate relationships. *The Canadian Journal of Human Sexuality*, 16(3-4), 89–100. DOI: 10.1177/01461672241257355

Oriza, I. I. D., & Hanipraja, M. A. (2020). Sexting and Sexual Satisfaction on Young Adults in Romantic Relationship. *Psychological Research on Urban Society*, 3(1), 30–39. DOI: 10.7454/proust.v3i1.61

Ostrager, B. (2010). SMS. OMG! LOL! TTYL: Translating the law to accommodate today's teens and the evolution from texting to sexting. *Family Court Review*, 48(4), 712–726. DOI: 10.1111/j.1744-1617.2010.01345.x

Parker, T. S., Blackburn, K. M., Perry, M. S., & Hawks, J. M. (2013). Sexting as an intervention: Relationship satisfaction and motivation considerations. *The American Journal of Family Therapy*, 41(1), 1–12. DOI: 10.1080/01926187.2011.635134

Patchin, J. W., & Hinduja, S. (2010). Cyberbullying and Self-Esteem. *The Journal of School Health*, 80(12), 614–621. DOI: 10.1111/j.1746-1561.2010.00548.x PMID: 21087257

Patchin, J. W., & Hinduja, S. (2019). The Nature and Extent of Sexting Among a National Sample of Middle and High School Students in the US. *Archives of Sexual Behavior*, 48(8), 1–11. DOI: 10.1007/s10508-019-1449-y PMID: 31309428

Patchin, J. W., & Hinduja, S. (2020). It is time to teach safe sexting. *The Journal of Adolescent Health*, 66(2), 140–143. DOI: 10.1016/j.jadohealth.2019.10.010 PMID: 31831321

Phippen, A. D., & Kennedy, C. (2018). *Sexting and sexting behaviour- "Oh you're all children, children do silly things. You'll be fine. Get over it!"*. Retrieved July 15, 2019, from https://pearl.plymouth.ac.uk/cgi/viewcontent.cgi?article=1008&context=sc-research

Renfrow, D. G., & Rollo, E. A. (2014). Sexting on campus: Minimizing perceived risks and neutralizing behaviors. *Deviant Behavior*, 35(11), 903–920. DOI: 10.1080/01639625.2014.897122

Reyns, B. W., Henson, B., & Fisher, B. S. (2014). Digital deviance: Low self-control and opportunity as explanations of sexting among college students. *Sociological Spectrum*, 34(3), 273–292. DOI: 10.1080/02732173.2014.895642

Ricciardelli, R., & Adorjan, M. (2019). 'If a girl's photo gets sent around, that'sa way bigger deal than if a guy's photo gets sent around': Gender, sexting, and the teenage years. *Journal of Gender Studies*, 28(5), 563–577. DOI: 10.1080/09589236.2018.1560245

Rice, E., Gibbs, J., Winetrobe, H., Rhoades, H., Plant, A., Montoya, J., & Kordic, T. (2014). Sexting and Sexual Behavior Among Middle School Students. *Pediatrics*, 134(1), 21–28. DOI: 10.1542/peds.2013-2991 PMID: 24982103

Rice, E., Rhoades, H., Winetrobe, H., Sanchez, M., Montoya, J., Plant, A., & Kordic, T. (2012). Sexually explicit cell phone messaging associated with sexual risk among adolescents. *Pediatrics*, 130(4), 667–673. DOI: 10.1542/peds.2012-0021 PMID: 22987882

Ricketts, M. L., Maloney, C., Marcum, C. D., & Higgins, G. E. (2015). The effect of internet related problems on the sexting behaviors of juveniles. *American Journal of Criminal Justice*, 40(2), 270–284. DOI: 10.1007/s12103-014-9247-5

Ringrose, J. (2010). Sluts, whores, fat slags and Playboy bunnies: Teen girls' negotiations of "sexy" on social networking sites and at school. In C. Jackson, C. Paechter, & E. Renold (Eds.), *Girls and education 3–16: Continuing concerns, new agendas* (pp. 170-182). Open University Press. DOI: 10.1080/00071005.2011.611290

Ringrose, J., Gill, R., Livingstone, S., & Harvey, L. (2012). *A qualitative study of children, young people and 'sexting': a report prepared for the NSPCC*. National Society for the Prevention of Cruelty to Children.

Ringrose, J., Harvey, L., Gill, R., & Livingstone, S. (2013). Teen girls, sexual double standards and 'sexting': Gendered value in digital image exchange. *Feminist Theory*, 14(3), 305–323. DOI: 10.1177/1464700113499853

Rosenberg, M. (1965). *Society and the adolescent self-image*. Princeton University Press. DOI: 10.1515/9781400876136

Scholes-Balog, K., Francke, N., & Hemphill, S. (2016). Relationships between sexting, self-esteem, and sensation seeking among Australian young adults. *Sexualization, Media, &. Society*, 2(2), 1–8. DOI: 10.1177/2374623815627790

Setty, E. (2019). Meanings of bodily and sexual expression in youth sexting culture: Young women's negotiation of gendered risks and harms. *Sex Roles*, 80(9-10), 586–606. DOI: 10.1007/s11199-018-0957-x

Silva, R. B., Teixeira, C. M., Vasconcelos-Raposo, J., & Bessa, M. (2016). Sexting: Adaptation of sexual behavior to modern technologies. *Computers in Human Behavior*, 64, 747–753. DOI: 10.1016/j.chb.2016.07.036

Simpson, B. (2013). Challenging childhood, challenging children: Children's rights and sexting. *Sexualities*, 16(5/6), 690–709. DOI: 10.1177/1363460713487467

Sorbring, E., Skoog, T., & Bohlin, M. (2014). Adolescent girls' and boys' well-being in relation to online and offline sexual and romantic activity. *Cyberpsychology (Brno)*, 8(1), 7. Advance online publication. DOI: 10.5817/CP2014-1-7

Strohmaier, H., Murphy, M., & Dematteo, D. (2014). Youth sexting: Prevalence rates, driving motivations, and the deterrent effect of legal consequences. *Sexuality Research & Social Policy*, 11(3), 245–255. DOI: 10.1007/s13178-014-0162-9

Temple, J. R., & Choi, H. (2014). Longitudinal association between teen sexting and sexual behavior. *Pediatrics*, 134(5), 1287–1292. DOI: 10.1542/peds.2014-1974 PMID: 25287459

Temple, J. R., Le, V. D., van den Berg, P., Ling, Y., Paul, J. A., & Temple, B. W. (2014). Brief report: Teen sexting and psychosocial health. *Journal of Adolescence*, 37(1), 33–36. DOI: 10.1016/j.adolescence.2013.10.008 PMID: 24331302

The National Campaign to Prevent Teen and Unplanned Pregnancy. (2008). *Sex and Tech: Results from a Survey of Teens and Young Adults*. Author.

Van Ouytsel, J., Van Gool, E., Walrave, M., Ponnet, K., & Peeters, E. (2017). Sexting: Adolescents' perceptions of the applications used for, motives for, and consequences of sexting. *Journal of Youth Studies*, 20(4), 446–470. DOI: 10.1080/13676261.2016.1241865

Van Ouytsel, J., Walrave, M., & Ponnet, K. (2019). Sexting within adolescents' romantic relationships: How is it related to perceptions of love and verbal conflict? *Computers in Human Behavior*, 97, 216–221. DOI: 10.1016/j.chb.2019.03.029

Van Ouytsel, J., Walrave, M., & Van Gool, E. (2014). Sexting: Between Thrill and Fear—How Schools Can Respond. *The Clearing House: A Journal of Educational Strategies, Issues and Ideas*, 87(5), 204–212. DOI: 10.1080/00098655.2014.918532

Vanden Abeele, M. V., Roe, K., & Eggermont, S. (2012). An exploration of adolescents' sexual contact and conduct risks through mobile phone use. *Communications*, 37(1), 55–77. DOI: 10.1515/commun-2012-0003

VandenAbeele, M., Campbell, S. W., Eggermont, S., & Roe, K. (2014). Sexting, Mobile Porn Use, and Peer Group Dynamics: Boys' and Girls' Self-Perceived Popularity, Need for Popularity, and Perceived Peer Pressure. *Media Psychology*, 17(1), 6–33. DOI: 10.1080/15213269.2013.801725

Villacampa, C. (2017). Teen sexting: Prevalence, characteristics and legal treatment. *International Journal of Law, Crime and Justice*, 49, 10–21. DOI: 10.1016/j.ijlcj.2017.01.002

Walker, S., Sanci, L., & Temple-Smith, M. (2013). Sexting: Young women's and men's views on its nature and origins. *The Journal of Adolescent Health*, 52(6), 697–701. DOI: 10.1016/j.jadohealth.2013.01.026 PMID: 23587784

Walrave, M., Heirman, W., & Hallam, L. (2014). Under pressure to sext? Applying the theory of planned behaviour to adolescent sexting. *Behaviour & Information Technology*, 33(1), 86–98. DOI: 10.1080/0144929X.2013.837099

Walrave, M., Ponnet, K., Van Ouytsel, J., Van Gool, E., Heirman, W., & Verbeek, A. (2015). Whether or not to engage in sexting: Explaining adolescent sexting behavior by applying the prototype willingness model. *Telematics and Informatics*, 32(4), 796–808. DOI: 10.1016/j.tele.2015.03.008

Watson, E., Milhausen, R., Smoliak, O., & Breen, A. (2018). *How Young Canadian Women Make Sense of their Experiences of Sexting*. Unpublished Doctoral dissertation, The University of Guelph, Guelph, Ontario, Canada. Retrieved July, 15, 2019, from https://atrium.lib.uoguelph.ca/server/api/core/bitstreams/ff78a7e2-8f12-4baa-8e88-f2c773b414d3/content

Wolak, J., & Finkelhor, D. (2011). 'Sexting: A typology'. *Research Bulletin, University of New Hampshire: Crimes Against Children Research Center*. Retrieved July, 15, 2013, from https://scholars.unh.edu/ccrc/48/

Woolard, A. (2011). *The frequency, attitudes, and beliefs of sexting among college students*. Unpublished Master's thesis, Eastern Illinois University. Retrieved July, 15, 2013, from https://thekeep.eiu.edu/cgi/viewcontent.cgi?article=1837&context=theses

Ybarra, M. L., & Mitchell, K. J. (2014). "Sexting" and its relation to sexual activity and sexual risk behavior in a national survey of adolescents. *The Journal of Adolescent Health*, 55(6), 757–764. DOI: 10.1016/j.jadohealth.2014.07.012 PMID: 25266148

Yoder, J., Hansen, J., & Precht, M. (2018). Correlates and outcomes associated with sexting among justice involved youth: The role of developmental adversity, emotional disinhibitions, relationship context, and dating violence. *Children and Youth Services Review*, 94, 493–499. DOI: 10.1016/j.childyouth.2018.08.020

Chapter 6
Digital Play Addiction Tendency Behaviors in Early Children Reflections in Social Environments:
Teachers' Perspective

Kadriye Selin Budak
https://orcid.org/0000-0002-8161-7074
Bilecik Şeyh Edebali University, Turkey

ABSTRACT

This chapter discusses children's digital play addiction tendencies and their impact on behavior in different social environments within the framework of microsystems. These tendencies affect children's developmental behaviors in various life areas. Interviews with 12 teachers revealed insights into how these tendencies manifest in classroom environments. The "Preschool Teachers' Opinions on the Reflections of Digital Play Addiction Tendencies" form was used for data collection. Digital play addiction has significant negative effects on development and learning, including distraction, reduced empathy, cooperation, and group participation. Children may imitate violent behaviors from digital play, increasing aggression. Addiction also causes attention problems, reduced academic success, and negatively impacts creative thinking and problem-solving skills, complicating classroom management and affecting other students' learning. Therefore, careful management of technology integration and guidance on potential risks are crucial for teachers.

INTRODUCTION

Over two-thirds of the world's population utilizes mobile devices, and by the end of 2023, the number of internet users will have surpassed 5 billion. These digital transformations continue to impact our lives, altering every aspect of human experience. Today, people spend approximately 25% of their waking hours in front of screens (We Are Social, 2023), as access to digital devices has become incredibly convenient, allowing people of all ages to connect easily. From a very young age, nearly all newborns and toddlers

DOI: 10.4018/979-8-3693-4191-9.ch006

are exposed to screens (Bergmann et al., 2022). Research indicates that 75% of young children between the ages of 6 months and 3 years regularly use touch screens (Bedford, 2016). Although it is generally advised against using digital devices at an early age (Radesky & Christakis, 2016; WHO, 2019), recent studies show that children aged 0 to 8 in various countries are increasingly accessing and using digital technology (Ofcom, 2023). New technologies have profoundly impacted and altered children's and adolescents' communication patterns, understanding of their surroundings, and worldviews (Puzio et al., 2022). A large-scale study involving 57,980 children found a negative correlation between screen time and developmental scores, with increased screen time from age 1 having a detrimental effect on future development (Yamamoto et al., 2023). Given the rising screen time and the increasing interaction of young children with digital play, it is imperative to prioritize research in this area. This is particularly important as excessive screen time in young children can lead to digital play addiction, a form of behavioral addiction

Digital Play Addiction Tendency

Behavioural addiction, although frequently associated with substance addiction, encompasses a broader range of concerns. Addiction is defined as a repetitive habit that negatively impacts an individual's health, leading to personal and social problems, and involves usage patterns that the individual cannot control (Griffiths, 2009; Marazziti et al., 2015). In the International Classification of Diseases (ICD) published by the World Health Organization(2024), the concept of "gaming disorder" is considered as gaming disorder and defined as follows; *"online is characterised by a pattern of persistent or recurrent gaming behaviour ('digital gaming' or 'video-gaming') that is primarily conducted over the internet and is manifested by; impaired control over gaming (e.g., onset, frequency, intensity, duration, termination, context); increasing priority given to gaming to the extent that gaming takes precedence over other life interests and daily activities; and continuation or escalation of gaming despite the occurrence of negative consequences. The behaviour pattern is of sufficient severity to result in significant impairment in personal, family, social, educational, occupational or other important areas of functioning."* In this context, behavioural addictions such as technology addiction, internet addiction, phone addiction, and gaming addiction have become the focus of many studies (Derevensky et al., 2019). While there is no standardized definition of "digital play addiction" (Schulz van Endert, 2021), Lemmens et al. (2009) describe play addiction as the persistent and uncontrolled use of digital tools that leads to social and emotional distress and disrupts daily routines. In their study developing the digital game addiction scale, they referenced the diagnostic criteria created by Griffiths and Davies (2005). These criteria include salience, which means that playing digital games becomes the most important activity in an individual's life, dominating their thoughts, feelings, and behaviours. The constant thought of interacting with digital games significantly affects the individual's life. Tolerance refers to the gradual increase in the time spent on the game. Mood modification is when individuals use games as an escape from daily life, finding relaxation in playing. Withdrawal is characterized by negative emotions and reactive behaviours resulting from a sudden reduction or restriction in game playing. When individuals cannot access the game, their desire to play increases and they may become tense. Relapse indicates the tendency to revert to game-playing behaviours despite unsuccessful attempts to control or reduce game use. Conflict arises from all interpersonal issues due to excessive game-playing. Finally, problems refer to the adverse effects of game addiction on an individual's school or work life and socialization activities. Budak & Işıkoğlu (2022) conducted a scale development study for children in early childhood. Regarding this research, the tendency of digital game addiction in early childhood causes children to neglect their responsibilities by moving away from daily life and social relationships as the time of playing games increases. This tendency leads to conflicts in family, friends and work/school life and becomes the centre of the individual's life with the constant desire to play games. It also includes the negative effects of game-playing behaviours on the quality of life of the individual and the awareness of these effects (Budak & Işıkoğlu, 2022). On the other hand, Yeşilay (2023) defines "technology addiction" as an uncontrollable desire to use the internet excessively, displaying nervous behaviour when deprived of internet access, and experiencing negative impacts on daily life. Uncontrolled digital play interactions that begin in early childhood and increase over time pose a risk of addiction in children (Işıkoğlu et al., 2024; Calhan & Goksu, 2024).

When examined from a historical perspective, before the concept of digital play addiction emerged, research primarily focused on children's screen time, with early studies concentrating on television viewing durations. In the 1980s, television was the primary source of screen time for children. However, from the 2000s onwards, the proliferation of digital devices such as computers, video game consoles, and mobile phones led to an increase in screen time and shifted the focus of research (Rideout et al., 2010). During this period, the initial focus was on children's screen time and the mediation strategies parents employed with digital tools (Livingstone & Helsper, 2008). Researchers sought to determine how parents managed and regulated their children's interactions with television (Valkenburg et al., 1999). Following these television-focused strategies, numerous approaches were developed for other digital devices (smartphones, tablets, computers, etc.) and internet usage, which had become integral to our lives (Brito et al., 2017; Clark, 2011).

By the 2010s, tablets and smartphones had become a central part of children's daily lives, leading research to prioritize examining the relationship between children's learning and development. The advantages and disadvantages of increased screen time became topics of significant discussion (Hastings et al., 2009; McArthur et al., 2022; Yalçın-Irmak & Erdoğan, 2016). Many researchers have highlighted that children's screen time significantly increased during the pandemic, affecting children internationally across many countries. Screen time for children aged 3-17 increased in 12 countries during the pandemic (Bergmann et al., 2022). Although tendencies toward digital play addiction appeared to decrease post-pandemic, there was still an observed increase compared to pre-pandemic levels (Işıkoğlu et al., 2024). Unfortunately, the current increase in screen time is a well-documented fact (Rosendo-Rios et al., 2022). In this context, rather than merely identifying screen time, preventing the negative consequences of increased screen time and supporting quality and effective mediation are deemed important. Therefore, identifying digital play addiction tendencies in children and intervening early, as well as raising awareness among parents, teachers, and policymakers on this issue, have become significant priorities.

Several factors contribute to the increased usage rates of digital tools, particularly those associated with the home environment. Significant factors include the nature of the parent-child relationship, parents' education levels, the guidance provided, household income, screen time, and attitudes toward technological advancements (Chaudron et al., 2018; Emiroğlu İlvan & Ceylan, 2023; Radesky et al., 2023; Rideout & Robb, 2020; Kabali et al., 2015; Lauricella et al., 2015). Regarding variables related to children, factors such as temperament, gender, school attendance duration, and the pandemic (Brito, 2016; Bergmann et al., 2022; Işıkoğlu et al., 2024) are found to directly impact children's screen time. Consequently, these factors contributing to increased screen time may lead to a tendency toward digital play addiction, which can negatively affect children's development.

Although the results are debated, some studies have observed that screen time varies according to children's gender (Atkins et al., 2014; Brito, 2016; Hastings et al., 2009). It has been found that boys tend to exhibit a higher tendency toward digital game addiction and have longer screen times compared to girls (Budak & Işıkoğlu, 2023). A longitudinal study emphasized that over four years, there was a significant increase in screen time among boys, particularly in activities such as digital gaming. In contrast, girls showed a greater increase in other screen activities, such as watching TV, using computers, and participating in online communication. However, the increase in screen time among boys still appears to be greater than that of girls (Thomas et al., 2020). This disparity is attributed to genetic differences, varying parental attitudes toward children based on gender, and cultural variations. Notably, parental attitudes play a critical role in regulating children's interactions with digital devices. Parental perspectives on digital interactions can influence children's digital literacy. The strategies that parents apply regarding their children's use of digital devices significantly shape and affect their digital engagement (Chen & MacCallum, 2023).

Factors such as the presence of digital devices in children's bedrooms, parents' perspectives on technological developments, the organization of outdoor activities in daily routines, and the encouragement of children to use digital tools in alternative environments significantly influence children's use of digital devices and their screen time (Brito et al., 2017; Fullerton et al., 2014; Lauricella et al., 2015; Lieberman et al., 2009; Schwarzer et al., 2022). Underlying these factors are those that shape the family environment, including parental employment status, income level, and education level. In a study by Lauricella, Wartella, and Rideout (2015), the relationship between digital device use by children aged 0-8 and their parents' digital habits was explored. The results indicate a strong correlation between the amount of time parents spend using digital devices and the time their children spend using them. Moreover, parental attitudes were found to significantly influence children's digital device usage. Similarly, research by Cingel and Krcmar (2013) and Chaudron et al. (2018) demonstrates a significant relationship between parents' attitudes and beliefs and the amount of time children spend with digital media. Studies on parental education levels, such as those by Livingstone et al. (2015), suggest that parents with higher education levels are more aware of the digital world and engage in more regulatory interventions concerning their children's digital interactions. This awareness is attributed to the fact that individuals with higher education levels are more cognizant of the risks and disadvantages associated with digital use. Conversely, research indicates that parents with lower education levels are more likely to prefer digital games for their children (Atkins et al., 2014; Işıkoğlu-Erdoğan et al., 2018; Rideout, 2011). These studies reveal that children from families with lower education levels are at a higher risk of excessive digital game use. Parental education level plays a critical role in determining how children interact with the digital world, and its impact on digital use can have significant implications for children's development and behavior. In terms of income level, studies have shown that children from low-income families spend twice as much time on screens as children from high-income families. Rideout (2011) notes that children from high-income families tend to use digital devices more consistently, while those from low-income families have more limited access. However, it is argued that, rather than income level alone, parents' awareness of digital tool use and methods may have a greater impact on these strategies (Livingstone et al., 2011). Rideout and Katz (2016) concluded that families with higher education and income levels are more likely to assist their children in digital interactions. In the United States, 97% of children aged six months to four years from low-income families use mobile devices, with most beginning to use them before their first birthday (Kabali et al., 2015). In summary, children of parents with lower income and education levels are exposed to more screen time with digital devices (Rideout & Robb, 2020).

A child can interact with digital tools for hours and play digital games if parental permission is granted (Emiroğlu İlvan & Ceylan, 2023). This is thought to be due to children's lower self-regulation mechanisms compared to adults (Vazsonyi & Huang, 2010). Excessive and inappropriate use of technology may lead to digital play addiction in individuals. However, instead of using the term "digital play addiction" directly for young children, the concept of "digital play addiction tendency" is preferred. This is because defining these behaviors as tendencies rather than labeling them as addictions is considered more appropriate for the child, allowing for early intervention and the avoidance of stigmatization during early childhood (Budak & Işıkoğlu, 2022).

The lack of consensus on screen time duration and the highly individualized nature of the question "How much is too much?" have made this a topic of debate among both parents and researchers. However, shaping screen time in early childhood according to the child's age, developmental stage, and individual characteristics, as well as considering the quality and educational value of the content, are crucial factors to be considered (UNICEF, 2017; Ponti, 2023; Puzio et al., 2022). The World Health Organization (2019) recommends zero screen exposure for children aged 0-1 and no sedentary screen time for those aged 1-2. For children aged 2 and older, it is emphasized that sedentary screen time should not exceed one hour. Consistent with findings that reveal an increase in screen time with age (Rideout & Robb, 2020; McArthur et al., 2022), it is suggested that screen time can be increased for children aged 3-4 and older, provided that content and duration controls are carefully managed.

The Effect of Digital Play Addiction Tendency on the Development of Early Childhood

Digital play addiction tendency, resulting from excessive exposure to technology, can negatively impact various aspects of an individual's life. Research focusing on early childhood indicates that the inappropriate use of digital tools is associated with conditions such as loneliness, poor social skills, obesity, sleep problems, short attention span, physical discomfort, low academic achievement, violence, peer bullying, and behavioral problems (Eirich et al., 2022; Mustafaoğlu & Yasacı, 2018; Şahin & Gözün Kahraman, 2021; Madigan et al., 2019). Specifically, the tendency toward digital play addiction can increase the frequency of behavioral problems, which not only causes issues in social contexts but also negatively impacts positive social behaviors (Gentile et al., 2011). Studies on digital play addiction tendency reveal results that align with screen time research, linking this tendency with variables such as parental attitudes (Emiroğlu İlvan & Ceylan, 2023), low social competence (Budak & Işıkoğlu, 2023), problematic behaviors (Budak & Işıkoğlu, 2023), negative digital parental mediation (Şenol et al., 2023; Çalhan & Goksu, 2024), children's orientation toward digital play (Budak & Işıkoğlu, 2023), pandemic-related changes (Işıkoğlu et al., 2024), and socio-emotional development (Şenol et al., 2023). The focus of the discussion should now shift from the effects of interaction to how to enhance positive interaction processes. This shift is crucial, as it is well-established that while daily interaction time with digital tools is increasing, the age at which children first interact with these tools is decreasing (Rideout & Robb, 2020).

Studies conducted worldwide have shown that mobile media has become an indispensable part of children's media experiences across all segments of society. In this context, Common Sense Media, which addresses and reflects this issue most comprehensively, has conducted periodic studies to determine the digital device usage habits of children aged 0-8 in the USA. Their latest report, published in 2020, provides a comparative analysis of these habits (Rideout & Robb, 2020). The 2017 report, which includes data from over 1,400 families, reveals that almost all children under the age of eight (98%) live in households with some type of mobile device, and this number has been steadily increasing since 2011. In line with the presence of digital devices in the home, it was found that children's digital device usage begins before the age of two and increases with age, ranging from 42 minutes to 180 minutes per day. In 2020, children from birth to eight years of age were found to spend approximately two and a half hours (2:24) per day using screen media, consistent with previous reports, with screen time increasing with age. In the United Kingdom, children in the same age group spend slightly less time in front of screens, averaging approximately 1.5 hours per day, with television still being the dominant medium (Ofcom, 2019). In East Asian countries such as Japan and South Korea, young children's average screen time exceeds three hours per day, with a significant portion of this time spent on educational apps and video games (Yamada et al., 2018). A study comparing the screen time of Canadian children (2:39) and Korean children (1:50) shows that both groups exceed the recommended time (Lee et al., 2021). Similar studies conducted in Turkey report that screen use begins before the age of 2 and that young children spend more than three hours a day in front of screens (Konca, 2022; Şimşek et al., 2023). The common finding across all these countries is that screen time has increased, exceeding three hours in early childhood, and the age of first use has decreased to as early as six months (Çelik et al., 2021; Konca, 2021; Işıkoğlu Erdoğan, 2019; Şimşek et al., 2023).

High media use in children is associated with impaired cognitive, language, and social-emotional skills (Schwarzer et al., 2022). Research indicates that prolonged exposure to screens can hinder the development of critical cognitive skills, such as problem-solving and attention control, which are crucial for academic success later in life (Lieberman et al., 2009; Gentile, 2009). Gentile (2009) investigated whether children aged 8-18 are addicted to video games. The results of the study emphasize that children who spend more time playing video games show lower academic achievement compared to those who spend less time on these games. Additionally, children who spend more time playing video games are associated with attention problems and attention deficit. Putnitk et al. (2023) found that children who spent more screen time between 12 and 36 months engaged less with peers during the same period, and this reduced peer interaction was linked to developmental delays in four of five developmental domains. Similarly, the American Academy of Pediatrics (AAP) recommends that screen time for children under the age of two should be minimized to foster healthy brain development. Excessive screen time at this age may disrupt essential interactions with caregivers, which are vital for language acquisition and social-emotional learning (AAP, 2016). In addition to cognitive impacts, high levels of screen time have been associated with delays in language development. Studies show that children who are frequently exposed to screens, especially without interactive content or adult mediation, tend to have smaller vocabularies and slower language processing skills compared to those with less screen exposure. A longitudinal study by Madigan et al. (2019) found that each additional hour of screen time at age two was associated with lower language scores at age three, emphasizing the importance of regulating screen time during critical periods of language development. The study also highlights the negative impact of background television, which can distract both children and caregivers, thereby reducing the quality and quantity of verbal interactions essential for language growth.

Screen time can also negatively impact children's physical health, particularly concerning obesity and motor skill development. Sedentary behavior associated with prolonged screen use is a significant risk factor for childhood obesity, as it often displaces physical activity (Fang et al., 2019; Fullerton et al., 2014). Fang et al. (2019) demonstrated in their meta-analysis that children with ≥2 hours of screen time per day are at a higher risk of overweight/obesity compared to those with <2 hours of screen time per day. For instance, Tremblay et al. (2015) found that children with higher screen time were less likely to meet physical activity guidelines, which are crucial for developing motor skills and overall physical health.

The impact of screen time on sleep patterns is another area of concern, as poor sleep can have far-reaching effects on a child's overall well-being. Numerous studies have shown that excessive screen time, especially before bedtime, can lead to difficulties falling asleep, shorter sleep duration, and poorer sleep quality. This is partly due to the blue light emitted by screens, which can interfere with the production of melatonin, a hormone that regulates sleep (Hale & Guan, 2015). Inadequate sleep can have cascading effects on a child's mood, behavior, and ability to concentrate, ultimately impacting their academic performance and emotional regulation. Chindamo et al. (2019) found that children with more screen time had shorter sleep durations, took longer to fall asleep, and were more likely to exhibit signs of hyperactivity and inattention, highlighting the importance of establishing healthy screen habits to support adequate sleep.

Finally, the social and emotional consequences of excessive screen time cannot be overlooked. Children who spend significant amounts of time engaging with screens, particularly through passive media consumption, may struggle with social interactions and emotional regulation. Anderson et al. (2010) conducted a meta-analysis examining studies on the relationship between violent video games and problem behaviors. The study, which included 136 research articles, concluded that exposure to violent digital content, specifically playing violent video games, increases aggressive behaviors. The literature review on video games reveals that violent video games contribute to an increase in problem behaviors among children and young adults. The analyses also showed that exposure to violent video games increases physiological arousal and aggression-related thoughts and feelings, while playing violent video games decreases positive social behaviors. Cho and Lee (2017) investigated the relationship between smartphone addiction tendencies, problematic behaviors, and emotional intelligence. They found that children in early childhood, due to their low self-control, tend to use digital devices more frequently. Additionally, smartphones contribute to problematic behaviors in children with addiction tendencies and hinder their emotional intelligence. Gentile et al. (2011) examined the digital game addictions of elementary and middle school children in a two-year longitudinal study and found that increased digital game use was associated with lower social competence and greater impulsivity. These findings underscore the need for parents and caregivers to actively manage and limit screen time to promote healthier social and emotional development.

Given the current state of research on the effects of digital media on children's development, a prudent and cautious approach to screen use among young age groups is essential. Although existing studies suggest that digital games can offer developmental benefits when used in a controlled and conscious manner, it is equally evident that uncontrolled and excessive use can have detrimental effects on children's development. In this context, parents, educators, and digital game producers must demonstrate the necessary commitment to ensuring the responsible use of digital games.

Reflection of Digital Play Addiction Tendency in Different Environments

The most crucial factor for a child's developmental stages to progress healthily is their relationship with the mother, father, and caregivers. Parents should provide age-appropriate activities that support the child's curiosity and learning, as these activities form the foundation of a positive parent-child relationship (Senemoğlu, 2011) and influence various aspects of children's lives. Parents mediate the opportunities available to children, shaping their understanding of play (Brito, 2016; Chaudron et al.,

2018; Yogman et al., 2018). Additionally, the home environment is where digital play interactions, which significantly impact today's understanding of play, first emerge (Ginsburg, 2007). Digital tools directly affect the parent-child relationship and, in turn, the entire family structure, which is the fundamental unit of society (Emiroğlu İlvan & Ceylan, 2023; Işıkoğlu et al., 2024; Chen & McCallum, 2023). The pervasive presence of digital tools increases children's digital interaction, and parents often struggle to balance digital life with real-life experiences. The bioecological development model provides a theoretical framework for understanding the impact of parental guidance strategies on young children's tendencies toward digital play addiction (Chen & McCallum, 2023). Bronfenbrenner (1995) posits that a child's development is influenced by a system of interconnected relationships across various environmental levels, from immediate settings such as family and school to broader cultural values, laws, and customs. The first layer of this theory, known as the microsystem, highlights the significant role of family, peers, school, and neighborhood in a child's development. On the other hand, Bandura's Social Learning Theory argues that individuals learn behaviors through observation and imitation. According to this theory, children learn by observing and imitating behaviors seen in digital play, which is why those who play violent games may exhibit violent behaviors in real life. Additionally, reinforcers such as winning and rewards in digital games can increase children's desire to play (Bandura & Hall, 2018). Social learning is a crucial factor in the development of digital play addiction tendencies, as increasing interaction with digital tools poses developmental risks, particularly regarding overuse and addiction. Considering that children's digital use is often modeled after and imitated from their parents, social learning is a significant variable influencing and increasing children's screen use (Chaudron et al., 2018; Chen & McCallum, 2023; Plowman & McPake, 2013).

In an increasingly digital world, parents are deeply concerned about their children (Radesky et al., 2023). There is a prevailing belief that children are not benefiting adequately from digital tools and may be harmed instead. Many parents worry about the risks their children may encounter in digital environments and believe that digital games negatively impact their children's development (Benedetto & Ingrassia, 2021; Papadakis et al., 2022). This concern often leads parents to impose bans and restrictions on their children's digital interactions (Chaudron et al., 2018; Palaiologou, 2016). However, despite concerns about the disadvantages, it is essential for children to stay abreast of technological advancements, adapt to the requirements of the age, and acquire digital literacy skills (Lange et al., 2021). Given these circumstances, parents are seen as the most crucial factor in managing and guiding their children's digital interactions (Brito et al., 2017). Therefore, parents should strive to regulate their children's use of digital tools, aiming to maximize the benefits of modern technology while minimizing its disadvantages (Livingstone & Helsper, 2008).

From an ecological perspective, the most important interaction environment for children, after family, is the school environment. School is a critical setting where children spend a significant amount of time and where their behavior is shaped (Thapa et al., 2013). The student's experience within the classroom, as well as interactions with teachers and peers, forms the basis of the child's behavior. When assessing whether a behavior is problematic, it is important to consider multiple interaction environments, such as the classroom or various play environments, where children express themselves and adopt behaviors. Long-term, unregulated screen use can negatively affect children's behavior. Early childhood children are particularly vulnerable in front of screens due to their developmental characteristics, as they may have difficulty distinguishing between imagination and reality, and between real and virtual experiences. Additionally, children may imitate behaviors of characters they see on screens and consider them role models (Plowman & McPake, 2013; Wernicke & Montag, 2022). Peer bullying, miscommunication, reactivity, and problem behaviors can be observed, especially in children who experience violent technology victimization. Overindulgence in digital games can lead to behavioral problems such as impatience, aggression, and inappropriate reactions in the classroom (Eirich et al., 2022). This can result in discipline problems and create difficulties for both teachers and other students. Furthermore, a tendency toward digital play addiction can lead children to withdraw from face-to-face social interactions and struggle with forming healthy relationships with peers, potentially causing feelings of loneliness and reluctance to participate in collaborative activities.

During the learning process, children may find it challenging to focus on the task at hand as they are preoccupied with thoughts of digital games, which can hinder their concentration in the classroom and shorten their overall attention span (Gentile et al., 2011). These distractions and concentration issues can negatively impact children's active participation in lessons and learning processes (Cheng & Siu, 2006), resulting in difficulties completing assignments and projects, lower test scores, and decreased overall academic achievement (Gentile, 2009; Hastings et al., 2009). Given that these repercussions can adversely affect children's educational processes and overall development, it is crucial for teachers and parents to recognize the signs of digital play addiction early, take necessary precautions, and provide guidance. Early childhood educators should be aware of both the advantages and disadvantages of digital games and understand the importance of guided use of technology and media tools (Hirsh-Pasek et al., 2015). Educators and parents need to be informed about the positive aspects of technology while also working to prevent and address addictive tendencies in children (Plowman et al., 2010).

METHOD

Research Model

The study adopted a basic qualitative research design. Basic qualitative research aims to reveal how individuals construct their understanding of the world because of their interactions with the world (Creswell, 2017). Within the scope of this research, preschool teachers' views on the reflections of digital play addiction tendencies in the classroom were taken.

Study Group

The study group for this research consists of twelve teachers currently employed in preschool education institutions in Turkey. Participants were selected using convenience sampling, a method that involves choosing respondents who are readily available and accessible at the time of the study. This approach facilitates the research process. While convenience sampling is commonly used in case studies, it does not support the generalization of results (Cohen et al., 2018).

The participants of the study were 16.5% male and 83.5% female, while 58% of the preschool teachers were between the ages of 25-30 and 42% were between the ages of 31-36. When the education levels of the participants are examined, it is seen that 75% of them are undergraduate graduates, while 25% are master's/doctorate graduates. When teachers were asked about their perspectives on digital games, 25% of them were positive, 17% were negative and 58% were neither positive nor negative.

Data Collection Tools

To collect data for the study, the researchers developed the 'Opinion Form on the Reflections of Digital Play Addiction Tendencies of Preschool Teachers.' Preliminary interviews were conducted with three teachers to inform the creation of this form. Based on these preliminary interviews, the form was reviewed by five field experts, and necessary revisions were made according to their feedback. The first section of the form includes variables related to the teachers themselves. The second section contains questions that require teachers to reflect on their observations of children in their classrooms who may exhibit tendencies toward digital play addiction. The form includes five questions, some of which are as follows: 'In your opinion, how are the developmental characteristics of children with tendencies toward digital play addiction reflected in your class? (Please detail the reflections in terms of cognitive, social, emotional, and physical development.)' and 'In your opinion, how does digital play addiction tendency reflect on the learning of children in your class?'.

Data Collection

The questions in the form were created using Google Forms. To collect the data, participants were informed about the purpose of the study. The form was then distributed to teachers working in preschool education institutions on a voluntary basis, and the data were collected accordingly

Data Analysis

The data obtained through Google Forms were transferred to Microsoft Excel. The transferred data were analyzed by the researcher using the content analysis method. First, codes were determined by carefully reading the participants' responses. Subsequently, categories and themes were established based on the content of these codes. Qualitative content analysis involves systematic procedures for meticulously analyzing, coding, replicating, making inferences, and verifying written data (Cohen et al., 2018; Gläser & Laudel, 2013). In the present study, teachers' opinions were presented with direct quotations without modification and were coded in accordance with ethical guidelines (Teacher 1: T1, Teacher 2: T2).

FINDINGS

The findings from the research, which aimed to determine preschool teachers' reflections on the classroom environment regarding children with addictive tendencies, were analyzed. The participants' responses to the questions were examined using content analysis, resulting in the identification of various themes and categories. In this context, the findings include teachers' views on technology integration in the classroom, reflections on the development and learning of children with tendencies toward digital play addiction, and the difficulties they encounter related to these reflections.

Technology Integration

Figure 1. Teacher opinions on the use of technology in the classroom

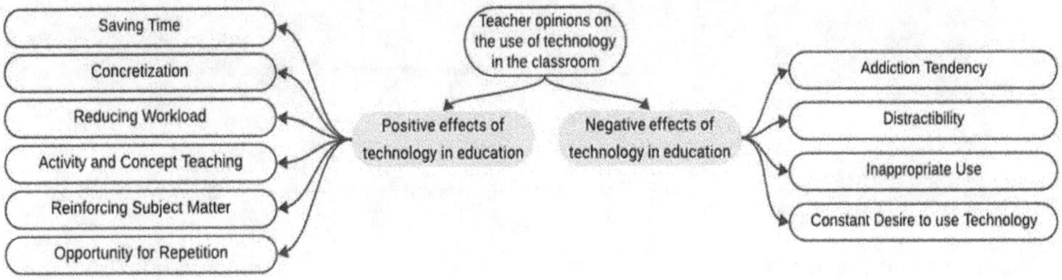

Analysis of teachers' perspectives on technology integration in the classroom reveals that opinions fall into two primary groups, with teachers expressing both advantages and disadvantages of the technology integration process. Interviews reflecting positive views indicated that technology made classroom activities more efficient and of higher quality, particularly during the integration process. Teachers noted that visual and auditory materials helped attract children's attention, saving time for both children and teachers while facilitating the repetition of concepts and learning. Additionally, it was emphasized that technology supports early childhood education by helping to concretize abstract concepts. Conversely, teachers also highlighted several negative aspects of technology integration. Issues such as addiction, distraction, inappropriate use, and children's constant desire to use digital devices were noted as drawbacks. Teachers reported that, when not managed properly, technology can become a significant source of distraction, leading to decreased focus on lessons, lower retention rates, and reduced participation in classroom activities. It was also stated that it may cause difficulties in adapting to structured learning activities that do not involve technology, which children constantly want to use, as T9 stated: *"While it is positive in terms of providing both visual and auditory support in activity and concept teaching, I observed that children who are exposed to technology too much present difficulties in focusing and paying attention to something for a long time."*.

The Impact of Dependency Tendency on Development

Figure 2. Possible effects of digital play addiction tendency on development according to teachers' opinions

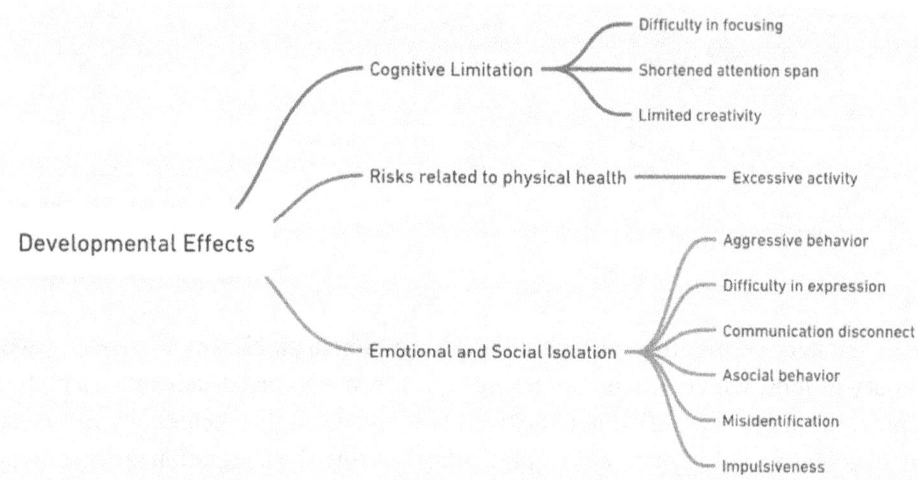

Evaluating teachers' views on the impact of children's addictive tendencies on their development in the classroom reveals that all participants have observed negative effects across various developmental areas. More specifically they state that it causes negative interactions in the field of social and emotional development and that it causes social regression (something that can also be seen in the statement of S5"*The most prominent negative features are in social emotional skills. The deficiencies in skills such as group consciousness, cooperation, waiting for their turn, empathy, etc. are clearly visible.*". Furthermore, participants stated that especially aggressive behaviors were shown within the framework of observations, while the majority expressed the idea that it was due to their identification with digital characters (T12 "*I think addiction negatively affects all developmental areas of children. Especially children imitate digital characters. We often encounter hitting behavior, swearing, aggression behaviors.*"). In terms of cognitive development, which constitutes an important dimension of developmental effects, it is seen that many children experience limitations, such as difficulty focusing their attention, short attention spans distraction and reduced creativity. In other words, it is possible to say that the limitations in cognitive development negatively affect their learning. As T3 stated: "*they cannot play, they wait for commands*", while according to T9:"*children have cognitive problems such as difficulty in focusing, very short attention span, difficulty in finishing the activity*". It is also noteworthy that teachers believe that these children show excessive mobility in the classroom environment.

The Impact of Addictive Tendencies on Learning

Figure 3.Possible effects of digital play addiction tendency on learning according to teachers' opinions

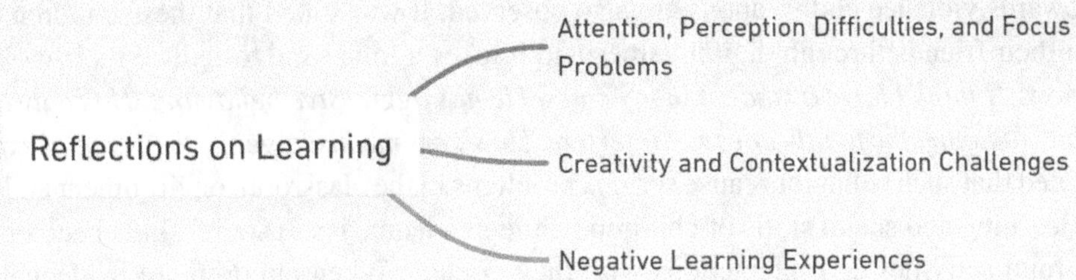

Analysis of the views on learning indicates that the reflections are predominantly negative and can be grouped into three main categories. Participants stated that children had attention, perception and focusing problems, creativity and contextualization difficulties, and negative learning experiences. Teachers tend to express that children got bored quickly, especially during the activities, and that they had difficulty maintaining and focusing their attention in activities that required larger attention span, asT9 explained "*The desired quality cannot be achieved in occasional activities because their attention span is very short and they have difficulty in focusing, they are constantly chatting about the games, and a child's question about a digital game during the activity completely distracts the attention of other children.*" Accordingly, T12 expressed the reflection of the addiction tendency on learning with the statement "*They have difficulty in perceiving the subject or activity because their attention span is short.*". Children who are prone to digital play addiction in early childhood may exhibit various attention and focusing problems, a view that T13 seems to agree with taking into consideration the statement "*...children's attention spans are very short compared to the past. I have a lot of difficulty especially in book reading activities.*". In the different activity contexts of these difficulties, it was observed that children had limited creativity and difficulty in establishing context between learning, as T6 stated "*Their creativity is gradually decreasing, they want to take everything ready-made. They have difficulty in establishing context by observing.*"

Challenges With Children With Addictive Tendencies

When examining the challenges faced by children with addictive tendencies, the categories of "Focus and Attention Problems," "Behavioral and Social Interaction Problems," and "Communication Issues with Family" emerged. It can be concluded that these difficulties are often rooted in negative aspects of the children's development and learning. Looking at the focusing problems, it is seen that children generally cannot focus their attention on an activity for a long time as T1 emphasized "*...adjustment problem, reluctance, leaving the activity halfway...*". Parallel to the symptoms of negative activation of learning, primarily when children have difficulty focusing, the learning process is weakened and this situation challenges teachers. T11 stated, "Since they have problems in focusing, they fall behind compared to other children." while according to T5 "*The biggest difficulty I experience is the focusing problems seen in these children.*". It is stated that children require one-to-one activities, have difficulty focusing and creating a sense of curiosity, and have difficulty forming long and connected sentences. This situation negatively affects children's learning processes and creates a significant obstacle for both them and their teachers. Furthermore, through participants' statements emphasize that activities should be repeated, and extra effort should be made to keep children's attention. Behavioral and Social Interaction Problems, on the other hand, are manifested by traits such as impatience, irritability, difficulty in making friends, and inability to regulate noise and volume. In addition, behaviors such as slang use, tendency towards violence and weapons are also observed. It was stated that these children tend to put pressure on their friends through digital games and it takes a long time to reduce their violent actions as T9 mentions "*I think I have a student in my class. He has aggressive behaviors. He is always playing with the tablet at home, the family does not interfere. He shows me his anger with his facial expressions.*" Teachers stated that such behaviors cause serious problems in the classroom environment and negatively affect both learning and social skills of children, while in adequacies in social skills become evident in children's group activities and interactions with their friends. When children are inadequate in group skills, they show problems in leaving the activities halfway and adaptation problems as it is seen through the statement of S9 "*I observe them throwing toys and not being able to play plays with their friends.*" This situation negatively affects the development of children's social skills and is seen as the difficulties that teachers face in carrying out the education process.

DISCUSSION

The formation of a digital ecosystem in early childhood underscores the crucial role of teachers in addressing significant issues such as digital play addiction tendencies (Plowman et al., 2010). Teachers can raise awareness among children as they explore the digital world, helping them balance their use of digital games (Hirsh-Pasek et al., 2015). Furthermore, integrating digital games into educational materials allows teachers to enhance students' learning experiences more effectively and efficiently. However, teachers must also highlight the potential risks of digital play and provide appropriate guidance. By doing so, they can support young children in exploring the digital world healthily and managing risks such as digital play addiction, thereby fostering more balanced and informed digital citizens. Technology integration has both positive and negative effects on children's learning processes (Prot et al., 2014; Yalçın-Irmak & Erdoğan, 2016). While incorporating technology into classroom activities can capture children's attention and make learning materials more accessible (Birds & Edwards, 2015), excessive and uncontrolled use of technology can exacerbate addictive tendencies and lead to distraction (Budak & Işıkoğlu, 2023). Therefore, it is crucial for teachers to ensure that children use these tools responsibly. In this context, teachers play a significant role (Neumann et al., 2018). Despite the recommendations for technology integration, it is important to consider that children who experience imbalanced and low-quality digital interactions at home may develop addictive tendencies. Being aware of the implications of digital play addiction is therefore essential.

Consistent with the literature, this study also considers teacher opinions, which suggest that digital play addiction tendencies in children create various negative effects on their development. This tendency towards addiction adversely affects children's social and emotional development, weakening their abilities to empathize, cooperate, and participate in group settings (Yalçın-Irmak & Erdoğan, 2016). Additionally, the imitation of violent behaviors seen in digital plays leads to an increase in aggressive behaviors (Anderson et al., 2010). This situation makes it difficult for children to establish healthy social relationships and become emotionally balanced individuals. Unfortunately, addiction tendencies are observed to negatively affect children's learning processes as well, according to teacher opinions, children have difficulty concentrating and cannot focus on long-term activities. This situation reduces efficiency in learning activities and is thought to negatively impact children's academic achievements, especially in tasks requiring high-level cognitive skills such as creative thinking and problem-solving.

Recommendations for Teachers

To mitigate the negative effects of children's tendencies towards digital play addiction, activities that support their social and emotional development should be planned, while teachers should organize group activities that develop social skills such as empathy, self-regulation skills, cooperation, and helping, and assist children in acquiring these skills. Additionally, it is important to limit the use of violent digital content and provide children with alternative opportunities for social interaction. Teachers should use various teaching strategies that capture children's attention and make learning materials engaging. Children should be given tasks that develop creative thinking and problem-solving skills. Teachers should make classroom arrangements to meet these children's individual attention needs and implement individualized education plans (Neumann et al., 2018). Additionally, clear rules should be established and encouraged to be followed to maintain discipline and order in the classroom. It is also recommended that meetings be organized at the beginning of the semester and at regular intervals so that teachers can convey to families the advantages and disadvantages of technology and the quality teaching opportunities on how it can be used. It is critical for teachers to increase their awareness of current technology integrations and their digital literacy. It is also important for them to reflect their digital literacy skills in the classroom in many contexts. Even though the importance of technology integration is emphasized, it is very important for teachers to frequently include outdoor activities in their classroom routines and for parents to direct their children to outdoor activities. It is recommended that they create a daily and monthly calendar of outdoor activities and make these activities a routine (Fenty et al., 2014; Lauricella et al., 2015; Nikolopoulou, 2024).

Recommendations for Parents

Parents should serve as positive role models to support their children's social development and direct them towards social plays instead of digital ones. To reduce the negative effects of addiction tendencies on learning, activities that develop children's attention and concentration skills should also be organized. Parents should actively participate in their children's learning processes and support them. To reduce the challenges faced with children who have addiction tendencies, teachers and parents should work collaboratively (Chen & MacCallum, 2023). Parents should limit their children's digital play time and direct them to activities that will develop their social skills. In this process, the rules they set together with their children regarding the processes of establishing digital interaction should be set and written/visual texts should be made, and it should be emphasized that the rules should be followed without using initiative. A balance should be established between digital interaction and other activities, and attention should be paid especially to their participation in outdoor activities. It is recommended that there should be areas for the use of digital tools in the home environment. It is recommended that children should not interact with any digital tools in their personal rooms (APA, 2016; Laurance et al., 2024; Lauricella et al., 2015; Nikolopoulou, 2024).

In this regard, both parents and teachers should work together and take on their respective responsibilities. Overall, a coordinated approach between parents and teachers is essential, as regular communication and collaboration can ensure that children receive consistent messages and support from both home and school environments. By working together, parents and teachers can create a well-rounded framework that supports children's social skill development and mitigates the potential negative effects of excessive digital play usage.

Recommendations for Policymakers

It is recognized that raising awareness among only teachers and parents is insufficient in addressing early childhood digital play addiction. Politicians, in particular, need to maintain comprehensive and holistic approaches to societal restructuring. First, national campaigns should be launched to increase awareness of digital play addiction. These campaigns should highlight the adverse effects of excessive digital game usage on children and provide educational materials to guide parents, teachers, and other community members. Digital literacy programs should be developed and implemented in educational institutions, aiming to instill healthy digital habits in children (Cho & Lee, 2017). Educational sessions should be organized for all stakeholders during the structuring of these programs. Parents' participation in these programs should be encouraged, emphasizing that this issue has critical societal impacts beyond individual effects. Moreover, regulatory policies on the content and playtime of digital games should be established and enforced to ensure age-appropriate access for children. Strengthening and educating families plays a crucial role in regulating a child's digital interactions within their immediate ecosystem. Support mechanisms for families should be established, offering activities that encourage parents to spend quality time with their children. Additionally, community centers and play areas should be expanded to promote social and physical activities over digital games. Policymakers can contribute to the healthy development of children by implementing these preventive and supportive measures to reduce early childhood digital play addiction tendencies. Given the importance of awareness among individuals planning to become parents, early intervention programs should be prepared and implemented to increase their digital literacy. This aligns with the World Health Organization's recommendations on screen time policies (Ofcom, 2023; WHO, 2019).

Considering all these suggestions, it is essential for all stakeholders to collaborate in reducing early childhood digital game addiction. This holistic approach will help create a healthy developmental environment for children, mitigating tendencies toward digital game addiction in early childhood.

CONCLUSION

To sum up, the increasing use of digital gaming in early childhood has led to significant concerns regarding its impact on child development, particularly by encouraging trends towards digital gaming addiction. While technology and digital tools provide numerous benefits, such as enhancing learning experiences and providing new opportunities for engagement, their excessive and irregular use can lead to harmful effects. Given these risks, it is crucial that educators, parents and policymakers collaborate to create balanced approaches to technology use. Educators should emphasize the importance of responsible digital interactions, while parents should play a critical role in setting boundaries and modeling healthy digital behaviors. Through a joint effort, the goal should be to harness the benefits of digital play while minimizing risks and ensuring that children develop into well-rounded and socially competent individuals.

REFERENCES

Anderson, C. A., Shibuya, A., Ihori, N., Swing, E. L., Bushman, B. J., Sakamoto, A., Rothstein, H. R., & Saleem, M. (2010). Violent video play effects on aggression, empathy, and prosocial behavior in eastern and western countries: A meta-analytic review. *Psychological Bulletin*, 136(2), 151–173. DOI: 10.1037/a0018251 PMID: 20192553

Atkin, A. J., Sharp, S. J., Corder, K., & van Sluijs, E. M.International Children's Accelerometry Database (ICAD) Collaborators. (2014). Prevalence and correlates of screen time in youth: An international perspective. *American Journal of Preventive Medicine*, 47(6), 803–807. DOI: 10.1016/j.amepre.2014.07.043 PMID: 25241193

Bandura, A., & Hall, P. (2018). Social learning theory. In MacBlain, S. (Ed.), *Learning theories for early years* (p. 78). SAGE Publications.

Bedford, R., Saez de Urabain, I. R., Cheung, C. H. M., Karmiloff-Smith, A., & Smith, T. J. (2016). Toddlers' fine motor milestone achievement is associated with early touchscreen scrolling. *Frontiers in Psychology*, 7, 1108. DOI: 10.3389/fpsyg.2016.01108 PMID: 27531985

Benedetto, L., & Ingrassia, M. (2021). Digital parenting: Raising and protecting children in media world. *Parenting: Studies By an Ecocultural and Transactional Perspective*, 127-148. https://doi.org/ DOI: 10.5772/intechopen.92579

Bergmann, C., Dimitrova, N., Alaslani, K., Almohammadi, A., Alroqi, H., Aussems, S., Barokova, M., Davies, C., Gonzalez-Gomez, N., Gibson, S. P., Havron, N., Horowitz-Kraus, T., Kanero, J., Kartushina, N., Keller, C., Mayor, J., Mundry, R., Shinskey, J., & Mani, N. (2022). Young children's screen time during the first COVID-19 lockdown in 12 countries. *Scientific Reports*, 12(1), 2015. DOI: 10.1038/s41598-022-05840-5 PMID: 35132065

Birds, J., & Edwards, S. (2015). Children learning to use technologies through play: A digital play framework. *British Journal of Educational Technology*, 46(6), 1149–1160. DOI: 10.1111/bjet.12191

Brauchli, V., Sticca, F., Edelsbrunner, P., Von Wyl, A., & Lannen, P. (2024). Are screen media the new pacifiers? The role of parenting stress and parental attitudes for children's screen time in early childhood. *Computers in Human Behavior*, 152, 108057. DOI: 10.1016/j.chb.2023.108057

Brito, R. (2016). "Who taught you how to play?", "I did!" Digital practices and skills of children under 6. *Medical Education*, 7(2), 281–302. DOI: 10.14605/MED721607

Brito, R., Francisco, R., Dias, P., & Chaudron, S. (2017). Family dynamics in digital homes: The role played by parental mediation in young children's digital practices around 14 european countries. *Contemporary Family Therapy*, 39(4), 271–280. DOI: 10.1007/s10591-017-9431-0

Bronfenbrenner, U. (1995). Developmental ecology through space and time: A future perspective. In Moen, P., Elder, G. H.Jr, & Lüscher, K. (Eds.), *Examining lives in context: Perspectives on the ecology of human development* (pp. 619–647). American Psychological Association. DOI: 10.1037/10176-018

Budak, K. S., & Işıkoğlu, N. (2022). Dijital oyun bağımlılık eğilimi ve ebeveyn rehberlik stratejileri ölçeklerinin geliştirilmesi [Development of children's digital play addiction tendency and parental mediation scales]. *Ankara University Journal of Faculty of Educational Sciences*, 55(3), 693–740. DOI: 10.30964/auebfd.939653

Budak, K. S., & Işıkoğlu, N. (2023). Erken çocuklukta dijital oyun bağımlılık eğilimi: Çocuk ve ebeveyn özelliklerinin etkileri. *Mehmet Akif Ersoy Üniversitesi Eğitim Fakültesi Dergisi*, 66(66), 1–25. DOI: 10.21764/maeuefd.1081497

Çalhan, C., & Göksu, İ. (2024). An effort to understand parents' media mediation roles and early childhood children's digital play addiction tendency: A descriptive correlational survey study. *Education and Information Technologies*, 29(14), 17825–17865. Advance online publication. DOI: 10.1007/s10639-024-12544-y

Çelik, E., Özer, Y., & Özcan, S. (2021). Okul öncesi dönem çocuklarının ekran süresinin ebeveynlerin ekran kullanım alışkanlıkları ve aile işlevleri ile ilişkisi. *Çukurova Tıp Dergisi, 46*(4), 343-351. DOI: 10.17826/cumj.780582

Chaudron, S., Di Gioia, R., & Gemo, M. (2018). Young Children (0-8) and digital technology - A qualitative study across Europe. Jrc Science for Policy Report. DOI: 10.2760/294383

Chen, R., & MacCallum, K. (2023). Parental perceptions on children's use of digital technology: A systematic review. *ASCILITE Publications*, 334-339. DOI: 10.14742/apubs.2023.715

Chindamo, S., Buja, A., DeBattisti, E., Terraneo, A., Marini, E., Gomez Perez, L. J., Marconi, L., Baldo, V., Chiamenti, G., Doria, M., Ceschin, F., Malorgio, E., Tommasi, M., Sperotto, M., Buzzetti, R., & Gallimberti, L. (2019). Sleep and new media usage in toddlers. *European Journal of Pediatrics*, 178(4), 483–490. DOI: 10.1007/s00431-019-03318-7 PMID: 30652219

Cho, K. S., & Lee, J. M. (2017). Influence of smartphone addiction proneness of young children on problematic behaviors and emotional intelligence: Mediating self- assessment effects of parents using smartphones. *Computers in Human Behavior*, 66, 303–311. DOI: 10.1016/j.chb.2016.09.063

Cingel, D. P., & Krcmar, M. (2013). Predicting media use in very young children: The role of demographics and parent attitudes. *Communication Studies*, 64(4), 374–394. DOI: 10.1080/10510974.2013.770408

Clark, L. S. (2011). Parental mediation theory for the digital age. *Communication Theory*, 21(4), 323–343. DOI: 10.1111/j.1468-2885.2011.01391.x

Derevensky, J., Hayman, V., & Gilbeau, L. (2019). Behavioral addictions: Excessive gambling, gaming, internet, and smartphone use among children and adolescents. *Pediatric Clinics of North America*, 66(6), 1163–1182. DOI: 10.1016/j.pcl.2019.08.008 PMID: 31679605

Eirich, R., McArthur, B. A., Anhorn, C., McGuinness, C., Christakis, D. A., & Madigan, S. (2022). Association of screen time with internalizing and externalizing behavior problems in children 12 years or younger: A systematic review and meta-analysis. *JAMA Psychiatry*, 79(5), 393–405. DOI: 10.1001/jamapsychiatry.2022.0155 PMID: 35293954

Emiroğlu İlvan, T., & Ceylan, R. (2023). Predicting preschool children's digital play addiction tendency during Covid-19 pandemic: Regarding the mother-child relationship, and child-and family-related factors. *Education and Information Technologies*, 28(12), 15687–15716. DOI: 10.1007/s10639-023-11802-9 PMID: 37361780

Fang, K. M. M., Liu, K., & He, Y. (2019). Screen time and childhood overweight/obesity: A systematic review and meta-analysis. *Child: Care, Health and Development*, 45(5), 744–753. DOI: 10.1111/cch.12701 PMID: 31270831

Fenty, N. S., & Anderson, E. M. (2014). Examining educators' knowledge, beliefs, and practices about using technology with young children. *Journal of Early Childhood Teacher Education*, 35(2), 114–134. DOI: 10.1080/10901027.2014.905808

Fullerton, S., Taylor, A. W., Grande, E. D., & Berry, N. (2014). Measuring physical inactivity: Do current measures provide an accurate view of "sedentary" video game time? *Journal of Obesity*, 1-5, 1–5. Advance online publication. DOI: 10.1155/2014/287013 PMID: 25002974

Gentile, D. (2009). Pathological video-play use among youth ages 8 to 18: A national study. *Psychological Science*, 20(5), 594–602. DOI: 10.1111/j.1467-9280.2009.02340.x PMID: 19476590

Gentile, D. A., Choo, H., Liau, A., Sim, T., Li, D., Fung, D., & Khoo, A. (2011). Pathological Video Game Use Among Youths: A Two-Year Longitudinal Study. *Pediatrics*, 127(2), 319–329. DOI: 10.1542/peds.2010-1353 PMID: 21242221

Ginsburg, K. (2007). The importance of play in promoting healthy child development and maintaining strong parent-child bonds. *Pediatrics*, 119(1), 182–191. DOI: 10.1542/peds.2006-2697 PMID: 17200287

Griffiths, M. D. (2009). Online computer gaming: Advice for parents and teachers. *Education for Health*, 27(1), 3–6. https://irep.ntu.ac.uk/id/eprint/20885/1/200593_6996%20Griffiths%20Publisher.pdf

Griffiths, M. D., & Davies, M. N. O. (2005). Videogame addiction: Does it exist? In Goldstein, J., & Raessens, J. (Eds.), *Handbook of computer game studies* (pp. 359–368). MIT Press.

Hale, L., & Guan, S. (2015). Screen time and sleep among school-aged children and adolescents: A systematic literature review. *Sleep Medicine Reviews*, 21, 50–58. DOI: 10.1016/j.smrv.2014.07.007 PMID: 25193149

Hastings, E. C., Karas, T. L., Winsler, A., Way, E., Madigan, A., Tyler, S. (2009). Young children's video/computer game use: Relations with school performance and behavior. *Issues in Mental Health Nursing, 30,* 638–649. DOI: 10.1080/01612840903050414

Hill, D., Ameenuddin, N., Reid Chassiakos, Y. L., Cross, C., Hutchinson, J., Levine, A., Boyd, R., Mendelson, R., Moreno, M., & Swanson, W. S.American Academy of Pediatrics. (2016). Media and young minds. *Pediatrics*, 138(5), e20162591. DOI: 10.1542/peds.2016-2591 PMID: 27940793

Hirsh-Pasek, K., Zosh, J. M., Golinkoff, R. M., Gray, J. H., Robb, M. B., & Kaufman, J. (2015). Putting education in "educational" apps: Lessons from the science of learning. *Psychological Science in the Public Interest*, 16(1), 3–34. DOI: 10.1177/1529100615569721 PMID: 25985468

Işıkoğlu, N., Budak, K. S., & Guzen, M. (2024). Longitudinal Study of Children's Digital Play Addiction Tendencies and Parental Guidance Strategies. *Early Childhood Education Journal*. Advance online publication. DOI: 10.1007/s10643-024-01633-9

Işıkoğlu Erdoğan, N., & Ergenekon, E. (2021). Bebeklerin teknolojik araçları kullanmalarıyla ilgili anne görüşleri. *Ankara University Journal of Faculty of Educational Sciences*, 54(1), 117–140. DOI: 10.30964/auebfd.767338

Johnson, G. M., & Puplampu, K. P. (2008). Internet use during childhood and the ecological techno-subsystem. *Canadian Journal of Learning and Technology*, 34(1). Advance online publication. DOI: 10.21432/T2CP4T

Kabali, H. K., Irigoyen, M. M., Nunez-Davis, R., Budacki, J. G., Mohanty, S. H., Leister, K. P., & Bonner, R. L.Jr. (2015). Exposure and use of mobile media devices by young children. *Pediatrics*, 136(6), 1044–1050. DOI: 10.1542/peds.2015-2151 PMID: 26527548

Kaye, L. K., Orben, A., Ellis, D. A., Hunter, S. C., & Houghton, S. (2020). The conceptual and methodological mayhem of "screen time". *International Journal of Environmental Research and Public Health*, 17(10), 3661. DOI: 10.3390/ijerph17103661 PMID: 32456054

Kebir, C., & Özkaya, H. (2023). 16-36 ay arası çocuklarda ekran maruziyetinin dil gelişimi üzerindeki etkisinin araştırılması. *Türkiye Aile Hekimligi Dergisi*, 27(2), 21–28. DOI: 10.54308/tahd.2023.21033

Keeley, B., & Little, C. (2017). *The State of the Worlds Children 2017: Children in a Digital World. UNICEF. 3.* Retrieved from https://eric.ed.gov/?id=ED590013

Konca, A. S. (2022). Digital technology usage of young children: Screen time and families. *Early Childhood Education Journal*, 50(7), 1097–1108. DOI: 10.1007/s10643-021-01245-7

Lange, B. P., Blaut, A., Becker, R., & Krämer, N. C. (2021). Digital literacy in children: The role of socio-demographic variables, cognitive abilities, and family characteristics. *Computers & Education*, 160, 104028. DOI: 10.1016/j.compedu.2020.104028

Laurence, P. G., de Melo Rodrigues, M., Tannus, M. C. B. L., Dekaney, E. M., & Macedo, E. C. (2024). Parental executive functions and motivations unveil variations in young children's screen media use. *Psicologia: Reflexão e Crítica : Revista Semestral do Departamento de Psicologia da UFRGS*, 37(1), 20. DOI: 10.1186/s41155-024-00289-z PMID: 38847965

Lauricella, A. R., Wartella, E., & Rideout, V. (2015). Young children's screen time: The complex role of parent and child factors. *Journal of Applied Developmental Psychology*, 36, 11–17. DOI: 10.1016/j.appdev.2014.12.001

Lee, E. Y., Song, Y. K., Hunter, S., Jeon, J., Kuzik, N., Predy, M., & Carson, V. (2021). Levels and correlates of physical activity and screen time among early years children (2–5 years): Cross-cultural comparisons between Canadian and South Korean data. *Child: Care, Health and Development*, 47(3), 377–386. DOI: 10.1111/cch.12850 PMID: 33463740

Lemmens, J. S., Valkenburg, P. M., & Peter, J. (2009). Development and validation of a play addiction scale for adolescents. *Media Psychology*, 12(1), 77–95. DOI: 10.1080/15213260802669458

Lieberman, D. A., Fisk, M. C., & Biely, E. (2009). Digital games for young children ages three tosix: From research to design. *Computers in the Schools*, 26(3), 299–313. DOI: 10.1080/07380560903360178

Livingstone, S., & Helsper, E. (2008). Parental mediation and children's internet use. *Journal of Broadcasting & Electronic Media*, 52(4), 581–599. DOI: 10.1080/08838150802437396

Livingstone, S., Mascheroni, G., Dreier, M., Chaudron, S., & Lagae, K. (2015). *How parents of young children manage digital devices at home: The role of income, education and parental style*. EU Kids Online, LSE. Retrieved from https://eprints.lse.ac.uk/63378/1/__lse.ac.uk_storage_LIBRARY_Secondary_libfile_shared_repository_Content_EU%20Kids%20Online_EU_Kids_Online_How%20parents%20manage%20digital%20devices_2016.pdf

Madigan, S., Browne, D., Racine, N., Mori, C., & Tough, S. (2019). Association Between Screen Time and Children's Performance on a Developmental Screening Test. *JAMA Pediatrics*, 173(3), 244–250. DOI: 10.1001/jamapediatrics.2018.5056 PMID: 30688984

Marazziti, D., Presta, S., Picchetti, M., & Dell'Osso, L. (2015). Behavioral addiction: Clinical and therapeutic aspects. *Official Journal of the Italian Society of Psychopathology*, 21, 72–84. DOI: 10.1017/S1092852913001041 PMID: 24589040

McArthur, B. A., Volkova, V., Tomopoulos, S., & Madigan, S. (2022). Global prevalence of meeting screen time guidelines among children 5 years and younger: A systematic review and meta-analysis. *JAMA Pediatrics*, 176(4), 373–383. DOI: 10.1001/jamapediatrics.2021.6386 PMID: 35157028

Mustafaoğlu, R., & Yasacı, Z. (2018). Dijital oyun oynamanın çocukların ruhsal ve fiziksel sağlığı üzerine olumsuz etkileri. *Bağımlılık Dergisi, 19*(3), 51-53. Retrieved from https://dergipark.org.tr/tr/pub/bagimli/issue/38282/447021#article_cite

Neumann, M. M., Merchant, G., & Burnett, C. (2018). Young children and tablets: The views of parents and teachers. *Early Child Development and Care*, 1–12. DOI: 10.1080/03004430.2018.1550083

Nikken, P., & Schols, M. (2015). How and why parents guide the media use of young children. *Journal of Child and Family Studies*, 24(11), 3423–3435. DOI: 10.1007/s10826-015-0144-4 PMID: 26472932

Ofcom (2023). *Children and parents: media use and attitudes report 2023*. Retrieved from https://www.ofcom.org.uk/media-use-and-attitudes/media-habits-children/children-and-parents-media-use-and-attitudes-report-2023/

Palaiologou, I. (2016). Children under five and digital technologies: Implications for early years pedagogy. *European Early Childhood Education Research Journal*, 24(1), 5–24. DOI: 10.1080/1350293X.2014.929876

Plowman, L., & McPake, J. (2013). Seven myths about young children and technology. *Childhood Education*, 89(1), 27–33. DOI: 10.1080/00094056.2013.757490

Plowman, L., Stevenson, O., Stephen, C., & McPake, J. (2010). Supporting young children's learning with technology at home and in preschool. *Research Papers in Education*, 25(1), 93–113. DOI: 10.1080/02671520802584061

Ponti, M. (2023). Screen time and preschool children: Promoting health and development in a digital world. *Paediatrics & Child Health*, 28(3), 184–202. DOI: 10.1093/pch/pxac125 PMID: 37205134

Prot, S., Anderson, C. A., Gentile, D. A., & Swing, E. L. (2014). The positive and negative effects of video play. In A. Jordan & D. Romer (Eds.), *Children and media* (pp. 109-128). Oxford University Press.

Putnick, D. L., Trinh, M. H., Sundaram, R., Bell, E. M., Ghassabian, A., Robinson, S. L., & Yeung, E. (2023). Displacement of peer play by screen time: Associations with toddler development. *Pediatric Research*, 93(5), 1425–1431. DOI: 10.1038/s41390-022-02261-y PMID: 35986149

Puzio, D., Makowska, I., & Rymarczyk, K. (2022). Raising the child—Do screen media help or hinder? The quality over quantity hypothesis. *International Journal of Environmental Research and Public Health*, 19(16), 9880. DOI: 10.3390/ijerph19169880 PMID: 36011514

Radesky, J. S., & Christakis, D. A. (2016). Increased screen time: Implications for early childhood development and behavior. *Pediatric Clinics of North America*, 63(5), 827–839. DOI: 10.1016/j.pcl.2016.06.006 PMID: 27565361

Radesky, J. S., Kaciroti, N., Weeks, H. M., Schaller, A., & Miller, A. L. (2023). Longitudinal associations between use of mobile devices for calming and emotional reactivity and executive functioning in children aged 3 to 5 years. *JAMA Pediatrics*, 177(1), 62–70. DOI: 10.1001/jamapediatrics.2022.4793 PMID: 36508199

Rideout, V. (2011). *Zero to eight: children's media use in America 2011*. Common Sense Media. Retrieved from https://www.commonsensemedia.org/sites/default/files/research/report/zero-to-eight-2013.pdf

Rideout, V., & Katz, V. S. (2016). *Opportunity for all? Technology and learning in lower-income families. A report of the Families and Media Project.* The Joan Ganz Cooney Center at Sesame Workshop. Retrieved from https://www.joanganzcooneycenter.org/wp-content/uploads/2016/01/jgcc_opportunityforall.pdf

Rideout, V., & Robb, M. B. (2020). *The common sense census: Media use by kids age zero to eight.* Retrieved from https://www.commonsensemedia.org/sites/default/files/research/report/2020_zero_to_eight_census_final_web.pdf

Rideout, V. J., Foehr, U. G., & Roberts, D. F. (2010). *Generation M2: Media in the Lives of 8- to 18-Year-Olds.* Henry J. Kaiser Family Foundation. Retrieved from https://files.eric.ed.gov/fulltext/ED527859.pdf

Rosendo-Rios, V., Trott, S., & Shukla, P. (2022). Systematic literature review online gaming addiction among children and young adults: A framework and research agenda. *Addictive Behaviors*, 129, 107238. DOI: 10.1016/j.addbeh.2022.107238 PMID: 35104738

Şahin, D., & Gözün Kahraman, Ö. (2021). Okul dönemi çocuklarının bilgisayar oyun bağımlılığı ile davranış problemleri arasındaki ilişkinin incelenmesi. *Milli Eğitim Dergisi*, 50(230), 13–28. DOI: 10.37669/milliegitim.682086

Schulz van Endert, T. (2021). Addictive use of digital devices in young children: Associations with delay discounting, self-control and academic performance. *PLoS One*, 16(6), e0253058. DOI: 10.1371/journal.pone.0253058 PMID: 34157026

Schwarzer, C., Grafe, N., Hiemisch, A., Kiess, W., & Poulain, T. (2021). Associations of media use and early childhood development: Cross-sectional findings from the LIFE Child study. *Pediatric Research*, 91(1), 247–253. DOI: 10.1038/s41390-021-01433-6 PMID: 33658656

Senemoğlu, N. (2011). *Gelişim, öğrenme ve öğretim; kuramdan uygulamaya*. Pegem Akademi Yayıncılık.

Şenol, Y., Şenol, F. B., & Can Yaşar, M. (2024). Digital play addiction of preschool children in the Covid-19 pandemic: Social emotional development and parental guidance. *Current Psychology (New Brunswick, N.J.)*, 43(1), 839–847. DOI: 10.1007/s12144-023-04323-8 PMID: 36819754

Şimşek, Z. C., Canbeldek, M., & Işıkoğlu, N. (2023). Ebeveynlerin pandemi sürecinde dijital ebeveynliğe yönelik deneyimleri. *Dokuz Eylül Üniversitesi Buca Eğitim Fakültesi Dergisi*, 55(55), 250–271. DOI: 10.53444/deubefd.1221315

Thapa, A., Cohen, J., Guffey, S., & Higgins-D'Alessandro, A. (2013). A Review of School Climate Research. *Review of Educational Research*, 83(3), 357–385. DOI: 10.3102/0034654313483907

Thomas, G., Bennie, J., Cocker, K., Ireland, M., & Biddle, S. (2020). Screen-based behaviors in Australian adolescents: Longitudinal trends from a 4-year follow-up study. *Preventive Medicine*, 106258, 106258. Advance online publication. DOI: 10.1016/j.ypmed.2020.106258 PMID: 33022322

Tremblay, M. S., Chaput, J. P., Adamo, K. B., Aubert, S., Barnes, J. D., Choquette, L., Duggan, M., Faulkner, G., Goldfield, G. S., Gray, C. E., Gruber, R., Janson, K., Janssen, I., Janssen, X., Jaramillo Garcia, A., Kuzik, N., LeBlanc, C., MacLean, J., Okely, A. D., & Carson, V. (2017). Canadian 24-hour movement guidelines for the early years (0–4 years): An integration of physical activity, sedentary behaviour, and sleep. *BMC Public Health*, 17(S5, Suppl 5), 874. DOI: 10.1186/s12889-017-4859-6 PMID: 29219102

Valkenburg, P. M., Krcmar, M., Peeters, A. L., & Marseille, N. M. (1999). Developing a scale to assess three styles of television mediation: "Instructive mediation," "restrictive mediation," and "social coviewing.". *Journal of Broadcasting & Electronic Media*, 43(1), 52–66. DOI: 10.1080/08838159909364474

Vazsonyi, A. T., & Huang, L. (2010). Where self-control comes from: On the development of self-control and its relationship to deviance over time. *Developmental Psychology*, 46(1), 245–257. DOI: 10.1037/a0016538 PMID: 20053021

We Are Social. (2023). *Global digital report 2023.* Retrieved from https://datareportal.com/reports/digital-2023-global-overview-report

Wernicke, J., & Montag, C. (2022). Linking gaming disorder tendencies in children to their personality and parental gaming behavior. *Frontiers in Psychiatry*, 12, 748195. DOI: 10.3389/fpsyt.2021.748195 PMID: 35250648

World Health Organization. (2019). *Guidelines on physical activity, sedentary behaviour and sleep for children under 5 years of age*. Retrieved from https://www.who.int/publications/i/item/9789241550536

World Health Organization. (2024) Retrived from https://icd.who.int/browse/2024-01/mms/en#338347362

Yalçın-Irmak, A. & Erdoğan, S. (2016). Ergen ve genç erişkinlerde dijital oyun bağımlılığı: güncel bir bakış. *Türk Psikiyatri Dergisi, 27*(2), 128-37. Retrieved from https://www.turkpsikiyatri.com/PDF/C27S2/07.pdf

Yamada, M., Sekine, M., & Tatsuse, T. (2018). Parental internet use and lifestyle factors as correlates of prolonged screen time of children in Japan: Results from the super Shokuiku school project. *Journal of Epidemiology*, 28(10), 407–413. DOI: 10.2188/jea.JE20170100 PMID: 29576604

Yamamoto, M., Mezawa, H., Sakurai, K., Mori, C., Kamijima, M., Yamazaki, S., Ohya, Y., Kishi, R., Yaegashi, N., Hashimoto, K., Mori, C., Ito, S., Yamagata, Z., Inadera, H., Nakayama, T., Sobue, T., Shima, M., Kageyama, S., Suganuma, N., & Katoh, T.Japan Environment and Children's Study Group. (2023). Screen time and developmental performance among children at 1-3 years of age in the Japan Environment and Children's Study. *JAMA Pediatrics*, 177(11), 1168–1175. DOI: 10.1001/jamapediatrics.2023.3643 PMID: 37721733

Yeşilay. (2023). Teknoloji bağımlılığı. Retrieved from https://www.yesilay.org.tr/tr/bagimlilik/teknoloji-bagimliligi

Yogman, M., Garner, A., Hutchinson, J., Hirsh-Pasek, K., & Golinkoff, R. (2018). The power of play: A pediatric role in enhancing development in young children. *Pediatrics*, 142(3), e20182058. DOI: 10.1542/peds.2018-2058 PMID: 30126932

Chapter 7
Online Gaming Addiction (OGA):
Influence on Learning and Socialization of Students With Disabilities

Stella Andreas Danou
https://orcid.org/0009-0001-5890-1683
Frederick University Cyprus, Cyprus

ABSTRACT

As a self-distracting behavior, online gaming addiction (OGA) has been discussed extensively during the recent years revealing both negative and positive effects on adolescents, that form complex and unique conditions. In this chapter, targeted thematic literature review is employed, to establish concrete thematic units that best describe the effects of OGA that touch aspects of learning and socialization. Research in the field argues for prevention and varied intervention practices as an avenue for reducing OGA for students with and without disabilities, including cognitive behavioral therapy, hypnotherapy, time management, and motivational interviewing. The rationality of labeling excessive online gaming as addiction and the individualistic character of OGA are also discussed so as to provide a thorough understanding of the subject. It is expected that interested parts utilize the presented material, thereby to increase students' maximum benefit and enjoyment of online gaming.

1. INTRODUCTION

In the International Classification of Diseases (ICD, 2019), World Health Organization classifies Online Game (or gaming) Addiction (OGA) as a mental disorder (Zatrahadi et al., 2021). Classified as internet addictive disorder, OGA is understood as a form of addiction developed by internet technology (Kurniawan, 2019). More specifically, it is described as a condition in which "*a person plays online games excessively and becomes enslaved to this habit*" (Augustini & Marleni, 2023, p. 374). Problematic Internet Use (PIU) is also a term used to describe internet addiction (Király & Demetrovics, 2020). OGA is used interchangeably in literature with terms such as game addiction, computer game addiction, and pathological game to describe Internet Gaming Disorder (IGD), a term introduced by the American Psychological Association (Purwaningsih & Nurmala, 2021). Many individuals addicted to internet hold previous experiences of video game addiction and the major internet use for individuals addicted to internet, is game (Yoo et al., 2004). Essentially, the very popular (Yilmaz et al., 2018) video games,

DOI: 10.4018/979-8-3693-4191-9.ch007

mentioned as the *"top leisure time occupation for children"* (Farchakh et al., 2020, p. 46) are being discussed in the overall context of addiction (e.g. Nadeem et al., 2023) while the term Gaming Disorder was also introduced in the ICD-11 by the World Health Organization in 2019 (Coutelle et al., 2021). All things considered, both gaming and internet addiction are discussed in this chapter as equally important, and all the aforementioned terms may be presented interchangeably, depending on the source.

2. LITERATURE REVIEW

2.1. Online Gaming Addiction (OGA) Prevalence in Individuals With Disabilities

Online Gaming Addiction is considered to be one of the *'deviant'* behaviors demonstrated by adolescents; online gaming is their way of life (Syari et al., 2023). Teenagers, either with disabilities or not, are able to experience endless playing against and with other individuals, which can be extensively rewarding, as well as psychologically absorbing; adolescents can only become addicted when they consistently receive rewards, during their engagement in a certain activity (Griffiths, 2010). Undoubtedly, games are assumed to be the most stimulating and direct rewarding activities on the internet. Griffiths (2010) stated that a small minority of adolescents exhibit OGA including individuals with disabilities. By contrast, latest facts support the raised existence of either online or offline addiction among individuals with and without different disabilities, implying for deviations from Griffith's statements.

For instance, a significant number of adolescents was recently identified as being addicted to online games (Syari et al., 2023). Particularly for individuals with disabilities, a significant proportion of individuals with visual impairment were reported to present a tendency to excessive gaming (Wrzesinska et al., 2021). In addition, in the study of Martinez (2015), individuals aged 18-32 with a motor kind of disability strongly preferred virtual social relationships as an *"escape and entertainment,"* while demonstrating higher levels of frequency and amount of time spent on the internet (p.21). They showed increased use and dependence on technology as motor disability is classified as a potential vulnerability factor for excessive use. At the same time, several studies mentioned that internet addiction is widespread among adolescents with Autism Spectrum Disorder (ASD). In specific, 45.5% of students with ASD were identified as being addicted to internet and the prevalence of internet addiction in the population of ASD was reported to be higher than in the general population. Also, 80% of students addicted to internet used portable games in contrast to non-addicted students (46.7%) (Kawabe et al., 2019) showing their favor upon games. Similarly, video game use among adolescents with ASD was reported to appear in high rates (Coutelle et al., 2021). Finally, in the systematic literature review of empirical research conducted by Murray et al. (2020) Autism Spectrum Disorder/ Autistic-Like traits (ASD/ALTs) were investigated in association with Problematic Internet Use (PIU)/ Gaming Disorder (GD). According to the results, a number of studies showed that ASD groups demonstrated significantly higher GD scores as compared to typical development (TD) groups of children and/ or adolescents. Finally, in the same review, five studies supported that autism was significantly related with GD.

Not unlike populations with visual impairments, motor disabilities, or with ASD, adolescents with ADHD show relevant characteristics, regarding internet addiction. In the study of Yoo et al. (2004) significant links were identified between the level of Attention Deficit Hyperactivity Disorder (ADHD) symptoms and internet addiction severity in Korean elementary children. Greater prevalence of internet addiction was identified in children with ADHD as compared to children without ADHD. The case was valid for both inattention and hyperactivity- impulsivity domains and findings argued for ADHD behaviors to potentially represent risk factors for internet addiction. Clinical observations of Yoo et al. (2004) tie well with their initial hypothesis that children and adolescents with ADHD tend to desire activities such as video games and surfing on the internet while hesitating to get involved in activities that require persistent mental efforts. To this end, perhaps, their cognitive style could provide an explanation, provided that internet use is reported to match the cognitive style of individuals with ADHD because internet use permits varied, multiple kinds of stimulation, and immediate reward (Yoo et al., 2021).

2.2. Brief Overview of Evidence on the Outcomes of Gaming

Previous evidence suggested that video games could bring benefits in health and education for different groups, including individuals with learning disabilities (Griffiths, 2010). Latest evidence particularly for students with disabilities, also lists varied positive results including cognitive abilities enhancement and emotional regulation (Kuo et al., 2024). On the other part, OGA is mentioned to bring negative effects on students like decrease on their enthusiasm for learning, (Agustini & Marleni, 2023) or weighing down of their daily activities, especially if they demonstrate low levels of time management skills (Suargani & Muslikah, 2021). Regarding students with disabilities, research noted that excessive use of video games puts them at risk for aggressive behavior and negative impact on academic performance (Kuo et al., 2024). Admittedly, each of the aforementioned outcomes could bring negative corresponding impact in learning and socialization of students with or without disabilities.

3. METHOD

3.1 Demonstration of the Epistemological Problem

There is data supporting the susceptibility of adolescents with disabilities on becoming addictive to the internet and related activities such as video gaming. The social skills profile of individuals with disabilities appears to play an important role. A study with participating adolescents of 11-18 years old with ADHD, revealed a significant association between social skills deficits and increased risk of Internet addiction. Significant associations were also identified between social skills deficits and Internet gaming or watching movies (Chou et al., 2017). Further, adolescents with disabilities in the study of Volkova et al. (2019) were identified as susceptible to addictive internet usage, and 25% of adolescents with ADHD in the study of Blasco-Fontecilla et al. (2023) demonstrated internet gaming disorder.

OGA on the part of students with disabilities brings changes that touch aspects of their learning and socialization in negative ways. Problems that come from internet excessive use often become complicated for boys, due to unhealthy interactions with their parents as the latter generally intensify the problems by mishandling practices (Verma, 2019). For example, taking mobile phones away and strict prohibits on the part of parents causes adolescent behavior that violates existing rules and norms (Syari et al., 2023). Given that online gaming holds both benefits and risks, it is essential to develop appropriate intervention practices to reduce OGA of students with disabilities and its negative effect on their learning and socialization.

3.2 Purpose

The purpose of this chapter is to utilize targeted thematic literature review in order to offer valuable evidence regarding the effects of OGA on students with disabilities with special concern on their learning and socialization; and to ultimately provide with working interventions to alternate the consequences of OGA.

3.3 Research Question

How can teachers and parents help students with disabilities maximize the benefits of online gaming?

4. RESULTS

Discussions about addictive internet use and potential consequences had started in the late 1990s (Purwaningsih & Nurmala, 2021). The effects of playing video games on students have also been discussed for a long time, with special attention on gamers' social lives (Yilmaz et al., 2018). More than a decade ago, Griffiths (2010) stated that interactive gaming technology holds more positives than negatives for children. More recently, ongoing discourse for and against the use of video games in educational and clinical settings assert that video games may benefit individuals with different abilities (Kuo et al., 2024) while excessive online gameplay has been linked to psychological conditions, social and physical health (Purwaningsih & Nurmala, 2021). The overall assumption is that playing online games may cause both positive and negative impacts (Syari, 2023) and may appear contradictive. For example, video games engagement is linked to lower academic achievement among American children, while other research suggests that video games may increase academic performance (Michalopoulou, 2023). Despite that extreme amount of time on online gameplay is mentioned to be adolescents' lifestyle (Purwaningsih & Nurmala, 2021) with potential benefits, OGA is considered to be a mental disorder (Zatrahadi et al., 2021) with increased risk of harm in the lives of individuals.

4.1. Benefits of Online Gaming

In a broad sense, today cyberspace is a place where teenagers feel competent, while online games consist of a way to alleviate boredom (Humayya et al. 2022). Less than a decade before, a study was conducted by Kovess-Masfety et al. (2016) in order to examine the relationship between the amount of time children spent on videogames and three factors named mental health, cognitive and social skills. Results supported high levels of video-gaming associated with decreases in problems regarding peer relationships and in prosocial deficits. These facts argue for the positive effects on young children. To put this further, visual spatial skills used during video games benefit students in the areas of math, science and technology, while they also enhance language skills, critical thinking, creativity, and problem-solving processes (Michalopoulou, 2023), all aspects directly involved in learning. What is more, "*millennials love playing games*," and this form of addiction can play a significant part in motivating and engaging students in the learning process (Nadeem et al., 2023, p. 1).

For individuals with disabilities, their access to online technology may ensure their inclusion and participation in life. Internet is expected to promote knowledge, service, employment, development, and social interactional opportunities available to people with intellectual disabilities (Chadwick et al., 2016). Virtual communication helps individuals with disabilities to overcome communication difficulties (Volkova et al., 2019) as internet communication assists their efforts to create intimate relationships or discuss similar health conditions (Seymour & Lupton, 2004). In the study of Chadwick et al. (2016) individuals without disabilities identified social and support related online activities as the most beneficial outcomes for individuals with intellectual disabilities. The perceived benefit ratings were higher for people with intellectual disabilities as compared to self ratings. Likewise, information and communication technologies of the 21st century permits participation in different aspects of life and promotes independence of individuals with sensory and intellectual impairments, which finally helps them overcome societal isolation (Volkova et al., 2019).

Playing video games also appears to bring several benefits for students with disabilities such as physical rehabilitation and psychological well-being, improved cognition and emotional regulation, chronic pain management and earned advantages from exercises (Kuo et al., 2024). Lastly, students with visual impairment may engage in computer games within haptic or hearing devices and benefit in areas of spatial and abstract reasoning, social interaction, and self- confidence (Wrzesinska et al., 2021). It is generally accepted that online and offline activities with the use of technology such as virtual communication and video gaming may bring positive results to young students with or without disabilities, in multiple areas related to learning and socialization.

4.2. Negative Effects of Online Gaming

Despite the numerous benefits of online activities, internet addiction is considered to be a 'global problem' with potential harm in individuals' mental health (De Pasquale et al., 2020; Purwaningsih & Nurmala, 2021; Yao et al., 2014) that can co-exist with psychiatric conditions like depression, insomnia, and social phobia (Kawabe et al., 2019). Likewise, internet gaming disorder has been tied with psychological distress, such as depression, anxiety, obsessive -compulsive behavior with inattention, hyperactivity, low self-esteem, loneliness, and social phobia (Andreassen et al., 2016; Lin et al., 2021; Purwaningsih, & Nurmala, 2021).

Individuals with disabilities are not only susceptible to online addiction (Volkova et al., 2019) as young individuals with motor disabilities may also hold a higher risk for being negatively affected by excessive internet use. In the study of Martinez (2015), internet use affected the daily lives of individuals with motor disabilities in ways that increased their anxiety during their disconnection to the internet thinking that their lives would be "dull and sad" (p.21). In fact, recently, behaviors like increased aggression, inactivity, and negative impact on academic performance are most expected by individuals with disabilities because they are thought to hold higher risk from excessive video game use (Kuo, et al., 2024).

As can be expected, Internet addiction is reported to bring psychological and physical effects on children with disabilities. For clarity, physical effects entail neglecting their meals or "*eat unhealthy foods, become obese (eating disorders), lose their sleep since many times they stay connected to the Internet for nights and days or the quality of their sleep becomes poor*" (Voulganis & Drigas, 2022, p. 102). Then, inappropriate use of internet on the part of children with disabilities can negatively affect the development of their personalities by decreasing their self-esteem and self-confidence and has the potential to further harm their personality due to excessive use which may lead to addiction (Voulganis & Drigas, 2022). Finally, increased game addiction levels in specially gifted children aged 9-14 years of age, were negatively associated with their life quality levels in four functioning sectors represented in the Pediatric Quality of Life Inventory: physical, emotional, social, and school (Yalcin et al., 2020). In another sense, past and recent research highlights that excessive online activity holds a risk for psychosomatic and physical harm to young individuals, especially for those with disabilities. Such conditions may extensively interfere with their learning and socialization in and out of school. Because this chapter aims at providing with concrete data regarding the effects of OGA on aspects of learning and socialization, such are immediately demonstrated in the following sections.

4.2.1. Effects in Cognition and Learning

Considering that OGA has the potential to decrease learning enthusiasm there can be a subsequent decrease in motivation to study as well as in classroom attentiveness (Agustini & Marlein, 2023). At the same time, falling down activities due to OGA (Suargani & Muslikah, 2021) raise questions about students' studying habits and keeping up with social activities, irrespectively of their disability status. Academic procrastination is a condition students experience that negatively affects their academic life (Saad, 2020). Specifically, students procrastinate when they avoid doing what they know they should be doing. For example, they may find it hard to start working or may be late (Devi & Dhull, 2019). Such behaviors could reflect their failure to start and complete their assigned homework or studying for their exams. In the study of Saad (2020), academic procrastination was positively correlated with smartphone addiction in students aged 13-14 years old, as individuals who cannot control the use of their smartphone demonstrated procrastination. In addition, there were confirmed correlations between and among the processes of self-regulated learning, academic procrastination, and smartphone addiction. Students with low risk for smartphone addiction could have higher average self-regulated learning. The upcoming result of such correlations indicate that excessive use of smartphones, which could involve internet usage, impedes students to achieve higher academic achievement and keeps them back on their academic work. The aspect of self-regulation skills is of great importance when dealing with adolescents with disabilities because their self-regulation deficiencies impede their self-control during online activities and thus raise concerns about potential negative impact of internet interaction on the physical and mental state (Volkova et al., 2019).

Available evidence from latest research approve that addictive habits could negatively affect students' learning because one of the aspects of addictive disorders is thought to be cognitive dysfunction. In the study of Jiang et al. (2020), neurocognitive deficits and social cognitive dysfunction in individuals under the age of 18 with Internet Gaming Disorder (IGD) resembled to those of methamphetamine-dependent individuals. In more specific, both groups (individuals with IGD and methamphetamine-dependent individuals) demonstrated impairments in working memory, decision-making dysfunction, executive defects, and personal perception restrictions. Aside from the aforementioned resemblance, in a cross-sectional study (Farchakh et al., 2020), the association between addiction to video games and cognitive abilities was examined among 566 children aged 9-13 years. Cognitive abilities included memory, attention and learning. Results supported a correlation between video games addiction and memory, attention, cognitive and academic abilities. Particularly, worse novel problem solving, and worse attention were significantly associated with higher levels of addiction to video gaming. Further, a systematic review conducted by Purwaningsih and Nurmala (2021) revealed that adolescents addicted to online gaming demonstrated increased chances to experience mental health disorders as compared to adolescents not addicted to online gaming. Those disorders included decreases in academic performance, physical and mental health issues, as well as problems in relationships with other adolescents. On the contrary, in a cross-sectional three-year study in Netherlands (Van Rooij et al., 2014), psychosocial functioning and grades were identified at lower levels for a small group of addictive gamers among adolescent population asserting that problems do not always come out as a logical consequence of addictive gaming. Nevertheless, addictive gaming was associated with alcohol, nicotine, and cannabis for boys (Van Rooij et al., 2014), conditions that require immediate response due to their expected harm on students' overall health.

4.2.2. Effects in Socialization

Online games consist of an alternative option for individuals who cannot succeed in finding others for cooperative games (Kuo et al., 2024). Gamers are expected to interact with each other in different ways to achieve their goals. Such experiences might not be exempted from producing undesired outcomes. It is argued that the ways in which peers engage in playing games may impact both their interactions and relationships. That is, competitive and cooperative play may influence aspects such as aggression, prosocial behavior, and feelings of empathy and trust. Such influence was evident when friendship quality was decreased after competitive gaming in the study of Verheijen et al. (2019). In the same study, participants' behavior during playing had changed depending on the mode of play. To sum up, friendship quality was thought to be determined by the mode of playing and the displayed behavior during gaming.

Online interaction may fulfill adolescents desire to be at home and engage online. Nevertheless, suppressing direct interaction and communication could potentially harm social interactions and development of communication skills. Such an assumption is relevant with the notion that video games addiction influence the development of relationship between video game addicts and others. Video game addicts in the study of Yilmaz (2018) appeared to struggle to communicate with others and to follow rules at school. They showed preference to spend more time at home playing video games rather than being at school and they felt more comfortable spending time with individuals with similar interests. Overall, data supported that playing videogames could influence the behavior of 10-year-old (or less) children with potential negative effects on the people that surround them. The negative effects of internet addiction are also evident in the social relationships of children with disabilities when they spend a lot of time on internet related activities. When the computer becomes "*the most important thing in their life*" they show indifference about their family (Voulganis & Drigas, 2022, p. 102). Likewise, impaired psychophysical development in adolescents with disabilities could potentially limit their opportunities for social interaction when their engagement in internet communication activities remains uncontrolled and under the risk of Problematic Internet Usage (PIU) (Volkova et al., 2019).

In a qualitative study conducted in Sweden (Löfgren-Mårtenson, 2008) individuals with disabilities mentioned to use internet for social and romantic reasons. However, their social surroundings expressed a worry about the risks that accompany internet usage. Individuals' reported expectations related to love and sexuality are often perceived to be strong and influence their behaviors and their willing to follow the so called "*netiquette rules*" (p. 136). Correspondingly, despite that teachers identified internet usage as a means to interact with others, they also stressed that their adolescent children with intellectual disabilities also run the risk of experiencing undesired situations (Molin et al. 2015). In line with previous research, individuals without intellectual disabilities reported their perceived risks of being online for individuals with intellectual disabilities. Higher rates were identified for risks including bullying, online threatening or harassing, sharing excessive personal information and vulnerability to online marketing scams. Participants rated risks higher for individuals with intellectual disabilities as compared with perceived risks about themselves (Chadwick et al., 2016). Indeed, research reveals that children and adolescents with special needs or special learning disabilities are vulnerable to online abuse (Voulganis & Drigas, 2022). Forty-two children and youth with ADHD and/ or Asperger's in the study of Kowalski and Fedina (2011) reported high rates of traditional and electronic bullying victimization. Internet may help students with disabilities relate to their peers, but several conditions may put them at risk for virtual (or real world) problems, like cyber bullying.

Undoubtedly, online gaming could bring great benefits to children and adolescents, with or without disabilities in learning and socialization. However, OGA could also harm their physical, psychological, and social health (Humayya et al., 2022) interfering with their studies, social life, and emotional health (Verma, 2019, p. 217). In the following sections, prevention and intervention practices are discussed, thereby to build an effective framework for preventing and reducing the negative effects of OGA for adolescents with disabilities.

4.3. Prevention of Online Gaming Addiction (OGA)

Prevention comes before the appearance of OGA and is considered to be essential against the consequences that OGA may bring to adolescent population. In this context, it is important to identify predicting factors that could support early detection processes regarding video gaming addiction in children (Farchakh et al., 2020). In the systematic review of Purwaningsih and Nurmala (2021), factors such as family disharmony, parental inconsistency, family dysfunction, poverty and problems in family relationships where thought to play a risk/ protective role associated with internet gaming disorder (Throuvala et al., 2019). Evidently, parents play an important role in the shaping of appropriate behaviors regarding the use of internet. Building a quality relationship with their children, spending adequate time together, and using the internet together are thought to prevent internet addiction in their children (Voulganis & Drigas, 2022). Furthermore, supervision, behavioral instruction and friendship establishment are suggested as practices to prevent online gaming addiction (Syari et al., 2023).

4.4. Intervention

On the condition that prevention is not accomplished, children or adolescents engage in excessive internet use which often results in OGA. Therefore, intervention practices are required, thereby to alternate inappropriate internet usage and related negative consequences. Yalcin and collaborates (2020) recommend the consideration of variables including appropriate internet use, time spent on online gaming, lesson activities and social-demographic characteristics in the development of interventions (Yalcin et al., 2020). Maternal occupational socioeconomic levels of the adolescents with ADHD seemed to play a role in the relationship between internet addiction and social skills deficits of adolescents with ADHD. In specific, occupational socioeconomic status of their parents was reported to moderate the association between social skills deficits and Internet addiction. Researchers of the study suggest that prevention and intervention programs should emphasize on social skills deficits for coping with Internet addiction among adolescents with ADHD (Chou et al., 2017). Finally, Griffiths (2003, 2010) lists five 'golden rules' for parents, practitioners, and psychologists when dealing with children and adolescent gaming.

These include a) checking content of gaming activity, b) encouraging group gaming, c) setting time limits for playing, d) follow game recommendations, and e) temporary prohibiting of gaming.

Cognitive Behavioral Therapy (CBT), Mindfulness, and Hypnotherapy are listed among several other behavior therapies for teenagers addicted to online games, while psychotherapy can also help with internet game addiction (Humayya et al., 2022) and certain antidepressants may be suitable for treatment (Zajac et al., 2017). Nevertheless, there is not substantial evidence to support the effectiveness of CBT, and evidence for family-based treatment is still not clear. Methodological concerns indicate that there are still no evidence-based treatments or a potentially worthwhile intervention for internet gaming disorder or Internet addiction (Zajac et al., 2017). Again though, research in the field has brought some light into the potential benefits of the aforementioned practices which will be straightforwardly presented in the following sections.

4.4.1 Self-Regulated Learning, Mindfulness, and Time Management

There are several factors that play out during the construction of addictive behaviors on the internet. As a matter of fact, self-regulated learning, mindfulness and time management skills may prove to be interrelated and beneficial in terms of intervention. Several studies examined the role of self-regulation with regard to addictive behaviors. According to Bandura (2005) self-regulation encompasses one's ability "*to regulate themselves, to influence their behavior by regulating the environment, to provide cognitive support, and to draw consequences for their behavior*" (Lay et al., 2021, p.532). In the same respect, researchers Lay et al. (2021) have identified the impact of self-regulation on online game addiction (both short-term and long-term) among individuals aged 12-24 in the city of Kupang. Pursuing this further, inability to self- regulated learning could point out internet or mobile phone use (Saad, 2020; Soror et al., 2012) and therefore, training students in effective self-regulation strategies may increase their skills to control the use of their smartphones (Saad, 2020). Finally, impulsivity in higher levels is related to lower levels of video game self-regulation, with consecutive higher levels of pathological video gaming (Liau et al., 2011). Consistent with self-regulation skills, mindfulness may provide essential benefits to gamers with online addiction. Mindfulness is accomplished when individuals act towards their goals and manage to fulfill them by exercising their self-control. On the contrary, disturbing (or intrusive) thoughts, typically indicate low levels of self-control (Fuadah, 2021; Humayya et al., 2022).

Time management is considered to be a key aspect of self-regulated learning, and protective element against internet gaming disorder (Chen et al., 2020; Wolters et al., 2017). The relevance between aspects of self-regulation and time management is well defined in the description of Chen et al. (2020): (Time management) "*is an individual's self-efficacy in accomplishing the difficult task of arranging their schedule, their self-control in avoiding engaging in time-wasting activities (which includes excessive or pathological play of online games), and their autonomy in making decisions regarding their daily activities*" (p. 5). Results of their study shed light into the patterns of parental interactions with their adolescent children and how those interactions influenced time management. Particularly, participating parents who interacted in a warm and accepting way, fostered self-control, self-efficacy, and autonomy in order to engage their children in effective time management (Chen at al., 2020).

Another significant assertion is that video game overuse that causes damage may be best attributed to poor time management or other health issues and hence, potential harm could be less related to the activity of video gaming itself (Wood, 2008). Consequently, teaching time management skills to students (Suargani & Muslikah, 2021) may decrease video game overuse. The lack of clinical data and increased attention on the negative impact of excessive video games shows that even the most damaging cases of video game overuse may be attributable to poor time management or underlying mental health issues, rather than being a primary problem stemming from video game involvement itself (Wood, 2008)

4.4.2. Cognitive Behavior Therapy (CBT)

In literature, interventions based on Cognitive Behavioral Therapy (CBT) are supported to provide effective coping with gaming addiction (e.g. Nugraha & Khasanah, 2023; Purwaningsih, & Nurmala, 2021). As a short-term treatment, CBT guides online gamers to be aware of emotions and behaviors that come with OGA and become able to avoid falling back in unwanted habits (Humayya et al., 2022; Stevens et al., 2018). The idea is that faulty cognitive processes take an important part in the construction and perseverance of maladaptive behaviors (King et al., 2010). Despite references in the positive impact on CBT on OGA, there are also some contradicting findings. For example, in the systematic review of Zajac et al. (2017) various intervention solutions for internet game disorder / internet addiction including pharmacotherapy, CBT- based psychotherapy, and other interventions such as speaking and writing course, family therapy, eclectic psychotherapy, and self- discovery camp provided insufficient evidence to support the effectiveness of CBT in internet addiction.

4.4.3. Hypnotherapy

Hypnosis is described as "*an altered state of consciousness*" which allows an outside individual to help or facilitate an imaginal experience (Hartman & Zimberoff, 2013, p. 6). It consists of a state of hyper-suggestibility (i.e. increased suggestibility) produced by narrowed consciousness and increased concentration (Doney, 1970). Hypnotherapy has been reported to be a complementary, cost-effective therapy, expected to influence behavior, and finally decrease OGA in children. It is supported to conquer bad habits and negative behaviors as individuals learn how to act more actively and concretely. In this context, parents and teachers are advised to learn hypnotherapy thereby to control gaming addiction (Syari et al., 2023). However, findings from a recent systematic review conducted by Conelly (2023) revealed that potential effectiveness of hypnosis as a treatment for internet addictive disorder is not documented in published research. Despite evidence from empirical studies that consider hypnosis-based therapies as a working therapeutic intervention for behavioral addiction and impulse control disorders, there is not any published literature (Conelly, 2023).

4.4.4. Motivational Interviewing

Motivation (or motivational) interviewing is a psychological intervention technique (Verma, 2019) or approach, capable of strengthening individual intrinsic motivation to reduce addictive behavior (Nugraha & Khasanah, 2023), although it is still insufficiently studied in the school environment (Afriwilda & Mulawarman, 2021). Existing evidence reveals positive outcomes for adolescent population in varied ways. As an illustration, an online-based motivational intervention was conducted by Dieris-Hirche et al. (2021) to reduce addictive internet use and to increase motivation for treatment of internet gaming disorder and internet use disorder (OMPRIS). The study included a diagnostic process, and a psychological intervention based on motivational interviewing, (internet-related) addiction therapy, behavioural therapy techniques and additional social counselling that lasted four weeks. 162 individuals aged at least

16 years old, participated in intervention and control groups. Results asserted that OMPRIS can be a more constructive process to work promptly with individuals with internet usage disorder and internet game disorder as compared with conventional approaches.

Another example is a case report developed by Verma (2019) where motivational techniques were utilized by a therapist for the management of a video game addicted teenager. Notably, very short attention was given on changing his cognitions (which is usually the case in CBT), but rather the process was collaborative and open towards the teenager's current state. Motivational interviewing distributed across 12 sessions that lasted two months was reported to decrease the child's depression, anxiety, anger, and addiction and the child was no longer addicted to video gaming (Verma, 2019). Finally, substantial changes were recognized in the psychological well-being of students aged 14 to 17 years old, after face-to-face counseling activities through motivational interviewing. The whole process was administered in several steps including: a) a pre-test prior to the intervention to determine students' psychological well-being, b) three sessions of motivational interviewing counseling interventions, c) a post-test to assess students' changes in psychological well-being and d), a post-test after two weeks. Therefore, based on the provided facts, counselors may utilize motivational interviewing counseling to intervene with students with online addictive disorder (Afriwilda & Mulawarman, 2021).

5. DISCUSSION

As illustrated in the Results section, OGA can bring both benefits and risks or harm to adolescents in the sectors of learning and socialization, while existing data support that adolescents with disabilities are more susceptible to experience negative effects. As documented in research in the field, addiction to gaming is associated with negative effects on adolescents' cognitive functioning which could unavoidably jeopardy important procedures of motivation (Agustini & Marlein, 2023), attention (Lin et al., 2021), working memory, decision-making, executive functioning, and perception (Farchakh et al., 2020). Rationally, there is an existing risk for harm on their academic abilities and subsequent learning. Not only consequences in academic performance, physical and mental health, but problems in relationships with other adolescents (Purwaningsih & Nurmala, 2021) are identified as well. The mode of playing and exhibited behavior during playing appears to influence friendship quality (Verheijen et al., 2019). Further, suppressing direct communication and interaction through online activities exclusively within home boarders could potentially harm the development of communication skills and social interactions of adolescents with disabilities (Yilmaz, 2018). Impaired psychophysical development consists of another factor that contributes to limited opportunities for social interaction when internet engagement is out of control (Volkova et al., 2019) and spending excessive time on internet may lead students with disabilities to disregard their families (Voulganis & Drigas, 2022). Several conditions such as self-regulated learning (Volkova et al., 2019), time management (Suargani & Muslikah, 2021), maternal socioeconomic status, and social skills deficits (Chou et al., 2017) are considered to play a significant role in the process of OGA and are therefore mentioned in the discussions regarding intervention practices. Other practices include CBT (Nugraha & Khasanah, 2023), mindfulness (Fuadah, 2021; Humayya et al., 2022), hypnotherapy (Syari et al., 2023), and motivational interviewing (Verma, 2019). Certainly, prevention comes first, beyond all intervention practices. To this end, parental role is increasingly discussed as essential through behavioral education of their children, supervision practices, guiding friends-establishment, and spending time together.

5.1. The Rationality of Labeling Excessive Online Gaming as Addiction

The process of intervening is not a one-way process but involves individuals from different backgrounds and characteristics, needs, and experiences. Hence, it is essential to distinguish cases of problematic (addictive) and non-problematic (non-addictive) games. The amount of time individuals spend playing video games if often used as a variable to measure excessive use (Purwaningsih & Nurmala, 2021). However, it is ascertained that individuals may play video games for more than 35 hours per week though, this behavior could not be identified as addictive. Further information is required to assess their behavior like general health functioning (e.g., physical exercise), lifestyle factors (e.g., hobbies,) and any co-morbid psychopathology (e.g., anxiety) (King et al., 2010). A literature review (Coutelle et al., 2021) on video game use among individuals with ASD demonstrated that high rates of video games engagement can be mainly explained by gaming addiction for boys and young males with ASD without intellectual disabilities. Nevertheless, restricted interest in video games could not be ignored, whilst addiction and interest aspects were expected to interact. Most importantly, excessive playing is not necessarily identified as addictive activity. The greatest portion of gamers who engage in gaming excessively, mention positive effects resulting from their gaming activity. In analogous way, children with disabilities often express enthusiasm rather than addiction (Griffiths, 2010). At this point, a screening tool could be employed to identify game disorder so as to provide the required professional help to individuals. Indicatively, the TIGTOC is considered to be a reliable tool to distinguish between problematic and non-problematic use of online games (Purwaningsih & Nurmala, 2021).

5.2. The Individualistic Character of Online Gaming Addiction

Internet addiction is described as a complex phenomenon with "*a range of behavioral problems and control over impulses*" (Neverkovich et al., p. 1493). Particularly, OGA is displayed within a number of physical, psychological, social, and spiritual symptoms described as 'clinical' (Humayya et al., 2022). On top of this complexity, in their discussion about addictive behavior of individuals with disabilities, Volkova et al. (2019) stated that addictive internet usage is mentioned to be individualistic, based on specific personal prerequisites that reflect the 'nature' of their particular developmental disorders. Rationally, adolescents with OGA differ in their causes, symptoms, effects, and corresponding psychotherapy (Humayya et al., 2022). Because different factors shape addictive internet usage among adolescents with disabilities, it is essential to develop individual prevention and intervention programmes for addictive internet usage that serve the individual needs of adolescents with disabilities (Volkova et al., 2019). Corresponding research has pointed the relationship between OGA and personality factors, indicating the role of individuals' personality traits on the progressive construction of OGA. Simply stated, games that involve role playing permit the adoption of different characters in imaginary contexts and such conditions could potentially decrease social anxiety feelings to certain individuals (Mehroof et al., 2010) with consequent changes on their internet usage patterns.

Existing knowledge about the differentiating online experiences among students with and without disabilities, points out the necessity to assess the existence of internet addiction when working with adolescents with psychiatric (Kawabe et al., 2019) or other disabilities. In this context, disorders such as ADHD, depression, insomnia, and social phobia should be assessed in depth and concurrent treatment of these disorders is expected to be beneficial during intervening for internet addiction. Indicatively, in the case when ADHD symptoms were strongly associated with internet addiction in adolescents with

ASD, internet addiction was suggested to be treated more thoroughly for adolescents with ASD and ADHD symptoms (Kawabe et al., 2019). In another study of Wrzesinska et al. (2021), the researchers aimed to identify the specific features of variables associated with gaming for adolescents with visual impairment. They stressed the importance of psychoeducational training for caregivers and adolescents in order to improve their skills on recognizing risky behaviors, places to ask for help, and using adaptive strategies to cope with difficulties.

Putting this further, without a doubt, addictive video gaming appears as a different experience among adolescents with ASD conceivably resulting from their need for structure, restricted interests, and social deficits. This for, the American Academy of Child and Adolescent Psychiatry (2015) lists several recommendations for parents in order to cope with addictive video game use in ASD. Indicatively, some include the determination of total screen time limits, experience sharing and discussion about game content, and encouragement of participation in other varied activities. Coutelle and collaborates (2021) stressed some points to take under consideration when intervening for individuals with ASD. Among others, firstly, they noted the importance of establishing rules that tie well with children's need for structure. Secondly, they supported that sometimes video games could reflect restricted interest and thus, should be maintained. A third point, was that because ASD is a social disability, asking children to play video games only in public places could be challenging.

5.3. Limitations and Future Research Directions

In the current chapter, evidence was illustrated regarding the effects of OGA with special attention to students with disabilities along with intervention practices suggested in literature, within a targeted thematic review. In view of the entire work, there are a few limitations determined. Firstly, in the current chapter, various terms have been employed (e.g. online gaming addiction, internet addiction, video gaming, addictive gaming), because multiple terms were identified in literature to describe similar online and gaming activities. However, this could bring confusion to the reader. Secondly, data was gathered from systematic reviews and published research. It would be of greatest significance to provide further concrete evidence on working practices in the areas of hypnotherapy (Syari et al., 2023), time management (Suargani & Muslikah, 2021), mindfulness (Fuadah, 2021; Humayya et al., 2022), and self-regulation (Volkova et al., 2019) for students with disabilities so that teachers and parents can act immediately. Thirdly, review was mainly focused on adolescent population and therefore, suggestions are limited to adolescent population. Finally, given that potential effectiveness of hypnosis as a treatment for internet addictive disorder is not documented in published research (Conelly, 2023) and that evidence to support the efficiency of CBT is reported to be insufficient (Zajac et al., 2017), more solid data is needed to provide with best working solutions for OGA in adolescent population.

In response to the aforementioned limitations, future research in the area of OGA is indicated to terms strictly associated with OGA so as to achieve maximum accuracy and validity in related academic descriptions. Additionally, further research in the areas of hypnotherapy, time management, mindfulness, and self-regulation for students with disabilities could give light to evidence-based practices for teachers and parents working with students with disabilities and OGA. Further, additional reviews concentrated in younger populations (aged 12 years or less) are expected to broaden our understanding of OGA phenomena and providing for responsive directions. Finally, the study of CBT as a treatment for OGA in diverse student populations, either in the school context or out of school boarders, is thought to bring valuable working solutions for OGA. Under the above considerations, combined research practices including case studies, qualitative studies utilizing focus groups, experimental designs, and program evaluations are recommended in the interest of bringing the best confrontation of OGA.

6. CONCLUSION

Internet can serve children with disabilities in educational and entertaining ways, given it is used moderately (Voulganis & Drigas, 2022). Depending on the context, both online and offline gaming can bring benefits or harm in learning and socialization of children and adolescents with disabilities. Influences of OGA are illustrated in literature, considering students' cognition and learning, as well as interaction and social relationships, among others. A series of intervention practices including self-regulated learning, mindfulness and time management, Cognitive Behavior Therapy (CBT), hypnotherapy, and motivational interviewing were described in this chapter aimed at improving prevention and intervention practices on the part of teachers and parents working with students who present OGA. The general perspective is that each case of OGA must be examined within an individualized lens to ensure accordance with students' individual profile. Provided that much of the research presented has been administered with participating adolescents without disabilities, findings may be employed with caution. Nevertheless, it can be ascertained that a vast number of findings presented in this chapter can be beneficial in the overall endeavors to reduce the negative impact of OGA in students with disabilities.

REFERENCES

Academy of Child and Adolescent Psychiatry. (2015). *Video games and children: playing withviolence*. https://www.aacap.org/AACAP/Families_and_Youth/Facts_for_Families/FFF-Guide/Children-and-Video-Games-Playing-with-Violence-091.aspx

Afriwilda, M. T., & Mulawarman, M. (2021). The effectiveness of motivational interviewing counseling to improve psychological well-being on students with online game addiction tendency. *Islamic Guidance and Counseling Journal*, 4(1), 106–115. DOI: 10.25217/igcj.v4i1.1235

Agustini, W., & Marleni, M. (2023). The impact of online game addiction on learning enthusiasm to promote the students' motivation to learn. *Esteem Journal of English Education Study Programme*, 6(2), 370–382. DOI: 10.31851/esteem.v6i2.12328

Andreassen, C. S., Billieux, J., Griffiths, M. D., Kuss, D. J., Demetrovics, Z., Mazzoni, E., & Pallesen, S. (2016). The relationship between addictive use of social media and video games and symptoms of psychiatric disorders: A large-scale cross-sectional study. *Psychology of Addictive Behaviors*, 30(2), 252–262. DOI: 10.1037/adb0000160 PMID: 26999354

Bandura. (2005). The Primacy of Self-Regulation in Health Promotion. Applied Psychology. *An International Review, 54*(2), 245-254.

Blasco-Fontecilla, H., Menéndez-García, Á., Sanchez-Sanchez, F., & Bella-Fernández, M. (2023). Lack of educational impact of video game addiction in children and adolescents diagnosed with ADHD: A cross-sectional study. *Frontiers in Psychiatry*, 14, 1136671. DOI: 10.3389/fpsyt.2023.1136671 PMID: 37151982

Chadwick, D. D., Quinn, S., & Fullwood, C. (2016). Perceptions of the risks and benefits of Internet access and use by people with intellectual disabilities. *British Journal of Learning Disabilities*, 45(1), 21–31. DOI: 10.1111/bld.12170

Chen, I. H., Lee, Z. H., Dong, X. Y., Gamble, J. H., & Feng, H. W. (2020). The influence of parenting style and time management tendency on internet gaming disorder among adolescents. *International Journal of Environmental Research and Public Health*, 17(23), 9120. DOI: 10.3390/ijerph17239120 PMID: 33291336

Chou, W. J., Huang, M. F., Chang, Y. P., Chen, Y. M., Hu, H. F., & Yen, C. F. (2017). Social skills deficits and their association with Internet addiction and activities in adolescents with attention-deficit/hyperactivity disorder. *Journal of Behavioral Addictions*, 6(1), 42–50. DOI: 10.1556/2006.6.2017.005 PMID: 28245666

Connelly, C. (2023). Hypnosis based treatments for internet addiction disorder: systematic review. *Journal of Addiction Research, 7*(1), 1-6.

Coutelle, R., Weiner, L., Paasche, C., Pottelette, J., Bertschy, G., Schröder, C. M., & Lalanne, L. (2021). Autism spectrum disorder and video games: Restricted interests or addiction? *International Journal of Mental Health and Addiction*, 1–22. DOI: 10.1007/s11469-021-00511-4

De Pasquale, C., Sciacca, F., Martinelli, V., Chiappedi, M., Dinaro, C., & Hichy, Z. (2020). Relationship of internet gaming disorder with psychopathology and social adaptation in Italian young adults. *International Journal of Environmental Research and Public Health*, 17(21), 8201. DOI: 10.3390/ijerph17218201 PMID: 33172015

Devi, R., & Dhall, P. (2017). Procrastination: A behavior need to be changed to have success. *International Education and esearch Journal, 3*(5), 475-476.

Dieris-Hirche, J., Bottel, L., Pape, M., Te Wildt, B. T., Wölfling, K., Timmesfeld, N., Neumann, A., Neusser, S., Beckers, R., Henningsen, P., & Herpertz, S. (2021). Effects of an online-based motivational intervention to reduce problematic internet use and promote treatment motivation in internet gaming disorder and internet use disorder (OMPRIS): Study protocol for a randomised controlled trial. *BMJ Open*, 11(8), e045840. DOI: 10.1136/bmjopen-2020-045840 PMID: 34344675

Doney, H. (1970). The theory and practice of hypnosis. *Canadian Family Physician Médecin de Famille Canadien*, 16(2), 52. PMID: 20468477

Farchakh, Y., Haddad, C., Sacre, H., Obeid, S., Salameh, P., & Hallit, S. (2020). Video gaming addiction and its association with memory, attention and learning skills in Lebanese children. *Child and Adolescent Psychiatry and Mental Health*, 14(1), 1–11. DOI: 10.1186/s13034-020-00353-3 PMID: 33308272

Fuadah, D. Z. (2021). Intervensi Mindfulness Attention Awareness untuk Mencegah Kecanduan Gadget pada Remaja Setingkat SMA. *Darmabakti: Jurnal Pengabdian dan Pemberdayaan Masyarakat, 2*(1), 38-45. DOI: 10.31102/darmabakti.2021.2.1.38-45

Griffiths, M. (2010). Excessive online computer use and learning disabilities. *Australian Journal of Dyslexia and Other Learning Disabilities*, 5, 31–34.

Hartman, D., & Zimberoff, D. (2013). Jung and hypnotherapy. *Journal of Heart-Centered Therapies*, 16(1), 3–52.

Humayya, A., Windarwati, H. D., & Winarni, I. (2022). Behavior therapy in those who are addicted to online games. *Journal of Nursing Science Update*, 10(1), 76–83. DOI: 10.21776/ub.jik.2022.010.01.10

Jiang, C., Li, C., Zhou, H., & Zhou, Z. (2020). Individuals with internet gaming disorder have similar neurocognitive impairments and social cognitive dysfunctions as methamphetamine-dependent patients. *Adicciones, 1342*(10.20882). https://doi.org/DOI: 10.20882/adicciones.1342

Kawabe, K., Horiuchi, F., Miyama, T., Jogamoto, T., Aibara, K., Ishii, E., & Ueno, S. I. (2019). Internet addiction and attention-deficit/hyperactivity disorder symptoms in adolescents with autism spectrum disorder. *Research in Developmental Disabilities*, 89, 22–28. DOI: 10.1016/j.ridd.2019.03.002 PMID: 30877993

King, D. L., Delfabbro, P. H., & Griffiths, M. D. (2010). Cognitive behavioral therapy for problematic video game players: Conceptual considerations and practice issues. *Journal of Cyber Therapy and Rehabilitation*, 3(3).

Király, O., & Demetrovics, Z. (2017). Inclusion of gaming disorder in ICD has more advantages than disadvantages: Commentary on: Scholars' open debate paper on the World Health Organization ICD-11 Gaming Disorder proposal (Aarseth et al.). *Journal of Behavioral Addictions*, 6(3), 280–284. DOI: 10.1556/2006.6.2017.046 PMID: 28816495

Kovess-Masfety, V., Keyes, K., Hamilton, A., Hanson, G., Bitfoi, A., Golitz, D., Koç, C., Kuijpers, R., Lesinskiene, S., Mihova, Z., Otten, R., Fremanian, C., & Pez, O. (2016). Is time spent playing video games associated with mental health, cognitive and social skills in young children? *Social Psychiatry and Psychiatric Epidemioly 51*, 349–357. https://link.springer.com/article/10.1007/s00127-016-1179-6?source=post_page5d49aeb02811&fbclid=IwAR0XGN_roQZCbXWDxArrTx52ocPN8QWWUslH3s5QktahdyL3amiodZ49D2c

Kuo, H. J., Yeomans, M., Ruiz, D., & Lin, C. C. (2024). Video games and disability—A risk and benefit analysis. *Frontiers in Rehabilitation Sciences*, 5, 1343057. DOI: 10.3389/fresc.2024.1343057 PMID: 38496777

Kurniawan, E. (2019). *Pengaruh Adiksi Bermain Game Online terhadap Pelaksanaan Ibadah Shalat Siswa Sekolah Menengah Atas Negeri 1 Siak kecamatan Siak kabupaten Siak* [Unpublished Doctoral dissertation, Universitas Islam Negeri Sultan Syarif Kasim Riau] https://repository.uin-suska.ac.id/22682/

Lay, A. R. S., Wijaya, R. P. C., & Keraf, M. A. (2021). A Study of Self-Regulation on Online Game Addiction in Kupang City. *Journal of Health and Behavioral Science*, 3(4), 524–535. DOI: 10.35508/jhbs.v3i4.4542

Liau, A. K., Neo, E. C., Gentile, D. A., Choo, H., Sim, T., Li, D., & Khoo, A. (2011). Impulsivity, self-regulation, and pathological video gaming among youth: Testing a mediation model. *Asia-Pacific Journal of Public Health*, 27(2), NP2188–NP2196. DOI: 10.1177/1010539511429369 PMID: 22199156

Lin, C. Y., Potenza, M. N., Broström, A., & Pakpour, A. H. (2021). Internet gaming disorder, psychological distress, and insomnia in adolescent students and their siblings: An actor-partner interdependence model approach. *Addictive Behaviors Reports*, 13, 100332. DOI: 10.1016/j.abrep.2020.100332 PMID: 33437860

Löfgren-Mårtenson, L. (2008). Love in cyberspace: Swedish young people with intellectual disabilities and the Internet. *Scandinavian Journal of Disability Research*, 10(2), 125–138. DOI: 10.1080/15017410701758005

Martínez, S. R. (2015). Disability in young people, increases the risk of excessive internet use? *Health and Addictions, 15*(1), 15-24. http://hdl.handle.net/10045/44528

Mehroof, M., & Griffiths, M. D. (2010). Online gaming addiction: The role of sensation seeking, self-control, neuroticism, aggression, state anxiety, and trait anxiety. *Cyberpsychology, Behavior, and Social Networking*, 13(3), 313–316. DOI: 10.1089/cyber.2009.0229 PMID: 20557251

Michalopoulou, V., Sarantiti, M., Chatzimbey, C., & Drigas, A. (2023). The effects of augmented reality and video games on mental skills of students with learning disabilities. *World Journal of Advanced Engineering Technology and Sciences*, 9(2), 324–337. DOI: 10.30574/wjaets.2023.9.2.0240

Molin, M., Sorbring, E., & Löfgren-Mårtenson, L. (2015). Teachers' and parents' views on the Internet and social media usage by pupils with intellectual disabilities. *Journal of Intellectual Disabilities*, 19(1), 22–33. DOI: 10.1177/1744629514563558 PMID: 25524596

Murray, A., Koronczai, B., Király, O., Griffiths, M. D., Mannion, A., Leader, G., & Demetrovics, Z. (2021). Autism, problematic internet use and gaming disorder: A systematic review. *Review Journal of Autism and Developmental Disorders*, 1–21. DOI: 10.1007/s40489-021-00243-0

Nadeem, M., Oroszlanyova, M., & Farag, W. (2023). Effect of digital game-based learning on student engagement and motivation. *Computers*, 12(9), 177. DOI: 10.3390/computers12090177

Neverkovich, S. D., Bubnova, I. S., Kosarenko, N. N., Sakhieva, R. G., Sizova, Z. M., Zakharova, V. L., & Sergeeva, M. G. (2018). Students' internet addiction: Study and prevention. *Eurasia Journal of Mathematics, Science and Technology Education*, 14(4), 1483–1495. DOI: 10.29333/ejmste/83723

Nugraha, Y. P., & Khasanah, F. U. (2023). Can motivational interviewing reduce video game addiction? Viewed from: Regulatory focus theory and interpersonal competence. *Jurnal Integrasi Sains dan Qur'an (JISQu), 2*(1), 141-155.

Purwaningsih, E., & Nurmala, I. (2021). The impact of online game addiction on adolescent mental health: A systematic review and meta-analysis. *Open Access Macedonian Journal of Medical Sciences (OAMJMS), 9*(F), 260-274. DOI: 10.3889/oamjms.2021.6234

Saad, M. A. E. (2020). Self-regulated learning and academic procrastination as predictors of smartphone addiction among second year-middle school learning disabled students. *Amazonia Investiga*, 9(26), 236–243. DOI: 10.34069/AI/2020.26.02.27

Seema, R., & Varik-Maasik, E. (2023, July). Students' digital addiction and learning difficulties: short-comings of surveys in inclusion. *Frontiers in Education, 8*, 1191817. Frontiers Media SA. DOI: 10.3389/feduc.2023.1191817

Soror, A. A., Steelman, Z. R., & Limayem, M. (2012, January 04-07). *Discipline yourself before life disciplines you: Deficient self-regulation and mobile phone unregulated use*. [Paper Presentation] 45th Hawaii International Conference on System Sciences, IEEE. https://ieeexplore.ieee.org/document/6148997

Stevens, M., King, D., Dorstyn, D., & Delfabbro, P. (2018). Cognitive–behavioral therapy for internet gaming disorder: A systematic review and meta-analysis. *Clinical Psychology & Psychotherapy*, 26(2), 191203. DOI: 10.1002/cpp.2341 PMID: 30341981

Suargani, G. (2021). Peer Conformity, Time Management and Online Game Addiction to High Schoolers. *Proceedings in6th International Conference on Science, Education and Technology (ISET 2020).* Atlantis Press.

Syari, W. R., Gusdiansyah, E., & Welly, . (2023). Hypnotherapy is Needed to Reduce Online Gaming Addiction in Adolescence. *Journal of Health Sciences and Epidemiology*, 1(1), 33–39. DOI: 10.62404/jhse.v1i1.7

Throuvala, M. A., Janikian, M., Griffiths, M. D., Rennoldson, M., & Kuss, D. J. (2019). The role of family and personality traits in Internet gaming disorder: A mediation model combining cognitive and attachment perspectives. *Journal of Behavioral Addictions*, 8(1), 48–62. DOI: 10.1556/2006.8.2019.05 PMID: 30739463

Van Rooij, A. J., Kuss, D. J., Griffiths, M. D., Shorter, G. W., Schoenmakers, T. M., & Van de Mheen, D. (2014). The (co-) occurrence of problematic video gaming, substance use, and psychosocial problems in adolescents. *Journal of Behavioral Addictions*, 3(3), 157–165. DOI: 10.1556/JBA.3.2014.013 PMID: 25317339

Verheijen, G. P., Stoltz, S. E., Van de Berg, Y. H., & Cillessen, A. H. (2019). The influence of competitive and cooperative video games on behavior during play and friendship quality in adolescence. *Computers in Human Behavior*, 91, 297–304. DOI: 10.1016/j.chb.2018.10.023

Verma, T. (2019). Managing online video gaming-related addictive behaviors through motivational interviewing. *Indian Journal of Social Psychiatry*, 35(3), 217–219. DOI: 10.4103/ijsp.ijsp_113_18

Volkova, I. P., Koroleva, N. N., Bogdanovskaya, I. M., Ikonnikova, G. Y., & Mashkova, A. V. (2019). Problematic internet usage by adolescents with disabilities. *Образование и наука, 21*(9), 98-121.

Vouglanis, T., & Drigas, A. (2022). The internet addiction and the impact on the cognitive, psychological and social side of people's personality with disabilities. *Technium Social Sciences Journal*, 35, 93–110. DOI: 10.47577/tssj.v35i1.7274

Wolters, C. A., Won, S., & Hussain, M. (2017). Examining the relations of time management and procrastination within a model of self-regulated learning. *Metacognition and Learning*, 12(3), 381–399. DOI: 10.1007/s11409-017-9174-1

Wood, R. T. A. (2008). Problems with the concept of video game "addiction": Some case study examples. *International Journal of Mental Health and Addiction*, 6(2), 169–178. DOI: 10.1007/s11469-007-9118-0

Wrzesińska, M. A., Tabała, K., & Stecz, P. (2021). Gaming Behaviors among Polish Students with Visual Impairment. *International Journal of Environmental Research and Public Health*, 18(4), 1545. DOI: 10.3390/ijerph18041545 PMID: 33561942

Yalcin, H., Guvener, E., & Kasal, D. (2020). Relationship between gifted children's internet gaming addiction and quality of life. *European Journal of Special Education Research*, 6(4), 1–21.

Yao, Y. W., Chen, P. R., Chen, C., Wang, L. J., Zhang, J. T., Xue, G., Deng, L.-Y., Liu, Q.-X., Yip, S. W., & Fang, X.-Y. (2014). Failure to utilize feedback causes decision-making deficits among excessive Internet gamers. *Psychiatry Research*, 219(3), 583–588. DOI: 10.1016/j.psychres.2014.06.033 PMID: 25024056

Yilmaz, E., Yel, S., & Griffiths, M. D. (2018). The Impact of Heavy(Excessive) Video Gaming Students on Peers and Teachers in the School Environment: A Qualitative Study, *5*(2), 147–161. https://core.ac.uk/download/pdf/161338199.pdf

Yoo, H. J., Cho, S. C., Ha, J., Yune, S. K., Kim, S. J., Hwang, J., Chung, A., Sung, Y. H., & Lyoo, I. K. (2004). Attention deficit hyperactivity symptoms and internet addiction. *Psychiatry and Clinical Neurosciences*, 58(5), 487–494. DOI: 10.1111/j.1440-1819.2004.01290.x PMID: 15482579

Zajac, K., Ginley, M. K., Chang, R., & Petry, N. M. (2017). Treatments for Internet gaming disorder and Internet addiction: A systematic review. *Psychology of Addictive Behaviors*, 31(8), 979–994. DOI: 10.1037/adb0000315 PMID: 28921996

Zatrahadi, M. F., Darmawati, D., & Yusra, N. N. (2021). The Effect of Online Game Addiction on Adjustment Social in Adolescents. *Indonesian Journal of Creative Counseling*, 1(1), 15–19. https://doi .org/http://doi.org/10.47679/ijcc.v1i1.93

Chapter 8
Technology Facilitated Sexual Violence in Adolescence:
Different Forms of the Phenomenon, Contributors to Perpetration and Victimization and Effects

Georgia Gkantona
https://orcid.org/0000-0001-5482-5225
University of Ioannina, Greece

Fotios Ntagkas
Centre of Systemic Therapy and Counselling, Greece

ABSTRACT

The following chapter explores technology facilitated sexual violence (TFSV) among adolescents with a particular focus on its conceptualization, prevalence, impact, and coping strategies. Various forms of TFSV are discussed, including online sexual harassment (OSH), image-based sexual abuse (IBSA), sexual aggression and coercion (SAC), and harassment based on gender and sexuality (HBGS). The gendered nature of TFSV is highlighted, with girls being more vulnerable to victimization and boys more likely to perpetrate. It also analyzes the detrimental effects of TFSV on adolescents' mental health, well-being, social and academic functioning. Additionally, the chapter draws attention to the challenges of identifying and researching TFSV due to underreporting and the evolving nature of technology. It concludes by emphasizing the need for comprehensive prevention and intervention strategies to address this pervasive and serious social phenomenon.

THE CONCEPTUAL FRAMEWORK OF TECHNOLOGY FACILITATED SEXUAL VIOLENCE

Over the past decade, digital communication has become the dominant form of communication among young people and nearly all teenagers are engaged in social networking to an extensive level globally (Englander, 2015). Text messaging is also widely used by three-quarters of teens with a high percentage

DOI: 10.4018/979-8-3693-4191-9.ch008

texting daily. This trend spans across all social classes, indicating widespread digital engagement. In fact, the preference for text messaging over other communication forms increased from 44% in 2010 to 62% in 2015 among teens (Englander, 2015). This shift underscores the pervasive influence of digital technology in the social interactions of youth, setting the stage for discussing the implications of such technologies on adolescents' lives including the appearance of online violence.

Online violence research uses various terms interchangeably to describe phenomena such as online stalking and cyberbullying. In recent years, terms such as "online aggression", "online harassment" and "cyberbullying" have been employed to encompass a wide range of online violent behaviors. Inevitably, studies shift their focus on the overlap between online victimization and sexual aggression, using terms such as "technology-based coercive behavior" to describe sexually explicit digital acts. The concept of "online victimization" for instance has been defined as pressure to submit to unwanted sexual cooperation or the sharing of sexual content without consent (Gámez-Guadix & Martínez-Bacaicoa, 2023). Similarly, "cyber victimization" includes receiving unsolicited sexual material, harassment and solicitation (Gámez-Guadix & Martínez-Bacaicoa, 2023). However, the literature often lacks precise categorization, broadly classifying various digital acts of sexual aggression with general terms such as "online sexual harassment" or "cyber harassment". This lack of standardized terminology poses a challenge to the field, hindering clear communication and comparison of research findings. It also underscores the need for a more nuanced understanding of the specific forms and manifestations of online sexual aggression, to develop targeted interventions and prevention strategies.

An initial effort to classify the various forms of online violence was attempted by Barak (2005), who tried to identify the ways in which offline sexual harassment were manifested digitally. He identified three types of harassment: Gender Harassment, Unwanted Sexual Attention and Sexual Coercion. Gender-based Harassment includes sexist actions targeting a person's gender to create distress, especially prevalent online. This type of harassment can be manifested in visual forms like degrading images or videos, or verbally through sexist jokes, unwanted emails, offensive usernames or exclusion from online platforms. Such actions aim to humiliate and marginalize individuals based on their gender contributing to a hostile online environment. Unwanted Sexual Attention includes the expression of sexual desires or intents which are unwanted by the person who receives them. It can take place in public as well as in private online spaces and can be either verbal or visual. According to Barak (2005) examples include sexualizing comments, unwanted photos and/or insulting statements with sexual content. The third type, Sexual Coercion, involves pressure or threats with the goal of obtaining some form of sexual gain. This could be in the form of theft of information to be used for threatening purposes or other forms of personal information to get something in return.

Other efforts to conceptualize online violence come from the work of Gámez-Guadix et al. (2015) where online sexual victimization was first defined as "the pressure to obtain sexual cooperation or the dissemination of a victim's sexual content through the internet" (Gámez-Guadix & Martínez-Bacaicoa, 2023 p.378). The authors suggest the following classification:

- Pressuring the victim to send explicit photos or videos against their wishes.
- Demanding the victim to disclose intimate details without their consent.
- Forcing the victim to engage in sexual acts online against their will.
- Coercing the victim into offline sexual encounters against their will.
- Threatening or manipulating the victim to send explicit content.
- Threatening or manipulating the victim to reveal intimate information.

- Threatening or manipulating the victim to perform sexual acts online.
- Threatening or manipulating the victim into offline sexual relations.
- Sharing explicit photos or videos of the victim online without consent.
- Spreading intimate details about the victim online without consent.

More recently, Powell & Henry (2019) made one of the most scientifically sound attempts to conceptualize the phenomenon by introducing the term Technology Facilitated Sexual Violence (TFSV) referring to the use of mobile or online technologies to threaten, control, coerce, harass, humiliate or violate in any form another person. Prior, a considerable challenge in effectively conceptualizing interpersonal online violence had been the construction or use of appropriate definitions which identify and describe terms such as "revenge pornography", "virtual rape", "online stalking/stalking" or "gendered hate speech". Before Henry & Powell conceptualized TFSV, most research on similar phenomena had focused on the different concepts and forms of online violence such as "abusive sexting". Within their framework however, Powell & Henry (2019) attempted to categorize these concepts more effectively, to understand the problem of definitions and what constitutes interpersonal online violence by focusing on its gendered and sexual dimension. Due to these conceptual inconsistencies, we chose the Powell & Henry classification as the basic conceptual framework in the present Chapter, while acknowledging its limitations (e.g. the lack of a cyberstalking conceptualization) (Champion et al., 2022). Moreover, adding to its strength, the classification proposed by Powell & Henry (2019) takes into consideration previous classifications such as those proposed by Barak et al. (2005) and Gámez-Guadix et al. (2015).

Therefore, the Powell & Henry conceptualization allows to study the gendered dimension of the phenomenon. This is crucial when examining TFSV as a form of violence, as it is not just digital violence of a sexual nature. It encompasses violence against individuals based on their constructed gender and sexual identity. Given that gender, as a social construct, creates hierarchies and inequalities that are also reproduced online, research can shed light on the extent TFSV is linked to power relations and control mechanisms exerted against women (Gkantona et al., 2024). Thus, the gender perspective helps us understand how social structures and gender stereotypes contribute to the perpetuation of violence against women, both in the real and digital worlds. A clearer understanding of TFSV, including the gendered impact and gender differences in perpetration and victimization, particularly among adolescents, will be explored in the following paragraphs. And while the assumption is that women and girls are more often the victims, men and boys can also experience sexual and gendered violence, an element which is also examined (Powell & Henry, 2019). Further exploration will delve into the gendered impact and differences in TFSV perpetration and victimization, particularly among adolescents, acknowledging that while women and girls are more often targeted, men and boys can also be victims. This holistic understanding is key to addressing the complex issue of TFSV and developing effective interventions.

The TFSV framework proposed by Powell & Henry (2019) incorporates various terminologies and categorizes online violence into four dimensions, presented as follows.

The first dimension is *Online Sexual Harassment (OSH).* OSH is defined as unwanted sexual behaviour carried out through electronic means such as emails and/or photos, online posts for example in social media, online discussion forums and digital worlds (Henry & Powell, 2015). Three distinct types of sexual harassment are introduced: Gender harassment (e.g. inappropriate sexual insults or the utilization of gender insensitive language), unwanted sexual attention (e.g. comments with sexual content) and sexual coercion (making requests for sexual acts) (Buchanan & Mahoney, 2022). In both online and offline environments sexual harassment might take the form of sexual jokes or sexual comments

(Ståhl & Dennhag, 2021). One of the main differences between online and offline sexual harassment is the differences in emotional consequences for the people that are subjected to these forms of violence (Ståhl & Dennhag, 2021). Overall, research studies by the Pew Research Center (2014) and Reed et al. (2019) indicate that OSH has been experienced by 6-59% of individuals. It is important to point out here that between 2-30% of individuals experiencing OSH are adolescents (Buchanan & Mahoney, 2022; Ybarra et al., 2015).

Regarding gender differences, several studies find that a high percentage of women have been subjected to OSH (Salerno-Ferraro et al., 2022). Additionally, women experience greater socioemotional impact following OSH, compared to men (Powell & Henry, 2019). These trajectories will be presented in more detail later in this chapter.

The second dimension is *Image-based Sexual Abuse (IBSA)*. This form of TFSV is defined as the distribution of nude or sexual intimate images of a person without their consent which is also known by the disputed term "revenge pornography" (Henry & Powell, 2015). This dimension has not been researched much and most empirical studies have focused on the exchange of intimate messages, which is known as "sexting". Sexting is defined as sending sexually explicit texts, images and/or videos using technological communication means (e.g. mobile to mobile or through chat apps with the use of the internet). A smaller pool of studies has conceptualized non-consensual or coercive sexting as "revenge pornography". Despite being widely used, this term is problematic. It excludes diverse forms of image-based abuse, disregards varying motives, and wrongly implies deliberate image creation linked to abusive behavior. Additionally, this term has been recently criticized as inadequate for describing the behavior's broad scope as outlined by Gkantona et al. (2024).

Another term later used was that of Image-Based Sexual Exploitation as an alternative to revenge porn or abusive sexting. Image-Based Sexual Exploitation is more adequate in that it captures a wide variety of motives driving the non-consensual distribution of intimate images, including that of revenge (Powell & Henry, 2019). Moreover, this term considers the wider context of where the image was initially produced (e.g. the person who experiences this form of violence has taken a selfie and shares it with someone else but has not consented to its further distribution, or a person does not know where the image was initially taken, or a person does not know that he/she/they has-have been photographed or filmed) (Powell & Henry, 2019). Finally, the term considers the fact that an image (intimate or not) is used as a form of sexual exploitation. The term "exploitation" was later replaced by the term "abuse" by Powell & Henry (2019), as the latter considers the broader socioemotional impact IBSA has on the person experiencing it.

The third dimension concerns *Sexual Aggression and Coercion (SAC)* and it includes three forms of behaviour. First, there is sexual coercion or "sextortion", a form of non-physical coercion, through bribery extortion and threats to the victim to perform virtual sexual acts or requiring the victim to send personal images or information (e.g. bribery, blackmail or threats to a person to be involved in virtual or interpersonal acts). The second form includes the utilization of technological communication means to perpetrate a sexual offending act, like organizing a meeting with a person through dating apps or apps like Facebook and Instagram to assault them. The third form according to Powell & Henry (2019) includes the extension of a sexual assault by taking and distributing images of this assault.

The fourth dimension is known as *Harassment Based on Gender and Sexuality (HBGS)*. This category of harassment can include posting pornographic content in public, chauvinistic jokes and gendered derogatory comments (Henry & Powell, 2015). Regarding the online environment, this phenomenon can occur in chat rooms, forums and social media. Despite the limited amount of empirical research in this area, these forms of aggressive behavior create a hostile environment, particularly for women and gender and/or sexual identity diverse groups. Studies show that both men and women can be victims and perpetrators of HBGS, but women are more likely to be targeted (Ballard & Welch, 2015; Megarry, 2014). Moreover, most of these studies indicate that young women especially are more likely to be subjected to some of these forms of online violence than their male peers (Ringrose et al., 2012).

TFSV AND ITS PREVALENCE OF PERPETRATION AND VICTIMIZATION IN ADOLESCENTS

Victimization From TFSV and TFSV-Related Forms

TFSV is a widespread phenomenon that occurs in many different countries regardless of socioeconomic level (Zagloul et al., 2022). The rapid spread of technology and the extensive use of social media (Instagram, Tiktok, Snapchat) have increased the chances of individuals being subjected to some forms of violence and/or harassment through different online and technological means especially since the coronavirus period. This is particularly pronounced and observable in countries with a lower Human Development Index (HDI), as observed in surveys conducted in similar countries (Pew Research Center, 2019).

While TFSV and its forms are widely researched in adult populations, research in adolescents is limited. This literature gap is surprising given that most people who have experienced different forms of violence tend to encounter them during their adolescence. For example, Powell & Henry (2019) indicate that 11.1% of their adult sample perpetrated sextortion before the age of 16. Similar results were observed by another study, where participants reported that a sexual message they had sent as adolescents was shared to other people without their consent (Strohmaier et al., 2014). Studies reveal a concerning prevalence of non-consensual sexting among adolescents, as 3% to 4.5% of adolescents have either had their own sexual images shared without permission or have shared images of others (Frankel et al., 2018; Van Ouytsel et al., 2019). While this behavior is more common among older adolescents, gender does not seem to play a role (Gámez-Guadix et al., 2022). Notably, research estimates that 12% of adolescents have perpetrated non-consensual sexting and 8.4% are reported to have been victims (Madigan et al., 2018). Notably, E. K. Englander & McCoy (2017) in a study conducted with 1,320 US adolescents identified a 25% prevalence rate of different TFSV forms.

With regards to Online Sexual Harassment (OSH) and other similar TFSV forms, some behaviours resemble cyberbullying and cybervictimization. OSH is more prevalent when these occur in a peer-to-peer context (Angela et al., 2023). As seen above, two different or more forms of TFSV could overlap. Taking a closer look into the forms of TFSV as categorized by Henry & Powell (2016) we can observe the differences, as well as the characteristics that these forms of violence share. In this framework, the prevalence of Online Sexual Harassment (OSH) varies across studies, with research on prevalence rates ranging from 1% to 68% (Reed et al., 2019). This wide range is likely due to differences in measurement tools, the specific types of OSH assessed, and the characteristics of the populations studied.

For example, a study of Croatian female adolescents found that 37.5% reported lifetime OSH, while 15.7% reported experiencing it in the past six months (Mitchell & Stulhofer, 2020). In Chile, lifetime prevalence was reported as 16.2%, with a higher rate among girls (24.7%) compared to boys (8.8%) and the 12-month prevalence was also higher in girls (16%) than boys (6.3%) (Guerra et al., 2021). Interestingly,

Reed et al. (2019) in their research with 159 US adolescent girls and a mean age of 17 years found that a significant 68% experienced some form of OSH. This harassment ranged from unwanted sexual texts or images (53%), requests for engaging in sexual acts (49%), coercion into sending sexual images (36%) to the non-consensual distribution of their sexual images (6%). In a nationally representative sample of US adolescents, 15% reported online sexual harassment victimization (Copp et al., 2021). While these findings underscore the need for consistent and comprehensive measures of OSH to facilitate comparisons across studies and populations, they also highlight gender differences, where adolescent girls are more likely to be victimized by Online Sexual Harassment compared to boys.

Concerning Image Based Sexual Abuse (IBSA), the literature shows that prevalence rates differ across cultures and countries. Pampati et al. (2020) found that 5.7% of boys and 4.8% of girls in the United States reported having a sexual photo shared without their permission. In a Norwegian sample, Pedersen et al. (2023) found that 2.9% of adolescents had experienced IBSA, which includes the nonconsensual distribution of sexual images. Moreover, in a Spanish sample, Gámez-Guadix et al. (2022) found that the prevalence of nonconsensual sexting victimization was 3.4%. In a Swedish sample, Sciacca et al. (2023) found that 6.5% of participants reported that their sexual pictures were shared without their consent at least once in their lifetime.

With regards to Sexual Aggression and/or Coercion (SAC), the most researched form of violence in this category is sextortion, which, as a form of sexual aggression and/or coercion can be connected to other forms of TFSV. Research shows that the prevalence of sextortion among adolescents varies. In U.S. samples, Patchin & Hinduja (2020) found that 5% of adolescents had been the victims of sextortion at some point in their lifetime, while Wolak et al. (2018) found that 47.5% of respondents aged 18-25 (young adults) reported that they had been victims of sextortion before the age of 18. In a Spanish sample, 2.6% of adolescents aged 12-17 had experienced sextortion victimization, and 0.7% self-reported perpetrating the behavior (Gámez-Guadix et al. (2022).

The last form of TFSV, Harassment Based on Gender and Sexuality (HBGS) shares the least characteristics with the other forms of TFSV. This form of violence almost exclusively targets the gender as well as the sexual orientation or sexual identities of the people subjected to it. Given that adolescents are in the process of gender and sexual identity construction, this form of TFSV can be critical to identity formation. Over the years, several studies have tried to map the phenomenon of HBGS, focusing exclusively on adolescents. In a study of Swiss and German adolescents, Castellanos et al. (2023) found that 17.3% of online victims reported being targeted due to their gender or gender identity. In another study conducted by Gámez-Guadix & Incera (2021) with 1779 adolescents (8.2% of whom were among sexual minorities), findings showed that 41.1% of the sample had experienced discrimination because of their sexual orientation and 28.4% had been subjected to gender-based victimization. From the 45.2% that experienced unwanted sexual attention, 9% experienced sextortion and 5.5% were victims/survivors of revenge porn (Gámez-Guadix & Incera, 2021). These findings share similarities with another related empirical data (Chaux & León, 2016; Kansok-Dusche et al., 2023).

Considering these prevalence rates, it is evident that victimization is higher for girls than boys. This observation supports the gender-based hypothesis about TFSV, and we can assume that girls are more vulnerable to TFSV victimization. Indeed, according to Gámez-Guadix & Martínez-Bacaicoa (2023), although men and women can both be victims of TFSV, women are more often targeted. The negative consequences of TFSV tend to be more severe for women than for men (Henry & Powell, 2016; Powell & Henry, 2019) possibly due to societal gender roles and sexual norms that expect women to be submissive (Henry & Powell, 2016). However, studies also exist where no significant gender differences were found in the types of TFSV experienced or the emotional consequences reported by victims (Champion et al., 2022). Men may also be victims of IBSA victimization (Powell & Henry, 2019).

It is important to mention that tere are several limitations for accessing TFSV victimization in adolescents. First, there is not a specific way to approach the issue. Most of the research available utilizes different methodology in approaching sexual violence. Therefore, is not possible to come to a specific conclusion about the forms of TFSV that adolescents are experiencing. Additionally, since research is done on a lot of different sociocultural contexts, all the tools utilized are developed on Western societies. Therefore, there is not a clear understanding of the difference in TFSV forms for adolescents coming from different countries.

Perpetration of TFSV and TFSV-Related Forms: Underlying Motivation and Risk Factors

Concerning IBSA, in a study conducted by Gámez-Guadix et al. (2022), the prevalence of TFSV perpetration was 4.7% for non-consensual sexting. Henry et al. (2019) found that 11.1% of respondents had perpetrated IBSA behaviours since the age of 16. It is important to note that studies utilize different methodologies to evaluate perpetration of TFSV among adolescents. In a natural study of 3,000 internet users aged 15 and above conducted by Eaton et al. (2017), 5.2% of participants reported to have perpetrated IBSA, mostly through text (44.7%), social media (18.9%), email (28%) or through websites (17%).

Cross-sectional studies on OSH perpetration also differ from one another. In a study conducted among a sample of 514 teenagers, only 12% admitted forwarding a sext without the sender's permission, while 8% said they had received a sext without requesting it and 4% said they had a sext forwarded without their permission (Naezer & van Oosterhout, 2021). Additionally, in a national survey of 5,568 middle and high school students in the United States, 3% admitted to threatening to share a sext (sexually explicit image) of another person without that person's consent (Patchin & Hinduja, 2018). Males were significantly more likely to report sextortion perpetration than females (4.1% vs. 1.9%). There was no significant difference in sextortion perpetration by race. While there was a statistically significant difference in sextortion perpetration by age, post-hoc analyses did not reveal any specific differences between age groups.

From the studies presented above with regards to perpetration, we observe several differences according to the forms of TFSV perpetrated by adolescents, as well as the countries in which the studies were conducted, and their sample sizes. The perpetration of TFSV from adolescents is not widely researched in terms of its prevalence, but perceptions towards it have been documented instead. This makes TFSV perpetration a challenging phenomenon for research. An important observation is that males engage more frequently in perpetrating TFSV, compared to females. This observation adds to the gendered hypothesis about TFSV overall. According to Gámez-Guadix & Martínez-Bacaicoa (2023) "…gender roles also play an important part in this by associating men with qualities related to power and domination that justify and normalize various forms of aggression" (p.383). This statement does not mean that girls do not perpetrate TFSV, rather they do so to a lesser extent compared to boys and TFSV can have a profound impact, particularly for minors experiencing it.

In summary, research on TFSV perpetration among adolescents indicates a higher prevalence among boys compared to girls. This disparity is observed across various forms of TFSV, including IBSA and OSH. While studies have reported different prevalence rates depending on the specific type of TFSV and the methodology used, a consistent pattern emerges highlighting boys' increased involvement in these harmful behaviours.

This gendered aspect of TFSV perpetration raises questions about the influence of societal norms and gender roles in shaping adolescents' behaviours. The findings emphasize the need for further investigation into the underlying factors contributing to this disparity, as well as the development of targeted interventions that address the specific needs and challenges faced by both male and female adolescents in relation to TFSV.

In regards with the limitations on research about perpetration, there is the issue of adolescents not perceiving some forms of violence as harmful, therefore, not reporting they have perpetrated it. Also, the sample methodology utilized in most of the cases is convenient sampling (where researchers are getting a grasp on the available population who is willing to complete the surveys) and not random sampling methodologies. Random sampling methodologies would provide a better grasp on the actual instances were adolescents who perpetrate TFSV are doing it in real-life situations.

THE CONTEXT OF TFSV: REASONS FOR ENGAGING IN TFSV

To fully understand the context in which TFSV occurs among adolescents, it's crucial to examine it within the broader framework of adolescent sexuality, sexual behaviour, and sexual violence. This includes exploring adolescents' attitudes towards sex, their motivations for engaging in sexually aggressive behaviours, and the reasons why they might become involved in TFSV either as victims or perpetrators.

Adolescence is a period of significant sexual development and exploration adolescents' attitudes towards sex being influenced by a variety of factors, including family, peers, media, and cultural norms (Boonmongkon et al., 2013; Fongkaew & Fongkaew, 2016; Yount et al., 2023). Family values and beliefs about sex can significantly influence adolescents' attitudes and behaviours. Open communication and parental support can promote healthy sexual development, while restrictive or negative messages can lead to shame and confusion. Peers also play a crucial role in shaping adolescents' sexual norms and expectations. Peer pressure to engage in sexual activity can increase the risk of TFSV, especially if adolescents feel unprepared or unable to set boundaries.

Furthermore, the media often portrays unrealistic and hypersexualized images of sex, which can influence adolescents' perceptions of what is normal or desirable. Exposure to sexually explicit or violent media can desensitize adolescents to sexual violence and contribute to a culture that normalizes it. Additionally, cultural norms around gender roles, sexuality, and relationships can impact adolescents' attitudes and behaviours. For example, restrictive gender norms or expectations around virginity can limit adolescents' ability to express their sexuality healthily and safely. In recent literature, it is stated that this new form of violence could be understood within the broader scope of gender-based violence. So, to grasp the context of TFSV and its perpetration to adolescents, this could be done by understanding the concept of adolescent sexual violence overall, both the one with the use of technological means as well as the violence happening in the real world.

Studies have consistently linked IBSA perpetration to the dark triad traits of narcissism, Machiavellianism, and psychopathy (Clancy et al., 2019; Karasavva, 2022; Pina, et al., 2017). Individuals who derive sexual gratification from exposing themselves are more likely to engage in cyber flashing, a type of IBSA involving sending unsolicited explicit images (Karasavva et al., 2023). Narcissism has been found to be associated with both exhibitionism and cyber flashing attitudes (March & Wagstaff, 2017;

Oswald et al. 2020). However, an overemphasis on individual personality traits like the "Dark Triad" risks overlooking the broader sociocultural factors that enable TFSV. Focusing solely on these traits may pathologize perpetrators while neglecting the influence of societal norms, power dynamics, and online disinhibition effects that contribute to the normalization of online harassment and abuse (Wykes & Gunter, 2019). This focus can limit the effectiveness of prevention and intervention strategies by failing to address the systemic issues that create fertile ground for TFSV to flourish.

Moral disengagement, the ability to justify harmful behaviours through cognitive distortions, emerges as a significant risk factor (Pina, Bell, Griffin, & Vasquez, 2021). Sexual compulsivity, often linked to sexual aggression and risky sexual behaviours, has also been implicated in IBSA perpetration (Garner, Brem, Shorey, Hamlin, & Stuart, 2022). Impulsivity, is another potential risk factor (Hare & Neumann, 2008). Substance use, particularly marijuana, alcohol, and opioids, has been found to be associated with technology-facilitated aggression, including IBSA (Seewald et al., 2022).

Beyond individual characteristics, the overlap between IBSA victimization and perpetration is noteworthy. Research suggests that individuals who have been victims of IBSA are more likely to perpetrate similar acts (Powell, Henry, Flynn, & Scott, 2019; 2022). Victim-perpetrators often exhibit higher levels of maladjustment, including moral disengagement, behavioural issues, and mental health problems (Holt et al., 2015; Shneyderman & Kiely, 2013).

Understanding the motivations behind IBSV perpetration is essential for effective prevention and intervention. While previous research has primarily focused on the forms of aggression, exploring the underlying functions or motives can provide valuable insights. Traditional research on violence often differentiates between proactive and reactive aggression. Proactive aggression refers to planned or premeditated actions, while reactive aggression is impulsive and driven by emotional states. However, this dichotomy is considered to be limited, as it fails to capture the full range of motivations that can underlie violent behaviour (Runions et al., 2018).

In the context of TFSV, research has identified various motivations that do not fit neatly into the proactive-reactive framework. Revenge, for instance, is a common motivation for engaging in online hate speech and can be carried out both impulsively and deliberately (Runions et al., 2018; Tanrikulu & Erdur-Baker, 2021; Wachs et al., 2022). The desire to fit into a social group is another motivation that can drive IBSV perpetration. This can be achieved through premeditated aggression or by simply following the dynamics of a group (Wachs et al., 2022).

These motivations can be linked to the risk factors identified in previous research on TFSV perpetration. For example, individuals with narcissistic personality traits may be more likely to engage in IBSV as a means of seeking attention and validation. Additionally, those with low moral disengagement may be more inclined to justify their actions and engage in revenge or other harmful behaviours. By exploring the interplay between motivations and risk factors, researchers can gain a deeper understanding of the factors that contribute to IBSV perpetration. This knowledge can inform the development of targeted prevention and intervention strategies.

IMPACTS OF TFSV VICTIMIZATION IN ADOLESCENTS

Empirical data reveal the severe negative impact of TFSV on victims' lives. Given that most of the literature focuses on the impact on adult populations and only a few studies reveal the impact of TFSV on adolescents, it is important to present the available empirical data in as much detail as possible.

Regarding IBSA, although research on the detrimental mental health effects among adolescents is limited, media reports reveal numerous instances in which teenagers have attempted to commit suicide following the nonconsensual sharing of their sexual images. Existing literature supports this concerning trend, indicating that being a victim of such abuse can have severe negative mental health consequences, comparable to those experienced by victims of in-person sexual abuse like assault or harassment (Sciacca et al., 2023). Studies with adults show that victims of various forms of IBSA, including nonconsensual sharing, creation, and sextortion often exhibit high levels of stress, depression, anxiety, suicidal thoughts, and unhealthy coping mechanisms such as substance abuse (Champion et al., 2022; Patel & Roesch, 2020).

Similarly, studies with adolescents indicate that IBSA is highly associated with bullying victimization and adolescents who were IBSA victims report high symptoms of anxiety as well as depression and display self-harm behaviors or suicidal ideation (Gámez-Guadix et al., 2022). Moreover, people who have experienced IBSA are likely to live in constant anxiety, not knowing whether their personal images or videos are on the Internet or not (Sciacca et al., 2023). Additionally, this form of violence has detrimental effects on the interpersonal relationships of the victims, to the point where they delete their social media information, in order not to be reminded of their IBSA experience (Bates, 2017).

Studies also tend to examine the different TFSV experiences retrospectively, instead of close to the time individuals were subjected to them. In many cases participants report to have been subjected to these forms of TFSV during adolescence and in some cases under the age of 16 (Powell & Henry, 2016). Very often adolescents who had been subjected to IBSA assumed the responsibility for what happened, implying that they made a bad choice by producing a sexual image and sending it to another person who later acted as a perpetrator (Sciacca et al., 2023). These self-blame feelings may lead to this increase in depressive symptoms, thus preventing adolescents from seeking help (Sciacca et al., 2023). Gradually, this often leads to the non-disclosure of the incident(s) and thus constituting the phenomenon as an underreported one (Mandau, 2021).

Regarding OSH, inconsistencies in measurement attempts prevent us from having a clear estimation of the impact on the individuals subjected to it. This could be linked to the ever-changing nature of the phenomenon that often leads to the introduction of new terms within the OSH terminology framework itself.

In a scoping review, Angela et al. (2023) report that OSH is likely to have a significant impact on mental health adjustment like self-esteem. Another study indicates intense anxiety and depressive symptoms in adolescent girls who have experienced OSH, while OSH correlations with mental health were not significant for boys (Ståhl & Dennhag, 2021), shedding light on the gendered nature of OSH. Moreover, the impact of OSH may be experienced by some even long after the TFSV incident has occurred. Adolescents who report having been subjected to OSH at least once in their lifetime and in the last 12 months prior to participating in the study reported higher levels of depressive symptoms compared to those who had not experienced it at all (Guerra et al., 2021).

Additionally, adolescents who have been repeatedly victims of OSH show higher levels of depressive symptoms (Guerra et al., 2021). It is also important to note that OSH as well as other forms of online violence often led to new forms of violence like cyberbullying, contributing to a cycle of violence. This also draws connection with the notion of peer victimization as highlighted in relevant research (Angela et al., 2023; Copp et al., 2021).

To effectively understand and evaluate the impact of the third dimension of TFSV, Sexual Aggression and Coercion (SAC), it is important to keep in mind that potentially all forms of TFSV could progressively lead to SAC. For example, IBSA could be used by the perpetrator to further harm the victim, by threatening to distribute the photos or videos that the perpetrator has taken with or without the victim being aware of it. Such forms of illegal behaviour fall into the three forms of SAC, as stated above.

Research on sextortion's effects has largely focused on the direct victimization process of the targeted adolescents (Gámez-Guadix et al., 2022; Patchin & Hinduja, 2020; Wolak et al., 2018). Self-compiled research literature similarly points out that severe mental, psychological, and social effects are associated with sextortion among adolescents, such as anguish, trauma, and social maladjustment. According to a study by Wolak et al. (2018), sextortion was indicated to also have serious social consequences, particularly among adolescence, as half of the victims were barred from their relationships. This highlights the detrimental social impact of the phenomenon, as the victims tend to isolate themselves from family and friends, because they experience it as shameful, embarrassing or they fear they will be judged by others. In this study, 30% of the adolescent victims also reported mental health issues. In the long term, severe consequences linked to sextortion are also mentioned. Victims may face difficulties in creating healthy relationships due to trust issues and fear of intimacy. They might also be unable to continue with academic and professional activities because of the continuous emotional pain and social loneliness. In some instances, the agony that people go through due to sextortion may result in self-harm or suicidal thoughts (Nilsson et al., 2019).

In a similar vein, practitioners working with girl-victims of sextortion list the mental effects that this form of violence yields (Dolev-Cohen et al., 2023). The counselors report that sextortion victims experience stress, worry, anxiety, and shame as after-effects. This emotional impact frequently results in adjustment problems or social difficulties such as missing school, distancing from friends and avoiding situations that require interactions with other people. Such findings support the severity of sextortion and how it impacts not only psychological health but also the victim's social and academic functioning.

In parallel with acknowledging that sextortion threatens directly the targeted person, it is necessary to mention that the effects of these forms of violence are not limited to the victims, but include relatives, friends, and sometimes even whole communities. As far as parents are concerned, they are likely to develop feelings of guilt, helplessness and anger, while siblings are likely to develop resentment and other negative attitudes towards the suffering sibling (Doley-Cohen et al., 2023). These negative consequences in the victim's social context create a further burden to the process of healing as they lead to a deterioration of the victims' mental health and social functioning. (Doley-Cohen et al., 2023).

As far as the fourth dimension of TFSV is concerned, Harassment Based on Gender and Sexuality (HBGS), relevant studies also highlight severe negative effects on victims' lives. HBGS is so prevalent that it poses equal harm to adolescents by disturbing their intrapersonal and interpersonal functioning (Wachs et al., 2022). Targeted individuals of this form of TFSV are usually subjected to gender or sexuality related comments, threats and discriminatory remarks until one's self esteem shatters and feelings of worthlessness set in (Beran et al., 2012). It is reported that victims develop anxious feelings, depression, difficulties sleeping and eating and an inability to concentrate in class, all of which hamper their academic and social lives. There is also evidence that students who are subjected to such forms of harassment may experience absenteeism eventually leading to low academic performance (Beran et al., 2012).

It is evident that the effects of HBGS are not just limited to the emotional realm but extend to the targeted individual's social life. Constant fear of being oppressed and discriminated results in the individuals isolating themselves from social networks and other online communities, all of which contribute to loneliness (Hendricks et al., 2020; Negi, 2023). For this reason, withdrawal can negatively affect one's potential to build as well as maintain healthy interpersonal online and offline relationships. In addition, the burden of being targeted can lead to victims' self-policing and limiting their ability to express themselves and contribute to online forums, chatrooms or other forms of technology-related communication (Parmar & Dutt, 2024). This negatively impacts their social development, since crucial processes of social and emotional development as well as identity formation are hindered. For example, Hendricks et al. (2020) showed that 'outing' was the most common form of cyber-harassment among the LGBTQIA+ youth and this may be very detrimental for those young people who have not yet decided to state their sexuality.

HBGS also presents long-term effects on victims, as even after the harassment has ceased, many victims report mental health related difficulties and emotional traumatization (Hatchel et al., 2017; K. J. Mitchell et al., 2014). This trauma could potentially lead to self-harm behaviors or suicidal ideation demonstrating why identification and help must be provided as soon as possible (Ybarra et al., 2015). Since cyber harassment imposes negative psychological and social impact on young people's development, it is imperative to create a tolerant and protection culture for users of the information space irrespective of the gender and sexual orientation.

There are a lot of things to consider in regards with TFSV impacts in adolescents. Firstly, since there is an underreporting of the phenomenon (in many cases due to the fear of secondary traumatization) there is not a specific way to effectively generalize the impacts, on adolescent populations. Another difficulty, which is similar to the assessment of the TFSV victimization, is that the models are developed in western societies. Thus, the ways that those models evaluate TFSV, in most of the cases are not appropriate to be utilized in different cultural settings, where TFSV experiences and impacts in adolescence might differ a lot. Moreover, no specific tools (e.g. screening tools, or questionnaires), are developed to access TFSV impact in adolescents. I the majority of research available, impact questionnaires are derived from studies utilizing them for other purposes (e.g. real-life sexual violence, or cyberbullying). Since it is established that TFSV is a form of violence with its unique characteristics, a lot of impact questionnaires might not be able to effectively grasp the phenomenon. The only questionnaire specifically designed to access the gender impacts on TFSV was created by Campion and his colleagues (2022) in a study for the gendered impacts of TFSV. This has also been adopted by other researchers to incorporate further impacts (e.g. the use of alcohol, or substance abuse) (Gkantona et al., 2024).

In summary, it is evident that the nature of TFSV, as evidenced by its detrimental effects, underscores the critical need for comprehensive prevention and intervention strategies. The emotional, psychological, and social consequences of TFSV can be devastating and long-lasting, affecting not only the direct victims but also their families, friends, and communities. As technology continues to evolve, the methods and platforms used for perpetrating TFSV are also likely to change, requiring ongoing research and the adaptation of prevention and intervention efforts.

COPING STRATEGIES OF TFSV VICTIMS

Given that TFSV is a phenomenon that not only is under-reported but also recently explored (Powell & Henry, 2019), evidence regarding adolescents subjected to TFSV and their coping behaviours is not extensive. In adult populations, an enlightening study by Bates, 2015 drew on Folkman & Moskowitz (2004) categorization of coping strategies (problem-focused, emotion-focused, meaning-focused and social coping/help seeking). Based on a series of interviews conducted with 18 people aged 18-54 who had been exposed to TFSV, it was discovered that many participants employed maladaptive coping strategies, like avoidance/denial or alcohol consumption trying to reduce negative emotions associated with the TFSV exposure. Additionally, some participants stated they had suicidal thoughts. Another maladaptive coping mechanism was the obsession about the situation and the worry of escalation. According to Bates (2015) "Participants could not understand how a person could do such a harmful thing...which resulted in an obsession and need to understand why they were victimized" (p.72). Participants however also engaged in positive coping mechanisms to manage their emotions after being victimized, such as seeing a therapist, displaying help-seeking behaviors, speaking out to friends and family and focusing on resuming a normal life again (Bates, 2015).

Fortunately, the existing limited data also indicates that despite the harmful effects of TFSV, adolescents demonstrate resilience and resourcefulness in coping with TFSV, employing active coping strategies to address the violent incident such as blocking perpetrators, deleting offensive content, adjusting privacy settings and seeking support from friends, family or professionals (Choi, 2020; Gilbert et al., 2023). While some individuals may choose to confront their harassers directly, others opt for more passive strategies, for example ignoring the harassment or withdrawing from online platforms. The effectiveness of these coping mechanisms can vary depending on individual characteristics, the severity of the harassment effects and the available support systems (Fox & Tang, 2017; Gilbert et al., 2023).

Concerning the forms of TFSV, research with adults who were subjected to OSH indicates that many survivors-victims cope actively (e.g. blocking the person who harassed them online) (Malanga, 2020). Many participants also mention having reported the incident to the police, however no actions were taken (Malanga, 2020). The finding may help explain why the phenomenon is underreported. When adolescents are confronted with OSH, some employ positive coping strategies (active coping) like reporting it to the authorities or the platforms, whereas many usually try to avoid the situation completely or resort to closing their accounts in the respective apps, sites, or forums they use, due to the fear of being exposed again to TFSV (Michikyan et al., 2014).

With respect to IBSA, the coping strategies adolescents utilize are quite unclear. Because the challenges that adolescents face are completely different to those of adults, common lines of action for adolescent victims-survivors of this form of violence could not be drawn from adult samples. Indicatively, a study conducted by Lunde & Joleby (2023) showed that none of the adolescents who participated in the study reported seeking help, even though they seemed to recognize the severity of the phenomenon.

Regarding CAS coping, Wang (2024) explored the coping mechanisms of 175 cyber sextortion victims (146 males and 29 females) who shared their experiences on the Reddit forum "r/sextortion"[3]. The study found that victims employed both emotion-focused coping (e.g., complying with demands, seeking emotional support, internalizing negative emotions) and problem-focused coping (e.g., blocking the perpetrator, reporting to authorities, deactivating accounts). Some victims transitioned from emotion-focused to problem-focused coping as the situation evolved, particularly after realizing that complying with demands did not resolve the issue. The study also revealed gender differences, with female victims more likely to experience non-financial requests and self-blame, while male victims were more often targeted for monetary gain.

The coping mechanisms employed by HBGS victims-survivors exhibit similar patterns. Survivors/victims of Gender-Based Harassment employ various coping strategies to navigate this type of online hostility. These strategies can be broadly categorized as engagement or disengagement. Engagement strategies involve actively addressing the harassment, such as confronting the perpetrator directly (Fox & Tang, 2017) or reporting the abuse to platform moderators or authorities (Ndlovu & Khupe, 2023). Disengagement strategies involve withdrawing from the online space either temporarily or permanently. This can be manifested as ignoring the harasser, blocking them or leaving the platform altogether (Fox & Tang, 2017). Some victims-survivors also take breaks from online platforms to safeguard their mental well-being (Uttarapong et al., 2021).

These strategies align with established coping mechanisms like social coping (seeking emotional support) and avoidance (mentally disengaging or physically distancing from the stressor) (Folkman & Moskowitz, 2004). Some victims may also resort to gender masking, adopting male or gender-neutral identities to avoid being targeted (Fox & Tang, 2017). While these coping mechanisms are emotion-focused and can offer temporary relief, they do not address the root of the problem and may have unintended consequences, such as reinforcing harmful stereotypes or silencing marginalized voices.

Similarly, various strategies of emotional coping were shown among people subjected to Sexuality-Based Harassment (e.g. people belonging to the LBGTQA+ community) (Uttarapong et al., 2021). These strategies include venting to close friends and family, seeking professional help through therapy or counselling, and engaging in activities that promote emotional release, such as crying or participating in enjoyable activities. However, according to existing literature, many LGBTQA+ adolescents who experience online harassment do not find social support from peers substantial enough to help them navigate through their experience. Thus, many of the employed coping strategies (which might be helpful for cis gendered heterosexual women (Fox & Tang, 2016), may not be helpful for LGBTQA adolescents for various reasons (for example exposure to peers who have stereotypical perspectives about diversity and lack empathy for youth who are different) (Ybarra et al., 2015).

As far as social coping strategies are concerned, help-seeking is an important strategy. This form of coping involves asking help from the community, experts or specialists, and their own social and family network (family and/or friends) to support them (Mclocklin et al., 2024). A particular dimension of TFSV victimization is that while other forms of violence are usually private, TFSV can be shared and spread widely online, making the victimization public. Due to social stigmatization as well as the fact that very often victims had received education in school about sexting and the consensual sending of images which implied victim-blaming, many adolescents might resort to self-blaming for finding themselves in such situations. Therefore, under these circumstances some victims believe that avoidance and/or non-disclosure of their victimizing helps them regulate their emotional distress and prevents them from being traumatized or re-traumatized (Mclocklin et al., 2024).

Similar findings indicate that adolescents are less likely to seek help from professionals after they had been subjected to some form of Sexual Aggression and/or Coercion, and they are more likely to seek help from friends and family instead to deal with their situation. This may be due to the distrust they have toward authorities (Howard, 2019). Additionally, there is the fear of stigmatization from reporting the situation. Moreover, due to the anonymity that online communication technologies provide, it might be difficult to identify the person who is coercing them, especially if they do not know the person's identity (Howard, 2019).

Regarding research in coping, there are several challenges where researchers could divert their focus on. For instance, most of the coping strategies in TFSV are not effectively researched. Research on coping has been conducted on sexting experiences (most recently defined as non-consensual sexting), but as we established in the beginning of the chapter, sexting does not effectively grasp the entirety of the TFSV phenomenon, rather than focuses only on a specific aspect of it.

In conclusion, the coping mechanisms employed by victims of TFSV are diverse and complex. While some individuals may actively confront the harassment through reporting or seeking help, others may disengage by blocking perpetrators or leaving online platforms. The choice of coping strategy can be influenced by various factors, including the severity of the harassment, individual resilience, and available support systems. However, there is a notable research gap on the specific coping mechanisms used by adolescents who have been subjected to TFSV. This highlights the need for further investigation into this understudied area not only to trace the phenomenon, but also to develop tailored interventions and support services for young victims. Accordingly, Mitchell & Štulhofer, (2021) showed that increasing reports of TFSV incidents before the age of 16 highlight the necessity of school-based interventions or intervention programs to build safe internet use skills and support adolescents subjected to OSH. Additionally, the existing literature suggests that many victims, both adolescents and adults, may not disclose their experiences or seek help due to the fear of stigma, self-blame, or lack of trust in the authorities. This underscores the importance of creating safe and supportive environments and services where victims feel empowered to report TFSV and access appropriate resources for healing and recovery.

BASIC PRINCIPLES FOR THE DEVELOPMENT OF TFSV PREVENTION PROGRAMS FOR ADOLESCENTS

Understanding the complex interplay of these influences is crucial for developing effective TFSV prevention programs (Yount et al., 2023). Programs should address the specific needs and challenges faced by adolescents in different contexts, considering the cultural norms and social pressures that may contribute to TFSV. By promoting healthy sexual development, open communication, and media literacy, prevention programs can empower adolescents to make informed choices, set boundaries, and seek help when needed. It is crucial to implement early education and prevention programs focused on the confrontation of TFSV, emphasizing healthy relationships, consent, and online safety (Gámez-Guadix & Martínez-Bacaicoa, 2023). These programs should be integrated into school curricula from a young age, ensuring that adolescents are equipped with the knowledge and skills to navigate the digital world safely and responsibly.

Incorporating digital literacy and media literacy components into prevention programs is essential. Adolescents need to be able to critically analyse online content, identify potentially harmful situations, and understand the consequences of their online actions. Bystander intervention training can empower adolescents to take an active role in preventing TFSV (Dolev-Cohen et al., 2023). By teaching them how to safely intervene when they witness harmful behaviours online, prevention programs can foster a culture of support and accountability among young people.

Gender-transformative approaches that challenge harmful gender norms and stereotypes should be central to TFSV prevention programs. By promoting healthy relationship dynamics and dismantling rigid gender roles, these programs can address the root causes of TFSV and foster a culture of respect and equality. A trauma-informed approach is also crucial in providing support services to adolescents who have experienced TFSV (Dolev-Cohen et al., 2023). This approach recognizes the potential impact of trauma on individuals' functioning and creates a safe and supportive environment for healing and recovery.

Collaboration among schools, parents, community organizations, and Law enforcement organizations is vital in creating a comprehensive support system for adolescents affected by TFSV. By working together, these stakeholders can ensure that prevention programs are effectively implemented and that victims have access to appropriate resources and support services. Continuous research and evaluation are critical to inform the development and improvement of TFSV prevention programs (Ståhl & Dennhag, 2021). By staying abreast of the latest research findings and evaluating program effectiveness, prevention efforts can be adapted to address the evolving nature of TFSV and the specific needs of adolescents.

DIFFICULTIES IN EFFECTIVELY IDENTIFYING AND RESEARCHING TFSV IN ADOLESCENTS

In recent years, despite the growing body of literature and research on TFSV, significant gaps remain. This might be due to the ever-changing nature of the phenomenon and the new ways that perpetrators utilize emerging technologies to cause harm to people. Moreover, some victims/survivors do not choose to disclose their experiences to anyone (Douglass et al., 2020). This finding is in line with Mclocklin et al. (2024) who also note "…reluctance to seek support like those who experience other forms of sexual violence..." (p.4). Many reasons that explain non-disclosure exist, and it is not easy to address all of them. Non-disclosure itself prevents researchers from understanding such reasons. Embarrassment and shame however are commonly listed as reasons for non-disclosure (Ruvalcaba & Eaton, 2020).

One major research effort to identify reasons for non-disclosure was by Mclocklin et al. (2024). Semi-structured interviews with victims/ survivors revealed that NCIBA is a stigmatizing experience, and this anticipating stigma prevents them from reporting. Other participants reported fear of judgment and embarrassment. According to Mclocklin et al. (2024) "Participant's concerns of being judged by others centred around either being viewed as "stupid" or "naïve" for sharing the images consensually or for being sexually promiscuous ("dirty," "immoral," "easy," "slut," "whore")" (p.9).

Another reason why victims/ survivors choose not to disclose TFSV incidents is likely a lack of knowledge around support services. Since non-disclosure and help-seeking regarding TFSV are not extensively researched in adults, reasons for non-disclosure require further investigation. This applies to adolescents as well. Worth noting is that most research on non-disclosure focuses on cyberbullying rather than specific forms of TFSV.

To increase disclosure of TFSV incidents, programs could be designed to target some of the reasons for non-disclosure mentioned above. Specifically, school-based interventions could be an answer to the situation. Additionally, strong connections between schools and the community are crucial to enhance trust in help-seeking and to make adolescents feel safe about reporting incidents to persons and organizations able to help them. Additionally, educating authorities, counsellors, therapists and parents about TFSV is needed. Finally naming TFSV as a situation that has always exists, instead of seeing it as merely a phenomenon of modern times.

Shifting from terms like cyberbullying (which has already been widely researched) and differentiating it from cyber-harassment, TFSV and other forms of violence, by targeting each of these specifically, would be a major step towards the eradication of this form of violence.

LIMITATIONS OF THE RESEARCH ON TFSV.

Several limitations within the current research on Technology-Facilitated Sexual Violence (TFSV) hinder a comprehensive understanding of this complex issue. These limitations span across various aspects of the phenomenon, including assessment of victimization, perpetration, impacts, and coping mechanisms.

- **Assessment of Victimization:**
  - o Lack of a Standardized Approach: The absence of a uniform methodology for assessing TFSV victimization makes it difficult to compare findings across studies and draw definitive conclusions about the specific forms of TFSV adolescents experience.
  - o Western-Centric Bias: Most research tools are developed in Western countries, limiting their applicability and understanding of TFSV experiences in diverse sociocultural contexts.
- **Assessment of Perpetration:**
  - o Underreporting and Misconceptions: Adolescents may not perceive certain harmful behaviors as violence, leading to underreporting of perpetration.
  - o Sampling Limitations: The use of convenience sampling instead of random sampling methodologies limits the generalizability of findings on TFSV perpetration.
- **Assessment of Impacts:**
  - o Underreporting and Generalizability: Fear of secondary traumatization often leads to underreporting of TFSV, making it difficult to address the impacts on adolescent populations.
  - o Western-Centric Models: Existing impact models are primarily developed in Western societies, limiting their relevance and applicability in different cultural settings where TFSV experiences and impacts may vary significantly.
- **Lack of Specific Tools:**
  - o The absence of specific tools for assessing TFSV impact in adolescents' forces researchers to rely on questionnaires designed for other purposes, potentially failing to capture the unique characteristics of TFSV.
- **Assessment of Coping:**
  - o Limited Research on Coping Strategies: Most research focuses on coping with sexting experiences, neglecting other aspects of TFSV and leaving a gap in understanding the broader range of coping strategies employed by adolescents.

Addressing these limitations is crucial for advancing the understanding of TFSV and developing effective prevention and intervention strategies. Future research should prioritize the development of standardized and culturally sensitive tools, cross-cultural comparisons, longitudinal studies, and qualitative research to explore the multifaceted nature of TFSV and its impact on adolescents.

TOWARDS A BROADER CONCEPTUALIZATION: INCLUDING OTHER FORMS AND RELATED DIMENSIONS OF TECHNOLOGY FACILITATED SEXUAL VIOLENCE

Considering the aforementioned information regarding TFSV conceptualization, as well as the limitations of assessing TFSV and its different aspects and socioemotional impacts, a broader scope is proposed addressing the difficulties related to understanding and effectively researching the phenomenon in adolescents.

While the TFSV framework proposed by Powell & Henry (2019) provides a valuable foundation for understanding technology-facilitated sexual violence, it necessitates further refinement to adequately address the unique experiences and vulnerabilities of adolescents in the digital age. To that end, we propose a broadened scope to its approach that builds upon their work, incorporating crucial elements to enhance its comprehensiveness and relevance to adolescent populations. This framework expands the dimensions of TFSV to include not only the original categories of Online Sexual Harassment (OSH), Image-Based Sexual Abuse (IBSA), Sexual Aggression and Coercion (SAC), and Harassment Based on Gender and Sexuality (HBGS), but also could explicitly incorporate Cyberstalking as a distinct dimension. This recognizes the severe impact of online stalking, which involves persistent online monitoring, unwanted contact, threats, and identity theft, often with sexual or gendered motivations.

Additionally, it would be crucial for Body Shaming to be incorporated to a broadened TFSV scope. Body shaming is directly linked to Technology-Facilitated Sexual Violence (TFSV). It reduces individuals to their physical appearance, judged against societal beauty standards (Henry & Powell, 2015). This objectification is a tool in TFSV to control, demean, and humiliate victims, using language or non-consensual image sharing to manipulate and degrade (Bates, 2017). Perpetrators exploit these insecurities to gain trust or silence victims. The normalization of body shaming online as harmless teasing creates a culture where disrespecting bodies is commonplace, facilitating TFSV (Ringrose et al., 2024). This links directly to image-based sexual abuse, where non-consensual images are used to body shame and humiliate, therefore TFSV models must recognize body shaming as a risk factor and incorporate it.

Furthermore, the broadened conceptualization could the evolving nature of online abuse by including the creation and distribution of deepfakes as a form of IBSA, highlighting the potential for severe emotional and reputational consequences for adolescent victims. Deepfakes (as a form of TFSV) is a new form of Artificial Intelligence (AI) generated sexual images utilizing photos from people that perpetrators know and making them perform sexual acts online (by incorporating the sexual aspects of other, many times real, pornographic images). Since it is not possible to differentiate fake from real, this form of violence should be incorporated, as according to the literature is a very serious form of sexual violence (Karasavva & Noorbhai, 2021).

Moreover, it is importance to emphasize on understanding TFSV within the context of adolescent development. Recognizing that adolescents are still developing their sense of self, navigate social relationships, and explore their sexuality, makes them particularly vulnerable to online exploitation, peer pressure, and the negative consequences of TFSV. Therefore, it is crucial to consider the influence of adolescent development on online behaviours, social dynamics, and vulnerability to abuse. For example, one aspect that could be incorporated into this model is the role of cyber-bystanders (Mainwaring et al., 2023). Cyber-bystanders in the aspects of technology facilitated sexual violence could involve the people who are aware of a TFSV situation that happened to a person, but do not take actions or do not recognize their responsibility in this (Mainwaring et al., 2023). Since, as mentioned previously, the role of peer and social relationships is crucial, the role of cyber-bystanders could be incorporated to broaden the aspects of TFSV incidents. However, since cyber-bystanders are not perpetrating, nor experiencing cyber violence themselves, they do not partake in abusive behaviours by themselves. However, their perception about a TFSV incident can possibly lead to secondary traumatization for people experiencing TFSV. Additionally, it can affect the impacts on the lives of people experiencing it.

Moreover, an informed model could consider the broader social and cultural context in which adolescent TFSV occurs, including the impact of gender norms, social media culture, peer pressure, and access to technology. It could consider how their age impacts their online behaviour, like younger teens being more susceptible to peer pressure around sexting, while older one's face risks on dating apps. It could also recognize how their brains are still developing, affecting their impulse control and understanding of consequences. This means teens might share explicit images without fully grasping the potential harm. The model also knows that teens use online spaces to explore their identity and social roles, making them vulnerable to manipulation. Finally, it would be beneficial to take into account how different online platforms, anonymity, and features like disappearing messages can contribute to TFSV.

Recognizing the diverse experiences of adolescents, a broader conceptualization could adopt an intersectional lens. It would be crucial to emphasize the importance of considering the intersecting identities of adolescents, such as gender, race, sexual orientation, socioeconomic status, and disability, to ensure that the framework captures the unique experiences and vulnerabilities of different groups. Finally, it acknowledges the dynamic and evolving nature of technology and online behaviours. By remaining flexible and adaptable, a broader model could incorporate new forms of TFSV and emerging online platforms as they arise. This idea could provide a more nuanced and comprehensive framework for understanding TFSV in adolescence and offers a valuable tool for researchers, educators, and policymakers to develop effective prevention strategies, interventions, and support services tailored to the unique needs of adolescents in the digital age.

IDEAS FOR FUTURE RESEARCH REGARDING TFSV EXPERIENCED BY ADOLESCENTS.

The following areas highlight key priorities for future research to address these limitations, to promote the new novel approach and advance our knowledge of TFSV among adolescents:

- **Incorporating the dimensions of Deep fakes, Cyber flashing and Body Shaming to TFSV:**
    - Broadening and enhancing the research tools: Future research could focus on the broader dimensions of TFSV (*Deep Fakes, Cyber Flashing and Body Shaming* alongside the 4 existing dimensions) and their incorporation to the existing tools utilized for the measurement of TFSV.
- **Addressing and Understanding the Role of the By-Standers:**
    - Future research should investigate the nuanced dynamics of the cyber-bystander role in adolescent TFSV, moving beyond simple categorizations of active intervention or passive observation to explore the diverse motivations, barriers, types, and effectiveness of interventions, the role of technology, and the ethical considerations involved
- **Standardization and Cross-Cultural Applicability:**

- Developing a standardized measurement tool: This would be important for comparison across studies and providing a clearer picture of the prevalence of TFSV and its forms. The tool could be developed in collaboration with experts, adolescent victims/ survivors, and representatives from various cultural backgrounds. It could contain questions with regard to specific online behaviors, such as cyberstalking, image-based abuse, online harassment, and grooming. Furthermore, translation and validation in multiple languages would ensure cultural sensitivity and relevance.
- Conducting cross-cultural comparative studies: This will help identify similarities and differences in how TFSV manifests in different parts of the world. For example, research could explore how cultural norms around gender roles, sexuality, and technology use influence adolescents' experiences of TFSV. These studies could employ mixed methods, combining quantitative data from the standardized tool with qualitative data from interviews and focus groups to gain a deeper understanding of cultural nuances.

- **Addressing Underreporting and the Misconceptions about TFSV:**
  - Investigating the reasons for underreporting: Research could explore the barriers that prevent adolescents from reporting TFSV victimization or perpetration. This could include fear of social stigma, lack of awareness about available resources, or distrust in authorities. Studies could also examine how different forms of TFSV are perceived by adolescents, and whether they are all recognized as harmful behaviors.
  - Evaluating the impact of educational interventions: It's important to assess whether TFSV awareness programs are effective in increasing adolescents' knowledge and recognition of different forms of TFSV. Research could focus on evaluating the effectiveness of different educational approaches, such as school-based programs, online resources, or peer-led initiatives.
- **Understanding the Impacts and Coping Mechanisms:**
  - Examining the short-term and long-term impacts: Research could investigate the full range of consequences associated with TFSV victimization, including mental health outcomes (e.g., anxiety, depression, PTSD), social difficulties, and academic problems. Longitudinal studies are particularly valuable for understanding the long-term effects and identifying potential risk and protective factors.
- **Investigating coping strategies:**
  - Research could explore the different ways adolescents cope with TFSV victimization, and whether certain strategies are more effective than others. This could include seeking social support, engaging in online help-seeking behaviors, or using self-soothing techniques. Studies could also examine how coping strategies vary across different cultural contexts.
- **Exploring the Role of Technology and Online Environments**
  - Examining the influence of online environments: Research could investigate how specific features of online platforms, such as anonymity, ease of access, and the permanence of online content, contribute to TFSV.
  - Evaluating technology-based interventions: Research could assess the effectiveness of using technology to prevent and address TFSV. This could include evaluating online safety campaigns, developing digital tools for reporting TFSV, or creating online support groups for victims.

By focusing on these areas, future research can significantly expand our understanding of TFSV and contribute to the development of more effective prevention and intervention strategies to protect adolescents worldwide.

CONCLUSION

TFSV is a complex and ever-changing phenomenon, which is often based on divergent definitions, different methodologies and in the various settings where this phenomenon takes place. Therefore, available empirical data vary, and it is difficult to make comparisons. On this basis, the chapter provides a review of the existing theoretical framework on TFSV, and the prevalence of victimization and perpetration regarding TFSV in adolescence. Additionally, the impact of TFSV victimization is described to highlight the importance of addressing the phenomenon as well as the coping strategies that victims-survivors utilize to deal with the situation. These insights are given to lay the ground for a more practical interventional approach to address the phenomenon and for research to focus on developing more suitable measurement tools. Finally, reasons for non-disclosure were reviewed and reveal the need to raise awareness among researchers, authorities, and specialists providing support to TFSV victims. This awareness is crucial in facilitating a comprehensive understanding of TFSV and promoting effective responses to its occurrence. It is essential to recognize the multifaceted nature of TFSV and acknowledge the various factors that contribute to its perpetuation. By delving into the theoretical underpinnings, examining prevalence rates, and analyzing the impact and coping strategies associated with TFSV, this chapter provides a comprehensive overview of the phenomenon. It emphasizes the need for further research, refined measurement tools, and enhanced support systems to effectively address TFSV and mitigate its devastating consequences.

REFERENCES

Ballard, M. E., & Welch, K. M. (2015). Virtual Warfare: Cyberbullying and Cyber-Victimization in MMOG Play. *Games and Culture*, 12(5), 466–491. DOI: 10.1177/1555412015592473

Barak, A. (2005). Sexual harassment on the internet. *Social Science Computer Review*, 23(1), 77–92. DOI: 10.1177/0894439304271540

Bates, S. (2015). *"Stripped": an analysis of revenge porn victims' lives after victimization* [MA Thesis]. Simon Fraser University. Retrieved from: https://summit.sfu.ca/item/15668

Bates, S. (2017). Revenge Porn and Mental Health: A Qualitative Analysis of the Mental Health Effects of Revenge Porn on Female Survivors. *Feminist Criminology*, 12(1), 22–42. DOI: 10.1177/1557085116654565

Beran, T. N., Rinaldi, C., Bickham, D. S., & Rich, M. (2012). Evidence for the need to support adolescents dealing with harassment and cyber-harassment: Prevalence, progression, and impact. *School Psychology International*, 33(5), 562–576. DOI: 10.1177/0143034312446976

Boonmongkon, P., Ojanen, T. T., Samakkeekarom, R., Samoh, N., Iamsilpa, R., Topananan, S., Cholratana, M., & Guadamuz, T. E. (2013). 'She met her (boy)friend online': Negotiating gender identity and sexuality among young Thai women in online space. *Culture, Health & Sexuality*, 15(10), 1162–1174. DOI: 10.1080/13691058.2013.809609 PMID: 23885969

Buchanan, N., & Mahoney, A. (2022). Development of a scale measuring online sexual harassment: Examining gender differences and the emotional impact of sexual harassment victimization online. *Legal and Criminological Psychology*, 27(1), 63–81. DOI: 10.1111/lcrp.12197

Castellanos, M., Wettstein, A., Wachs, S., Kansok-Dusche, J., Ballaschk, C., Krause, N., & Bilz, L. (2023). Hate speech in adolescents: A binational study on prevalence and demographic differences. *Frontiers in Education*, 8, 1076249. DOI: 10.3389/feduc.2023.1076249

Champion, A. R., Oswald, F., Khera, D., & Pedersen, C. L. (2022). Examining the Gendered Impacts of Technology-Facilitated Sexual Violence: A Mixed Methods Approach. *Archives of Sexual Behavior*, 51(3), 1607–1624. DOI: 10.1007/s10508-021-02226-y PMID: 35182285

Chaux, E., & León, M. (2016). Homophobic Attitudes and Associated Factors Among Adolescents: A Comparison of Six Latin American Countries. *Journal of Homosexuality*, 63(9), 1253–1276. DOI: 10.1080/00918369.2016.1151697 PMID: 26861958

Choi, N. Y. (2020). The Correlations on Coping with Cyberviolence, Attribution Method and Social Support among Middle School Students. *Asia-Pacific Journal of Convergent Research Interchange*, 6(8), 31–39. DOI: 10.47116/apjcri.2020.08.04

Copp, J. E., Mumford, E. A., & Taylor, B. G. (2021). Online sexual harassment and cyberbullying in a nationally representative sample of teens: Prevalence, predictors, and consequences. *Journal of Adolescence*, 93(1), 202–211. DOI: 10.1016/j.adolescence.2021.10.003 PMID: 34801812

Dolev-Cohen, M., Nezer, I., & Abu Zumt, A. (2023). A Qualitative Examination of School Counselors' Experiences of Sextortion Cases of Female Students in Israel. *Sexual Abuse*, 35(8), 903–926. DOI: 10.1177/10790632221145925 PMID: 36510813

Douglass, C. H., Wright, C. J. C., Davis, A. C., & Lim, M. S. C. (2020). Non-consensual sharing of personal sexually explicit imagery among young people in Australia: Results from an online survey. *Sexual Health*, 17(2), 182–186. DOI: 10.1071/SH19147 PMID: 32135074

Eaton, A. A., Jacobs, H. E., & Ruvacalba, Y. (2017). *2017 Nationwide Online Study of Nonconsensual Porn Victimization and Perpetration.* Cyber Civil Rights Initiative. Retrieved from: https://www.cybercivilrights.org/wp-content/uploads/2017/06/CCRI-2017-Research-Report.pdf

Englander, E. (2015). Coerced Sexting and Revenge Porn Among Teens. *Bullying, Teen Aggression & Social Media, 1*(2), 19–21. https://vc.bridgew.edu/psychology_fac/69

Englander, E. K., & McCoy, M. (2017). Pressured sexting and revenge porn in a sample of Massachusetts adolescents. *International Journal of Technoethics*, 8(2), 16–25. DOI: 10.4018/IJT.2017070102

Folkman, S., & Moskowitz, J. T. (2004). Coping: Pitfalls and promise. *Annual Review of Psychology*, 55(1), 745–774. DOI: 10.1146/annurev.psych.55.090902.141456 PMID: 14744233

Fongkaew, W., & Fongkaew, K. (2016). My space, my body, my sexual subjectivity: Social media, sexual practice and parental control among teenage girls in urban Chiang Mai. *Culture, Health & Sexuality*, 18(5), 597–607. DOI: 10.1080/13691058.2015.1091948 PMID: 26489939

Fox, J., & Tang, W. Y. (2017). Women's experiences with general and sexual harassment in online video games: Rumination, organizational responsiveness, withdrawal, and coping strategies. *New Media & Society*, 19(8), 1290–1307. DOI: 10.1177/1461444816635778

Franceschi, A. (2024, December). Rodríguez-deArriba María-Luisa, Annalaura Nocentini, & Ersilia Menesini. (2023). Online Sexual Harassment in Adolescence: A Scoping Review. *Sexuality Research & Social Policy*, 21(4), 1480–1499. Advance online publication. DOI: 10.1007/s13178-023-00869-1

Frankel, A. S., Bass, S. B., Patterson, F., Dai, T., & Brown, D. (2018). Sexting, Risk Behavior, and Mental Health in Adolescents: An Examination of 2015 Pennsylvania Youth Risk Behavior Survey Data. *The Journal of School Health*, 88(3), 190–199. DOI: 10.1111/josh.12596 PMID: 29399839

Gámez-Guadix, M., & Incera, D. (2021). Homophobia is online: Sexual victimization and risks on the internet and mental health among bisexual, homosexual, pansexual, asexual, and queer adolescents. *Computers in Human Behavior*, 119, 106728. DOI: 10.1016/j.chb.2021.106728

Gámez-Guadix, M., & Martínez-Bacaicoa, J. (2023). Technology-Facilitated Sexual Violence: Typologies, Prevalence, and Associated Variables. *Handbook of Anger, Aggression, and Violence*, 375–389. DOI: 10.1007/978-3-031-31547-3_20

Gámez-Guadix, M., Mateos-Pérez, E., Wachs, S., Wright, M., Martínez, J., & Íncera, D. (2022). Assessing image-based sexual abuse: Measurement, prevalence, and temporal stability of sextortion and nonconsensual sexting ("revenge porn") among adolescents. *Journal of Adolescence*, 94(5), 789–799. DOI: 10.1002/jad.12064 PMID: 35719041

Garner, A. R., Brem, M. J., Shorey, R. C., Hamlin, J., & Stuart, G. L. (2022). Negative urgency moderates the association between compulsive sexual behaviors and sending unsolicited sexts among men in residential treatment for substance use disorders. *Computers in Human Behavior*, 136, 107385. DOI: 10.1016/j.chb.2022.107385

Gilbert, M., Fernet, M., & Hébert, M. (2023). Diversity of Profiles and Coping Among Adolescent Girl Victims of Sexual Dating Violence. *Article in Journal of Child Sexual Abuse*. DOI: 10.1080/10538712.2023.2195856

Gkantona, G., Arbyrou, K., Giannopoulou, M. D., Zapantis, R., Karakoula, P., Kitsiou, A., Kogka, G., Nikolakopoulos, S., Ntagkas, F., Patrinou, S., & Rekka, E. (2024). *Cyber Violence against Women & Girls in Greece*. Kentro Ereunon gia Themata Isotitas (K.E.T.H.I.). Ioannina, Greece. Retrieved from: https://www.kethi.gr/ereunes-meletes/diadiktyaki-bia-kata-ton-gynaikon-synoptiki-ekthesi

Guerra, C., Pinto-Cortez, C., Toro, E., Efthymiadou, E., & Quayle, E. (2021). Online sexual harassment and depression in Chilean adolescents: Variations based on gender and age of the offenders. *Child Abuse & Neglect*, 120, 105219. DOI: 10.1016/j.chiabu.2021.105219 PMID: 34315004

Hare, R. D., & Neumann, C. S. (2008). Psychopathy as a clinical and empirical construct. *Annual Review of Clinical Psychology*, 4(1), 217–246. DOI: 10.1146/annurev.clinpsy.3.022806.091452 PMID: 18370617

Hatchel, T., Espelage, D. L., & Huang, Y. (2018). Sexual harassment victimization, school belonging, and depressive symptoms among LGBTQ adolescents: Temporal insights. *The American Journal of Orthopsychiatry*, 88(4), 422–430. DOI: 10.1037/ort0000279 PMID: 28617003

Hendricks, K., Tsibolane, P., & van Belle, J. P. (2020). Cyber-Harassment Victimization Among South African LGBTQIA+ Youth. *Responsible Design, Implementation and Use of Information and Communication Technology: 19th IFIP WG 6.11 Conference on e-Business, e-Services, and e-Society, I3E 2020, Skukuza, South Africa, April 6–8, 2020Proceedings*, 12067(Part II), 135–146. DOI: 10.1007/978-3-030-45002-1_12

Henry, N., & Powell, A. (2015). Beyond the "sext": Technology-facilitated sexual violence and harassment against adult women. *Australian and New Zealand Journal of Criminology*, 48(1), 104–118. DOI: 10.1177/0004865814524218

Henry, N., & Powell, A. (2016). Technology-Facilitated Sexual Violence: A Literature Review of Empirical Research. *Trauma, Violence & Abuse*, 19(2), 195–208. DOI: 10.1177/1524838016650189 PMID: 27311818

Holt, M. K., Vivolo-Kantor, A. M., Polanin, J. R., Holland, K. M., DeGue, S., Matjasko, J. L., Wolfe, M., & Reid, G. (2015). Bullying and suicidal ideation and behaviors: A meta-analysis. *Pediatrics*, 135(2), e496–e509. DOI: 10.1542/peds.2014-1864 PMID: 25560447

Howard, T. (2019). Sextortion: Psychological Effects Experienced and Seeking Help and Reporting Among Emerging Adults. *Walden Dissertations and Doctoral Studies*. Retrieved from: https://scholarworks.waldenu.edu/dissertations/6584

Kansok-Dusche, J., Ballaschk, C., Krause, N., Zeißig, A., Seemann-Herz, L., Wachs, S., & Bilz, L. (2023). A Systematic Review on Hate Speech among Children and Adolescents: Definitions, Prevalence, and Overlap with Related Phenomena. *Trauma, Violence & Abuse*, 24(4), 2598–2615. DOI: 10.1177/15248380221108070 PMID: 35731198

Karasavva, V., Brunet, L., Smodis, A., Swanek, J., & Forth, A. (2023). Putting the Y in cyberflashing: Exploring the prevalence and predictors of the reasons for sending unsolicited nude or sexual images. *Computers in Human Behavior*, 140, 107593. Advance online publication. DOI: 10.1016/j.chb.2022.107593

Karasavva, V., & Forth, A. (2022). Personality, attitudinal, and demographic predictors of non-consensual dissemination of intimate images. *Journal of Interpersonal Violence*, 37(21–22), NP19265–NP19289. DOI: 10.1177/08862605211043586 PMID: 34507500

Karasavva, V., & Noorbhai, A. (2021). The Real Threat of Deepfake Pornography: A Review of Canadian Policy. *Cyberpsychology, Behavior, and Social Networking*, 24(3), 203–209. DOI: 10.1089/cyber.2020.0272 PMID: 33760666

Klettke, B., Hallford, D. J., Clancy, E., Mellor, D. J., & Toumbourou, J. W. (2019). Sexting and Psychological Distress: The Role of Unwanted and Coerced Sexts. *Cyberpsychology, Behavior, and Social Networking*, 22(4), 237–242. DOI: 10.1089/cyber.2018.0291 PMID: 30855187

Lunde, C., & Joleby, M. (2023). Being Under Pressure to Sext: Adolescents' Experiences, Reactions, and Counter-Strategies. *Journal of Research on Adolescence*, 33(1), 188–201. DOI: 10.1111/jora.12797 PMID: 36059189

Madigan, S., Ly, A., Rash, C. L., Van Ouytsel, J., & Temple, J. R. (2018). Prevalence of Multiple Forms of Sexting Behavior Among Youth: A Systematic Review and Meta-analysis. *JAMA Pediatrics*, 172(4), 327–335. DOI: 10.1001/jamapediatrics.2017.5314 PMID: 29482215

Mainwaring, C., Scott, A. J., & Gabbert, F. (2023). Behavioural Intentions of Bystanders to Image-Based Sexual Abuse: A Preliminary Focus Group Study with a University Student Sample. *Journal of Child Sexual Abuse*, 32(3), 318–339. DOI: 10.1080/10538712.2023.2190734 PMID: 36921125

Malanga, D. (2020). *Tackling Gender-Based Cyber Violence against Women and Girls in Malawi Amidst the COVID-19 Pandemic*. African Internet Rights. Retrieved from: https://africaninternetrights.org/sites/default/files/Donald_ Flywell.pdf

Mandau, M. B. H. (2021). "Snaps", "screenshots", and self-blame: A qualitative study of image-based sexual abuse victimization among adolescent Danish girls. *Journal of Children and Media*, 15(3), 431–447. DOI: 10.1080/17482798.2020.1848892

March, E., & Wagstaff, D. L. (2017). Sending nudes: Sex, self-rated mate value, and trait Machiavellianism predict sending unsolicited explicit images. *Frontiers in Psychology*, 8, 2210. Advance online publication. DOI: 10.3389/fpsyg.2017.02210 PMID: 29326632

Mclocklin, G., Kellezi, B., Stevenson, C., & Mackay, J. (2024). Disclosure Decisions and Help-Seeking Experiences Amongst Victim-Survivors of Non-Consensual Intimate Image Distribution. *Victims & Offenders*, 1–27. DOI: 10.1080/15564886.2024.2329107

Megarry, J. (2014). Online incivility or sexual harassment? Conceptualising women's experiences in the digital age. *Women's Studies International Forum, 47*(PA), 46–55. DOI: 10.1016/j.wsif.2014.07.012

Michikyan, M., Lozada, F. T., Weidenbenner, J. V., & Tynes, B. M. (2014). Adolescent coping strategies in the face of their "worst online experience.". *International Journal of Gaming and Computer-Mediated Simulations*, 6(4), 1–16. DOI: 10.4018/ijgcms.2014100101

Mitchell, K., & Štulhofer, A. (2021). Online sexual harassment and negative mood in Croatian female adolescents. *European Child & Adolescent Psychiatry*, 30(2), 225–231. DOI: 10.1007/s00787-020-01506-7 PMID: 32162054

Mitchell, K. J., Ybarra, M. L., & Korchmaros, J. D. (2014). Sexual harassment among adolescents of different sexual orientations and gender identities. *Child Abuse & Neglect*, 38(2), 280–295. DOI: 10.1016/j.chiabu.2013.09.008 PMID: 24148274

Ndlovu, M., & Khupe, N. A. (2023). *Online Harassment of Journalists in Zimbabwe: Experiences, Coping Strategies and Implications*. 95–111. DOI: 10.1007/978-3-031-23625-9_6

Negi, C. (2023). An Overview of Worldwide Cyberbullying and Cyberviolence Against Women, Teenagers, LGBTQ on Social Media: Facebook, Instagram, Telegram, WhatsApp, Snapchat, YouTube, LinkedIn and Twitter. *SSRN*. Advance online publication. DOI: 10.2139/ssrn.4529613

Nilsson, M. G., Pepelasi, K. T., Ioannou, M., & Lester, D. (2019). Understanding the link between Sextortion and Suicide. *International Journal of Cyber Criminology*, 13(1), 55–69. https://pure.hud.ac.uk/en/publications/understanding-the-link-between-sextortion-and-suicide

Oswald, F., Lopes, A., Skoda, K., Hesse, C. L., & Pedersen, C. L. (2020). I'll show you mine so you'll show me yours: Motivations and personality variables in photographic exhibitionism. *Journal of Sex Research*, 57(5), 597–609. DOI: 10.1080/00224499.2019.1639036 PMID: 31318606

Pampati, S., Lowry, R., Moreno, M. A., Rasberry, C. N., & Steiner, R. J. (2020). Having a Sexual Photo Shared Without Permission and Associated Health Risks: A Snapshot of Nonconsensual Sexting. *JAMA Pediatrics*, 174(6), 618–619. DOI: 10.1001/jamapediatrics.2020.0028 PMID: 32202601

Parmar, S., & Dutt, S. (2024). Impact of Cyberbullying and Cyber Victimisation on Adolescents Well-being. *International Journal of Interdisciplinary Approaches in Psychology, 2*(5), 823-852. https://www.psychopediajournals.com/index.php/ijiap/article/view/366

Patchin, J. W., & Hinduja, S. (2018). Sextortion Among Adolescents: Results From a National Survey of U.S. *Youth*, 32(1), 30–54. DOI: 10.1177/1079063218800469 PMID: 30264657

Patchin, J. W., & Hinduja, S. (2020). Sextortion Among Adolescents: Results From a National Survey of U.S. Youth. *Sexual Abuse*, 32(1), 30–54. DOI: 10.1177/1079063218800469 PMID: 30264657

Patel, U., & Roesch, R. (2020). The Prevalence of Technology-Facilitated Sexual Violence: A Meta-Analysis and Systematic Review, *23*(2), 428–443. DOI: 10.1177/1524838020958057

Pedersen, W., Bakken, A., Stefansen, K., & von Soest, T. (2023). Sexual Victimization in the Digital Age: A Population-Based Study of Physical and Image-Based Sexual Abuse Among Adolescents. *Archives of Sexual Behavior*, 52(1), 399–410. DOI: 10.1007/s10508-021-02200-8 PMID: 35059946

Pew Research Center. (2014). *Online Harassment*. Retrieved from: https://www.pewresearch.org/internet/2014/10/22/online-harassment/

Pew Research Center. (2019). *Mobile Technology and Home Broadband 2019*. Retrieved from: https://www.pewresearch.org/internet/wp-content/uploads/sites/9/2019/06/PI_2019.06.13_Mobile-Technology-and-Home-Broadband_FINAL2.pdf

Pina, A., Bell, A., Griffin, K., & Vasquez, E. (2021). Image Based Sexual Abuse proclivity and victim blaming: The role of dark personality traits and moral disengagement. *Oñati Socio-Legal Series*, 11(5), 1179–1197. DOI: 10.35295/osls.iisl/0000-0000-0000-1213

Powell, A., & Henry, N. (2016). Technology-Facilitated Sexual Violence Victimization: Results From an Online Survey of Australian Adults. *Journal of Interpersonal Violence*, 34(17), 3637–3665. DOI: 10.1177/0886260516672055 PMID: 27697966

Powell, A., Henry, N., Flynn, A., & Scott, A. J. (2019). Image-based sexual abuse: The extent, nature, and predictors of perpetration in a community sample of Australian residents. *Computers in Human Behavior*, 92, 393–402. DOI: 10.1016/j.chb.2018.11.009

Powell, A., Scott, A. J., Flynn, A., & McCook, S. (2022). Perpetration of Image-Based Sexual Abuse: Extent, Nature and Correlates in a Multi-Country Sample. *Journal of Interpersonal Violence*, 37(23-24), NP22864–NP22889. DOI: 10.1177/08862605211072266 PMID: 35184577

Reed, E., Salazar, M., Behar, A. I., Agah, N., Silverman, J. G., Minnis, A. M., Rusch, M. L. A., & Raj, A. (2019). Cyber Sexual Harassment: Prevalence and association with substance use, poor mental health, and STI history among sexually active adolescent girls. *Journal of Adolescence, 75*, 53. DOI: 10.1016/j.adolescence.2019.07.005

Ringrose, J., Betsy, M., Tanya, H., & Kaitlynn, M. (2024). Postdigital Bodies: Young People's Experiences of Algorithmic, Tech-Facilitated Body Shaming and Image-Based Sexual Abuse during and after the COVID-19 Pandemic in England. *Youth*, 4(3), 1058–1075. DOI: 10.3390/youth4030066

Ringrose, J., Gill, R., Livingstone, S., & Harvey, L. (2012). *A qualitative study of children, young people and "sexting": a report prepared for the NSPCC*. National Society for the Prevention of Cruelty to Children. Retrieved from http://eprints.lse.ac.uk/id/eprint/44216

Runions, K. C., Salmivalli, C., Shaw, T., Burns, S., & Cross, D. (2018). Beyond the reactive-proactive dichotomy: Rage, revenge, reward, and recreational aggression predict early high school bully and bully/victim status. *Aggressive Behavior*, 44(5), 501–511. DOI: 10.1002/ab.21770 PMID: 29956340

Ruvalcaba, Y., & Eaton, A. A. (2020). Nonconsensual pornography among U.S. adults: A sexual scripts framework on victimization, perpetration, and health correlates for women and men. *Psychology of Violence*, 10(1), 68–78. DOI: 10.1037/vio0000233

Salerno-Ferraro, A. C., Erentzen, C., & Schuller, R. A. (2022). Young Women's Experiences With Technology-Facilitated Sexual Violence From Male Strangers. *Journal of Interpersonal Violence*, 37(19–20), NP17860–NP17885. DOI: 10.1177/08862605211030018 PMID: 34271829

Sciacca, B., Mazzone, A., Loftsson, M., O'Higgins Norman, J., & Foody, M. (2023). Nonconsensual Dissemination of Sexual Images Among Adolescents: Associations With Depression and Self-Esteem. *Journal of Interpersonal Violence*, 38(15-16), 9438–9464. DOI: 10.1177/08862605231165777 PMID: 37073923

Seewald, L., Walsh, T. B., Tolman, R. M., Lee, S. J., Reed, L. A., Ngo, Q., & Singh, V. (2022). Technology-facilitated abuse prevalence and associations among a nationally representative sample of young men. *Annals of Family Medicine*, 20(1), 12–17. DOI: 10.1370/afm.2758 PMID: 35074762

Shneyderman, Y., & Kiely, M. (2013). Intimate partner violence during pregnancy: Victim or perpetrator? Does it make a difference? *BJOG*, 120(11), 1375–1385. DOI: 10.1111/1471-0528.12357 PMID: 23786367

Ståhl, S., & Dennhag, I. (2021). Online and offline sexual harassment associations of anxiety and depression in an adolescent sample. *Nordic Journal of Psychiatry*, 75(5), 330–335. DOI: 10.1080/08039488.2020.1856924 PMID: 33347341

Strohmaier, H., Murphy, M., & DeMatteo, D. (2014). Youth sexting: Prevalence rates, driving motivations, and the deterrent effect of legal consequences. *Sexuality Research & Social Policy*, 11(3), 245–255. DOI: 10.1007/s13178-014-0162-9

Tanrikulu, I., & Erdur-Baker, Ö. (2021). Motives behind cyberbullying perpetration: A test of uses and gratifications theory. *Journal of Interpersonal Violence*, 36(13-14), NP6699–NP6724. DOI: 10.1177/0886260518819882 PMID: 30608015

Uttarapong, J., Cai, J., & Wohn, D. Y. Y. (2021). Harassment experiences of women and LGBTQ live streamers and how they handled negativity. *IMX 2021 - Proceedings of the 2021 ACM International Conference on Interactive Media Experiences*, 7–19. DOI: 10.1145/3452918.3458794

Van Ouytsel, J., Walrave, M., & Ponnet, K. (2019). An Exploratory Study of Sexting Behaviors Among Heterosexual and Sexual Minority Early Adolescents. *The Journal of Adolescent Health*, 65(5), 621–626. DOI: 10.1016/j.jadohealth.2019.06.003 PMID: 31473082

Wachs, S., Castellanos, M., Wettstein, A., Bilz, L., & Gámez-Guadix, M. (2023). Associations Between Classroom Climate, Empathy, Self-Efficacy, and Countering Hate Speech Among Adolescents: A Multilevel Mediation Analysis. *Journal of Interpersonal Violence*, 38(5-6), 5067–5091. DOI: 10.1177/08862605221120905 PMID: 36148972

Wachs, S., Gámez-Guadix, M., & Wright, M. F. (2022). Online Hate Speech Victimization and Depressive Symptoms Among Adolescents: The Protective Role of Resilience. *Cyberpsychology, Behavior, and Social Networking*, 25(7), 416–423. DOI: 10.1089/cyber.2022.0009 PMID: 35639126

Wang, F. (2024). Breaking the silence: Examining process of cyber sextortion and victims' coping strategies. *International Review of Victimology*. Advance online publication. DOI: 10.1177/02697580241234331

Wolak, J., Finkelhor, D., Walsh, W., & Treitman, L. (2018). Sextortion of Minors: Characteristics and Dynamics. *The Journal of Adolescent Health*, 62(1), 72–79. DOI: 10.1016/j.jadohealth.2017.08.014 PMID: 29055647

Ybarra, M. L., Mitchell, K. J., Palmer, N. A., & Reisner, S. L. (2015a). Online social support as a buffer against online and offline peer and sexual victimization among U.S. LGBT and non-LGBT youth. *Child Abuse & Neglect*, 39, 123–136. DOI: 10.1016/j.chiabu.2014.08.006 PMID: 25192961

Ybarra, M. L., Mitchell, K. J., Palmer, N. A., & Reisner, S. L. (2015b). Online social support as a buffer against online and offline peer and sexual victimization among U.S. LGBT and non-LGBT youth. *Child Abuse & Neglect, 39*, 123. DOI: 10.1016/j.chiabu.2014.08.006

Yount, K. M., Gram, L., & Peterman, A. (2024). Is intimate partner violence declining? It's still an open question. *The Lancet. Global Health*, 12(4), e559. DOI: 10.1016/S2214-109X(23)00599-5 PMID: 38485422

Zagloul, N. M., Farghaly, R. M., ELKhatib, H., Issa, S. Y., & El-Zoghby, S. M. (2022). Technology facilitated sexual violence: A comparative study between working and non-working females in Egypt before and during the COVID-19 pandemic. *Egyptian Journal of Forensic Sciences*, 12(1), 1–11. DOI: 10.1186/s41935-022-00278-2 PMID: 35433051

KEY TERMS AND DEFINITIONS

Cybervictimization: It refers to the experience of being harmed or exploited through digital means. It encompasses a range of offenses, including online harassment, fraud, and identity theft, that are perpetrated with technology.

Gendered Phenomenon: A social, cultural, or behavioural occurrence in which gender plays a significant role in shaping experiences, outcomes, or expectations

Non-Disclosure: The act of withholding or concealing information, often through formal agreements or unspoken understandings.

Revenge Porn: The online, sometimes offline, non-consensual distribution or sharing, of explicit images of someone else by ex-partners, partners, others or hackers seeking revenge or entertainment.

Sexting: The exchange of sexually suggestive messages, photos, or videos, typically through digital platforms. The term was used before IBSA.

Sextortion: A term that falls under the umbrella of Sexual Aggression and/or Coercion from TFSV. Sextortion is a criminal act involving the threat of disseminating sexually explicit material in exchange for financial gain, sexual favors, or other forms of compliance.

Solicitation: The act of seeking or requesting something, often with the implication of persuasive or persistent efforts.

Unsolicited Sexual Material: The transmission of sexually explicit content, such as images or messages, without the recipient's consent or desire.

ENDNOTES

1 Assistant Professor of Counselling Psychology, University of Ioannina, Ioannina, Greece, email: gkantona@uoi.gr

[2] Child & Adolescent Psychologist, Centre of Systemic Therapy & Counselling, Ioannina, Greece, email: f.ntagkas@gmail.com

[3] "r/" is the abbreviation for Reddit forums. R stands for the reddit platform. So accordingly, this Reddit thread was about experiences of people who were victims/survivors of sextortion.

Chapter 9
Decoding Adolescents' Internet Addiction, Academic Achievement, and Empathy Levels:
Untangling Complex Associations

Sena Meral
MEF University, Turkey

Servet Altan
https://orcid.org/0000-0001-6331-7556
MEF University, Turkey

ABSTRACT

This study explores the relationships between internet addiction, academic achievement, and empathy levels among 179 eighth-grade students. Using regression analyses, the research investigates how internet addiction impacts academic performance and empathy, and whether gender plays a role in internet addiction. Results indicate no statistically significant correlation between internet addiction and either academic achievement or empathy levels. However, a moderate positive correlation is found between empathy and academic performance. These findings suggest that internet addiction may not be a strong predictor of academic or empathic outcomes in adolescents. The study underscores the importance of promoting empathy to enhance academic success and highlights the need for balanced internet use. Future research should consider longitudinal designs and diverse samples to further explore these complex relationships. Implications for educational practices include integrating social-emotional learning programs to foster empathy and support students' overall well-being.

DOI: 10.4018/979-8-3693-4191-9.ch009

1. INTRODUCTION

The Internet has become a part of people's daily lives all over the world, and each innovation that becomes a part of people has a variety of psychological and social repercussions on them. The use of the internet for children aged 6 - 15 has started to increase rapidly in recent years. Technology use, which was 50.8% in 2013, increased to 82.7% in just 5 years (Nazanin, 2015). Although technology and the internet benefit human life when used appropriately, inappropriate, and excessive use causes internet addiction. Internet addiction has garnered increasing attention in recent years, particularly concerning its effects on adolescents' academic achievement and empathy levels. Since technology innovation is gradually gaining supremacy in todays' society, students' study habits are rapidly disappearing. Also, with the increasing reliance on the internet, children may not develop their empathetic skills appropriately.

Internet addiction, also known as problematic internet use or pathological internet use, refers to an excessive and compulsive use of the internet that interferes with an individual's daily life and responsibilities (Young, 1998). It is characterized by a preoccupation with internet activities, withdrawal symptoms when internet use is curtailed, and continued use despite negative consequences such as impaired social relationships, academic decline, or physical health issues. Internet addiction can manifest in various forms, including excessive gaming, social media use, or browsing, and is often associated with difficulties in regulating the amount of time spent online (Young, 1998). This chapter delves into the intricate relationships between internet addiction, academic success, and empathy levels among adolescents, seeking to uncover how these dimensions interact and influence each other in the context of contemporary digital environments.

1.1. Internet Addiction and Academic Achievement

A myriad of studies have examined the impact of internet addiction on students' academic performance. Findings from studies indicate in what ways internet addiction may deter students from excessive internet use and how internet use can be moderated in favor academic achievement. Guo et al. (2021) explored the association between emotional and behavioral problems and internet use among Chinese young adults, involving 30,581 undergraduates. The study found that emotional problems, conduct problems, hyperactivity, and peer problems were positively associated with prolonged internet use and problematic internet use (PIU), while prosocial behavior was negatively associated with internet use. Academic performance moderated these associations, with stronger associations found among students with poor academic performance. The findings suggest that interventions should focus on emotional and behavioral regulation and abnormal internet use, particularly for students with poor academic performance or emotional and behavioral problems (Guo, Shi, Du, Wang, Guo, & Lu, 2021).

Similarly, longitudinal research conducted by Lam and Peng (2010) over three years revealed a consistent negative correlation between internet addiction and academic achievement among adolescents. Similarly, meta-analytical findings by Tsitsika et al. (2014) confirmed a significant association between internet addiction and lower academic performance across diverse age groups and geographical locations. Zhang et al. (2018) studied the impact of internet addiction on academic achievement among Chinese adolescents, focusing on the mediating role of academic engagement. The study involved 2407 students and found that internet addiction negatively affects academic achievement through decreased academic engagement. The classroom achievement norm moderated the association between academic disaffection and achievement. The study suggests that interventions to increase engagement and improve classroom norms can mitigate the negative effects of internet addiction on academic achievement (Zhang, Qin, & Ren, 2018).

Kim (2011) explored the effects of internet use on the academic achievement and behavioral adjustment of South Korean adolescents, emphasizing parental influences. The study includes 609 10th and 11th graders from Seoul. Findings indicated that internet use for educational purposes positively correlates with academic achievement, while social and recreational use correlates negatively. The study also highlighted significant gender differences in internet use patterns, with girls more likely to engage in educational activities and boys more in gaming. The quality of parent-child relationships played a crucial role in moderating these effects, suggesting that strong parental involvement can mitigate the adverse impacts of non-educational internet use (Kim, 2011).

In another study by Lei et al. (2022), the intricate relationships between internet addiction, social isolation, and academic achievement among adolescents were investigated. Findings from this study revealed that academic engagement serves as a key mediator between internet addiction and academic performance. Furthermore, the study investigated the role of classroom achievement norms in moderating this relationship, discovering that in classrooms with high achievement norms, the negative effects of internet addiction on academic performance are less severe. Thus, fostering a high-achievement academic environment can help alleviate some of the detrimental effects of internet addiction on students' academic outcomes (Lei et al., 2022).

The literature consistently demonstrates a strong association between internet addiction and negative academic outcomes, such as academic procrastination and decreased achievement, particularly among adolescents and young adults. Aznar-Díaz et al. (2020) found that internet addiction significantly correlates with academic procrastination among university students in Mexico and Spain, with daily internet and electronic device use identified as key risk factors. Differences in problematic internet use (PIU) were noted between countries, emphasizing the need for further research to establish causal links and develop targeted interventions.

Similarly, Traş and Gökçen (2020) discovered that academic procrastination and social anxiety are significant predictors of internet addiction in high school students. The study indicated that students with high social anxiety are more prone to internet addiction, suggesting that anxiety related to evaluation in both social and online settings contributes to this behavior. The authors recommend larger sample sizes and qualitative methods to establish more reliable cause-and-effect relationships, underscoring the complex interplay between internet addiction, procrastination, and academic performance.

Demir and Kutlu (2018) further examined the impact of internet addiction on academic motivation, procrastination, and school attachment among adolescents. Findings from this study indicated higher levels of internet addiction correlate with lower academic motivation and increased academic procrastination, which negatively affect academic performance. However, the study also highlighted the protective role of school attachment, showing that adolescents who feel more connected to their school are less likely to suffer the negative academic consequences of internet addiction. This underscores the importance of fostering strong school attachment to mitigate the adverse effects of internet addiction.

The mechanisms underlying the relationship between adolescents' internet addiction and academic achievement have also been explored extensively. Kandell (1998) proposed that internet addiction can disrupt students' study habits and time management skills, leading to procrastination and reduced engagement in academic activities. Moreover, Morrison and Gore (2010) suggested that excessive internet use may exacerbate stress and anxiety levels, further compromising students' cognitive functioning and academic success. Additionally, theoretical models have highlighted the role of psychological factors in mediating the relationship between internet addiction and academic achievement. Zhou et al. (2011) proposed a model wherein internet addiction negatively influences self-regulation and motivation, ultimately impairing students' ability to concentrate and perform well academically. Karacic and Oreskovic (2017) further emphasized the detrimental effects of internet addiction on self-esteem and self-efficacy, which are essential determinants of academic success.

1.2. Internet Addiction and Empathy Levels

In addition to its impact on academic achievement, internet addiction has been implicated in the erosion of empathy levels among adolescents. Research by Yen et al. (2007) demonstrated that individuals with internet addiction exhibited lower levels of empathy compared to their non-addicted counterparts. Similarly, Kim et al. (2016) found a negative correlation between internet addiction and empathic concern among college students, highlighting the pervasive nature of this phenomenon across different age groups and educational settings.

Verrastro et al. (2021) examined these relationships across early and late adolescence, finding that empathy and social self-efficacy impact PIU and POG (Problematic Online Gaming) differently depending on the age group. The study, involving 1585 Italian students, highlights that PIU and POG decrease in late adolescence while empathic concern increases in the 15-17 age group. Empathy and social self-efficacy play distinct roles in the development of PIU and POG, with prosocial behaviors mediating the relationship between empathy and PIU/POG. The findings suggest that middle adolescence is a crucial period where significant transformations related to empathy, social self-efficacy, and prosocial behaviors take place. The study underscores the importance of age-specific prevention and intervention strategies to address PIU and POG among adolescents (Verrastro, Albanese, Ritella, Gugliandolo, & Cuzzocrea, 2021).

Servidio et al. (2019) conducted a study to explore the factors influencing Internet addiction among Italian adolescents and validated the Internet Related Experiences Questionnaire (IREQ-I) to assess Internet addiction risk. The research involved 838 Italian students and found that lower self-esteem and more time spent online were associated with a higher risk of Internet addiction. The study suggests that intrapersonal factors, such as self-esteem, are more associated with Internet abuse than interpersonal factors. The IREQ-I proved to be a valuable instrument for measuring Internet abuse, with implications for developing prevention strategies and educational programs for adolescents. The study emphasizes the need for an integrated conceptual framework that includes both intrapersonal and interpersonal conflicts to understand Internet addiction among adolescents (Servidio, Bartolo, Palermiti, Casas, Ruiz, & Costabile, 2019).

Kiss et al. (2020) further explored the risk and protective factors related to problematic internet and smartphone use. They conducted a study to identify user profiles based on risk and protective factors related to problematic internet and smartphone use among Hungarian youth. Using cluster analysis, the researchers identified four distinct user profiles characterized by varying levels of vulnerability and protection. Sensation seeking, boredom proneness, and flow experience were found to contribute to vulnerability, while self-esteem and self-regulation served as important protective factors. The study recommended cognitive-behavioral interventions to modify attitudes towards digital devices and emphasized the importance of self-esteem, self-regulation, and resilience in prevention efforts. However, the researchers noted the limitation of generalizability due to the online convenience sampling method used (Kiss, Fitzpatrick, & Piko, 2020).

Yen et al. (2007) and Kim et al. (2016) provided evidence that internet addiction negatively impacts empathy levels among adolescents. Yen et al. (2007) found that individuals with internet addiction exhibited lower levels of empathy compared to their non-addicted counterparts. Similarly, Kim et al. (2016) identified a negative correlation between internet addiction and empathic concern among college students, highlighting the pervasive nature of this phenomenon across different age groups and educational settings. These findings underscore the detrimental impact of excessive internet use on adolescents' empathic abilities.

Theoretical perspectives suggest that excessive internet use may undermine the development of empathy by reducing opportunities for face-to-face interactions and interpersonal communication (Nie & Erbring, 2002). As individuals immerse themselves in virtual environments, they may become desensitized to others' emotions and less adept at understanding and sharing their feelings, thereby diminishing their empathic abilities. Furthermore, the content and context of online activities have been implicated in shaping individuals' empathic responses. Anderson et al. (2010) demonstrated that exposure to violent video games and antisocial online behaviors can desensitize individuals to real-life emotions and interpersonal relationships, fostering a culture of indifference and apathy. Kraut et al. (1998) further highlighted the role of social media in promoting superficial interactions and shallow relationships, which may impede the development of genuine empathy and compassion among adolescents.

The literature provides compelling evidence of the detrimental impact of internet addiction on students' academic achievement and empathy levels. Excessive internet use has been associated with lower academic performance, impaired study habits, and diminished empathic abilities among adolescents. Understanding these relationships is crucial for developing targeted interventions and educational programs aimed at promoting healthy digital behaviors and enhancing students' overall well-being.

1.3. The present study

The purpose of the current investigation was to expand our understanding of the reciprocal relationships among adolescents' internet addiction, academic achievement, and empathy levels. We conducted this investigation in private and public schools located in İstanbul, Türkiye. Our research was guided by the following questions:

1. To what extent students' internet addiction impacts their academic achievement?
2. To what extent students' internet addiction impacts their empathy levels?
3. What role does gender play in internet addiction among adolescents, if any?

We hypothesized that as internet addiction increases, academic achievement would decrease. Similarly, we hypothesized that increase in internet addiction would lead to lower levels of empathy. We also hypothesized that gender would play a role in internet addiction.

2. METHODS

2.1. Participants

Participants for this study were selected based on their willingness to participate and parent approval as they were under the age of 18 by the time of study. Researchers had no particular criteria apart from studying at 8th grade. Invitations to private and public schools located in İstanbul, Türkiye were sent and overall, a total of 179, 8th-grade students participated in this study comprising self-identified 82 female and 97 male students. The mean age for both female ($M = 13.1$, SD = 0.445) and male ($M = 13.1$, SD = 0.522) participants was 13.1 years. Data from all participants was analyzed apart from participant 108's data, which deemed unanalysable, was excluded from the dataset.

2.2. Measures

Demographic Information Form. The demographic form was used to learn about participants' age, gender, school, and CGPA (which belongs to 7th grade), which demonstrate academic achievement.

Internet Addiction Test (IAT). The Turkish version of the Internet Addiction Test was used to measure students' internet addiction. IAT is the most used scale among all internet addiction scales (Boysan et al., 2017). It was originally developed by Kimberly Young (1998) and translated into Turkish. It is a symptom-measuring tool. IAT consists of 20 items, and it is a six-point Likert-type scale with high internal consistency ($\alpha = 0.93$). There are questions such as "Do you neglect household chores to spend more time online?'' 50 points or above has been proposed as indicating problematic internet use, and 80 or above as pathological use. IAT typically indicates strong reliability and validity for the scale (Boysan et al., 2017).

Adolescent Measure of Empathy and Sympathy (AMES). The Adolescent Measure of Empathy and Sympathy (AMES) is a questionnaire used to assess sympathy and empathy in adolescents. It has 12 items and is scored on a five-point Likert scale. The Cronbach's alpha (α) reliability coefficients ranged between 0.63 and 0.75 for three subscales that were used to construct AMES. AMES is considered as a reliable and valid measurement tool of empathy and sympathy for Turkish adolescents (Zengin et al., 2017). It provides a significant advantage compared to existing measurement tools by distinguishing affective empathy, cognitive empathy and sympathy. There are questions such as ''When my friend is sad, I become sad too''.

Data collection

The data collection process commenced with the selection of schools for study implementation. A parental approval letter was distributed to all 8th-grade students in the designated private and public schools located in İstanbul. The letter explicitly communicated that the study posed no physical, emotional, or psychological harm to the students. Parents were informed that participation was voluntary, and their child's information would remain anonymous. Additionally, it was emphasized that students could withdraw from the study at any point, and collected data could be promptly expunged from the system. Participants were selectively taken from their classes with approval from the designated educator for that class. Subsequently, the specified inventories were administered to each group. Initially, participants completed the Demographic Information Form. Subsequently, the Internet Addiction Test (IAT) was administered in the second stage, followed by the third stage involving the Adolescent Measure of Empathy and Sympathy Test (AMES).

2.3. Data Analysis

Data analysis in this study involved the use of regression analysis to explore the relationships between internet addiction and two distinct outcome variables: academic achievement and empathy levels among adolescents. The analytical process began with the systematic entry of raw data into Microsoft Excel following the completion of the initial data collection phase. This raw data was meticulously coded to facilitate analysis. Subsequently, the coded dataset was imported into the statistical software IBM SPSS Version 26 for further examination.

Before proceeding with regression analysis, a thorough check for normality was conducted to ensure that the data met the necessary assumptions for valid statistical testing. Separate regression analyses were then performed to investigate the specific relationships between internet addiction and each of the two outcome variables: academic achievement and empathy levels.

The decision to conduct separate regression analyses was intentional, allowing for a detailed understanding of how internet addiction impacts each outcome variable independently. This approach provided insights into the distinct ways in which internet addiction may influence academic performance and levels of empathy among adolescents. By analyzing these relationships separately, we aimed to elucidate the nuanced effects of internet addiction on these critical aspects of adolescent development.

3. RESULTS

This section presents and discusses the main results of this study; what is IA's impact on academic achievement, if there is a relationship between IA and empathy and what is the role of gender in IA. Three hypotheses were tested; (1) as internet addiction increases, academic achievement would decrease, (2) increase in internet addiction would lead to lower levels of empathy, and (3) gender would play a role in internet addiction.

3.1. Relationship between internet addiction and academic achievement

In order to investigate the impact of IA on participants' academic achievement, first the model was checked.

Table 1. Model Summary

Model	R	R Square	Adjusted R Square	Std. Error of the Estimate
1	.056	.003	-.002	11.29085

The correlation coefficient, indicating a very weak positive correlation ($R = .056$) between internet addiction (IAT) and grades. Only 0.3% of the variance in grades is explained by the IAT scores. This is very low, indicating that IAT is not a strong predictor of grades. The adjusted R Square (-.002) corrects the R Square for the number of predictors in the model. Here, it slightly decreases, suggesting that the predictor (IAT) does not improve the model's fit.

Table 2. ANOVA Table

Model	Sum of Squares	df	Mean Square	F	Sig.
1	71.704	1	71.704	.562	.454
Residual	22692.046	178	127.483		
Total	22763.750	179			

The F-test determines whether the model is a good fit for the data. Here, the p-value is 0.454, which is greater than 0.05, indicating that the model is not statistically significant. Therefore, IAT does not significantly predict grades.

Table 3. Coefficients Table

Model	Unstandardized Coefficients (B)	Std. Error	Standardized Coefficients (Beta)	*t*	Sig.
1	(Constant) 86.199	2.312		37.277	.000
IAT	-.843	1.124	-.056	-.750	.454

When the IAT score is zero, the expected grade is 86.199. This value is statistically significant. For each one-unit increase in the IAT score, the grade decreases by 0.843 units on average. However, this result is not statistically significant ($p = .454$). Based on these results, there is no statistically significant evidence to support the hypothesis that internet addiction (IAT) impacts academic achievement (grades).

3.2. Relationship Between Internet Addiction and Empathy Levels

In order to investigate the impact of IA on participants' empathy levels, first the model was checked.

Table 4. Model Summary

Model	R	R Square	Adjusted R Square	Std. Error of the Estimate
1	.095	.009	.003	.57217

The correlation coefficient (R) indicates a very weak negative correlation (.095) between internet addiction (IAT) and empathy levels (AMES). This means that only 0.9% of the variance in empathy levels is explained by the IAT scores. This is very low, indicating that IAT is not a strong predictor of empathy levels. The adjusted R Square corrects the R Square for the number of predictors in the model. Here, it slightly decreases (.003), suggesting that the predictor (IAT) does not improve the model's fit significantly.

Table 5. ANOVA Table

Model	Sum of Squares	df	Mean Square	F	Sig.
1	.528	1	.528	1.613	.206
Residual	58.273	178	.327		
Total	58.801	179			

The F-test determined whether the model is a good fit for the data. Here, the p-value is 0.206, which is greater than 0.05, indicating that the model is not statistically significant. Therefore, IAT does not significantly predict empathy levels.

Table 6. Coefficients Table

Model	Unstandardized Coefficients (B)	Std. Error	Standardized Coefficients	*t*	Sig.
1	(Constant) 3.613	.117		30.830	.000
IAT	-.072	.057	-.095	-1.270	.206

When the IAT score is zero, the expected empathy level is 3.613. This value is statistically significant. For each one-unit increase in the IAT score, the empathy level decreases by 0.072 units on average. However, this result is not statistically significant ($p = .206$). Based on these results, there is no statistically significant evidence to support the hypothesis that internet addiction (IAT) impacts empathy levels (AMES).

3.3. The Role of Gender in Internet Addiction Among Adolescents

In order to find out the role of gender in internet addiction, we conducted one-way ANOVA and investigated coefficients.

Table 7. ANOVA analysis

ANOVA	Sum of Squares	df	Mean Square	F	Sig.
Regression	1.001	1	1.001	1.784	.183
Residual	99.928	178	.561		
Total	100.929	179			

The regression model is not statistically significant ($F = 1.784$, $p = .183$), suggesting that Gender does not significantly predict internet addiction scores.

Table 8. Coefficients table

Coefficients	Unstandardized Coefficients	Standardized Coefficients	*t*	Sig.
Constant	1.689		9.428	< .001
Gender	.147	.100	1.336	.183

The coefficient of .147 suggests that, on average, being in a different gender category (if coded as 0 and 1) is associated with an increase of .147 units in IAT scores, but this effect is not statistically significant ($t = 1.336$, $p = .183$). Overall, gender does not appear to have a statistically significant effect on internet addiction scores (IAT) among adolescents in your dataset. This conclusion is supported by both the regression analysis ($p = .183$) and bootstrap results ($p = .214$).

3.4. Correlation Analyses

As looking for correlations between dependent and your independent variable could provide additional insights, especially if regression results are not significant, we further investigated the correlations between our variables.

Table 9. Correlation matrix

	Internet Addiction (IAT)	Empathy (AMES)	Academic Achievement (Grade)
Internet Addiction (IAT)	1.00	-.095	-.056
Empathy (AMES)	-.095	1.00	.320**
Academic Achievement (Grade)	-.056	.320**	1.00

Notes. ** indicates that the correlation is significant at the 0.01 level (2-tailed).

There is a very weak negative correlation between Internet Addiction and Empathy. However, this relationship is not statistically significant ($p > .05$), indicating that there is no strong evidence to suggest a linear relationship between these variables in the population. There is a very weak negative correlation between Internet Addiction and Academic Achievement. This relationship is also not statistically significant ($p > .05$), suggesting no strong evidence of a linear relationship between these variables. There is a moderate positive correlation between Empathy and Academic Achievement, which is statistically significant ($p < .01$). This suggests that higher empathy levels are associated with higher academic achievement.

Finally, findings obtained from participants who underwent the Internet Addiction Test provided us valuable insights. Scoring in IAT is conducted sequentially as 0, 1, 2, 3, 4, 5. Accumulating a total score of 80 or above is defined as "Pathological Internet Use" Scores ranging from 50 to 79 are categorized as "Problematic Internet Use" while individuals scoring 49 or below are classified as "Average Internet Users" without experiencing issues related to internet use. Based on the IAT scores, 41 out of 179 participants were classified as exhibiting "Problematic Internet Use," while the remaining participants fell within the category of "Average Internet Users". There were no instances of pathological usage identified. The maximum score observed is 79, which is one point below the threshold indicative of pathological use and the minimum score is 4.

4. DISCUSSION

The primary objective of this study was to explore the intricate relationships between adolescents' internet addiction, academic achievement, and empathy levels. Despite the statistically non-significant findings in the regression analyses, the study offers valuable insights into the dynamics of these variables.

4.1. Internet Addiction and Academic Achievement

The results indicated a very weak and non-significant relationship between internet addiction and academic achievement. This finding contrasts with several previous studies, such as those by Lam and Peng (2010) and Tsitsika et al. (2014), which reported significant negative correlations between these variables. The weak correlation suggests that other factors might be influencing academic performance more strongly than internet addiction in this sample. This could include variables such as socio-economic status, parental involvement, and intrinsic motivation, which were not controlled for in this study.

4.2. Internet Addiction and Empathy Levels

Similarly, the relationship between internet addiction and empathy levels was found to be very weak and non-significant. This result is not in line with previous research, such as Yen et al. (2007) and Kim et al. (2016), which highlighted significant negative correlations. The non-significant findings might be attributed to the cultural context of the study, as cultural differences can impact both internet usage patterns and the expression of empathy. Additionally, the use of self-report measures might have introduced bias, as participants could have underreported their internet addiction or overestimated their empathy levels.

The correlation analyses revealed a significant positive [moderate] correlation between empathy and academic achievement, suggesting that students with higher empathy levels tend to perform better academically. This finding aligns with previous research indicating that social-emotional skills, including empathy, contribute to better academic outcomes (Elias & Weissberg, 2000).

4.3. Gender and Internet Addiction

The study also found no significant effect of gender on internet addiction, which aligns with some studies but contradicts others that suggest gender differences in internet usage patterns. The lack of significant findings here could be due to the relatively balanced gender distribution in the sample or other moderating variables not accounted for in this study, such as the type of internet activities engaged in by boys and girls.

4.4. Implications

Despite the non-significant regression results, this study has several important implications for educators, policymakers, and researchers. Given the significant [moderate] correlation between empathy and academic achievement, educational programs that foster empathy and other social-emotional skills might indirectly improve academic outcomes.

Educational programs that integrate social-emotional learning (SEL) into curricula can significantly enhance academic performance and overall student well-being (Elias & Weissberg, 2000). Schools should incorporate SEL programs that focus on developing empathy, self-regulation, and interpersonal skills. Additionally, implementing workshops and activities specifically designed to cultivate empathy among students, such as role-playing, perspective-taking exercises, and community service projects, can effectively enhance empathy.

It is crucial to differentiate between educational and non-educational internet use. Promoting positive internet use through educational initiatives that emphasize the benefits of using the internet for research, collaborative learning, and accessing educational content can mitigate the negative impacts of internet addiction on academic achievement (Zhang et al., 2018). Schools and parents should work together to monitor and manage students' screen time, ensuring a balance between online and offline activities. Programs that teach time management skills and self-regulation can help students use the internet responsibly.

Addressing internet addiction and academic procrastination requires the development of early intervention programs to identify and support students at risk. Counseling services, digital detox programs, and workshops on effective study habits can be beneficial (Díaz et al., 2020). Providing additional academic support, such as tutoring and study groups, can help students struggling with procrastination and poor time management. Creating a supportive academic environment can encourage better study habits and reduce dependency on the internet for leisure (Gökçen, 2020).

Interventions should be tailored to the cultural context of the students. Understanding cultural differences in internet usage patterns, empathy expression, and academic motivations can help design more effective and relevant programs (Servidio et al., 2019). Encouraging cross-cultural research to explore how different cultural contexts influence the relationships between internet addiction, academic achievement, and empathy can help develop universal strategies while acknowledging local specificities.

While this study found no significant gender differences in internet addiction, other studies suggest that boys and girls may engage in different types of online activities. Tailoring interventions to address these differences can be more effective in mitigating internet addiction and promoting healthy internet use habits (Díaz et al., 2020). Schools should adopt inclusive policies that address the diverse needs of all students, considering gender differences in internet use and its impact on academic and social-emotional development.

Future research directions include conducting longitudinal studies to better understand the causal relationships between internet addiction, academic achievement, and empathy. This can provide deeper insights into how these variables interact over time and inform more effective intervention strategies. Utilizing qualitative research methods to explore students' personal experiences and perspectives on internet use, academic challenges, and empathy can uncover nuanced insights that quantitative data alone may not reveal. Collaborating across disciplines, including psychology, education, and technology, can help develop comprehensive strategies addressing the multifaceted nature of internet addiction and its impacts.

By implementing these practical ideas and recommendations, educators and policymakers can better support students in managing their internet use, enhancing their academic performance, and fostering essential social-emotional skills.

4.5. Limitations

Several limitations should be noted. The sample size, while adequate, limits the generalizability of the findings. Future studies should include larger, more diverse samples to enhance the robustness and applicability of the results. The use of self-report questionnaires may introduce response biases, such as social desirability or inaccurate self-assessment. Incorporating multiple methods of assessment, including behavioral measures and reports from parents or teachers, could provide a more comprehensive picture. The cross-sectional nature of the study precludes any conclusions about causality. Longitudinal studies are needed to better understand the temporal relationships between internet addiction, academic achievement, and empathy. Important variables such as socio-economic status, parental involvement, and the quality of internet use were not controlled for, which could have influenced the results. Future research should consider these factors to provide a more detailed understanding of the relationships studied.

5. CONCLUSION

The digital age presents a complex landscape for adolescents, offering both substantial opportunities and notable challenges. This study's findings imply that the direct impact of internet addiction on academic and empathic outcomes might be less pronounced than previously assumed. Rather than focusing exclusively on mitigating internet addiction, it is crucial to promote balanced and constructive internet use. Encouraging healthy online behaviors, combined with fostering empathy and addressing a range of factors influencing academic and emotional development, should be prioritized.

Educators, parents, and policymakers can adopt a holistic approach to support adolescents. This includes integrating SEL programs that enhance empathy, self-regulation, and interpersonal skills into the educational curriculum. Additionally, initiatives that promote balanced internet use and effective time management can help students navigate the digital landscape more responsibly. Schools and families should collaborate to create environments that balance online and offline activities, providing students with the skills needed to thrive in both realms.

Future research should address the limitations of this study, including the need for more diverse and representative samples, and explore these relationships across different cultural and socio-economic contexts. Longitudinal studies could offer deeper insights into the long-term effects of internet use on academic and emotional development. Moreover, qualitative research methods could reveal more nuanced understandings of how adolescents experience and manage internet use, academic pressures, and empathy. By examining these factors across various settings and populations, researchers can develop more comprehensive and context-sensitive strategies to support adolescent development in the digital age.

Ultimately, by focusing on promoting empathy, balanced internet use, and a broad range of developmental factors, stakeholders can better equip adolescents to achieve academic success and emotional well-being. A comprehensive and informed approach will help navigate the complexities of the digital world, supporting adolescents in their growth and development as they face the unique challenges and opportunities of the 21st century.

REFERENCES

Anderson, C. A., Shibuya, A., Ihori, N., Swing, E. L., Bushman, B. J., Sakamoto, A., Rothstein, H. R., & Saleem, M. (2010). Violent video game effects on aggression, empathy, and prosocial behavior in Eastern and Western countries: A meta-analytic review. *Psychological Bulletin*, 136(2), 151–173. DOI: 10.1037/a0018251 PMID: 20192553

Aznar-Díaz, I., Romero-Rodríguez, J.-M., García-González, A., & Ramírez-Montoya, M.-S. (2020). Mexican and Spanish university students' Internet addiction and academic procrastination: Correlation and potential factors. *PLoS One*, 15(5), e0233655. DOI: 10.1371/journal.pone.0233655 PMID: 32442238

Chen, P.-C., & Chen, Y.-H. (2023). Social media addiction and academic engagement as serial mediators between social anxiety and academic performance among college students. *BMC Psychology*, 11, 144. DOI: 10.1186/s40359-023-01110-2

Corp, I. B. M. (2019). *IBM SPSS Statistics for Windows (Version 26.0)* [Computer software]. IBM Corp.

Demir, Y., & Kutlu, M. (2018). The relationship among internet addiction, academic motivation, academic procrastination and school attachment in adolescents. *International Online Journal of Educational Sciences*, 9(3), 65–78. DOI: 10.15345/iojes.2018.05.020

Guo, L., Shi, G., Du, X., Wang, W., Guo, Y., & Lu, C. (2021). Associations of emotional and behavioral problems with Internet use among Chinese young adults: The role of academic performance. *Journal of Affective Disorders*, 287, 214–221. DOI: 10.1016/j.jad.2021.03.050 PMID: 33799040

Kandell, J. J. (1998). Internet addiction on campus: The vulnerability of college students. *Cyberpsychology & Behavior*, 1(1), 11–17. DOI: 10.1089/cpb.1998.1.11

Karacic, S., & Oreskovic, S. (2017). Internet addiction through the phase of adolescence: A questionnaire study. *JMIR Mental Health*, 4(2), e11. DOI: 10.2196/mental.5537 PMID: 28373154

Kim, J. U., Kim, Y. J., & Choi, S. H. (2016). The effect of internet addiction on college students' empathy: The mediating effects of social support. *Journal of the Korean Data Analysis Society*, 18(4), 1995–2007. DOI: 10.30773/pi.2018.08.07.2

Kim, S. (2011). *Effects of internet use on academic achievement and behavioral adjustment among South Korean adolescents: Mediating and moderating roles of parental factors* (Doctoral dissertation, Syracuse University).

Kiss, H., Fitzpatrick, K. M., & Piko, B. F. (2020). The digital divide: Risk and protective factors and the differences in problematic use of digital devices among Hungarian youth. *Children and Youth Services Review*, 108, 104612. DOI: 10.1016/j.childyouth.2019.104612

Kormas, G., Critselis, E., Janikian, M., Kafetzis, D., & Tsitsika, A. (2011). Risk factors and psychosocial characteristics of potential problematic and problematic internet use among adolescents: A cross-sectional study. *BMC Public Health*, 11(1), 595. DOI: 10.1186/1471-2458-11-595 PMID: 21794167

Kraut, R., Patterson, M., Lundmark, V., Kiesler, S., Mukopadhyay, T., & Scherlis, W. (1998). Internet paradox: A social technology that reduces social involvement and psychological well-being? *The American Psychologist*, 53(9), 1017–1031. DOI: 10.1037/0003-066X.53.9.1017 PMID: 9841579

Lam, L. T., & Peng, Z. W. (2010). Effect of pathological use of the internet on adolescent mental health: A prospective study. *Archives of Pediatrics & Adolescent Medicine*, 164(10), 901–906. DOI: 10.1001/archpediatrics.2010.159 PMID: 20679157

Lam, L. T., & Wong, E. M. Y. (2015). Stress Moderates the Relationship Between Problematic Internet Use by Parents and Problematic Internet Use by Adolescents. *The Journal of Adolescent Health*, 56(3), 300–306. DOI: 10.1016/j.jadohealth.2014.10.263 PMID: 25703319

Liao, H., Lei, L., Wang, Y., & Huang, X. (2022). Exploring the relationship between internet addiction, social isolation, and academic achievement in adolescents: A study in China. *International Journal of Environmental Research and Public Health*, 19(3), 1243. DOI: 10.3390/ijerph19031243 PMID: 35162266

Morrison, C. M., & Gore, H. (2010). The relationship between excessive internet use and depression: A questionnaire-based study of 1,319 young people and adults. *Psychopathology*, 43(2), 121–126. DOI: 10.1159/000277001 PMID: 20110764

Nie, N. H., & Erbring, L. (2002). Internet and society: A preliminary report. *ITandSociety*, 1(1), 275–283.

Restrepo, A., Scheininger, T., Clucas, J., Alexander, L., Salum, G. A., Georgiades, K., Paksarian, D., Merikangas, K. R., & Milham, M. P. (2020). Problematic internet use in children and adolescents: Associations with psychiatric disorders and impairment. *BMC Psychiatry*, 20(1), 252. DOI: 10.1186/s12888-020-02640-x PMID: 32456610

Servidio, R., Bartolo, M. G., Palermiti, A. L., Casas, J. A., Ruiz, R. O., & Costabile, A. (2019). Internet addiction, self-esteem and the validation of the Italian version of the Internet Related Experiences Questionnaire. *European Review of Applied Psychology*, 69(2), 51–58. DOI: 10.1016/j.erap.2019.03.003

Traş, Z., & Gökçen, G. (2020). Academic Procrastination and Social Anxiety as Predictive Variables Internet Addiction of Adolescents. *International Education Studies*, 13(9), 23–35. DOI: 10.5539/ies.v13n9p23

Tsitsika, A., Janikian, M., Schoenmakers, T. M., Tzavela, E. C., Ólafsson, K., Wójcik, S., Macarie, G. F., Tzavara, C., & Richardson, C. (2014). Internet addictive behavior in adolescence: A cross-sectional study in seven European countries. *Cyberpsychology, Behavior, and Social Networking*, 17(8), 528–535. DOI: 10.1089/cyber.2013.0382 PMID: 24853789

Verrastro, V., Albanese, C. A., Ritella, G., Gugliandolo, M. C., & Cuzzocrea, F. (2021). Empathy, Social Self-Efficacy, Problematic Internet Use, and Problematic Online Gaming Between Early and Late Adolescence. *Cyberpsychology, Behavior, and Social Networking*, 24(12), 806–814. DOI: 10.1089/cyber.2021.0042 PMID: 34515543

Yen, J. Y., Ko, C. H., Yen, C. F., Wu, H. Y., & Yang, M. J. (2007). The comorbid psychiatric symptoms of internet addiction: Attention deficit and hyperactivity disorder (ADHD), depression, social phobia, and hostility. *The Journal of Adolescent Health*, 41(1), 93–98. DOI: 10.1016/j.jadohealth.2007.02.002 PMID: 17577539

Young, K. S. (1998). Internet addiction: The emergence of a new clinical disorder. *Cyberpsychology & Behavior*, 1(3), 237–244. DOI: 10.1089/cpb.1998.1.237

Zengin, H., Çaka, Y. S., & Çınar, N. (2017). AMES is a reliable and valid measurement tool of empathy and sympathy for Turkish adolescents. It provides a significant advantage compared to existing measurement tools by distinguishing affective empathy, cognitive empathy and sympathy. *Anatolian Journal of Psychiatry*, 19(2), 184–192. DOI: 10.5455/apd.262004

Zhang, Y., Qin, X., & Ren, P. (2018). Adolescents' academic engagement mediates the association between Internet addiction and academic achievement: The moderating effect of classroom achievement norm. *Computers in Human Behavior*, 89, 299–307. DOI: 10.1016/j.chb.2018.08.018

Chapter 10

Unfolding the Association Between the Multiple Determinants of Sexting Behaviors and Relationship Satisfaction in University Students: Theoretical and Clinical Implications

Panagiotis Parpottas
https://orcid.org/0000-0002-4448-6589
European University Cyprus, Cyprus

Iliada Spyrou
Cyprus Social Welfare Services, Cyprus

ABSTRACT

Technological advances have brought a revolution in communication, which in turn has influenced many aspects of personal relationships. According to the literature, young adults utilize the newest technological means in their communications and sexting has become a frequent means of sexual communication in romantic relationships. On the one hand, sexting is captured as a tremendous concern due to its possible negative effects on individual and relational level, but on the other, it is seen as part of normal sexual development which could also promote partners' sexuality and satisfaction. The aim of this chapter is to build on the existing literature to explore the determinants of sexting, as well as the effects of sexting on romantic relationships, by focusing on young university adults. The chapter will conclude with implications for education, clinical practice, and policy, which could facilitate practitioners' work, as well as others who directly and indirectly relate to young university students.

DOI: 10.4018/979-8-3693-4191-9.ch010

INTRODUCTION

With the rapid growth of technology, people are directed to utilize the newest means of communication in almost all facets of their lives. The literature suggests that, primarily young adults among other populations, use the communication technology in their personal interactions (Olson et al., 2011; Vasilescu et al., 2020). Furthermore, as changes have been observed in the use of communication, it can be argued that the dynamics, the trajectories and even the qualities of personal relationships, may have been reformed. In the face of technological advancements in communication, romantic relationships have not remained unaffected (Goodman-Dean et al., 2016; Gomes et al., 2021; Weiss & Samenow, 2010).

Communication can have a large impact on the quality of a romantic relationship and more researchers and clinicians nowadays aim to explore the use of technology on relational communication, as well as the consequences of a technological assisted communication on relationship satisfaction (Lapierre & Custer, 2021; Vauclair et al., 2023). More specifically, an aspect of communication which is conditioned by technology and gathers important research and clinical interest, is sexual communication. Sexual communication is a way of exploring one's sexual identity and also the expression of sexual interests to partners and/or potential partners (Šmahel & Subrahmanyam, 2014; Valkenburg & Peter, 2007, 2009; Walrave et al., 2015).

With the increased use and advancements of technology, sexting has become a frequent mean of sexual communication and exploration, mainly within the adolescent and young adult population (Agustina & Gómez-Durán, 2012; Drouin, 2015; Morelli et al., 2023; Walrave et al., 2015). Additionally, it looks that sexting has rapidly become part of the dating process (Lenhart, 2009; Van Ouytsel et al., 2020) and is even frequently featured in popular media as a mean which could improve relationship and sexual satisfaction but also romantic relationship dynamics in general (Beckmeyer 2024; Fratti, 2018; Roth, 2015). Nevertheless, more evidence is needed to empirically support and test such claims, considering several factors on both individual (e.g., personality characteristics, demographics, relational patterns etc.) and context specific levels (e.g., sociocultural influences, content and motivations of sexting, type and status of romantic relationship and satisfaction types). Furthermore, researchers' interests are directed in exploring sexting as a method of developing and communicating sexual interests. On the one hand, the attention of the literature has initially captured sexting as a major concern due to its possible negative psychological and social effects (Currin et al., 2017; Day, 2010; Richards & Calvert, 2009), with the most recognized risks associated to sexual exploitation, the legality of exchanging sexually explicit photos/videos without the consent of both involved adults and also its link to potential sexual harassment and digital sexual victimization (Ross et al., 2019; Strassberg et al., 2013). On the other hand, sexting can be seen as part of normal sexual development and research suggested that consensual sexting may provide free expression and sexual exploration which could promote partners' sexuality and even relationship satisfaction (Beckmeyer, 2024; Gordon-Messer et al., 2013; Le et al., 2023).

Although several studies explore the phenomenon of sexting (Mori et al., 2020), less research has thoroughly investigated the positive and negative impacts of sexting on university students' relationship satisfaction. Additionally, there is limited research referring to the use of sexting as a method of sexual exploration in promoting relational satisfaction or as an intervention which might be a beneficial therapeutic strategy to increase affection and connectedness in intimate relationships (Parker et al., 2013). Thus, the available literature does not assure full comprehension of the effects of sexting in romantic relationships among the general young adult population.

The aim of this chapter is to build on the existing literature and understand the determinants of sexting as well as the effects of sexting on romantic relationships by focusing on young university adults. Initially, we will introduce the concept of sexting and its relevant behaviors and attitudes. Then, appropriate links between theory and research will be provided in order to recognize the motivations and determinants of sexting but also the characteristic patterns of individuals who are involved in sexting. Furthermore, we will draw on recent research evidence to understand sexting and its effects on relationship satisfaction among young adult university students. Given that the scope of our chapter targets a specific population, we will only use studies representing young heterosexual adults and limit our focus within the context of romantic relationships. Although we scarcely use studies relevant to other populations, characteristics and contexts (i.e., children, adolescent, non-heterosexual partners, individuals with disabilities, casual relationships and non-university students), we will explicitly mention them when available. Ultimately, this chapter will present valuable clinical implications from which, practitioners who work with university students could draw upon to inform prevention strategies and their interventions, with the purpose of facilitating reflection and even enhancing a safer utilization of sexting in romantic relationships. Moreover, we believe that some considerations for addressing sexting behaviors may also be informative for others who relate to university students.

As noted earlier, research concerning possible links between sexting and relationship satisfaction is limited. Additionally, although it is widely agreed that young adults are most likely to engage in sexting behaviors and use technology more often in romantic relationships, the majority of the available studies explore these associations in older adult populations (McDaniel & Drouin, 2015; Parker et al., 2013; Thorne et al., 2024; Walrave et al., 2015; Whitney et al., 2020). We consider that focusing on younger adults is of utmost importance, since the developmental life stage of young adulthood is associated with early patterns of forming intimate relationships. This implies that being able to understand the dynamic aspect of communication, especially in the early beginning of the development of intimate romantic relationships, could help clinicians and researchers to better comprehend the trajectories of relational growth and satisfaction. Furthermore, the transition to university coincides with a developmental phase during which young adults leave the family home. In their attempt to adjust and maintain a balanced university life, come across to new life conditions, new sexual and romantic explorations and even new ways of sexual communication. These challenges may impose threats to their adaptation and quality of life and inevitably will bring changes in their relational patterns which could also affect their relationships. Moreover, being able to comprehend how attitudes, motivations, relational, personality and other characteristics may impact sexual behaviors, as well as the exploration of what may consist a "risky sexting" behavior, can help us demystify the effects of sexting on romantic relationships among university students. Therefore, we believe that this chapter will contribute in our understanding of how the technological advancements in communication reformed sexual and romantic relationship expectations between young adults.

THE PHENOMENON OF SEXTING: ATTITUDES, BEHAVIORS AND MOTIVATIONS

The term sexting which was coined in the early 2000s, is the combination of "sex" and "texting". Sexting is the act of sending sexually explicit messages (text, images and videos), through cell phones, applications, emails or social networking (Renfrow & Rollo, 2014). Two major criticisms regarding sexting, is firstly the inconsistency in its definition and secondly how the phenomenon is approached to serve each study's research purpose. After gathering data from the available studies, as well as considering the current advances in technology, from our point of view sexting can be understood as a sexually explicit or implicit message in the form of text, image and video. Moreover, this message could be transmitted via mobile phones, computers, applications, emails, social networking and any other available technological mean of communication. Finally, engagement with sexting refers to the act of sending, receiving or forwarding a message with explicit or implicit sexual content, as a form of sexual expression and communication.

Concerning the prevalence of sexting, studies reveal that the rate of sexting among young and emerging adults is estimated at about more than a third of that research population, defining sexting as a common behavior in this age group. More specifically, according to Drouin et al. (2017) most studies report that the prevalence of sexting in the young adult population is estimated between 12% to 88% depending on multiple factors (e.g., type of sext, direction of transmission, participants' gender and relationship context), whereas the most recent evidence, to our knowledge, concerning young adults aged 18-29 suggests a prevalence of 38.3% for sending, 41.5% for receiving and 47.7% for engagement in reciprocal sexting (Mori et al., 2020). In addition, we caution readers in interpreting the association between age and prevalence of sexting in young adults, as the evidence from comparisons between young adults and other age groups seems rather inconclusive. Specifically, a study revealed that young adults reported greater levels of technology use, more online encounters of sexual content specifically during their college experience, and finally more frequent engagements in sending/receiving sexts, than older adults (Garcia et al., 2012). Similarly, a study comparing young adults aged 19 to 24 with older adults aged 25 to 50+, reported that the prevalence of sending nude photos significantly decreased as age inclined (Wysocki & Childers, 2011). Yet, the systematic review conducted by Klettke et al. (2014) reported that the frequency of sexting increases with age among adolescents and young adults, while it either remains stable or reduces with age when comparing young and old adults. Finally, contrary to all previous findings, a number of studies did not find any significant links between age and prevalence of sexting in young adults (Benotsch et al., 2013; Dir et al., 2013; Giroux, 2011; Gordon-Messer et al., 2013). Therefore, these findings cannot be conclusive enough, especially due to their limitations such as differences on how the content, the type and the direction of transmission (sending or receiving) of sexting are perceived in each study, as well as in the context of other important factors that we will discuss later in this chapter (e.g., social, cultural, etc.).

One interesting fact about sexting, is that although it's been around for more than 20 years it is arguably considered something of a media construction, as opposed to researchers' reports which reveal that young people rarely use this term (Phippen & Bond, 2023). Similarly, there is a chasm in its interpretation, acknowledgment and acceptance by the wide population. We believe that this chasm originates in people's understanding of, and attitudes towards, sexting. More specifically, sending, receiving or forwarding sexual content, creates remarkably different perceptual approaches towards the act of sexting, from being a deviant behavior and even a mean of victimization, to a natural expression of normative sexual behavior (Klettke et al. 2014). While these perceptions may contribute in shaping sexting behaviors, it is logical to expect differences across various populations. At the same time, it must be acknowledged that sexting is not merely a modern phenomenon among youngsters, but as we argue throughout this chapter, sexting presents a unique complexity which can only be unfolded by utilizing a pluralistic framework of understanding the individual within the overall context.

One of the most prominent pluralistic theory that places the individual within the wider context, is the Socio-ecological model (Bronfenbrenner, 1979). We observe that this model is progressively adopted in sexting research, as it illustrates the importance of networks and their interaction with individual factors on influencing a person's behavior. Briefly, this model consists of individual factors (demographics) and a number of systems namely, the microsystem (everyone in a person's immediate environment), the mesosystem (the interaction of the microsystem structures), the exosystem (larger social systems such as community, media etc.) and the macrosystem (culture, politics, religion etc.). To begin our exploration on what drives the differences in sexting attitudes and behaviors among young adults, we firstly turn our attention to the larger picture which includes the cultural and social contexts.

Sociocultural Influences on Sexting Attitudes and Behaviors

According to Schwartz and Boehnke (2004), cultural values can influence daily practices, attitudes and behaviors in a society, and systems such as schools, family and media support and reinforce these values. A growing body of research highlights the influence of cultural values on sexuality, sexual behavior and gender roles which seems to differently shape attitudes towards sexting from early ages. The most prevalent comparisons in the literature, lie between traditional and non-traditional countries or cultures, revealing significant differentiations between permissive (liberal and more openly acceptive) and conservative (traditional and restrictive) attitudes towards sexual behaviors. More specifically, past studies have demonstrated that traditional values may heavily limit adolescents' sexual behavior (Sharabany et al., 2008; Widmer et al., 1998), whereas permissive sexual attitudes may lead to an inclination towards participation in sexual activities (Petersen & Hyde, 2010). Furthermore, these results extended to sexting research with studies confirming that more sexually permissive attitudes and lower traditionalism are positively associated to sexting behaviors (Baumgartner et al., 2014; Gil-Llario et al., 2020; Gil-Llario et al., 2021). According to the above, we hypothesize that different sexting attitudes may also contribute in how emerging adults engage in sexting behavior and although the literature points in that direction, a more complex picture is presented when cultural values are studied in combination with other variables.

As previously mentioned, the literature on the impact of culture on adult sexting attitudes and behaviors, more or less, depicts similar findings to adolescent studies, with permissive attitudes being linked with acceptance and engagement in sexting and conservative attitudes being negatively associated with sexting (Dodaj et al., 2024; Samimi & Anderson, 2014). However, a cross-cultural examination on this topic reveals interesting findings with the addition of other sociocultural variables such as individualism-collectivism, religion, country-specific characteristics like technological advancements in digital communication and also individual factors such as gender and age. It must be stressed that although we found a small number of studies specifically focusing on young adults, there is an overall significant lack of cross-cultural comparisons in this area. Additionally, a number of cross-cultural studies which involved both adolescents and adults, provide us contradictive data for sexting prevalence (because of methodological limitations i.e., differences in design, in measurement, small sampling, etc.). This makes any comparisons between young adults and minors inconclusive, yet a higher prevalence of sexting is found in non-traditional countries such as USA (54.4%) compared to countries with less sexually liberal attitudes or inflexible gender roles such as Uganda (16.9%) and China (14.3%) (Morelli et al., 2021).

We begin with studies conducted in Europe. It is interesting to note, that while European countries share many similarities also have important differences concerning cultural values, with northern European countries exhibiting more sexually permissive attitudes compared to southern or north-eastern European countries (Widmer et al., 1998). One would expect that such differences would also be reflected in sexting attitudes and behaviors, something that has been confirmed by some adolescent studies (Baumgartner et al., 2014; Morelli et al., 2020), however, the scant number of cross-cultural studies on young adults does not allow such generalization. The two existing cross-cultural studies conducted in western Balkan countries, found a link between sexting behavior and cultural values (Dodaj et al., 2022; Dodaj & Sesar, 2023). More specifically, both studies revealed that individuals from Croatia had higher scores on the dimension of individualism and displayed more positive attitudes towards sexting and a higher likelihood in engaging in sexting, compared to individuals from Bosnia and Herzegovina who demonstrated a stronger collectivist orientation. From these studies is understood that, perhaps modern cultures may be characterized by individualistic values such as focusing on individual freedom and independence which resemble liberal and more permissive attitudes on sexuality and sexting, while the more conservative cultures may be guided by collectivistic values such as traditionalism, strong influence by family and group norms, and hence have more restrictive sexual attitudes especially towards sexting behaviors.

Differences on sexting between individualistic and collectivistic cultural values, may also appear in well economically developed countries. Although it is evident that such countries show enormous progression in technology, with digital communication being more prevalent among the general population, cultural values may differently influence sexting. We begin with a relatively recent study comparing US and Chinese college students (Qu et al., 2022), which could provide some degree of cultural consideration. Although this study omitted to report sexting prevalence rates, among other serious limitations (e.g., sampling and data collection inconsistencies), overall findings revealed that American students were more likely to experience sexting victimization compared to Chinese. These results could be culturally contextualized, since these two countries are characterized by distinct cultural traditions. Specifically, American students may perceive sexting as more harassing compared to Chinese, perhaps because of their more individualistic/permissive attitudes and inclination to risk-taking behaviors, which may lead them in a higher involvement to sexting and thus having more chances to experience the negative consequences of sexting. Conversely, the traditional-collectivistic upbringing background of Chinese which embraces strong family and societal values, obedience to norms and rules for social harmony as well as avoidance of risk-taking behaviors, may act as a deterrent against engaging in the same sexting practices as Americans. As this is, to our knowledge, currently the only available cross-cultural study among purely Western and Eastern traditions, more studies are needed to present conclusive evidence on the topic. A clearer picture is provided in two more studies comparing university students from USA and Poland (Marganiski, 2017; Marganiski & Fauth, 2013). These studies revealed that while the two countries share similarities in technology integration in everyday life, students from Poland are more conservative in sexuality and sexual relationships compared to their American counterparts who show more permissive attitudes and report more sexting engagement than Polish students. Additionally, in the same study of Marganiski (2017), gender and nationality differences were found in perceptions of normalizing technologically-mediated intimate behaviors, such as sexting and risk exposure, with males and Americans scoring higher in normalization and women and Americans scoring higher in risk exposure than their counterparts, thus calling for future studies exploring gender and cultural interactions on sexting.

As mentioned earlier, cultural values are also influential on attitudes about gender norms, stereotypes and sexual expectations which in turn could shape both the perceptions and practice of sexting. While several studies were conducted to explore the association between gender and participation in adult sexting behavior, when the variable of gender is taken on its own the findings are mixed. For example, a number of studies found that women were more likely to send sexts than men and also that men were more likely to receive sexts than women (AP-MTV, 2011; Dir et al., 2013; Dodaj & Sesar, 2023; Englander, 2012; Gordon-Messer et al., 2013; Mori et al., 2020; Reyns et al., 2014; Wysocki & Childers, 2011; Ybarra & Mitchell, 2014). On the contrary, a number of studies report that men in general are more inclined to participate in sexting behaviors compared to women (Delevi & Weisskirch, 2013; Hudson, 2011; Jonsson et al., 2014; Morelli et al., 2016; Strassberg et al., 2013). Moreover, Winkelman et al. (2014) observed minimal disparity between men and women in terms of general sexting behavior, while six other studies did not find any differences on sexting according to gender (Benotsch et al., 2013; Dir et al., 2013; Drouin et al., 2017; Drouin & Landgraff, 2012; Giroux, 2011; Henderson & Morgan, 2011). Although findings on gender differences in sexting among young adults look inconclusive, the relevant cross-cultural studies we present in the next paragraph confirm that culture and gender interact in several ways, providing us a more in-depth understanding of the phenomenon.

Countries with traditional values are known for holding conservative beliefs, maintain gender inequality and adhere to strict attitudes towards sexuality (Boehnke, 2011; Wood & Eagly, 2012). Such traditional values require women to be more sexually passive than men and encourage free sexual expression and engagement predominately in men, reinforcing double standards which restrict women's sexuality who also face more judgment and scrutiny (Dodaj & Sesar, 2021). On the other hand, countries with more sexually permissive attitudes accept women's free sexual expression and also women are equally accepted as sexually active as men (Petersen & Hyde, 2010). The available cross-cultural research on young adults, highlights the interaction of culture and gender in sexting which reflects broader sociocultural attitudes towards sexuality.

Beginning with a study comparing Indian and Australian young adults, a link was found between sexting and cultural values which varied by gender (Klettke et al., 2018). More specifically, Australians had significantly higher rates of engagement in sexting compared to Indians, and separate comparisons revealed that Australian men significantly send more sexts than Indian men, while Australian women significantly send and received more sexts than Indian women. Furthermore, gender differences were analyzed by country and showed significant differences in India but not in Australia, with Indian men engaging in sexting more than women. Although this study had several limitations such as significant differences in the gender profile and the recruitment procedure, it can be postulated that Australia as a country with more liberal values could have embraced a freer engagement in sexual online behaviors for both young men and women. While India's traditionalism could prevent young people from engaging in sexting behaviors, the same traditional gender norms and sexual attitudes could support the appropriateness and acceptance of sexual expression in men than in women.

Similar results were found in another cross-cultural study, with Spanish university students reporting higher sexting practices than Mexican students and also with men sexting more than women in both countries (García-González et al., 2021). From our understanding, Spain is characterized by more liberal attitudes in accepting sexting than Mexico, yet the higher tendency of men in practicing sexting is shared by the two countries. While it seems that this shared difference between men and women in both countries may be culturally-driven, as it reflects values of accepting men's sexual freedom compared to women, what may differentiate the two is that Mexico may be driven by more conservative and religious views on sexuality and greater gender inequality than Spain (Gil-Llario et al., 2017). Finally, another cross-cultural comparison showed that American university students (men and women) send more sexts than Spanish (55% vs 35.8%), while Spanish students (men and women) receive greater number of sexts than Americans (57.6% vs 40.9%) (Gassó et al., 2021a). Once again, although this study had important limitations (e.g., incomparable sample between cohorts and unequal gender participation), it can be claimed that even between countries with liberal attitudes sexting can be differently practiced. This finding does not only suggest differentiations between countries with relatively similar attitudes, but also that some other unique macrosystem influences can highly interact with cultural values and shape some in-country attitudinal trends. This, may be more applicable especially in countries where diverse communities and ethnic groups thrive. One of the most common macrosystem characteristics which highly correlate with cultural values and shape behaviors that express sexuality, is religion.

Many studies have examined the relationship between religiosity and sexual behavior (Moon, 2021; Schmitt & Fuller, 2015), indicating that sexual behavior choices as well as the expression of sexuality are influenced by religion. Religion is responsible to establish moral rules for acceptable and unacceptable behavior and this in turn shapes societal perceptions of sexuality by either encouraging or discouraging certain sexual behaviors (Alwin & Felson, 2010; Masters et al., 2006). In relation to religious beliefs, it is also important to consider the moral incongruence theory in the context of online sexual activity (Roberts, 1985). Applying this theory, we consider that users may believe that engaging in online sexual behavior is morally or religiously wrong, yet still participate, potentially leading to heightened emotional symptoms and reduced self-esteem.

According to studies on the association between religion and sexting, the practice of sexting is influenced by the individual's level of religiousness from young age (Strassberg et al., 2017). Furthermore, in a study with adults in USA it was found that a higher degree of religiosity negatively associated with sexting, whereas religious/spiritual struggles positively influenced sexting behaviors (Upenieks et al., 2024). Results from studies with young adult university/college students, generally show a positive association between sexting and low religiosity (Dodaj & Sesar, 2023; García-González et al., 2021; Ricon & Dovel-Cohen, 2024). Similarly, a prior study by Baugh and Paradis (2016) revealed that individuals with stronger religious beliefs are less inclined to engage in exchanging sexual messages, indicating that individuals who feel a stronger connection to a particular religion are more inclined to endorse the beliefs of that religion and adhere to its principles regarding sexual conduct. Moreover, Holmes et al. (2021) found that more religious college students rated more negatively their sexting experience and also reported that they would be less likely to be involved in future sexting compared to less religious participants. Therefore, is clear that those who adhere to higher and stricter religious moral principles tend to hold unfavorable views of sexting and tend to abstain or even minimally participate in sexting.

Interestingly, one study revealed that sexting could be seen as an alternative mean of physical sexual expression for individuals who find it challenging to express their sexuality due to religion. More specifically, in the study of Hall et al. (2020) religious undergraduate women, but not men, reported of utilizing sexting as a form of non-physical sexual interaction. Thus, according to this finding, it can be assumed that although strong religious beliefs come with values that emphasize sexual abstinence and view relevant behaviors as inappropriate, participation in sexting may still be possible as a social or a relational interaction rather than purely sexual. Additionally, we believe that individual interpretations of religious teachings, along with other social influences, personal attitudes towards sexuality and certain personality characteristics, might morally question religious attitudes on some sexual practices, like sexting, which could be perceived more flexibly. According to the study of Hall et al. (2020), this applies to religious women but not men, however, as this was found only in one study it is not clear whether this is solely a gendered phenomenon or not. Similarly, we may logically assume that sexting could be practiced between religious partners, within the security of their committed romantic relationship as a form of intimate communication, especially if it's consensual. Moreover, one could also argue that sexting between young people could be a normative practice in the 21st century, not only used for initiation of sexual courtship but also for establishing a relational connection with the recipient, free of any moral inhibitions or religious restrictions. Hence, it may be difficult to conceptualize such a contemporary behavior in traditional or religious terms, and even more difficult to be understood and accepted by those who have been raised in an era where sexual and relational communication was different. Nevertheless, more studies are needed to test such hypotheses but also to further understand the interaction of other factors with religious variables and its impact on sexting attitudes and behaviors.

As we already stressed so far, it's important to remind that conceptualizing the relation between sexting attitudes and behaviors with socio-cultural factors is not always straightforward. Young people establish complex emotional and sexual relationships; hence, sexting must not be simply perceived as a risk factor that needs to be tackled, especially without understanding it holistically. Instead, a more pluralistic approach should be applied, by exploring additional characteristics that may contribute to the global understanding of sexuality and sexting from a socio-cultural perspective. For example, the increasing economic developments, the exposure to technological advancements and the integration of the newest communication technology in daily life, as well as the different sociodemographic features which can be found in different ethnic and religious groups within the same country, may gradually and in the long-term replace sexual norms and gender stereotypes, even in countries with relatively strong traditional or religious values. Finally, considered that many studies report a significant fortification of societal and cultural values by important figures and systems in a person's life (e.g., family, peers, schools, communities, media etc. - for a review see Mansor et al., 2023), we believe that the necessity to understand their role in shaping sexting behaviors from early ages, remains an essential aim of causational and longitudinal empirical research on the topic, as these behaviors could be reflected in their future sexual practices in young adulthood.

According to the information we presented so far, people hold diverse attitudes towards sexting. Besides the influential factors and its significance in shaping sexting attitudes and behaviors, and regardless to if young people received at least a rudimentary sexual education in life or not, we consider that sexting is a phenomenon which draws a great deal of interest across disciplines. Moreover, watching the technological progression as well as its prevalence among the young population, we understand that sexting is rapidly replacing traditional forms of sexual communication. This is excellently depicted in the "sexual access timeline" found in the editorial paper of Weiss and Samenow (2010), which shows a constant evolution from the expression of sexuality in cave art (prehistorical times), to phone sex (90s) and use of smartphones/social media (currently), to virtual multisensory experiences in the future. Interestingly, looking at the existing sexting literature, most of us usually address the current trends in digital communication, and we rightly do so as it represents the lived experience and the challenges of the present time. Nevertheless, to understand progression and development we need to refer to the past and answer questions such as: how technological advancements in communication have changed sexual behaviors and we got to sexting? Therefore, the brief historical overview which follows aims to answer this question and shed some light on how the exponential growth of technology altered the way of expression and communication which have facilitated the evolution of sexting behaviors.

Evolution of Sexting Behaviors via the Cultivation of a Digital Culture. As early as the 14th-15th century, a major social phenomenon called printing press, opened the horizon of written communication and created the need for learning to read and write (Licata, 2024). Around the 20th century with the expansion of literacy, more people were able to read and write, especially in the early-industrialized countries. As seen from the stats, the worldwide prevalence of individuals from the age of 15 and above who were able to read and write, was estimated at 12% during 1820, raised at 21% in 1900 and climbed to 81% in 2000 (Roser & Ortiz-Ospina, 2024). According to these evolutions, people gradually became prone to use technological means in their interactions, something which changed the way of communicating thoughts and feelings in interpersonal relationships (Paldam, 2017). For example, the exchange of erotic letters between partners, can be seen as an early form of sexual communication, which could have also served as a form of an alternative expression of verbal communication. Still, direct verbal communication was the main communication preference back then, with written communication between a couple taking place during periods apart, or between couples in secret relationships not known to their parents.

Later developments such as the rise of photo technology, allowed people to exchange intimate photographs, while the discovery of the telephone created new opportunities for sexual conversations with the use of analog technology. Once again it seems that the communication trends reshaped the behavior, as the inclusion of photographs and videos introduced the visual sexual communication. Furthermore, the use of the telephone as a medium for sexual communication (e.g., phone-sex), brought changes in the mode of communication and also participation was not only limited between partners, but also openly and diversely expanded among strangers compared to the past (Flowers, 2010).

Nevertheless, the most influential development in the use of technological advancements in sexual communication took place in the late 90s with the entrance to the digital era. The wide access to computers, the invention and use of the internet, as well as the development of the mobile technology, brought a revolution in communication which transformed some of the previous forms of traditional sexual communication. The access to the cyberspace together with the use of computers, allowed digital exchanges of sexual content but also participation in online chat rooms and hence opened the door to social networking. The later which was very prominent during the millennium, reshaped once more the interpersonal and sexual interactions as well as the communication patterns. People were able to satisfy psychological needs such social interaction, need for belonging, flirting and even relational fulfillment, through social network. The digital era marked a turning point for relational and sexual communication not only for users but also for scholars, with more researchers studying the internet use, misuse and abuse on sexual behaviors and relationships (Bankov, 2022; Cooper et al., 2000; Rotunta et al., 2003).

Furthermore, the use of cellphones and specifically the function of sending and receiving short messages (SMS) and later the invention of an integrated camera which allowed to send multimedia messages (MMS), increased the capabilities in sexual communication, and It can be said that this development might have established what we call today sexting (Weisskirch & Delevi, 2011). Additionally, the introduction of smartphones brought an incredible development in sexual communication. These devices were able to connect to the internet at any time and later the blooming use of apps with functions that could have been imaginable in the past (e.g., real time communication and geolocation), provided more options in sexting practices. A systematic review of the literature, showed that dating apps and platforms increased online dating and sexing, thus confirming once again the transformation of traditional ways of communication, socialization and relation to romantic/sexual partners (Castro & Barrada, 2020) especially in young adults (Thorne et al., 2024). Finally, a not very well researched topic that we foresee to gradually grow, is the use of emerging technologies such as Virtual Reality (VR) and Artificial Intelligence (AI) and its potential impact on future sexual communication and sexting practices. What is already known, is the potential rise of apps specifically developed for sexting which are mainly promoted in popular media (e.g., Kibbe & Thomas, 2024), as well as the existence of hardware technologies such as sex bots and VR technologies (Bankov, 2022) that could be easily used for sexting purposes. For example, AI-driven chatbots (or Sext-bots) will have the ability to analyze conversations and generate sexting responses, while VR can be used to create customizable fantasy environments to assist users express themselves according to their personalized desires. These, features suggest that both real-person and non-human interactions can be involved in sexting, indicating a potentially new cultural shift. Thus, we believe that placing sexting nowadays at the heart of romantic relationships and technological advancements in sexual communication, can provide us a better understanding of its current use and misuse, as well as its effects on individual and dyadic level. Nonetheless, as relationships and communication are also constantly evolving, we must keep in mind that our current understanding may change in the next 25 years or more.

Under the scope of this chapter, we believe that sexting is rightly placed in the sexual and communicational behavior repertoire. Therefore, it is crucial to empirically demystify the link between the motives and the function of sexting for young adults. Although the content of sexting can be anything, from a psychological perspective the motivation to sext can be better understood in the context of individual differences. At this point, we will draw our attention on what motivates young people to sext. By utilizing a pluralistic theoretical formulation, we will try to enhance our understanding which will ultimately lead us in the next section of this chapter, that of comprehending the characteristic differences of young adults who engage in sexting.

Sexting Motivations

One may wonder why do young people sext and we begin with the most obvious reason. The growing accessibility in technology and the cultivation of a digital culture, enables more individuals, especially youngsters, to adopt technological means in their everyday communications. Actually, studies reveal that young people are more receptive in using technology (Ostrager, 2010) and with the ubiquity of communication technology, sexting may have become a more accessible method to communicate sexual topics. Additionally, the alternate personal state which is constructed in platforms and social media, the so-called "online self" (Hongladarom, 2011), can allow individuals to use sexting as an easier and a more convenient way to communicate sexual desires, thoughts or feelings, which would have been otherwise challenging to communicate verbally and face-to-face. Hence, technological advancements in communication have largely contributed in enabling younger people utilize sexting in discussing and exploring sexual interests.

During emerging adulthood individuals leave from home and make attempts to earn their individuation and establish their identity. This period is marked by experimentation and formation of new life experiences, including sexual exploration and development (Boislard et al., 2016). As a matter of fact, a few studies confirmed that young adults can experiment with sexting as a way to communicate, discuss and explore sexual topics in intimate committed romantic relationships, in dating relationships and even in casual sexual contexts (Drouin et al., 2013; Henderson & Morgan, 2011; Yeung et al., 2014). According to these studies, sexting can be utilized as a purely experimental method to familiarize themselves or see what feels "right" in sex. In addition, sexting can be used as a significant component of a sexual relationship, aiming to initiate or maintain sexual activity between partners, while at other times it can be used as a safer alternative to real life sexual activity. However, these results should be cautiously interpreted due to their limitations which comprise of relatively small samples, cross-sectional design, and collection of data mainly in western cultures using convenience sampling and with disproportioned participation among men and women.

Sexuality can also be explored out of the concept of intimate sexual relationships or direct sexual encounters. In fact, a number of qualitative studies have found a significant link between sexting and the opportunities provided to peers share and explore their sexual experiences (Albury & Crawford, 2012; Burkett, 2015; Lippman & Campbell, 2014; Ringrose et al., 2012). It must be stressed here, that these findings cannot be representative of the young adult population nor can be generalized due the methodological approach which was followed and the fact that this research was carried out in USA, yet these qualitative studies are able to provide us a deeper understanding of participants' attitudes on sexting than quantitative studies. The main reasons for engagement in sexting according to these young adults, is that it helps peers turn to peers to share, discuss and receive feedback, either for their personal sexual experiences or for aesthetic purposes regarding their appearance and even for boosting their self-esteem. Therefore, under the umbrella of motivations described in the literature as *reactive sexting* (Dodaj & Sesar, 2020), young adults may sext to explore, experiment and communicate their sexuality with peers (and partners).

Another relevant motive for sexting, is the conveyance of specific signals which reveal sexual or romantic interest. These signals which can be overt or covert in nature, are communicated aiming to form an intimate relationship or just to initiate courtship. We refer to an essential aspect of human interaction, flirting (Henningsen, 2004). In the online communication age, the practice of flirting takes different forms and has different rules (Whitty, 2003). In the context of sexting, flirting can be perceived under the category of *relational sexting* (Dodaj & Sesar, 2020) aiming at signaling sexual attraction, creating interaction and play and ultimately initiate and maintain intimacy and connection between partners. A number of studies reveal that sexting is an alternative to face-to-face flirtation, both with new and current partners in casual and committed relationships (Dir et al., 2013; Drouin et al., 2013; Drouin & Tobin, 2014; Garcia et al., 2016; Yeung et al., 2014). Finally, there are studies which revealed that although sexting was used for flirting, no association was found with positive attitudes among participants (Dodaj et al., 2022; Dodaj et al., 2023). Regardless the participants' reactions or the relational context in which mediated flirting takes place, the practices used to achieve sexual interplay, either purely sexual, sexually concealed or just for social fun (Speer, 2017), are nowadays evident and strongly associated with sexting among young adults.

Under *relational sexting*, we also see another strong motivation for young adults, that of the anticipation of positive relationship consequences, such as the preservation of a connection and intimacy between partners. Weisskirch and Delevi (2011) found that young adults have positive attitudes towards sexting as it could enhance their romantic relationships. When sexting takes place in committed relationships, partners report being more comfortable and see more sexual and emotional benefits in their relationship, compared to casual ones (Drouin et al., 2017). Additionally, in a more recent study Falconer et al. (2023) confirmed that sexting in committed relationships is used as a way to improve intimacy and relationship commitment, but also to maintain and improve relationship satisfaction. Moreover, some of the existing studies emphasize on the role of sexting in long-distance relationships (Beckmeyer et al., 2022; Currin et al., 2020; Drouin et al., 2013; Falconer et al., 2023; Hudson & Marshal, 2018). These studies revealed that conditions such as the temporary absence of a partner or an established long-distance relationship, become strong motives to engage in sexting and as a result, sexting maintains connectedness and intimacy and even enhances the long-distance relationships.

Further to relationship enhancement, researchers have also found that sexting is positively related to sexual satisfaction in romantic relationships (Falconer et al., 2023; Galovan et al., 2018; Oriza & Hanipraja, 2020; Parker et al., 2013; Stasko & Geller, 2015). As is widely known, sexual satisfaction has a key role in maintaining quality and general relationship satisfaction (Beaulieu et al., 2023; Sprecher et al., 2004). Under this scope, sexting is a sexual behavior and a mean of sexual communication utilized by partners because of its potential benefits, such as the increase of their sexual and general relationship satisfaction. At the same time, we must note that the positive relation between sexting and sexual satisfaction among adult/young adult couples may exist under specific conditions such as gender, age, relationship status and attachment insecurity which will be further analyzed in other sections of this chapter.

Attempting to explore sexting in the context of close relationships, most of us are drawn into understanding primarily its sexual aspect, especially because we are led by its prefix "sex". However, sex is not only related to behaviors (e.g., kisses, arousal, penile-vaginal intercourse, anal/oral sex, etc.) or actions to initiate those behaviors (e.g., flirting, sexual invitations, etc.), but it also has a complex psychosexual aspect (e.g., pleasure, amusement, excitement, relief of sexual frustration, fantasy, etc.). Therefore, beyond the already presented motivations for utilizing sexting, we believe that attention should be also directed to a state of mind, often neglected or misunderstood in adulthood, playfulness.

As Van Vleet and Feeney (2015) discuss in their paper, play serves an important function in adulthood and especially in the context of close relationships, as it has a highly interactive element between participants resulting in immediate and long-term positive outcomes. Play involves different kind of activities, aiming to create amusement, excitement and fun. Although there are many studies which report a link between fun and sexting (e.g., Gewirtz-Meydan et al., 2018; Lippman & Campbell, 2014), we only used data from studies with young adults as we consider that "fun" is differently perceived by adolescents and younger children. These studies confirmed that young people utilize sexting because it is fun and exciting (Burkett, 2015; Falconer et al., 2023; Kalish, 2023; Yeung et al., 2014; Weisskirch & Delevi, 2011). More specifically, young adults describe sexting as a gratifying experience which results in mood elevations, mental stimulation of sexual desire and feelings of pleasure. At the same time, during the exchange (playfulness) of sexts and flirting, partners feel thrilled, excited and mentally stimulated. On the other hand, sexting may be used just as a joke within the peer context and such behaviors are considered funny and humorous rather than sexual in nature. Similarly, sexting can be fun and playful without a direct sexual element which will lead to sex, and is seen as something rather pleasurable, balanced, without risks and not taken too far as being offensive (Renfrow & Rollo, 2014). Therefore, this aspect of sexting which seems to have a playful element, drives many young adults into enthusiasm and leads to amusement and fun during the interaction between senders and receivers.

Unfortunately, motivations and reasons to sext do not always come with good intentions and now we will turn our attention to the reasons which draw young people to the so-called *violent* (intentionally harmful with abusive and illegal elements) and *forced* (coerced and unwanted) sexting (Dodaj & Sesar, 2020). Although most research conducted on the perils of sexting typically presents it as a risky and deviant behavior among youngsters, we will attempt to go beyond these simplistic views. Our aim is to further understand the complexity of this issue, by formulating the themes we recognized as motivations, reasons or motivational determinants to sext, with the utilization of both research and theory.

Beginning with the first theme, we must note that relevant studies justify sexting as a risk-taking behavior in both adult and adolescent populations. However, risks are differently interpreted when sexting is placed in the context of illegality. Firstly, the illegality of sexting differs according to the country and its existing laws. For example, in Scotland, Singapore, Canada, in the UK and in some states in USA, although the word sexting is not used in legislations, sending unsolicited sexual images is criminalized (Evans et al., 2022; Gov.uk 2024; Penal Code 1871, Section 377BF, Singapore; Protecting Canadians from online criminal act, 2014; Sexual Offences Scotland Act, 2009). Elsewhere, and more specifically in Australia, Japan and many European countries, any online behavior or technologically facilitated sexual violence such as invasion of privacy, revenge porn, cyberviolence, blackmailing and sexual harassment, could be considered illegal or malicious (Crofts & Lievens, 2018; eSafety Commissioner, 2024a,b,c; Krieger, 2017; Matsoui, 2015). Secondly, the legality of sexting is arguable due to many factors which must be considered case by case (e.g., consent, content, age of senders-recipients, existence of abuse, etc.) but when it contains child material and pornography or imperils a child's welfare, there is no doubt that is illegal (Bradley et al., 2020; Lorang et al., 2016; Wolak et al., 2012). However, even this interpretation dramatically changes according to the age of participants and the intent of sexting. Looking at the existing literature, it is clear that anyone who is considered legally underaged and has in their possession sexual content of themselves or others (with or without their consent), or is involved in exchanges of such content (send, receive or forward) with other minors or adults, then is committing an illegal act and could be charged with a crime (Call, 2023). What is also clear according to O'Connor et al. (2017), is the lack of agreement on how to handle sexting cases involving minors, since many countries internationally do not have laws to specifically tackle sexting and mostly rely on child pornography laws. Even though it is not in the scope of our chapter to further analyze the legal frameworks or risks for minors, it is understood that the legislation on sexting is very inconsistent not only for minors but for adults too. After a thorough search of the literature, we could not find many papers which discuss the existing laws on sexting for adults, yet we conclude that sexting is not a criminal act between consenting users given that they are over age 18 (O'Connor & Drouin, 2020). More importantly, there is a need to conceptualize young adult sexting in the legal context as a multidimensional phenomenon. Therefore, we will delve into such matters by looking at the harmful effects of sexting as well as the motivations of those involved in harmful sexting. This is neatly described in the work of Wolak and Finkelhor (2011), who talk about two relevant sexting categories, the *aggravated* and the *experimental*.

According to these authors, *aggravated sexting* is the possession, creation and transmission or reception of child sexual images. *Aggravated sexting* takes place between adults and minors but also between minors and has criminal intentions such as deception, threats, extortion, abuse and production of child pornography. On the other hand, *experimental sexting* takes place willingly between young people for flirting purposes and to establish a romantic relationship. It can also occur for any other reason but without the intention of malice or criminal behavior and generally speaking in the absence of any element of the *aggravated sexting*. These two categories could be easily applied for (young) adults too and help us distinguish between purely sexual/romantic motives to sext and intentional behaviors to harm which are also deemed malicious/illegal. Self-control and opportunity theory (Gottfredson & Hirschi, 2017) can color this understanding, as it suggests that individuals with low self-control are more prone to engage in illegal behaviors by seeking riskier experiences, something which could be reinforced by the relevant opportunities that arise. Therefore, it would be reasonable to consider that low self-control, as well as the exposure and availability to engage in risky and illegal behaviors, may facilitate aggravated sexting.

Another motive we see in sexting but in a more grayish area of legality, is the willingness to take risks while something internal doesn't feel totally right and nevertheless pushes in that direction. For example, we use the study of Walker et al. (2013), which found that young adults reported that they were driven by the thrill to engage in sexting, while knowing that this behavior was potentially illegal. This behavior can be explained by theories such as the type *T personality* (Farley, 1986) and *sensation seeking* (Zuckerman, 1990). According to the theory of *T personality*, the individual is motivated to take risks and engage in uncertain experiences because of the thrill of it. Furthermore, according to the theory of *sensation seeking*, there is a willingness to take risks for the sake of experiences which create intense sensations. Therefore, it can be understood that some young adults may be motivated to sext by taking risks just for the thrill of it or because of intense (physical or psychological) stimulation and regardless of its negative or legal consequences. This behavior seems to be generally associated with younger age and the educational status (i.e., college-university) of young adults (Sarshar et al., 2019).

The second theme of "negatively charged" intentions for sexting, relates to coercion to sext. Our focus on pressures to sext, aims to unfold the motivations behind such actions, as well as the expected outcomes which may drive young people to engage in this "double helix" situation. A romantic relationship between two people is described by complex dynamics, where each partner brings in to the play their own psychosynthesis and both partners develop mutually in the ongoing and continuous change of this co-created relational experience. Under this scope, behavior unfolds in a dynamically continuous pattern of responses (and even interpretation of responses) arising from reflections upon the current relationship as well as from previous significant relationships. Therefore, it can be said that either "it takes two to tango", and they do it in accordance, or you need only one who will do it irrespective of their partner's will or presence. The same juxtaposition can apply to sexting, which may take place with the consensus of both partners or be forced by the one to the other.

Considering the findings of the available research literature on sexting, we stress that coercion to sext, either direct or indirect, with or without consent, leads to relationship entrapment. This pitfall applies when sexting is demanded only by the one partner, regardless to if the sext-content remains between the couple or is forwarded/leaked to others. However, to understand the reasons firstly for individuals who concede under pressure and secondly for individuals who use coercion to lure others into sexting and then share, forward or leak these sexts, we firstly turn to the work of Calver (2009) who distinguished sexting as *primary* and *secondary*. *Primary sexting*, has to do with self-produced material which is send by the owner and creator to the receiver(s), and most times this is consensual. *Secondary sexting*, has to do with material created by and related to others than those who share/forward it, to third parties (other than the originator) and most times is not consensual.

Under the category of coerced *primary sexting*, we find studies that report consensual but unwanted sexting (Burkett, 2015; Drouin et al. 2013; Falconer et al., 2023; Roberts et al., 2021; Thorne et al., 2024; Walker et al., 2013). This unwanted and coerced sexting, reflects a variety of motivational determinants for the consenting partner and the partner who coerces, which can be either individual (i.e., gender, age, personality traits, attitudes/perceptions) or contextual (i.e., relational dynamics, cultural values, religion) (Sesar et al., 2019). Based on the literature, we recognized the following intrinsic motivations for individuals who are pressured by their partners and finally accept to engage in sexting, (i) wanting to please the partner, (ii) need for acceptance and attention, (iii) naivety or irresponsibility, (iv) sexual or relational compliance/passiveness, (v) fear of the partner, (vi) low self-control and (vii) low self-confidence. These motivational factors which "guide" an individual to accept the coercion and consent to unwanted sexting, may also lead to their victimization (Cornelius et al., 2020). Moreover, the literature suggests that those who coerce their partners to sext, are characterized by: (i) hostility, (ii) physical and psychological aggression, (iii) manipulation, (iv) psychopathology and (v) history of previous sexual coercion (Gamez-Guadix et al., 2011; Gassó et al., 2021b; Gassó & Duran, 2021; Ross et al., 2016).

A strong motivational determinant that we frequently encountered in the literature and is specifically linked to unwanted and coerced sexting, is gender. Although gender cannot be considered a motivation, it can help us understand the conditions which drive an individual to coerce in sexting and another to accept it. In their study, Walker et al. (2013) found that pressure to sext was defined by gender dynamics, where young men forced, threatened and even bribed young women to engage in sexting. In another study, college women reported feeling more pressured to sext than men and men were more likely to pressure others to sext (Springston, 2017). Coercion to sext under pressure and threat, appeared also for women more than men (Laird et al., 2021; Thorne et al., 2024), while in the study of Gassó et al. (2020) women reported feeling more pressured and threatened to sext than men. Finally, a very recent scoping review revealed that most relevant studies indicate that men and young adults are more likely to be involved in image-base sexual abuse perpetration which also includes coerced sexting (Henry & Beard, 2024). What is interesting from these studies, is the emerge of gender stereotype effects on coercion to sexting, which we discuss under the double standard, the egalitarian sexual standard and the post-feminism approach.

The double standard (Endendijk et al., 2020) of sexual reputation, can be used to explain the findings of the link between pressure to sext and gender. According to the double standard, it can be understood that men's masculinity can reinforce and be reinforced by sexting, whereas women may lose their reputation as they could be derogatively labeled, stigmatized and even face peer disapproval –If we look at it from a different point view, someone could actually say that the fear of reputational loss, can be a risk-reducer motivator to avoid participation in unwanted, coerced and non-consensual sexting, not only for women but also for anyone–. Although a number of studies support the existence of the double standard in sexting, other studies claim that this is a traditional view which gave its place to contemporary views, especially for the recent generation adults. Therefore, beyond the double standard, there is the egalitarian standard which de-emphasizes the traditional gender attitudes and roles, indorsing more balanced and equal ones. Similarly, the post-feminism is a neoliberal approach suggesting that there is a freedom of choice and that women are sexual, in a full control of their sexuality and also can take sexual decisions without being stopped by societal obstacles (Gill, 2007, 2008). These positions are seen in the study of Harvey et al. (2020) which empirically did not support the endorsement of the double standard in sexting. Also, in another study it was found that those who hold egalitarian gender role attitudes in sexting, are less likely to receive sexts and perceive sexting as a form of intimacy without relenting in pressures (Springston, 2017). Interestingly, the study of Cornelius et al. (2020) found that coercion in consensual sexting relationship, is equal for men and women. Finally, in the study of Kalish (2023) it was found that women engage in various forms of sexting and enjoy it, and although they are aware of the double standard which makes them protective of their reputations, they criticize it and deliberately make choices to protect their privacy and safeguard their reputation. Thus, we see that depending on the theoretical frame which is used to interpret results, motivations for coerced sexting according to gender may vary.

The gender issue in the sexting literature has multiple dimensions and another one is to look at it under the context of *secondary sexting*. More specifically, coercion to sext does not happen only between couples and is not only employed by men and used against women. Research reveals a pressure to forward a sext within the peer context. This is especially prevalent among young men (Henry & Beard, 2024; Roberts et al., 2021; Yeung et al., 2014; Walker et al., 2013). Although such an action can be seen as an unethical secondary and non-consensual sexting, which we will analyze later on, our emphasis here is on the coercion between peers. The reasons which motivate men to share their partners' sexts, under the coercion of their peers may be the following, (i) feeling excluded if they don't share a sext, (ii) direct or indirect pressure to be part of the group, (iii) brag, (iv) impress and (v) gain reputation among peers. Looking at these factors, we believe that masculinity comes into the play as a buffer, aiming to minimize the effects of the psychological pressure between peers. Indeed, the study of Roberts et al. (2021) found that when sexting with peers, as well as with women, men presented perceptions of wanting to demonstrate a masculine status and objectify women, but at the same time they reported modest perceptions too. For example, to counterbalance their masculine perceptions, they reported "masculine-inclusive" practices such as recognition of bad behavior, demonstration of respect to women and the need to build trust and mutuality in their relations with women. Nevertheless, participants prioritized respect between "committed girlfriends" and "other girls" and shared information and sexts with peers mostly for casual partners and one-night stands. According to this study, men may rely on masculinity-type perceptions, which promote gender inequality, and although they may struggle with this and want to find ways out of it, they do not fully adopt progressive perceptions, especially when they have to face their peers. Finally, a word about heterosexual peer coercion to send same gender sexts, although we did not come across many relevant studies, the aforementioned motivations for men and women do not entirely apply in this example and we would tentatively hypothesize that such an exchange can be seen under a group of motivations related to fun, teasing and gossip (Burkett, 2015; Clancy et al., 2020).

Consensual but unwanted sexting, may take place with the promise to delete. Either this happens and is ok(ish) between the couple, or it goes totally wrong as the other partner leaks a sexting, it is a humiliating situation which brings issues of trust and commitment in the relationship. Research shows, that specifically in casual and cheating relationships, there is a greater risk for easier sext leakage due to lower trust and intimacy (Drouin et al., 2013), as well as higher chances of betrayal (Burkett, 2015). Exactly this is where the line is crossed, as an originally created personal and private moment, loses its private status either during unstable relationship conditions or after relationship break-ups.

Another significant motivational determinant which appears implicitly and explicitly in studies (e.g., Bonilla et al., 2021; Burkett, 2015; Ravn et al., 2021), is called hypersexualization or a highly sexualized culture (Choi & DeLong, 2019). The hyper-sexualized culture has many elements. One is that there is a tendency to promote women's sexual objectification and men's predatory status. In other words, the female body, or parts of the body, can be used as a sexual tool and also a person's value depends on their sexuality. In the same line, there is an expectation especially for young women to promote their femininity as highly sexualized. Men on the one hand, are considered lucky to be the "consumers" of this and at the same time, are also positioned as sexual predators. Additionally, while many in the industry of popular media and products present the aforementioned women's sexualization and objectification, there are studies revealing that men are sexualized too, yet women are hypersexualized compared to men (Hatton & Trautner, 2011; Ward, 2016; Urman & Makhortykh, 2024). More specifically, as in women, men's sexualization focuses on body parts, where men are presented shirtless with their sexiness being also highly related to muscularity (Dotson, 2021; Fasoli et al., 2017). Arguably, this element of hypersexualization promotes a culture of symbols who are either presented as "weak", "sexual", "perpetrators" or "driven by passions" and unfortunately inflate unnecessarily and unfairly double sexual standards. Another aspect of the hypersexualized culture, is that we are daily bombarded with sexual content through media and also sexual content is nowadays more available everywhere, especially digitally. Pornography was once a taboo, but nowadays is being fashioned as something neutral or trendy with the many "influencers" or "social media icons" significantly contributing to this. Soft porn, is another "simple" element of this hypersexualized culture. This can be seen or perceived as a norm, since youngsters use technology to share and express their sexual behaviors with others and even earn money out of it (e.g., OnlyFans, Patreon, etc.). The transformation of the naked body, or sexual act, that were once private, to public, and then by hitting the "share button" to even more public, is paradoxically considered "OK" but at the same time is being perceived in terms of risk. Therefore, it can be understood that these elements of the hypersexualized culture can reinforce all the aforementioned motivations for sexting.

We now move from the consensual and unwanted, to the non-consensual sexting. This may be one of the most unethical sexting practices, as the person acts selfishly and independently of others' wishes and consent. Such behaviors take two forms, the first is the intentional leakage of others' sexual content to third parties (*secondary sexting*) and the second is the intentional act to send sexts to people who have not consented or wanted to receive it (*primary sexting*). As we previously mentioned under the theme of coerced consensual sexting, there are occasions of material leakage which do not entirely fall under the non-consensual sexting. Nevertheless, the possession of sexual material which originated from a coerced consensual but unwanted sexting and hence its subsequent leakage to others, can be seen as an extension of the unethical secondary and non-consensual sexting. Although non-consensual sexting has a coercive element, it goes even further beyond this. Such a practice is very dangerous and can seriously harm others, as the motivations behind it may consist of (i) intention, (ii) deception, (iii) unethical entertainment, (iv) retaliation, (v) revenge and jealousy, (vi) humiliation and denigration, and (vii) bullying to gain power over others. These motivations could result in blackmailing and sextortion (another form of blackmailing including threats to leak sexual information or photos unless the victim complies with financial, sexual or other demands), cyberbullying, sexual abuse, revenge porn and generally victimization (Barrense-Dias et al., 2020; Branch et al., 2017; Burkett, 2015; Clancy et al., 2021; Clancy et al., 2023; Falconer et al., 2023; Matthews et al., 2018; Medrano et al., 2018; Reyns et al., 2011; Walker et al., 2013). From these, the unintentional forward of a sext is excluded, specifically those cases where something has gone entirely wrong either because sexual material had mistakenly sent to the wrong recipient or because the device was compromised (hacked or stolen). Nevertheless, when this random recipient or hacker, who has it in their possession leaks the sext, then the unethical and intentional element of secondary sexting re-applies.

The second form of such a non-consensual behavior, which has been explored by many studies in the young adult population, is *unsolicited sexting* which actually is being send to unsuspected receivers without their consent (Courtice et al., 2021; Howard et al., 2024; Karasavva et al., 2022; Mandau, 2020; Matthews et al., 2018; Nicklin et al., 2020; Sparks et al., 2023). According to these studies, unsolicited sexting generates different reactions to receivers according to gender. For example, men found such sexts as flattering, complementing, humorous and a way to show off, while women found such sexts intrusive, threatening, inappropriate, harassing and violating of trust and privacy (Mandau, 2020; Matthews et al., 2018). In addition, previous higher exposure to sexual content was linked to rating unsolicited sexting as funnier compared to mild and no exposure, whereas previous higher exposure to violent content was linked with ratings of unsolicited sexting as more amusing and exciting (Nicklin et al., 2020). Another form of unsolicited sexting is cyberflashing, which basically is the dissemination of a picture of an individual's genitals to unsuspected persons (Karassava et al., 2022; Karasavva et al., 2023; Sparks et al., 2023). Cyberflashing is associated with sexual abuse but also with personality traits such as narcissism and psychopathy. Other motives for cyberflashing can be the following, (i) flirt or demonstration of sexual interest to partners, (ii) transactional: sending with the expectation and hope to receive sexual favors in return, (iii) enjoyment of the behavior because it is sexually and personally gratifying, something which is also correlated to narcissism, (iv) being proud of their body and want to show off and (v) exert power and control over others, since the recipient passively receives it and is unable to say no. This is a way to exploit potential fear or discomfort from others, leading to intimidation and sexual harassment.

Lastly, an entirely different category of negatively charged sexting motivations, either falling under coerced, unsolicited or consensual sexting are associated to higher report of alcohol and drug use (Benotsch et al., 2013; Dir et al., 2013) and impulsive behavior (Dir et al., 2013). Other times, there are just simple motivations without any negative intentions, such as forwarding sext because of assuming that others want to receive it, for showing off, as a joke, because is funny or because of boredom (Associated press [AP]-MTV digital abuse survey, 2011; Barrense-Dias et al., 2020; Drouin et al., 2013).

Independently to if a sexting is coerced, non-consensual or unsolicited, recent studies show possible links with victimization of young adults (Garrido-Macías et al., 2023; Marcum et al., 2022). While most studies agree that sexting victimization is more prevalent in adolescents and young adults, and also differences exist according to culture and country, there is a slightly higher rate of victimization in women than men (Gassó et al., 2021b; Noorishad & Trottier, 2022; Qu et al., 2021). This does not mean that men are not coerced or victimized, but on the contrary they can be deeply influenced, yet less eager to report it as found in the study of Notté (2024) which studied young men's experiences of image-based sextortion. Furthermore, in a large international study including individuals aged 16-64, it has been found that image-based sexual abuse was associated to higher victimization in younger adults aged 20-29, with very similar rates in men (37.4%) and women (38.1%) (Powell et al., 2020). Finally, we stress here that although sexting in general cannot directly be linked with health consequences, the effects of sexting practices which lead to victimization can have a negative impact on mental health which includes among other lower well-being, life satisfaction and self-esteem, stress, anxiety, depression, suicidal ideation and PTSD symptoms (Drouin et al., 2015; Gassó et al., 2021b; Klettke et al., 2019; Medrano et al., 2018; Patel & Roesch, 2022). Given the overall number of studies on young adults' sexting, the existence of empirical studies on causal relationships and longitudinal studies on the negative effects of sexting are either very scant or do not exist. Additionally, adolescent studies show mixed longitudinal evidence on the relation between sexting, victimization and negative outcomes (Hu et al., 2023). Thus, there is a need for more studies to better understand the long-term effects of negative sexting on mental health and general well-being.

CHARACTERISTICS OF INDIVIDUALS INVOLVED IN SEXTING

Recently, sexting has been the focus of numerous studies, which have primarily looked into the prevalence of this behavior. However, taking into consideration individual characteristics of people who engage in sexting, such as personality traits and attachment styles, are important to understand and approach the phenomenon of sexting more holistically. Thus, in this section we present the individual characteristics of young adult university students who engage in sexting.

Personality Traits

Personality traits could play a role in understanding the phenomenon of sexting on a broader scale. Research from De Wit (2009), has found a connection between impulsivity and engaging in risky behaviors, indicating that individuals with poor impulse control may be more likely to participate in sexting without considering the potential outcomes. Additionally, according to Ferguson (2011) sexting was linked to engaging in unprotected intercourse and finding pleasure in sexual activities during college years. Moreover, the reception of sexually suggestive images among young adults, was found to be three times higher for sexually active individuals compared to those who didn't receive such images (Gordon-Messer et al., 2013). Furthermore, research has demonstrated a correlation between sexting and deficiencies in emotional competencies (Houck et al., 2014), as well as a limited capacity for self-control (Dir et al., 2013; Kerstens & Stol, 2014) and impulsiveness (Baumgartner et al., 2014; Dir et al., 2013; Temple & Choi, 2014). Therefore, it can be said that personality traits may influence individuals' decisions to engage in risky sexting behaviors.

Another group of studies focused specifically on two primary personality traits, outlined in the literature as sensation seeking and negative urgency. Sensation seeking, is defined as the inclination to pursue novel and thrilling experiences (Whiteside & Lynam, 2001) which was associated to sexual risk-taking behaviors (e.g., Donohew et al., 2000; Hoyle et al., 2000; Justus et al., 2000; Paul et al., 2000; Veléz-Blasini, 2008) and sexting (Dir et al., 2013b). Negative urgency, refers to the inclination to act impulsively when experiencing intense negative emotions (Whiteside & Lynam, 2001). Research by Deckman and DeWall (2011) and Dir et al. (2013b) has linked negative urgency to both sexual behaviors and sexting. Finally, it seems that acting impulsively without any planning is characterized by the tendency to act without any forethought, which was also found as a significant risk factor for sexting (Kahn et al., 2002; Khurana et al., 2012).

The correlation between several other personality traits and engagement in sexting among emerging adults, was also confirmed by another group of studies. Specifically, Mori et al. (2020) found that extraversion was strongly associated with visual forms of sexting behavior. Additionally, the study by Englander (2019) proposed a noteworthy link between sexting and extraversion, neuroticism, conscientiousness and agreeableness. Specifically, the findings of this study indicated that individuals with high levels of extraversion and neuroticism were more inclined to engage in sexting behavior. It was also found that individuals with lower scores in conscientiousness and agreeableness were less likely to participate in sexting. Moreover, histrionic characteristics were found to predict sexting and more specifically sending and receiving nude and erotic photos (Ferguson, 2011). The study of Hassan et al. (2023) found that honesty/humility had a positive correlation with the perceived risk of sexting attitudes and a negative correlation with the fun and carefree and relational expectations of sexting attitudes. This study, also revealed that emotionality had a negative relationship, while conscientiousness had a positive relationship, with perceived risk of sexting attitudes. Furthermore, it was discovered that self-control was positively associated with perceived risk and negatively associated with the fun and carefree aspects of sexting attitudes. Finally, it was indicated that honesty/humility negatively predicted relational expectations in young adults and also significant differences were identified between employed and unemployed young adults in terms of sexting frequency, personality types and sexting attitudes.

Attachment Styles

Attachment is a rich theory which can provide a unique understanding of individual differences in intimacy and affect regulation (Mikulincer et al., 2002). Attachment styles were heavily researched in the young adult university population, however, only a few studies have explored the relationship between attachment and sexting (e.g., Drouin & Langraff, 2012; Drouin & Tobin, 2014; Drouin et al., 2014; Guest & Denes, 2022; Trub & Starks, 2017; Weisskirch & Delevi, 2011; Weisskirch et al., 2017). Most of these studies, reveal a positive association between attachment styles and sexting which will be further explained, yet two studies present a slightly different picture.

For starters, Weisskirch and Delevi (2011) conducted an in-depth investigation of the association between sexting attitudes, sexting behavior and attachment styles. They found that only attachment anxiety was a strong predictor of favorable sexting attitudes. This finding indicates that, individuals with higher attachment anxiety view sexting as a natural aspect of a relationship, consider it to be beneficial for the relationship and anticipate receiving sexually suggestive content through text messages. Additionally, it was found that attachment anxiety was significantly associated with one specific type of sexting behavior, the act of proposing sex to their partners through messages. Although this study suffered from several limitations, such as very small sample and disproportionate participation of men and women, its results were confirmed by the study of Drouin and Langraff (2012) who examined the relationship between sexting practices and attachment styles in college students. Anxious attachment was found to predict sending sex text messages, whereas attachment avoidance predicted sending both sex text messages and pictures. Interestingly, they also discovered that attachment avoidant men were more likely to send sex text messages and pictures to their relationship partners than women. Furthermore, Trub and Starks (2017) found that both attachment anxiety and avoidance correlated with sexting, however, the association between attachment anxiety and sexting was mediated by the difficulty of controlling impulses during emotional distress. Moreover, Drouin and Tobin (2014) found that women with higher attachment anxiety were more likely to consent to unwanted sexting and this was mediated by the avoidance of arguments, while Drouin et al. (2014) found that attachment avoidance predicted lying during sexting.

Finally, contrary to these findings, a study with a very small sample (N=133) reported that attachment avoidance was negatively correlated with sending and receiving sext messages and no significant correlation was found between attachment anxiety and sexting (Guest & Denes, 2022). Similarly, in the study of Weisskirch et al. (2017) attachment avoidance was found to negatively correlate with sending a sexually suggestive photo or video, a photo or video with underwear/lingerie, a sexually suggestive text and a text to propose sex, while attachment anxiety correlated positively only with sending a photo or video with underwear/lingerie.

The findings from all these studies, can be conceptualized in the rich context of attachment theory. According to attachment theory (Mikulincer et al., 2002), individuals with anxious/preoccupied attachment styles are characterized by the use of hyperactivation strategies. Such strategies are utilized not only to regulate difficult emotions caused in the interaction with their partners but also to minimize any emotional distance, by excessively depending on them to elicit support. Conversely, those with an avoidant attachment style are characterized by the use of deactivating strategies which involve suppression of emotional distress and compulsive self-reliance. Therefore, previous results on the positive association between attachment anxiety and sexting, as well as the negative association between attachment avoidance and sexting, can be interpreted accordingly. More specifically, anxiously attached individuals will tend to use sexting as a hyper-stimulating strategy to fulfil their innate desire for intimacy and closeness, whereas individuals higher in attachment avoidance would use sexting in such a way to satisfy their sexual needs by maintaining emotional distance from partners.

In addition, it was found that controlling impulses during emotional distress, could explain the association between anxious attachment style and sexting as well as the engagement of anxiously attached women in unwanted sexting in order to avoid arguments. As a matter of fact, poor emotional regulation in young adults, was also found to be generally associated with sexting (Ricon & Dovel-Cohen, 2024). To be able to control impulses and difficult emotions, individuals need to exhibit the necessary coping mechanisms. Such a skill, is emotional regulation which is also an important element of attachment styles. Emotional regulation involves a set of cognitive processes that affect an individual's emotional reactions, including initiation and inhibition or modification of various aspects of emotional functioning (Gross, 1998). As we know, people with anxious attachment tend to get very emotional when dealing with relational rejection or loss, while individuals with avoidant attachment tend to distance themselves from emotional situations (Ferraro & Taylor, 2021). Therefore, it is understood that these characteristic patterns could influence how individuals participate in sexual communication and also how they manage their emotions in the context of sexting in relationships.

Concerning the content of sexting (texts, photos and videos), for which variations were found according to attachment styles, we believe that no definite conclusions can be drawn due to the limited number of existing studies and contradictive results. However, from an attachment theory perspective, these findings were not entirely unexpected. For example, individuals higher in attachment anxiety would be more likely to send sexual videos, photos and text for the same reasons they would be motivated to engage in sexual relationships, such as to please their partners, to gain reassurance but also to reduce emotional distance and avoid being rejected (Segovia et al., 2019). In addition, the double scenario of the positive association between attachment avoidance with photos and texts in the first study and the negative association in the other, can be explained by the characteristic pattern of defensive deactivation and minimization of relational intimacy. On the one hand, avoidantly attached individuals would be less engaged in sharing sexts because of the lack of trust they generally feel in intimate relationships (Obegi & Berant, 2010). Therefore, sharing sexual photos or revealing their sexual feelings and thoughts to others would be considered as quite intimate and frustrate them. As a response, they would activate their defense of keeping others at a distance and choose not to send a sext. On the other hand, avoidantly attached individuals may want to send sexual texts (presumably very short and superficial in content, not revealing emotions yet being purely sexual in nature) as well as photos, aiming to initiate sex and nothing more. This can be explained by previous research which found that, avoidantly attached individuals are mainly motivated for casual sex just for pleasure and with the least possible emotional closeness (Segovia et al., 2019). Finally, it seems that gender differences appeared in the link of attachment styles to the content of sexting and this was also expected, since previous research has found a higher prevalence of avoidant attachment in men and attachment anxiety in women (Kirkpatrick & Davis, 1994; Sprecher, 2013; Weber et al., 2022).

RESEARCH EVIDENCE ON SEXTING AND ITS EFFECTS ON RELATIONSHIP SATISFACTION AMONG YOUNG ADULT UNIVERSITY STUDENTS

As we already mentioned, technology is nowadays deeply integrated into nearly all aspects of our daily lives, including the formation and preservation of intimate relationships (Murray & Campbell, 2015). Sexting is a common practice in intimate relationships. Couples often utilize mobile phones to share loving text messages and this has been linked to positive communication, positive emotional attachment and increased satisfaction within the relationship (Novak et al., 2016; Schade et al., 2013).

Overall, there are several types of romantic/sexual relationships that could form during the university/college years, such as casual relationships (e.g., hookups and friends with benefits) and committed/romantic relationships. Although casual relationships are highly prevalent during university life and although they have been associated to sexting, the focus of our attention will be only on committed romantic relationships. The reason is because we are interested in relationship satisfaction which develops in time and has those conditions which are best understood in committed relationships (Sternberg, 1986), something that casual relationships cannot provide.

Before we present the relevant results, we need to say that while there is not much research to investigate the associations between sexting and relationship satisfaction, the limited existing studies were conducted on samples with a bit higher mean age than we would normally expect to see in university

students. Hence, we present these studies and at the same time we suggest that readers keep a critical stance in the evaluation and interpretation of these results on our target population. Generally, this stream of studies shows, that positive attitudes towards sexting could enhance the romantic relationship (Weisskirch & Delevi, 2011). Additionally, people in committed relationships report to be less affected by the potential negative consequences of sexting (Dir et al., 2013; Drouin et al., 2017). Specifically, committed relationship couples seem to experience better outcomes, such as more sexual and emotional benefits, but also report being more comfortable with sexting and have more positive sexting encounters compared to couples in casual relationships (Drouin et al., 2017; Galovan et al., 2018). Moreover, Parker et al. (2013) found that married and dating couples reported a positive significant relationship between sexting and relationship satisfaction. Similarly, the studies of McDaniel and Drouin (2015) and McDaniel et al. (2017) revealed that sexting was positively related to relationship satisfaction among cohabiting couples, but under the conditions of partners' gender and attachment styles.

A different stream of studies has shown a connection between sexting and sexual fulfillment (Beaulieu et al., 2023; Sprecher et al., 2004). Additionally, many researchers have found that sexting is positively related to sexual satisfaction in romantic relationships (Galovan et al., 2018; Oriza & Hanipraja, 2020; Parker et al., 2013; Stasko & Geller, 2015). Finally, Falconer et al. (2023) confirmed that sexting for people in committed relationships is a way to improve intimacy as well as maintain the relationship sexual satisfaction. Under this scope, sexting is a sexual behavior and a mean of sexual communication between partners which seems to be beneficial in terms of significantly increasing a couple's sexual satisfaction. However, at the same time we still wonder if there could be a causal relationship between these variables and relationship satisfaction.

In contrast to previous studies, there is a stream of research which reveals that neither sexting does necessarily promote commitment, nor is related to satisfaction, but also that it could even lower relationship satisfaction. Beginning with the study of Galovan et al. (2018), they found that although sexters reported higher sexual satisfaction, higher sexting was associated with lower levels relationship commitment. In addition, they did not find any differences in relationship satisfaction between the study's four types of sexters (non-sexters, world-only, frequent and hypersexters). The study of Currin et al. (2016) reported that relationship satisfaction was lower among women who received but did not send a sext, compared to non-sexter women, and no other associations or significant findings were found in this study. Finally, Jeanfreau et al. (2019) found that sexting was unrelated to relationship satisfaction and similarly Matotek et al. (2021) found a strong correlation between the level of commitment and relationship satisfaction, yet they did not find a significant relationship between sexting and commitment or between sexting and relationship satisfaction.

From the studies we presented in this section, it is understood that commitment is a crucial factor in relationship satisfaction for young adults, but there are mixed findings concerning the association between sexting and relationship satisfaction. Although sexual satisfaction was found to be an important element of the couple's relationship which is related to sexting, exchanging sexual messages with a partner is not entirely linked to the quality of the relationship. Consequently, it is possible that there could be an overstatement of the potential benefits of sexting on relationship satisfaction and definitely more research is needed to further explore and understand this.

IMPLICATIONS FOR EDUCATION, CLINICAL PRACTICE AND POLICY

Drawing from available research evidence and considering the theoretical richness used to understand the phenomenon of sexting in the young adult population, we are directed now to present some implications for educators and mental health practitioners who work with university students. We consider that the following implications can be seen as recommendations and less as intervention protocols or definite lines for action. It is of utmost importance, that university and college counselling centers act as the front line in addressing this phenomenon and together with the organization's teaching personnel and administration involve the entire academic community to join the efforts for healthier utilization, prevention and even intervention. Moreover, other non-campus-based professionals within the specialties of mental health, education, social work and other medical areas, who work with young adult university students, may also consider these practice implications. Finally, we believe that some considerations for addressing sexting behaviors may also inform university students themselves and many others who directly or directly relate to them.

Prevention

"*Prevention is better than cure*" Hippocrates (460-370 BC); Desiderius Erasmus (1466–1536)

It may be a cliché to say that prevention is the best solution before any intervention, nevertheless, generally speaking this is a true fact and a fundamental principle behind public health. If you look prevention as a method to tackle the upstream of several problems, the same could be applied for the negative outcomes which are caused by the harmful use of sexting. We caution professionals during the design and use of prevention programs, firstly to consider all the possible causes of negative outcomes in the utilization of sexting in romantic relationships and secondly to clearly understand their target population so that they tailor these programs according to their needs. Finally, prevention programs should be evidence-based and equally important, their application and achieved outcomes must be easily measurable and open for feedback and redesign if needed.

Comprehensive Sexual Education. Sexual education is a big chapter in life, as is the education on the use of safe internet and mediated digital communication (Finkelhor et al., 2021). These programs begin from younger age and occur in different settings (Goldfarb & Lieberman, 2021; Lameiras-Fernández et al., 2021). Whether these programs are effective or equally provided to all youngsters, it seems that during the period of university young adults are faced with a "life examination" which requires from them to apply their previously acquired skills. Therefore, one prevention strategy could be the incorporation of courses related to sexual education in the university curriculum.

The aim of such courses is to familiarize students with relevant research and enhance awareness on issues of sexuality. These courses, are not meant only to provide basic information but also to act as refreshers of previous knowledge. However, we must not assume that all university students have received a sexual education during schooling and for those who did, perhaps previous knowledge may not always be accurate or up-to-date. Additionally, as research indicates, educational and pedagogical presentations of sexting as something negative, dangerous, harmful and "forbidden", as well as strategies targeting the reduction/elimination of the behavior by focusing on sexting abstinence and controversial fear/shame tactics, have already failed (Ojeda & Del Rey, 2022; Patchin & Hinduja, 2019). Such teachings and strategies, do not promote healthy discussions on ethics, consent or agency, but reinforce stigmatization as well as erroneous attitudes and behaviors towards sexting. Therefore, particular attention must be provided on the associations between sexuality and dangerous online sexual behavior, including the negative motives and risks of sexting (e.g., non-consensual dissemination and coerced sexting). The ultimate objective of such courses is to develop effective decision-making strategies, encourage critical thinking and promote self-awareness on sexuality and sexual behaviors.

These courses are recommended to be offered soon in the students' academic path, either as a free general education elective or as a tutorial/seminar course. The first one, is more comprehensive as it will cover a broad range of information on sexual behavior and will be part of the study program, lasting one entire academic semester. It will have specific learning outcomes and follow a formal procedure of assessment which will be developed in such ways so that upon completion of the course, will allow students demonstrate the extent to which the intended learning outcomes have been achieved. The second proposed course, takes the form of a tutorial which will be more informal but still structured concerning its content. It will be offered on a short-term basis and will be open for enrollment throughout the academic year for all university students. The aim of such a tutorial course is to provide the space to engage with the material more actively, as it will be designed for small groups of students. Students will have the opportunity to participate in discussions around a topic, voice their opinions and test their ideas.

Training and Personal Development Events. This category includes one-off seminars/webinars, presentations, day camps, experiential workshops, campaigns and awareness weeks. The aim of these events, if we look at them on a continuum, is on the one end to expose (large) audience to specific topics and provide necessary general information for awareness increase and on the other end to learn practical skills by using hands-on experience to encourage a mindset of continuous growth. These events could be provided to students, staff and others out of the university community. Appropriate methods to apply and achieve the aforementioned goals, could be the following: (i) presentation of material and information, (ii) information resources with real testimonials, (iii) interactive lectures, (iv) simulations, (v) use of case studies analyses-vignettes which reflect different scenarios on which participants can present their thoughts, attitudes, beliefs, emotions and solutions, (vi) use of video and online sources for debates, (vii) open discussions without judgments, (viii) group discussions and (ix) utilization not only of experts to deliver such trainings and events, but also university students who can act as peer-educators.

One important area that could be covered by training and personal development events, is the definition of the aspects of sexting. Information could be given on what is a sexting, its uses, the motivations behind it and how it is utilized in the context of intimate relationships. Distinctions should be made between aggravated and experimental sexting, consensual and non-consensual practices but also attention should be given to non-consensual sext dissemination. Additionally, it is also important to present the legal implications of sexting and explain the potential risks and consequences of harmful sexting practices. These should come along with information on online safety and personal data, as well as the rights and responsibilities while using the internet and digital technology in general.

Specific emphasis should be given in educating about sexual coercion and sexting. A related issue, is the negotiation of consent within online sexual experiences. Thus, programs should be directed to contrasting and analyzing several communication and negotiation strategies and practices. Accordingly, on the same line of discussion, sextortion should be introduced by formulating its associated risks and legal consequences, and also focus in developing the necessary skills to recognize, and deal with, such occurrences. Moreover, it is vital to explain how sexting could increase individuals' victimization but also to go a step further to be able to identify the characteristics of potential perpetrators and victims. By introducing vulnerability factors, such as high extraversion, low conscientiousness and willingness to comply with prevailing peer pressure and norms, awareness could be raised to build healthy defenses for harm-minimization and protection such as, help-seeking behaviors and other skills to deal with online sexual harassment. Prevention programs, should also emphasize on finding ways to resist peer pressure and address normative expectations around harmful sexting. In addition, concerning perpetrators, it is important to list deviant behaviors and personality characteristics which are linked to cyberflashing such as T-behavior, narcissism and psychopathy. On the same page, it is understandable that perpetrators (or potential perpetrators) could be present among the audience and might also be imperative to present both the healthy and unhealthy expression of such characteristics. By doing this, we may be realistically able to sow the seed of sublimation which would ideally and in the best scenario, encourage reflection on alternative options such as participation in healthier risk-taking behaviors (e.g., extreme sports).

Campus campaigns and awareness days/week within the wider topic of sexuality, could be designed to illustrate the positive aspects of sexting but also challenge norms such as "sexting is trivial", "men can do it but women are sluts", "women are victims and men perpetrators", "If I don't send back I will be punished", etc. Awareness events can also be used to educate people on the abusive/harmful side of sexting such as leaking and sharing unwanted nude photos and its negative effects. Ultimately, such actions could play an important role in acknowledging, validating and even legitimizing the experience of victims. Thus, this way universities can demonstrate their inclusive, humanistic and socially responsive character, which could empower their students feel safe and come out of the refusal, fear and awkwardness to talk to friends, family and mental health specialists.

Another area of sexting which needs to be tackled and openly discussed with university students, is sexual relationship ethics. The aim of such opportunities is to build skills on how to maintain an intimate and ethical romantic/sexual relationship. One aspect of this issue, is sexting with people out of the romantic relationship and what is already known, is the leakage of sexts to third parties out of the current relationship. Nevertheless, we now also know, that one of the two partners may engage in sexting with unknown people, peers and even ex-partners but with the sext content relating only to their own sexual material and not their partners (Hertlein & Twist, 2017). Because the university setting is a new environment, where students are able to meet new people, and because during this period they developmentally establish their attitudes towards sexuality, technology makes it easier for some to expose themselves to diverse sexual information and explore new potential sexual endeavors (e.g., invitation for friendship may lead to online dating, use of Tinder for hook-ups, etc.). Therefore, these reasons together with the anonymity that sometimes is provided by the technological advances, can accommodate their desires and enable them to participate in such interactions, bringing issues of trust and commitment in their current relationships. These are matters which can create distress and need to be explored.

Within the sexual ethics framework, opportunities should be given for discussions to analyze sex and relationships but also to challenge gender and power dynamics on the use of sexting in intimate romantic relationships. In addition, because sexting was found to relate to body-esteem and self-esteem, prevention programs can be utilized to improve knowledge on how media present the ideal body image and deconstruct such stereotypes. Moreover, as nowadays many universities host international students, is important to understand how sexting practices can be utilized by students from different socio-cultural backgrounds. Research indicates that students from countries of collectivistic background, are more conservative concerning sexuality and less likely to engage in sexting, compared to students from individualist countries. Additionally, men of conservative backgrounds have an advantage over women in the frequency and content of sexual activities, while women are often stigmatized for exactly the same activities and attitudes. Furthermore, individualistic cultures are associated with lower gender inequality but greater willingness to take sexual risks. Having said these, promotion of sexual ethics should not involve conversations on what is right or wrong but rather to provide the space to generate ideas and elaborate on topics such as gender roles and stereotypes (masculinity, femininity, sexual double standards etc.), body shaming, diverse cultural practices and expectations on sex and relationships. Finally, personal opinions are welcomed and respected and can be safely compared, contrasted and debated within a space for reflection and development.

Clinical Implications

Many of the areas covered in prevention programs, can be used to take further actions on a therapeutic level too. Saying this, we do not imply that psychological therapy/counselling should be provided, necessarily, as a second step because of the failure of the first. Therapeutic interventions provided on and off campus, according to any therapeutic model which works better with young adults, can be beneficial either as ancillary to sexting prevention programs or as a primary method to tackle the most serious problems and distress caused by the perils of sexting. Our aim here, is to use the material that was generously offered to us by research, to inform firstly our clinical assessment and secondly our decisions to intervene on specific target areas.

Clinical Assessment. One of the most difficult, psychologically-wise, outcomes resulted by a negative experience with sexting, is victimization. There are strong associations of victimization with coerced sexting, non-consensual dissemination of sexual material, threats, sextortion, revenge porn and other types of sexual harassment. Thus, is of outmost importance to assess possible vulnerability factors which could enhance victimization such as the following personality traits: (i) high extraversion, (ii) low conscientiousness, (iii) low self-control, (iv) high permissiveness, (v) great willingness for compliance, (vi) passiveness, (viii) histrionic characteristics, (ix) neuroticism and (x) shyness. Except of personality traits, other vulnerability factors for victimization could also be the following: (i) low self-esteem, (ii) negative body-esteem, (iii) previous traumatic experiences, (iv) multiple sexual partners, (v) substance use, (vi) impulsivity, (vii) difficulties in detecting emotion and (viii) poor emotional regulation.

The experience of psychological and social consequences for the victim after such a negative exchange, could be PTSD, panic attacks, depression and suicidal ideation. In addition, the person may fear subsequent neglect, bullying or harassment by peers. During the assessment, the clinician should also look after symptoms of anxiety, social withdrawal and isolation, anger, low self-esteem and self-harm behaviors. Due to reputation damage, but also guilt and shame caused by the experience, depressive symptoms may develop as well. Therefore, a careful risk assessment with a focus on suicidality is considered clinically appropriate for such cases. Assessment in these cases requires a non-threatening and non-judgmental attitude to help build a strong rapport, so that clients feel comfortable to disclose embarrassing experiences. The most suitable approach in assessment, is to embrace Person-Centered conditions such as active listening to build context of understanding their experience, congruence, unconditional positive regard and empathy.

At other occasions, the client may not present any distress directly related to sexting, but we may want to assess the client's sexuality, including any experiences with sexting. The first important thing to consider, is not to dive into assessment with predetermined judgments or make any premature assumptions that just because we deal with young adults they must be sexually active. Sexting may be, or not, part of an active sex life. Thus, do not assume that if a client does not report an active sex-life, they are not involved in sexting, or the contrary. Sometimes, questions which target sexual content may seem uncomfortable to both the clinician and the client. Therefore, it might be easier to ask closed questions, while other times it may be better to inquire explicitly about certain behaviors by utilizing open questions. This is a clinical judgment that the clinician should take, considering factors such as ease and flow of the conversation, evaluation of moment-to-moment rapport, how talkative and reflective the client is and the client's openness in discussing sexual matters. Open questions must be treated with professionalism and neutrality, without demonstrating any countertransferential reactions in the room, such as interest with excitement, surprise, challenge, approval or disapproval of the experience. Sometimes, it's easier to explore sexual behaviors in the context of assessing the relationship quality or dating issues.

Another important element of the assessment, is to wonder about normalizations or rationalizations of experiences with sexting. It is advisable to pay attention to the flow of the conversation and the connection of storytelling with the affect and body language. Sometimes, coercion in sexting for example, could be concealed and the clinician must be prepared to read between the lines. Other times, the client's developmental history can reveal significant information about their sexual behavior patterns. Additionally, we can use inferences from research to inform our clinical exploration. For example, as research specifies, previous experience of sexting in adolescence or earlier, can be indicative of future online risk behaviors, especially when considering that the prevalence of sexting inclines in young adulthood (Hu et al., 2023). Finally, some other factors to consider which may be linked to sexting are the following: (i) digital efficiency and being highly active in social media and dating apps, (ii) alcohol and drug use/abuse, (iii) high sexual activity, (iv) sexualized discourse, (v) poor impulse control, (vi) sensation seeking, (viii) thrill seeking and risk-taking behaviors, (ix) impulsive sex, (x) unprotected sex and (xi) insecure attachment.

An area of specific attention for clinicians, which relates both to the assessment and intervention phase (will be discussed in the following subsection), is ethics. Psychologists, psychotherapists and counsellors, are legally and ethically bound to protect clients' confidentiality and only in extraordinary cases, where their clients' or others' life or welfare (including minors) is at stake, confidentiality must be breached and safeguarding actions are to be taken (ACA, 2015; APA, 2017; BPS, 2021). While in some cases it may be clear how the clinician should proceed (e.g., suicidal actions, intention to harm another person, child abuse, child pornography, etc.), the subject of sexting can create some ethical dilemmas. Our intention here, is not to thoroughly discuss this matter, on which we could even devote a whole chapter, but to point out some dilemmas we consider that practitioners could encounter in their work with young adults. The following dilemmas, are based on real case examples from our clinical experience with university students:

- Case 1: Your client mentions that s/he is sexting with her/his partner but s/he is highly anxious that her/his photos could be leaked by the partner, even though s/he has no such indications.
- Case 2: Your 19-year-old client tells you that s/he is sexting with her/his partner who currently resides in another country and with whom s/he has been in relationship for three years now. Furthermore, s/he reveals that the partner is a 16-year-old high school student.
- Case 3: Your client who was referred by their instructor for depression, reveals that s/he has forwarded her/his partner's naked photo to a friend. S/he regretted for her/his action and after s/he revealed it to her/his partner they broke up.
- Case 4: Your client tells you that s/he met someone at a campus party, with whom they began to text in social media from the day after. S/he also told you that while just texting each other through the week, this person sent photos of her/his genitals without consent and also asked for your client's nude photos. Your client had not replied but disapproved her/his actions. However, in the

session s/he was rather upset and confused, not knowing what to do, as on the one hand s/he liked that person but on the other, s/he considered his/her action inappropriate for the little time they knew each other.

A multiple dilemma that could arise from these four scenarios, is questioning the necessity, the timing and circumstances under which we could breach confidentiality and report sexting. Although the answer is fairly easy when sexting takes place voluntarily and consensually between adults, unfortunately it may get complicated depending on the laws (for criminalizing sexting), or the absence of these, in each country. Additionally, for scenarios that include coercion or unsolicited sexting without consent, and even in cases where allegedly the client could be the victim or the perpetrator, although practitioners are mandated to breach confidentiality it may be questionable if and when this action can cause more harm than benefit clients and others. Moreover, sexting discussions may also get very complicated in the case where an adult engages in sexting with an underaged person, however, any decision for breaching confidentiality (or not), might depend on the legal age that someone is considered a minor. Therefore, it can be argued that although the answer should have been fairly easy because we are dealing with adult sexting, the matter of beneficence and nonmaleficence could clash with the law or its interpretation which can sometimes be very rigid and not necessarily on the benefit of the client.

Our recommendation, is firstly practitioners to be clearly informed of the local laws and their responsibilities on how to handle such matters. Secondly, they should refer to their professional associations or professional regulating bodies for advice. Thirdly, we believe that training and professional organizations should create relevant guidelines and offer continuing education courses to psychologists, psychotherapists and counsellors for such matters. Fourthly, supervision can be a "safe heaven" for professionals, as they could openly discuss their ethical dilemmas and find appropriate solutions. Last but not least, according to the existing literature legislations may suffer on many levels concerning sexting for both adolescents and adults. Hence, mental health professionals and researchers should be involved, with other stakeholders, in the process of updating or developing relevant laws, so that these could more accurately represent the phenomenon in the current era.

Areas of Potential Interventions. As previously mentioned, clinicians may use the therapeutic model of their choice. The findings from their assessment, can be used to produce tailor-made formulations which must not only include clinical and relational information, but also consider these in the wider context of their clients' social and cultural values. This pluralistic formulation-approach, will guide their interventions which could focus on the following target areas:

- Awareness of legal issues (underage sexual content, harassment, revenge porn, etc.), risks for self and others, and the duty to report or break confidentiality when necessary.
- Stress management in interpersonal relationships.
- Protection of the body image, body-esteem and self-esteem.
- Long-Distance relationships create anxiety, loss and separation issues that need to be addressed. Therapists could focus on building and strengthening communication skills to achieve better connection with partner, maintain intimacy and attraction.
- Raise awareness and provide psychoeducation of online risk behaviors: the social, legal and psychological risks of sexting must be clearly presented. Statistics can be useful, however are meaningful only when the client understands them on a personal level.
- Work on resilience-building especially for potential victims.

- Develop assertiveness and skills to resist peer pressure.
- Work with the fear of rejection and abandonment.
- Alleviate the distress caused by the conflicts related to students' sociocultural backgrounds, values and attitudes which may be very different to those of their partners. Additional stressors might be the customs and the relational/sexual/dating patterns of the country in which they are currently studying.

Finally, as Parker et al. (2013) report, sexting can be an intervention in relationships for the following reasons:

- for those who may have a difficulty in engaging in physical sexual activity, either because of lack of previous sexual experiences or hesitations and restrictions because of cultural, religious background and other personal fears. For them, sexting can be an easier and safer way to express initial interest, feelings and even sexual desires as opposed to face-to-face direct communication.
- Sexting as an intervention could be promoted by clinicians with clients who want to enhance the sexual satisfaction of their relationship.
- Suggestions for sexting utilization in romantic relationships should be made in such way that does not unethically disturbs the person's psychosynthesis.
- Therapists should avoid suggestions on how to sext and present alternatives to the exchange of nude images with perhaps a suggestive or sexually implicit text message. A text message is a mean of communication that partners can use in secrecy without others knowing. This could actually add a flirtatious element in their communication. Nevertheless, it is important to explore and define with couples what feels more comfortable for them.
- Another important aspect is to emphasize on consent and help the person determine if their partner is open and willing to participate in sexting.
- Sexting can initiate sexual behavior only under mutual agreement and without coercion.
- Partners must be able to assess the expectations of the partner who asks for a sexting and even their own expectations when they agree to engage in sexting.
- Sexting can be a medium for safe expression and exploration of sexuality (preferences, desire, arousal, sexual fantasies) only when there are potential mutual benefits for partners and realistic expectations without the element of risk.
- Increasing the couple's secure attachment will lead to safe sexual practices which could then strengthen intimacy and increase relationship and sexual satisfaction.

IMPLICATIONS FOR USERS AND OTHER STAKEHOLDERS

This subsection, is not intended to provide any safe sexting advice or tips, but on the contrary, it presents some parameters on the features of apps and platforms which can be used for sexting. Our goal is to inform users on such matters, so that they develop a critical stance which can guide their choice of a technological medium for sexting. At the same time, we stress the need for policymakers and other stakeholders to see the possibilities to further enhance the security and privacy of these technological means of communication.

As already presented in the chapter, sexting can be performed in many ways, with one frequently featured in young adult studies being the utilization of a variety of social media, dating apps and communication apps (Thorne et al., 2024). Some of these mediums, provide simple functions such as sending and receiving texts, videos and photos, while other offer more advanced features. Although not well examined, some factors which could influence young adults' choice of a medium, are the relational context in which sexting will take place and the platform's specific features. For example, studies indicate that single young adults might prefer to initially sext in dating apps (e.g., Tinder and Bumble) and then use other mediums, while couples and peers may use social media and communication apps instead (e.g., Messenger, WhatsApp, Snapchat, etc.) (Mori et al., 2020; Van Ouytsel et al., 2020).

The use of such apps and platforms, come with a number of potentials, challenges and limitations that users should acknowledge before making their final choice. One of the main challenges has to do with safety and privacy. An important element of safety and privacy, is the end-to-end encryption which appears that not all apps/platforms can offer. As Adatoga et al. (2024) argue in their paper, end-to-end encryption is critically important as it ensures that the content remains only between the users, however, approaches taken by different regions vary significantly. Additionally, they discuss that while some apps/platforms clearly declare the existence or absence of this function, users should be very careful as a number of apps might partly offer it, while others may have unclear policies on such a function. A second challenge, is the boundaries on how the content can be used and by whom (Geeng et al., 2020). More specifically, some apps provide functions such as the ability to erase content after posting, or setting a time-lapse for the content's availability and even activating a limitation on the number of views by others. Such functions can be unilateral (e.g., only the sender can adjust the time-lapse availability of a photo), bilateral (e.g., both users may be able to delete a content) or automatic (e.g., ability to activate automatic deletion). Furthermore, additional functions such as the option to blur faces in images containing nudity, but also the ability to password-protect stored sexual content, aim to further enhance users' privacy and allow them to better control the exchange and storage of sexting material. Finally, another major challenge which comes in the use of apps/platforms in sexting, is the protection from unsolicited forwarding. Two important functions to tackle this issue, are the control against screenshots and the detection and blockage of unwanted content. However, such functions are only offered in a very limited number of apps/platforms (Franco et al., 2024).

From the above, it is understood that while we are talking about a "state-of-the-art" technology in nowadays (sexual) communication, there is still a long way to go until platforms and apps become sexting-friendly. While there is a variety of mediums to choose from, young adults must carefully consider all the aforementioned features, challenges and limitations before making their final choice. Moreover, platforms need to establish clearer policies and better guidelines concerning boundaries, privacy and safe-use, especially for sexting. Developers of such technological mediums, could be directed in creating more efficient features to tackle unsolicited sexting and even support users in cases of abuse. Finally, we hope that policymakers and other stakeholders (e.g., commissioners, consumer associations) will consider the challenges that young people face in the digital age in a more informed and sensitive way, and also better approach this complex issue by taking appropriate actions in the regulation of apps and platforms. Ultimately, we believe that such considerations and actions could minimize the negative social and mental health consequences of harmful sexting.

CONCLUSION

This chapter attempted to provide an illustration of how sexting is perceived and utilized among young adults. It is evident from the current research literature, that over a third of young adults utilize sexting as a mean of sexual communication within romantic (and other) relationships. One could argue that the online world is a close a reflection of the offline word. In other words, many of the practices which are reported in the existing studies (e.g., flirting, initiation of sexual courtship, sexual experimentation, coercion, deception, harassment and victimization, etc.) were originally initiated on a conventional face-to-face basis (and still are), but with the progression of technology the same practices are nowadays heavily incorporated in peoples' digital exchanges. Therefore, we believe that by placing sexting at the heart of romantic relationships and the technological advancements in sexual communication, we can better understand its current use and misuse. Studies on the topic of sexting and romantic relationships, highlight several motives and reasons for utilizing sexting among young adults. They also point a number of individual, contextual, relational and sociocultural influences on sexting. On this basis, we can clearly conclude that sexting seems to have many faces which are transformed accordingly. Definitely, sexting is not merely a modern phenomenon among youngsters, but as we argued in this chapter, it presents a unique complexity which can only be unfolded by utilizing a pluralistic framework of understanding the individual within the overall context. Still, a significant gap continues to exist in accurate prevalence data, in common ways to approach and measure sexting, in cross-cultural and longitudinal explorations of the phenomenon, and more importantly in the investigation of sexting's effects on romantic relationships among young university students.

Having reached this point and coming to an end of writing this chapter, we hope to have helped the readers comprehend the role of sexting in young adults' lives. Importantly, we would like to consider that implications presented some ideas on how to utilize education, prevention and clinical interventions when working with university students who share with us their thoughts, attitudes, emotions, challenges and generally their experience with sexting. Finally, we hope that some of the discussed notions will inform young adults' attitudes towards the development of a critical approach to the phenomenon of sexting. This approach, should not be one that restricts their autonomy to freely decide whether or not or when to engage in sexting, but a one which encourages agency and ownership of thoughtful and mature actions that respect themselves and others. Lastly, we truly wish that policymakers and other stakeholders view adult sexting more pluralistically and in the context of contemporary relational and sexual communication. This can allow them to develop (or reshape) more inclusive and appropriate policies concerning adult sexting, that reflect a respectful stance towards young adults' autonomy and at the same time safeguard privacy and promote physical and mental health in the wider society.

REFERENCES

Agustina, J. R., & Gómez-Durán, E. L. (2012). Sexting: Research criteria of a globalized social phenomenon. *Archives of Sexual Behavior*, 41(6), 1325–1328. DOI: 10.1007/s10508-012-0038-0 PMID: 23080397

Albury, K., & Crawford, K. (2012). Sexting, consent and young people's ethics: Beyond Megan's story. *Continuum (Perth)*, 26(3), 463–473. DOI: 10.1080/10304312.2012.665840

Alwin, D. F., & Felson, J. L. (2010). Religion and child-rearing. In Ellison, C. G., & Hummer, R. A. (Eds.), *Religion, families, and health: Population-based research in the United States* (pp. 40–60). Rutgers University Press.

American Counseling Association. (2014). *2014 ACA code of ethics*. https://www.counseling.org/docs/default-source/default-document-library/ethics/2014-aca-code-of-ethics.pdf

American Psychological Association. (2017). *Ethical principles of psychologists and code of conduct* (2002, amended effective June 1, 2010, and January 1, 2017). https://www.apa.org/ethics/code/

Associated Press-MTV. (2011, September 2). *Digital Abuse Survey*. Retrieved April 3, 2024, from http://surveys.associatedpress.com/data/KnowledgeNetworks/AP_DigitalAbuseSurvey_ToplineTREND_2nd%20story%20WITHOUT%20hacking.pdf

Atadoga, A., Farayola, O. A., Ayinla, B. S., Amoo, O. O., Abrahams, T. O., & Osasona, F. (2024). A comparative review of data encryption methods in the USA and Europe. *Computer Science & IT Research Journal*, 5(2), 447–460. DOI: 10.51594/csitrj.v5i2.815

Bankov, K. (2022). *The digital mind: semiotic explorations in digital culture* (Vol. 22). Springer Nature. DOI: 10.1007/978-3-030-92555-0

Barrense-Dias, Y., Akre, C., Auderset, D., Leeners, B., Morselli, D., & Surís, J. C. (2020). Non-consensual sexting: Characteristics and motives of youths who share received-intimate content without consent. *Sexual Health*, 17(3), 270–278. DOI: 10.1071/SH19201 PMID: 32594970

Baugh, C., & Paradis, G. (2016, April). *The relationship between sexting and religiosity* [Poster presentation]. *96th Annual Convention of the Western Psychological Association*, Long Beach, CA, United States.

Baumgartner, S. E., Sumter, S. R., Peter, J., Valkenburg, P. M., & Livingstone, S. (2014). Does country context matter? Investigating the predictors of teen sexting across Europe. *Computers in Human Behavior*, 34, 157–164. DOI: 10.1016/j.chb.2014.01.041

Beaulieu, N., Bergeron, S., Brassard, A., Byers, E. S., & Péloquin, K. (2023). Toward an integrative model of intimacy, sexual satisfaction, and relationship satisfaction: A prospective study in long-term couples. *Journal of Sex Research*, 60(8), 1100–1112. DOI: 10.1080/00224499.2022.2129557 PMID: 36205506

Beckmeyer, J. J. (2024). Sexting and the Dynamics of Emerging Adults' Romantic Partnerships. *Sexuality & Culture*, 28(2), 447–463. DOI: 10.1007/s12119-023-10125-8

Beckmeyer, J. J., Herbenick, D., & Eastman-Mueller, H. (2022). Sexting with romantic partners during college: Who does it, who doesn't and who wants to. *Sexuality & Culture*, 26(1), 48–66. DOI: 10.1007/s12119-021-09878-x

Benotsch, E. G., Snipes, D. J., Martin, A. M., & Bull, S. S. (2013). Sexting, substance use, and sexual risk behavior in young adults. *The Journal of Adolescent Health*, 52(3), 307–313. DOI: 10.1016/j.jadohealth.2012.06.011 PMID: 23299017

Boehnke, M. (2011). Gender role attitudes around the globe: Egalitarian vs. traditional views. *Asian Journal of Social Science*, 39(1), 57–74. DOI: 10.1163/156853111X554438

Boislard, M. A., Van de Bongardt, D., & Blais, M. (2016). Sexuality (and lack thereof) in adolescence and early adulthood: A review of the literature. *Behavioral Sciences (Basel, Switzerland)*, 6(1), 8. Advance online publication. DOI: 10.3390/bs6010008 PMID: 26999225

Bonilla, S., McGinley, M., & Lamb, S. (2021). Sexting, power, and patriarchy: Narratives of sexting from a college population. *New Media & Society*, 23(5), 1099–1116. DOI: 10.1177/1461444820909517

Bradley, N., Gilea, B., Overton, S., & O'Neill, R. (2020). Sexting between minors: Ethical, legal, and clinical considerations. *Journal of Counselor Practice*, 11(2), 1–20. DOI: 10.22229/sbm1122020

Branch, K., Hilinski-Rosick, C. M., Johnson, E., & Solano, G. (2017). Revenge porn victimization of college students in the United States: An exploratory analysis. *International Journal of Cyber Criminology*, 11(1), 128–142. DOI: 10.5281/zenodo.495777

British Psychological Society. (2021). *Code of Ethics and Conduct* (amended effective December 12, 2021). DOI: 10.53841/bpsrep.2021.inf94

Bronfenbrenner, U. (1979). *The ecology of human development: Experiments by nature and design*. Harvard University Press. DOI: 10.4159/9780674028845

Burkett, M. (2015). Sex(t) talk: A qualitative analysis of young adults' negotiations of the pleasures and perils of sexting. *Sexuality & Culture*, 19(4), 835–863. DOI: 10.1007/s12119-015-9295-0

Call, C. (2023). Public perceptions and legal dimensions of juvenile sexting. *Journal of Social, Behavioral and Health Sciences*, 17(1), 196–216. DOI: 10.5590/JSBHS.2023.17.1.14

Castro, Á., & Barrada, J. R. (2020). Dating apps and their sociodemographic and psychosocial correlates: A systematic review. *International Journal of Environmental Research and Public Health*, 17(18), 6500. Advance online publication. DOI: 10.3390/ijerph17186500 PMID: 32906632

Choi, D., & DeLong, M. (2019). Defining Female Self Sexualization for the Twenty-First Century. *Sexuality & Culture*, 23(4), 1350–1371. DOI: 10.1007/s12119-019-09617-3

Clancy, E. M., Hallford, D., March, E., Howard, D., Toumbourou, J. W., & Klettke, B. (2023). The role of consent and motivations in sext dissemination. *Journal of Interpersonal Violence*, 38(15-16), 9315–9342. DOI: 10.1177/08862605231163886 PMID: 37067003

Clancy, E. M., Klettke, B., Crossman, A. M., Hallford, D. J., Howard, D., & Toumbourou, J. W. (2021). Sext dissemination: Differences across nations in motivations and associations. *International Journal of Environmental Research and Public Health*, 18(5), 2429. Advance online publication. DOI: 10.3390/ijerph18052429 PMID: 33801431

Clancy, E. M., Klettke, B., Hallford, D. J., Crossman, A. M., Maas, M. K., & Toumbourou, J. W. (2020). Sharing is not always caring: Understanding motivations and behavioural associations with sext dissemination. *Computers in Human Behavior*, 112, 106460. Advance online publication. DOI: 10.1016/j.chb.2020.106460

Cooper, A., Delmonico, D. L., & Burg, R. (2000). Cybersex users, abusers, and compulsives: New findings and implications. *Sexual Addiction & Compulsivity*, 7(1-2), 5–29. DOI: 10.1080/10720160008400205

Cornelius, T. L., Bell, K. M., Kistler, T., & Drouin, M. (2020). Consensual sexting among college students: The interplay of coercion and intimate partner aggression in perceived consequences of sexting. *International Journal of Environmental Research and Public Health*, 17(19), 7141. Advance online publication. DOI: 10.3390/ijerph17197141 PMID: 33003567

Courtice, E. L., Czechowski, K., Noorishad, P. G., & Shaughnessy, K. (2021). Unsolicited pics and sexual scripts: Gender and relationship context of compliant and non-consensual technology-mediated sexual interactions. *Frontiers in Psychology*, 12, 673202. Advance online publication. DOI: 10.3389/fpsyg.2021.673202 PMID: 34349699

Crofts, T., & Lievens, E. (2018). Sexting and the Law. In M. Walgrave, J. Van Oytsel, K., Ponnet, & J. R. Temple (Eds.), *Sexting. Motives and risk in online sexual self*-representation (pp.119–136). Palgrave Macmillan Cham. *https://doi.org/*DOI: 10.1007/978-3-319-71882-8_8

Currin, J. M., Hubach, R. D., Sanders, C., & Hammer, T. R. (2017). Sexting leads to "risky" sex? An analysis of sexting behaviors in a nonuniversity-based, older adult population. *Journal of Sex & Marital Therapy*, 43(7), 689–702. DOI: 10.1080/0092623X.2016.1246390 PMID: 27732509

Currin, J. M., Jayne, C. N., Hammer, T. R., Brim, T., & Hubach, R. D. (2016). Explicitly pressing send: Impact of sexting on relationship satisfaction. *The American Journal of Family Therapy*, 44(3), 143–154. DOI: 10.1080/01926187.2016.1145086

Currin, J. M., Pascarella, L. A., & Hubach, R. D. (2020). "To feel close when miles apart": Qualitative analysis of motivations to sext in a relationship. *Sexual and Relationship Therapy*, 35(2), 244–257. DOI: 10.1080/14681994.2020.1714024

Day, T. (2010). The New Digital Dating Behavior-Sexting: Teens' Explicit Love Letters: Criminal Justice or Civil Liability. *Hastings Communication & Entertainment Law Journal*, 33(1), 69–96.

De Wit, H. (2009). Impulsivity as a determinant and consequence of drug use: A review of underlying processes. *Addiction Biology*, 14(1), 22–31. DOI: 10.1111/j.1369-1600.2008.00129.x PMID: 18855805

Deckman, T., & DeWall, C. N. (2011). Negative urgency and risky sexual behaviors: A clarification of the relationship between impulsivity and risky sexual behavior. *Personality and Individual Differences*, 51(5), 674–678. DOI: 10.1016/j.paid.2011.06.004

Dir, A. L., Coskunpinar, A., Steiner, J. L., & Cyders, M. A. (2013). Understanding differences in sexting behaviors across gender, relationship status, and sexual identity, and the role of expectancies in sexting. *Cyberpsychology, Behavior, and Social Networking*, 16(8), 568–574. DOI: 10.1089/cyber.2012.0545 PMID: 23675996

Dir, A. L., Cyders, M. A., & Coskunpinar, A. (2013). From the bar to the bed via mobile phone: A first test of the role of problematic alcohol use, sexting, and impulsivity-related traits in sexual hookups. *Computers in Human Behavior*, 29(4), 1664–1670. DOI: 10.1016/j.chb.2013.01.039

Dodaj, A., & Sesar, K. (2020). Sexting categories. *Mediterranean Journal of Clinical Psychology*, 8(2). Advance online publication. DOI: 10.6092/2282-1619/mjcp-2432

Dodaj, A., & Sesar, K. (2021). Social Ecological Approach to Sexting Behaviour. *Central European Journal of Paediatrics*, 17(2), 145–156. Advance online publication. DOI: 10.5457/p2005-114.303

Dodaj, A., & Sesar, K. (2023). Individual and cross-cultural predictors of sexting among adults from Bosnia and Herzegovina and Croatia. *Sexuality Research & Social Policy*, 20(4), 1537–1551. DOI: 10.1007/s13178-023-00807-1

Dodaj, A., Sesar, K., Bošnjak, L., & Vučić, M. (2024). Theory of planned behaviour and sexting intention of college student. *Emerging Adulthood*, 12(2), 163–174. DOI: 10.1177/21676968231208343

Dodaj, A., Sesar, K., & Novak, T. (2022). A Cross-Cultural Examination of the Sexting Motives and Attitudes: Bosnia and Herzegovina vs. Croatia. *Human Behavior and Emerging Technologies*, 2022(1), 7606949. Advance online publication. DOI: 10.1155/2022/7606949

Dodaj, A., Sesar, K., Pérez, M. O., Del Rey, R., Howard, D., & Speno, A. G. (2023). Using vignettes in qualitative research to assess young adults' perspectives of sexting behaviours. *Human Technology*, 19(1), 103–120. DOI: 10.14254/1795-6889.2023.19-1.7

Donohew, L., Zimmerman, R., Cupp, P. S., Novak, S., Colon, S., & Abell, R. (2000). Sensation seeking, impulsive decision-making, and risky sex: Implications for risk-taking and design of interventions. *Personality and Individual Differences*, 28(6), 1079–1091. DOI: 10.1016/S0191-8869(99)00158-0

Dotson, E. (2021). *Behold the man: The hype and selling of male beauty in media and culture*. Routledge. DOI: 10.4324/9781315865362

Drouin, M. (2015). Sexual communication in the digital age. In L. D. Rosen, C. Nancy & L. M. Carrier (Eds.), *The Wiley handbook of psychology, technology, and society*, (pp. 176–191). John Wiley & Sons. DOI: 10.1002/9781118771952.ch10

Drouin, M., Coupe, M., & Temple, J. R. (2017). Is sexting good for your relationship? It depends…. *Computers in Human Behavior*, 75, 749–756. DOI: 10.1016/j.chb.2017.06.018

Drouin, M., & Landgraff, C. (2012). Texting, sexting, and attachment in college students' romantic relationships. *Computers in Human Behavior*, 28(2), 444–449. DOI: 10.1016/j.chb.2011.10.015

Drouin, M., Ross, J., & Tobin, E. (2015). Sexting: A new, digital vehicle for intimate partner aggression? *Computers in Human Behavior*, 50, 197–204. DOI: 10.1016/j.chb.2015.04.001

Drouin, M., & Tobin, E. (2014). Unwanted but consensual sexting among young adults: Relations with attachment and sexual motivations. *Computers in Human Behavior*, 31, 412–418. DOI: 10.1016/j.chb.2013.11.001

Drouin, M., Tobin, E., & Wygant, K. (2014). "Love the way you lie": Sexting deception in romantic relationships. *Computers in Human Behavior*, 35, 542–547. DOI: 10.1016/j.chb.2014.02.047

Drouin, M., Vogel, K. N., Surbey, A., & Stills, J. R. (2013). Let's talk about sexting, baby: Computer-mediated sexual behaviors among young adults. *Computers in Human Behavior*, 29(5), 25–30. DOI: 10.1016/j.chb.2012.12.030

Endendijk, J. J., van Baar, A. L., & Deković, M. (2020). He is a stud, she is a slut! A meta-analysis on the continued existence of sexual double standards. *Personality and Social Psychology Review*, 24(2), 163–190. DOI: 10.1177/1088868319891310 PMID: 31880971

Englander, E. (2012). *Low risk associated with most teenage sexting: A study of 617 18-year-olds*. https://vc.bridgew.edu/marc_reports/6

Englander, E. (2019). What do we know about sexting, and when did we know it? *The Journal of Adolescent Health*, 65(5), 577–578. DOI: 10.1016/j.jadohealth.2019.08.004 PMID: 31648755

eSafety Commissioner. (2024a). *Police and Legal Help*. https://www.esafety.gov.au/key-topics/image-based-abuse/police-and-legal-help

eSafety Commissioner. (2024b). *Receiving Unwanted Nudes*. https://www.esafety.gov.au/young-people/receivingunwanted-nudes

eSafety Commissioner. (2024c). *What Is Illegal and Restricted Online Content?*https://www.esafety.gov.au/report/what-is-illegal-restricted-content

Evans, A. E., Currin, J. M., Garos, S., Stokes, A., Cox, K., & Meyer, C. L. (2022). 'Wasn't this already considered sexual harassment?': Exploring the confusion around the law mandating consent to receive a nude sext message. *American Journal of Sexuality Education*, 17(3), 343–367. DOI: 10.1080/15546128.2021.2025181

Falconer, T. A., Humphreys, T. P., O'Hagan, F. T., & Johnson, J. R. (2023). Influences on sexting in an intimate relationship: Motivations, risks, communication, personality traits, and relationship variables. *The Canadian Journal of Human Sexuality*, 32(3), 275–288. DOI: 10.3138/cjhs.2022-0052

Farley, F. (1986). The big T in personality. *Psychology Today*, 20(5), 44–52.

Fasoli, F., Durante, F., Mari, S., Zogmaister, C., & Volpato, C. (2018). Shades of sexualization: When sexualization becomes sexual objectification. *Sex Roles*, 78(5-6), 338–351. DOI: 10.1007/s11199-017-0808-1

Ferguson, C. J. (2011). Sexting behaviors among young Hispanic women: Incidence and association with other high-risk sexual behaviors. *The Psychiatric Quarterly*, 82(3), 239–243. DOI: 10.1007/s11126-010-9165-8 PMID: 21153441

Ferraro, I. K., & Taylor, A. M. (2021). Adult attachment styles and emotional regulation: The role of interoceptive awareness and alexithymia. *Personality and Individual Differences*, 173, 110641. Advance online publication. DOI: 10.1016/j.paid.2021.110641

Finkelhor, D., Walsh, K., Jones, L., Mitchell, K., & Collier, A. (2021). Youth internet safety education: Aligning programs with the evidence base. *Trauma, Violence & Abuse*, 22(5), 1233–1247. DOI: 10.1177/1524838020916257 PMID: 32242503

Flowers, A. (2010). *The fantasy factory: An insider's view of the phone sex industry*. University of Pennsylvania Press.

Franco, M., Gaggi, O., & Palazzi, C. E. (2023). Can messaging applications prevent sexting abuse? A technology analysis. *IEEE Transactions on Mobile Computing*, 23(2), 1613–1626. DOI: 10.1109/TMC.2023.3238189

Fratti, M. (2018, April 4). *Why sexting is something you should definitely do in a relationship*. https://hellogiggles.com/why-sexting-is-something-you-should-definitely-do-in-a-relationship/

Galovan, A. M., Drouin, M., & McDaniel, B. T. (2018). Sexting profiles in the United States and Canada: Implications for individual and relationship well-being. *Computers in Human Behavior*, 79, 19–29. DOI: 10.1016/j.chb.2017.10.017

Gámez-Guadix, M., Straus, M. A., & Hershberger, S. L. (2011). Childhood and adolescent victimization and perpetration of sexual coercion by male and female university students. *Deviant Behavior*, 32(8), 712–742. DOI: 10.1080/01639625.2010.514213

Garcia, J. R., Gesselman, A. N., Siliman, S. A., Perry, B. L., Coe, K., & Fisher, H. E. (2016). Sexting among singles in the USA: Prevalence of sending, receiving, and sharing sexual messages and images. *Sexual Health*, 13(5), 428–435. DOI: 10.1071/SH15240 PMID: 27470210

Garcia, J. R., Reiber, C., Massey, S. G., & Merriwether, A. M. (2012). Sexual hookup culture: A review. *Review of General Psychology*, 16(2), 161–176. DOI: 10.1037/a0027911 PMID: 23559846

García-González, A., Romero-Rodríguez, J. M., Ramírez-Montoya, M. S., & Aznar-Díaz, I. (2021). The Phenomenon of Sexting Among Mexican and Spanish University Students: A Multigroup Model. *Sexuality & Culture*, 25(3), 939–959. DOI: 10.1007/s12119-020-09802-9

Garrido-Macías, M., Herrera, A., Alonso-Ferres, M., & Herrera, C. M. (2023). Sexting is not always wanted: Consequences on satisfaction and the role of sexual coercion and online sexual victimization. *Anales de Psicología*, 39(3), 354–363. DOI: 10.6018/analesps.514431

Gassó, A. M., Agustina, J. R., & Goméz-Durán, E. (2021). Cross-cultural differences in sexting practices between American and Spanish university students. *International Journal of Environmental Research and Public Health*, 18(4), 2058. Advance online publication. DOI: 10.3390/ijerph18042058 PMID: 33672448

Gassó, A. M., & Gómez-Durán, E. (2021). Psychopathological profile of sexting coercion perpetrators. *Spanish Journal of Legal Medicine*, 47(4), 157–163. DOI: 10.1016/j.remle.2021.02.003

Gassó, A. M., Mueller-Johnson, K., & Gómez-Durán, E. L. (2021). Victimization as a result of non-consensual dissemination of sexting and psychopathology correlates: An exploratory analysis. *International Journal of Environmental Research and Public Health*, 18(12), 6564. Advance online publication. DOI: 10.3390/ijerph18126564 PMID: 34207211

Gassó, A. M., Mueller-Johnson, K., & Montiel, I. (2020). Sexting, online sexual victimization, and psychopathology correlates by sex: Depression, anxiety, and global psychopathology. *International Journal of Environmental Research and Public Health*, 17(3), 1018. Advance online publication. DOI: 10.3390/ijerph17031018 PMID: 32041115

Geeng, C., Jevan, H., & Franziska, R. (2020, August 10–11). *Usable Sexurity: Studying People's Concerns and Strategies When Sexting* [Symposium presentation]. Sixteenth Symposium on Usable Privacy and Security, Virtual Conference. https://www.usenix.org/system/files/soups2020-geeng.pdf

Gewirtz-Meydan, A., Mitchell, K. J., & Rothman, E. F. (2018). What do kids think about sexting? *Computers in Human Behavior*, 86, 256–265. DOI: 10.1016/j.chb.2018.04.007

Gil-Llario, M. D., Gil-Juliá, B., Morell-Mengual, V., Cárdenas-López, G., & Ballester-Arnal, R. (2021). Analysis of demographic, psychological and cultural aspects associated with the practice of sexting in Mexican and Spanish adolescents. *International Journal of Intercultural Relations*, 82, 197–206. DOI: 10.1016/j.ijintrel.2021.03.013

Gil-Llario, M. D., Giménez, G., Ballester-Arnal, R., Cárdenas-López, G., & Durán-Baca, X. (2017). Gender, Sexuality, and Relationships in Young Hispanic People. *Journal of Sex & Marital Therapy*, 43(5), 456–462. DOI: 10.1080/0092623X.2016.1207732 PMID: 27366863

Gil-Llario, M. D., Morell-Mengual, V., Jiménez-Martínez, M. C., Iglesias-Campos, P., Gil-Julia, B., & Ballester-Arnal, R. (2020). Culture as an influence on sexting attitudes and behaviors: A differential analysis comparing adolescents from Spain and Colombia. *International Journal of Intercultural Relations*, 79, 145–154. DOI: 10.1016/j.ijintrel.2020.08.010

Gill, R. (2007). Post-Feminist Media Culture: Elements of a Sensibility. *European Journal of Cultural Studies*, 10(2), 147–166. DOI: 10.1177/1367549407075898

Gill, R. (2008). Culture and Subjectivity in Neoliberal and Post-Feminist Times. *Subjectivity*, 25(1), 432–445. DOI: 10.1057/sub.2008.28

Giroux, A. M. (2011). *Sexting: Connections to sexual and social development.* [Unpublished honors thesis]. The University of Arizona.

Goldfarb, E. S., & Lieberman, L. D. (2021). Three decades of research: The case for comprehensive sex education. *The Journal of Adolescent Health*, 68(1), 13–27. DOI: 10.1016/j.jadohealth.2020.07.036 PMID: 33059958

Gomes, M., Vasconcelos-Raposo, J., & Teixeira, C. M. (2021). The impact of technology usage on love and intimacy satisfaction among Portuguese adults. *Computers in Human Behavior Reports*, 4, 100084. Advance online publication. DOI: 10.1016/j.chbr.2021.100084

Goodman-Deane, J., Mieczakowski, A., Johnson, D., Goldhaber, T., & Clarkson, P. J. (2016). The impact of communication technologies on life and relationship satisfaction. *Computers in Human Behavior*, 57, 219–229. DOI: 10.1016/j.chb.2015.11.053

Gordon-Messer, D., Bauermeister, J. A., Grodzinski, A., & Zimmerman, M. (2013). Sexting among young adults. *The Journal of Adolescent Health*, 52(3), 301–306. DOI: 10.1016/j.jadohealth.2012.05.013 PMID: 23299018

Gottfredson, M. R., & Hirschi, T. (2017). Self-control and opportunity. In Britt, C. L., & Gottfredson, M. R. (Eds.), *Control Theories of Crime and Delinquency* (1st ed., pp. 5–20). Routledge. DOI: 10.4324/9781351323727-1

Gov.uk. (2024, January 31). *Cyberflashing, Epilepsy Trolling and Fake News to Put Online Abusers Behind Bars from Today* [Press release]. https://www.gov.uk/government/news/cyberflashing-epilepsy-trolling-and-fake-news-to-put-online-abusers-behindbars-from-today

Guest, C., & Denes, A. (2022). Too much too soon?: Perceived appropriateness of sexting across stages of relationship development and attachment tendencies among emerging adults. *Computers in Human Behavior*, 137, 107429. Advance online publication. DOI: 10.1016/j.chb.2022.107429

Hall, M., Williams, R. D., Ford, M. A., Cromeans, E. M., & Bergman, R. J. (2020). Hooking-up, religiosity, and sexting among college students. *Journal of Religion and Health*, 59(1), 484–496. DOI: 10.1007/s10943-016-0291-y PMID: 27468909

Harvey, C. A., Harvey, T. A., & Thompson, A. E. (2020). The "sextual" double standard: An experimental examination of variations in judgments of men and women who engage in computer-mediated sexual communication. *Sexuality & Culture*, 24(3), 712–732. DOI: 10.1007/s12119-019-09658-8

Hassan, H., Tariq, K., Nasir, M., & Ayub, S. (2023). Personality Traits, Self-Control, and Sexting Attitudes Among Young Adults. *Pakistan Journal of Psychological Research*, 38(1), 147–164. DOI: 10.33824/PJPR.2023.38.1.10

Hatton, E., & Trautner, M. N. (2011). Equal Opportunity Objectification? The Sexualization of Men and Women on the Cover of Rolling Stone. *Sexuality & Culture*, 15(3), 256–278. DOI: 10.1007/s12119-011-9093-2

Henderson, L., & Morgan, E. (2011). Sexting and sexual relationships among teens and young adults. *McNair Scholars Research Journal*, 7, 31–39.

Henningsen, D. D. (2004). Flirting with meaning: An examination of miscommunication in flirting interactions. *Sex Roles*, 50(7-8), 481–489. DOI: 10.1023/B:SERS.0000023068.49352.4b

Henry, N., & Beard, G. (2024). Image-based sexual abuse perpetration: A scoping review. *Trauma, Violence, & Abuse. Trauma, Violence & Abuse*, 15248380241266137(5), 3981–3998. Advance online publication. DOI: 10.1177/15248380241266137 PMID: 39078000

Hertlein, K. M., & Twist, M. L. C. (2017). Sexting Behavior Among College Students: Implications for College Clinicians. *Journal of College Student Psychotherapy*, 31(3), 215–230. DOI: 10.1080/87568225.2016.1277814

Holmes, L. G., Nilssen, A. R., Cann, D., & Strassberg, D. S. (2021). A sex-positive mixed methods approach to sexting experiences among college students. *Computers in Human Behavior*, 115, 106619. Advance online publication. DOI: 10.1016/j.chb.2020.106619

Hongladarom, S. (2011). Personal identity and the self in the online and offline world. *Minds and Machines*, 21(4), 533–548. DOI: 10.1007/s11023-011-9255-x

Houck, C. D., Barker, D., Rizzo, C., Hancock, E., Norton, A., & Brown, L. K. (2014). Sexting and sexual behavior in at-risk adolescents. *Pediatrics*, 133(2), e276–e282. DOI: 10.1542/peds.2013-1157 PMID: 24394678

Howard, D., Ryter, S., Hu, Y., Clancy, E. M., Klettke, B., & Klas, A. (2024). Unsolicited Sexting and Help-Seeking Behaviours among Australian Adults: A Mixed-Methods Study. *Social Sciences (Basel, Switzerland)*, 13(6), 289. Advance online publication. DOI: 10.3390/socsci13060289

Hoyle, R. H., Fejfar, M. C., & Miller, J. D. (2000). Personality and sexual risk taking: A quantitative review. *Journal of Personality*, 68(6), 1203–1231. DOI: 10.1111/1467-6494.00132 PMID: 11130738

Hu, Y., Clancy, E. M., & Klettke, B. (2023). Longitudinal Sexting Research: A Systematic Review. *Psych*, 5(2), 526–544. DOI: 10.3390/psych5020035

Hudson, H. K. (2011). *Factors affecting sexting behaviors among selected undergraduate students.* [Unpublished doctoral dissertation]. Southern Illinois University at Carbondale.

Hudson, H. K., & Marshall, S. A. (2018). Consequences and predictors of sexting among selected southern undergraduates. *International Journal of Sexual Health, 30*(1), 20–27. . 2017. 14045 40DOI: <ALIGNMENT.qj></ALIGNMENT>10.1080/ 19317 611

Jeanfreau, M. M., Wright, L., & Noguchi, K. (2019). Marital satisfaction and sexting behavior among individuals in relationships. *The Family Journal (Alexandria, Va.)*, 27(1), 17–21. DOI: 10.1177/1066480718819868

Jonsson, L. S., Priebe, G., Bladh, M., & Svedin, C. G. (2014). Voluntary sexual exposure online among Swedish youth–social background, Internet behavior and psychosocial health. *Computers in Human Behavior*, 30, 181–190. DOI: 10.1016/j.chb.2013.08.005

Justus, A. N., Finn, P. R., & Steinmetz, J. E. (2000). The influence of traits of disinhibition on the association between alcohol use and risky sexual behavior. *Alcohol, Clinical and Experimental Research*, 24(7), 1028–1035. DOI: 10.1111/j.1530-0277.2000.tb04646.x PMID: 10924006

Kahn, J. A., Kaplowitz, R. A., Goodman, E., & Emans, S. J. (2002). The association between impulsiveness and sexual risk behaviors in adolescent and young adult women. *The Journal of Adolescent Health*, 30(4), 229–232. DOI: 10.1016/S1054-139X(01)00391-3 PMID: 11927234

Kalish, R. (2023). Sexting in a post-feminist society: Balancing agentic empowerment and the sexual double standard. *Women's Studies International Forum*, 98, 1–8. DOI: 10.1016/j.wsif.2023.102726

Karasavva, V., Brunet, L., Smodis, A., Swanek, J., & Forth, A. (2023). Putting the Y in cyberflashing: Exploring the prevalence and predictors of the reasons for sending unsolicited nude or sexual images. *Computers in Human Behavior*, 140, 107593. Advance online publication. DOI: 10.1016/j.chb.2022.107593

Karasavva, V., Swanek, J., Smodis, A., & Forth, A. (2022). Expectations VS reality: Expected and actual affective reactions to unsolicited sexual images. *Computers in Human Behavior*, 130, 107181. Advance online publication. DOI: 10.1016/j.chb.2022.107181

Kerstens, J., & Stol, W. (2014). Receiving online sexual requests and producing online sexual images: The multifaceted and dialogic nature of adolescents' online sexual interactions. *Cyberpsychology (Brno)*, 8(1), 1–12. DOI: 10.5817/CP2014-1-8

Khurana, A., Romer, D., Betancourt, L. M., Brodsky, N. L., Giannetta, J. M., & Hurt, H. (2012). Early Adolescent Sexual Debut: The mediating role of working memory ability, sensation seeking, and impulsivity. *Developmental Psychology*, 48(5), 1416–1428. DOI: 10.1037/a0027491 PMID: 22369334

Kibbe, K., & Thomas, S. S. (2024, May 24). *The 10 best sexting apps that should already be on your phone*. https://www.cosmopolitan.com/sex-love/a28137017/sexting-apps/

Kirkpatrick, L. A., & Davis, K. E. (1994). Attachment style, gender, and relationship stability: A longitudinal analysis. *Journal of Personality and Social Psychology*, 66(3), 502–512. Advance online publication. DOI: 10.1037/0022-3514.66.3.502 PMID: 8169762

Klettke, B., Hallford, D. J., & Mellor, D. J. (2014). Sexting prevalence and correlates: A systematic literature review. *Clinical Psychology Review*, 34(1), 44–53. DOI: 10.1016/j.cpr.2013.10.007 PMID: 24370714

Klettke, B., Mellor, D., Silva-Myles, L., Clancy, E., & Sharma, M. K. (2018). Sexting and mental health: A study of Indian and Australian young adults. *Cyberpsychology (Brno)*, 12(2), 2. Advance online publication. DOI: 10.5817/CP2018-2-2

Krieger, M. A. (2017). Unpacking "sexting": A systematic review of non-consensual sexting in legal, educational, and psychological literatures. *Trauma, Violence & Abuse*, 18(5), 593–601. DOI: 10.1177/1524838016659486 PMID: 27436858

Laird, J., Klettke, B., Clancy, E., & Fuelscher, I. (2021). Relationships between coerced sexting and differentiation of self: An exploration of protective factors. *Sexes*, 2(4), 468–482. DOI: 10.3390/sexes2040037

Lameiras-Fernández, M., Martínez-Román, R., Carrera-Fernández, M. V., & Rodríguez-Castro, Y. (2021). Sex education in the spotlight: What is working? Systematic review. *International Journal of Environmental Research and Public Health*, 18(5), 2555. Advance online publication. DOI: 10.3390/ijerph18052555 PMID: 33806507

Lapierre, M. A., & Custer, B. E. (2021). Testing relationships between smartphone engagement, romantic partner communication, and relationship satisfaction. *Mobile Media & Communication*, 9(2), 155–176. DOI: 10.1177/2050157920935163

Le, L., Goegan, L. D., & Daniels, L. M. (2023). The impact of autonomous and controlled sexting motivations on subjective well-being and relationship quality. *Archives of Sexual Behavior*, 52(1), 243–254. DOI: 10.1007/s10508-022-02361-0 PMID: 35881253

Lenhart, A. (2009, December 15). *Teens and sexting: How and why minor teens are sending sexually suggestive nude or nearly nude images via text messaging*. Pew Internet & American Life Project.

https://www.pewinternet.org/2009/12/15/teens-and-sexting/

Licata, N. (2024). The Digital Era Will Prompt Revolutions - as Did the Print Era. *CounterPunch*, 1–5.

Lippman, J. R., & Campbell, S. W. (2014). Damned if you do, damned if you don't...if you're a girl: Relational and normative contexts of adolescent sexting in the United States. *Journal of Children and Media*, 8(4), 371–386. DOI: 10.1080/17482798.2014.923009

Lorang, M. R., McNiel, D. E., & Binder, R. L. (2016). Minors and sexting: Legal implications. *The Journal of the American Academy of Psychiatry and the Law*, 44(1), 73–81. PMID: 26944746

Mandau, M. B. H. (2020). 'Directly in your face': A qualitative study on the sending and receiving of unsolicited 'dick pics' among young adults. *Sexuality & Culture*, 24(1), 72–93. DOI: 10.1007/s12119-019-09626-2

Mansor, N., Ahmad, N., & Zulkefli, N. A. M. (2023). Intrinsic and Extrinsic Factors Associated with Sexting Behavior Among Young People: A Systematic Review. *Malaysian Journal of Public Health Medicine*, 23(1), 42–56. DOI: 10.37268/mjphm/vol.23/no.1/art.1485

Marcum, C. D., Zaitzow, B. H., & Higgins, G. E. (2002). The role of sexting and related behaviors to victimization via nonconsensual pornography: An exploratory analysis of university students. *Journal of Aggression, Conflict and Peace Research*, 14(1), 43–60. DOI: 10.1108/JACPR-02-2021-0578

Marganski, A. (2017). Sexting in Poland and the United States: A comparative study of personal and social-situational factors. *International Journal of Cyber Criminology*, 11(2), 183–201. DOI: 10.5281/zenodo.1037385

Marganski, A., & Fauth, K. (2013). Socially Interactive Technology and Contemporary Dating: A Cross-Cultural Exploration of Deviant Behaviors Among Young Adults in the Modern, Evolving Technological World. *International Criminal Justice Review*, 23(4), 357–377. DOI: 10.1177/1057567713513797

Masters, N. T., Norris, J., Stoner, S. A., & George, W. H. (2006). How does it end? Women project the outcome of a sexual assault scenario. *Psychology of Women Quarterly*, 30(3), 291–302. DOI: 10.1111/j.1471-6402.2006.00297.x

Matotek, L., Howard, D., Clancy, E. M., Fuelscher, I., & Klettke, B. (2021). Sexting and relationship satisfaction among emerging adults: Dispelling the myth. *Sexuality & Culture*, 25(4), 1192–1203. DOI: 10.1007/s12119-021-09832-x

Matsui, S. (2015). The criminalization of revenge porn in Japan. *Washington International Law Journal*, 24, 289–317.

Matthews, S. J., Giuliano, T. A., Thomas, K. H., Straup, M. L., & Martinez, M. A. (2018). Not cool, dude: Perceptions of solicited vs. unsolicited sext messages from men and women. *Computers in Human Behavior*, 88, 1–4. DOI: 10.1016/j.chb.2018.06.014

McDaniel, B. T., & Drouin, M. (2015). Sexting among married couples: Who is doing it, and are they more satisfied? *Cyberpsychology, Behavior, and Social Networking*, 18(11), 628–634. DOI: 10.1089/cyber.2015.0334 PMID: 26484980

McDaniel, B. T., Drouin, M., & Cravens, J. D. (2017). Do You Have Anything to Hide? Infidelity-Related Behaviors on Social Media Sites and Marital Satisfaction. *Computers in Human Behavior*, 66, 88–95. DOI: 10.1016/j.chb.2016.09.031 PMID: 28439148

Medrano, J. L. J., Lopez Rosales, F., & Gámez-Guadix, M. (2018). Assessing the links of sexting, cybervictimization, depression, and suicidal ideation among university students. *Archives of Suicide Research*, 22(1), 153–164. DOI: 10.1080/13811118.2017.1304304 PMID: 28287925

Mikulincer, M., Gillath, O., & Shaver, P. R. (2002). Activation of the attachment system in adulthood: Threat-related primes increase the accessibility of mental representations of attachment figures. *Journal of Personality and Social Psychology*, 83(4), 881–895. Advance online publication. DOI: 10.1037/0022-3514.83.4.881 PMID: 12374442

Moon, J. W. (2021). Why are world religions so concerned with sexual behavior? *Current Opinion in Psychology*, 40, 15–19. DOI: 10.1016/j.copsyc.2020.07.030 PMID: 32877834

Morelli, M., Bianchi, D., Baiocco, R., Pezzuti, L., & Chirumbolo, A. (2016). Not-allowed sharing of sexts and dating violence from the perpetrator's perspective: The moderation role of sexism. *Computers in Human Behavior*, 56, 163–169. DOI: 10.1016/j.chb.2015.11.047

Morelli, M., Chirumbolo, A., Bianchi, D., Baiocco, R., Cattelino, E., Laghi, F., Sorokowski, P., Misiak, M., Dziekan, M., Hudson, H., Marshall, A., Nguyen, T. T. T., Mark, L., Kopecky, K., Szotkowski, R., Demirtaş, E. T., Van Ouytsel, J., Ponnet, K., Walrave, M., & Drouin, M. (2020). The role of HEXACO personality traits in different kinds of sexting: A cross-cultural study in 10 countries. *Computers in Human Behavior*, 113, 106502. Advance online publication. DOI: 10.1016/j.chb.2020.106502

Morelli, M., Plata, M. G., Isolani, S., Zabala, M. E. Z., Hoyos, K. P. C., Tirado, L. M. U., Gracia, M. S. R., Barbosa, C. P., Pistella, J., Zuffianò, A., Gerbino, M., Laghi, F., Pastorelli, C., & Baiocco, R. (2023). Sexting behaviors before and during COVID-19 in Italian and Colombian young adults. *Sexuality Research & Social Policy*, 20(4), 1515–1527. DOI: 10.1007/s13178-023-00798-z PMID: 37363349

Mori, C., Cooke, J. E., Temple, J. R., Ly, A., Lu, Y., Anderson, N., Rash, C., & Madigan, S. (2020). The prevalence of sexting behaviors among emerging adults: A meta-analysis. *Archives of Sexual Behavior*, 49(4), 1103–1119. DOI: 10.1007/s10508-020-01656-4 PMID: 32072397

Murray, C. E., & Campbell, E. C. (2015). The pleasures and perils of technology in intimate relationships. *Journal of Couple & Relationship Therapy*, 14(2), 116–140. DOI: 10.1080/15332691.2014.953651

Nicklin, L. L., Swain, E., & Lloyd, J. (2020). Reactions to unsolicited violent, and sexual, explicit media content shared over social media: Gender differences and links with prior exposure. *International Journal of Environmental Research and Public Health*, 17(12), 4296. Advance online publication. DOI: 10.3390/ijerph17124296 PMID: 32560142

Noorishad, P.-G., & Trottier, D. (2022). Investigating the relationships between sexting and sexual coercion. *Sexologies*, 31(1), e8–e15. DOI: 10.1016/j.sexol.2021.11.004

Notté, R. J. (2024). Exploring the impact of sextortion on adult males: A narrative approach. *Technology in Society*, 78, 102167. Advance online publication. DOI: 10.1016/j.techsoc.2024.102617

Novak, J. R., Sandberg, J. G., Jeffrey, A. J., & Young-Davis, S. (2016). The impact of texting on perceptions of face-to-face communication in couples in different relationship stages. *Journal of Couple & Relationship Therapy*, 15(4), 274–294. DOI: 10.1080/15332691.2015.1062452

O'Connor, K., & Drouin, M. (2020). Sexting and social concerns. *The Palgrave Handbook of International Cybercrime and Cyberdeviance*, 1087–1108. DOI: 10.1007/978-3-319-78440-3_50

O'Connor, K., Drouin, M., Yergens, N., & Newsham, G. (2017). Sexting legislation in the United States and abroad: A call for uniformity. *International Journal of Cyber Criminology*, 11(2), 218–245. DOI: 10.5281/zenodo.1037397

Obegi, J. H., & Berant, E. (Eds.). (2010). *Attachment theory and research in clinical work with adults.* Guilford press.

Ojeda, M., & Del Rey, R. (2022). Lines of action for sexting prevention and intervention: A systematic review. *Archives of Sexual Behavior*, 51(3), 1659–1687. DOI: 10.1007/s10508-021-02089-3 PMID: 34791584

Olson, K. E., O'Brien, M. A., Rogers, W. A., & Charness, N. (2011). Diffusion of Technology: Frequency of Use for Younger and Older Adults. *Ageing International*, 36(1), 123–145. DOI: 10.1007/s12126-010-9077-9 PMID: 22685360

Oriza, I. I. D., & Hanipraja, M. A. (2020). Sexting and sexual satisfaction on young adults in romantic relationship. *Psychological Research on Urban Society*, 3(1), 30–39. DOI: 10.7454/proust.v3i1.61

Ostrager, B. (2010). SMS. OMG! LOL! TTYL: Translating the law to accommodate today's teens and the evolution from texting to sexting. *Family Court Review*, 48(4), 712–726. DOI: 10.1111/j.1744-1617.2010.01345.x

Parker, T. S., Blackburn, K. M., Perry, M. S., & Hawks, J. M. (2013). Sexting as an intervention: Relationship satisfaction and motivation considerations. *The American Journal of Family Therapy*, 41(1), 1–12. DOI: 10.1080/01926187.2011.635134

Patchin, J. W., & Hinduja, S. (2020). It is time to teach safe sexting. *The Journal of Adolescent Health*, 66(2), 140–143. DOI: 10.1016/j.jadohealth.2019.10.010 PMID: 31831321

Patel, U., & Roesch, R. (2022). The prevalence of technology-facilitated sexual violence: A meta-analysis and systematic review. *Trauma, Violence & Abuse*, 23(2), 428–443. DOI: 10.1177/1524838020958057 PMID: 32930064

Paul, E. L., McManus, B., & Hayes, A. (2000). "Hookups": Characteristics and correlates of college students' spontaneous and anonymous sexual experiences. *Journal of Sex Research*, 37(1), 76–88. DOI: 10.1080/00224490009552023

Penal Code. 1871, Section 377BF, Singapore. Sexual exposure. https://sso.agc.gov.sg/Act/PC1871?ProvIds=pr377BF-

Petersen, J. L., & Hyde, J. S. (2010). A meta-analytic review of research on gender differences in sexuality, 1993–2007. *Psychological Bulletin*, 136(1), 21–38. Advance online publication. DOI: 10.1037/a0017504 PMID: 20063924

Phippen, A., & Bond, E. (2023). *Policing teen sexting: Supporting children's rights while applying the law.* Springer Nature., DOI: 10.1007/978-3-031-31455-1

Powell, A., Scott, A. J., Flynn, A., & Henry, N. (2020). *Image-Based Sexual Abuse: An International Study of Victims and Perpetrators*. Summary Report. Melbourne: RMIT University. https://doi:DOI: 10.13140/RG.2.2.35166.59209

Protecting Canadians from Online Crime Act. (2014). S.C., c, 31. https://laws-lois.justice.gc.ca/

Qu, J., Shen, S., Sun, I. Y., Farmer, A. K., & Xue, J. (2022). Sexting victimization among dating app users: A comparison of US and Chinese college students. *Journal of Interpersonal Violence*, 37(19-20), NP17109–NP17132. DOI: 10.1177/08862605211028281 PMID: 34182820

Ravn, S., Coffey, J., & Roberts, S. (2021). The currency of images: Risk, value and gendered power dynamics in young men's accounts of sexting. *Feminist Media Studies*, 21(2), 315–331. DOI: 10.1080/14680777.2019.1642229

Renfrow, D. G., & Rollo, E. A. (2014). Sexting on campus: Minimizing perceived risks and neutralizing behaviors. *Deviant Behavior*, 35(11), 903–920. DOI: 10.1080/01639625.2014.897122

Reyns, B. W., Burek, M. W., Henson, B., & Fisher, B. S. (2011). The unintended consequences of digital technology: Exploring the relationship between sexting and cybervictimization. *Journal of Crime and Justice*, 36(1), 1–17. DOI: 10.1080/0735648X.2011.641816

Reyns, B. W., Henson, B., & Fisher, B. S. (2014). Digital deviance: Low self-control and opportunity as explanations of sexting among college students. *Sociological Spectrum*, 34(3), 273–292. DOI: 10.1080/02732173.2014.895642

Richards, R. D., & Calvert, C. (2009). When sex and cell phones collide: Inside the prosecution of a teen sexting case. *Hastings Communication & Entertainment LJ, 32*, Article 1.

Ricon, T., & Dolev-Cohen, M. (2024). Sexting behavior by young adults: The correlation between emotion regulation and moral judgment. *American Journal of Sexuality Education*, 19(2), 211–229. DOI: 10.1080/15546128.2023.2212189

Ringrose, J., Gill, R., Livingstone, S., & Harvey, L. (2012). *A qualitative study of children, young people and 'sexting': A report prepared for the NSPCC*. National Society for the Prevention of Cruelty to Children. https://eprints.lse.ac.uk/44216/1/__Libfile_repository_Content_Livingstone%2C%20S_A%20qualitative%20study%20of%20children%2C%20young%20people%20and%20%27sexting%27%20%28LSE%20RO%29.pdf

Roberts, R. C. (1985). Carl Rogers and the Christian virtues. *Journal of Psychology and Theology*, 13(4), 263–273. DOI: 10.1177/009164718501300403

Roberts, S., Ravn, S., Maloney, M., & Ralph, B. (2021). Navigating the tensions of normative masculinity: Homosocial dynamics in Australian young men's discussions of sexting practices. *Cultural Sociology*, 15(1), 22–43. DOI: 10.1177/1749975520925358

Roser, M., & Ortiz-Ospina, E. (2024, March). *Literacy.*https://ourworldindata.org/literacy

Ross, J. M., Drouin, M., & Coupe, A. (2019). Sexting coercion as a component of intimate partner polyvictimization. *Journal of Interpersonal Violence*, 34(11), 2269–2291. DOI: 10.1177/0886260516660300 PMID: 27443412

Roth, M. (2015). *Here's Why Sexting May Be Good For Your Relationship – MTV*. http://www.mtv.com/news/2238267/sexting-relationship-study/

Rotunda, R. J., Kass, S. J., Sutton, M. A., & Leon, D. T. (2003). Internet use and misuse: Preliminary findings from a new assessment instrument. *Behavior Modification*, 27(4), 484–504. DOI: 10.1177/0145445503255600 PMID: 12971124

Samimi, P., & Alderson, K. G. (2014). Sexting among undergraduate students. *Computers in Human Behavior*, 31, 230–241. DOI: 10.1016/j.chb.2013.10.027

Sarshar, M., Farley, F., Fiorello, C. A., & DuCette, J. (2019). T behavior: Psychological implications of thrill-seeking/risk-taking. *Current Psychology (New Brunswick, N.J.)*, 1–8. DOI: 10.1007/s12144-019-00557-7

Schade, H. M., Hülür, G., Infurna, F. J., Hoppmann, C. A., & Gerstorf, D. (2016). Partner dissimilarity in life satisfaction: Stability and change, correlates, and outcomes. *Psychology and Aging*, 31(4), 327–339. Advance online publication. DOI: 10.1037/pag0000096 PMID: 27294715

Schmitt, D. P., & Fuller, R. C. (2015). On the varieties of sexual experience: Cross-cultural links between religiosity and human mating strategies. *Psychology of Religion and Spirituality*, 7(4), 314–326. DOI: 10.1037/rel0000036

Schwartz, S. H., & Boehnke, K. (2004). Evaluating the structure of human values with confirmatory factor analysis. *Journal of Research in Personality*, 38(3), 230–255. DOI: 10.1016/S0092-6566(03)00069-2

Segovia, A. N., Maxwell, J. A., DiLorenzo, M. G., & MacDonald, G. (2019). No strings attached? How attachment orientation relates to the varieties of casual sexual relationships. *Personality and Individual Differences*, 151, 109455. Advance online publication. DOI: 10.1016/j.paid.2019.05.061

Sesar, K., Dodaj, A., & Šimić, N. (2019). Motivational determinants of sexting: Towards a model integrating the research. *Psihologijske Teme*, 28(3), 461–482. DOI: 10.31820/pt.28.3.1

Sexual Offences (Scotland) Act 2009. https://www.legislation.gov.uk/asp/2009/9/section/6

Sharabany, R., Eshel, Y., & Hakim, C. (2008). Boyfriend, girlfriend in a traditional society: Parenting styles and development of intimate friendships among Arabs in school. *International Journal of Behavioral Development*, 32(1), 66–75. DOI: 10.1177/0165025407084053

Šmahel, D., & Subrahmanyam, K. (2014). Adolescent sexuality on the internet: A developmental perspective. In Saleh, F. M., Grudzinskas, A., & Judge, A. M. (Eds.), *Adolescent sexual behavior in the digital age* (pp. 62–85). Oxford University Press.

Sparks, B., Stephens, S., & Trendell, S. (2023). Image-based sexual abuse: Victim-perpetrator overlap and risk-related correlates of coerced sexting, non-consensual dissemination of intimate images, and cyberflashing. *Computers in Human Behavior*, 148, 107879. Advance online publication. DOI: 10.1016/j.chb.2023.107879

Speer, S. A. (2017). Flirting: A designedly ambiguous action? *Research on Language and Social Interaction*, 50(2), 128–150. DOI: 10.1080/08351813.2017.1301297

Sprecher, S. (2013). Attachment style and sexual permissiveness: The moderating role of gender. *Personality and Individual Differences*, 55(4), 428–432. DOI: 10.1016/j.paid.2013.04.005

Sprecher, S., & Cate, R. M. (2004). Sexual Satisfaction and Sexual Expression as Predictors of Relationship Satisfaction and Stability. In Harvey, J. H., Wenzel, A., & Sprecher, S. (Eds.), *The handbook of sexuality in close relationships* (pp. 235–256). Lawrence Erlbaum Associates Publishers.

Springston, K. M. (2017). Gender differences in participation in and motivations for sexting: The effects of gender role attitudes, masculinity, and femininity. *Butler Journal of Undergraduate Research, 3*(1), Article 9.

Stasko, E. C., & Geller, P. A. (2015, August 6-9). *Reframing sexting as a positive relationship behavior* [Conference presentation]. In 123rd American Psychological Association Annual Convention, Toronto, Ontario, Canada.

Sternberg, R. J. (1986). A triangular theory of love. *Psychological Review*, 93(2), 119–135. Advance online publication. DOI: 10.1037/0033-295X.93.2.119

Strassberg, D. S., Cann, D., & Velarde, V. (2017). Sexting by high school students. *Archives of Sexual Behavior*, 46(6), 1667–1672. DOI: 10.1007/s10508-016-0926-9 PMID: 28050742

Strassberg, D. S., McKinnon, R. K., Sustaita, M. A., & Rullo, J. (2013). Sexting by high school students: An exploratory and descriptive study. *Archives of Sexual Behavior*, 42(1), 15–21. DOI: 10.1007/s10508-012-9969-8 PMID: 22674035

Temple, J. R., & Choi, H. (2014). Longitudinal association between teen sexting and sexual behavior. *Pediatrics*, 134(5), e1287–e1292. DOI: 10.1542/peds.2014-1974 PMID: 25287459

Thorne, E., Babchishin, K. M., Fisico, R., & Healey, L. (2024). Sexting in Young Adults: A Normative Sexual Behavior. *Archives of Sexual Behavior*, 53(2), 593–609. DOI: 10.1007/s10508-023-02728-x PMID: 38082175

Trub, L., & Starks, T. J. (2017). Insecure attachments: Attachment, emotional regulation, sexting and condomless sex among women in relationships. *Computers in Human Behavior*, 71, 140–147. DOI: 10.1016/j.chb.2017.01.052

Upenieks, L., Chakraborty, R., & Hill, T. D. (2024). Sin in the Digital Flesh? Religiosity and the Sexting Behavior of Women and Men in the United States. *Journal of Religion and Health*, 63(4), 1–29. DOI: 10.1007/s10943-024-02059-8 PMID: 38753133

Urman, A., & Makhortykh, M. (2024). "Foreign beauties want to meet you": The sexualization of women in Google's organic and sponsored text search results. *New Media & Society*, 26(5), 2932–2953. DOI: 10.1177/14614448221099536

Valkenburg, P. M., & Peter, J. (2007). Preadolescents' and adolescents' online communication and their closeness to friends. *Developmental Psychology*, 43(2), 267–277. DOI: 10.1037/0012-1649.43.2.267 PMID: 17352538

Valkenburg, P. M., & Peter, J. (2009). The effects of instant messaging on the quality of adolescents' existing friendships: A longitudinal study. *Journal of Communication*, 59(1), 79–97. DOI: 10.1111/j.1460-2466.2008.01405.x

Van Ouytsel, J., Punyanunt-Carter, N. M., Walrave, M., & Ponnet, K. (2020). Sexting within young adults' dating and romantic relationships. *Current Opinion in Psychology*, 36, 55–59. DOI: 10.1016/j.copsyc.2020.04.007 PMID: 32480021

Van Vleet, M., & Feeney, B. C. (2015). Young at heart: A perspective for advancing research on play in adulthood. *Perspectives on Psychological Science*, 10(5), 639–645. DOI: 10.1177/1745691615596789 PMID: 26386001

Vasilescu, M. D., Serban, A. C., Dimian, G. C., Aceleanu, M. I., & Picatoste, X. (2020). Digital divide, skills and perceptions on digitalisation in the European union-towards a smart labour market. *PLoS One*, 15(4), e0232032. Advance online publication. DOI: 10.1371/journal.pone.0232032 PMID: 32324786

Vauclair, C.-M., Rudnev, M., Hofhuis, J., & Liu, J. H. (2023). Instant messaging and relationship satisfaction across different ages and cultures. *Cyberpsychology (Brno)*, 17(3), 8. Advance online publication. DOI: 10.5817/CP2023-3-8

Velez-Blasini, C. J. (2008). Evidence against alcohol as a proximal cause of sexual risk taking among college students. *Journal of Sex Research*, 45(2), 118–128. DOI: 10.1080/00224490801987408 PMID: 18569533

Walker, S., Sanci, L., & Temple-Smith, M. (2013). Sexting: Young women's and men's views on its nature and origins. *The Journal of Adolescent Health*, 52(6), 697–701. DOI: 10.1016/j.jadohealth.2013.01.026 PMID: 23587784

Walrave, M., Ponnet, K., Van Ouytsel, J., Van Gool, E., Heirman, W., & Verbeek, A. (2015). Whether or not to engage in sexting: Explaining adolescent sexting behaviour by applying the prototype willingness model. *Telematics and Informatics*, 32(4), 796–808. DOI: 10.1016/j.tele.2015.03.008

Ward, L. M. (2016). Media and sexualization: State of empirical research, 1995–2015. *Journal of Sex Research*, 53(4-5), 560–577. DOI: 10.1080/00224499.2016.1142496 PMID: 26979592

Weber, R., Eggenberger, L., Stosch, C., & Walther, A. (2022). Gender Differences in Attachment Anxiety and Avoidance and Their Association with Psychotherapy Use-Examining Students from a German University. *Behavioral Sciences (Basel, Switzerland)*, 12(7), 204. Advance online publication. DOI: 10.3390/bs12070204 PMID: 35877274

Weiss, R., & Samenow, C. P. (2010). Smart Phones, Social Networking, Sexting and Problematic Sexual Behaviors—A Call for Research. *Sexual Addiction & Compulsivity*, 17(4), 241–246. DOI: 10.1080/10720162.2010.532079

Weisskirch, R. S., & Delevi, R. (2011). "Sexting" and adult romantic attachment. *Computers in Human Behavior*, 27(5), 1697–1701. DOI: 10.1016/j.chb.2011.02.008

Weisskirch, R. S., Drouin, M., & Delevi, R. (2017). Relational anxiety and sexting. *Journal of Sex Research*, 54(6), 685–693. DOI: 10.1080/00224499.2016.1181147 PMID: 27247026

Whiteside, S. P., & Lynam, D. R. (2001). The five factor model and impulsivity: Using a structural model of personality to understand impulsivity. *Personality and Individual Differences*, 30(4), 669–689. DOI: 10.1016/S0191-8869(00)00064-7

Whitney, J., Maslyanskaya, S., & Hultgren, M. (2020). Technology/Sexting/Social Media. In Titchen, K., & Miller, E. (Eds.), *Medical Perspectives on Human Trafficking in Adolescents* (pp. 113–125). Springer., DOI: 10.1007/978-3-030-43367-3_6

Whitty, M. T. (2003). Cyber-flirting: Playing at love on the Internet. *Theory & Psychology*, 13(3), 339–357. DOI: 10.1177/0959354303013003003

Widmer, E. D., Treas, J., & Newcomb, R. (1998). Attitudes toward nonmarital sex in 24 countries. *Journal of Sex Research*, 35(4), 349–358. DOI: 10.1080/00224499809551953

Winkelman, S. B., Smith, K. V., Brinkley, J., & Knox, D. (2014). Sexting on the College Campus. *The Electronic Journal of Human Sexuality*, 17.

Wolak, J. & Finkelhor, D. (2011). *Sexting: A typology*. Crimes against Children Research Center.

Wolak, J., Finkelhor, D., & Mitchell, K. (2012). How often are teens arrested for sexting? Data from a national sample of police cases. *Pediatrics*, 129(1), 4–12. DOI: 10.1542/peds.2011-2242 PMID: 22144707

Wood, W., & Eagly, A. H. (2012). Biosocial construction of sex differences and similarities in behavior. *Advances in Experimental Social Psychology*, 46, 55–123. DOI: 10.1016/B978-0-12-394281-4.00002-7

Wysocki, D. K., & Childers, C. D. (2011). "Let my fingers do the talking": Sexting and infidelity in cyberspace. *Sexuality & Culture*, 15(3), 217–239. DOI: 10.1007/s12119-011-9091-4

Ybarra, M. L., & Mitchell, K. J. (2014). "Sexting" and its relation to sexual activity and sexual risk behavior in a national survey of adolescents. *The Journal of Adolescent Health*, 55(6), 757–764. DOI: 10.1016/j.jadohealth.2014.07.012 PMID: 25266148

Yeung, T. H., Horyniak, D. R., Vella, A. M., Hellard, M. E., & Lim, M. S. (2014). Prevalence, correlates and attitudes towards sexting among young people in Melbourne, Australia. *Sexual Health*, 11(4), 332–339. DOI: 10.1071/SH14032 PMID: 25087581

Zuckerman, M. (1990). The psychophysiology of sensation seeking. *Journal of Personality*, 58(1), 313–345. DOI: 10.1111/j.1467-6494.1990.tb00918.x PMID: 2198341

Chapter 11
Impact of Sexting, Inappropriate Content Sharing, and Cyberbullying on Youth Education

José-María Romero Rodríguez
https://orcid.org/0000-0002-9284-8919
University of Granada, Spain

Blanca Berral-Ortiz
https://orcid.org/0000-0001-8139-8468
University of Granada, Spain

Juan José Victoria Maldonado
University of Granada, Spain

Alejandro Martínez Menéndez
https://orcid.org/0009-0006-2506-5144
University of Granada, Spain

ABSTRACT

The lives of present-day young learners are more influenced by relationships built in the digital world than ever before. Although it is undeniable that a proper use of these resources may return relevant learning and developmental benefits, their misuse can build up new forms of personal attack and harassment that tend to be unknown to a victim's immediate context. Throughout this chapter, some of the most prominent forms of online risk behaviors involving privacy invasion, mainly cyberbullying and sexting, will be conceptualized alongside their main effects on the academic life of potential victims. Furthermore, the immediate need and relevant characteristics of prevention and response protocols will be discussed, as well as the role played by educational personnel and relatives in relation to both preventing and dealing with these phenomena. This chapter, therefore, highlights the urgency of these situations, as well as the relevance and contemporaneity of the matter.

DOI: 10.4018/979-8-3693-4191-9.ch011

INTRODUCTION

In the current digital era, marked by the ubiquity of electronic devices and social media platforms, we have witnessed an unprecedented revolution in the social and cultural landscape. This change has been particularly noticeable among young people, whose lives are intrinsically intertwined with digital technology (Rai, 2020). These media have not only altered the way young users relate to each other, but also their perception of the world around them and, ultimately, of themselves (Sovacool & Del Río, 2020). From how they communicate to how they construct their identity, the influence of technology on youth is undeniable.

Never before in history has the youth been so immersed in a digital world. The technological revolution has radically transformed the way young people relate to one another and perceive their environment. For example, social media has redefined the idea of friendship and community, allowing young people to connect instantly with individuals worldwide and share their life experiences virtually. Communication has become more instant and visual with emojis, GIFs, and memes becoming integral parts of the youth's digital language.

Furthermore, the omnipresence of electronic devices has created a culture of multitasking and instant gratification, where young people expect quick responses and are constantly exposed to a barrage of information and stimuli. This has led to significant changes in how young people process information and construct their identity, with a greater reliance on external validation through likes, comments, and followers on social media.

Ultimately, technology has created a world where young people are constantly connected but can also feel lonely and misunderstood. The gap between online and offline life has become increasingly blurred, and young people face unique challenges in navigating this ever-evolving digital landscape.

This paper aims to explore and understand in depth the complex interplay between digital technology, social behaviours and educational outcomes, focusing specifically on the phenomena of sexting, inappropriate sharing and cyberbullying among young people. In examining these issues, this study will address whether inappropriate sharing is an aspect of sexting and, if so, how it can escalate into forms of cyberbullying.

A crucial point to clarify is whether the impact of these phenomena will be analysed individually or primarily through the lens of sexting, considering inappropriate sharing as an extension of sexting that can lead to cyberbullying. This decision will significantly shape the organisation of the sub-chapters and the interpretation of the findings. Furthermore, this study addresses a well-defined population (adolescents and young adults) and provides a focused analysis of the risks and challenges presented by digital technology for this age group. Ultimately, the aim is to propose effective strategies to mitigate these risks within this demographic.

However, behind the apparent connectivity and opportunities for self-expression that these technological advances offer, there are also a number of risks and challenges that can profoundly affect young people's well-being and development (Redmond et al., 2020). One such phenomenon is sexting, an increasingly common behaviour among adolescents and young adults. Although often perceived as an intimate or sexual form of communication, sexting is not always initiated within trusting or exclusive relationships, nor is it necessarily a simple, consensual gesture.

The literature on sexting shows that it can arise from a variety of relational dynamics and motives and, under certain conditions (such as non-consensual sharing, forced participation or leaking of content), can become a problematic situation leading to cyberbullying or victimisation. Given the risks involved, this trend poses significant challenges for parents, educators and society, and requires a nuanced understanding of the contexts and mechanisms in which sexting can cause harm.

Moreover, cyberbullying has become a growing concern in the digital age (Sezer and Tunçer, 2021). Through tactics such as spreading rumours, sending threatening messages or creating fake profiles, bullies can inflict deep emotional and psychological harm on their victims. This type of bullying can not only have devastating effects on young people's mental and emotional health, but can also negatively affect their academic performance and participation in school life (Odgers and Jensen, 2020).

In this context, sexting and cyberbullying are interconnected risks within digital interactions. For example, inappropriate sharing of sexting content can serve as a form of cyberbullying in some types of relationships, blurring the boundaries between personal communication and aggressive behaviours. While technology offers a wide range of opportunities and benefits for young people, the dual nature of these interactions must be recognised and addressed effectively to prevent the negative outcomes that can arise when sexting becomes a pathway to cyberbullying.

SEXTING AND THE EXCHANGE OF INAPPROPRIATE CONTENT: DEFINITION AND MANIFESTATIONS

Sexting, a term derived from the combination of sex and texting, encompasses a wide spectrum of behaviors involving the exchange of sexually explicit content via digital platforms (Molla-Esparza et al., 2020). This can range from the sharing of suggestive messages, intimate photographs, or explicit videos through popular social media apps such as Snapchat, Instagram, or WhatsApp. Although initially perceived by some as a means of fostering intimacy and trust within romantic relationships, the implications of sexting extend far beyond its immediate context, such as long-distance relationships not only of a sexual or intimate nature but also extending to friendships that arise at a distance from common hobbies or at school itself as first approaches to practices of a sexual nature (Hollá et al., 2018) However, it is important to take different elements into account, as aspects such as the existence of excessive rules or the ability to communicate in an effective way with the person with whom these practices are performed are more frequent (Confalonieri et al., 2020).

The prevalence of sexting among adolescents has surged in recent years, driven by factors such as increased access to smartphones, the normalization of online dating culture, and the blurring of boundaries between public and private spaces in the digital realm (Bozzola et al., 2022). A study conducted by Van Ouytsel et al. (2014) found that approximately 70% of teenagers reported engaging in sexting behaviors by the age of 18, highlighting the pervasive nature of this phenomenon among youth during this stage of development, the presence of norms especially imposed by parents without full knowledge of the environments where their children interact generate disruptive behaviors. (Confalonieri et al., 2020)

Certainly, the prevalence of sexting among adolescents underscores its significance as a common sexual behavior within this demographic, as noted by Bonilla et al. (2021). This phenomenon has permeated youth culture, facilitated by the widespread accessibility of digital communication tools and platforms. In particular, it is especially interesting how most of the studies focus on North America (Mori et al., 2020) highlighting how images and videos are common practices although text messages are the most common form of sexting (Mori et al., 2022).

This percentage of students who practice sexting varies according to the country, with the United States being the country where most cases occur and where the most studies have been carried out (Molla-Esparza et al., 2020). Another important aspect is the age, because despite the fact that the United States is the country with the highest rate, also due to the fact that it is the most studied, what is shown is that up to 14 years of age sexting does not present worrying quantities, while from 16 years of age onwards it exceeds 25% of the population (Molla-Esparza et al., 2020).

Consequently, researchers and scholars have endeavored to categorize sexting into distinct typologies to better understand its nuances and implications, as articulated by Dodaj & Sesar (2020):

- relational sexting: this type of sexting involves the exchange of intimate images between individuals who are in a personal romantic relationship. Here, the sending of explicit sexual content occurs within the context of an established relationship, with the purpose of strengthening intimacy and emotional connection between the involved parties.
- reactive sexting: in contrast to relational sexting, reactive sexting occurs without a pre-existing personal romantic relationship. Thus, the individuals involved in this activity send images hoping to initiate or develop an emotional or romantic connection with the recipient. This type of sexting may arise as a response to perceived attraction or as a search for attention and affection.
- forced sexting: despite its name, forced sexting does not necessarily involve coercion or direct threats. In this case, there is no explicit extortion or blackmail for the dissemination of intimate images. However, there is an implicit pressure or emotional obligation to send such content, conditioning the relationship with the other person. The failure to send images may be perceived as a challenge to the relationship or as a potential threat to its continuation.
- violent sexting: in this modality of sexting, blackmail or coercion is used as means to obtain intimate images from the victim. Although initially presented as an attempt to establish an intimate relationship, pressure and emotional manipulation characterize this type of interaction. The victim is compelled to engage in the exchange of explicit sexual content under the threat of public dissemination or negative repercussions for their reputation and well-being.

However, the consequences of sexting can be far-reaching, especially within educational environments. What may begin as a seemingly harmless exchange of flirtatious messages or provocative images can quickly spiral into situations of cyberbullying, coercion, or even legal ramifications. The shared content, once disseminated without consent, can become fodder for online harassment, leading to feelings of victimization, humiliation, and social ostracization among students. Moreover, the pressure to conform to societal expectations of attractiveness and desirability in the digital age can exacerbate the risks associated with sexting, particularly for vulnerable individuals. Bradley et al. (2020) suggests that minors who suffer a non-contentious sharing of pictures, texts, or other kinds of private media as they navigate the complex terrain of online relationships and self-presentation, may experience heightened levels of anxiety, depression, and self-esteem issues.

In light of these complexities, educators and parents play a pivotal role in addressing the challenges posed by sexting and promoting responsible digital citizenship among young people. By fostering open dialogue, providing comprehensive sex education, and advocating for consent-based approaches to intimacy, they can empower students to make informed decisions about their online behavior and navigate the digital landscape with confidence and resilience.

Seen from this point of view, there are two differentiated approaches, the psychological one with positive and negative implications in which the people who carry out these practices have a relationship with very differentiated roles within the relationship (not necessarily loving) and the educational one, having as main form of approach to the activities of sexual character for the students having a negative repercussion in the academic performance and with the possibility of an intervention starting from a correct sexual education (Resett et al., 2022). From the positive perspective on sexting posits that it can bolster students' self-esteem. Engaging in these sexual practices may engender feelings of acceptance by society and being sexually desired among those who participate (Coduto, 2024; Hollá, 2020). This outlook suggests that sexting, when approached consensually and responsibly, could serve as a platform for individuals to explore and affirm their sexuality in a safe and supportive environment. It may provide an avenue for self-expression, intimacy, and validation, particularly for adolescents navigating the complexities of identity formation and social acceptance. This positive perspective on sexting should be considered, as mentioned earlier, as a sexual practice that is quite widespread, especially among adolescents and young adults. Furthermore, as previously outlined, sexting exists as a consensual sexual practice and as a form of sexual development within a relationship.

Nonetheless, due to its nature, sexting is considered a risky sexual behavior, especially during the youthful stage of development when various factors come into play. This is the stage in life when one develops many aspects which underpin the formation of families and healthy relationships. It can rarely be the period of first relationships or first love, however it is usually the time when two people start living together for the first time, discuss their future endeavors as a couple, hence a fundamental stage concerning the establishment of a couple a (Rhoades et al., 2009). This implies that during this period, both parties in the relationship tend to idealize each other, which can lead to problems and a change in the type of sexting used. It is estimated that around 15% of young adults () have been victims of the non-consensual dissemination of explicit images following an idealized relationship, with men being more susceptible to this problem due to their greater tendency to share explicit content (Van Ouytsel et al., 2020).

Specifically, the non-consensual dissemination of explicit content and blackmail can severely impact the educational environment, often becoming catalysts for bullying (Fajardo-Caldera et al., 2013). Such issues have various implications on education, which we will explore in detail later.

Additionally, it is essential to understand how sexting may influence students' academic performance. To this end, educational proposals have been put forward, such as the one developed in Romania, the Youth Risk Behavior Surveillance System (YRBSS) (Ruvalcaba et al., 2023) instument by means of which major problems related to other types of problems such as buylling, mental problems or drug use have been avoided after having suffered sexting. Thus, it has been determined that sexting does indeed have an influence on academic performance.

So much so, that it is one of the main reasons justifying school changes and dropouts (Hernández et al., 2022). Another example that supports and reinforces this idea is expressed in Torices (2023), where it is argued that students who have experienced sexting during pre-university stages of university often also suffer from sexting, which results in the majority of students who have experienced buylling during their teenage years not completing higher education.

However, the multifaceted impact of sexting extends beyond the practice itself, especially when considering its intersection with terms such as bullying or cyberbullying (Burke & Norvilitis, 2022). In many cases, sexting can become a cyber expression of bullying, where images or messages of a sexual nature are used as a tool for manipulation, humiliation, or control. This occurs when privately shared intimate material is disseminated without consent or is threatened, generating feelings of shame, fear and vulnerability in the victim.

CYBERBULLYING AND ONLINE HARASSMENT: IMPACT ON THE SCHOOL ENVIRONMENT

Cyberbullying involves the use of electronic means to harass, intimidate, or humiliate others (Kintonova et al., 2021). This may include sending threatening messages, spreading rumors, or creating fake profiles to harass someone. Cyberbullying has a devastating impact on students' mental health and emotional well-being, leading to feelings of anxiety, depression, and even suicidal thoughts. Additionally, it can negatively affect academic performance by distracting students and causing them significant stress.

To effectively address cyberbullying in educational settings, it is essential not only to understand its nature and changing dynamics but also to identify how it relates to other digital behaviors, such as sexting. In this context, sexting can be considered a form of cyberbullying when it involves coercion, non-consensual sharing, or the dissemination of inappropriate content. Although inappropriate content sharing need not be discussed separately, it will be analyzed within the context of behaviors such as 'secondary sexting,' 'unsolicited sexting,' and 'forced sexting,' all of which carry significant social and psychological risks.

A comprehensive understanding of cyberbullying includes exploring how it manifests in different settings, such as classrooms, social media platforms, and other online environments. To develop effective intervention and prevention strategies, it is essential to consider how different forms of cyberbullying affect students' well-being, adapting these strategies to protect them emotionally and psychologically. Ultimately, addressing cyberbullying requires a holistic approach involving educators, school administrators, parents, and the wider community to create a safe and supportive environment where all individuals feel respected and protected.

Building on this framework, Neyra (2021) examines the psychological factors associated with cyberbullying, identifying it as a precursor to serious consequences, such as violent forms of sexting (Giménez-Gualdo et al., 2022) and even tragic cases of victim suicide (Buelga et al., 2022). Research has documented how cyberbullying not only alters the emotional and psychological well-being of affected students but also significantly impairs academic performance, social relationships, and self-esteem.

The profound and potentially irreversible impact of cyberbullying highlights the urgency of addressing it from a disciplinary, psychological, and social support perspective. By understanding the psychological mechanisms underlying cyberbullying and its connections to related and concerning behaviors, educators and policymakers can implement preventive measures to foster safer and more supportive learning environments. In doing so, they contribute to mitigating the harmful effects of cyberbullying on students' mental health, which helps reduce instances of academic underachievement and dropout.

In summary, the influence of cyberbullying on academic performance is clear, understanding that this issue has a negative impact both socially and academically. The onset of bullying can significantly diminish students' motivation and academic performance. Studies have shown that victims of bullying and cyberbullying often experience a decline in academic achievement, lower grades, and decreased engagement in school activities (American Psychological Association, n.d.).

The constant fear and stress associated with being targeted by bullies can erode students' self-confidence and enthusiasm for learning (Foody et al., 2017). This negative emotional state can lead to decreased concentration, lower academic motivation, and a reluctance to participate in classroom activities (Piotrowski, 2012). Victims of bullying and cyberbullying may also experience symptoms of depression, anxiety, and social withdrawal, further exacerbating the impact on their academic performance (American Psychological Association, n.d.; Foody et al., 2017).

Moreover, the pervasive atmosphere of intimidation and harassment created by bullying can foster a sense of unease within the school environment (Foody et al., 2017). This undermines students' ability to thrive in a supportive and nurturing educational setting, with far-reaching consequences beyond just academic performance (Piotrowski, 2012).

To address this issue, schools and communities must implement comprehensive anti-bullying programs that promote a positive school climate, provide support for victims, and educate students on the importance of respect and empathy (American Psychological Association, n.d.). By creating a safe and inclusive environment, educators can help mitigate the detrimental effects of bullying and cyberbullying on students' motivation and academic success.

Cyberbullying, broadly defined as repeated and intentional bullying through digital media, has a markedly negative impact on young students, particularly underage students (Piotrowski, 2012; Van Ouytsel et al., 2020). Research consistently links cyberbullying to decreased academic performance, increased dropout rates, and other detrimental educational outcomes. In educational settings, cyberbullying can be exacerbated by related behaviors, such as sexting and sharing inappropriate content, which often intersect with instances of cyberbullying to intensify students' emotional distress.

Therefore, educational institutions should implement initiatives to detect and address potential cyberbullying, especially cases that are disseminated through digital platforms (ICT). Schools are encouraged to develop strategies that combine internal resources, such as counseling services and digital literacy programs, with external support networks to provide comprehensive assistance to students affected by any form of digital bullying. This approach emphasizes the importance of addressing cyberbullying within the educational system to protect students and promote a positive and inclusive school environment.

CHALLENGES AND ETHICAL DILEMMAS FOR EDUCATORS AND SCHOOL ADMINISTRATORS

Traditional forms of bullying and blackmailing within educational centers already have their own set of complex relationships and implications that must be dealt with when tackling them, either within the scope of the household or the teaching body. Nevertheless, and as digital evolutions from these concepts, cyberbullying and revolve around a three-way axis of aspects to be considered regarding successful interventions that benefit all parts within such critical environments. These, mainly, include the sheer nature of the online world and the anonymous character of potential aggressors, the barrier between the victims' online and offline life, and the training necessities that effectively resolving such scenarios requires.

People posting private content online slowly create an online identity, which may or not be a direct reflect of their actual self, that may be visible to every person within the online world, without an actual true ability to limit potential consumers of this information (Camacho et al., 2012). Therefore, and firstly, following Ybarra and Mitchell (2004), in most victimization cases regarding online risk behaviors the attacker either does not personally know the victim and just aimed to hurt them according to content reviewed online or is actually well aware of their in-real-life identity, and chooses to hide their personal information and identity. Although it is true that certain services and social media applications offer privacy settings to avoid such risks, hurtful practices may originate even from actual offline personal relationships via online means (Yisa & Orji, 2024). As Wei et al. (2024) affirm, not even being proficient in online privacy preservation necessarily means being immune to falling victim to this kind of invasive practices. As such, it could be said that every individual, regardless of their age and socio-affective situation, may be a potential victim at any given point in their lives to the aforementioned online risk activities.

Secondly, as Sharma et al. (2024) declare, individuals prone to take part in these activities tend to create *online personas*, i.e. made up and fairly exaggerated ideal self-identification based on socially accepted traits, in an attempt to build barriers between their offline selves and the practices they get into within the online world. After all, interactions developed between potential victims and related aggressors and/or attackers even if developed on online platforms, take place within a sense of personal privacy that direct messages and closed social groups are able to offer (Kopecký et al., 2022). As a result, users may behave freely and under a feeling of trust with other persons with whom they may have established close personal online relationships, not expecting others external to that limited context to view, access or comment on said behaviors and media (Yisa & Orji, 2024).

Shattering these limitations by exposing the actions developed under the guise of these personas, directly revealing them to relatives and any other given form of close relationships, leads to severe embarrassment and feelings of invasion (Nazarov & Averbukh, 2023). Therefore, although most authorities related to affected users may opt for direct intervention-based strategies when tackling these issues, in truth, such procedures may end up worsening the mental health state of these individuals, deeply complicating their recovery and trust building process after such incidents (Mladenović et al., 2021). As Rodríguez-Castro et al. (2021) point out, what victims of these activities fear most is the revelation of their personal, supposedly private, online acting to their close ones and relatives, which may lead external help to be deemed undesired and ill-intended.

Finally, and perhaps being the most worrying dimension of this handful of challenges, a relatively ample section of the current teaching body does not have a well-defined and proper conception of online learner privacy, as detailed in a study conducted by Leatham (2017). This apparent ignorance, following Marín et al. (2021), can be traced back to blindly devoting oneself to policies developed by institutions of a higher administrative order, without taking the time to carefully study them or being repelled by the frighteningly complex concepts of online risk and security. The subjacent lack of preparation regarding how to address privacy and protection in educational environments, as Sciacca et al. (2021) point out, often leads to educators feeling reserved about introducing learners to the reality of inadequate social media use and its respective consequences, associating it with crossing the line between the student's personal and academic life.

Now, it is in the conflicting verge of these three aspects where the actual role of educators regarding such issues lies within an ethically ambiguous paradigm, as the dilemma here is not based around the need for intervention or not, but rather the approach that should be considered when trying to intervene in such phenomena (Smith, 2015). Currently, as Gudmundsdottir et al. (2020) describe it, teachers opt to assume the duty of an advising figure, based on empathy and comprehension towards the student, avoiding overstepping into the individual's privacy while acting as an external yet close guide. As previously outlined, even if direct intervention would be most efficient in order to put an end to victimization scenarios based on explicit and intimate extortion, following Kopecký et al. (2022), it is indeed the duty of a teacher to look out both for the learners' safety and well-being, having to consider their sense of identity and right to privacy as a crucial aspect of that very notion.

In this line of thought, and as Tackie (2022) recommends, educators should deal with such situations by establishing close personal pedagogical relationships with their students based on mutual trust and accessibility, which can facilitate dealing with personal traumas and developing socioemotional skills. However, not every educator may feel up to the task of addressing learners as equals from a socioemotional perspective, especially considering antecedents of learners exploiting and taking advantage of the intimate character of this kind of relationships to humiliate or make fun of educators (Adorjan & Ricciardelli, 2023).

In this paradigm based on indirect intervention, the teacher should, in sum, adopt the role of a close personal figure, that has been trained regarding varied strategies and notions regarding the preservation of privacy while understanding the need for help and companionship of their learners, is able to guide pupils from both expert knowledge and experience through the realm of both offline and online trust, while being careful enough not to get too involved in the pupils' personal affairs.

It is in this very same context where the notion of *pedagogical love* arises. Following Gonzalez and Holdgate (2023), this idea could be understood as a form of altruist and sustained care and support towards one's own learners, in line with the basic responsibilities and goals of the teaching guild itself. In other words, following Moller (2023), this approach would be entirely based on adopting education as a self-existent dimension, without acting as a subjacent practice towards activities of a higher order, having the sole goal of devoting oneself to the pupil's overall wellbeing.

Now, as Chen (2023) outlines, developing such a close professional teacher-learner relationship can be key in supporting learners when dealing with their drawbacks and negative vital aspects that may hinder their educational and developmental process, naturally including risk online behaviors. This paradigmatic approach, different from sheer teaching vocation, entails addressing the child as an autonomous being, who presents a set of necessities to be fulfilled not simply by offering academic contents or insights, but by acting as true role-model mentors though proximity and personal support (Andaya et al., 2024).

However, one must take into consideration that, as pupils grow and become mature human beings from a socioemotional and cognitive perspective, they tend to feel more reserved towards the teaching staff with regard to their personal beliefs and affairs (Desrosiers et al., 2012). This, eventually, may create unpleasant situations in which, although educators maintain the aforementioned notion of close professionalism regarding their students, learners may actually deem said practices to be intrusive, invasive of their personal privacy, or even offensive (Mâ ă, 2022). As underscored by Liu (2020), the act of trying to mediate between young users' actual reality and their online selves can be actually perceived by this population to be more of a privacy invasion than an aiding practice, leading to further engaging in potential addictive and risk behaviors.

Conclusively, careful planning and thought must necessarily lead teachers' action regarding interventions within students' personal lives and events, having to walk on the critical, rather thin, line between acting as a close yet distant mentor regarding the establishment of an online identity in youngsters' first years of use of social media (Daher et al., 2022), and overdoing such behavior and eventually breaking into one's own students' personal reality, mostly without any ill ulterior intention, but still negatively affecting young pupils' sense of protection and right to privacy (Sari et al., 2024), these being fundamental developmental milestones within their vital sojourn.

PREVENTION AND RESPONSE STRATEGIES IN EDUCATIONAL ENVIRONMENTS

Before delving into the different insights and interpretations that lie within both existing legislation and the body of scientific literature regarding prevention and intervention, one should analyze the conceptual reality of these notions from an educational and administrative view. Following Corcoran et al. (2015), it has been an all-time issue by now that cyberbullying, given its prevalence and relevance within educational settings, has been generally linked in a one-to-one equivalence of meaning to cyberaggression, which includes a far more diverse variety of problematic situations associated with online activity.

Nevertheless, the lack of a clear interpretation of this terminology is further proved by the tendency within the scientific educational research field to consider sexting, the second main behavior addressed in this chapter, as a fully negative or detrimental practice (Rübner et al., 2019). In reality, as previously indicated and as detailly commented on Van Ouytsel et al.'s (2020) work, sexting does not have an innate negative effect on teenagers and young adults, as it can act as a beneficial and enriching way to enjoy one's own intimacy towards trusted partners. As these authors state, students are in dire need of experiencing adequate and elaborate sexual education practices related to the potential risks of conducting sexting with individuals with whom one does not have a close or trustworthy connection. This, eventually, leads the potential victimization derived from inadequate sexting practices to be included into this field of cyberaggression (Bacaksiz et al., 2020; Corcoran et al., 2015).

It should be worth noting, however, that in order to establish a clear differentiation between malevolent sexting practices and healthy intimate exchanges, authors such as Henry and Beard (2024) opt for using the term *Image-Based Sexual Abuse Perpetration*, in order to refer to the former while underscoring its detrimental effects over their targets. For the purposes of analyzing the existing literature about on preventing and acting in these activities, in order to clear up potential misconceptions, the term cyberaggression and cybervictimization will be used to refer to the wide group of risk and harmful activities in which one could include detrimental sexting and cyberbullying.

Having addressed these basic legalese ambiguous delimitations, and given the severity of long-term exposure to cyberaggression, establishing effective, clear and non-invasive action-prevention protocols must be a priority for any given educational administrator or organism. "Teachers are in a position of controlling information access of a vulnerable population and for which they are duty bound to protect the best interests of the student" (Leatham, 2017, p. 72). It, therefore, becomes essential for administrations to limit the extent of involvement of staff when such risk behaviors are directly related to any given educational community. As it is stated in the Convention on the Rights of the Child (United Nations, 1989), the privacy of a child should not be meddled with on account of unlawful or arbitrary reasons. This establishes the need to intervene in such scenarios with care regarding personal data and information that may be involved.

This is the general course of action followed in American legislation, in which avoiding issues such as "online bullying [...] sexual exploitation and abuse" (Kids Online Safety Act, 2023, p. 60) is an explicit top priority. Accessing a child's personal information can only be conducted without consent, even if trying to receive it is, nonetheless, mandatory; in order to safeguard the safety of the user in any given platform (Children's Online Privacy Protection Rule, 2013). Similarly, the European legislation establishes that the processing of data and information regarding children is considered lawful, among a plethora of reasons, if it is essential to protect the utmost benefit of the user or individuals related to them, as well as participate in legal activities of public interest (Regulation (EU) 2016/679 of the European

Parliament and of the Council of 27 April 2016 on the protection of natural persons with regard to the processing of personal data and on the free movement of such data, and repealing Directive 95/46/EC).

Hypothetical action-prevention protocols should, nonetheless, be preceded by the development of training and mentalization activities and/or courses aimed at educating on its proper, formal, and respectful use (Ojeda & Del Rey, 2022). It is only in this way how both potential victims and aggressors may be reached, as the core of every educational action towards a negative behavior shall have eradicating it via social transformation rather than penalization as its aim. The Spanish legislation, as a leading example, allows educational centers to establish specific protocols in order to tackle episodes of cybervictimization in which, as a last resort, educational authorities may recover proof of the committed acts (Ley Orgánica 8/2021, de 4 de junio, de protección integral a la infancia y la adolescencia frente a la violencia), although training aimed at the prevention of said stages is preferred, as "public administrations will guarantee [...] the learning of a safe use of digital resources, respectful with [...] personal privacy and [...] personal data" (p. 68683).

Overall, the mainstream line of thought regarding the design of preparation programs assumes that the online space is a complex environment with concepts that need to be understood and addressed (Bozza & Vinha, 2023). Moreover, great advancements have been designed in the field of anonymous and automated risk behavior detection, such as the federated deep learning interface proposed by Samee et al. (2023), trained with pre-labelled iterations linked, or not, to cyberbullying that can even add data noise to hide the users' identity. Similarly, and intending to make good use of the benefits of peer tutoring and advise, training programs with a purpose linked to both reeducation and prevention such as *Safety.net*, developed by Ortega-Barón et al. (2024), tend to recruit actual victims, of a similar age to the target population, of either cyberbullying, harmful sexting experiences and inappropriate content sharing so that pupils are able to accommodate and integrate these discourses to their own day-to-day life.

When it comes to potential intervention proposals on already occurring cases of any given form of cyberaggression, considering the profound ethical dilemmas that tackling them may entail as previously underscored, researchers such as Dully et al. (2023) incite practitioners to assist regarding the matter to address these situations from a communicative, collaborative and mutually interactive perspective, that is, openly discussing the sequence of events and the reasoning behind them. Learners should be presented with strategies not only to avoid cyberaggression, but also to fight against it should it arise (Yurdakul & Ayhan, 2023), building on their self-esteem as a protective factor against the influence of attackers as well as temptation to harm other users (Touloupis & Athanasiades, 2022). Apart from providing safe havens in order to report falling victim to such critical situations, authors like Vijayarani et al. (2024) propose establishing intervention procedures based, not only on clearly establishing grave consequences for perpetrators, but on teaching coping strategies to victims as well. It is well-known that falling victim to either a cyberbullying or ill-purpose sexting practices may scarce victims for life, independently of their ability to safely report their situation to higher authorities, therefore, assisting them towards self-regulation and personal development is essential in order to fully overcome these dark and traumatic experiences.

Valuing victims' own experiences instead of repeatedly referring to not having followed basic prevention strategies, as Aulia et al. (2024) expose, leads to fluent communication as well as reconstruction of self-security and self-esteem, subsequent to avoiding demonization of involvement within these scenarios and irrelevant reiteration of potential preventive courses of action that could no longer benefit actual victims. It is precisely within this field of respect and understanding of mistakes that already led to severe consequences that the role of peer mediators is presented. The role of the *cyberbystander* is broader than reporting on potential scenarios of cybervictimization, since, following, Chicote-Beato et al. (2024), acting as social references to the affected pupils, making sure that they will not lose any of the social networks that they are already a part of, can be essential when facing the aftermath behind solving such cases. Equally, Daniels et al. (2024) advise against directly restricting youngsters' access to online means of establishing personal relationships, as such a categorical course of action, while avoiding experiences leading to possibly negative consequences, brutally conflicts with the natural need for communication and relationships that is akin to individuals within these age gaps.

It should be noted, nonetheless, that action programs should not only aim to aid in the personal restoration of the victims' psychological state out of their own wellbeing, which naturally represents a vastly important area to be taken into account and that should guide every proposal at hand, but rather to avoid internally damaged victims to end up evolving into future perpetrators out of anger and desire for revenge. Although this phenomenon is especially common when it comes to sexting, mainly because it frequently involves mutual sharing of explicit images and other media that could be used in retaliation by the opposite person in response to a prior threat or blackmail (Henry & Beard, 2024), it has been determined to be a relation that applies to cyberbullying as well, leading once-were victims to be future probable perpetrators (Chan & Wong, 2020), in a sense of implicit disregard or disappointment towards the very notion of justice and social harmony.

The harsh reality about the flip side of this normative and educational coin, however, is that even if educators believe in the necessity of such policies and courses, in practice, they feel either unprepared or at unease when conversing about such matters in the school environment (York et al., 2021). As exposed in García-Martínez and García-Zabaleta's (2024) study, there is a clear lack of actually defined action protocols when it comes to tackling existing cases, and most of the established ones require external intervention that frequently excludes both educators and administrative personnel. This, unfortunately, is also linked to how teachers may suffer from subjective bias when being part of these activities, focusing them, as Sciacca et al. (2021) state, on a hypothetical carelessness of the victim, especially when it comes to girls. Moreover, as the authors claim, this can cause the educational community to even obviate the boys' state of affairs as victims of these behaviors, having remarked influence in the case of sexting.

ROLE OF PARENTS AND THE EDUCATIONAL COMMUNITY IN STUDENT PROTECTION

Despite the establishment of the previously mentioned measures, the prevalence of deciding not to report cybervictimization neither to educators nor institutions, especially among older learners, is still surprisingly high (Iorga et al., 2022). This, within a plethora of reasons, could mainly be due to a lack of faith in potential action, associated with how student victims often conceive educational agents employed within formal learning environments as insufficiently empathetic towards issues and spiky situations seemingly exclusively akin to newer generations (Dully et al., 2023), or simply out of embarrassment (York et al., 2021). This proves that there is still a latent need to assist victims of these modern-day phenomena to the best of our possibilities beyond those protocols, adding a personal component that can point towards inner healing and wellbeing.

Turning the family household into a space for open and intimate conversation (Daher et al., 2022), where discussing implications of connecting with people online, accompanied by emotional support and assistance (Fazil et al., 2023) is possible and favored, acts as an essential step towards that goal. As

Verrastro et al. (2023) point out, establishing family relationships on developing a child's positive self-concept, as well as being willing to have more disclosure about personal predicaments with trusted adults, can prevent children from engaging in inappropriate online interactions and activities. This idea is in line with the findings reported by Turzák et al. (2020), who studied a sample comprised of 790 adolescents between the ages of twelve and eighteen, showing that having a poor relationship with one's own family can act as a catalyst for getting involved, either as a victim or perpetrator, in sexting, one of the online risk behaviors that is connected the most to self-esteem and validation. Such considerations are of key relevance during both the teenage and young adulthood stages, as it is during these developmental phases when the desire for personal independence and parental authority conflict the most (Cabrera et al., 2024).

There is, however, a blatant need to move on from parental tendencies based on strict monitoring of children's online activities since, as Orosco et al. (2022) claim, they do not influence the users' online patterns neither in a positive nor negative way. Conversely, establishing parenting styles based on affection and experience sharing has been proved to be a negative predictor for participation in cyberbullying situations, leading children to consult their parents more frequently about uncertainties when establishing online social contact (Pallarés-Piquer et al., 2022; Yépez-Tito et al., 2020). In this way, as established by Bolognesi and Bukhalovskaya (2022), educators, institution managers, relatives and other agents close to young internet users should not act as restrictive forces, but rather establish a compromise towards their educational and model roles regarding pupils, no matter their age.

Families, nevertheless, are not expected to be knowledgeable about aspects with such educational implications right from the get-go. Ultimately, they are part of an educational community comprised of a variety of stakeholders, including administrators and community agents apart from teachers themselves, who can act as role models when navigating these constantly changing themes (Gudmundsdottir et al., 2020). Cortés-Pascual et al. (2020) offer results pointing out at the high significance of positive and collaborative relationships between the household environment and the potentially involved educational centers when it comes to both preventing and taking action regarding these activities. As such, educational centers should act as reference and coordination spaces regarding the joint efforts of all the stakeholders involved in them, as their role as key socialization agents should be extended to communications of a nature that transcends academic settings (Pallarés-Piquer et al., 2022).

The role of external agents, however, should never go unnoticed, as specialists in such recent and relevant practical topics are essential to impregnate a sense of responsibility and urgency of action amongst teachers and relatives alike, who should equally participate under a learning role in such recent, ever-changing and complex topics (Bolognesi & Bukhalovskaya, 2022). Furthermore, administrative staff and service-providers employed within educational centers could actually play a key role acting as informers and mediators as well since, as declared by García-Martínez and García-Zabaleta (2024), they conform one of the sectors within the educational community that spends the most time with potential victims and perpetrators, therefore acting as recipients of interest regarding training and action-based intervention. A great example of growth opportunities lies in contacting the social services agencies of one's own territory, as they are able to offer valuable insights to pupils and stakeholders alike based on previous cases and past/personal experiences that are, usually, not within the reach of the majority of educators and families (Cabrera et al., 2024).

Finally, although often overlooked due to being allocated within the very same social group of both victims and aggressors alike, having a well-established and defined group of friends may be of great assistance when avoiding participance altogether in the aforementioned online risk behaviors. As Cortés-Pascual et al. (2020) point out, the quality and number of friendships developed by teenagers within educational environments acts a negative predictor of likely taking on both of the roles involved in these scenarios. A game-based intervention conducted by Ferreira et al. (2022) in Secondary Education showed that young learners involuntarily tend to act in a mob-like way supporting aggressive behaviors towards individuals external to their group, and that if not properly mentalized, they may understand such behaviors as not worth noting.

Apart from the sheer positive influence of feeling cared about and accompanied, being able to share insights derived from potential experiences linked to cyberaggression scenarios with others can be of great assistance as to acknowledge indicators that pinpoint the actions of not-yet detected perpetrators, given that individuals with different sociocultural backgrounds may not hold a unanimous conception of cyberaggression (Elbedour et al., 2020). However, and considering that some learners that may currently end up becoming victims to these forms of cyberaggression tend not to have deeply rooted friendships networks, advancements in the field of computer-based tutoring and mentoring have allowed diverse pupils to have their own advisement network, adapted to their personal needs and traits, via programming and generative software (Ferrer et al., 2024).

In relation to this community collaborative perspective, Zhao et al. (2022) describe teachers as substitute parents for learners during their time at formal education placements, which allows them to detect unique nonverbal cues that can be key to detect cybervictimization and prevent it from taking place. Respectively, families have deep knowledge about children's behavioral tendencies, personalities, and mentalities. Following Ortega-Barón et al. (2022), educational centers should not only act as training stations for practitioners and educational experts but should also take on the responsibility of offering the whole educational community, including third parties, a haven for communication and mutual learning. Proposals in this line can build up common guidelines and conclusions that complement the separate knowledge of each participant, guaranteeing both the online and offline safety of the pupils (Martín et al., 2023). In the end, there is no better way to prevent cyberbullying and harmful cyberbullying scenarios than promoting harmonious coexistence amongst peers (Rodríguez-Álvarez et al., 2022), a function close to both counselors and psychologists, as professional agents, and personal mentors, embodied within the close collaboration between practitioners and caregivers, or even similar age peers of reference.

CONCLUSIONS

Having compiled relevant and varied scientific information regarding the reality of two of the most prevalent online risk behaviors of our days, it could be safely affirmed that, even if online applications in general, and social media in particular, have been reported to be quite beneficial regarding both the educational and academic vital and developmental aspects of pupils, handling the vast amount of private data and information that one could, voluntarily or not, communicate through these channels, with utmost care and under selective and informed trust criteria must be an essential pillar when it comes to mediation between young learners and the ubiquitous online world.

As a result, throughout this chapter, the often blurry and pervasive concepts of cyberbullying and sexting have been clearly delimited, further expanding on their potential effect and influence over pupils. Furthermore, an analysis of the three most relevant challenging axis that appear when attempting to intervene in such situations, alongside the deep ethical dilemmas existing behind them, was conducted. Finally, the main trends regarding prevention/intervention protocols were critically appraised and commented on, taking into consideration the unique and essential role that every educational stakeholder presents, or rather should occupy, within them.

One of the main ideas that can be extracted out of this comprehensive literature-based discourse is, essentially, that even if both sexting and cyberbullying hold such importance and interest in the current-day educational setting, much more research and conceptualization work is still needed in order to fully be aware of what educational agents may actually be up against. Apart from the unique complications that the anonymity of this digital world already provides, still holding mild perspectives on these matters may be one of the factors hindering the normalization of occurrence, and therefore assimilation of urgency of intervention, the most. Administrators and practitioners alike need to understand the complex factorial network existing behind these risk online behaviors, as well as avoid stereotypes based on giving more relevance to their traditional forms, if they truly aim to design useful and effective protocolar courses of action.

As it has been widely explored, educators and relatives need to move on from the more traditional restrictive and punishing forms of actuation towards such scenarios, as in most cases teens and young adults simply engage in them out of their natural and pure desire to communicate with others and establish personal relationships with their peers. Therefore, a new action paradigm based on the notion of *knowing how to properly use* instead of *banning the possibility of interaction* should gradually become the new established and common norm so as to guarantee training fully autonomous, critical thinking and capable digital humans.

The current interventional paradigm within the educational and psychological research world, as it has been extensively explored, is mostly based around focusing on intervention via comprehension of the negative aspects linked to being either a victim or aggressor in such practices. Even if it is true that evading this typology of dreadful online risk behaviors to ever taking place is preferred over having to attend scarred students, the lack of well-defined collaborative and dialogue-based intervention approaches is indeed quite alarming. Dealing with the immediate consequences of risk behaviors linked to inappropriate internet use and social network use requires delicate action undertaken by teachers, families, and educational administrators alike, as abrupt invasion of privacy can take a toll on students' mental wellbeing and sense of vulnerability.

Current literature appears to suggest that there is such trust in the robustness of prevention protocols to eradicate the emerging possibility of these behaviors, that educators lack actual training and preparation in order to effectively tackle them when they happen to take place. As a direct consequence of this, further studies and literature reviews should be developed regarding the effectiveness of intervention protocols in order to determine the existence of a potentially grave theoretical-practical research gap within the field of educational services, tutoring, counselling and school organization.

Opting for outright rejection and technological avoidance towards these scenarios, while ensuring absolute safety of young students, will be equally effective in building up a sense of isolation, impossibility of contact and general lack of trust within these future adults, out of sheer fear of being exposed, blackmailed or made fun of. In an era of always-advancing technological products and innovations, in which youngsters most likely are more proficient regarding access to technology and digital media than their referent adults of trust, the establishment of close personal mentorships regarding their introduction to the world of socialization and personal connections, though altered, is still one of the most necessary and irreplaceable educative actions in the current-day digitally pervasive educational ecosystem.

REFERENCES

Adorjan, M., & Ricciardelli, R. (2023). Educators and synoptic prudentialism: Educator reflections on educator training, student surveillance and using technology for student outreach. *Canadian Review of Sociology*, 60(3), 367–384. DOI: 10.1111/cars.12441 PMID: 37278202

American Psychological Association. (n.d.). Bullying. https://www.apa.org/topics/bullying

Andaya, A. M., Andea, J. M. G., & Gallego, E. J. B. (2024). The Experience of the Love for Children in Teaching. *Psychology and Education: A Multidisciplinary Journal, 21*(1), 28-32. DOI: 10.5281/zenodo.12168019

Aulia, N., Syamsuddin, H., Irawansah, D., Tiara, Ramadhan, S., & Syahrudin, I. (May 27, 2024). *Protection of ITE Law Against Sexting By Teenagers* [Conference paper]. ICORHESTECH 2024, Situbondo, East Java, Indonesia. https://journal.ibrahimy.ac.id/index.php/icorhestech/article/view/5665/2408

Bacaksiz, F. E., Eskici, G. T., & Seren, A. K. H. (2020). "From my Facebook profile": What do nursing students share on Timeline, Photos, Friends, and About sections? *Nurse Education Today*, 86, 104326. DOI: 10.1016/j.nedt.2019.104326 PMID: 31945672

Bolognesi, S., & Bukhalovskaya, A. (2022). Acoso escolar en la red: ciberacoso datos, prevención e intervención [School bullying online: cyberbullying data, prevention and intervention]. *Etic@net, 22*(2), 216-240. DOI: 10.30827/eticanet.v22i2.23791

Bonilla, S., McGinley, M., & Lamb, S. (2021). Sexting, power, and patriarchy: Narratives of sexting from a college population. *New Media & Society*, 23(5), 1099–1116. DOI: 10.1177/1461444820909517

Bozza, T. C. L., & Vinha, T. P. (2023). Cyberbullying, cyber agressão e riscos on-line: Como a escola pode atuar diante dos problemas da (cyber)convivência. *Revista Ibero-Americana De Estudos Em Educação*, 18(00), e023059. DOI: 10.21723/riaee.v18i00.18444

Bradley, N., Gilea, B., Overton, S., & O'Neill, R. (2020). Sexting between minors: Ethical, legal, and clinical considerations. *Journal of Counselor Practice*, 11(2), 1–20. DOI: 10.22229/sbm1122020

Buelga-Vázquez, S., Cava-Caballero, M. J., Moreno-Ruiz, D., & Ortega-Barón, J. (2022). Cyberbullying y conducta suicida en alumnado adolescente: Una revisión sistemática. *Review of Education*, 397, 43–67. DOI: 10.4438/1988-592X-RE-2022-397-539

Burke, G., & Norvilitis, J. M. (2022). The relationships between cyberbullying, sexting, and college student well-being. In *Research Anthology on Combating Cyber-Aggression and Online Negativity* (pp. 789–802). IGI Global. DOI: 10.4018/978-1-6684-5594-4.ch043

Cabrera, M. C., Larrañaga Rubio, E., & Yubero, S. (2024). Variables sociofamiliares en adolescentes ciberacosadores: prevención e intervención desde el Trabajo Social [Socio-family variables in adolescent cyberbullies: prevention and intervention from Social Work]. *Alternativas. Cuadernos de Trabajo Social*, 31(2), 378–408. DOI: 10.14198/ALTERN.24774

Camacho, M., Minelli, J., & Grosseck, G. (2-5 February 2012). *Self and Identity: Raising Undergraduate Students' Awareness on Their Digital Footprints. 4th World Conference on Educational Sciences (WCES-2012)*, Barcelona, Spain. DOI: 10.1016/j.sbspro.2012.06.032

Chan, H. C., & Wong, D. S. W. (2020). The overlap between cyberbullying perpetration and victimisation: Exploring the psychosocial characteristics of Hong Kong adolescents. *Asia Pacific Journal of Social Work*, 30(3), 164–180. DOI: 10.1080/02185385.2020.1761436

Chen, S. (2023). Modeling the effect of loving pedagogy dispositions and teacher self-efficacy on teacher burnout. *Frontiers in Psychology*, 14, 1157324. DOI: 10.3389/fpsyg.2023.1157324 PMID: 37251022

Chicote-Beato, M., González-Víllora, S., Bodoque-Osma, A. R., & Navarro, R. (2024). Cyberbullying intervention and prevention programmes in Primary Education (6 to 12 years): A systematic review. *Aggression and Violent Behavior*, 77, 101938. DOI: 10.1016/j.avb.2024.101938

Children's Online Privacy Protection Rule. 16 C.F.R. § 312 (2013). Retrieved from https://www.ecfr.gov/current/title-16/chapter-I/subchapter-C/part-312

Chiza-Lozano, D., Vásquez-Mendoza, D., & Ramírez-Vega, C. (2021). Adicción a redes sociales y ciberbullying en los adolescentes. *Revista Muro de la Investigación*, 6(1), 34–44. DOI: 10.17162/rmi.v6i1.1437

Coduto, K. D. (2024). Channel affordances for sexting: Social presence relates to improved self-esteem, sexual gratification, and sexting certainty. *Sexuality & Culture*, 28(1), 228–242. DOI: 10.1007/s12119-023-10112-z

Confalonieri, E., Cuccì, G., Olivari, M. G., Parise, M., Borroni, E., & Villani, D. (2020). What are you sexting? Parental practices, sexting attitudes and behaviors among Italian adolescents. *BMC Psychology, 8*(1), 63 1-11. https://doi.org/DOI: 10.1186/s40359-020-00425-1

Corcoran, L., Guckin, C. M., & Prentice, G. (2015). Cyberbullying or Cyber Aggression?: A Review of Existing Definitions of Cyber-Based Peer-to-Peer Aggression. *Societies (Basel, Switzerland)*, 5(2), 245–255. DOI: 10.3390/soc5020245

Cortés-Pascual, A., Cano-Escorianza, J., Elboj-Saso, C., & Iñiguez-Berrozpe, T. (2020). Positive relationships for the prevention of bullying and cyberbullying: A study in Aragón (Spain). *International Journal of Adolescence and Youth*, 25(1), 182–199. DOI: 10.1080/02673843.2019.1602064

Daher, W., Omar, A., Swaity, H., Allan, B., Issa, S. D., Amer, Z., & Halabi, A. (2022). Upper-Basic Schoolteachers' Beliefs about Their Students' Awareness of Digital Citizenship. *Sustainability (Basel)*, 14(19), 12865. DOI: 10.3390/su141912865

Daniels, E. A., Dajches, L., Terán, L., Gahler, H., Choi, H. J., Speno, A., & Stevens, J. (2024). The Sexual Landscape of Youth: How Adolescents From the U.S. Make Sense of Sexting. *Journal of Adolescent Research*. Advance online publication. DOI: 10.1177/07435584241231448

Desrosiers, H., Japel, C., Singh, P. R. P., & Tétreault, K. (2012). *Positive Teacher-Student Relationships: Associations with Child Characteristics and Academic Achievement in Elementary School*. Institut de la Statistique Québec. https://www.jesuisjeserai.stat.gouv.qc.ca/publications/ELDEQ_fasc6no2_an.pdf

Dodaj, A., & Sesar, K. (2020). Sexting categories. *Mediterranean Journal of Clinical Psychology*, 8(2), 1–26. DOI: 10.6092/2282-1619/mjcp-2432

Dully, J., Walsh, K., Doyle, C., & O'Reilly, G. (2023). Adolescent experiences of sexting: A systematic review of the qualitative literature, and recommendations for practice. *Journal of Adolescence*, 95(6), 1077–1105. DOI: 10.1002/jad.12181 PMID: 37157169

Elbedour, S., Alqahtani, S., El Sheikh Rihan, I., Bawalsah, J. A., Booker-Ammah, B., & Turner, J. F.Jr. (2020). Cyberbullying: Roles of school psychologists and school counselors in addressing a pervasive social justice issue. *Children and Youth Services Review*, 109, 104720. DOI: 10.1016/j.childyouth.2019.104720

Fajardo-Caldera, M. I., Gordillo-Hernández, M., & Regalado-Cuenca, A. B. (2013). Sexting: Nuevos usos de la tecnología y la sexualidad en adolescentes. *International Journal of Developmental and Educational Psychology*, 1(1), 521–533.

Fazil, A. W., Hakimi, M., Sajid, S., Quchi, M. M., & Khaliqyar, K. Q. (2023). Enhancing Internet Safety and Cybersecurity Awareness among Secondary and High School Students in Afghanistan: A Case Study of Badakhshan Province. *American Journal of Education and Technology*, 2(4), 50–61. DOI: 10.54536/ajet.v2i4.2248

Ferreira, P. C., Simão, A. M. V., Paiva, A., Martinho, C., Prada, R., & Rocha, J. (2022). Serious Game-based Psychosocial Intervention to Foster Prosociality in Cyberbullying Bystanders. *Psychosocial Intervention*, 31(2), 83–96. DOI: 10.5093/pi2022a5 PMID: 37360059

Ferrer, R., Ali, K., & Hughes, C. (2024). Using AI-Based Virtual Companions to Assist Adolescents with Autism in Recognizing and Addressing Cyberbullying. *Sensors (Basel)*, 24(12), 3875. DOI: 10.3390/s24123875 PMID: 38931659

Foody, M., Samara, M., & O'Higgins-Norman, J. (2017). Bullying and cyberbullying studies in the school-aged population on the island of Ireland: A meta-analysis. *The British Journal of Educational Psychology*, 87(4), 535–557. DOI: 10.1111/bjep.12163 PMID: 28555753

García-Martínez, S., & García-Zabaleta, E. (2024). El acoso escolar en España: Revisión y análisis de los protocolos de actuación por comunidades autónomas [Bullying in Spain: review and analysis of action protocols by autonomous communities]. *Contextos Educativos: Revista De Educación*, 33(33), 193–217. DOI: 10.18172/con.5765

Giménez-Gualdo, A. M., Sánchez-Romero, E. I., & Torregrosa Díez, M. (2022). El lado oscuro de internet.¿ Predice el cyberbullying la participación en sexting? *Revista Latinoamericana de Psicología*, 54, 112–119. DOI: 10.14349/rlp.2022.v54.13

Giumetti, G. W., & Kowalski, R. M. (2022). Cyberbullying via social media and well-being. *Current Opinion in Psychology, 45*(101314), 1-8. https://doi.org/DOI: 10.1016/j.copsyc.2022.101314

Gonzalez, S.-J., & Holdgate, H. (2023). Is there a place for love in early childhood education and care in England? Early years educators' beliefs. *Research in Teacher Education*, 13(1), 44–48. DOI: 10.1016/j.compedu.2020.103877v

Gudmundsdottir, G. B., Gassó, H. H., Colomer, J. C., & Hatlevik, O. E. (2020). Student teachers' responsible use of ICT: Examining two samples in Spain and Norway. *Computers & Education*, 152, 103877. DOI: 10.1016/j.compedu.2020.103877

Hendry, B. P., Hellsten, L.-A. M., McIntyre, L. J., & Smith, B. R. R. (2023). Recommendations for cyberbullying prevention and intervention: A Western Canadian perspective from key stakeholders. *Frontiers in Psychology, 14*. DOI: 10.3389/fpsyg.2023.1067484

Henry, N., & Beard, G. (2024). Image-Based Sexual Abuse Perpetration: A Scoping Review. *Trauma, Violence & Abuse*, 25(5), 3981–3998. DOI: 10.1177/15248380241266137 PMID: 39078000

Hernández-León, M. L., Rodríguez-Fernández, M. C., & Cruz-Martínez, I. (2022). Consecuencias psicológicas del sexting y relación con el estrés académico. *Medisan (Santiago de Cuba)*, 26(4), e4093.

Hollá, K., Jedlickova, P., & Seidler, P. (2020). Sexting types and motives detected among Slovak adolescents. *European Journal of Mental Health*, 15(2), 75–92. DOI: 10.5708/EJMH.15.2020.2.1

Iorga, M., Pop, L. M., Croitoru, I., Hanganu, E., & Anton-Păduraru, D. T. (2022). Exploring the Importance of Gender, Family Affluence, Parenting Style and Loneliness in Cyberbullying Victimization and Aggression among Romanian Adolescents. *Behavioral Sciences (Basel, Switzerland)*, 12(11), 457. DOI: 10.3390/bs12110457 PMID: 36421753

Kids Online Safety Act, S. 1409, 118th Cong. (2023). Retrieved from https://www.congress.gov/118/bills/s1409/BILLS-118s1409rs.pdf

Kintonova, A., Vasyaev, A., & Shestak, V. (2021). Cyberbullying and cyber-mobbing in developing countries. *Information and Computer Security*, 29(3), 435–456. DOI: 10.1108/ICS-02-2020-0031

Kopecký, K., Szotkowski, R., Krejčí, V., & Gómez-García, G. (2022). Digital safety and its importance in teacher education. Analysis of children's online behaviour in the Czech and Polish context. *Revista Interuniversitaria de Formación del Profesorado, 98*(36.2), 79-92. DOI: 10.47553/rifop.v98i36.2.94062

Leatham, H. (2017). *Digital privacy in the classroom: an analysis of the intent and realization of Ontario policy in context*. Unpublished Master's thesis, Ontario Tech University. Ontario Tech University - eScholar. https://hdl.handle.net/10155/816

Ley Orgánica 8/2021, de 4 de junio, de protección integral a la infancia y la adolescencia frente a la violencia [Organic Law 8/2021, of the 4th of June, of integral protection of infancy and adolescence towards violence]. *Boletín Oficial del Estado, 134*, of the 5th of June 2021, 68657-68730. https://www.boe.es/boe/dias/2021/06/05/pdfs/BOE-A-2021-9347.pdf

Liu, Y.-L. (2020). Maternal mediation as an act of privacy invasion: The association with internet addiction. *Computers in Human Behavior*, 112, 106474. DOI: 10.1016/j.chb.2020.106474

Marín, V. I., Carpenter, J. P., & Tur, G. (2021). Pre-service teachers' perceptions of social media data privacy policies. *British Journal of Educational Technology*, 52(2), 519–535. DOI: 10.1111/bjet.13035

Martin, F., Bacak, J., Polly, D., Wang, W., & Ahlgrim-Delzell, L. (2023). Teacher and School Concerns and Actions on Elementary School Children Digital Safety. *TechTrends*, 67(3), 561–571. DOI: 10.1007/s11528-022-00803-z PMID: 36249671

Mâ ă, L. (2022). Ethical Rules of Online Communication Between University Teachers and Students. In Mâ ă, L. (Ed.), *Ethical Use of Information Technology in Higher Education* (pp. 99–112). Springer. DOI: 10.1007/978-981-16-1951-9_7

Mladenović, M., Ošmjanski, V., & Stanković, S. V. (2021). Cyber-aggression, cyberbullying, and cyber-grooming: A survey and research challenges. *ACM Computing Surveys*, 54(1), 1–42. DOI: 10.1145/3424246

Molla-Esparza, C., Losilla, J.-M., & López-González, E. (2020). Prevalence of sending, receiving and forwarding sexts among youths: A three-level meta-analysis. *PLoS One*, 15(12), e0243653. DOI: 10.1371/journal.pone.0243653 PMID: 33284862

Moller, V. (2023). Leading for Love, Life, Wisdom, and Voice in Steiner Schools: Constraints and Conditions of Possibility. In K. E. Reimer, S. Windsor, & S. Kemmis (Eds.), *Living Well in a World Worth Living in for All: Volume I. Current Practices of Social Justice, Sustainability and Wellbeing* (pp. 69-86). Springer.

Mori, C., Cooke, J. E., Temple, J. R., Ly, A., Lu, Y., Anderson, N., Rash, C., & Madigan, S. (2020). The prevalence of sexting behaviors among emerging adults: A meta-analysis. *Archives of Sexual Behavior*, 49(4), 1103–1119. DOI: 10.1007/s10508-020-01656-4 PMID: 32072397

Mori, C., Park, J., Temple, J. R., & Madigan, S. (2022). Are youth sexting rates still on the rise? A meta-analytic update. *The Journal of Adolescent Health*, 70(4), 531–539. DOI: 10.1016/j.jadohealth.2021.10.026 PMID: 34916123

Nazarov, V. L., & Averbuch, N. V. (2023). Traditional bullying and cyberbullying: Bystander strategies. *The Education and Science Journal*, 25(9), 80–117. DOI: 10.17853/1994-5639-2023-9-80-117

Neyra, O. (2021). Ciberbullying: El acoso escolar en el ciberespacio e implicancias psicológicas. *Hamut'ay*, 8(1), 67–74. DOI: 10.21503/hamu.v8i1.2238

Odgers, C. L., & Jensen, M. R. (2020). Annual research review: Adolescent mental health in the digital age: Facts, fears, and future directions. *Journal of Child Psychology and Psychiatry, and Allied Disciplines*, 61(3), 336–348. DOI: 10.1111/jcpp.13190 PMID: 31951670

Ojeda, M., & Del Rey, R. (2022). Lines of action for sexting prevention and intervention: A systematic review. *Archives of Sexual Behavior*, 51(3), 1–29. DOI: 10.1007/s10508-021-02089-3 PMID: 34791584

Ojeda, M., & Del Rey, R. (2022). Lines of action for sexting prevention and intervention: A systematic review. *Archives of Sexual Behavior*, 51(3), 1659–1697. DOI: 10.1007/s10508-021-02089-3 PMID: 34791584

Orosco, J. R., Huaytalla, R. P., Rosales, A. M., & Alania, N. R. (2022). Ciberbullying en estudiantes del nivel secundario de la Sierra Central de Perú [Cyberbullying in Secondary Education learners in Sierra Central, Perú]. *Ciencias Pedagógicas e Innovación*, 10(1), 11–20. DOI: 10.26423/rcpi.v10i1.439

Ortega-Barón, J., Buelga, S., Cava, M.-J., & Iranzo, B. (2022). Eficacia del programa Prev@cib 2.0 en cyberbullying, conductas de ayuda y percepción de ayuda del professor [Effectiveness of the Prev@cib 2.0 program in cyberbullying, helping behaviors and perception of teacher help]. *Electronic Journal of Research in Educational Psychology*, 20(2), 427–448. DOI: 10.25115/ejrep.v20i57.6684

Pallarés-Piquer, M., Salvador-García, C., Maravé-Vivas, M., Esteve-Sancho, M., & Cabero-Fayos, I. (2022). Acción pedagógica como prevención de ciberagresiones [Pedagogical action to prevent cyber-aggressions]. *Espiral: Cuadernos del Profesorado*, 15(31), 22–31. DOI: 10.25115/ecp.v15i31.7125

Piotrowski, C. (2012). Cyber-bullying in school settings: A research citation analysis. ERIC, ED525783. https://files.eric.ed.gov/fulltext/ED525783.pdf

Rai, A. (2020). Explainable AI: From black box to glass box. *Journal of the Academy of Marketing Science*, 48(1), 137–141. DOI: 10.1007/s11747-019-00710-5

Redmond, P., Lock, J. V., & Smart, V. (2020). Developing a cyberbullying conceptual framework for educators. *Technology in Society*, 60, 101223. DOI: 10.1016/j.techsoc.2019.101223

Regulation (EU) 2016/679 of the European Parliament and of the Council of 27 April 2016 on the protection of natural persons with regard to the processing of personal data and on the free movement of such data, and repealing Directive 95/46/EC. *Official Journal of the European Union, L119*, of the 4th of May 2010, 119/1-119/88. https://eur-lex.europa.eu/legal-content/EN/TXT/PDF/?uri=CELEX:32016R0679

Resett, S., González Caino, P., & Mesurado, B. (2022). Problemas emocionales, personalidad oscura, sexting y grooming en adolescentes: El rol del género y la edad. *CES Psicología*, 15(2), 23–43. DOI: 10.21615/cesp.6132

Rhoades, G. K., Stanley, S. M., & Markman, H. J. (2009). Couples' reasons for cohabitation: Associations with individual well-being and relationship quality: Associations with individual well-being and relationship quality. *Journal of Family Issues*, 30(2), 233–258. DOI: 10.1177/0192513X08324388 PMID: 19756225

Rodríguez-Álvarez, J. M., Navarro, R., Yubero, S., & Larrañaga, E. (2022). Apoyo social, competencias socioemocionales y cibervictimización: Estudio longitudinal en estudiantes de Educación Primaria [Social support, socio-emotional skills and cybervictimization: longitudinal study in students of Primary Education]. *Review of Education*, 397, 125–152. DOI: 10.4438/1988-592X-RE-2022-397-542

Rodríguez-Castro, Y., Martínez-Román, R., Alonso-Ruido, P., Adá-Lameiras, A., & Carrera-Fernández, M. V. (2021). Intimate partner cyberstalking, sexism, pornography, and sexting in adolescents: New challenges for sex education. *International Journal of Environmental Research and Public Health*, 18(4), 1–14. DOI: 10.3390/ijerph18042181 PMID: 33672240

Rübner, C., Weckesser, A., Turner, J., & Wade, A. (2019). Young people's views on sexting education and support needs: Findings and recommendations from a UK-based study. *Sex Education*, 19(1), 25–40. DOI: 10.1080/14681811.2018.1475283

Ruvalcaba, Y., Mercer Kollar, L. M., Everett Jones, S., Mercado, M. C., Leemis, R. W., & Ma, Z.-Q. (2023). Adolescent sexting, violence, and sexual behaviors: An analysis of 2014 and 2016 Pennsylvania Youth Risk Behavior survey data. *The Journal of School Health*, 93(8), 690–697. DOI: 10.1111/josh.13290 PMID: 36544265

Samee, N. A., Khan, U., Khan, S., Jamjoom, M. M., Sharif, M., & Kim, D. H. (2023). Safeguarding Online Spaces: A Powerful Fusion of Federated Learning, Word Embeddings, and Emotional Features for Cyberbullying Detection. *IEEE Access : Practical Innovations, Open Solutions*, 11, 124524–124541. DOI: 10.1109/ACCESS.2023.3329347

Sari, G. C., Krutka, D. G., & Smits, R. M. (2024). Why is There a Picture of Me on Snapchat?: Educational Approaches to Overposting. *TechTrends*, 68(4), 682–692. DOI: 10.1007/s11528-024-00970-1

Sciacca, B., Mazzone, A., Norman, J. O., & Foody, M. (2021). Blame and responsibility in the context of youth produced sexual imagery: The role of teacher empathy and rape myth acceptance. *Teaching and Teacher Education*, 103, 103354. DOI: 10.1016/j.tate.2021.103354

Sharma, R., Sharma, M., & Joshi, S. (2024). Social media mirage-the two actual selves of an individual: Conceptualization and scale development. *Technological Forecasting and Social Change*, 206, 123502. DOI: 10.1016/j.techfore.2024.123502

Smith, L. J. (2015). Minors' Right to Confidentiality: Addressing the Issue of Bullying and the Ethical Obligation to Prevent Harm. *Journal of Human Behavior in the Social Environment*, 25(7), 746–755. DOI: 10.1080/10911359.2015.1032649

Sovacool, B. K., & Del Rio, D. D. F. (2020). Smart home technologies in Europe: A critical review of concepts, benefits, risks and policies. *Renewable & Sustainable Energy Reviews*, 120, 1–22. DOI: 10.1016/j.rser.2019.109663

Tackie, H. N. (2022). (Dis)Connected: Establishing Social Presence and Intimacy in Teacher–Student Relationships During Emergency Remote Learning. *AERA Open*, 8(1), 1–14. DOI: 10.1177/23328584211069525

Torices-Colpisa, A. (2023, mayo 21). *Nueve de cada diez universitarios que sufren "sexting" dejan la carrera. Heraldo de Aragón.* Retrieved from https://www.heraldo.es/noticias/sociedad/2023/05/21/nueve-de-cada-diez-universitarios-que-sufren-sexting-dejan-la-carrera-1653084.html

Touloupis, T., & Athanasiades, C. (2022). Evaluation of a cyberbullying prevention program in elementary schools: The role of self-esteem enhancement. *Frontiers in Psychology*, 13, 980091. DOI: 10.3389/fpsyg.2022.980091 PMID: 36211905

Turzák, T., Kurincová, B., Hollá, C., & Zelená, D. (2020). Sexting and family environment of children and adolescents. *Ad Alta*, 10(2), 326–330.

United Nations. (1989). *Convention on the Rights of the Child.* Retrieved from https://treaties.un.org/doc/Treaties/1990/09/19900902%2003-14%20AM/Ch_IV_11p.pdf

Van Ouytsel, J., Punyanunt-Carter, N. M., Walrave, M., & Ponnet, K. (2020). Sexting within young adults' dating and romantic relationships. *Current Opinion in Psychology*, 36, 55–59. DOI: 10.1016/j.copsyc.2020.04.007 PMID: 32480021

Vásquez-Idrovo, J. H., García-Herrera, D. G., Ochoa-Encalada, S. C., & Erazo-Álvarez, J. C. (2020). Ciberbullying y sus factores de riesgo. *Episteme Koinonia*, 3(1), 577. DOI: 10.35381/e.k.v3i1.1028

Verrastro, V., Saladino, V., Eleuteri, S., Barberis, N., & Cuzzocrea, F. (2023). Sexting, Self-esteem, and Social Media: A Comparison among Frequent, Occasional, and Non-sexting Italian Adolescent Girls. *Psychology in Russia : State of the Art*, 16(4), 3–20. DOI: 10.11621/PIR.2023.0401 PMID: 38162809

Vijayarani, M., Balamurugan, G., Sevak, S., Gurung, K., Bhuvaneswari, G., Sangeetha, X., Thenmozhi, P., & Tamilselvi, S. (2024). Silent Screams: A Narrative Review of Cyberbullying Among Indian Adolescents. *Cureus*, 16(8), e66292. DOI: 10.7759/cureus.66292 PMID: 39238690

Wei, H.-S., Hsieh, Y.-P., Chen, Y.-F., Ma, J. K.-H., & Lin, Y.-S. (2024). (in press). Prevalence and associated factors of sexting among Taiwanese adolescents. *Behavioral Sciences & the Law*. Advance online publication. DOI: 10.1002/bsl.2697 PMID: 39267296

Ybarra, M. L., & Mitchell, K. J. (2004). Online aggressor/targets, aggressors, and targets: A comparison of associated youth characteristics. *Journal of Child Psychology and Psychiatry, and Allied Disciplines*, 45(7), 1308–1316. DOI: 10.1111/j.1469-7610.2004.00328.x PMID: 15335350

Yépez-Tito, P., Ferragut, M., & Blanca, M. J. (2020). Sexting in adolescence: The use of technology and parental supervision. *Revista Latinoamericana de Psicología*, 52, 115–130. DOI: 10.14349/rlp.2020.v52.12

Yisa, V., & Orji, R. (2024). Hidden desires, echoed distress: Dissecting Nigeria's sexting landscape and its ties to depression. *Computers in Human Behavior*, 161, 108420. DOI: 10.1016/j.chb.2024.108420

York, L., MacKenzie, A., & Purdy, N. (2021). Sexting and institutional discourses of child protection: The views of young people and providers of relationship and sex education. *British Educational Research Journal*, 47(6), 1717–1734. DOI: 10.1002/berj.3751

Yurdakul, Y., & Ayhan, A. B. (2023). The effect of the cyberbullying awareness program on adolescents' awareness of cyberbullying and their coping skills. *Current Psychology (New Brunswick, N.J.)*, 42(28), 24208–24222. DOI: 10.1007/s12144-022-03483-3 PMID: 35935748

Zhao, H., Weng, H., Weng, Q., Huang, Z., & Soon, K. C. (2022). Teachers' management of cyberbullying on China's social media sites: A case study in Shandong Province, China. *Cogent Education, 9*(1), 2127502. https://doi.org/mw5p

Chapter 12
Empowering Students in the Digital Age Through Psychoeducational Programs

Eirini Karakasidou
https://orcid.org/0000-0003-2946-8275
Panetion University, Greece

Athanasios Tapeinos
https://orcid.org/0000-0001-5952-9468
National and Kapodistrian University of Athens, Greece

Maria Christina Pylioti
https://orcid.org/0009-0008-7421-8383
National and Kapodistrian University of Athens, Greece

Anna Papadimitriou
Panteion University, Greece

ABSTRACT

This chapter is an in-depth overview of the critical role that psychoeducational programs play in training students to negotiate the complexity of the digital age. In response to the growing issues provided by online hazards, this chapter examines the design, implementation, and impact of programs designed to provide students with the necessary information. Based on educational psychology concepts, the chapter gives practical recommendations for educators and facilitators looking to develop programs that not only inform but also actively involve students in critical discussions about responsible online behavior. The chapter underlines the importance of interactive techniques in addressing the psychoeducational components of online behavior via the perspective of experiential learning. As schools aspire to create a digitally empowered generation, this chapter is a great resource for educators, providing concrete insights for designing meaningful programs that prepare students with the resilience and knowledge needed to navigate the ever-changing digital landscape responsibly.

DOI: 10.4018/979-8-3693-4191-9.ch012

INTRODUCTION

Psychoeducational programs are structured interventions designed to educate individuals about psychological and educational topics. In the context of addressing online risk behaviors, these programs are tailored to equip students with the knowledge and skills necessary to navigate the digital world safely and responsibly (Bandura, 1977). As the digital age introduces new and complex challenges, such as cyberbullying, online privacy issues, and exposure to inappropriate content, the role of psychoeducational programs becomes increasingly critical (Prensky, 2010).

The significance of these programs lies in their comprehensive approach to education and behavior modification. By combining psychological insights with educational strategies, psychoeducational programs address not only the cognitive aspects of learning but also the emotional and social dimensions. This holistic approach is essential for fostering a deep understanding of online risks and encouraging positive behavior change among students (Piaget, 1952).

These programs aim to raise awareness by educating students about various online risks and the potential consequences of unsafe online behaviors (Wenger, 1998). The second goal is to develop students' skills and equip them with the ability to recognize, avoid, and respond to online threats (Kolb, 1984). The final goal is to promote responsible behavior and foster a sense of digital citizenship, encouraging students to engage in positive and responsible online activities (Boud et al., 1985).

OVERVIEW OF THE CHAPTER'S FOCUS ON EMPOWERING STUDENTS THROUGH EXPERIENTIAL LEARNING

This chapter focuses on the empowering potential of psychoeducational programs through the lens of experiential learning (Smith & Doe, 2024). Experiential learning, a process through which students develop knowledge, skills, and values from direct experiences, is particularly effective in teaching about online behaviors. The chapter explores how hands-on activities, interactive discussions, and real-life simulations can engage students more deeply than traditional didactic methods (Johnson & Lee, 2023; Smith & Doe, 2024). By incorporating experiential learning techniques, psychoeducational programs can enhance engagement, build critical thinking and foster emotional connection: Enhancing engagement can be built with interactive and hands-on activities capture students' interest and ma1ke learning more memorable. Building critical thinking can be succeeded with real-life scenarios and problem-solving tasks help students develop critical thinking and decision-making skills (Johnson & Lee, 2023). Fostering emotional connection can be achieved with experiential learning, which often involves reflective exercises that allow students to connect emotionally with the material, leading to more meaningful and lasting behavior change (Smith & Doe, 2024).

The chapter outlines practical recommendations for educators and facilitators looking to develop and implement effective psychoeducational programs, through presenting a wide range of relative interventions that have already been applied in the past (Smith & Doe, 2024). By comprehensively presenting selected interventions it emphasizes the importance of designing content that is not only informative but also engaging and relevant to students' lives. Empowering students with the necessary knowledge and skills, psychoeducational programs play a pivotal role in preparing them to navigate the digital landscape responsibly and confidently (Johnson & Lee, 2023; Smith & Doe, 2024).

THEORETICAL FOUNDATIONS OF PSYCHOEDUCATIONAL PROGRAMS

Educational psychology provides the foundational principles that guide the design and implementation of effective psychoeducational programs. Understanding how students learn and what motivates them is crucial for developing programs that are both engaging and impactful. Several key principles from educational psychology are particularly relevant:

Constructivism: This theory posits that learners construct their own understanding and knowledge of the world through experiences and reflection on those experiences. Psychoeducational programs that encourage active participation and critical thinking help students build their own understanding of online behaviors and risks (Piaget, 1952).

Social Learning Theory: Proposed by Albert Bandura, this theory emphasizes the importance of observing and modeling the behaviors, attitudes, and emotional reactions of others. Programs that include peer learning, role-playing, and group discussions can effectively leverage this theory to teach responsible online behavior (Bandura, 1977).

Cognitive-Behavioral Theory: This approach focuses on the interplay between thoughts, feelings, and behaviors. Psychoeducational programs can use cognitive-behavioral strategies to help students identify and change negative thought patterns related to online interactions, thereby influencing their behavior positively (Beck, 1967).

Developmental Psychology: Understanding the cognitive and emotional development stages of children and adolescents is crucial. Programs tailored to the developmental levels of students can more effectively address their specific needs and capabilities, ensuring that content is age-appropriate and engaging (Berk, 2018).

CONNECTION BETWEEN EXPERIENTIAL LEARNING AND EMPOWERING STUDENTS IN THE DIGITAL AGE

Experiential learning, as conceptualized by David Kolb, is a process through which students gain knowledge by experiencing and reflecting on their activities (Kolb, 1984). This learning model is particularly powerful in the context of psychoeducational programs for several reasons:

Active Engagement: Experiential learning involves students in active problem-solving and critical thinking. Activities such as simulations of online scenarios, interactive workshops, and hands-on projects allow students to engage deeply with the material, making learning more impactful (Kolb & Kolb, 2005).

Real-World Relevance: By incorporating real-life situations and practical exercises, experiential learning bridges the gap between theoretical knowledge and real-world application. This relevance helps students understand the importance of responsible online behavior and how it applies to their daily lives (Chapman et al., 1995).

Reflective Practice: A core component of experiential learning is reflection. After engaging in an activity, students reflect on their experiences, which helps them internalize lessons and develop personal insights. This reflective practice is essential for fostering a deeper understanding and long-term retention of safe online behaviors (Boud et al., 1985).

Personal Connection: Experiential learning often involves collaborative and interactive elements, which can create a sense of community and shared learning. This personal connection and social interaction enhance motivation and commitment to learning (Wenger, 1998).

By integrating experiential learning into psychoeducational programs, educators can empower students to navigate the digital age with confidence and competence. Programs designed with these principles not only inform students about online risks but also actively involve them in learning processes that develop critical thinking, problem-solving, and responsible decision-making skills. This approach helps build a digitally literate generation capable of managing the complexities of the digital world effectively (Prensky, 2010).

IDENTIFYING TARGETED LEARNING OBJECTIVES- STRATEGIES FOR DEVELOPING INTERACTIVE AND RELEVANT PROJECT CONTENT.

For psychoeducational programs to be effective, it is essential to define clear and specific learning objectives that align with overarching psychoeducational goals (Bandura, 1977). These objectives serve as the foundation for curriculum design and implementation, guiding educators in what students should achieve by the end of the program (Piaget, 1952). Key learning objectives might include awareness, skills development, behavioral change, critical thinking, and emotional regulation (Kolb, 1984). The awareness objective aims to increase students' understanding of various online risks, including cyberbullying, privacy breaches, and exposure to inappropriate content (Prensky, 2010). Skill development involves equipping students with practical skills for safe online navigation, such as recognizing phishing attempts, setting strong passwords, and managing digital footprints (Berk, 2018). Encouraging positive online behavior and digital citizenship, promoting empathy, respect, and responsible communication, may lead to behavioral change (Beck, 1967). Enhancing critical thinking is achieved by developing students' ability to critically evaluate online information and sources, discerning between reliable and unreliable content (Wenger, 1998). Finally, emotional regulation aims to help students manage their emotional responses to online interactions, reducing the likelihood of negative behaviors such as retaliatory cyberbullying (Boud, Keogh, & Walker, 1985).

TAILORING OBJECTIVES TO ADDRESS DIVERSE ONLINE RISK BEHAVIORS AND CHALLENGES

Different age groups and student populations face varied online risks and challenges. Tailoring learning objectives to these specific contexts ensures that the psychoeducational program is relevant and effective.

For elementary students, the primary objective is to help them understand basic online safety rules, with a focus on recognizing trusted adults for help and protecting their privacy by not sharing personal information (Piaget, 1952). As students' progress to middle school, the objective shifts to identifying and responding to cyberbullying, emphasizing the importance of building empathy, understanding the impact of online words and actions, and knowing how to report and seek help (Bandura, 1977). By high school, the focus becomes more complex, with the objective of helping students navigate online interactions and manage their digital footprints. High schoolers are encouraged to think critically about online content, maintain a positive digital presence, and understand the legal and ethical implications of their online behavior (Prensky, 2010).

DESIGNING ENGAGING PROGRAM CONTENT

Creating engaging content is crucial for the success of psychoeducational programs, especially when it comes to addressing online safety. The content must be interactive, age-appropriate, and relevant to students' digital experiences to foster greater engagement and learning retention. Interactive activities play a pivotal role in promoting connections among students, helping them build social bonds and learn collaboratively (Mayer, 2009). For instance, simulations and role-playing scenarios, such as those that involve practicing responses to cyberbullying or other online risks, allow students to engage in experiential learning in a safe, controlled environment (Kolb, 1984). These immersive techniques not only enhance understanding but also provide opportunities to practice appropriate responses to common online challenges (Smith et al., 2015).

Gamification is another powerful strategy for engaging students, making learning more fun and motivating through elements like points, badges, and leaderboards (Gee, 2003). When combined with multimedia resources—such as videos, animations, and sound—these game-like features can enhance the educational experience by providing diverse, stimulating ways to absorb information (Clark & Mayer, 2016). For example, using videos to explain complex concepts like digital footprints or phishing scams helps break down intricate ideas into digestible, relatable formats (Sung et al., 2017). Similarly, interactive quizzes and polls offer real-time feedback, reinforcing learning while keeping students actively engaged.

Collaborative projects also serve as an excellent means of promoting student interaction and fostering friendship. Activities such as group discussions and debates encourage students to critically reflect on online behaviors and ethical dilemmas, thus promoting perspective-taking and problem-solving skills (Johnson & Johnson, 1999). Peer education programs, where older students educate younger ones about online safety, reinforce learning and cultivate a sense of responsibility (Bandura, 1977).

Real-life case studies, drawn from both positive and negative online experiences, allow students to contextualize the consequences of online behavior, making the lessons more tangible and relatable (Brown, 2008).

Hands-on workshops that teach practical skills, such as setting up privacy settings or recognizing phishing emails, further empower students by providing them with the tools they need to navigate the digital world safely (Dabbagh & Kitsantas, 2012). Such workshops employ an active learning approach where students learn by doing, rather than passively consuming information (Bonwell & Eison, 1991).

Creative projects, such as developing posters, videos, or other digital content to promote safe online behaviors, engage students in applying their knowledge creatively and promoting digital citizenship (Ribble, 2015).

By defining clear learning objectives and tailoring the content to address the various online risks students face, psychoeducational programs can effectively empower students to navigate the digital landscape responsibly. This approach not only enhances their knowledge and skills but also builds the confidence necessary to manage online interactions with greater awareness and caution (Prensky, 2010).

ADAPTING WORKSHOP CONTENT AND APPROACHES FOR DIFFERENT AGE GROUPS.

When designing psychoeducational programs, it's crucial to consider the developmental stages and varying digital literacy levels of students. Tailoring content to these factors ensures that the material is accessible, engaging, and effective for all learners.

Developmental Stages

Early Childhood (Ages 5-7):

Cognitive Development: At this stage, children are concrete thinkers and have a limited attention span (Piaget, 1971).

Content Focus: Basic concepts of online safety, such as recognizing trusted adults, understanding the difference between public and private information, and simple rules like not talking to strangers online.

Engagement Methods: Use colorful visuals, simple language, interactive games, and storytelling to convey messages (Mayer, 2001).

Middle Childhood (Ages 8-11):

Cognitive Development: Children begin to develop logical thinking and can understand cause and effect (Vygotsky, 1978).

Content Focus: Introduction to cyberbullying, basic digital etiquette, and privacy settings.

Engagement Methods: Incorporate role-playing activities, group discussions, and age-appropriate videos that depict real-life scenarios (Prensky, 2001).

Adolescence (Ages 12-18):

Cognitive Development: Adolescents develop abstract thinking and can engage in more complex problem-solving (Piaget, 1971).

Content Focus: Critical thinking about digital content, managing digital footprints, understanding legal and ethical aspects of online behavior, and dealing with online peer pressure.

Engagement Methods: Use debates, case studies, interactive workshops, and peer-led sessions to foster engagement and critical thinking (Palfrey & Gasser, 2008).

Digital Literacy Levels

Low Digital Literacy:

Content Focus: Basic navigation skills, understanding internet safety fundamentals, identifying trustworthy sources, and basic privacy settings (Palfrey & Gasser, 2008).

Engagement Methods: Hands-on workshops, step-by-step tutorials, and guided practice sessions with ample support.

Intermediate Digital Literacy:

Content Focus: More advanced topics such as recognizing and avoiding phishing scams, managing digital footprints, and understanding social media privacy policies.

Engagement Methods: Interactive activities, simulations, and project-based learning where students apply what they have learned in practical scenarios.

High Digital Literacy:

Content Focus: Complex issues like ethical hacking, digital rights and responsibilities, advanced privacy techniques, and content creation with an emphasis on ethical considerations.

Engagement Methods: Advanced workshops, collaborative projects, peer teaching opportunities, and involvement in community outreach programs.

Implementation in Educational Settings

Practical Considerations for Integrating Programs into the School Curriculum

Integrating psychoeducational programs into the school curriculum requires strategic planning and collaboration. Here are some practical considerations:

Curriculum Alignment:

Integration: Ensure the program aligns with existing curriculum standards and learning objectives. Integrate digital safety topics into subjects like health, social studies, or computer science (Prensky, 2001).

Flexibility: Design the program to be flexible, allowing teachers to adapt content to fit their schedules and classroom needs.

Resource Allocation:

Training: Provide training for educators on how to deliver the program effectively. This includes understanding the content, using interactive tools, and managing discussions about sensitive topics.

Materials: Ensure that all necessary materials, such as lesson plans, multimedia resources, and interactive tools, are readily available and easily accessible.

Scheduling:

Regular Sessions: Plan regular sessions to reinforce learning over time. For example, weekly or biweekly classes can help maintain continuity and retention.

Workshops and Assemblies: Organize special workshops or assemblies featuring guest speakers, such as cybersecurity experts or psychologists, to provide additional insights and inspiration.

Collaborative Efforts Involving Educators, School Counselors, and Technology Specialists

Successful implementation requires a collaborative approach:

Educators:

Role: Teachers play a central role in delivering the content, facilitating discussions, and providing support to students.

Collaboration: Work with other teachers to integrate digital safety into various subjects and share best practices.

School Counselors:

Role: Counselors can provide emotional and psychological support to students dealing with online issues. They can also help design and deliver content related to mental health and well-being in the digital age.

Collaboration: Partner with educators to identify students at risk and develop targeted interventions.

Technology Specialists:

Role: Technology specialists ensure that the necessary digital tools and platforms are available and functioning properly. They can also teach advanced digital literacy skills and provide technical support.

Collaboration: Work with educators to integrate technology seamlessly into the curriculum and troubleshoot any technical issues that arise.

Measuring Impact and Effectiveness

Assessment Tools:

Develop comprehensive assessment tools to measure students' knowledge, attitudes, and behaviors before and after program participation.

Use surveys, quizzes, and reflective journals to gather data.

Evaluating Outcomes:

Assess changes in students' digital competencies, such as their ability to identify online risks and use privacy settings effectively.

Evaluate behavioral changes, such as a reduction in incidents of cyberbullying or an increase in positive online interactions.

Continuous Improvement:

Use feedback from students, educators, and parents to continuously improve the program.

Stay updated on emerging digital trends and risks to ensure the program remains relevant and effective.

By addressing developmental nuances, considering digital literacy levels, and implementing collaborative and practical strategies, psychoeducational programs can effectively prepare students to navigate the digital world responsibly and safely (Palfrey & Gasser, 2008).

PRACTICAL CONSIDERATIONS FOR INTEGRATING PROGRAMS INTO THE SCHOOL CURRICULUM

Successful implementation of psychoeducational programs in schools' hinges on a collaborative approach that leverages the expertise of educators, school counselors, and technology specialists. Each group plays a critical role in ensuring that the programs are comprehensive, relevant, and effective.

The role of educators, particularly teachers, in psychoeducational programs is central to content delivery, student engagement, and collaboration across disciplines. Teachers are tasked with delivering program content, fostering active discussions, and seamlessly integrating digital safety lessons into their existing curriculum (Livingstone, 2012). By creating an engaging learning environment, teachers encourage students to critically examine online behaviors, promoting a culture of reflective thinking about digital safety (Berson & Berson, 2005). Additionally, interdisciplinary collaboration enhances the integration of digital safety themes across diverse subjects like literature, social studies, and science, allowing for a comprehensive approach to digital ethics (Greenhow, 2011). This approach enables students to understand the relevance of digital safety across various contexts, enhancing their overall digital literacy. Professional development is another critical component for teachers, as staying current with evolving online risks and effective strategies for teaching digital safety is essential (Bauer & Kenton, 2005). Through regular training, teachers can continuously adapt their teaching methods to align with the latest online challenges.

School counselors play an equally crucial role, focusing on the emotional support of students. They offer psychological assistance to those affected by issues like cyberbullying, anxiety, or online addiction (Patchin & Hinduja, 2012). School counselors contribute to program development by ensuring that the emotional and social dimensions of online interactions are adequately addressed. They work closely with teachers to assess students' needs, identifying those who may require additional support and designing tailored interventions (Durlak et al., 2011). Parent engagement is another key area, where counselors conduct workshops and provide parents with the tools to better understand online risks and support their children effectively (Staksrud, 2013). This ensures a more holistic approach to digital safety, extending the program's impact beyond the classroom and into students' homes.

Technology specialists, meanwhile, provide the technical backbone required for these programs to function. Their role includes ensuring that the digital tools and platforms used for content delivery are operational and accessible to both teachers and students (Grunewald, 2009). In addition, they offer advanced training in digital literacy and cybersecurity, equipping students and staff with the knowledge to use technology responsibly (Martin, 2018). Technology specialists also collaborate with educators to develop and maintain interactive digital resources, such as online safety tutorials and simulations, ensuring that the content remains dynamic and engaging (Livingstone, 2012). Troubleshooting technical issues that arise during program implementation is another critical function, enabling seamless learning experiences.

Assessing the impact and effectiveness of psychoeducational programs is essential to ensure that they are meeting their objectives. This process involves employing various assessment tools, such as pre- and post-program surveys to measure students' understanding of online risks and safe digital practices (Valcke et al., 2011). Quizzes and tests further evaluate students' ability to apply these concepts in real-world scenarios, such as identifying phishing attempts or adjusting privacy settings (Elliott et al., 2013). Reflective journals serve as a qualitative tool, allowing students to document their personal insights and experiences related to online interactions (Lewison et al., 2002). These assessment strategies provide a multifaceted view of student progress, capturing both their cognitive and emotional development in relation to digital safety.

Evaluating outcomes from these programs focuses on several key areas, including digital competencies, behavioral changes, and emotional and social impacts. Pre- and post-assessments help measure changes in students' digital skills, such as their ability to recognize online threats and navigate privacy settings (Livingstone, 2014). Behavioral surveys and incident tracking offer insights into shifts in online behavior, such as reduced instances of cyberbullying or inappropriate content sharing (Patchin & Hinduja, 2012). Emotional well-being surveys and counselor reports further highlight the program's impact on students' mental health and social relationships, providing a comprehensive view of its effectiveness (Cross et al., 2015).

For continuous improvement, feedback mechanisms are essential. Collecting feedback from students, educators, and parents helps identify areas of strength and opportunities for program enhancement (Greenhow, 2011). This feedback informs the updating of content to reflect emerging online risks and advances in educational technology, ensuring that the program remains relevant and responsive to students' needs. Longitudinal studies offer an additional layer of evaluation by assessing the long-term impact of these programs on students' digital literacy and online behavior, ensuring that the program evolves in step with the changing digital landscape (Staksrud, 2013).

By fostering collaboration among educators, school counselors, and technology specialists, while systematically measuring outcomes, psychoeducational programs can be continually refined. This approach empowers students with the knowledge and skills they need to safely navigate the complexities of the digital world, preparing them for responsible digital citizenship in a technology-driven society.

INTERVENTIONS IN ADDRESSING ONLINE RISK BEHAVIORS AND LEARNING APPROPRIATE INTERNET SKILLS

The programs we present are rooted in a comprehensive philosophy aimed at addressing the multifaceted nature of cyberbullying and related online risks. While cyberbullying has garnered significant attention due to its pervasive and harmful impact on youth, the interventions we explore go beyond merely mitigating this phenomenon. These programs are designed to cultivate a range of essential skills and protective factors that support adolescents in navigating the digital world safely and responsibly. The aim of these programs is versatile. Among them, the interventions' purposes are to raise students' awareness about cyberbullying and its consequences, increase empathy, reduce moral disengagement, develop social norms regarding positive online communication, define behavioral expectations in social network, encourage positive digital footprints, address online safety concerns, foster responsible digital citizenship, empower digital literacy and promote critical thinking skills.

Central to these interventions is the enhancement of empathy and emotional intelligence. By fostering a deeper understanding of others' feelings and perspectives, these programs aim to reduce aggressive behaviors and promote a more supportive online environment (Goleman, 1995). Empathy training not only helps prevent cyberbullying but also encourages positive social interactions, contributing to a more inclusive and respectful school climate (Salmivalli, 2010). In addition to addressing cyberbullying, these programs focus on broader internet safety and digital literacy. They equip students with the skills to recognize and avoid various online dangers, such as online grooming, sexting, and problematic internet use. By improving digital competencies, these interventions empower adolescents to make informed decisions and engage in healthier online behaviors (Livingstone et al., 2017). By fostering improved digital competencies, these interventions empower adolescents to make informed decisions and engage in healthier online behaviors, further contributing to their overall well-being in the digital landscape (Jones & Mitchell, 2016).

Furthermore, the programs integrate elements of cognitive-behavioral therapy (CBT), psychoeducation, and social skill development. These components are instrumental in helping students build resilience, enhance self-esteem, and develop effective coping strategies for managing stress and peer pressure (Beck, 2011). The holistic approach of these interventions ensures that students are not only safeguarded from immediate risks but are also equipped with the emotional and psychological tools necessary to thrive in the digital age (Willard, 2007).

Overall, the philosophy underpinning these programs is one of comprehensive prevention and empowerment. By targeting a range of psychological, social, and behavioral factors, they aim to create a safer, more empathetic, and supportive online community for adolescents.

Interventions

The Tabby Improved Prevention and Intervention Program (TIPIP) (Sorrentino, Baldry & Farrington, 2018)

The Tabby Improved Prevention and Intervention Program (TIPIP) aims to reduce cyberbullying and cybervictimization among students. TIPIP is the first program in this field that combines the Ecological Systems Theory and the Threat Assessment Approach. To assess the program, an experimental design was used with 759 Italian students (aged 10-17 years), who were randomly assigned by their classes to an Experimental Group and a Control Group. The study involved 759 Italian students aged 10-17 years. Repeated measures ANOVA analyses showed a significant reduction in both cyberbullying and cybervictimization among students who received the intervention, with a six-month follow-up period. The program was more effective for boys than for girls. TIPIP includes four main components: (i) educational activities for teachers, (ii) school conferences with parents, (iii) online materials for students, teachers, and parents, and (iv) classroom activities with students. The educational activities for teachers included a three-day training with an additional day for legal issues, while classroom activities included group discussions and assignments to understand and avoid cyberbullying. The findings highlight the importance of fully implementing and promoting such programs to effectively reduce these issues.

The Asegúrate Program (Del Rey, Ortega-Ruiz & Casas, 2019)

The Asegúrate program aims to reduce cyberbullying among students by leveraging the theory of normative social behavior, self-regulation skills, and adolescents' beliefs. The program includes a comprehensive package of strategies and resources designed for teachers to integrate into the regular curriculum. The evaluation involved 4779 students (48.9% girls) from primary and secondary education in Spain, using a quasi-experimental methodology with pre-test and post-test measures.

The study found that involvement in cyberbullying as a cyber-victim, cyber-aggressor, and cyber-bully-victim increased without intervention but decreased when teachers who received specific training used the Asegúrate materials. The program was particularly effective in reducing traditional forms of bullying behavior adapted to the online environment, such as insults, threats, social exclusion, and spreading rumors. However, it was less effective for more specific forms of cyberbullying like identity theft or manipulating multimedia.

The Asegúrate program consists of eight sessions covering various aspects of online behavior and cyberbullying. Each session includes activities designed to raise awareness, enhance self-regulation, and promote safe online interactions. The program also provides audiovisual materials and resources for teachers and families to support these efforts. Despite its effectiveness, the study suggests that additional training and materials focusing on specific digital behaviors could further enhance the program's impact. The results emphasize the crucial role of teacher involvement in effectively implementing anti-cyberbullying programs and improving the overall social climate in schools.

The TEI (Tutoría Entre Iguales) Program (Ferrer-Cascales, Albaladejo-Blázquez, Sánchez-SanSegundo, Portilla-Tamarit, Lordan & Ruiz-Robledillo, 2019)

The TEI (Tutoría Entre Iguales) program aims to reduce bullying and cyberbullying and improve school climate among students aged 11 to 16 years. The program is based on the Ecological Systems Theory and integrates principles of emotional intelligence and positive psychology. The intervention involves the entire school community, including teachers, students, and parents, and is implemented through peer tutoring. A quasi-experimental study was conducted with 2057 Spanish students from 22 schools, randomly assigned to either the experimental group (10 schools, 987 students) or the control group (12 schools, 1070 students). Data were collected at two points: pre-intervention (T1) and post-intervention (T2) after seven months. The program includes several stages: dissemination and awareness where information about the program is shared with the school community and families are encouraged to participate, teacher training which consists of a 30-hour program (10 hours in-person and 20 hours online) creating a coordinating group for the intervention, student tutors training with three initial training sessions of 1 hour each followed by quarterly follow-up sessions, pairing students based on age and interpersonal skills with older students tutoring younger ones, intervention development with ongoing training and activities including formal and informal tutorials aimed at developing specific skills, and a closing stage with a final joint activity to deliver diplomas to all participants. The final analysis included 2057 students (49.6% female, 50.4% male) aged 11-16 years, with an average age of 13.08 years. Significant reductions in bullying, peer victimization, fighting, cyberbullying, and cybervictimization were observed in the experimental group. Additionally, improvements in school climate factors such as satisfaction, sense of belonging, cooperation, and communication between family and school were noted in the experimental group. The TEI program effectively reduces bullying and cyberbullying and improves the overall school climate. The program's success is attributed to its comprehensive approach, involving all members of the school community, and its emphasis on peer support and emotional intelligence. These results highlight the importance of implementing peer tutoring programs to foster a positive school environment and reduce violence.

A Cognitive Behavioral Therapy (CBT) Program in Reducing Cyberbullying Behavior Among Adolescents During the COVID-19 Pandemic (Nuzulawati & Astuti, 2022)

The study aimed to determine the effectiveness of cognitive behavioral therapy (CBT) in reducing cyberbullying behavior among adolescents during the COVID-19 pandemic. This quasi-experimental study involved an experimental group and a control group, each consisting of five adolescents aged 13-18 years who engaged in moderate to high levels of cyberbullying. Conducted online using Zoom, the research utilized the Cyber Bullying Scale based on Willard's aspects of cyberbullying to collect data. The main goal was to compare the levels of cyberbullying before and after administering CBT in the experimental group and to measure differences between the experimental and control groups. Participants were from SMP Negeri X Brebes, and data were collected through pre-test and post-test measurements. The experimental group received CBT sessions, while the control group did not receive any therapy. Analysis revealed significant differences in cyberbullying levels between the experimental and control groups post-intervention, with the Mann Whitney U-test showing a post-test Z score of -2.619 ($p = 0.009$), indicating lower cyberbullying levels in the experimental group. The Wilcoxon Rank test results demonstrated significant differences within the experimental group between pre-test and post-test scores ($Z = -2.527$, $p = 0.012$) and between post-test and follow-up ($Z = -2.217$, $p = 0.027$), confirming a decrease in cyberbullying behavior after CBT. The study concluded that CBT effectively reduces cyberbullying behavior among adolescents by increasing awareness and changing their thinking patterns. The therapy helped participants recognize and correct cognitive distortions, leading to reduced aggressive behavior. These findings underscore the potential of CBT as a therapeutic intervention for addressing cyberbullying, suggesting its broader application in similar contexts. However, limitations included the focus on WhatsApp group interactions and the small sample size, which may affect the generalizability of the results.

The Safe Surfing Anti-Cyberbullying Program (Aizenkot & Kashy-Rosenbaum, 2020)

The Safe Surfing program aims to reduce both online and offline bullying while improving students' perceived popularity and self-esteem. Based on the Theory of Planned Behavior (TPB), the intervention was implemented among 1,550 students (53% male) from 69 classes across 19 public schools in Israel, covering grades 3 to 11. The program involved eight weekly lesson plans addressing cyberbullying definitions, implications, bystander roles, relevant laws, self-monitoring skills, and school rule formulation through collaborative workshops.

The study utilized pre- and post-intervention questionnaires to measure exposure to cyberbullying and traditional bullying, perceived popularity, and self-esteem. Results showed significant reductions in both online and offline bullying following the intervention, with a notable association between decreased bullying and improved perceived popularity and self-esteem, particularly among primary school students. However, middle and high school students did not show significant changes in these areas.

The intervention demonstrated that school-based anti-cyberbullying programs could positively influence students' social behaviors and emotional well-being, reinforcing the importance of comprehensive approaches to bullying that address both virtual and physical environments. The findings suggest that integrating these programs into school curricula can contribute to reducing bullying and enhancing students' overall social experiences and mental health.

The Cyberprogram 2.0 Study (Garaigordobil & Martínez-Valderrey, 2016, 2018)

The Cyberprogram 2.0 aims to prevent and reduce cyberbullying during adolescence through a combination of a structured program and a cooperative videogame, Cybereduca 2.0. The intervention, based on cognitive-behavioral principles, includes 25 classroom activities that focus on understanding bullying and cyberbullying, recognizing their severe consequences, and developing strategies to prevent and address these behaviors. The program's objectives are to educate students on bullying and cyberbullying, raise awareness about the harm caused, teach preventive measures, and foster social and emotional skills such as empathy, cooperation, and communication. The program's activities provide students with strategies to prevent and deal with bullying in all its forms and promote cognitive restructuring of the roles involved, with victims learning to defend themselves and observers learning to intervene in favor of the victims.

The study involved 176 adolescents aged 13-15 from the Basque Country, Spain, divided into experimental (93 students) and control (83 students) groups. Over a school year, the experimental group participated in weekly one-hour sessions, while the control group continued their usual activities. Pretest and posttest assessments were conducted using eight different instruments to measure variables such as victimization, aggression, social behaviors, conflict resolution, self-esteem, and empathy. The intervention sessions followed a structure that included explaining the activity's objectives, watching a video, cooperative action, and a final debate or discussion.

Results indicated significant reductions in both face-to-face and cyberbullying behaviors among the experimental group compared to the control group. Improvements were noted in students' perceptions of school violence, reductions in impulsive and premeditated aggressiveness, and increases in positive social behaviors, self-esteem, and empathy. The program was particularly effective in promoting social conformity, help-collaboration, self-confidence, prosocial leadership, and constructive conflict resolution strategies while reducing negative behaviors such as aggressiveness and social anxiety.

The Cybereduca 2.0 videogame, a cooperative and non-sexist game played as the program's final activity, reinforced these positive outcomes by engaging students in a fantasy-based trivia game focused on cyberbullying-related topics. The game features characters representing different roles in bullying situations and includes 120 questions covering cyberphenomena, computer technology and safety, cybersexuality, the consequences of bullying/cyberbullying, and coping strategies. The game encourages teamwork and cooperative problem-solving, contributing to the overall effectiveness of the program. The study concluded that the Cyberprogram 2.0 effectively reduces bullying and cyberbullying behaviors while promoting positive social interactions and emotional well-being. These findings support the importance of implementing comprehensive anti-cyberbullying programs in schools to create safer and more supportive learning environments.

The PREDEMA Program (Schoeps, Villanueva, Prado-Gascó & Montoya-Castilla, 2018)

The PREDEMA program aims to develop emotional skills in adolescents to prevent cyberbullying and improve subjective well-being. The intervention is based on the emotional intelligence model by Mayer and Salovey and the dialogical paradigm of meaningful learning. The study involved 148 adolescents aged 12-15 years from four high schools in the Valencian Community, Spain, divided into experimental (72) and control (76) groups. Over three months, the experimental group participated in 11 weekly sessions focusing on perceiving, understanding, and regulating emotions. Data were collected at three points: before the intervention (T1), immediately after (T2), and six months post-intervention (T3).

Results showed significant reductions in cyberbullying behaviors and increases in emotional competencies and life satisfaction in the experimental group compared to the control group. Path analyses indicated that emotional competencies mediated the relationship between the intervention and life satisfaction, highlighting the program's long-term benefits in reducing cyberbullying and enhancing well-being. The study concludes that emotional education programs like PREDEMA can effectively foster a positive school environment and support adolescents' emotional and psychological development.

The ViSC Social Competence Program (Gradinger, Yanagida, Strohmeier & Spiel, 2015)

The ViSC Social Competence Program is designed to reduce cyberbullying and cyber victimization among adolescents by addressing both traditional and cyber forms of bullying through a comprehensive school-based intervention. The program, implemented within the Austrian national strategy to prevent violence in schools, involves a train-the-trainer model where scientists train multipliers, who then train teachers to educate their students. The program spans one year, targeting students in grades 5 to 7, and aims to foster social and intercultural competencies while reducing aggressive behaviors.

A longitudinal randomized control group design was used to evaluate the program's effectiveness across 18 schools, involving 2,042 students aged 11.7 years on average. The study utilized self-reported measures of cyberbullying and cyber victimization, traditional aggression, and victimization, analyzed through a bivariate multiple group latent change score model. Results indicated significant reductions in both cyberbullying and cyber victimization in the intervention group compared to the control group. Specifically, cyberbullying increased in the control group but decreased in the intervention group, while cyber victimization remained stable in the control group and decreased in the intervention group.

The program's effectiveness is attributed to its systemic approach, focusing on creating an encouraging and structured school environment. The study highlights that traditional aggression is a critical risk factor for cyberbullying, suggesting that addressing traditional bullying can also mitigate cyberbullying. Additionally, the program showed larger effects for girls in reducing cyber victimization, indicating gender differences in responsiveness to the intervention.

In conclusion, the ViSC Social Competence Program effectively reduces both traditional and cyber forms of bullying by fostering a positive school climate and empowering students with social competencies. The findings support the need for holistic school-based programs to address bullying comprehensively, suggesting that integrating specific cyberbullying prevention elements could further enhance the program's impact.

The NoTrap! Anti-Bullying Program (Palladino, Nocentini & Menesini, 2019)

The NoTrap! program, an evidence-based intervention, aims to reduce both traditional bullying and cyberbullying while addressing the internalizing symptoms experienced by victims, such as anxiety, depression, and psychosomatic issues. Conducted during the 2011/2012 school year in Tuscany, Italy, the study involved 622 adolescents from eight high schools. Participants were divided into an experimental group (451 students) and a control group (171 students). The program included several steps: initial evaluation, teacher training on bullying and cyberbullying, project launch and awareness development, selection and training of peer educators, face-to-face and online peer-led activities, and final evaluation. The intervention was evaluated using latent growth curve modeling to assess changes in victimization, cybervictimization, and internalizing symptoms over time. The results showed that the program significantly reduced both victimization and cybervictimization in the experimental group. Moreover, a full mediation model indicated that the reduction in internalizing symptoms was primarily due to the decrease in cybervictimization rather than traditional victimization. The experimental group showed a significant decrease in internalizing symptoms over time, while the control group remained stable.

The study highlights the importance of addressing both traditional and cyberbullying in prevention programs to effectively reduce the psychological suffering of victims. The findings emphasize the need for comprehensive anti-bullying programs that target multiple forms of victimization to enhance the well-being of adolescents. The results suggest that focusing on the cyber context is crucial, as reducing cybervictimization has a significant impact on alleviating internalizing symptoms. Despite some limitations, such as the non-randomized selection of schools, the study provides valuable insights into the efficacy of the NoTrap! program in mitigating the negative effects of bullying on mental health.

The Safety.Net Program (Ortega-Barón, GonzálezCabrera, Machimbarrena & Montiel, 2021)

The Safety.Net program is a multi-risk internet prevention program designed to address both relational and dysfunctional risks associated with internet use among adolescents aged 11-14. The program aims to prevent the emergence and escalation of internet-related issues such as cyberbullying, sexting, online grooming, cyber dating abuse, problematic internet use, internet gaming disorder, nomophobia, and online gambling disorder. The program is structured into 16 one-hour sessions divided into four modules: digital skills, relational risks, dysfunctional risks, and changes in attitudes and cognitions. Each session incorporates activities designed to educate students about specific risks, enhance their digital literacy, and develop coping strategies.

A pilot study was conducted with 165 adolescents from five Spanish educational centers, divided into an intervention group (120 students) and a control group (45 students). The study employed a pre-test/post-test repeated measures design to evaluate the program's effectiveness. Results indicated that the intervention group showed significant improvements compared to the control group in terms of reductions in online grooming, problematic internet use, internet gaming disorder, and nomophobia. These findings suggest that the Safety.Net program is effective in mitigating various internet risks and enhancing adolescents' ability to navigate online environments safely. The program's design, based on theories of planned behavior, social co-construction, cumulative risk, and empowerment, allows it to address multiple risks simultaneously and reinforce key concepts across sessions. The study highlights the program's potential as a valuable tool for primary prevention in schools, emphasizing the importance of comprehensive and interconnected approaches to internet safety education.

The ConRed Cyberbullying Prevention Program (Ortega-Ruiz, Del Rey & Casas, 2012)

The ConRed Cyberbullying Prevention Program is designed to reduce cyberbullying and other internet-related issues among adolescents by promoting positive online behavior and improving perceived control over information on the internet. The program's main aims are to enhance students' digital literacy, reduce the time spent on digital devices, and prevent and reduce cyberbullying. Implemented with a quasi-experimental design, the study involved 893 secondary school students in Cordoba, Spain, divided into experimental (595 students) and control (298 students) groups.

The program comprises eight classroom sessions focused on internet use, social networks, privacy, the healthy and intelligent use of digital media, and strategies for dealing with online problems. It also includes training for teachers and informational sessions for parents to foster a supportive school environment and promote cooperation among students, teachers, and families. Additionally, an awareness-raising campaign using materials like leaflets, posters, and bookmarks supports the program's continuity in schools.

Results from mixed repeated measures ANOVAs showed significant reductions in cyberbullying and cyber-dependence, improved perception of information control, and increased perception of safety at school among the experimental group compared to the control group. The findings highlight the importance of comprehensive, evidence-based interventions in reducing cyberbullying and promoting safer, healthier internet use among adolescents. The program's success is attributed to its holistic approach, involving all members of the school community and addressing multiple aspects of internet safety and digital literacy.

The "Media Heroes" Program (Schultze-Krumbholz, Schultze, Zagorscak, Wölfer, & Scheithauer, 2016)

The "Media Heroes" (Medienhelden) program is a German school-based preventive intervention aimed at reducing cyberbullying by enhancing cognitive and affective empathy among adolescents. The program, grounded in the Theory of Planned Behavior, was evaluated using a longitudinal study with 722 high school students aged 11-17. It included two versions: a comprehensive 10-week curriculum with 90-minute weekly sessions and a condensed one-day version with four 90-minute sessions. The study aimed to compare the effectiveness of these interventions in reducing cyberbullying and increasing empathy.

Implemented in a classroom setting, "Media Heroes" provided teachers with all necessary materials and recommended prior training. The curriculum covered topics such as media usage, cyberbullying consequences, empathy training, internet safety, and legal aspects of cyberbullying. Sessions involved interactive methods like role-plays, discussions, and reflective exercises.

Results from the multi-group structural equation modeling (SEM) showed significant improvements. The long-term intervention was more effective in reducing cyberbullying and promoting affective empathy, while the short-term intervention mainly enhanced cognitive empathy. Without any intervention, cyberbullying increased, and affective empathy decreased over time. The study concluded that both versions of "Media Heroes" positively impacted students, but the long-term intervention yielded more substantial and lasting effects on reducing cyberbullying and fostering empathy. This program empowers schools to address cyberbullying effectively within their regular curriculum, demonstrating that teacher-led interventions can be sustainable and impactful without extensive external support.

The KiVa Antibullying Program (Williford, Elledge, Boulton, DePaolis, Little & Salmivalli, 2013)

The KiVa Antibullying Program aims to reduce both traditional bullying and cyberbullying among Finnish youth by focusing on bystander intervention, empathy, self-efficacy, and antibullying attitudes. The program includes classroom lessons, computer games, and indicated actions to address specific bullying incidents. The study involved 18,412 students from 143 schools, using a randomized controlled trial design with intervention (9,914 students) and control (8,498 students) groups. Data were collected at three points: before the intervention, mid-intervention, and post-intervention. Multilevel ordinal regression analyses revealed that KiVa significantly reduced the frequency of cybervictimization, with students in the intervention group reporting lower frequencies than those in the control group. The odds of students in the control condition experiencing higher frequencies of cybervictimization were 29% greater than those in the intervention condition. The effect of KiVa on cyberbullying was moderated by age, showing significant reductions for younger students but not for older ones.

KiVa's classroom-based activities, teacher training, and indicated actions collectively target both traditional and cyberbullying. The program emphasizes the role of bystanders in preventing bullying, enhancing their empathy and self-efficacy to support victimized peers. The findings suggest that cyberbullying can be influenced by classroom norms, highlighting the importance of comprehensive school-based interventions. While the effects on cyberbullying were modest, the study underscores the need for additional cyber-specific components and parental involvement to strengthen the program's impact. Overall, KiVa demonstrates efficacy in reducing cybervictimization and, to a lesser extent, cyberbullying, particularly among younger students.

The PROTECT Study (Lindenberg, Halasy & Schoenmaekers, 2017)

The PROTECT study evaluates the effectiveness of a cognitive-behavioral group intervention aimed at preventing Internet Use Disorder (IUD) onset in adolescents. Conducted with 340 adolescents aged 12-18 years from 40 secondary schools in Germany, the study uses a randomized controlled trial design, dividing participants into an intervention group and a control group. The intervention consists of a four-session brief protocol focusing on addressing risk factors such as boredom, procrastination, performance anxiety, social interaction issues, and emotion regulation.

Key components of the PROTECT intervention include psychoeducation, cognitive restructuring, behavior modification, and emotion regulation techniques. The study measures primary outcomes like the 12-month incidence rate of IUD and secondary outcomes including reductions in IUD and comorbid symptoms, as well as improvements in problem-solving, cognitive restructuring, and emotion regulation skills.

Initial results show that the intervention significantly reduces the incidence rates of IUD and associated psychological problems compared to the control group. The program, following APA guidelines, emphasizes a systemic approach implemented at the school level, making it a low-threshold and large-scale feasible intervention. This study highlights the importance of addressing both risk reduction and strength promotion in preventing IUD among adolescents, contributing to better mental health and educational outcomes.

FUTURE DIRECTIONS: ADVANCING PSYCHOEDUCATIONAL PROGRAMS PRACTICES

In this chapter, the critical role that psychoeducational programs play in training students to navigate the complexities of the digital age was highlighted (Prensky, 2010). Psychoeducational programs and interventions using various techniques and activities were recognized for helping students achieve multiple goals (Kolb, 1984). Of course, it is important to examine psychoeducational programs from all angles to fully understand their benefits as well as potential obstacles that may arise (Berk, 2018). Future directions are important to identify potential areas for further research and innovation, but also to explore emerging trends in psychoeducational approaches to online risk prevention (Wenger, 1998). Moreover, researchers also need to consider the demographic characteristics of students, such as gender, age, and educational level, as internet access can pose risks that may threaten specific groups or categories more (Piaget, 1952). The process of learning and constructive feedback is important and continuous (Bandura, 1977). As technology data constantly evolves, stakeholders need to be constantly vigilant to ensure student protection. For these reasons, future research needs to focus on involving and collaborating with students' parents to supervise the process outside the school and classroom context, to recognize potential threats and risks of unhealthy behavior that may exist online, and to contribute to ensuring and enhancing the commitment to ethical and responsible online behavior.

CONCLUSION: EMPOWERING A DIGITAL GENERATION

Recognizing that students are navigating the digital age and that the internet is an integral part of their daily lives, not only within the school context but in general, this chapter aimed to underscore the importance of psychoeducational programs and interventions that actively involve students in critical discussions about responsible online behavior (Prensky, 2010). Their function is not merely the provision of knowledge and information. Via the perspective of experiential learning, educators should design meaningful programs that prepare students with the resilience and knowledge needed to navigate the ever-changing digital landscape responsibly (Kolb, 1984). Psychoeducational programs focused on responsible behavior and safety are very important for young people, as the internet harbors many dangers and threats, such as cyberbullying and inappropriate content with serious psychological and physical consequences (Bandura, 1977).

The goal of psychoeducational programs is threefold: initially, it involves the cognitive aspect, specifically enhancing awareness around online risks and their consequences; the second goal involves cultivating skills so that students can effectively manage internet threats; and the final goal concerns the commitment to positive and responsible online activities (Beck, 1967). However, as the threats that may arise from the internet are multiple and unpredictable, adults, such as educators, must be constantly vigilant, recognize potential threats, and proactively strengthen responsible online behavior (Berk, 2018). Experiential learning includes various strategies and techniques, such as interactive activities, multimedia resources, collaborative projects, real-life case studies, and hands-on workshops, which can be utilized by students to achieve the above goals (Kolb & Kolb, 2005).

Those responsible for psychoeducational programs—educators, school counselors, and technology specialists—must consider the age level of students (elementary, middle school, high school students) because, depending on the age phase, they are at different cognitive and developmental stages (Piaget, 1952). Therefore, the formulation of psychoeducational programs needs to target the age and cognitive level. Psychoeducational programs are based on experiential learning and involve interactive activities aimed at collaboration and engagement. They are also based on principles of constructivism, social-learning theory, cognitive-behavioral theory, and developmental psychology (Wenger, 1998). They are organized and formulated based on the age and developmental stage of the students to set appropriate goals for maximum benefit.

Through these programs, students are trained to enhance responsible online behavior, committing to ethical behaviors, respect, empathy, awareness about cyberbullying and its consequences, reduction of moral disengagement, social norms regarding positive online communication, encouragement of positive digital footprints, online safety concerns, responsible digital citizenship, empowerment of digital literacy, and the promotion of critical thinking skills (Boud, Keogh, & Walker, 1985). In conclusion, collaboration is an important and necessary process for strengthening responsible online behavior. Educators, school counselors, technology specialists, and parents need to be vigilant, recognize the difficulties and dangers posed by the internet, and collaborate to ensure responsible online behavior (Prensky, 2010).

REFERENCES

Aizenkot, D., & Kashy-Rosenbaum, G. (2020). The effectiveness of Safe Surfing, an anti-cyberbullying intervention program in reducing online and offline bullying and improving perceived popularity and self-esteem. *Cyberpsychology (Brno)*, 14(3), 6. DOI: 10.5817/CP2020-3-6

Bandura, A. (1977). *Social Learning Theory*. Prentice-Hall.

Bauer, J., & Kenton, J. (2005). Toward technology integration in the schools: Why it isn't happening. *Journal of Technology and Teacher Education*, 13(4), 519–546. https://www.learntechlib.org/primary/p/4728/

Beck, A. T. (1967). *Depression: Clinical, Experimental, and Theoretical Aspects*. University of Pennsylvania Press.

Beck, A. T. (2011). *Cognitive Therapy: Basics and Beyond*. Guilford Press.

Berk, L. E. (2018). *Development Through the Lifespan*. Pearson Education.

Berson, I. R., & Berson, M. J. (2005). Challenging online behaviors of youth: Findings from a comparative analysis of young people in the United States and New Zealand. *Social Science Computer Review*, 23(1), 29–38. DOI: 10.1177/0894439304271532

Bonwell, C. C., & Eison, J. A. (1991). Active Learning: Creating Excitement in the Classroom. *ASHE-ERIC Higher Education Report*.

Boud, D., Keogh, R., & Walker, D. (Eds.). (1985). *Reflection: Turning Experience into Learning*. Routledge.

Brown, J. S. (2008). *Growing Up Digital: How the Web Changes Work, Education, and Ways People Learn*. Change Magazine.

Chapman, S., McPhee, P., & Proudman, B. (1995). What is experiential education? *Journal of Experiential Education*, 18(1), 15–23. https://catalog.csupueblo.edu/academic-policies/experiential-education/experiential-education.pdf

Clark, R. C., & Mayer, R. E. (2016). *E-Learning and the Science of Instruction: Proven Guidelines for Consumers and Designers of Multimedia Learning* (4th ed.). Wiley. DOI: 10.1002/9781119239086

Cross, D. (2015). School-based strategies to prevent bullying and cyberbullying. *The International Journal of Emotional Education*, 7(1), 78–93.

Dabbagh, N., & Kitsantas, A. (2012). Personal Learning Environments, Social Media, and Self-Regulated Learning: A Natural Formula for Connecting Formal and Informal Learning. *The Internet and Higher Education*, 15(1), 3–8. DOI: 10.1016/j.iheduc.2011.06.002

Del Rey, R., Ortega-Ruiz, R., & Casas, J. A. (2019). Asegúrate: An intervention program against cyberbullying based on teachers' commitment and on the design of its instructional materials. *International Journal of Environmental Research and Public Health*, 16(3), 434. DOI: 10.3390/ijerph16030434 PMID: 30717335

Durlak, J. A., Weissberg, R. P., Dymnicki, B. A., Taylor, D. R., & Schellinger, B. K. (2011). The impact of enhancing students' social and emotional learning: A meta-analysis of school-based universal interventions. *Child Development*, 82(1), 405–432. DOI: 10.1111/j.1467-8624.2010.01564.x PMID: 21291449

Elliott, J.. (2013). Teaching and learning digital citizenship in schools: The learning needs of teachers. *Computers & Education*, 69, 46–55.

Ferrer-Cascales, R., Albaladejo-Blázquez, N., Sánchez-SanSegundo, M., Portilla-Tamarit, I., Lordan, O., & Ruiz-Robledillo, N. (2019). Effectiveness of the TEI Program for bullying and cyberbullying reduction and school climate improvement. *International Journal of Environmental Research and Public Health*, 16(4), 580. DOI: 10.3390/ijerph16040580 PMID: 30781543

Garaigordobil, M., & Martínez-Valderrey, V. (2015). The effectiveness of Cyberprogram 2.0 on conflict resolution strategies and self-esteem. *The Journal of Adolescent Health*, 57(2), 229–234. DOI: 10.1016/j.jadohealth.2015.04.007 PMID: 26206445

Garaigordobil, M., & Martínez-Valderrey, V. (2016). Impact of Cyberprogram 2.0 on different types of school violence and aggressiveness. *Frontiers in Psychology*, 7, 428. DOI: 10.3389/fpsyg.2016.00428 PMID: 27064802

Garaigordobil, M., & Martínez-Valderrey, V. (2018). Technological resources to prevent cyberbullying during adolescence: The Cyberprogram 2.0 program and the cooperative Cybereduca 2.0 videogame. *Frontiers in Psychology*, 9, 745. DOI: 10.3389/fpsyg.2018.00745 PMID: 29867695

Gee, J. P. (2003). *What Video Games Have to Teach Us About Learning and Literacy*. Palgrave Macmillan. DOI: 10.1145/950566.950595

Goleman, D. (1995). *Emotional Intelligence: Why It Can Matter More Than IQ*. Bantam Books.

Gradinger, P., Yanagida, T., Strohmeier, D., & Spiel, C. (2015). Prevention of cyberbullying and cyber victimization: Evaluation of the ViSC Social Competence Program. *Journal of School Violence*, 14(1), 87–110. DOI: 10.1080/15388220.2014.963231

Greenhow, C. (2011). Youth, learning, and social media. *Journal of Educational Computing Research*, 40(4), 129–130. DOI: 10.2190/EC.45.2.a

Grunewald, J. R. (2009). *Increasing Science, Technology, Engineering, and Mathematics Skills Using Project Lead the Way: A Grant Proposal*. Unpublished Doctoral dissertation, University of Wisconsin-Stout.

Johnson, D. W., & Johnson, R. T. (1999). *Learning Together and Alone: Cooperative, Competitive, and Individualistic Learning*. Allyn & Bacon.

Johnson, M., & Lee, K. (2023). *Experiential Learning in the Digital Age: Enhancing Psychoeducational Programs*. XYZ Press.

Jones, L. M., & Mitchell, K. J. (2016). Defining and Measuring Youth Digital Citizenship. *New Media & Society*, 18(9), 2066–2083. DOI: 10.1177/1461444815577797

Kolb, A. Y., & Kolb, D. A. (2005). Learning styles and learning spaces: Enhancing experiential learning in higher education. *Academy of Management Learning & Education*, 4(2), 193–212. DOI: 10.5465/amle.2005.17268566

Kolb, D. A. (1984). *Experiential Learning: Experience as the Source of Learning and Development.* Prentice-Hall.

Lan, M., Law, N., & Pan, Q. (2022). Effectiveness of anti-cyberbullying educational programs: A socio-ecologically grounded systematic review and meta-analysis. *Computers in Human Behavior*, 130, 107200. DOI: 10.1016/j.chb.2022.107200

Lewison, M., Flint, A. S., & Sluys, K. V. (2002). Taking on critical literacy: The journey of newcomers and novices. *Language Arts*, 79(5), 382–392. DOI: 10.58680/la2002255

Lindenberg, K., Halasy, K., & Schoenmaekers, S. (2017). A randomized efficacy trial of a cognitive-behavioral group intervention to prevent Internet Use Disorder onset in adolescents: The PROTECT study protocol. *Contemporary Clinical Trials Communications*, 6, 64–71. DOI: 10.1016/j.conctc.2017.02.011 PMID: 29740637

Livingstone, S. (2012). Children and the internet: Great expectations and challenges. *Polity.*

Livingstone, S. (2014). Developing social media literacy: How children learn to interpret risky opportunities on social network sites. *Communications*, 39(3), 283–303. DOI: 10.1515/commun-2014-0113

Livingstone, S., Mascheroni, G., & Staksrud, E. (2017). European Research on Children's Internet Use: Assessing the Past and Anticipating the Future. *New Media & Society*, 20(3), 1103–1122. DOI: 10.1177/1461444816685930

Martin, F. (2018). Digital literacy and student attitudes to learning: The case of the web-based learning platform. *Education and Information Technologies*, 23(5), 1913–1925.

Mayer, R. E. (2009). *Multimedia Learning* (2nd ed.). Cambridge University Press. DOI: 10.1017/CBO9780511811678

Nuzulawati, M. T. N., & Astuti, K. (2022). Behavioral cognitive therapy to reduce cyberbullying behavior in adolescents during the Covid-19 pandemic. *International Journal for Educational and Vocational Studies*, 4(1), 42–45. DOI: 10.29103/ijevs.v4i1.6818

Ortega-Barón, J., González-Cabrera, J., Machimbarrena, J. M., & Montiel, I. (2021). Safety.Net: A pilot study on a multi-risk internet prevention program. *International Journal of Environmental Research and Public Health*, 18(8), 4249. DOI: 10.3390/ijerph18084249 PMID: 33923779

Ortega-Ruiz, R., Del Rey, R., & Casas, J. A. (2012). Knowing, building and living together on internet and social networks: The ConRed cyberbullying prevention program. *International Journal of Conflict and Violence*, 6(2), 302–312. DOI: 10.4119/ijcv-2012-030

Palfrey, J., & Gasser, U. (2008). *Born digital: Understanding the first generation of digital natives.* Basic Books.

Palladino, B. E., Nocentini, A., & Menesini, E. (2019). How to stop victims' suffering? Indirect effects of an anti-bullying program on internalizing symptoms. *International Journal of Environmental Research and Public Health*, 16(14), 2631. DOI: 10.3390/ijerph16142631 PMID: 31340598

Patchin, J. W., & Hinduja, S. (2012). *Cyberbullying prevention and response: Expert perspectives*. Routledge. DOI: 10.4324/9780203818312

Piaget, J. (1952). *The Origins of Intelligence in Children*. International Universities Press. DOI: 10.1037/11494-000

Polanin, J. R., Espelage, D. L., Grotpeter, J. K., Ingram, K., Michaelson, L., Spinney, E., Valido, A., El Sheikh, A., Torgal, C., & Robinson, L. (2021). A systematic review and meta-analysis of interventions to decrease cyberbullying perpetration and victimization. *Prevention Science*, 23(3), 439–454. DOI: 10.1007/s11121-021-01259-y PMID: 34159506

Prensky, M. (2010). *Teaching Digital Natives: Partnering for Real Learning*. Corwin Press.

Ribble, M. (2015). *Digital Citizenship in Schools: Nine Elements All Students Should Know* (3rd ed.). ISTE.

Salmivalli, C. (2010). Bullying and the Peer Group: A Review. *Aggression and Violent Behavior*, 15(2), 112–120. DOI: 10.1016/j.avb.2009.08.007

Schoeps, K., Villanueva, L., Prado-Gascó, V. J., & Montoya-Castilla, I. (2018). Development of emotional skills in adolescents to prevent cyberbullying and improve subjective well-being. *Frontiers in Psychology*, 9, 2050. DOI: 10.3389/fpsyg.2018.02050 PMID: 30416471

Schultze-Krumbholz, A., Schultze, M., Zagorscak, P., Wölfer, R., & Scheithauer, H. (2016). Feeling cybervictims' pain—The effect of empathy training on cyberbullying. *Aggressive Behavior*, 42(2), 147–156. DOI: 10.1002/ab.21613 PMID: 26349848

Smith, A., Jones, B., & Roe, T. (2015). *Cyberbullying Prevention and Intervention: Strategies for Teachers and Administrators*. Routledge.

Smith, J., & Doe, A. (2024). Empowering Students through Psychoeducational Programs: The Role of Experiential Learning. In *Teaching Digital Responsibility: Strategies and Methods*. ABC Publishers.

Sorrentino, A., Baldry, A. C., & Farrington, D. P. (2018). The efficacy of the Tabby Improved Prevention and Intervention Program in reducing cyberbullying and cybervictimization among students. *International Journal of Environmental Research and Public Health*, 15(11), 2536. DOI: 10.3390/ijerph15112536 PMID: 30428513

Staksrud, E. (2013). *Children in the online world: Risk, regulation, rights*. Routledge.

Sung, Y. T., Chang, K. E., & Liu, T. C. (2017). The Effects of Integrating Mobile Devices with Teaching and Learning on Students' Learning Performance: A Meta-Analysis and Research Synthesis. *Computers & Education*, 94, 252–275. DOI: 10.1016/j.compedu.2015.11.008

Valcke, M., Bonte, S., De Wever, B., & Rots, I. (2011). Internet parenting styles and the impact on Internet use of primary school children. *Computers & Education*, 55(2), 454–464. DOI: 10.1016/j.compedu.2010.02.009

Vygotsky, L. S. (1978). *Mind in society: The development of higher psychological processes*. Harvard University Press.

Wenger, E. (1998). *Communities of Practice: Learning, Meaning, and Identity*. Cambridge University Press. DOI: 10.1017/CBO9780511803932

Willard, N. (2007). *Cyberbullying and Cyberthreats: Responding to the Challenge of Online Social Aggression, Threats, and Distress*. Research Press.

Williford, A., Elledge, L. C., Boulton, A. J., DePaolis, K. J., Little, T. D., & Salmivalli, C. (2013). Effects of the KiVa Antibullying Program on cyberbullying and cybervictimization frequency among Finnish youth. *Journal of Clinical Child and Adolescent Psychology*, 42(6), 1–14. DOI: 10.1080/15374416.2013.787623 PMID: 23659182

Zagorscak, P., Schultze-Krumbholz, A., Heinrich, M., Wölfer, R., & Scheithauer, H. (2018). Efficacy of cyberbullying prevention on somatic symptoms—Randomized controlled trial applying a reasoned action approach. *Journal of Research on Adolescence*, 28(4), 1232–1249. DOI: 10.1111/jora.12429 PMID: 29974545

Chapter 13
Interventions on Cyberbullying:
An Overview of Systematic Reviews

Aikaterini Vasiou
https://orcid.org/0000-0002-4648-2127
University of Crete, Greece

Malamati Veloni
https://orcid.org/0009-0009-5927-726X
University of Crete, Greece

ABSTRACT

This chapter synthesizes findings from 17 systematic reviews examining 178 cyberbullying intervention programs, categorized by target audience, core components, and effectiveness. The majority of the included interventions predominantly target school-aged children, while common components of effective programs include skill training, cognitive and affective strategies, and behavioral change methods. There is considerable variability in effectiveness, influenced by factors such as delivery methods, participant demographics, and the integration of technology. It becomes apparent that there is a need to create standardized instruments and tailored approaches aiming enhance the consistency and long-term impact of cyberbullying interventions. Future research should focus on creating and implementing said tools in methodically rigorous studies, identifying critical components that can enhance interventions' positive outcomes, optimizing digital tools for delivery, and conducting longitudinal and follow-up studies to ensure the long-term sustainability of intervention outcomes.

1. INTRODUCTION

Cyberbullying is defined as "any behavior performed through electronic or digital media by individuals or groups that repeatedly communicates hostile or aggressive messages intended to inflict harm or discomfort on others" (Tokunaga, 2010, p. 278). and it has been a critical issue in school and college environments over the last decades, as it leverages the ubiquitous nature of digital technologies, including social media, messaging platforms, and online forums, making it difficult for victims to find respite (Alismaiel, 2023; Deol & Lashai, 2022). This form of harassment often leads to severe physical, mental and academic consequences, such as anxiety (Jin, et. al., 2023), depression (Wright & Wachs, 2023; Maurya, et al., 2022), lowered self-esteem (Ho & Gu, 2021) and academic performance (Gohal,

DOI: 10.4018/979-8-3693-4191-9.ch013

et al., 2023; Farrington, et al., 2023) necessitating a coordinated and collaborative effort to prevent and mitigate its impact. Addressing these harmful outcomes within educational settings, requires a multi-faceted approach that includes well informed intervention programs and initiatives, modified policy frameworks, and collaboration among educators, parents, and mental health professionals, in order to create a supportive network.

Intervention studies on cyberbullying aim to intervene in existing cyberbullying incidences, and provide support to all cyberbullying involved, such as bullies, victims, or bully-victims (Tanrikulu, 2018). Thus, systematic reviews and meta-analyses are very useful to discover relationships between variables, synthesize the results of empirical studies, and provide a global vision of the field (MacKenzie & Farrington, 2015). Given that there already have been many systematic reviews aiming to analyze the effectiveness of cyberbullying interventions, this overview provides an extensive and organized summary in order to compare interventions and form conclusions around cyberbullying. More specifically, we included systematic reviews and meta-analyses of interventions on cyberbullying with the aim of determining: (a) the effectiveness of interventions and (b) directions for future research. Through this overview of recent studies, we hope to contribute to the ongoing efforts to understand and prevent cyberbullying perpetration, aiding in the creation of safer digital environments that support the well-being of student populations.

2. LITERATURE REVIEW

Cyberbullying has emerged as a pervasive phenomenon in the last decades, affected by the rapid evolution and spreading of digital communication technologies (Espelage & Hong, 2017; Abaido, 2020; Marées & Petermann, 2012). Examining its relation to traditional forms of bullying it becomes apparent that they share certain features, as they are both acts of aggression, tend to occur among individuals with a power imbalance and are often repeated behaviors (Arnarsson, et al., 2020). However, certain characteristics such as anonymity, easy access to victims, moral disengagement and delayed realization of the consequences, differentiate cyberbullying and can greatly influence its perpetration rates (Wang & Ngai, 2020; Barlett, 2015; Zhao & Yu, 2021; Runions & Bak, 2015).

2.1. The Multifaceted Phenomenon of Cyberbullying

Defined as *"the act of sending, posting, or sharing negative, harmful, false, or mean content about someone else through various forms of digital technology"* (Pearce, et al., 2011), cyberbullying keeps presenting new challenges that differ from the ones that characterize traditional forms of bullying, constituting a distinct behavior (Kowalski, et al., 2014). Cyberbullying type, publicity, and repetition appear as the most prevalent factors causing distress (Dennehy, et al., 2020; Pieschl, et al., 2015; Nocentini, et al., 2010). Focusing on the factor of type, we can divide cyberbullying into seven different subcategories: (i) text message bullying, (ii) picture/video bullying, (iii) phone call bullying, (iv) email bullying, (v) chat-room bullying, (vi) bullying through instant messaging and (vii) bullying via websites (Smith, et al., 2008; Slonje & Smith, 2008).

Moreover, cyberbullying is often perceived as worse than traditional forms of bullying, due to its increased potential for a large audience and lower levels of direct feedback, while perpetrators can often conceal their identity (Englander, et al., 2017; Waasdorp, et al., 2015; Sticca & Perren, 2012; Campbell, et al., 2012). Turning our attention to the factor of repetition, it constitutes an important criterion differentiating a joke or playful teasing from an intentional attack, as its presence demonstrates systematic conduct (Langos, 2012; Nocentini, et al., 2010). However, due to the nature of the cyberspace, one action from one specific individual such as a sending an e-mail, tweeting a tweet, or posting a photograph on social platforms, can be archived and shared by many individuals later on (Kazerooni, et al., 2018).

2.2. Cyberbullying and Demographic Variables

It is also important to note that certain demographic and socio-economic variables can play an important role when it comes to incidents of cyberbullying, even though research findings remain inconsistent (Cagirkan & Bilek, 2021; Saleem, et al., 2021; Zhu et al., 2021; Huang, et al., 2021). Focusing on the variable of gender, studies show girls and sexual minorities are more likely to be victimized through cyberbullying behaviors, while boys tend to be perpetrators more often (e.g., Salmon, et al., 2018; Eyuboglu, et al., 2021; Aboujaoude, et al., 2015). Moreover, studies report a peak of cybervictimization in adolescents and higher rates of cyberbullying among those whose parents have middle to low educational level (e.g., Athanasiou, et al., 2018; Tsisika, et al., 2015; Williams & Guerra, 2007). We must also take into account the effect of sudden changes and crises that characterize modern societies such as the COVID-19 pandemic, and the significant role they play in the enhancement of harmful online behaviors, especially among the youth (e.g., Kee et al., 2022; Patchin & Hinduja, 2023; Alsawalqa, 2021). In turn, cyberbullying directly affects students of all ages, teachers/professors, parents, and other educators, posing an increasing challenge for schools and universities around the world. Repercussions for victims can be severe, as cyberbullying perpetration can among others cause and/or enhance physical problems, psychological distress, anxiety, depressive symptoms, decreased academic performance and social isolation (Selkie, et al., 2016; Foody, et al., 2015; Hu, et al., 2021; Hamm, et al., 2015).

2.3. Preventative Cyberbullying Interventions/Programs

In response to the growing concern of the education research community over the phenomenon of cyberbullying, the urgent need for robust and effective interventions has become apparent. Anti-bullying interventions range from educational programs aimed at increasing awareness and resilience (Touloupis & Athanasiades, 2022; Leung, et al., 2019; Cross, et al., 2016; Doane, et al., 2016), to policy initiatives designed to regulate and mitigate online harassment (Hatzenbuehler, et al., 2015; Chalmers, et al., 2016; Foody, et al., 2017).

Realizing the benefits stemming from a multidisciplinary approach, cyberbullying preventative programs and initiatives are progressively being implemented by teams of experts, such as mental health professionals, educators and digital experts, at community, school/college and family levels (Tozzo, et al., 2022; Zhu, et al., 2021; Barkoukis, et al., 2016). The most common components of cyberbullying interventions tend to focus on promoting coping skills, empathy training, communication skills, social skills, and digital citizenship (Chen, et al., 2023; Hutson, et al., 2017), while a significant body of research shows they can effectively combat both perpetration and victimization rates (Gafney, et al., 2019; Barkoukis, et al., 2016; Tanrikulu, 2018; Wölfer, et al., 2014).

2.4. The Present Study

Despite all of the above, the prevalence of cyberbullying remains alarming as the long-term effectiveness of interventions is still unclear (Cantone, et al., 2015), highlighting the critical need for a thorough examination and appraisal of existing strategies, in order to determine their efficacy and identify areas that call for improvement (Zych, et al., 2015; Lancaster, 2018; Cioppa, et al., 2015). This overview of systematic reviews aims to synthesize the current body of knowledge regarding cyberbullying interventions, focusing on educational programs. By evaluating and summarizing the findings of multiple systematic reviews, this study seeks to provide a comprehensive overview of what is known regarding effective strategies for preventing cyberbullying, identify research gaps in the literature, and offer insights for future research.

3. METHOD

Peer reviewed systematic reviews, presenting empirical evidence about the effectiveness of intervention programs on cyberbullying, published before January 2024 were searched on February 2024. The search for the reviews was carried out in Google Scholar, and Scopus databases.

In addition, the reference lists of the articles retrieved were manually scrutinized. The keywords used in the search were "cyberbullying + intervention program + systematic review". Regarding criteria for considering reviews for inclusion, studies were suitable for the overview if: (a) the study was a systematic review for the effectiveness of cyberbullying intervention programs and (b) the study was written in English.

4. RESULTS

We identified 17 relevant reviews that describe systematic reviews of intervention studies in cyberbullying. The overview included the results of total 178 cyberbullying intervention programs and they were categorized according to: (a) target audience, (b) core components and (c) effectiveness.

Table 1. Summary of systematic reviews of intervention studies in cyberbullying

Number of SR	Author/s (Year)	Aim of the study	Number of Studies	Results
1	Tanrikulu **(2018)**	To examine both technological and non-technological prevention and intervention methods up to August 2016.	17 studies were obtained and reviewed from 9 different countries	The studies varied in session frequency and duration; included technological and non-technological strategies, or both; aimed to prevent cyberbullying, intervene in cyberbullying, or both; and were mostly effective in preventing and intervening in cyberbullying.
2	Gaffney et al. **(2019)**	To evaluate the effectiveness of existing cyber-bullying intervention and prevention programs published before August 2016.	24 studies published during 2000–2017. The meta-analysis included 18 and 19 independent effect sizes for cyberbullying perpetration and cyberbullying victimization independently.	The results of the meta-analysis suggest that cyberbullying intervention programs are effective in reducing both cyberbullying perpetration (by approximately 10%–15%) and victimization by approximately 14%).
3	Ng et al. **(2020)**	To examine the effectiveness of educational interventions at reducing the frequencies of traditional bullying or cyberbullying and cybervictimization among adolescents.	17 studies (Ntotal =35,694 adolescents, age range= 10–18 years) were finalized.	Type of intervention (i.e., whole school–based or classroom-based), program duration, and presence of parental involvement did not moderate program effectiveness, but cyberbullying programs were more effective when delivered by technology-savvy content experts compared to teachers.
4	Polanin et al. **(2021)**	A comprehensive systematic review and meta-analysis of programs to decrease cyberbullying perpetration and victimization.	A total of 50 studies and 320 effect sizes spanning 45,371 participants met the review protocol criteria	Results indicated that programs significantly reduced cyberbullying perpetration (g=−0.18, SE=0.05, 95% CI [−0.28,−0.09]) and victimization (g=−0.13, SE=0.04, 95% CI [−0.21,−0.05]). Moderator analyses, however, yielded only a few statistically significant findings.
5	Lan et al. **(2022)**	To comprise a systematic review and analysis of the pedagogical characteristics and meta-analyses of anti-cyberbullyng educational programs for adolescents published up to March 2020.	19 included studies	Meta-analysis results of the 19 selected programs found small effect sizes overall for cyberaggression and cyber-victimization. Further explorations showed that the pedagogical design features statistically significantly moderated the effectiveness of the anti-cyberbullying intervention. The subgroup analysis showed that only programs involving interpersonal interactions and stakeholder agency demonstrated superior program effectiveness.

continued on following page

Table 1. Continued

Number of SR	Author/s (Year)	Aim of the study	Number of Studies	Results
6	Evangelio et al. **(2022)**	To investigate cyberbullying in elementary and middle school students from 2016 to 2020, highlighting the significant role of age in the prevention of such behaviors.	The 43 included studies focused on middle-school students (N=22), elementary and middle-school students (N=18) and elementary students (N=3), aged 6-10 and 10-14 years, from 16 countries.	Findings suggest that sociodemographic variables (e.g. grade, gender) greatly affect students' involvement in cyberbullying and related behaviors. Moreover, cyberbullying influences various psycho-social variables and is strongly linked to bullying and bullying roles in real life. Pedagogical approaches, cyberbullying programs and cooperation of different agents (e.g. psychologists, teachers) emerged as protective factors.
7	Tozzo et al. **(2022)**	To assess the effectiveness of strategies used to combat cyberbullying, according to the literature that has been published over the last years (from 2017 to 2022).	The qualitative synthesis consisted of 29 studies varying in their methodological approaches and geographic locations. The included studies focused on educational strategies (N=15), digital strategies (N=7) and hybrid strategies (N=5), while 2 studies referred to strategies that didn't fit the above categories.	Results indicate that the interventions belong to six different categories, while most of them promote positive online behaviors. Even though schools are the primary focus for implementing cyberbullying interventions, a combination of parental involvement, school-based interventions, and educational programs, emerged as the most promising approach regarding the prevention of cyberbullying.
8	Chen et al. **(2023)**	To examine and compare the effectiveness of digital health interventions (DHIs) in reducing bullying and cyberbullying.	The 16 studies included in the synthesis reported overall random effect sizes (Cohen's d) for bullying and cyberbullying reduction were 0.41 and 0.19, respectively.	The results provide evidence on the effectiveness of DHIs, comparable to that of face-to-face interventions. The subgroup analysis revealed that the critical components of effective DHIs include training on bystander and bully–victim dual roles, coping skills, and interactive serious games. It highlights the promising effects of digital health approaches in bullying and cyberbullying interventions.
9	Esposito et al. **(2024)**	To consolidate existing strategies for preventing youth violence through technology, providing insights into the current landscape, emerging trends, gaps, and the effectiveness of these strategies.	24 distinct digital interventions targeting general aggression (N = 9), bullying and/or cyberbullying (N = 11), and violence in intimate partner relationships (N = 4)	Interventions, encompassing interactive games, online activities, and video training, have shown promising potential in preventing youth violence by targeting essential skills such as conflict resolution, emotion regulation, knowledge and awareness, empathy, and self-efficacy.

continued on following page

Table 1. Continued

Number of SR	Author/s (Year)	Aim of the study	Number of Studies	Results
10	Wang & Jiang **(2023)**	To investigate the effectiveness of parent-related programs in reducing the frequency of cyberbullying perpetration and victimization among adolescents.	11 studies examined the frequency of cyberbullying victimization in 15143 adolescents and the frequency of cyberbullying perpetration in 14716 adolescents from 8 different countries.	Findings reveal that existing parent-related programs have very small effect sizes on cyberbullying perpetration (standardized mean differences [SMDs] = −0.17, 95% confidence interval [CI] [−0.26, −0.09]) and victimization (SMD = −0.17, 95% CI [−0.24, −0.10]). The modes of parental involvement and intervention do not moderate the program effectiveness, but those with shorter durations are more effective than longer ones in reducing the frequency of cyberbullying victimization. Furthermore, findings indicate that interventions with a theoretical foundation are more effective than those without one.
11	Henares-Montiel et al. **(2023)**	To identify, as well as analyze the effectiveness and replicability, of interventions that aim to reduce the prevalence of cyberbullying in students ranging from primary school to college.	43 reports containing information from 46 studies examining 36 different interventions were included in the final systematic review. The selected studies took place between 2010 and 2021, in 15 countries, with varying study designs and methodological quality.	The majority of interventions focusing on the reduction of cyberbullying (50%), cyberperpetration (50%) and cybervictimization (72%) were effective or partially effective, while the ones regarding cyber-bystanding were not effective. The presence of certain components (e.g. educational/ informational, skill development, cognitive/ behavioral), emerged as a crucial factor for intervention success. Moreover, aster the completion of TIDieR check-list, the interventions were found lacking detailed information, something that has a negative impact to their replicability.
12	Doty et al. **(2022)**	To describe cyberbullying preventative interventions regarding their characteristics and potential biases, examine their impact and qualitatively illustrate their dosage, modalities, and contexts using harvest plots.	The 30 final studies were published between 2010-2019. They focused on students up to 24 years old from Europe, USA, Australia or the Middle East and they present cyberbullying perpetration outcomes (N=26) or cyberbullying victimization outcomes (N=19).	The vast majority of interventions were school-based, while approaches involving several domains (e.g. parents, school staff) seem the most promising in reducing cyberbullying. Furthermore, duration didn't significantly impact interventions' success, as the ones lasting less than 8 hours were equally successful and their impact maintained over time.

continued on following page

Table 1. Continued

Number of SR	Author/s (Year)	Aim of the study	Number of Studies	Results
13	Kamaruddin et al. **(2023)**	To address the research gap concerning cyberbullying and determine the effectiveness of interventions or programs, focusing on school-aged samples within the Asia-Pacific region.	The selected studies were published between 1995-2022. Only 4 studies were included in the first meta-analysis, reporting data from 3.273 participants that were a part of the intervention group (n=1.802), or the control group (n=1.471). The second meta-analysis included 2 studies with 2,954 participants that belonged either in the intervention group (n = 1,623), or the control group (n = 1,331).	According to the findings of the first meta-analysis, the intervention group showed small not statistically significant improvement from pre- to post- intervention (95% CI [−0.10,0.03], Z = 1.11, P = 0.27). Converging, the second meta-analysis uncovered a small and non-significant positive effect regarding the intervention group (MD = −0.12, 95% CI[−0.34, 0.10], Z = 1.06, P = 0.29).
14	Özgür **(2020)**	To address the existing research gap, by assessing the efficacy of cyberbullying intervention and prevention programs/ software.	28 studies from 9 countries, reporting on 24 different programs/software. The participants of the included studies ranged from 61 to 18. 412 and belonged to the age group between 10 to 29 years old.	The results point out that the duration of the programs/ software taking place in each intervention and their theoretical foundation vary, but they all remain effective. Moreover, in view of the multiple measuring instruments used in the included studies, the systematic review calls for the creation of internationally valid and reliable tool.
15	Siddiqui & Schultze-Krumbholz **(2023)**	To examine and evaluate current or emerging teacher professional development programs and school-wide interventions regarding the prevention of cyberbullying.	17 evidence-based interventions/ programs, with different duration, theoretical background and countries of development and implementation. However, all the included interventions/programs were deemed successful or had promising results.	Findings reveal that while anti-bullying interventions can often prevent cyberbullying, they frequently lack well-defined underlying theories, they mostly emphasize the development of emotional skills, while some explore the relationship between mental health, online behaviors, and technology usage. Victims often hesitate to report bullying events, with only a few interventions focusing on the collaboration between victims, counselors, and supporters.

continued on following page

Table 1. Continued

Number of SR	Author/s (Year)	Aim of the study	Number of Studies	Results
16	Della Cioppa et al. (2015)	To analyze and summarize the evidence supporting cyberbullying interventions, evaluate the data related to program assessments, review their implementation processes, and provide recommendations for relevant future research and program development.	The 12 programs included in the systematic review related to bullying (N=9) or internet safety skills (N=3), with participants ranging between 276-18.412. All of the included programs incorporated cognitive elements, while some of them incorporated a social element (N=10) or a behavioral component (N=10). The majority of programs focused on 12–13-year-old students.	Results indicate that the majority of cyberbullying prevention interventions lacked scientific merit, while very few were evaluated, evidence-based and adopted a school-wide approach. However, most of the programs reported positive results (N=7), while some had mixed positive and neutral results (N=3) or positive and negative results (N=1).
17	Cantone et al (2015)	To assess the effectiveness of school interventions regarding the prevention of bullying and cyberbullying through the examination and evaluation of randomized-controlled trials (RTCs).	17 studies conducted in te USA (N=8), Europe (N=6) or Australia (N=3) between 2000-2013. Most of them focused on primary school (N=12), while some examined adolescents (N=4) or teenagers (N=1).	The results reveal that even though 80% of the studies report improvement in the experimental group, these effects are not preserved long-term. Moreover, results tend to be greatly affected by factors such as the gender, age and socio-economic status of the participants. Internal inconsistency, the application of different methodologies and the lack of standardized measures, remain significant obstacles in the field.

4.1. Target Audience

A significant number of the studies we examine cater towards school-aged children. More specifically, Evangelio et al. (2022) composed a systematic review of 43 articles ranging from 2016-2020, focusing on programs for early prevention specifically designed for middle-school students, emphasizing the importance of timely interventions. Similarly, Esposito et al. (2024) examined 24 interventions applied on children and adolescents up to 18 years old, covering a broad age range. Through their review of 29 articles published between 2017-2022, Tozzo et al. (2022) highlight strategies that involve schools and families, underlining the significance of a collaborative approach. Polanin et al. (2021) reviewed 50 relative studies aiming to assess the effectiveness of K-12 school-based prevention programs, providing insights into broad educational settings. Moreover, the review by Della Cioppa et al. (2015) focused on 12 programs that adopted school-wide approaches aiming at 12–13-year-old students, while Cantone et al. (2015) included 17 studies pointing out the significance of such interventions on students in both primary and secondary education. Finally, the meta-analysis of Kamaruddin et al. (2023) addresses a general range of school-aged children, proposing interventions applicable across various educational stages.

Redirecting our attention to the reviews regarding adolescents and emerging adults, Henares-Montiel et al. (2023) examined 46 studies aiming to address cyberbullying interventions that span from primary school students to college-level individuals. Converging, Doty et al. (2022) extend their focus to 30 studies published between 2010-2019 regarding school-based interventions on students up to 24 years old, encompassing both traditional adolescent and young adult populations. However, Lan and his colleagues (2022) concentrate specifically on adolescents, reviewing 19 studies in order to provide targeted strategies for this critical developmental stage, while Ng et al. (2020) narrow their focus to 17 interventions aimed at adolescents aged 10-18 years, investigating age-appropriate approaches within this narrower age range.

However, several studies have explored various aspects of cyberbullying interventions across the general population or age groups that don't necessarily fit into a certain category. More specifically, Özgür (2020) examined 28 studies from 9 countries reporting on 24 programs/software, targeting individuals between 10-29 years old he highlights the diverse age range affected by cyberbullying, while Siddiqui & Schultze-Krumbholz (2023) focused on 17 successful interventions/programs, including teachers' professional development, preventative measures for adolescents, and school-wide programs aiming to mitigate cyberbullying. Moreover, Wang & Jiang (2023) investigated 11 studies dealing with parent-related programs and their effectiveness in reducing cyberbullying among adolescents, emphasizing the important role of family involvement. Chen et al. (2023) extended their research to 16 studies referring to both school-aged children and college students, showcasing the need for interventions across educational stages. On the other side, Tanrikulu (2018) examined 17 studies regarding prevention and intervention methods, but did not specify a target audience, while Gaffney et al. (2019) discussed 24 publications about general cyberbullying intervention programs, without narrowing their focus to specific age groups. Together, these studies underscore the multifaceted approaches necessary to effectively address the phenomenon of cyberbullying.Τέλος φόρμας

4.2. Core components

Systematic reviews addressing cyberbullying prevention, present programs/interventions that include a wide range of different components. A significant number of interventions adopt a skill training/education component that they implement through various approaches, as it can be seen through the study of Lan et al. (2022) who focused on intrapersonal and interpersonal processes, as well as community-oriented events, providing a broad framework for skill development. Furthermore, Chen et al. (2023) highlighted skill training by targeting bystander and bully–victim dual roles along with coping skills, utilizing interactive serious games and online forums to engage participants. Polanin et al. (2021) reviewed programs that incorporated skill-building and training, often using structured curricula and multimedia materials to enhance learning outcomes, while Kamarudin et al. (2023) found that most studies included educational components, such as curricula and prepared materials, as well as skill-building activities promoting digital citizenship. Together, the abovementioned studies reflect a multifaceted approach to educating individuals on cyberbullying, blending traditional and interactive methods aiming to foster effective skill development.

Furthermore, many programs/interventions include cognitive and affective components, such as the study by Esposito et al. (2024) which emphasized the promotion of both affective and cognitive skills, targeting areas such as emotion regulation, conflict resolution, empathy, knowledge about bullying and cultivation of coping strategies, through interactive games, online activities and video training. Complementarily, Tozzo et al. (2022) integrated cognitive components (e.g. police information) with affective components (e.g. emotional regulation and literacy, empathy, assertiveness) adopting a multidimensional approach. Their approach also incorporated skill training focused on communication, conflict resolution, group cohesion, and fostering values of coexistence and non-violence. On the other hand, Siddiqui & Schultze-Krumbholz (2023) advocated for a comprehensive framework that merges educational efforts

-such as disseminating information and employing educational materials- with affective components, emphasizing the importance of emotional skills, empathy and skill-building elements. By encompassing practical, cognitive, and behavioral skills, all of the above-mentioned studies underline the importance of a multi-faceted approach when it comes to developing essential interpersonal skills.

Redirecting our focus towards studies that encompass a behavioral change aspect, Doty et al. (2022) examined the behavioral changes of students within school settings, while Wang & Jiang (2023) combined cognitive (e.g. awareness, knowledge, competencies), and affective components (e.g. empathy, resilience) with behavioral control aspects, such as self-management. Furthermore, Henares-Montiel et al. (2023) identified that the majority of interventions they reviewed incorporated elements of information dissemination, cognitive development, behavioral change, and skill development. Converging, Della Cioppa et al. (2015) find that most programs combine cognitive components, such as sharing information and promoting awareness, with social elements like relationship development and perspective-taking, and behavioral activities including role-playing and presentations. Cantone et al. (2015) focused on the development of social, cognitive, and emotional skills, as well as pro-social behaviors, by integrating affective elements aimed at promoting empathy and addressing low self-esteem, anxiety, and depression.

However, some systematic reviews do not seem to come to a conclusion regarding common components in the studies they included, such as Tanrikulu (2018) who conducted an examination of existing programs but did not find a clear pattern of common components. Similarly, Ng et al. (2020), Evangelio et al. (2022), and Özgür (2020) did not specify common components in their reviews of interventions regarding the prevention of cyberbullying incidents. Through the examination of these studies, it becomes obvious that there is often a lack of consensus or clear identification of shared elements across various programs, suggesting a diverse range of approaches without a standardized set of features.

4.3. Effectiveness

Numerous recent studies have focused on the phenomenon of cyberbullying, highlighting the effectiveness of various programs and interventions in mitigating both perpetration and victimization. However, as it will be discussed in this subsection, the success of these interventions varies considerably, influenced by a broad array of factors. More specifically, Gaffney et al. (2019) synthesized findings from a significant body of publications, revealing reductions in cyberbullying behaviors through diverse interventions, while Polanin et al. (2021) reported substantial declines in both perpetration and victimization as a result of preventative cyberbullying programs/interventions. Converging, Henares-Montiel et al. (2023) found that interventions were either effective or partially effective in mitigating cyberbullying, while Esposito et al. (2024) concluded that relative interventions that deploy new technologies can turn out to be just as effective in preventing youth violence and cyberbullying. Through their study, Doty et al. (2022) emphasized that school-based interventions, even of brief durations, demonstrated enduring effectiveness over time, something that is also supported by Özgür (2020), who suggested that despite their theoretical and practical differences, interventions were generally effective.

Despite the abovementioned effective programs/interventions, we should not fail to mention that many studies that adopt diverse approaches report varying degrees of effectiveness. A characteristic example of that can be found in the systematic reviews of Siddiqui & Schultze-Krumbholz (2023) and Della Cioppa et al. (2015), which demonstrated positive outcomes, even though studies often lacked an advanced and well-defined theoretical foundation that could support their findings. Moreover, Chen et al. (2023) reported that the studies they examined showed greater effectiveness when cyberbullying programs were delivered by technology-savvy content experts, rather than teachers, while Tanrikulu (2018) observed mixed effectiveness of combined technological and non-technological methods. Attempting to examine if the inclusion of different components could affect an interventions' effectiveness, Lan et al. (2022) identified 19 critical areas contributing to the success of digital health interventions. On the other side, Evangelio et al. (2022) examined the possible significance of participants' age, concluding that programs/interventions can positively influence cyberbullying prevention from a young age, while Tozzo et al. (2022) centered their study around various educational strategies involving school units and families and reported mixed results. Collectively, these findings suggest that while many cyberbullying interventions can be greatly beneficial, their success is influenced by factors such as the chosen delivery method, the adoption of technology, the involvement of different experts, participants' age and the inclusion of certain critical components.

Lastly, we ought to mention that cyberbullying interventions can also exhibit small or non-significant effect sizes, as we can observe by examining the discouraging findings of Ng et al. (2020) that showed small effect sizes for overall cyberaggression and cyber-victimization. Similarly, Wang & Jiang (2023) reported very small effect sizes regarding parent-related programs aimed at reducing cyberbullying perpetration, while Kamaruddin et al. (2023) noted that improvements from pre- to post-intervention were small and not statistically significant. Moreover, Cantone et al. (2015) concluded that although there were improvements, cyberbullying programs/interventions often lacked long-term sustainability, with factors such as participants' age, gender, and socioeconomic status significantly influencing outcomes. Taking all of the above into consideration, it becomes apparent that there is significant variability in the effectiveness of cyberbullying interventions, suggesting that their impact can be influenced by factors such as their overall design, the demographic characteristics of participants and other contextual elements that researchers should pay regard to when creating and applying relative programs/interventions. A checklist for the summarizing of systematic reviews of intervention studies in cyberbullying is provided in Table 1.

5. DISCUSSION

This overview synthesizes findings from a wide range of recent systematic reviews and categorizes them in order to come to conclusions regarding their target audience, core components, and effectiveness. As it is concluded through this procedure, most of the examined interventions target school-aged children emphasizing the importance of early prevention and the implementation of multifaceted collaborative approaches. Although many reviews underline a lack of consensus regarding standard components that are critical for the interventions' success, core components that were common in effective programs include skill training, cognitive and affective strategies and behavioral change methods. Furthermore, effectiveness varies significantly between programs/interventions, influenced by factors such as delivery methods, participant demographics and the inclusion of technology. Overall, while many programs show great promise, the variability in their impact underscores the need for standardized instruments and tailored approaches, as well as further research in order to identify and implement effective elements, ensuring the long-term sustainability of intervention outcomes.

5.1. Suggestions for Future Research

Given the diverse approaches and variable effectiveness of cyberbullying programs/interventions, future research should focus on several key areas to enhance the understanding and efficacy of these programs. Firstly, there is a need for more thorough investigations into the specific components that contribute to successful outcomes, particularly how skill training, cognitive, affective, and behavioral strategies can be optimized and integrated. Comparative studies with representative samples across different geographical locations, age groups and educational stages, would help clarify how interventions can be tailored to the developmental needs of participants, from young children to emerging adults (Ng et al., 2020; Lan et al., 2022; Evangelio et al., 2022; Esposito et al., 2024). Moreover, it would be of interest to conduct studies comparing and contrasting programs/interventions that focus on traditional forms of bullying and cyberbullying respectively (Gaffney et al., 2019; Polanin et al., 2021). Additionally, research should explore the role of technology and digital tools in delivering these programs, identifying best practices for engaging and educating participants in the digital age (Gaffney et al., 2019; Tozzo et al., 2022; Esposito et al., 2024; Doty et al., 2022).

Redirecting our focus to methodological approaches that could be adopted in order to gain insight regarding the multidimensional phenomenon of cyberbullying, systematic reviews employing the PRISMA guidelines along with randomized controlled trials (RCTs), can offer significant advantages. More specifically, PRISMA (Preferred Reporting Items for Systematic Reviews and Meta-Analyses) ensures a transparent and rigorous methodology for identifying, selecting and critically appraising relevant studies (Page et al., 2021; Nee et al., 2023; Zhu et al., 2021). This approach can also minimize bias and enhance the reliability of the final conclusions (Liu et al., 2019; Bo et al., 2021). Meanwhile, RCTs with random sampling can provide robust data on the efficacy of said interventions by reducing confounding variables and enabling generalizable results (Bright et al., 2022; Miller et al., 2020; Gaffney et al., 2019), while they can also help to avoid biases, allowing the identification og causal effects between variables (Doleac et al., 2020). Together, these methods can identify effective strategies and gaps in existing research, guiding future studies to improve the design and implementation of cyberbullying interventions. Their combined application ensures that recommendations for future research adopt reliable and rigorous methodological approaches, promoting the development of more effective and targeted solutions to combat cyberbullying.

We also ought to mention that longitudinal studies, follow-up studies and/or studies implementing maintenance strategies are essential to assess the sustainability of intervention effects over time and to determine how factors like socioeconomic status and family involvement influence long-term outcomes (Chen et al., 2023; Wang & Jiang, 2023; Della Cioppa et al., 2015; Cantone et al., 2015). Finally, developing standardized tools and a detailed theoretical framework for conducting methodologically rigorous studies evaluating the effectiveness of cyberbullying interventions could facilitate more consistent and actionable insights, enabling researchers and practitioners to refine and adapt programs based on robust evidence (Tanrikulu, 2018; Henares-Montiel et al., 2023; Kamaruddin et al., 2023).

5.2. Limitations

Despite its signifant contributions, this study has certain limitations that we ought to mention. Firstly, the overview is limited to 17 studies that were accessed through two main databases, potentially missing some pertinent studies. Another key limitation of this overview can be traced to our choice to incorporate only English-language studies, resulting in the exclusion of relevant research conducted in other languages and perhaps leading to incomplete results.

It is also important to note that there was a reduced number of anti-cyberbullying programs/interventions for children and adolescents in geographical regions such as Asia and Africa, something that could possibly reduce the generalizability of our results. Converging, the wide range of heterogeneity observed in the examined studies (e.g. differences regarding methodological foundations, target populations, means of delivery, duration) can limit the generalizability of the findings. Lastly, we must not fail to point out that there was a significant lack of studies with longitudinal design or follow-ups, something that could lead to an incomplete understanding of long-term trends and outcomes, potentially resulting in biased or inaccurate conclusions.

6. CONCLUSION

The current study synthesized the main results regarding the effectiveness of intervention programs through an overview of all the systematic reviews on cyberbullying published to date. The overview, bringing together a summary of reviews in one place, highlights the effectiveness of cyberbullying intervention programs. These findings can be useful to improve anti-cyberbullying programs, policy and practice. Nevertheless, due to the small number of studies that provided data on long-term programs and sustained accessibility. Further research is also needed to identify key moderators that enhance educational programs or aid in the development of alternative forms of interventions, considering cultural factors during intervention design or shifting school–family patterns to reduce cyberbullying.

REFERENCES

Abaido, G. (2020). Cyberbullying on social media platforms among university students in the United Arab Emirates. *International Journal of Adolescence and Youth*, 25(1), 407–420. DOI: 10.1080/02673843.2019.1669059

Aboujaoude, E., Savage, M., Starcevic, V., & Salame, W. (2015). Cyberbullying: Review of an Old Problem Gone Viral. *The Journal of Adolescent Health*, 57(1), 10–18. DOI: 10.1016/j.jadohealth.2015.04.011 PMID: 26095405

Alismaiel, O. (2023). Digital Media Used in Education: The Influence on Cyberbullying Behaviors among Youth Students. *International Journal of Environmental Research and Public Health*, 20(2), 1370. DOI: 10.3390/ijerph20021370 PMID: 36674128

Alsawalqa, R. O. (2021). Cyberbullying, social stigma, and self-esteem: The impact of COVID-19 on students from East and Southeast Asia at the University of Jordan. *Heliyon*, 7(4), e06711. DOI: 10.1016/j.heliyon.2021.e06711 PMID: 33869877

Ang, R. P. (2015). Adolescent cyberbullying: A review of characteristics, prevention and intervention strategies. *Aggression and Violent Behavior, 25*(A), 35-42. DOI: 10.1016/j.avb.2015.07.011

Arnarsson, Á., Nygren, J., Nyholm, M., Torsheim, T., Augustine, L., Bjereld, Y., Markkanen, I., Schnohr, C., Rasmussen, M., Nielsen, L., & Bendtsen, P. (2020). Cyberbullying and traditional bullying among Nordic adolescents and their impact on life satisfaction. *Scandinavian Journal of Public Health*, 48(5), 502–510. DOI: 10.1177/1403494818817411 PMID: 30672390

Athanasiou, K., Melegkovits, E., Andrie, E., Magoulas, C., Tzavara, C., Richardson, C., Greydanus, D., Tsolia, M., & Tsitsika, A. (2018). Cross-national aspects of cyberbullying victimization among 14–17-year-old adolescents across seven European countries. *BMC Public Health*, 18(1), 800. DOI: 10.1186/s12889-018-5682-4 PMID: 29986687

Barkoukis, V., Lazuras, L., Ourda, D., & Tsorbatzoudis, H. (2016). Tackling psychosocial risk factors for adolescent cyberbullying: Evidence from a school-based intervention. *Aggressive Behavior*, 42(2), 114–122. DOI: 10.1002/ab.21625 PMID: 26350445

Barlett, C. P. (2015). Anonymously hurting others online: The effect of anonymity on cyberbullying frequency. *Psychology of Popular Media Culture*, 4(2), 70–79. DOI: 10.1037/a0034335

Bo, A., Hai, A., Chen, D., & Hammock, K. (2021). Risk of bias assessments in systematic reviews and meta-analyses of behavioral interventions for substance use outcomes. *Journal of Clinical Epidemiology*, 139, 20–27. DOI: 10.1016/j.jclinepi.2021.06.012 PMID: 34166755

Bright, M. A., Sayedul Huq, M., Patel, S., Miller, M. D., & Finkelhor, D. (2022). Child Safety Matters: Randomized Control Trial of a School-Based, Child Victimization Prevention Curriculum. *Journal of Interpersonal Violence*, 37(1-2), 538–556. DOI: 10.1177/0886260520909185 PMID: 32249651

Cagirkan, B., & Bilek, G. (2021). Cyberbullying among Turkish high school students. *Scandinavian Journal of Psychology*, 62(4), 608–616. DOI: 10.1111/sjop.12720 PMID: 33719100

Campbell, M., Spears, B., Slee, P., Butler, D., & Kift, S. (2012). Victims' perceptions of traditional and cyberbullying, and the psychosocial correlates of their victimisation. *Emotional & Behavioural Difficulties*, 17(3-4), 389–401. DOI: 10.1080/13632752.2012.704316

Cantone, E., Piras, A. P., Vellante, M., Preti, A., Daníelsdóttir, S., D'Aloja, E., ... Bhugra, D. (2015). Interventions on bullying and cyberbullying in schools: A systematic review. *Clinical Practice and Epidemiology in Mental Health, 11*(Suppl 1), 58-76. DOI: 10.2174/1745017901511010058

Chalmers, C., Campbell, M. A., Spears, B. A., Butler, D., Cross, D., Slee, P., & Kift, S. (2016). School policies on bullying and cyberbullying: Perspectives across three Australian states. *Educational Research*, 58(1), 91–109. DOI: 10.1080/00131881.2015.1129114

Chen, Q., Chan, K. L., Guo, S., Chen, M., Lo, C. K. M., & Ip, P. (2023). Effectiveness of digital health interventions in reducing bullying and cyberbullying: A meta-analysis. *Trauma, Violence & Abuse*, 24(3), 1986–2002. DOI: 10.1177/15248380221082090 PMID: 35446724

Cioppa, V., O'Neil, A., & Craig, W. (2015). Learning from traditional bullying interventions: A review of research on cyberbullying and best practice. *Aggression and Violent Behavior*, 23, 61–68. DOI: 10.1016/j.avb.2015.05.009

Cross, D., Shaw, T., Hadwen, K., Cardoso, P., Slee, P., Roberts, C., Thomas, L., & Barnes, A. (2016). Longitudinal impact of the Cyber Friendly Schools program on adolescents' cyberbullying behavior. *Aggressive Behavior*, 42(2), 166–180. DOI: 10.1002/ab.21609 PMID: 26351263

Della Cioppa, V., O'Neil, A., & Craig, W. (2015). Learning from traditional bullying interventions: A review of research on cyberbullying and best practice. *Aggression and Violent Behavior*, 23, 61–68. DOI: 10.1016/j.avb.2015.05.009

Dennehy, R., Meaney, S., Walsh, K., Sinnott, C., Cronin, M., & Arensman, E. (2020). Young people's conceptualizations of the nature of cyberbullying: A systematic review and synthesis of qualitative research. *Aggression and Violent Behavior*, 51, 101379. DOI: 10.1016/j.avb.2020.101379

Deol, Y., & Lashai, M. (2022). Impact of Cyberbullying on Adolescent Mental Health in the midst of pandemic – Hidden Crisis. *European Psychiatry : the Journal of the Association of European Psychiatrists*, 65(S1), S432. DOI: 10.1192/j.eurpsy.2022.1096

Doane, A., Kelley, M., & Pearson, M. (2016). Reducing cyberbullying: A theory of reasoned action-based video prevention program for college students. *Aggressive Behavior*, 42(2), 136–146. DOI: 10.1002/ab.21610 PMID: 26349445

Doleac, J., Temple, C., Pritchard, D., & Roberts, A. (2020). Which prisoner reentry programs work? Replicating and extending analyses of three RCTs. *International Review of Law and Economics*, 62, 105902. DOI: 10.1016/j.irle.2020.105902

Doty, J. L., Girón, K., Mehari, K. R., Sharma, D., Smith, S. J., Su, Y. W., Ma, X., Rijo, D., & Rousso, B. (2021). The dosage, context, and modality of interventions to prevent cyberbullying perpetration and victimization: A systematic review. *Prevention Science*, 23(4), 523–537. DOI: 10.1007/s11121-021-01314-8 PMID: 34714506

Englander, E., Donnerstein, E., Kowalski, R., Lin, C., & Parti, K. (2017). Defining Cyberbullying. *Pediatrics*, 140(Supplement_2), 148–151. DOI: 10.1542/peds.2016-1758U PMID: 29093051

Espelage, D., & Hong, J. (2017). Cyberbullying Prevention and Intervention Efforts: Current Knowledge and Future Directions. *Canadian Journal of Psychiatry*, 62(6), 374–380. DOI: 10.1177/0706743716684793 PMID: 28562094

Esposito, C., De Masi, F., Dragone, M., & Bacchini, D. (2024). Technology-Based Interventions for Preventing Youth Violence: A Systematic Review of Programs, Tools, and Evidence. *Adolescent Research Review*, 9(2), 165–192. DOI: 10.1007/s40894-023-00222-y

Evangelio, C., Rodriguez-Gonzalez, P., Fernandez-Rio, J., & Gonzalez-Villora, S. (2022). Cyberbullying in elementary and middle school students: A systematic review. *Computers & Education*, 176, 104356. DOI: 10.1016/j.compedu.2021.104356

Eyuboglu, M., Eyuboglu, D., Pala, S. C., Oktar, D., Demirtas, Z., Arslantas, D., & Unsal, A. (2021). Traditional school bullying and cyberbullying: Prevalence, the effect on mental health problems and self-harm behavior. *Psychiatry Research*, 297, 113730. DOI: 10.1016/j.psychres.2021.113730 PMID: 33486274

Farrington, D. P., Zych, I., Ttofi, M. M., & Gaffney, H. (2023). Cyberbullying research in Canada: A systematic review of the first 100 empirical studies. *Aggression and Violent Behavior*, 69(2), 101811. DOI: 10.1016/j.avb.2022.101811

Foody, M., Samara, M., & Carlbring, P. (2015). A review of cyberbullying and suggestions for online psychological therapy. *Internet Interventions : the Application of Information Technology in Mental and Behavioural Health*, 2(3), 235–242. DOI: 10.1016/j.invent.2015.05.002

Foody, M., Samara, M., El Asam, A., Morsi, H., & Khattab, A. A. (2017). Review of cyberbullying legislation in Qatar: Considerations for policy makers and educators. *International Journal of Law and Psychiatry*, 50, 45–51. DOI: 10.1016/j.ijlp.2016.10.013 PMID: 27837914

Gaffney, H., Farrington, D. P., Espelage, D. L., & Ttofi, M. M. (2019). Are cyberbullying intervention and prevention programs effective? A systematic and meta-analytical review. *Aggression and Violent Behavior*, 45, 134–153. DOI: 10.1016/j.avb.2018.07.002

Gohal, G., Alqassim, A., Eltyeb, E., Rayyani, A., Hakami, B., Al Faqih, A., Hakami, A., Qadri, A., & Mahfouz, M. (2023). Prevalence and related risks of cyberbullying and its effects on adolescent. *BMC Psychiatry*, 23(1), 39. DOI: 10.1186/s12888-023-04542-0 PMID: 36641459

Hamm, M., Newton, A., Chisholm, A., Shulhan, J., Milne, A., Sundar, P., Ennis, H., Scott, S., & Hartling, L. (2015). Prevalence and Effect of Cyberbullying on Children and Young People: A Scoping Review of Social Media Studies. *JAMA Pediatrics*, 169(8), 770–777. DOI: 10.1001/jamapediatrics.2015.0944 PMID: 26098362

Hatzenbuehler, M., Schwab-Reese, L., Ranapurwala, S., Hertz, M., & Ramirez, M. (2015). Associations Between Antibullying Policies and Bullying in 25 States. *JAMA Pediatrics*, 169(10), e152411. DOI: 10.1001/jamapediatrics.2015.2411 PMID: 26437015

Henares-Montiel, J., Pastor-Moreno, G., Ramírez-Saiz, A., Rodríguez-Gómez, M., & Ruiz-Pérez, I. (2023). Characteristics and effectiveness of interventions to reduce cyberbullying: A systematic review. *Frontiers in Public Health*, 11, 1219727. DOI: 10.3389/fpubh.2023.1219727 PMID: 37711240

Henares-Montiel, J., Pastor-Moreno, G., Ramírez-Saiz, A., Rodríguez-Gómez, M., & Ruiz-Pérez, I. (2023). Characteristics and effectiveness of interventions to reduce cyberbullying: A systematic review. *Frontiers in Public Health*, 11, 1219727. DOI: 10.3389/fpubh.2023.1219727 PMID: 37711240

Ho, T. T. Q., & Gu, C. (2021). Cyberbullying victimization and depression: Self-esteem as a mediator and approach coping strategies as moderators. *Journal of American College Health*, 71(1), 94–101. DOI: 10.1080/07448481.2021.1877718 PMID: 33650940

Hu, Y., Bai, Y., Pan, Y., & Li, S. (2021). Cyberbullying victimization and depression among adolescents: A meta-analysis. *Psychiatry Research*, 305, 114198. DOI: 10.1016/j.psychres.2021.114198 PMID: 34537540

Huang, J., Zhong, Z., Zhang, H., & Li, L. (2021). Cyberbullying in Social Media and Online Games among Chinese College Students and Its Associated Factors. *International Journal of Environmental Research and Public Health*, 18(9), 4819. DOI: 10.3390/ijerph18094819 PMID: 33946441

Hutson, E., Kelly, S., & Militello, L. (2017). Systematic Review of Cyberbullying Interventions for Youth and Parents With Implications for Evidence-Based Practice. *Worldviews on Evidence-Based Nursing*, 15(1), 72–79. DOI: 10.1111/wvn.12257 PMID: 28859246

Jin, X., Zhang, K., Twayigira, M., Gao, X., Xu, H., Huang, C., Luo, X., & Shen, Y. (2023). Cyberbullying among college students in a Chinese population: Prevalence and associated clinical correlates. *Frontiers in Public Health*, 11, 110006. DOI: 10.3389/fpubh.2023.1100069 PMID: 36908470

Kamaruddin, I. K., Ma'rof, A. M., Mohd Nazan, A. I., & Ab Jalil, H. (2023). A systematic review and meta-analysis of interventions to decrease cyberbullying perpetration and victimization: An in-depth analysis within the Asia Pacific region. *Frontiers in Psychiatry*, 14, 1014258. DOI: 10.3389/fpsyt.2023.1014258 PMID: 36778634

Kazerooni, F., Taylor, S., Bazarova, N., & Whitlock, J. (2018). Cyberbullying Bystander Intervention: The Number of Offenders and Retweeting Predict Likelihood of Helping a Cyberbullying Victim. *Journal of Computer-Mediated Communication*, 23(3), 146–162. DOI: 10.1093/jcmc/zmy005

Kee, D. M. H., Al-Anesi, M. A. L., & Al-Anesi, S. A. L. (2022). Cyberbullying on social media under the influence of COVID-19. *Global Business and Organizational Excellence*, 41(6), 11–22. DOI: 10.1002/joe.22175

Kowalski, R., Giumetti, G., Schroeder, A., & Lattanner, M. (2014). Bullying in the digital age: A critical review and meta-analysis of cyberbullying research among youth. *Psychological Bulletin*, 140(4), 1073–1137. DOI: 10.1037/a0035618 PMID: 24512111

Lan, M., Law, N., & Pan, Q. (2022). Effectiveness of anti-cyberbullying educational programs: A socio-ecologically grounded systematic review and meta-analysis. *Computers in Human Behavior*, 130, 107200. DOI: 10.1016/j.chb.2022.107200

Lancaster, M. (2018). A Systematic Research Synthesis on Cyberbullying Interventions in the United States. *Cyberpsychology, Behavior, and Social Networking*, 21(10), 593–602. DOI: 10.1089/cyber.2018.0307 PMID: 30334647

Langos, C. (2012). Cyberbullying: The Challenge to Define. *Cyberpsychology, Behavior, and Social Networking*, 15(6), 285–289. DOI: 10.1089/cyber.2011.0588 PMID: 22703033

Leung, A., Wong, N., & Farver, J. (2019). Testing the Effectiveness of an E-Course to Combat Cyberbullying. *Cyberpsychology, Behavior, and Social Networking*, 22(9), 569–577. DOI: 10.1089/cyber.2018.0609 PMID: 31526296

Liu, H., Zhou, X., Yu, G., & Sun, X. (2019). The effects of the PRISMA statement to improve the conduct and reporting of systematic reviews and meta-analyses of nursing interventions for patients with heart failure. *International Journal of Nursing Practice*, 25(3), e12729. DOI: 10.1111/ijn.12729 PMID: 30790391

MacKenzie, D. L., & Farrington, D. P. (2015). Preventing future offending of delinquents and offenders: What have we learned from experiments and meta-analyses? *Journal of Experimental Criminology*, 11(4), 565–595. DOI: 10.1007/s11292-015-9244-9

Marées, N., & Petermann, F. (2012). Cyberbullying: An increasing challenge for schools. *School Psychology International*, 33(5), 467–476. DOI: 10.1177/0143034312445241

Maurya, C., Muhammad, T., Dhillon, P., & Maurya, P. (2022). The effects of cyberbullying victimization on depression and suicidal ideation among adolescents and young adults: A three-year cohort study from India. *BMC Psychiatry*, 22(1), 599. DOI: 10.1186/s12888-022-04238-x PMID: 36085004

Miller, C., Smith, S., & Pugatch, M. (2020). Experimental and quasi-experimental designs in implementation research. *Psychiatry Research*, 283, 112452. DOI: 10.1016/j.psychres.2019.06.027 PMID: 31255320

Nee, C., Samsudin, N., Chuan, H., Ridzuan, M., Boon, O., Mohamad, A., & Scheithauer, H. (2023). The digital defence against cyberbullying: A systematic review of tech-based approaches. *Cogent Education*, 10(2), 2288492. DOI: 10.1080/2331186X.2023.2288492

Ng, E. D., Chua, J. Y. X., & Shorey, S. (2022). The effectiveness of educational interventions on traditional bullying and cyberbullying among adolescents: A systematic review and meta-analysis. *Trauma, Violence & Abuse*, 23(1), 132–151. DOI: 10.1177/1524838020933867 PMID: 32588769

Nocentini, A., Calmaestra, J., Schultze-Krumbholz, A., Scheithauer, H., Ortega, R., & Menesini, E. (2010). Cyberbullying: Labels, Behaviours and Definition in Three European Countries. *Australian Journal of Guidance & Counselling*, 20(2), 129–142. DOI: 10.1375/ajgc.20.2.129

Özgür, H. (2020). A Systematic Review on Cyberbullying Interventions and Preventions. *Shanlax International Journal of Education*, 9(1), 11–26. DOI: 10.34293/education.v9i1.3373

Page, M. J., McKenzie, J. E., Bossuyt, P. M., Boutron, I., Hoffmann, T. C., Mulrow, C. D., Shamseer, L., Tetzlaff, J. M., Akl, E. A., Brennan, S. E., Chou, R., Glanville, J., Grimshaw, J. M., Hróbjartsson, A., Lalu, M. M., Li, T., Loder, E. W., Mayo-Wilson, E., McDonald, S., & Moher, D. (2021). The PRISMA 2020 statement: An updated guideline for reporting systematic reviews. *International Journal of Surgery*, 88, 105906. DOI: 10.1016/j.ijsu.2021.105906 PMID: 33789826

Patchin, J. W., & Hinduja, S. (2023). Cyberbullying Among Asian American Youth Before and During the COVID-19 Pandemic. *The Journal of School Health*, 93(1), 82–87. DOI: 10.1111/josh.13249 PMID: 36221854

Pearce, N., Cross, D., Monks, H., Waters, S., & Falconer, S. (2011). Current evidence of best practice in whole-school bullying intervention and its potential to inform cyberbullying interventions. *Australian Journal of Guidance & Counselling*, 21(1), 1–21. DOI: 10.1375/ajgc.21.1.1

Pieschl, S., Kuhlmann, C., & Porsch, T. (2015). Beware of Publicity! Perceived Distress of Negative Cyber Incidents and Implications for Defining Cyberbullying. *Journal of School Violence*, 14(1), 111–132. DOI: 10.1080/15388220.2014.971363

Polanin, J. R., Espelage, D. L., Grotpeter, J. K., Ingram, K., Michaelson, L., Spinney, E., & Robinson, L. (2021). A systematic review and meta-analysis of interventions to decrease cyberbullying perpetration and victimization. *Prevention Science*, 23(3), 439–454. DOI: 10.1007/s11121-021-01259-y PMID: 34159506

Runions, K., & Bak, M. (2015). Online Moral Disengagement, Cyberbullying, and Cyber-Aggression. *Cyberpsychology, Behavior, and Social Networking*, 18(7), 400–405. DOI: 10.1089/cyber.2014.0670 PMID: 26167839

Saleem, S., Khan, N., & Zafar, S. (2021). Prevalence of cyberbullying victimization among Pakistani Youth. *Technology in Society*, 65, 101577. DOI: 10.1016/j.techsoc.2021.101577

Salmon, S., Turner, S., Taillieu, T., Fortier, J., & Afifi, T. O. (2018). Bullying victimization experiences among middle and high school adolescents: Traditional bullying, discriminatory harassment, and cybervictimization. *Journal of Adolescence*, 63(1), 29–40. DOI: 10.1016/j.adolescence.2017.12.005 PMID: 29268108

Selkie, E. M., Fales, J. L., & Moreno, M. A. (2016). Cyberbullying Prevalence Among US Middle and High School-Aged Adolescents: A Systematic Review and Quality Assessment. *The Journal of Adolescent Health*, 58(2), 125–133. DOI: 10.1016/j.jadohealth.2015.09.026 PMID: 26576821

Siddiqui, S., & Schultze-Krumbholz, A. (2023). Successful and emerging cyberbullying prevention programs: A narrative review of seventeen interventions applied worldwide. *Societies (Basel, Switzerland)*, 13(9), 212. DOI: 10.3390/soc13090212

Slonje, R., & Smith, P. (2008). Cyberbullying: Another main type of bullying? *Scandinavian Journal of Psychology*, 49(2), 147–154. DOI: 10.1111/j.1467-9450.2007.00611.x PMID: 18352984

Smith, P. K., Mahdavi, J., Carvalho, M., Fisher, S., Russell, S., & Tippett, N. (2008). Cyberbullying: Its nature and impact in secondary school pupils. *Journal of Child Psychology and Psychiatry, and Allied Disciplines*, 49(4), 376–385. DOI: 10.1111/j.1469-7610.2007.01846.x PMID: 18363945

Sticca, F., & Perren, S. (2012). Is Cyberbullying Worse than Traditional Bullying? Examining the Differential Roles of Medium, Publicity, and Anonymity for the Perceived Severity of Bullying. *Journal of Youth and Adolescence*, 42(5), 739–750. DOI: 10.1007/s10964-012-9867-3 PMID: 23184483

Tanrikulu, I. (2018). Cyberbullying prevention and intervention programs in schools: A systematic review. *School Psychology International*, 39(1), 74–91. DOI: 10.1177/0143034317745721

Tokunaga, R. S. (2010). Following you home from school: A critical review and synthesis of research on cyberbullying victimization. *Computers in Human Behavior*, 26(3), 277–287. DOI: 10.1016/j.chb.2009.11.014

Touloupis, T., & Athanasiades, C. (2022). Evaluation of a cyberbullying prevention program in elementary schools: The role of self-esteem enhancement. *Frontiers in Psychology*, 13, 980091. DOI: 10.3389/fpsyg.2022.980091 PMID: 36211905

Tozzo, P., Cuman, O., Moratto, E., & Caenazzo, L. (2022). Family and educational strategies for cyberbullying prevention: A systematic review. *International Journal of Environmental Research and Public Health*, 19(16), 10452. DOI: 10.3390/ijerph191610452 PMID: 36012084

Tsitsika, A., Janikian, M., Wójcik, S., Makaruk, K., Tzavela, E., Tzavara, C., Greydanus, D., Merrick, J., & Richardson, C. (2015). Cyberbullying victimization prevalence and associations with internalizing and externalizing problems among adolescents in six European countries. *Computers in Human Behavior*, 51, 1–7. DOI: 10.1016/j.chb.2015.04.048

Waasdorp, T., & Bradshaw, C. (2015). The overlap between cyberbullying and traditional bullying. *The Journal of Adolescent Health*, 56(5), 483–488. DOI: 10.1016/j.jadohealth.2014.12.002 PMID: 25631040

Wang, L., & Jiang, S. (2023). Effectiveness of parent-related interventions on cyberbullying among adolescents: A systematic review and meta-analysis. *Trauma, Violence & Abuse*, 24(5), 3678–3696. DOI: 10.1177/15248380221137065 PMID: 36458864

Wang, L., & Ngai, S. S.-y. (2020). The effects of anonymity, invisibility, asynchrony, and moral disengagement on cyberbullying perpetration among school-aged children in China. *Children and Youth Services Review*, 119, 105613. DOI: 10.1016/j.childyouth.2020.105613

Williams, K. R., & Guerra, N. G. (2007). Prevalence and Predictors of Internet Bullying. *The Journal of Adolescent Health*, 41(6), S14–S21. DOI: 10.1016/j.jadohealth.2007.08.018 PMID: 18047941

Wölfer, R., Schultze-Krumbholz, A., Zagorscak, P., Jäkel, A., Göbel, K., & Scheithauer, H. (2014). Prevention 2.0: Targeting Cyberbullying @ School. *Prevention Science*, 15(6), 879–887. DOI: 10.1007/s11121-013-0438-y PMID: 24122481

Wright, M., & Wachs, S. (2023). Cyberbullying Involvement and Depression among Elementary School, Middle School, High School, and University Students: The Role of Social Support and Gender. *International Journal of Environmental Research and Public Health*, 20(4), 2835. DOI: 10.3390/ijerph20042835 PMID: 36833529

Zhao, L., & Yu, J. (2021). A Meta-Analytic Review of Moral Disengagement and Cyberbullying. *Frontiers in Psychology*, 12, 681299. DOI: 10.3389/fpsyg.2021.681299 PMID: 34916984

Zhu, C., Huang, S., Evans, R., & Zhang, W. (2021). Cyberbullying Among Adolescents and Children: A Comprehensive Review of the Global Situation, Risk Factors, and Preventive Measures. *Frontiers in Public Health*, 9, 634909. DOI: 10.3389/fpubh.2021.634909 PMID: 33791270

Zych, I., Ortega-Ruiz, R., & Rey, R. (2015). Systematic review of theoretical studies on bullying and cyberbullying: Facts, knowledge, prevention, and intervention. *Aggression and Violent Behavior*, 23, 1–21. DOI: 10.1016/j.avb.2015.10.001

Chapter 14
Alice and the Risky Wonderland:
Pedagogical Agents in Dual Roles

Aristea Mavrogianni
https://orcid.org/0000-0002-5926-0363
University of Crete, Greece

Eleni Vasilaki
https://orcid.org/0009-0000-9152-5862
University of Crete, Greece

ABSTRACT

The authors designed pedagogical agents with dual roles to be integrated into the Geo-Histor learning environment: preventing risky behavior and promoting reading strategies aimed at improving adolescent students' metacognitive awareness. In order to reduce risky behaviors, they have incorporated the use of pedagogical agents that are deemed to be appropriate for the learning environment. To inform their design, they considered the latest research on agent anthropomorphism and voices. The preferences of 53 10th graders who participated in the preliminary study were considered in the initial design phase. During the main research project, comparisons were made between the experimental group using the interactive learning environment and the control group. The use of pedagogical agents during the interactive intervention resulted in the students' focus on the academic material and not on useless internet wandering. There was an increase in comprehensive knowledge of history, distance from parroting, deeper understanding, and consolidation of the material, followed by an increase in performance.

1. THEORETICAL SECTION

1.1. Internet Misuse and Psychological Consequences

The increasing number of internet users has correspondingly led to a rise in concerns regarding the possible adverse consequences of excessive internet usage, and the inquiry into whether such usage can genuinely be classified as an addiction. The availability of internet access to people of all socioeconomic

DOI: 10.4018/979-8-3693-4191-9.ch014

levels has given rise to a relatively recent and concerning phenomenon known as "internet addiction," mostly impacting adolescents and young adults.

The available research data, generated since 1990, is clear and unambiguous in its description of internet addiction as an impulse-control disorder, similar to other pathological disorders (Young, 1999). Studies have established a correlation between internet usage and various psychological symptoms such as social isolation, stress, and depression (Akin & Iskender, 2011; Kandasamy et al., 2019; Kawabe et al., 2016; Murali & George, 2007). Furthermore, persons who excessively use the internet often display elevated levels of anxious mood, fear, and tension, together with insomnia, low self-esteem, and anxiety disorders (Bahrainian et al., 2014; Goel et al., 2013; Saikia et al., 2019; Younes et al., 2016). They also experience reduced life satisfaction, sensation seeking, poor mental health, and impaired family functioning (Armstrong et al., 2000; Kraut, 1998).

Several studies have investigated the connections between problematic internet use and the conception of paranoid ideas, as well as the emergence of hostility among students (Alavi et al, 2010; Xiuqin et al., 2010). A study carried out by Odacı and Kalkan (2010) demonstrates a direct relationship between Internet addiction and feelings of isolation, challenges in communication, anxiety related to social interactions, and physical symptoms. Furthermore, Singh et al. (2020) and Jaiswal et al. (2020) have shown that internet addiction significantly impacts the ability to predict social anxiety, social support, and loneliness in college students.

Research conducted by Ranjan et al. (2021) documented that students demonstrated a tendency to use the internet as a strategy to reduce stress, anxiety, and depression. The aforementioned phenomenon was noted in correlation with a proclivity for excessive internet usage, potentially influenced by various emotional conditions such as low mood, insomnia, fear, guilt, hopelessness, tension, anxious mood, and mental decline. Their research uncovered a notable positive association between internet addiction and symptoms of total anxiety and somatic anxiety among undergraduate students.

1.2. Risky Behavior in Adolescence

As internet use becomes more prevalent among younger demographics, so too does the incidence of risky online behavior. It should be noted, however, that adolescents may not perceive the aforementioned behaviors as risky. Paluckaitė et al. (2017) demonstrated that students perceive a variety of online behaviors to be risky. There are three factors that influence the way in which students perceive risk online: gender, age and engagement with online risk-taking behaviors. Girls, younger adolescents and those who engage less with risky online behaviors perceive behaviors as riskier than boys, older adolescents and those who engage more frequently. Consequently, older male students and students who engage in risky online behaviors are less likely to recognize and perceive behaviors on the Internet as such when compared to other demographic groups.

As asserted by Notten and Nikken (2014), adolescence represents a period characterized by identity experimentation, which can be attributed to a number of factors, including heightened sensation seeking, a lack of self-regulation and a proclivity for risk-taking behaviors (Reyna et al., 2015). Therefore, these developmental aspects may be associated with adolescents' inclination to engage in risky online activities (Livingstone & Smith, 2014; Valkenburg & Peter, 2011).

Cognitive development is an important consideration in adolescents' proclivity towards engagement in risky behaviors (Noll et al., 2013). This is due to the fact that adolescents' interpretations of behavioral options diverge from those of adults (Reyna et al., 2015). According to the theory of active risk-reward systems (Reyna et al., 2015; Steinberg & Chein, 2015), which supplements the adolescent need to make risky decisions to receive reward, adolescents may be likely to take part in risky activities (Mitchell et al., 2008).

The decision to engage in risky behavior or not is primarily contingent on adolescents' capacity to accurately assess the potential risks involved (Mitchell et al., 2008). It is posited that during middle adolescence, adolescents are more prone to seek sensation due to deficiencies in self-regulation skills. This trajectory is referred to as the dual system model (Steinberg et al., 2008). In line with this model, one might posit that adolescents' risk-taking behavior is predominantly linked to, and contingent upon, their cognitive functioning and reward sensitivity systems (Duell et al., 2016; Shulman et al., 2016), including in online environments.

Furthermore, the role of peers in influencing adolescent risky online behavior merits consideration. As adolescents begin to doubt the authority of adults and are inclined to align themselves with the opinions of their peers in order to belong to their social group or to gain attention. As posited by Baumgartner, Valkenburg and Peter (2010), adolescents may be more likely to engage in risky sexual online behaviors if they perceive their peers to be engaging in such activities.

Additionally, it is evident from existing research that there are age and gender-related differences in adolescents' engagement with online risky behaviors. The majority of researchers concur that older male adolescents are more inclined to engage in risky behaviors online (Baumgartner et al., 2010; Notten et al., 2016). As evidenced by research conducted by Livingstone, Kalmus and Talves (2013), males are more likely to engage in online gaming and visit pornographic websites, whereas females are more inclined to utilize social networking platforms.

Bullying represents one of the most prevalent and severe forms of problematic conduct observed among pupils with prevalent manifestations ridicule and name-calling. Furthermore, it is notable that there has been an observable increase in the prevalence of cyberbullying directed at educators via the internet. This phenomenon encompasses a range of behaviors, such as posting disparaging remarks or images in online discussion groups or sharing sensitive information on social media (Chrienová et al., 2019).

Technology may be used to develop effective pedagogical agents that can serve as a peer group, influencing adolescents to avoid the negative and dangerous consequences of modern technology, thereby mitigating risky behaviors. Here, we outline our endeavor to develop four Pedagogical Agents for use in Interactive Learning Environments to enhance learning and deter risky behavior.

1.3. Pedagogical Agents as an Essential Element of Interactive Learning Environments

Interactive learning environments (ILE) are contemporary digital tools that facilitate novel approaches to learning and teaching through the senses of sight, hearing and touch (Clark & Mayer, 2016; Woo, 2009). They aim to optimize the advantages of information and communication technologies while minimising the risks associated with the Internet. These computer-based, multi-sensory, learner-centred tools have become common practice in teaching a variety of learning subjects in both secondary and higher education (Blevins, 2018; Huang et al., 2019; Ilhan & Oruc, 2016; Kapi et al., 2017). These technologies have attracted significant research interest internationally (Lubis, 2019; Norbekova et al., 2019; Xefteris et al., 2018; Xia, 2020) due to their ability to provide users with a comprehensive and enjoyable learning experience. In particular, Geographic Information Systems (GIS) technologies offer particular potential for the creation of ILE for teaching and learning History (Antoniou et al., 2018; Groshans et al., 2019).

The primary criticism of computers as educational tools is that they lack a social learning environment, which results in a "cold" and "detached" character (Dinçer & Doğanay, 2017: p. 74). This has led to the design and use of Animated Pedagogical Agents (APA), which enable the computer's otherwise impersonal environment to resemble an actual classroom (Mayer & DaPra, 2012). APA can motivate students more than any other learning environment to try and comprehend the learning material (Choi & Clark, 2006), such as to prevent students' online risk behaviors and Problematic Use of the Internet (PUI). The "Wonderland of the Internet," despite its apparent advantages, in reality, disguise a dimension of PUI, which refers to the inability to maintain the useful parts of the Internet's use, avoiding the possibility of resulting in emotional, psychological, and social difficulties (Fernandes et al., 2019). Empirical studies have demonstrated a correlation between PUI and various adverse outcomes, including loneliness, depressive mood, diminished well-being, and reduced academic performance (Olenik Shemesh et al., 2023).

The function of the Animated Pedagogical Agent (APA) is of particular interest in the design and development of these environments (Liew et al., 2017; Lowe & Schnotz, 2014). The APA is used as a tool to assist students in interacting with the environment, supporting them in the learning process and preventing risky behaviors. These agents are suitable for open and distance learning courses, stimulating the learning efforts of anyone not physically present in a classroom. They can equally support the learning process through multimedia learning environments for secondary school as well as university students. They make up for the lack of social learning environment and remove a sense of loneliness on the part of the student, which is considered a disadvantage of these environments (Dinçer & Doğanay, 2017). The utilisation of Animated Pedagogical Agents (APA) has the potential to: a) create an environment that resembles an actual classroom, thus overcoming the limitations of a computer-based learning environment (Mayer & DaPra, 2012); b) encourage students to engage with the learning material in a more active manner than is possible in any other learning environment (Choi & Clark, 2013); c) motivate students to actively participate in the learning process (Liew et al., 2017), thereby reducing the likelihood of risky behaviors associated with the use of the Internet (García, et al., 2020; Lin et al., 2013).

The efficacy of pedagogical agents has not been demonstrably superior to other forms of instruction, prompting further investigation. The research findings indicate that pedagogical agents are more effective and efficient when they exhibit anthropomorphic characteristics with an emphasis on the real-life human voice. The anthropomorphic personas of digital agents have been demonstrated to facilitate learning and increase students' motivation (Schroeder et al., 2017; Woo, 2009). The research evidence indicates that pedagogical agents should be designed based on the actual teaching strategies, interact with the learner, and provide feedback through various forms of expression (Dinçer & Doğanay, 2017).

It is possible that pedagogical agents could function effectively in learning environments by providing the necessary assistance to the learner and strengthening the learning process. Indeed, they are frequently employed in learning environments as "scaffolds" (Zheng, 2016), offering a range of forms of assistance to the learner, including strategies, metacognitive commentary, motives or guides (Bendou et al., 2017; Simons & Klein, 2007; ter Beek et al., 2018; 2019), which have the potential to facilitate advanced thinking and more effective learning. In order to support students in acquiring higher levels of understanding (Bendou et al., 2017), the role model (whether it is a human teacher or a digital pedagogical agent) may work by providing one of the "scaffold" types (Zheng, 2016). Hannafin, Land and Oliver (1999) classified four "scaffold" types: metacognitive; procedural; strategic; and conceptual. In the case of fading scaffolding, students gradually assimilate to their model through observation and imitation, thus

self-identifying and self-regulating. This process results in a gradual decrease in the need for guidance, which is then gradually diminished. Consequently, in the design and structuring of a pedagogical agent in an ILE, fading guidance is implemented as a mechanism for guiding students. In this context, fading guidance may be associated with the adoption of effective study practices, including the utilisation of learning strategies and the avoidance of risky online behaviors (Lin et al., 2013).

The pedagogical agent is a human-like entity that embodies certain characteristics associated with humans. Consequently, the pedagogical agent's type determines the specific behaviors that are externalized through extra-linguistic and paralinguistic elements, such as ways of expression, hand movements, and facial expressions (Dinçer & Doğanay, 2017). Consequently, the pedagogical agent interacts with the learners and provides them with the necessary feedback to enhance their learning actions. It is thus possible to design an agent based on the strategies of actual teaching and learning in order to effectively assist students in focusing on study objectives and avoiding the distractions of the Internet. In a manner analogous to Odysseus's avoidance of the alluring song of the Sirens, which could have led to the destruction of himself and his crew, the modern users of the Internet can similarly avoid the negative aspects of the Internet that could have disastrous consequences by limiting their own actions and making appropriate choices, which the pedagogical agent encourages them to make.

To avoid increased cognitive effort (Wang et al., 2020) and to achieve optimal learning conditions, elements from both dual coding theory (Clark & Paivio, 1991; Paivio, 1991) and cognitive load theory (Sweller, 2011) are used in the design and development of agents, as they are used in the context of multimedia learning theory (Mayer, 2014). Furthermore, the personalisation principle is the primary guiding principle in the design of digital learning environments (Mayer & Moreno, 2002). This principle ensures that information is presented in a friendly and intimate manner, rather than in a formal and distant way (Mayer, 2014).

It is clear that presenting the agent in human form is the best way to create better learning conditions. This is because the student feels that they are in an interpersonal conversation, which activates the cognitive processes of selection, organisation and integration to a greater extent (Dinçer & Doğanay, 2017; Mayer & DaPra). Recent research findings (Schroeder et al., 2017) confirm that anthropomorphism makes agents more likeable to students and more effective in learning. The agents' form is defined or selected by the student users from an initial list. The appropriate voice synchronisation software with facial movements is then entered into the system (Dinçer & Doğanay, 2017). This creates the impression that the agents are realistically narrating the text. Finally, a video file is created containing both the recording and the necessary graphics for the agent in a setting that enhances anthropomorphism, such as the Instagram social media environment.

The dynamic of agents in ILE is related to their ability to provide the necessary user-supportive context of fading guidance for the use of learning strategies. This guidance can lead to the internalisation, automation and autonomous application of strategies by their users to transform them into skills (Daradoumis & Arguedas, 2020; Lin et al., 2020). A crucial aspect of the term "strategies" is that it refers to the internal cognitive processes involved in managing, monitoring, and directing attention and control (Moore, 2014). These processes function as a set of systematic actions to complete a cognitive task. In particular, metacognitive strategies relate to the monitoring and control of the learning process and contribute to the individual's ability to gradually reorient themselves in relation to goals and criteria of a learning task (Mitsea & Drigas, 2019). Consequently, metacognitive strategies are associated with the individual's motivation to monitor learning conditions, coordinate and correct potential omissions and errors, as well as evaluate the cognitive outcome (Kostaridou-Euklidi, 2011).

Empirical studies have demonstrated that metacognitive strategies play a pivotal role in facilitating learning, as students effectively approach the texts they study through the design, implementation and evaluation of strategies at various stages, including the pre-, during- and post-reading phases (Koulianou et al., 2020; Mastrothanasis et al., 2018; Mastrothanasis, 2019; Mokhtari et al., 2018). It has been demonstrated that these strategies are linked to specific demands and serve specific goals, and that they positively correlate with reading comprehension (Muhid et al., 2020). In essence, these strategies are purposeful and demanding actions, which can be flexibly manipulated to improve learning outcomes and performance (Becker et al., 2021; Brevik, 2019). Indeed, it has been demonstrated that they can enhance reading comprehension in students with and without learning difficulties (Koulianou et al., 2019).

1.4. Designing Agents for the Interactive Learning Environment Geo-Histor

The interactive learning environment of this research project was constructed on the Story Map Journal platform of ArcGIS. It leverages Geographic Information Systems technology by further enriching the digital text with multimedia and agent integration to improve multimedia learning (Mavrogianni, 2023; Mavrogianni et al, 2023), as well as prevent and diminish risky behavior. The learning environment was named Geo-Histor because it refers to the relation between Geography and History. The structure of the environment was based on two main functions of the educational process: teaching/learning and assessment of the student. The embedded agents within the learning environment facilitate the training of students in the use of learning strategies, the avoidance of risky behaviors and the learning of History in an interactive manner. Subsequent to this, the student's performance is assessed digitally through the completion of reliable performance evaluation tools.

In the educational tool Geo-Histor, scaffolding is provided through narrative agents who share ideas about the use of reading strategies and risky behaviors prevention. This makes it a metacognitive "scaffold." The objective was to design pedagogical agents to be part of the Geo-Histor multimedia learning environment, with the goal of enhancing students' use of reading strategies and their overall metacognitive development in order to improve performance. In designing the agents, we considered the latest research findings on their anthropomorphism (Martha & Santoso, 2019) and voices (Craig & Schroeder, 2017), as well as the preferences of all 53 10th-graders who participated in the preliminary project for the construction of the agents. Digital assistants are perceived as members of society similar to humans. Consequently, they are more efficacious in motivating students in ILE, where social interaction is necessary (Mayer & DaPra, 2012). Therefore, we elected to simulate digital communication conditions that are familiar to teenagers by creating a version of Instagram as the environment where the agents converse.

According to cognitive load theory, pedagogical agents accompanied by graphics and texts require more visual and cognitive resources (Choi & Clark, 2006; Moreno et al., 2001; Moreno, 2010; Paas & Sweller, 2011; 2014). Consequently, we elected to exclude the agents' verbal utterances from the on-screen text. In contrast, our agents serve as narrative agents engaged in discourse with one another in a manner analogous to that of a group of peers. This approach was selected in order to provide procedural facilitation regarding how students can act before, during, and after reading the digital expository text. However, we ensured that students' questions could be addressed by documenting relevant queries based on elements from actual teaching conditions from the previously referenced one-year course. The dialogues between the agents were designed in such a way that the questions posed by the students were answered.

The objective of the videos is to encourage students to utilize more reading strategies and to refrain from Internet surfing that could potentially lead to risky behavior. This approach is common in innovative educational multimedia, where technology is used to address specific learning needs (Christensen et al., 2008) and to avoid Internet traps (García, et al., 2020). A number of researchers have employed videos as fading guidance tools for learners in a variety of ways (Guo et al., 2014; Pan et al., 2012; Rismark & Sølvberg, 2019). The primary objective of the agent design for the Geo-Histor environment (Mavrogianni, 2023) was to provide fading guidance to address the pedagogical need for students to adopt more learning strategies and avoid risky online behaviors.

The ability to select the desired agent has been demonstrated to enhance user satisfaction and motivation (Kim & Baylor, 2016). In this context, the students themselves selected the 3D anthropomorphic animations (Johnson, et al., 2013). The potential of agents in supporting learning is related to the resemblance of the impersonal digital environment with a real classroom learning environment (Mayer & DaPra, 2012). Agents can motivate, activate, and encourage students to understand and consolidate learning material, thereby preventing risky behaviors (García, et al., 2020). The objective of the study was to create a pedagogical agent, Alice, for risky behavior prevention, as a member of an agent's peer group, with the aim of reinforcing the students' effective learning strategies. Students interact with the learning environment and progress through the stages of cognitive processes effectively when they treat the learning environment as a friend (Liew et al., 2017).

The peer group of Alice consists of three narrative pedagogical agents, representing the group of everyday peers, who appear in six dialogue videos (Mavrogianni et al., 2019). The three agents are as follows: a) Iris, named after the ancient Greek divine messenger, represents "declarative knowledge" and knows "what to do" to learn effectively; b) Sifis, named after the 1898-1913 Cretan State period represents "procedural knowledge," or the knowledge of how to use reading strategies, as an inexperienced reader who requires guidance on this topic. The period is also associated with Thomas, named after Jesus' doubting disciple, who represents "conditional knowledge," or the knowledge of why to do something, as a skeptical reader who questions learning paths.

By allowing students to identify with their preferred agent, we could potentially reduce anxiety and increase motivation to learn. The use of animated agents, which resemble familiar characters, has been shown to effectively enhance the learning process, as indicated by Johnson, Shaw, and Ganeshan in 1998, as referenced in Ergül and Koç (2013). The agents, Iris, Sifis, and Thomas, facilitate the learning process through their friendly dialogues, which suggest specific learning strategies to students. In the creation of the dialogues, several key elements were considered. These included the adoption of a plausible and humorous style, the practical application of strategies based on the preliminary project, the importance of respecting copyright, the judicious use of the Internet, and the necessity of collaboration to achieve common learning goals. Additionally, the potential for overloading students' working memory based on cognitive load theory (Paas & Sweller, 2014) was also taken into account.

The dialogues are based on the thirty statements from the MARSI 1.0 Metacognitive Awareness of Reading Strategies Scale (Mokhtari & Reichard, 2002). The statements were subsequently adapted into Greek (Mavrogianni et al., 2018; 2020). The statements were grouped into three categories: before, during, and after reading strategies. These categories were further transformed based on the types of knowledge: declarative, procedural, and conditional. This creative adaptation was developed to facilitate a realistic dialogue among peers (Mavrogianni et al., 2019). In order to construct engaging and humorous dialogues, insights were drawn from observations made during the preliminary project, and direct quotes from 53 10th-grade students were incorporated. These quotes addressed the students' reading methods, challenges, and uncertainties in adopting new learning strategies. Examples of quotes include, "No link should be missing from the knowledge chain...," "I don't like following orders...," and "I'm bored of dictionaries...."

Furthermore, we augmented the dialogues by implementing strategies proposed by the students. For example, in dialogue 4, as Sifis becomes increasingly assertive, he counsels: "In the event that the text is not intelligible, it would appear that consulting a dictionary is the only viable option." In dialogue 5, Iris, demonstrating her reading proficiency, shares the following: "I created a timeline where I write down every new piece of information and attach notes in order not to overlook anything." In dialogue 6, Thomas, who is moving away from the "low-level student" stereotype, recognizes that the learning process advances through mistakes. He states, "If we guessed wrong and abstracts don't include all the important stuff, we should learn from that mistake."

In the dialogues, we also highlighted the following points:

a) Respect for copyright (THOMAS – I made a misstep in the classroom when Mrs Mavrogianni activated the projector and I had copied the entire website... SIFIS – Have you not been informed of the necessity to respect copyright? It is not possible to copy the thoughts of others.
b) The sensible use of the Internet requires that one does not trust everything that is online. THOMAS: "One for all, and all for one." The collective strength of a group is greater than the strength of any individual.

2. RESEARCH METHODOLOGY

The research project is part of an educational field research program that has been approved by the Ethics Committee of the University of Crete (decision 2/2018/13-03-2018) and the Greek Ministry of Education (No. 89964/D2/01-06-2018). The study was conducted at a General Lyceum in Heraklion, Crete, during the 2018-2019 as part of the research work course, conducted in real classroom conditions.

The study involved two groups of 10th-grade students participating in a "Project Method Activity" course over the course of three months. The topic of "The XXX State period (1898-1913)" from the twelfth-grade Humanities-oriented History textbook was taught using either Geo-Histor or traditional methods, through the schoolbook. The study included 54 10th-grade students from General Lyceum, with 51.9% being male and 48.1% female. The students were selected at random from eight classes at the same school. A second random selection was conducted to determine the experimental and control groups. The experimental group (N=27) engaged in experimental interactive teaching with the Geo-Histor environment, which involved embedded agent dialogues. In contrast, the control group (N=27) was taught with traditional teaching methods using the schoolbook. The participants were a representative sample of the diverse abilities, skills, and performance found in classrooms (Bryman, 2017). Prior to their participation, students and their parents or guardians were informed of the nature of the study and provided with the necessary consent forms. It should be noted that none of the students had any diagnosed learning difficulties.

The assessment of students' historical knowledge was conducted using closed-ended criteria, including multiple-choice and true-false questions. The assessment included the following components:

a) A test of 15 comprehensive questions to gauge students' pre-existing knowledge about the specific historical period of the Cretan State (1898-1913).
b) Historical knowledge tests were given after each of the 10 modules, including 3 to 7 questions (a total of 44 questions across the 10 units).
c) A 25-question evaluation criterion was created out of the above 44 questions, in order to measure the students' historical knowledge of the taught material at the end of the 10-module intervention and at the retest one month later.

In order to ensure the reliability of the aforementioned assessment criteria, a Cronbach's alpha coefficient reliability test was conducted on all participants from both the experimental and control groups (N=54). The general classifications of acceptable (0.60-0.69), good (0.70-0.79), very good (0.80-0.89), and excellent (0.90-1.00) were employed for the alpha index (Blunch, 2008; DeVellis, 2012; Field, 2013; George & Mallery, 2003; Kline, 2000; Tavakol & Dennick, 2011). The Cronbach's alpha values are predominantly classified as "very good to excellent," as evidenced by the following examples: a. test of 15 comprehensive questions: .758-.888, 44 questions: .869, 25-question evaluation criterion: .815-.931. The statistical processing of the survey data was conducted using the statistical software package SPSS 24.0 (Field, 2013). The threshold for statistical significance was set at $p < .05$.

3. RESEARCH QUESTIONS

The following research questions will be addressed:

1. Did the pedagogical agents that instructed learning strategies and avoidance of risky behavior have a positive effect on performance?
2. Did the interactive instruction have a positive effect on students' achievement in history?
3. Does interactive teaching result in better performance than traditional teaching methods?
4. Does interactive teaching result in better historical knowledge retention compared to traditional teaching methods?

4. PROCEDURE

In both cases, the fading guidance method was employed to facilitate the students' familiarity with the reading strategies. This type of instruction is classified as metacognitive "scaffolding" (Hannafin et al., 1999). In the interactive teaching using the Geo-Histor environment, the provision of fading guidance on the use of learning strategies was delivered through the dialogues of the narrative agents (Iris, Sifis, and Thomas), while the instructions for avoiding attention destruction were provided by Alice. In traditional teaching, the dialogic method was employed to instruct students in the use of strategies. Initially, the teacher elucidated the strategies, and subsequently, students applied them during the processing of the expository text.

Both teaching methods included ten teaching modules, and the students' performance was evaluated at the end of each module and at the end of the project. One month later, a second test was administered to determine the efficacy of the instructional approach and the retention of historical information. The project spanned a period of four months. In the Geo-Histor environment, students engaged in interactive teaching watched videos featuring dialogues between peers, agents, before commencing each teaching unit. The students studied the expository text by reading it on a screen and listening to it in a podcast with a human voice. Furthermore, they had access to explanations in pop-up windows and active websites for further comprehension. The role of the tutor was primarily to familiarize the students with the interface and address any technical issues that may have arisen.

Six of the videos feature dialogues between three agents, designated as Iris, Sifis, and Thomas. The agents are depicted as equals engaged in a discussion of their strategies within an Instagram-like environment (Figure 1) (Mavrogianni et al., 2019).

Figure 1. Agents discussing the efficacy of reading strategies in an Instagram environment

In a subsequent video, the agent Alice, who represents gender equality through her gender and multiculturalism through her foreign name, advises students to prioritize their reading goals in order to circumvent the necessity of conducting searches on active websites (Figure 2). Additionally, the agent cautions students to exercise caution when navigating the Internet, emphasizing the potential risks associated with online activities. The videos are accessible in all ten teaching modules via the "Help" option.

Figure 2. Screenshot of the Geo-Histor environment with Alice providing guidance on goal-oriented navigation

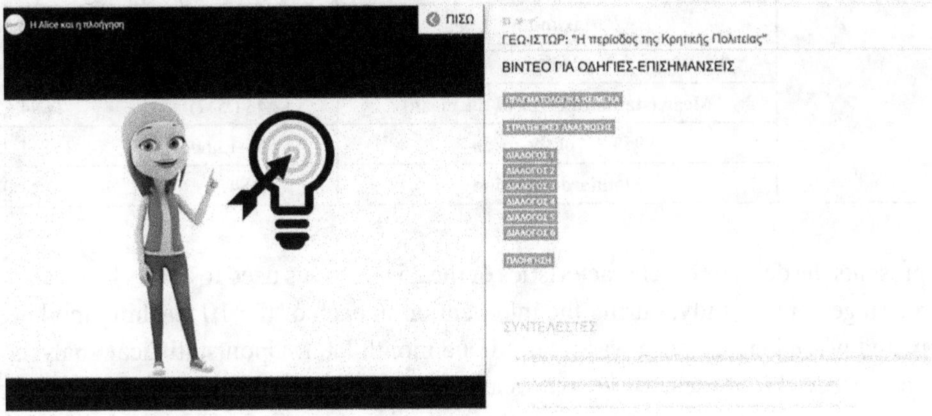

5. DATA ANALYSIS AND RESULTS

Following the collection of data, comparisons were made between the two groups, initially prior to the commencement of the research study (pre-test), subsequently following its completion (post-test), and finally at a subsequent retest conducted one month later.

Table 1. Descriptive statistics

Stage	Statistical quantity	Control group	Experimental group
During intervention (10 modules)	**Minimum**	8,00	18,00
	Maximum	23,00	25,00
	Median	16,00	23,00
	Mean (standard error of the mean)	16,96 (,685)	22,78 (,355)
	95% CI of the mean	15,556-18,370	22,047-23,508
	Standard deviation	3,557	1,847
Post-test	**Minimum**	8,00	24,00
	Maximum	19,00	25,00
	Median	12,00	25,00
	Mean (standard error of the mean)	12,70 (,554)	24,96 (,037)
	95% CI of the mean	11,565-13,843	24,887-25,039
	Standard deviation	2,880	,192

continued on following page

Table 1. Continued

Stage	Statistical quantity	Control group	Experimental group
Retest	**Minimum**	7,00	19,00
	Maximum	18,00	25,00
	Median	13,00	25,00
	Mean (standard error of the mean)	12,48 (,547)	24,44 (,308)
	95% CI of the mean	11,355-13,608	23,811-25,078
	Standard deviation	2,847	1,601

Table 1 presents the descriptive characteristics of the 25 questions used to assess historical knowledge over the three stages of the study: during the intervention in each of the 10 teaching modules, after the intervention, and when performance was retested one month later. Upon statistical analysis of the two groups, it was observed that there were significant differences between the control and experimental groups.

Table 2. Frequencies and percentages (%) of the ratings of the assessment criterion (25 questions) on the historical knowledge taught

Stage	Score	Control group$	Intervention group$
During intervention	**low**	2 (7,4%)	0 (0,0%)
	medium	19 (70,4%)	3 (11,1%)
	high	6 (22,2%)	24 (88,9%)
Post test	**low**	10 (37,0%)	0 (0,0%)
	medium	17 (63,0%)	0 (0,0%)
	high	0 (0,0%)	27 (100,0%)
Retest	**low**	11 (40,7%)	0 (0,0%)
	medium	16 (59,3%)	2 (7,4%)
	high	0 (0,0%)	25 (92,6%)

$ Frequency percentages are reported in the same group (summed vertically at 100%).

Table 2 presents the frequencies and percentages of the assessment criterion of historical knowledge taught at the three stages of the study (during and after the intervention and at the retest) for the control (traditional teaching) and experimental (interactive teaching) groups. The distribution of scores in the experimental group differs significantly from that of the control group (7.4%-70.4%-22.2% vs. 0.0%-11.1%-88.9%). Following the intervention, the differences in distribution are further accentuated (control group: 37%-63%-0.0% vs. experimental group: 0.0%-0.0%-100%). A comparable outcome with marginal discrepancies is observed at the retest. The control group demonstrated a distribution of 40.7%, 59.3%, and 0%, while the experimental group demonstrated a distribution of 0%, 7.4%, and 92.6%.

The findings of this study align with those of previous research in the field of education. It has been observed that students in traditional teaching groups tend to perform well in shorter lessons but struggle to retain information when the material is more extensive. This phenomenon is commonly referred to as the "forgetting curve." However, this observation is reversed in the experimental group, with the absolute concentration of scores in the high category not only after the intervention (post-test) but also at the retest.

Table 3. Comparison between the control (N=27) and the intervention (N=27) groups.

Stage	Comparison[$] of control-experimental groups
During Intervention	U=48,500 *p*<,001[*1]
Post test	U=,000 *p*<,001[*1]
Retest	U=,000 *p*<,001[*1]

[$] Mann-Whitney U test was used.
* Indicates statistical significance (p<.05).
[1] Experimental group > control group (SPSS output not shown here)

Table 3 presents the results of a comparison between the control and experimental groups based on their scores on the 25-question criterion for assessing learned historical knowledge. The data indicate that the experimental group demonstrated statistically significant differences from the control group at all three stages of the study. The scores are consistently higher in the experimental group than in the control group, as indicated by the ranking. In traditional teaching, historical reasoning appears to be underutilized, potentially due to the lack of diverse sources of historical information and the emphasis on the use of prescribed textbooks, which constrains the manner in which students interact with the text and the learning process (Moje et al., 2011). In contrast, an interactive learning environment, through the provision of supportive scaffolding and the utilization of pedagogical agents and multiple sources of historical information that address both visual and auditory channels, facilitates the development of essential skills and the acquisition of knowledge that does not diminish over time.

Table 4. Comparison of the scores of the assessment criterion (25 questions) conducted separately for the control (N=27) and experimental (N=27) groups at different stages of the study.

Comparison[$]stages	Control group	Experimental group
During intervention - Post-intervention	Z=-3,974 *p*<,001[*1]	Z=-4,121 *p*<,001[*2]
Post-intervention - Retest	Z=-,284 *p*=,776	Z=-1,730 *p*=,084
During intervention - Retest	Z=-4,141 *p*<,001[*3]	Z=-2,975 *p*=,003[*3]

[$] The Wilcoxon Signed Ranks test was used and the negative, positive and equal ranks matrix was utilized.
* Indicates statistical significance (p<.05).
[1] During intervention >Post intervention.
[2] Post intervention >During intervention.
[3] During intervention >Retest.

Table 4 presents the results of the comparison of the scores on the criterion for assessing the historical knowledge taught, separately for the control and experimental groups, between the two phases of the study. The following observations can be made: The pairs that demonstrate statistically significant differences for both groups are "during intervention-post intervention" and "during intervention-retest." In contrast, the "post-intervention-retest" pairs demonstrate no statistically significant differences for either group.

However, an examination of the ranking table reveals a pronounced disparity between the two groups. In the control group, the scores for each of the ten teaching modules are higher in the "during intervention" phase than in the "post-intervention" phase. In the case of interactive teaching, the highest scores are observed in the "post-intervention" phase, which encompasses all material taught in the form of revision for a test.

6. CONCLUSIONS: REVERSING THE NEGATIVE CONSEQUENCES OF RISKY BEHAVIOR

As posited by Hollá and Hanuliaková (Niklová, 2020), the prevention of online risk behavior in educational settings can be achieved through two distinct avenues. The formal approach is to be employed during lessons, with the incorporation of discussions, lectures, exchanges of ideas and workshops, among other techniques. The non-formal way, which refers to the informal, unstructured curriculum that exists within a school, including factors such as the school's atmosphere and the relationships between students and teachers. This approach involves implementing activities outside of the traditional teaching setting, with the goal of fostering positive interactions and a supportive learning environment for students. Furthermore, the implementation of a supportive environment can be achieved through the utilization of digital learning environments, where pedagogical agents are employed to provide support (Mavrogianniet al., 2023). Pedagogical agents aim not only to enhance learning and academic performance through the simulation of a social learning environment, but also to prioritize the learning process and minimize the likelihood of students engaging in risky online behaviors by limiting their exposure to online websites and social networking sites.

Risky behaviors not only impede student learning but also have consequences for individuals and their peers, including emotional harm (Hessler & Katz, 2010; Weiss et al., 2015), interpersonal distress (Chen et al., 2020; Copeland et al., 2007), social deterioration (Hoff et al., 2012), and victimization (Windle, 1994). The creation of a supportive and safe learning environment has consistently been a pivotal objective in both offline and online educational contexts. It is recommended that greater emphasis be placed on the education of adolescents regarding risky online behaviors. Consequently, it is imperative to comprehend the manifestations of risky behaviors in internet-based learning environments and to identify strategies for the prevention and intervention of such behaviors among students.

In their study, Gökçearslan and Seferoğlu (2016) examined middle school students' computer and Internet use in terms of, among other things, risky Internet behavior. Although the prevalence of risky Internet behavior was not particularly high, students did engage in certain types of risky online activities. Overall, their findings suggest that students, families, and various institutions have a responsibility to address online risks. The development of effective solutions to these problems will require the collaboration of all stakeholders (Gökçearslan & Seferoğlu, 2016).

Huang et al. (2023) highlight that, while online learning environments may have positive effects (Chou & Liu, 2005; El-Sabagh, 2021; Piccoli et al., 2001), they can also have negative effects on cognitive functioning (Britt et al., 2019) and impaired reasoning and thinking skills (Axelsson et al., 2021; Bago et al., 2020). They posit that parents of millennials and Generation Z lack the requisite technological expertise to effectively delineate and support their children in today's fully digitized world. Indeed, as demonstrated by Luo et al. (2023), 80% of children begin interacting with information and communication technologies (ICT) before the age of 6, despite the fact that half of the parents believe these interactions should commence at a later age. One potential solution is to enhance internet-based learning environments with pedagogical agents that educate children about the potential risks associated with the internet. Given the significant influence that peer groups exert during adolescence, particularly in shaping attitudes towards internet safety, it is crucial to develop agents that can serve as a protective influence within the learning environment.

From our study it can be concluded that the enhanced cognitive performance of the students contributed to the structuring of the interactive Geo-Histor environment. Special attention was paid to the activation of the visual and auditory channels based on the theory of dual coding (Paivio, 1991), to the adoption of the appropriate principles of multimedia learning (Mayer, 2014a), and to the avoidance of cognitive overload (Paas & Sweller, 2014; Sweller, 1994; 2006; 2011). As evidenced by the findings of other studies (Gen & Žahin, 2016), the utilization of multimedia in social studies—which encompasses history—has been demonstrated to result in a notable enhancement in academic performance.

The traditional teaching group demonstrated proficiency in the day's lesson (during the intervention stage), but when the material to be tested was extended (re-testing of all 10 teaching units), they exhibited a decline in performance. As time passed (re-testing stage), they demonstrated a lack of retention of other information that they likely had not assimilated in depth. In contrast, the interactive teaching group demonstrated a clear concentration of scores in the high category, both after the intervention and at the retest stage.

It can be concluded that the use of the interactive learning environment Geo-Histor, which addressed both the visual and auditory channels, and the provision of procedural facilitation by the pedagogical agents, Alice, Iris, Sifis and Thomas, contributed to the prevention of risky behavior, more effective learning and better cognitive performance. This is supported by numerous other studies that have employed multimedia learning environments (Al-Hariri & Al-Hattami, 2017; Chen & Xia, 2012; Dalacosta et al., 2009; Kingsley & Boone, 2008; Shah & Khan, 2015).

The data indicated that students who received interactive teaching demonstrated a departure from the exclusive focus on textbook content observed in previous research on Greek students (Bikos, 2018; Bonidis, 2004). The students sought out supplementary materials to facilitate more in-depth learning, which resulted in enhanced performance. The findings of our research corroborate the assertion that the emergence of agents (Johnson et al., 2013; Schroeder et al., 2017), their "character" and discourse content (Veletsianos, 2010), as well as their ability to match with different types of learning levels of an adolescent peer group, were found to be important factors in the effective functioning of digital assistants (Guo & Goh, 2016). This was demonstrated by the pedagogical agents' ability to assist students in avoiding risky behaviors and successfully adopting learning strategies that led to higher achievement. The user's interaction with the ILE (Liew et al., 2017) was brought to life by Alice and her peer group, which enhanced the student's active role, increased the use of learning strategies, and protected students from the Internet Sirens. This finding is consistent with the results of other studies (Dincer & Doganay, 2017; García, et al., 2020; Pifarré et al., 2014; Yilmaz & Kilic-Cakmak, 2012).

It can be concluded that pedagogical agents that provide guidance to students enhance their learning strategies, prevent them from engaging in unnecessary Internet browsing and risky behaviors, and encourage them to focus on academic material, which in turn contributes to improved cognitive performance. The implementation of pedagogical agents led to an improvement in comprehensive historical knowledge, moving away from rote learning and towards a deeper understanding and consolidation of the material.

This was followed by an increase in performance and the longer retention of historical information. The results are consistent with those of other studies that have utilized multimedia learning environments, thereby confirming the significant impact of multimedia tools in education (Aloraini, 2012; Barzegar et al., 2012; Jian-Hua, 2012; Keengwe et al., 2008; Kingsley & Boone, 2008).

7. LIMITATIONS OF THE STUDY

As the study was conducted in a classroom setting, certain limitations must be acknowledged. Firstly, the sample size was limited due to the proportionality of the number of students in two school divisions. The study was conducted among high school students, and the degree to which the results can be generalized to other educational levels was not examined. The study was limited to expository history texts, which precludes the generalizability of the results for different textual genres or different subject areas and other learning contexts. Finally, due to the structure of the Geo-Histor ILE, the cognitive assessment was limited to closed-ended questions and did not include more complex forms of assessment such as the analysis of historical resources.

REFERENCES

Akin, A., & Iskender, M. (2011). Internet addiction and depression, anxiety and stress. *International Online Journal of Educational Sciences*, 3(1), 138–148.

Al-Hariri, M. T., & Al-Hattami, A. A. (2017). Impact of students' use of technology on their learning achievements in physiology courses at the University of Dammam. *Journal of Taibah University Medical Sciences*, 12(1), 82–85. DOI: 10.1016/j.jtumed.2016.07.004 PMID: 31435218

Alavi, S. S., Alaghemandan, H., Maracy, M. R., Jannatifard, F., Eslami, M., & Ferdosi, M. (2012). Impact of addiction to internet on a number of psychiatric symptoms in students of Isfahan universities, Iran, 2010. *International Journal of Preventive Medicine*, 3(2), 122–127. PMID: 22347609

Aloraini, S. (2012). The impact of using multimedia on students' academic achievement in the College of Education at King Saud University. *Journal of King Saud University-Languages and Translation*, 24(2), 75–82. DOI: 10.1016/j.jksult.2012.05.002

Antoniou, V., Ragia, L., Nomikou, P., Bardouli, P., Lampridou, D., Ioannou, T., Kalisperakis, I., & Stentoumis, C. (2018). Creating a story map using geographic information systems to explore geomorphology and history of Methana Peninsula. *ISPRS International Journal of Geo-Information*, 7(12), 1–15. DOI: 10.3390/ijgi7120484

Armstrong, L., Phillips, J. G., & Saling, L. L. (2000). Potential determinants of heavier internet usage. *International Journal of Human-Computer Studies*, 53(4), 537–550. DOI: 10.1006/ijhc.2000.0400

Axelsson, C. A. W., Guath, M., & Nygren, T. (2021). Learning how to separate fake from real news: Scalable digital tutorials promoting students' civic online reasoning. *Future Internet*, 13(3), 1–18. DOI: 10.3390/fi13030060

Bago, B., Rand, D. G., & Pennycook, G. (2020). Fake news, fast and slow: Deliberation reduces belief in false (but not true) news headlines. *Journal of Experimental Psychology. General*, 149(8), 1608–1613. DOI: 10.1037/xge0000729 PMID: 31916834

Bahrainian, S. A., Alizadeh, K. H., Raeisoon, M. R., Gorji, O. H., & Khazaee, A. (2014). Relationship of Internet addiction with self-esteem and depression in university students. *Journal of Preventive Medicine and Hygiene*, 55(3), 86–89. PMID: 25902574

Barzegar, N., Farjad, S., & Hosseini, N. (2012). The effect of teaching model based on multimedia and network on the student learning (case study: Guidance schools in Iran). *Procedia: Social and Behavioral Sciences*, 47, 1263–1267. DOI: 10.1016/j.sbspro.2012.06.809

Baumgartner, S. E., Valkenburg, P. M., & Peter, J. (2010). Assessing causality in the relationship between adolescents' risky sexual online behavior and their perceptions of this behavior. *Journal of Youth and Adolescence*, 39(10), 1226–1239. DOI: 10.1007/s10964-010-9512-y PMID: 20177962

Becker, L. B., Welter, V. D. E., Aschermann, E., & Großschedl, J. (2021). Comprehension-Oriented Learning of Cell Biology: Do Different Training Conditions Affect Students' Learning Success Differentially? *Education Sciences*, 11(8), 1–31. DOI: 10.3390/educsci11080438

Bendou, K., Megder, E., & Cherkaoui, C. (2017). Animated Pedagogical Agents to Assist Learners and keep them motivated in Online Learning Environments (LMS or MOOC). *International Journal of Computer Applications*, 168(6), 46–53. DOI: 10.5120/ijca2017914477

Blevins, B. (2018). Teaching digital literacy composing concepts: Focusing on the layers of augmented reality in an era of changing technology. *Computers and Composition*, 50, 21–38. DOI: 10.1016/j.compcom.2018.07.003

Brevik, L. M. (2019). Explicit reading strategy instruction or daily use of strategies? Studying the teaching of reading comprehension through naturalistic classroom observation in English L2. *Reading and Writing*, 32(9), 2281–2310. DOI: 10.1007/s11145-019-09951-w

Britt, M. A., Rouet, J. F., Blaum, D., & Millis, K. (2019). A reasoned approach to dealing with fake news. *Policy Insights from the Behavioral and Brain Sciences*, 6(1), 94–101. DOI: 10.1177/2372732218814855

Chen, R., Peng, K., Liu, J., Wilson, A., Wang, Y., Wilkinon, M. R., Wen, S., Cao, X., & Lu, J. (2020). Interpersonal trauma and risk of depression among adolescents: The mediating and moderating effect of interpersonal relationship and physical exercise. *Frontiers in Psychiatry*, 11, 194. DOI: 10.3389/fpsyt.2020.00194 PMID: 32351408

Chen, S., & Xia, Y. (2012). Research on application of multimedia technology in college physical education. *Procedia Engineering*, 29, 4213–4217. DOI: 10.1016/j.proeng.2012.01.645

Choi, S., & Clark, R.E. (2006). Cognitive and affective benefits of an animated pedagogical agent for learning English as a second language. *Journal of Educational Computing Research, 34*(4), 441-466. DOI: 10.2190/A064-U776-4208-N145

Chou, S. W., & Liu, C. H. (2005). Learning effectiveness in a Web-based virtual learning environment: A learner control perspective. *Journal of Computer Assisted Learning*, 21(1), 65–76. DOI: 10.1111/j.1365-2729.2005.00114.x

Chrienová, M., Majerová Kropáčová, K., Oster, J., & Osterová, I. (2019). Výskyt nežiadúcich javov v základných školách v okrese Lučenec. Retrieved from https://preventista.sk/info/prieskum-lucenec.

Christensen, C. M., Horn, M. B., & Johnson, C. W. (2008). *Disrupting class. How disruptive innovation will change the way the world learns.* McGraw-Hill companies.

Clark, J. M., & Paivio, A. (1991). Dual coding theory and education. *Educational Psychology Review*, 3(3), 149–210. DOI: 10.1007/BF01320076

Clark, R. C., & Mayer, R. E. (2016). *E-Learning and the Science of Instruction: Proven Guidelines for Consumers and Designers of Multimedia Learning*. John Wiley & Sons. DOI: 10.1002/9781119239086

Copeland, W. E., Keeler, G., Angold, A., & Costello, E. J. (2007). Traumatic events and posttraumatic stress in childhood. *Archives of General Psychiatry*, 64(5), 577–584. DOI: 10.1001/archpsyc.64.5.577 PMID: 17485609

Craig, S. D., & Schroeder, N. L. (2017). Reconsidering the voice effect when learning from a virtual human. *Computers & Education*, 114, 193–205. DOI: 10.1016/j.compedu.2017.07.003

Dalacosta, K., Kamariotaki-Paparrigopoulou, M., Palyvos, J. A., & Spyrellis, N. (2009). Multimedia application with animated cartoons for teaching science in elementary education. *Computers & Education*, 52(4), 741–748. DOI: 10.1016/j.compedu.2008.11.018

Daradoumis, T., & Arguedas, M. (2020). Cultivating Students' Reflective Learning in Metacognitive Activities through an Affective Pedagogical Agent. *Journal of Educational Technology & Society*, 23(2), 19–31. https://www.jstor.org/stable/26921131

Dinçer, S., & Doğanay, A. (2017). The effects of multiple-pedagogical agents on learners' academic success, motivation, and cognitive load. *Computers & Education*, 11, 74–100. DOI: 10.1016/j.compedu.2017.04.005

Duell, N., Steinberg, L., Chein, J., Al-Hassan, S. M., Bacchini, D., Lei, C., Chaudhary, N., Di Giunta, L., Dodge, K. A., Fanti, K. A., Lansford, J. E., Malone, P. S., Oburu, P., Pastorelli, C., Skinner, A. T., Sorbring, E., Tapanya, S., Uribe Tirado, L. M., & Alampay, L. P. (2016). Interaction of reward seeking and self-regulation in the prediction of risk taking: A cross-national test of the dual systems model. *Developmental Psychology*, 52(10), 1593–1605. DOI: 10.1037/dev0000152 PMID: 27598251

El-Sabagh, H. A. (2021). Adaptive e-learning environment based on learning styles and its impact on development students' engagement. *International Journal of Educational Technology in Higher Education*, 18(1), 53. DOI: 10.1186/s41239-021-00289-4

Fernandes, B., Maia, B. R., & Pontes, H. M. (2019). Internet addiction or problematic internet use? Which term should be used? *Psicologia USP, 30,* 1-8(e190020). DOI: 10.1590/0103-6564e190020

García, G. G., Jiménez, C. R., & Marín, J. A. M. (2020). The transcendence of Augmented Reality in student motivation. A systematic review and meta-analysis. *Alteridad*, 15(1), 36–46. DOI: 10.17163/alt.v15n1.2020.03

Gen, O. I. & žahin, O. (2016). Effect of the use of multimedia on students' performance: A case study of social studies class. *Educational Research Review*, 11(8), 877–882. DOI: 10.5897/ERR2016.2741

Goel, D., Subramanyam, A., & Kamath, R. (2013). A study on the prevalence of internet addiction and its association with psychopathology in Indian adolescents. *Indian Journal of Psychiatry*, 55(2), 140–143. DOI: 10.4103/0019-5545.111451 PMID: 23825847

Gökçearslan, Ş., & Seferoğlu, S. S. (2016). The use of the Internet among middle school students: Risky behaviors and opportunities. *Kastamonu Education Journal*, 24(1), 383–404.

Groshans, G., Mikhailova, E., Post, C., Schlautman, M., Carbajales-Dale, P., & Payne, K. (2019). Digital story map learning for STEM disciplines. *Education Sciences*, 9(2), 75. DOI: 10.3390/educsci9020075

Guo, P. J., Kim, J., & Rubin, R. (2014). How video production affects student engagement: An empirical study of MOOC videos. In *Proceedings of the first ACM conference on Learning@ Scale conference*, L@S'14, 41-50. DOI: 10.1145/2556325.2566239

Guo, Y. R., & Goh, D. H. L. (2016). Evaluation of affective embodied agents in an information literacy game. *Computers & Education*, 103, 59–75. DOI: 10.1016/j.compedu.2016.09.013

Hannafin, M., Land, S. M., & Oliver, K. (1999). Open learning environments: foundations, methods, and models. In Reigeluth, C. M. (Ed.), *Instructional design theories and models* (pp. 115–140). Lawrence Erlbaum Associates.

Hessler, D. M., & Katz, L. F. (2010). Brief report: Associations between emotional competence and adolescent risky behavior. *Journal of Adolescence*, 33(1), 241–246. DOI: 10.1016/j.adolescence.2009.04.007 PMID: 19481247

Hoff, C. C., Chakravarty, D., Beougher, S. C., Neilands, T. B., & Darbes, L. A. (2012). Relationship characteristics associated with sexual risk behavior among MSM in committed relationships. *AIDS Patient Care and STDs*, 26(12), 738–745. DOI: 10.1089/apc.2012.0198 PMID: 23199191

Huang, C. L., Alimu, Y., Yang, S. C., & Kang, S. (2023). What you think is a joke is actually cyberbullying: The effects of ethical dissonance, event judgment and humor style on cyberbullying behavior. *Computers in Human Behavior*, 142(4), 107670. DOI: 10.1016/j.chb.2023.107670

Huang, T. C., Chen, M. Y., & Lin, C. Y. (2019). Exploring the behavioral patterns transformation of learners in different 3D modeling teaching strategies. *Computers in Human Behavior*, 92, 670–678. DOI: 10.1016/j.chb.2017.08.028

Ilhan, G. O., & Oruc, S. (2016). Effect of the Use of Multimedia on Students' Performance: A Case Study of Social Studies Class. *Educational Research Review*, 11(8), 877–882. DOI: 10.5897/ERR2016.2741

Jaiswal, A., Manchanda, S., Gautam, V., Goel, A. D., Aneja, J., & Raghav, P. R. (2020). Burden of internet addiction, social anxiety and social phobia among University students, India. *Journal of Family Medicine and Primary Care*, 9(7), 3607–3612. DOI: 10.4103/jfmpc.jfmpc_360_20 PMID: 33102337

Jian-Hua, S., & hong, L. (2012). Explore the effective use of multimedia technology in college physics teaching. *Energy Procedia*, 17, 1897–1900. DOI: 10.1016/j.egypro.2012.02.329

Johnson, A. M., DiDonato, M. D., & Reisslein, M. (2013). Animated agents in K-12 engineering outreach: Preferred agent characteristics across age levels. *Computers in Human Behavior*, 29(4), 1807–1815. DOI: 10.1016/j.chb.2013.02.023

Kandasamy, S., Buhari, A. M., & Janaki, S. (2019). A study on anxiety disorder among college students with internet addiction. *International Journal of Community Medicine and Public Health*, 6(4), 1695–1700. DOI: 10.18203/2394-6040.ijcmph20191407

Kapi, A. Y., Osman, N., Ramli, R. Z., & Taib, J. M. (2017). Multimedia education tools for effective teaching and learning. *Journal of Telecommunication, Electronic and Computer Engineering (JTEC), 9*(2-8), 143-146.

Kawabe, K., Horiuchi, F., Ochi, M., Oka, Y., & Ueno, S. I. (2016). Internet addiction: Prevalence and relation with mental states in adolescents. *Psychiatry and Clinical Neurosciences*, 70(9), 405–412. DOI: 10.1111/pcn.12402 PMID: 27178110

Keengwe, J., Onchwari, G., & Wachira, P. (2008). The use of computer tools to support meaningful learning. *AACE Review (formerly AACE Journal), 16*(1), 77-92. Retrieved from https://www.learntechlib.org/primary/p/23647/

Kim, Y., & Baylor, A. L. (2016). Research-based design of pedagogical agent roles: A review, progress, and recommendations. *International Journal of Artificial Intelligence in Education*, 26(1), 160–169. DOI: 10.1007/s40593-015-0055-y

Kingsley, K. V., & Boone, R. (2008). Effects of multimedia software on achievement of middle school students in an American history class. *Journal of Research on Technology in Education*, 41(2), 203–221. DOI: 10.1080/15391523.2008.10782529

Kostaridou-Eukleidi, A. (2011). *Cognitive Psychology. From the representation of cognition to memory and action*. Pedio.

Koulianou, M., Mastrothanasis, K., Roussos, P., & Samartzi, S. (2020). Greek adaptation and psychometric validation of the Jr. MAI scale for the assessment of metacognitive learning strategies in adolescent students with and without specific learning difficulties. *Education Sciences*, SI-1, 20–29.

Koulianou, M., Roussos, P., & Samartzi, S. (2019). Metacognitive reading strategies: A Greek adaptation of the MARSI tool and a comparative study in adolescent students with and without specific learning difficulties. *Psychology (Irvine, Calif.)*, 24(1), 138–156. DOI: 10.12681/psy_hps.22391

Kraut, R., Patterson, M., Lundmark, V., Kiesler, S., Mukophadhyay, T., & Scherlis, W. (1998). Internet paradox: A social technology that reduces social involvement and psychological well-being? *The American Psychologist*, 53(9), 1017–1031. DOI: 10.1037/0003-066X.53.9.1017 PMID: 9841579

Liew, T. W., Mat Zin, N. A., & Sahari, N. (2017). Exploring the affective, motivational and cognitive effects of pedagogical agent enthusiasm in a multimedia learning environment. *Human-centric Computing and Information Sciences*, 7(1), 1–21. DOI: 10.1186/s13673-017-0089-2

Lin, L., Atkinson, R., Christopherson, R., Joseph, S., & Harrison, C. (2013). Animated agents and learning: Does the type of verbal feedback they provide matter? *Computers & Education*, 67, 239–249. DOI: 10.1016/j.compedu.2013.04.017

Livingstone, S., Kalmus, V., & Talves, K. (2013). Girls' and boys' experiences of online risk and safety. In *The Routledge Companion to Media & Gender* (pp. 190-200). Routledge.

Livingstone, S., & Smith, P. K. (2014). Annual research review: Harms experienced by child users of online and mobile technologies: The nature, prevalence and management of sexual and aggressive risks in the digital age. *Journal of Child Psychology and Psychiatry, and Allied Disciplines*, 55(6), 635–654. DOI: 10.1111/jcpp.12197 PMID: 24438579

Lowe, R. K., & Schnotz, W. (2014). Animation principles in multimedia learning. *The Cambridge handbook of multimedia learning, 2*, 513-546.

Lubis, H., Rivai, M., Yushar, Y., & Nasution, M. (2019, December). Interactive Map of Historical Sites: The Media of History Learning on the 21st Century in North Sumatra. In *Proceedings of the 2nd International Conference on Social Sciences and Interdisciplinary Studies (formerly ICCSSIS), ICCSIS 2019*. DOI: 10.4108/eai.24-10-2019.2290580

Luo, Y. F., Yang, S. C., Chou, K. Y., & Lee, H. T. (2023). Taiwanese parents' perspectives on young children's use of information communication technology. *Frontiers in Psychology*, 14, 1248863. DOI: 10.3389/fpsyg.2023.1248863 PMID: 37799529

Martha, A. S. D., & Santoso, H. B. (2019). The Design and Impact of the Pedagogical Agent: A Systematic Literature Review. *The Journal of Educators Online*, 16(1). Advance online publication. DOI: 10.9743/jeo.2019.16.1.8

Mastrothanasis, K. (2019). Development and psychometric validation of self-reflection of reading comprehension strategies for bilingual students. *Preschool & School Education*, 7(2), 116–138. DOI: 10.12681/ppej.20212

Mastrothanasis, K., Koulianou, M., Katsifi, S., & Zouganeli, A. (2018). The use of Metacognitive knowledge and regulation strategies' of students with and without special learning difficulties. *International Journal of Special Education*, 33(1), 191–207.

Mavrogianni, A. (2023). *Development of Metacognitive Strategies and Interactive Learning Systems: Designing, Implementing and Evaluating an Interactive Learning Environment for Teaching Expository Texts.* [Doctoral Thesis, University of Crete, Greece]. EKT.

Mavrogianni, A., Vasilaki, E., Spantidakis, I., Papadaki-Michailidi, E., & Linardakis, M. (2018, May). Adaptation to the Greek population of the Metacognitive Awareness of Reading Strategies Inventory (MARSI) version 1.0. *Poster session presented at the 5th Hellenic Cognitive Science Society Conference*, Leukes, Paros.

Mavrogianni, A., Vasilaki, E., Spantidakis, I., Sarris, A., Papadaki Michaelides, E., & Yahnakis, E. (2019). Narrative pedagogical agents to enhance reading strategies in the multimedia learning environment Geo-Histor. *In Proceedings of the 10th International Conference on Open and Distance Education, ICODL* 2019, 22-24 November, Athens, Greece.

Mavrogianni, A., Vassilaki, E., Spantidakis, G., Sarris, A., Papadaki-Michailidi, E., & Yachnakis, E. (2020). An alternative factorization of the metacognitive awareness of reading strategies inventory associated with the Greek national curriculum and its psychometric properties. *Creative Education*, 11(8), 1299–1323. DOI: 10.4236/ce.2020.118096

Mavrogianni, A., Vassilaki, E., & Spantidakis, I. (2023). Pedagogical Agents as Facilitators of Instructional Guidance for the Development of Metacognitive Strategies. Dialogues. *Theory and Practice in Education Sciences*, 9, 90–114. DOI: 10.12681/dial.36288

Mayer, R. E. (2014). *The Cambridge Handbook of Multimedia Learning* (2nd ed.). Cambridge University Press. DOI: 10.1017/CBO9781139547369

Mayer, R. E., & DaPra, C. S. (2012). An Embodiment Effect in Computer-Based Learning with Animated Pedagogical Agents. *Journal of Experimental Psychology*, 18(3), 239–252. DOI: 10.1037/a0028616 PMID: 22642688

Mayer, R. E., & Moreno, R. (2002). Aids to computer-based multimedia learning. *Learning and Instruction*, 12(1), 107–119. DOI: 10.1016/S0959-4752(01)00018-4

Mitchell, S. H., Schoel, C., & Stevens, A. A. (2008). Mechanisms underlying heightened risk taking in adolescents as compared with adults. *Psychonomic Bulletin & Review*, 15(2), 272–277. DOI: 10.3758/PBR.15.2.272 PMID: 18488639

Mitsea, E., & Drigas, A. (2019). A journey into the metacognitive learning strategies. *International Journal of Online & Biomedical Engineering*, 15(14), 4–19. DOI: 10.3991/ijoe.v15i14.11379

Moje, E. B., Stockdill, D., Kim, K., & Kim, H. J. (2011). The role of text in disciplinary learning. *Handbook of Reading Research, Volume IV*, 453-486. https://doi.org/DOI: 10.3991/ijoe.v15i14.11379

Mokhtari, K., Dimitrov, D. M., & Reichard, C. A. (2018). Revising the Metacognitive Awareness of Reading Strategies Inventory (MARSI) and testing for factorial invariance. *Studies in Second Language Learning and Teaching*, 8(2), 219–246. DOI: 10.14746/ssllt.2018.8.2.3

Mokhtari, K., & Reichard, C. A. (2002). Assessing Students' Metacognitive Awareness of Reading Strategies. *Journal of Educational Psychology*, 94(2), 249–259. DOI: 10.1037/0022-0663.94.2.249

Moore, K. D. (2014). *Effective instructional strategies: From theory to practice*. Sage Publications.

Moreno, R. (2010). Cognitive load theory: More food for thought. *Instructional Science*, 38(2), 135–141. DOI: 10.1007/s11251-009-9122-9

Moreno, R., Mayer, R. E., Spires, H. A., & Lester, J. C. (2001). The case for social agency in computer-based teaching: Do students learn more deeply when they interact with animated pedagogical agents? *Cognition and Instruction*, 19(2), 177–213. DOI: 10.1207/S1532690XCI1902_02

Muhid, A., Amalia, E. R., Hilaliyah, H., Budiana, N., & Wajdi, M. B. N. (2020). The Effect of Metacognitive Strategies Implementation on Students' Reading Comprehension Achievement. *International Journal of Instruction*, 13(2), 847–862. DOI: 10.29333/iji.2020.13257a

Murali, V., & George, S. (2007). Lost online: An overview of internet addiction. *Advances in Psychiatric Treatment*, 13(1), 24–30. DOI: 10.1192/apt.bp.106.002907

Niklová, M. (2020). Prevention of online risk behavior in schools with regard to the socioeducational activity of the school social pedagogue. *Pedagogická Orientace*, 30(4), 542–554. DOI: 10.5817/PedOr2020-4-542

Noll, J. G., Shenk, C. E., Barnes, J. E., & Haralson, K. J. (2013). Association of maltreatment with high-risk internet behaviors and offline encounters. *Pediatrics*, 131(2), e510–e517. DOI: 10.1542/peds.2012-1281 PMID: 23319522

Norbekova, G., Safarova, D., Bazarov, B., & Yakubov, F. (2019). Interactive Learning Environment in the English Language Teaching with the help of Computer Technology. *Mental Enlightenment Scientific-Methodological Journal*, 2019(1), 5.

Notten, N., & Nikken, P. (2016). Boys and girls taking risks online: A gendered perspective on social context and adolescents' risky online behavior. *New Media & Society*, 18(6), 966–988. https://psycnet.apa.org/doi/10.1177/1461444814552379. DOI: 10.1177/1461444814552379

Odacı, H., & Kalkan, M. (2010). Problematic Internet use, loneliness and dating anxiety among young adult university students. *Computers & Education*, 55(3), 1091–1097. DOI: 10.1016/j.compedu.2010.05.006

Olenik Shemesh, D., Heiman, T., & Wright, M. F. (2023). Problematic Use of the Internet and Well-Being among Youth from a Global Perspective: A Mediated-Moderated Model of Socio-Emotional Factors. *The Journal of Genetic Psychology*, 1–23. DOI: 10.1080/00221325.2023.2277319 PMID: 37933515

Paas, F., & Sweller, J., (2011). An Evolutionary Upgrade of Cognitive Load Theory: Using the Human Motor System and Collaboration to Support the Learning of Complex Cognitive Tasks. *Educational Psychology Review, 24*(1), 27–45. DOI: 10.1007/s10648-011-9179-2

Paas, F., & Sweller, J. (2014). Implications of cognitive load theory for multimedia learning. In Mayer, R. E. (Ed.), *The Cambridge handbook of multimedia learning* (2nd ed., pp. 27–42). Cambridge University Press. DOI: 10.1017/CBO9781139547369.004

Paivio, A. (1991). Dual Coding Theory: Retrospect and Current Status. *Canadian Journal of Psychology*, 45(3), 255–287. DOI: 10.1037/h0084295

Paluckaitė, U., & Žardeckaitė-Matulaitienė, K. (2017). Adolescents' perception of risky behavior on the internet. *European Proceedings of Social and Behavioral Sciences*, 30, 284–292. DOI: 10.15405/epsbs.2017.09.27

Pan, G., Sen, S., Starrett, D. A., Bonk, C. J., Rodgers, M. L., Tikoo, M., & Powell, D. V. (2012). Instructor-Made Videos as a learner scaffolding tool. *Journal of Online Learning and Teaching*, 8(1), 298–311. https://citeseerx.ist.psu.edu/viewdoc/summary?doi=10.1.1.297.4017

Piccoli, G., Ahmad, R., & Ives, B. (2001). Web-based virtual learning environments: A research framework and a preliminary assessment of effectiveness in basic IT skills training. *Management Information Systems Quarterly*, 25(4), 401–426. DOI: 10.2307/3250989

Pifarré, M., Cobos, R., & Argelagós, E. (2014). Incidence of group awareness information on students' collaborative learning processes. *Journal of Computer Assisted Learning*, 30(4), 300–317. DOI: 10.1111/jcal.12043

Ranjan, L. K., Gupta, P. R., Srivastava, M., & Gujar, N. M. (2021). Problematic internet use and its association with anxiety among undergraduate students. *Asian Journal of Social Health and Behavior*, 4(4), 137–141. DOI: 10.4103/shb.shb_30_21

Reyna, V. F., Wilhelms, E. A., McCormick, M. J., & Weldon, R. B. (2015). Development of risky decision making: Fuzzy-trace theory and neurobiological perspectives. *Child Development Perspectives*, 9(2), 122–127. DOI: 10.1111/cdep.12117 PMID: 25983859

Rismark, M., & Sølvberg, A. M. (2019). Video as a Learner Scaffolding Tool. *International Journal of Learning. Teaching and Educational Research*, 18(1), 62–75. DOI: 10.26803/ijlter.18.1.5

Saikia, A. M., Das, J., Barman, P., & Bharali, M. D. (2019). Internet addiction and its relationships with depression, anxiety, and stress in urban adolescents of Kamrup District, Assam. *Journal of Family & Community Medicine*, 26(2), 108–112. DOI: 10.4103/jfcm.JFCM_93_18 PMID: 31143082

Schroeder, N. L., Romine, W. L., & Craig, S. D. (2017). Measuring pedagogical agent persona and the influence of agent persona on learning. *Computers & Education*, 109, 176–186. DOI: 10.1016/j.compedu.2017.02.015

Schunk, D. H. (2012). *Learning Theories. An Educational Perspective* (6th ed.). Pearson.

Shah, I., & Khan, M. (2015). Impact of multimedia-aided teaching on students' academic achievement and attitude at elementary level. *US-China Education Review A*, 5(5), 349–360. DOI: 10.17265/2161-623X/2015.05A.006

Shulman, E. P., Smith, A. R., Silva, K., Icenogle, G., Duell, N., Chein, J., & Steinberg, L. (2016). The dual systems model: Review, reappraisal, and reaffirmation. *Developmental Cognitive Neuroscience*, 17, 103–117. DOI: 10.1016/j.dcn.2015.12.010 PMID: 26774291

Simons, K. D., & Klein, J. D. (2007). The impact of scaffolding and student achievement levels in a problem-based learning environment. *Instructional Science*, 35(1), 41–72. DOI: 10.1007/s11251-006-9002-5

Singh, A., Khess, C. R. J., Kj, M., Ali, A., & Gujar, N. M. (2020). Loneliness, social anxiety, social support, and internet addiction among postgraduate college students. *Open Journal of Psychiatry & Allied Sciences*, 11(1), 10–13. DOI: 10.5958/2394-2061.2020.00002.6

Steinberg, L., Albert, D., Cauffman, E., Banich, M., Graham, S., & Woolard, J. (2008). Age differences in sensation seeking and impulsivity as indexed by behavior and self-report: Evidence for a dual systems model. *Developmental Psychology*, 44(6), 1764–1778. DOI: 10.1037/a0012955 PMID: 18999337

Steinberg, L., & Chein, J. M. (2015). Multiple accounts of adolescent impulsivity. *Proceedings of the National Academy of Sciences of the United States of America*, 112(29), 8807–8808. DOI: 10.1073/pnas.1509732112 PMID: 26150513

Sweller, J. (2011). Cognitive load theory. *Psychology of Learning and Motivation*, 55, 37–76. DOI: 10.1016/B978-0-12-387691-1.00002-8

ter Beek, M., Brummer, L., Donker, A. S., & Opdenakker, M.-C. J. L. (2018). Supporting secondary school students' reading comprehension in computer environments: A systematic review. *Journal of Computer Assisted Learning*, 34(5), 557–566. DOI: 10.1111/jcal.12260

ter Beek, M., Opdenakker, M.-C., Spijkerboer, A. W., Brummer, L., Ozinga, H. W., & Strijbos, J.-W. (2019). Scaffolding expository history text reading: Effects on adolescents' comprehension, self regulation, and motivation. *Learning and Individual Differences*, 74, 101749. DOI: 10.1016/j.lindif.2019.06.003

Valkenburg, P. M., & Peter, J. (2011). Online communication among adolescents: An integrated model of its attraction, opportunities, and risks. *The Journal of Adolescent Health*, 48(2), 121–127. DOI: 10.1016/j.jadohealth.2010.08.020 PMID: 21257109

Wang, C., Fang, T., & Gu, Y. (2020). Learning performance and behavioral patterns of online collaborative learning: Impact of cognitive load and affordances of different multimedia. *Computers & Education*, 143, 103683. DOI: 10.1016/j.compedu.2019.103683

Weiss, N. H., Sullivan, T. P., & Tull, M. T. (2015). Explicating the role of emotion dysregulation in risky behaviors: A review and synthesis of the literature with directions for future research and clinical practice. *Current Opinion in Psychology*, 3, 22–29. DOI: 10.1016/j.copsyc.2015.01.013 PMID: 25705711

Windle, M. (1994). Substance use, risky behaviors, and victimization among a US national adolescent sample. *Addiction (Abingdon, England)*, 89(2), 175–182. DOI: 10.1111/j.1360-0443.1994.tb00876.x PMID: 8173483

Woo, H. L. (2009). Designing multimedia learning environments using animated pedagogical agents: Factors and issues. *Journal of Computer Assisted Learning*, 25(3), 203–218. DOI: 10.1111/j.1365-2729.2008.00299.x

Xefteris, S., Palaigeorgiou, G., & Tsorbari, A. (2019). A Learning Environment for Geography and History Using Mixed Reality, Tangible Interfaces and Educational Robotics. In Auer, M., & Tsiatsos, T. (Eds.), *The Challenges of the Digital Transformation in Education. ICL 2018. Advances in Intelligent Systems and Computing* (Vol. 917). Springer. DOI: 10.1007/978-3-030-11935-5_11

Xia, X. (2020). Learning behavior mining and decision recommendation based on association rules in interactive learning environment. *Interactive Learning Environments*, 1–16. DOI: 10.1080/10494820.2020.1799028

Xiuqin, H., Huimin, Z., Mengchen, L., Jinan, W., Ying, Z., & Ran, T. (2010). Mental health, personality, and parental rearing styles of adolescents with Internet addiction disorder. *Cyberpsychology, Behavior, and Social Networking*, 13(4), 401–406. DOI: 10.1089/cyber.2009.0222 PMID: 20712498

Yilmaz, R., & Kilic-Cakmak, E. (2012). Educational interface agents as social models to influence learner achievement, attitude and retention of learning. *Computers & Education*, 59(2), 828–838. DOI: 10.1016/j.compedu.2012.03.020

Younes, F., Halawi, G., Jabbour, H., El Osta, N., Karam, L., Hajj, A., & Rabbaa Khabbaz, L. (2016). Internet addiction and relationships with insomnia, anxiety, depression, stress and self-esteem in university students: A cross-sectional designed study. *PLoS One*, 11(9), e0161126. DOI: 10.1371/journal.pone.0161126 PMID: 27618306

Young, K. S. (1999). Internet addiction: Evaluation and treatment. *BMJ (Clinical Research Ed.)*, 319(Suppl S4), 9910351. Advance online publication. DOI: 10.1136/sbmj.9910351

Zheng, L. (2016). The effectiveness of self-regulated learning scaffolds on academic performance in computer-based learning environments: A meta-analysis. *Asia Pacific Education Review*, 17(2), 187–202. DOI: 10.1007/s12564-016-9426-9

Chapter 15
The Role of Psychodrama in the Prevention of Cyberbullying:
School Psychologists' Perspective

Konstantinos Mastrothanasis
https://orcid.org/0000-0002-8703-9607
National and Kapodistrian University of Athens, Greece

Maria Kladaki
University of Aegean, Greece

Alexia Andreopoulou
General Hospital of Kozani, Mamatsio, Greece

ABSTRACT

The study investigates the effectiveness of psychodrama as an intervention method for preventing cyberbullying in schools. Its aim is to highlight the need for new approaches that address the social and emotional needs of students, as traditional prevention methods often fail to fully address the complexity of cyberbullying. Psychodrama, a therapeutic approach that uses drama and role-playing, is identified as an effective tool for promoting empathy, self-awareness, and emotional expression among students. Through a series of semi-structured interviews with school psychologists, the chapter examines their views on psychodrama, the techniques they consider most effective, and the obstacles they experience in implementing it for cyberbullying prevention. The findings reveal that psychodrama helps make schools safer and more supportive and that psychologists need regular training and support to use it well.

INTRODUCTION

Cyberbullying constitutes an important problem that affects students' mental health, academic performance, and social interactions in a negative way (Alkhayat, 2023; Bali et al., 2023; Touloupis & Athanasiades, 2022a). It is a type of bullying that happens through electronic devices, and it uses technology to harass, intimidate, or hurt individuals or groups (Campbell & Bauman, 2017; Shapiro, 2022; Touloupis et al., 2024). Since bullying go from face-to-face forms to online spaces, the need for

DOI: 10.4018/979-8-3693-4191-9.ch015

prevention strategies becomes even more important (Andreou et al., 2022; Faccio et al., 2014; Touloupis, 2024; Touloupis & Campbell, 2024; Vassou et al., 2017). Moreover, traditional strategies against bullying do not involve the experiences and emotional needs of students, even though they should (Gaffney et al., 2021), since using different strategies according to the needs of each student is very important for addressing cyberbullying (Diamanduros et al., 2008).

Psychodrama is a method that uses drama techniques to help students through potential problems they face, to better express their feelings, to improve their behaviour and relationships (Orkibi et al., 2023; Orkibi & Feniger-Schaal, 2019), as well as a method against cyberbullying (Joronen et al., 2012; Lyngstad et al., 2022; Orkibi et al., 2023). It is considered effective, since it provides ways for students to interact with other ones properly (Howie & Bagnall, 2015, 2020; Mavroudis & Bournelli, 2016; Ulusoy et al., 2023; Yosep et al., 2023). School psychologists use it as a supporting strategy against cyberbullying, since it is personalized according to the needs of each student that encounters it.

The current study aims to test how psychodrama prevents cyberbullying. To do so, the opinions of school psychologists who have used it in schools are investigated. The paper is structured as follows: in Section 1, a literature review on cyberbullying and existing prevention programs in a school context is presented. Section 2 analyzes the use of applied theatre forms in interventions for cyberbullying prevention, citing relevant examples from various countries. Section 3 introduces psychodrama as an expression of applied theatre, analyzing its basic principles, the phases of therapeutic process and the techniques used. Section 4 refers to the purpose and method of the research, while section 5 presents the study results. Finally, sections 6-7 discuss the findings and present the conclusions, highlighting the need for future research and the development of training programs that incorporate psychodramatic approaches for cyberbullying prevention.

Cyberbullying as an Online Risk

Cyberbullying is defined as the repeated infliction of harm on an individual or a group of individuals through digital means, which includes actions such as insults and threats. This form of bullying differs from traditional bullying due to its digital nature, which often allows perpetrators to remain anonymous and reach a wider audience (Shapiro, 2022; Touloupis, 2024; Touloupis & Athanasiades, 2022a, 2022b).

Recently, the prevalence rates of cyberbullying have increased, although they remain lower compared to traditional bullying. According to a critical review and meta-analysis of research on cyberbullying among young people by Kowalski and colleagues (2014), there are varying degrees of prevalence, which are characterized as high and range between 10-40%.

Cyberbullying is not just a recent social phenomenon, but also a threat that affects its victims both psychologically and socially. Since messages and photos of the internet can remain accessible for long periods of time, its harmful potential is amplified. This causes emotional exhaustion and upheaval to victims, who have to live again and again their traumatic experience every time the offending material is further disseminated or remains visible.

Considering cyberbullying an inherent risk in the use of the internet, we can be better prepared to deal with and mitigate its effects. The continuous development of technology creates new spaces and platforms where cyberbullying can occur, making it more difficult to detect and deal with it, despite efforts to develop technological tools to combat it (Teng et al., 2024).

The school has to adapt and adopt prevention strategies, taking into account both the psychosocial consequences and the technological infrastructures which allow the phenomenon to persist. Having a better understanding of cyberbullying as one of the main dangers of the internet, the educational community can better prepare students to safely navigate the digital world and reduce the impact of this phenomenon.

School Prevention Programs for Cyberbullying

The effects of cyberbullying on mental health and development of young people are significant. A review of the existing literature reveals the complex interplay of psychosocial risk factors associated with cyberbullying, including its potential to trigger psychiatric and psychosomatic problems in adolescents (Sourander et al., 2010). Victims may experience long-term mental health problems, risks of self-harm, and in some cases, suicidal tendencies (Alkhayat, 2023; Deol & Lashai, 2022). These consequences highlight the urgent need for preventive measures and interventions that will ensure the well-being of adolescents and young people, with schools playing an important role in preventing cyberbullying among students using various strategies. One of the key approaches is the development and implementation of comprehensive anti-bullying policies that define cyberbullying, establish reporting procedures, and involve stakeholders in the development of policies (Ganca & Kyobe, 2023). Furthermore, encouraging positive behavior from bystanders and training teachers on cyberbullying are essential elements for effectively addressing the problem (Hou, 2023).

Many school-based cyberbullying prevention programs have been developed on this basis and evaluated for their effectiveness. An example of a prevention program is UPRIGHT, which was developed to build resilience and promote the mental well-being of adolescents, or the CREEP program designed to support schools in early detection of cyberbullying incidents and educate students on managing such behaviors (Gabrielli et al., 2021). Another effective prevention program is the TABBY program, which was developed to increase the self-esteem of elementary school students with and without special educational needs (Touloupis & Athanasiades, 2022b).

In most implemented programs, the aim is to strengthen certain basic psychological functions such as self-esteem, self-awareness, and resilience to prevent cyberbullying, as they have been linked to reducing the occurrence and intensity of such phenomena (Chamizo-Nieto et al., 2024; Chen et al., 2022; Chicote-Beato et al., 2024; Gaffney et al., 2021). Teachers and school psychologists play an important role in developing and implementing effective prevention programs within the school environment, as they can promote awareness, assess the prevalence and severity of the problem within the school, and develop interventions for the entire school community (Burlet & Panahon, 2022; Diamanduros et al., 2008; Grădinariu & Diac, 2023; Moreno & Vaillancourt, 2017).

Do Drama and Theatre matter in cyberbulling prevention programs?

Prevention programs against cyberbullying that use drama and theatre as intervention methods have been deemed effective in raising awareness and understanding of bullying (Elpus & Carter, 2016; Goodwin et al., 2019; Gourd & Gourd, 2011; Grădinariu & Diac, 2023; Lambert et al., 2023; Lyngstad et al., 2022; Mavroudis & Bournelli, 2016; O'Toole & Burton, 2005; Shiakou & Piki, 2020; Yan et al., 2019). Arts and theatre contribute to awareness and understanding (Asimidou et al., 2021; Kladaki & Mastrothanasis, 2022; Mastrothanasis et al., 2024), allowing participants to examine conflict from different perspectives (Berceanu et al., 2020; Folostina et al., 2015; Karaosmanoğlu, 2024), develop empathy (Goldstein, 2024; Lenakakis & Koltsida, 2017; Mastrothanasis, Kladaki, et al., 2023), engage with humanitarian values (Grammatas et al., 2023; Mastrothanasis & Grammatas, 2022) and gain a deeper understanding of other's feelings and experiences (Mastrothanasis & Kladaki, 2020; Papakosta et al., 2020; Vasiou et al., 2023).

Over in Australia, research showed that the Friendly Schools Program, which involved a combination of theatre activities and role-playing with skills training, led to a reduction in the numbers of incidents of bullying (Cross et al., 2011). In Australia, the Acting against Bullying program also produced large effects on increasing awareness about bullying and decreasing its prevalence through drama and theatre techniques incidents (Burton & O'Toole, 2009). In Australia, the Brisbane DRACON program had been using drama to help students understand and manage conflicts and incidents of bullying in their schools (O'Toole & Burton, 2005). Through dramatic techniques and peer teaching, students were trained to recognize the causes of conflicts and manage them effectively. The program achieved a significant reduction in bullying incidents and helped resolve conflicts, especially in multicultural schools, where drama was used as a tool to cultivate understanding and acceptance of different cultures. The Dare to Care: Bully Proofing Tour School Program involved in discussions and skits and role-playing games in Canada (Beran & Tutty, 2002). An assessment of the program showed a marked reduction in bullying incidents. In Ireland, the Bullying Prevention Pack, which includes role-playing games, showed a 53% reduction in victimization and increased students' awareness of the nature and consequences of bullying and boosted the confidence and self-esteem of those who were victims (Donohoe, 2016; Donohoe & O'Sullivan, 2015). Research by Goodwin et al. (2019) and Lyngstad et al. (2022) indicated that students view theatre as an engaging medium for realistically representing the dynamics of bullying, which enhances their understanding of it's complex aspects. However, they noted the need for consistent and ongoing efforts within schools to maintain the benefits.

Research highlights that the integration of such programs into a broader strategy involving teachers, parents, and the wider school community is significant for their success (Grădinariu & Diac, 2023; Stives et al., 2021). Studies suggest that drama and theatre programs can promote emotional intelligence and reduce bullying incidents when implemented consistently and continuously (Goodwin et al., 2019; Gourd & Gourd, 2011; Joronen et al., 2011; Qiao et al., 2023; Roberts et al., 2017; White et al., 2019). Simultaneously, there is a gap in the literature regarding the use of these methods to the prevention of cyberbullying (Froeschle Hicks et al., 2016). Although drama techniques, role-playing games and theatre methods can raise awareness and promote empathy, their effectiveness in the context of cyberbullying has not yet been thoroughly evaluated, and their implementation remains limited (Goodwin et al., 2019; Mavroudis & Bournelli, 2016). A related empowerment program in Turkey used online drama workshops to address the issue of cyberbullying among young people aged 12 to 14 (Karaosmanoğlu, 2024). Participants used improvisation and other dramatic techniques through Web 2.0 tools, examining cyberbullying from different perspectives. The evaluation of the effectiveness of the program demonstrated that these techniques help to understand the phenomenon, increasing empathy and offering an experiential way to express emotions and find solutions to reduce internet risk.

Froeschle Hicks et al. (2016) suggests that incorporating drama and its techniques can foster empathy and thus reduce aggressive behaviors among youth involved in cyberbullying. Theatre and drama can contribute to the reduction of online dangers and risks through the development of empathy, psychosocial empowerment and understanding (Karaosmanoğlu, 2024). Prevention programmes that incorporate theatrical activities allow participants to explore the emotions of others and understand the impact of their actions in a safe, symbolic environment (Shiakou & Piki, 2020). This not only enhances empathy, but also helps reduce aggressive behaviours and conflicts in the digital environment.

Psychodrama and School Prevention Applications

Psychodrama, a form of group psychotherapy developed by psychiatrist Jacob Levy Moreno, is a method based on applied theatre for exploring individuals' psyches through dramatization (Gonzalez, 2023; Orkibi & Feniger-Schaal, 2019). In this process, participants reenact events from their lives, providing a deeper understanding of their emotions, thoughts, and coping mechanisms (Kende, 2017). Psychodrama encourages spontaneity, action and creativity, essential elements for a healthy life according to Moreno, functioning cathartically and educationally (El-Mazahy, 2023; Şimşek et al., 2019; Zaragas, 2021).

The main contributors of psychodrama include the protagonist, the psychodramatist, the auxiliary egos, the audience, and the stage. The protagonist represents the individual's experience, the psychodramatist directs and guides the session, while the auxiliary egos support the enactment by playing roles from the protagonist's environment. The stage is the space where the session takes place, allowing the protagonist to fully express themselves.

The process of psychodrama involves three distinct phases, namely the warm-up, the psychodramatic enactment, and the sharing phase. The warm-up phase helps to boost spontaneity and strengthen group cohesion. During the enactment, the protagonist expresses their emotions through action, supported by auxiliary egos, while various psychodramatic techniques are implemented. Among the basic techniques used in psychodrama are the double and the mirroring techniques. The double acts as the protagonist to observe their own behaviour through another person. Other important techniques include role reversal and role-plays, where individuals explore the roles of others, thereby enhancing empathy and understanding. Finally, during the sharing phase, participants discuss their personal experiences, which enhances individual introspection and understanding.

In educational and counseling settings, psychodrama for adolescents offers advantages for addressing and preventing bullying. This approach helps in solving problems, improving interpersonal relationships, and increasing self-awareness. Dramatizing personal and relational issues through guided role-play, have shown efficacy in reducing social anxiety and improving emotional regulation (Chang et al., 2022; Goldstein, 2009; Goldstein & Bloom, 2011; Hadley et al., 2019; Mastrothanasis, Zervoudakis, et al., 2023; McDonald et al., 2020; Orkibi & Feniger-Schaal, 2019). Groups can consist of individuals of the same age or with common issues, providing a safe environment for expression and seeking solutions, allowing for emotional expression, acquiring new knowledge, and practicing new behavioural patterns (Bucharová et al., 2020; El-Mazahy, 2023).

In an educational setting, school psychologists can implement psychodrama to prevent and address important issues like cyberbullying, as well as to enhance resilience and students' emotional well-being. Psychodrama has been used effectively in suicide prevention programs for high school and middle school students and has also used for various issues such as eating disorders, substance abuse, risky behaviors, academic difficulties, and violence prevention (Park et al., 2019; Park & Kim, 2022; Şimşek et al., 2019). Particularly encouraging, are the results of using psychodrama in reducing symptoms of post-traumatic stress disorder in elementary school students living in earthquake-affected areas (Hamidi & Sobhani Tabar, 2021). Psychodramatic techniques have been applied to boost students' self-efficacy too (Permana & Suwarjo, 2022). Furthermore, psychodrama has been applied in high schools and universities to improve teaching and learning processes and address student's social and psychological needs (Maya

& Maraver, 2020; Zaragas, 2021). Especially for women who have experienced abuse, psychodrama has been found to be an effective method for enhancing resilience and promoting adaptive strategies (Bucuţă et al., 2018). Moreover, its implementation in various healthcare settings has helped support professionals and patient care outcomes (Testoni et al., 2020).

The effectiveness of psychodrama has been explored in group therapy sessions, showing its potential to improve feelings of loneliness and anxiety among psychiatric patients (Ron, 2018). Additionally, it has been examined as an intervention to reduce loneliness, particularly in the context of health crises, such as the COVID-19 pandemic (Usakli, 2021).

Despite these positive indications, there is a need for further investigation into the effectiveness of psychodrama as an intervention method for the prevention of cyberbullying, considering the perspectives of school psychologists who have used psychodrama in an educational setting. Although psychodrama and theater techniques are used to prevent and deal with bullying at a more general level, the same methods can be adapted to target specific issues related to cyberbullying (Karaosmanoğlu, 2024; Shiakou & Piki, 2020; White et al., 2019). Using drama allows students to act out situations and examine the emotions of those involved, which is equally effective in the prevention and understanding of cyberattacks. Thus, this intervention, while focusing on tackling bullying in general, can also contribute to the prevention of cyberbullying through the development of empathy and conflict management in the digital environment.

Aim and Research Questions of the Study

The aim of the present study is twofold. On the one hand, to investigate the effectiveness of psychodrama as an intervention method for preventing cyberbullying and on the other hand, to clarify how this method can be effectively integrated into school practice, from the perspective of school psychologists. School psychologists are considered as main contributors to the prevention, assessment, and intervention in cases of cyberbullying, highlighting the importance of dealing with behaviours associated with cyberbullying both at individual and at a class level (Burlet & Panahon, 2022). They can play a vital role in overcoming the barriers that hinder effective strategies to prevent cyberbullying at schools (Burlet & Panahon, 2022; Diamanduros et al., 2008). Furthermore, exploring the perceptions of school psychologists is crucial, as, according to the Theory of Planned Behavior (Ajzen, 1991), their attitudes and beliefs shape their intentions, which in turn influence their actions and the implementation of practices. Given their role in applying prevention programs in schools, understanding their perceptions is key, as these directly impact the effectiveness of their interventions (Ajzen, 2011).

Based on the above purpose, the following research questions are formulated:

(1) How do school psychologists assess the importance of preventing cyberbullying in the school environment?
(2) To what extent are school psychologists familiar with psychodrama, and how do they use it in their practice?
(3) Which psychodrama techniques prove to be most effective for developing empathy and conflict management skills among students in the prevention of cyberbullying?
(4) What are the barriers to implementing psychodrama in schools, and what strategies do school psychologists recommend for overcoming them in the prevention of cyberbullying?

METHOD

Participants

A total of 9 Greek school psychologists, selected through public invitation by the research team, participated in this study. Due to the fact that participants needed to have certain characteristics according to the criteria that had been set, in order for an individual to be included in the research, the sampling focused on the composition of homogeneous samples (Mertler, 2018). Criteria for one's participation in it were the following: a) to work as school psychologists in primary or secondary education and b) to be familiar or have used psychodrama as a psychotherapeutic method.

Among the 9 participants, 6 (67%) were females and 3 (33%) were males, with a mean work experience as school psychologists of 6.56 years (standard deviation= 5.39 years), and a mean overall work experience in the field of psychology of 16.33 years (standard deviation= 5.61 years). Regarding the age distribution of participants, 56% (N=5) belonged to the 40-49 age group and 22% (N=2) to the age group > 50.

Regarding the educational level of the participants, 67% (N=6) held a master's degree, 22% (N=2) held a doctorate, and 11% (N=1) did not have any additional degree beyond the basic one. Additionally, 67% (N=6) had some additional training or education in dealing with issues of cyber bullying or other type of bullying.

Research design

The data of the present study were collected using semi-structured interviews with school psychologists, based on the principles of phenomenology. This type of interview was chosen because it allows for the adaptation of questions according to the feedback of the respondents and the possibility to examine specific topics in a deeper way, offering flexibility (Knott et al., 2022).

The semi-structured interviews used a predetermined guide of questions as a basis, in order to investigate the appropriate thematic sections which are related to the importance of cyberbullying prevention, the use of psychodrama as a therapeutic method and the barriers that may arise during its implementation in schools.

The interviews were conducted from distance using Skype, lasted from 15 to 25 minutes and were recorded. After this, the audio files were transcribed word to word, using Mishler's (1991) transcription guidelines, to ensure that the content is accurate and complete, taking also into consideration non-verbal elements such as intonation and speech rate.

Data analysis began by importing the transcribed dialogues into ATLAS.ti software. The constant comparison approach guided the electronic coding of the verbal data, with the aim of highlighting and saturating categories. The coding followed three phases.

During the open coding phase, the data were explored to identify and highlight significant words or phrases, which signalled key concepts and led to the creation of initial codes. This was followed by axial coding, where relevant codes were combined to create more conceptually complex categories, allowing conceptual networks to be created between them. The process was repeated until theoretical saturation of the categories was achieved.

The final phase of selective coding involved the integration and concise interpretation of categories into a unified thematic framework. During this phase, the second researcher independently analysed the data, identifying and grouping into higher-level systems. The agreement between the two researchers regarding the allocation of codes to categories was recorded as high, with a Fleiss Kappa coefficient >0.90, providing a significant indicator of the reliability of the coding process (Fleiss, 1971).

This coding methodology allowed the emergence of the core category "Psychodrama and prevention of cyberbullying", which incorporated the main thematic structures of the interviews. The goal of the analysis was to provide a documented narrative of the research data, offering a deep and coherent understanding of the experiences and perspectives of the participants.

The above procedures resulted in 147 reports classified in 37 codes, which belong to 10 low-order categories and correspondingly to 3 high-order categories. The main higher-order category "Psychodrama and cyberbullying prevention" emerged through the process of selective coding and formed the core upon which the interpretive framework, of how all higher-order categories were interconnected, was based. The ultimate goal of this process was informed narrative and the emergence of a fundamental meaning from the research data.

Finally, it is noted that the quantification of the reports, topics and categories of low and high order followed, in order to allow the calculation of the frequencies of occurrence and the prevalence rates of the above.

Ethical Statement

The present study was conducted in accordance with ethical standards and guidelines established for the protection of participants. All school psychologists who participated in the research were fully informed about the aim and methodology of the study and gave their consent to participate. Personal data and information collected were maintained with strict confidentiality and used solely for the purposes of the research. This research was designed in accordance with the ethical principles of the Declaration of Helsinki, respecting the dignity, rights and well-being of the participants and received approval by the Institute of Educational Policy of the Greek Ministry of Education.

RESULTS

The qualitative analysis of the data revealed three high-order categories that refer to: a) the perceptions related to the importance of cyberbullying prevention in the school environment, b) the use of psychodrama as a method of preventing and empowering students against cyberbullying, and c) the barriers and proposals for the effective implementation of psychodrama in the school community.

Perceptions Related to the Importance of Cyberbullying Prevention.

Regarding the perceptions of school psychologists, concerning the importance they attribute to cyberbullying prevention in schools, two main thematic categories emerged through thematic analysis of the responses: a) the importance of prevention and b) the prevention techniques, in total 27 codes (see Table 1).

Table 1. Categories, codes, frequencies (N), and percentage frequences (N%) of references regarding the importance of cyberbullying prevention in the school environment.

Categories	Codes	N	N%	Code explanation
Prevention importance	Safe school environment	7	47%	Cyberbullying prevention contributes to creating a safe environment for students.
	Education and awareness	5	33%	There is an emphasis on the need for educating students about the consequences of cyberbullying.
	Mental health of students	3	20%	Preventing cyberbullying affects positively the mental health of students.
Prevention techniques	Workshops and seminars	6	50%	Workshops and seminars as tools to strengthen cyberbullying prevention.
	Group activities	4	33%	Group activities promoting empathy and social solidarity.
	Drama techniques	2	17%	Using drama techniques to help students explore cyberbullying situations from various perspectives.

In the category "prevention importance", three codes were identified. The code "safe school environment", with the most references from participants, refers to the necessity of prevention to create a safe and supportive atmosphere in the school environment, where students are not afraid to express themselves or participate in school activities (N=7.47%). One participant emphasized: "*Preventing cyberbullying is crucial for creating a safe and supportive school environment*" (participant 2). Secondly, the code "education and awareness" highlights the need for informing and educating students about the consequences and management tactics of cyberbullying (N = 5, 33%). Another participant pointed: "*We aim to educate students about the consequences of cyberbullying and equip them with necessary skills to deal and avoid it*" (participant 2). Thirdly, the code "psychological well-being" underscores the importance of cyberbullying prevention for students' mental health, as this form of bullying can have deep and long-lasting effects on their psychological well-being (N=3,20%). One participant characteristically said: "*This form of bullying can have long-term effects on their psychological well-being*" (participant 9).

Continuing with the category "prevention techniques", various techniques were mentioned that could be utilized for preventing cyberbullying. The majority of participants mentioned the implementation of awareness-raising workshops and seminars on cyberbullying prevention (N=6,50%), as well as group activities that could be conducted in this direction (N=4,33%), to enhance empathy, critical thinking, and social solidarity among students. As one participant stated:

> For the prevention of cyberbullying, we occasionally organize workshops on emotional awareness, seminars on internet safety, and discussions within the group or various group activities. Our goal is to develop empathy and strengthen conflict resolution skills through experiential engagement… (participant 5).

Lastly, the use of dramatic and theatrical techniques is mentioned as methodologies for exploring and processing emotions and situations (N = 2, 17%), as they provide the necessary safety for approaching sensitive issues. Regarding this, one of the participants said: "*I use theatre techniques to approach sensitive issues like this one*" (participant 1).

Perceptions Regarding the Utilization of Psychodrama in Cyberbullying Prevention

Regarding the perceptions of school psychologists on the utilization of psychodrama in cyberbullying prevention, four main thematic categories emerged, which encompassed: a) their familiarity with psychodrama, b) the importance they attribute to it for cyberbullying prevention, c) the techniques of psychodrama and the psychodramatic approaches that can be utilized in this direction, and d) the approaches that can be used complementary to optimise the efficiency of the method in cyberbullying prevention, through a total of 91 codes (see Table 2).

Table 2. Categories, codes, frequencies (N), and percentage frequencies (N%) regarding the utilization of psychodrama in the prevention of cyberbullying

Category	Codes	N	N%	Code description
Familiarization with psychodrama as a form of psychotherapy	Utilization in practice	7	78%	Participants actively utilizing psychodrama in their work
	Basic knowledge	2	22%	Participants with basic knowledge of psychodrama
The significance of psychodrama in the prevention of cyberbullying	Importance of approach	9	26%	The participants consider the approach of psychodrama in the prevention of cyberbullying to be significant
	Empathy	8	23%	It develops the empathy of the participants
	Sensitization	4	11%	It promotes sensitization through “safe” experiential situations.
	Self-awareness	3	9%	Promotes Self-Awareness
	Experience	3	9%	It promotes understanding of relationship dynamics through experience
	Emotional management	2	6%	It promotes the management and expression of emotions
	Self-esteem	2	6%	It contributes to the development of self-esteem
	Intrapersonal conflicts	2	6%	It promotes the management of intrapersonal conflicts
	Reservations	2	6%	Expression of reservations regarding utilization in a school setting or preferences for alternative approaches
Psychodrama techniques and approaches	Role reversal	10	26%	The adoption of opposite roles for understanding the others’ emotions
	Mirroring	9	23%	Utilization of the technique for self-awareness.
	Role-play	8	21%	Participatory enactment for empathy
	Drama scenarios	5	13%	The utilization of dramatic scenarios depicting cyberbullying
	Double	4	10%	Activity to enhance understanding of multiple perspectives
	Reflection	2	5%	Analysis of the role-related thoughts and feelings
	Monodrama	1	3%	Utilization of monodrama
Supplementary approaches	Information on safe internet usage	5	63%	Information on safe internet use as a complement to psychodramatic sessions
	Technological integration	2	25%	The use of technology is recommended to enhance the psychodramatic approach
	Psychological support	1	13%	The complementary utilization of individual psychological support sessions is recommended

Initially, in the category "Familiarization with psychodrama as a form of therapy", two main codes emerged. The content and the absolute frequency of references to the code "utilization in practice" (N=7,78%) indicate that most participants actively use psychodrama in their work, highlighting its value as a therapeutic tool. Regarding this, one participant noted: "*I am familiar with psychodrama and have extensively used it in my practice*" (participant 4). The code "basic knowledge" (N = 2, 22%) reflects the general knowledge that some participants have about psychodrama ("*I only know the basic principles of psychodrama, but I am looking for opportunities to utilize it more...*" participant 9).

Regarding the category "The importance of psychodrama in cyberbullying prevention", it was revealed that psychodrama is a significant approach in cyberbullying prevention (N=9,26%) ("*What excites me about psychodrama is its ability to move children from simple discussions to real, experiential situations*", participant 8). According to the school psychologists, its implementation primarily facilitates the development of empathy (N=8,23%) ("*...in its value as a tool for developing empathy...*", participant 4). It also promotes awareness through "safe" experimental situations (N=4,11%), fosters self-awareness (N=3,9%), and facilitates emotion management /expression (N=2,6%) ("*...encourages participants to express and process their emotions through theatrical play*", participant 7). With 3 mentions (9%), its ability to enhance the self-esteem of participants, as well as their understanding of relationship dynamics through dramatic experience, was noted. Only 2 mentions (6%) expressed some reservations about its use in the school context, preferring other approaches in cyberbullying prevention ("*Although psychodrama may have its place in promoting empathy, I am not convinced it is the best approach for cyberbullying prevention given the tome we have available. I prefer more targeted educational approaches*" participant 3). Regarding psychodramatic techniques and action methods that can facilitate cyberbullying prevention, the technique of role reversal was highly mentioned (N=10,26%), focusing on assuming opposite roles to understand the feelings of others. The mirroring technique (N=9,23%), as well as the approach of role-play as a form of participatory representation to enhance self-perception and empathy among students. As one participant mentions:

> *The techniques of role reversal and mirroring are two of my favourite tools in psychodrama. In general, anything related to role-playing because it enhances understanding and empathy, which is crucial for addressing cyberbullying, especially in high school where things have gotten out of hand...* (participant 8).

Other useful and effective techniques mentioned include the Double (N=4,10%), the use of drama scenarios related to cyberbullying issues (N=2,5%) and monodrama (N=1,3%). Finally, school psychologists recommend other important strategies that complement psychodramatic sessions, such as the use of informational sessions on safe internet use (N=5,63%), the use of technological tools in prevention (N=2.25%, "*...utilization of virtual educational games...*", participant 1), and the use of individual psychological support sessions (N=1,13%), in order to provide a comprehensive prevention program.

Obstacles and Proposals for the Implementation of Psychodrama in the School Community

Regarding the reported obstacles and proposals made by school psychologists for the implementation of psychodrama in the school community, four main thematic categories were identified: a) perceived difficulties in implementing psychodrama in the school community, b) proposed solutions and actions to address the difficulties of utilizing psychodrama in the school community, c) the need for training, d) strategies to enhance interdisciplinary collaboration in implementing cyberbullying prevention programs, through a total of 29 codes (see Table 3).

Table 3. Categories, codes, frequencies (N), and percentage frequencies (N=%) references related to obstacles and proposals in the implementation of psychodrama in the school community.

Category	Code	N	N%	Description
Obstacles	Limited time	4	40%	The work of psychologists in many schools makes implementation difficult.
	Lack of experience	2	20%	The inexperience in psychologists in psychodrama is considered a significant obstacle.
	Community resistance	2	20%	Resistance from the school community.
	Challenges in implementation within large groups	1	10%	Issues with implementing psychodrama in large groups.
	Difficulty in management	1	10%	Difficulty managing sensitive topics in a school environment.
Suggestions	Workshops	7	88%	Organizing workshops for the training and information of educators and parents
	Information sessions	1	12%	Organizing informative seminars to address resource shortages of resistance.
Training needs	Necessary	9	100%	The expressed need for continuous training of school psychologists in psychodrama.
Collaboration	Educational activities	1	50%	Training activities to strengthen collaboration between psychologists, educators, and parents.
	Network formation	1	50%	Creation of support networks among stakeholders

In the category of "obstacles" the most common obstacle mentioned regarding the implementation of psychodrama interventions for the prevention of cyberbullying in the school community is the limited time due to the work of psychologists in many schools (N = 4, 40%). As characteristically mentioned by one of the participants "*My constant movement between several schools makes it difficult to initiate and continue long-term psychodrama interventions. Psychodrama requires a constant presence and development of relationship*", participant 9). Furthermore, important obstacles include the lack of experience of psychologists (N = 2, 20%) in psychodrama ("*...inexperience of the psychologist*", participant 3), the possible resistance from the school community (N = 2, 20%), the difficulties arising from applying psychodrama in multi-member student groups (N = 1, 10%) and difficulties arising from the management of sensitive issues in the school environment (N = 1, 10%).

Regarding the suggestions of school psychologists, the most frequent suggestion concerns the organization of workshops for teachers and parents in schools (N = 7, 88%) that offer an educational framework for integrating psychodrama into the daily routine of schools. Information days and cooperation with organisms are also suggested as strategies to strengthen cyberbullying prevention programs (N = 1, 12%), with all research participants agreeing on the need for continuous training in psychodramatic approaches (N = 9, 100%). Finally, the development of interdisciplinary collaboration networks with regular meetings (N = 1, 50%) and supportive practices among teachers, psychologists, parents and other professionals (N = 1, 50%) emerges as a priority strategy ("*Collaboration can be strengthened through the organization of common workshops, sharing experiences and practices...*", participant 2).

DISCUSSION

The present study examined the perceptions of school psychologists on the effectiveness of psychodrama in preventing cyberbullying, as well as the barriers and strategies they may use to integrate it into school practice. The results highlight important aspects related to supporting students' psychological resilience and social empathy through a psychodramatic approach.

The views of school psychologists about the importance of cyberbullying prevention are important and can contribute to a great extent in the assessment and development of preventive programs in schools. According Diamanduros et al (2008), school psychologists can play an important role in the early detection and intervention of bullying behaviors. The findings also support that the contribution of psychodrama is important in creating a safe and supportive school environment, where students express themselves without any hesitations and participate in school life in an active way. School psychologists highlight the value of psychodrama and support that it is a powerful tool that can promote understanding, develop empathy among students and helps resolving interpersonal conflicts (Howie & Bagnall, 2015, 2020; Orkibi et al., 2023).

Additionally, it is important to recognize cyberbullying as an inherent risk of internet use. The increasing use of online platforms by students makes cyberbullying a constant threat to their mental and emotional health. Incorporating psychodrama into prevention strategies can help reduce the risks associated with online behavior. Using techniques such as role reversal and reflection, students can gain a better understanding of the effects of cyberbullying and develop the skills needed to safely navigate in the digital world.

Using psychodrama techniques assists developing empathy and skills related to conflict management within the school community, evidencing the advantages for the prevention and management of cyberbullying. More specifically, the technique of role reversal is one of the most powerful methods of psychodrama for preventing cyberbullying (Şimşek et al., 2019). When this technique is used, students are asked to take on the roles of other people which helps them have a deeper understanding of the thoughts, feelings, and behaviors of others, increasing empathy and reducing the possibility of aggressive or deviant behaviors (Joronen et al., 2012). The mirroring technique plays also an important role in developing self-awareness and self-esteem, as it allows student to see themselves through the eyes of others, offering a safe place for self-criticism and reflection (Blatner, 1996; Kende, 2017; Shutenko et al., 2020; Wan, 2023). Role-playing and drama games give students the opportunity to explore and process social situations in a controlled environment, allowing them to discuss and analyse the consequences of different actions and behaviors (Lyngstad et al., 2022; Mastrothanasis, Kladaki, et al., 2023).

The potential of psychodrama to promote empathy and conflict resolution in the school setting is also important for internet safety. By enhancing empathy, students can develop a more self-aware and responsible attitude towards their online behavior, which can help reduce aggressive and delinquent behaviors in cyberspace. Psychodrama, as a prevention tool, is not limited only to the traditional form of bullying, but can also be adapted to address the difficulties associated with cyberbullying, making it an art-based tool which promotes internet safety.

Regarding the familiarity of school psychologists with psychodrama, participants confirmed that the need for further training is necessary, although the majority of them were familiar of or had already used psychodrama as a psychotherapeutic method. This element highlights the importance of continuous professional training in this method of psychotherapy, confirming the relevant literature that emphasizes the need for lifelong training and professional development for school psychologists (Diamanduros et al., 2008; Gonzalez, 2023).

The main obstacles that school psychologist encounter in implementing psychodrama in a school setting include limited availability of time, lack of experience, and possible resistance from some members of the community. The limited availability of time is a broader issue of school psychologists' workload. The school is a space where there are multiple needs and demands and the time for implementing specialized programs, such as psychodrama, is often limited (Moreno & Vaillancourt, 2017). Also, the lack of experience in psychodrama indicates that there is a gap in school psychologists' educational training and ongoing professional development (Diamanduros et al., 2008). Finally, resistance from community members may reflect hesitations or misunderstandings about the methods and goals of psychodrama. The proposals that have emerged are related to organizing workshops, conferences and interdisciplinary collaborations and aim to overcome these barriers, facilitating the integration of psychodrama into daily school practice (Grădinariu & Diac, 2023). These actions can help the educational community members to understand the value of psychodrama and can reduce resistance by providing the practical skills required for its implementation. Collaborations with organizations/universities that are specialized in psychodrama can provide the necessary support and expertise for its implementation at the school level (Mahatme et al., 2020; Permana & Suwarjo, 2022).

CONCLUSION

The present study examined the role of psychodrama in the prevention of cyberbullying, highlights the practical significance and the supportive dynamics of this art-based approach. Research findings support that psychodrama can play an important role in strengthening students by increasing levels of empathy, social solidarity, and self-awareness (Orkibi et al., 2023; Orkibi & Feniger-Schaal, 2019; Şimşek et al., 2019). Due to its experiential and applied nature, psychodrama allows students to explore and express their emotions in a safe environment, improving their ability to manage interpersonal conflicts and their understanding of human dynamics (Howie & Bagnall, 2015).

Moreover, this study highlights the importance of incorporating psychodrama as a means of reducing the risks associated with the use of the internet. By recognizing cyberbullying as an inherent risk of the internet, psychodrama provides students with the necessary tools to manage cyber threats with greater empathy and responsibility.

Furthermore, research suggests that psychodrama, as a more art-based participatory approach can be effectively incorporated into cyberbullying prevention programs, in school settings (El-Mazahy, 2023; Joronen et al., 2012). It has the ability to incorporate direct experiences using role-playing and dramatic enactments helps students analyze and perceive both the bully's and the victim's behavior. Thus, it provides the way to have a deeper understanding of cyberbullying and develop effective strategies to reduce it (Lyngstad et al., 2022; Orkibi & Feniger-Schaal, 2019).

The findings of this study highlight the need for non-traditional intervention methods that incorporate active, applied and experiential elements that help children develop life skills (Berceanu et al., 2024; Goodwin et al., 2019; Gourd & Gourd, 2011; Kassis et al., 2023; Touloupis et al., 2023). The use of psychodrama, in addition to preventing bullying, can also make a significant contribution to internet safety, reducing the risks that students face while surfing. This element underlines the practical value of psychodrama as a cyberbullying prevention strategy, which can be implemented and adapted in various

school settings in order to improve social coexistence and school climate (Grădinariu & Diac, 2023; Permana & Suwarjo, 2022).

Although the study provides important evidence about the effectiveness of psychodrama in preventing cyberbullying in a school context, there are some limitations that need to be mentioned. The first one concerns the small number of school psychologists with specific characteristics participated in the study. This might have affected the generalization of the findings. Furthermore, another limitation is related to methodology and is the fact that the study relied only on semi-structured interviews for data collection.

For further research, it is suggested that studies with larger and more diverse samples should be conducted in order to examine the influence of psychodrama in different school environments or cultural contexts in a more extensive way. It would also be useful to apply mixed evaluation methods. Finally, the combined use of psychodrama with other intervention methods could also be examined to enhance the effectiveness of cyberbullying prevention strategies, or even its effectiveness in addressing emergency incidents involving young students.

REFERENCES

Ajzen, I. (1991). The theory of planned behavior. *Organizational Behavior and Human Decision Processes*, 50(2), 179–211. DOI: 10.1016/0749-5978(91)90020-T

Ajzen, I. (2011). The theory of planned behaviour: Reactions and reflections. *Psychology & Health*, 26(9), 1113–1127. DOI: 10.1080/08870446.2011.613995

Alkhayat, L. S. (2023). The effects of cyberbullying on primary-stage students. *Pastoral Care in Education*, 1–15. DOI: 10.1080/02643944.2023.2292139

Andreou, E., Vasiou, A., Xafakos, E., & Korona, A. (2022). Animal abuse and bullying/victimization in a community sample of school-age children. *Society & Animals*, 32(4), 1–18. DOI: 10.1163/15685306-bja10104

Asimidou, A., Lenakakis, A., & Tsiaras, A. (2021). The contribution of drama pedagogy in developing adolescents' self-confidence: A case study. *NJ Drama Australia Journal*, 45(1), 45–58. DOI: 10.1080/14452294.2021.1978145

Bali, D., Pastore, M., Indrio, F., Giardino, I., Vural, M., Pettoello-Mantovani, C., Pop, T. L., & Pettoello-Mantovani, M. (2023). Bullying and cyberbullying increasing in preadolescent children. *The Journal of Pediatrics*, 261, 113565. DOI: 10.1016/j.jpeds.2023.113565 PMID: 37329977

Beran, T., & Tutty, L. (2002). *An evaluation of the Dare to Care: Bully proofing your school program.* Resolve.

Berceanu, A. I., Matu, S., & Macavei, B. I. (2020). Emotional and cognitive responses to theatrical representations of aggressive behavior. *Frontiers in Psychology*, 11, 1785. Advance online publication. DOI: 10.3389/fpsyg.2020.01785 PMID: 32922328

Berceanu, A. I., Papasteri, C., Sofonea, A., Boldasu, R., Nita, D., Poalelungi, C., Froemke, R., & Carcea, I. (2024). Oxytocin predicts positive affect gains in a role-play interaction. *Frontiers in Psychology*, 15, 1258254. Advance online publication. DOI: 10.3389/fpsyg.2024.1258254 PMID: 38873527

Blatner, A. (1996). *Acting-in: Practical applications of psychodramatic methods* (3rd ed.). Springer Publishing Co.

Bucharová, M., Malá, A., Kantor, J., & Svobodová, Z. (2020). Arts therapies interventions and their outcomes in the treatment of eating disorders: Scoping review protocol. *Behavioral Sciences (Basel, Switzerland)*, 10(12), 188. DOI: 10.3390/bs10120188 PMID: 33316926

Bucuţă, M. D., Dima, G., & Testoni, I. (2018). "When you thought that there is no one and nothing": The value of psychodrama in working with abused women. *Frontiers in Psychology*, 9, 1518. Advance online publication. DOI: 10.3389/fpsyg.2018.01518 PMID: 30190692

Burlet, R. E., & Panahon, C. J. (2022). Cyberbullying prevention and intervention: Current practices in schools. *Journal of Prevention and Health Promotion*, 3(2), 258–267. DOI: 10.1177/26320770221087454

Burton, B., & O'Toole, J. (2009). Power in their hands: The outcomes of the acting against bullying research project. *Applied Theatre Research*, 2009, 1–15.

Campbell, M., & Bauman, S. (2017). Cyberbullying: Definition, consequences, prevalence. In M. Campbell & S. Bauman (Eds.), *Reducing cyberbullying in schools* (pp. 3–16). Elsevier. DOI: 10.1016/B978-0-12-811423-0.00001-8

Chamizo-Nieto, M. T., Wallace, A., & Rey, L. (2024). Anti-cyberbullying interventions at school: Comparing the effectiveness of gratitude and psychoeducational programmes. *The Journal of Positive Psychology*, 19(2), 291–300. DOI: 10.1080/17439760.2023.2170821

Chang, W.-L., Wang, E., Chang, W.-H., Hu, H., Chang, T.-Y., Wu, Y., Wang, Y., Liang, Y., Wang, Y., & Kues, S. (2022). Study on the effect of psychodrama therapy on the emotional regulation of college teachers during the epidemic of Covid-19 coronavirus disease. *The International Journal of Neuropsychopharmacology*, 25(Supplement_1), A5–A6. DOI: 10.1093/ijnp/pyac032.006

Chicote-Beato, M., González-Víllora, S., Bodoque-Osma, A. R., & Navarro, R. (2024). Cyberbullying intervention and prevention programmes in Primary Education (6 to 12 years): A systematic review. *Aggression and Violent Behavior*, 77, 101938. DOI: 10.1016/j.avb.2024.101938

Cross, D., Monks, H., Hall, M., Shaw, T., Pintabona, Y., Erceg, E., Hamilton, G., Roberts, C., Waters, S., & Lester, L. (2011). Three-year results of the Friendly Schools whole-of-school intervention on children's bullying behaviour. *British Educational Research Journal*, 37(1), 105–129. DOI: 10.1080/01411920903420024

Deol, Y., & Lashai, M. (2022). Impact of Cyberbullying on adolescent mental health in the midst of pandemic – Hidden Crisis. *European Psychiatry : the Journal of the Association of European Psychiatrists*, 65(S1), S432. DOI: 10.1192/j.eurpsy.2022.1096

Diamanduros, T., Downs, E., & Jenkins, S. J. (2008). The role of school psychologists in the assessment, prevention, and intervention of cyberbullying. *Psychology in the Schools*, 45(8), 693–704. DOI: 10.1002/pits.20335

Donohoe, P. (2016). *Teacher utilisation of role-play to reduce bullying in a primary school setting*. Trinity.

Donohoe, P., & O'Sullivan, C. (2015). The Bullying Prevention Pack: Fostering vocabulary and knowledge on the topic of bullying and prevention using role-play and discussion to reduce primary school bullying. *Scenario: A Journal of Performative Teaching, Learning. Research*, 9(1), 97–113. DOI: 10.33178/scenario.9.1.6

El-Mazahy, H. (2023). Psychodrama games: A framework for heterogenous psychodrama groups with children from Egypt. *Zeitschrift für Psychodrama und Soziometrie*, 22(2), 365–376. DOI: 10.1007/s11620-023-00736-6

Elpus, K., & Carter, B. A. (2016). Bullying victimization among music ensemble and theatre students in the United States. *Journal of Research in Music Education*, 64(3), 322–343. DOI: 10.1177/0022429416658642

Faccio, E., Iudici, A., Costa, N., & Belloni, E. (2014). Cyberbullying and Interventions Programs in School and Clinical Setting. *Procedia: Social and Behavioral Sciences*, 122, 500–505. DOI: 10.1016/j.sbspro.2014.01.1382

Fleiss, J. L. (1971). Measuring nominal scale agreement among many raters. *Psychological Bulletin*, 76(5), 378–382. DOI: 10.1037/h0031619

Folostina, R., Tudorache, L., Michel, T., Erzsebet, B., Agheana, V., & Hocaoglu, H. (2015). Using Play and Drama in Developing Resilience in Children at Risk. *Procedia: Social and Behavioral Sciences*, 197, 2362–2368. DOI: 10.1016/j.sbspro.2015.07.283

Froeschle Hicks, J., Le Clair, B., & Berry, S. (2016). Using solution-focused dramatic empathy training to eliminate cyber-bullying. *Journal of Creativity in Mental Health*, 11(3–4), 378–390. DOI: 10.1080/15401383.2016.1172533

Gabrielli, S., Rizzi, S., Carbone, S., & Piras, E. M. (2021). School interventions for bullying–cyberbullying prevention in adolescents: Insights from the UPRIGHT and CREEP Projects. *International Journal of Environmental Research and Public Health*, 18(21), 11697. DOI: 10.3390/ijerph182111697 PMID: 34770212

Gaffney, H., Ttofi, M. M., & Farrington, D. P. (2021). Effectiveness of school-based programs to reduce bullying perpetration and victimization: An updated systematic review and meta-analysis. *Campbell Systematic Reviews*, 17(2), e1143. Advance online publication. DOI: 10.1002/cl2.1143 PMID: 37131921

Ganca, S.-S., & Kyobe, M. (2023). The Effectiveness of school anti-cyberbullying policies and their compliance with South African laws: A conceptual framework. In Mytton, O., & Thom, L. (Eds.), *School cyberbullying policies and practices* (pp. 234–248). Springer. DOI: 10.1007/978-3-031-28472-4_15

Goldstein, T. R. (2009). Psychological perspectives on acting. *Psychology of Aesthetics, Creativity, and the Arts*, 3(1), 6–9. DOI: 10.1037/a0014644

Goldstein, T. R., & Bloom, P. (2011). The mind on stage: Why cognitive scientists should study acting. *Trends in Cognitive Sciences*, 15(4), 141–142. DOI: 10.1016/j.tics.2011.02.003 PMID: 21398168

Gonzalez, A.-J. (2023). Psychodrama in Portugal. *Zeitschrift für Psychodrama und Soziometrie*, 22(1), 67–75. DOI: 10.1007/s11620-023-00717-9

Goodwin, J., Bradley, S. K., Donohoe, P., Queen, K., O'Shea, M., & Horgan, A. (2019). Bullying in schools: An evaluation of the use of drama in bullying prevention. *Journal of Creativity in Mental Health*, 14(3), 329–342. DOI: 10.1080/15401383.2019.1623147

Gourd, K. M., & Gourd, T. Y. (2011). Enacting democracy: Using Forum Theatre to confront bullying. *Equity & Excellence in Education*, 44(3), 403–419. DOI: 10.1080/10665684.2011.589275

Grădinariu, T., & Diac, G. (2023). New perspectives in developing teachers' social-emotional skills to prevent bullying: The role of Forum Theatre. *Review of Artistic Education*, 25(1), 137–147. DOI: 10.2478/rae-2023-0020

Grammatas, T., Mastrothanasis, K., & Papakosta, A. (2023). *The values of Ancient Greek Drama and Theatre in Space and Time: The Presence of the values* (Andreou, A., Trans.). National and Kapodistrian University of Athens Press.

Hadley, W., Houck, C., Brown, L. K., Spitalnick, J. S., Ferrer, M., & Barker, D. (2019). Moving beyond Role-Play: Evaluating the use of virtual reality to teach emotion regulation for the prevention of adolescent risk behavior within a randomized pilot trial. *Journal of Pediatric Psychology*, 44(4), 425–435. DOI: 10.1093/jpepsy/jsy092 PMID: 30551157

Hamidi, F., & Sobhani Tabar, S. (2021). Effect of psychodrama on post-traumatic stress disorder symptoms in primary school students living in earthquake-stricken areas. *Majallah-i Ravanpizishki va Ravanshinasi-i Balini-i Iran*, 26(4), 400–417. DOI: 10.32598/ijpcp.26.3.3190.2

Hou, D. (2023). The factors, impact, and interventions of cyberbullying in schools. *Journal of Education. Humanities and Social Sciences*, 8, 345–353. DOI: 10.54097/ehss.v8i.4272

Howie, P. C., & Bagnall, R. (2015). The transmogrification of warm-up: From drama to psychodrama. *The Arts in Psychotherapy*, 44, 35–44. DOI: 10.1016/j.aip.2014.11.004

Howie, P. C., & Bagnall, R. G. (2020). A criterial framework for concept evaluation in social practice and scholarship. *Sociological Methods & Research*, 49(3), 719–741. DOI: 10.1177/0049124118769104

Joronen, K., Häkämies, A., & Åstedt-Kurki, P. (2011). Children's experiences of a drama programme in social and emotional learning. *Scandinavian Journal of Caring Sciences*, 25(4), 671–678. DOI: 10.1111/j.1471-6712.2011.00877.x PMID: 21362006

Joronen, K., Konu, A., Rankin, H. S., & Astedt-Kurki, P. (2012). An evaluation of a drama program to enhance social relationships and anti-bullying at elementary school: A controlled study. *Health Promotion International*, 27(1), 5–14. DOI: 10.1093/heapro/dar012 PMID: 21385761

Kassis, W., Vasiou, A., Govaris, C., Favre, C., Aksoy, D., & Graf, U. (2023). Social and individual factors predicting students' resilience: A multigroup structural equation model. *Education Sciences*, 14(1), 15. DOI: 10.3390/educsci14010015

Kende, H. (2017). *Psychodrama with Children: Healing Children Through Their Own Creativity*. Routledge.

Knott, E., Rao, A. H., Summers, K., & Teeger, C. (2022). Interviews in the social sciences. *Nature Reviews. Methods Primers*, 2(1), 1–15. DOI: 10.1038/s43586-022-00150-6

Kowalski, R. M., Giumetti, G. W., Schroeder, A. N., & Lattanner, M. R. (2014). Bullying in the digital age: A critical review and meta-analysis of cyberbullying research among youth. *Psychological Bulletin*, 140(4), 1073–1137. DOI: 10.1037/a0035618 PMID: 24512111

Lambert, L., Joshanloo, M., Warren, M. A., Christiani, K., Lomas, T., Cody, B., Al Sabah, I., El Chalabi, A., & Kruchlik, G. (2023). Promoting Kindness Through the Positive Theatrical Arts: Assessing Kuwait's Boomerang Programme. *Psychological Studies*, 68(1), 101–113. DOI: 10.1007/s12646-022-00706-2

Lenakakis, A., & Koltsida, M. (2017). Disabled and non-disabled actors working in partnership for a theatrical performance: A research on theatrical partnerships as enablers of social and behavioural skills for persons with disabilities. *Research in Drama Education*, 22(2), 251–269. DOI: 10.1080/13569783.2017.1286975

Lyngstad, M. B., Baraldsnes, D., & Gjærum, R. G. (2022). Process drama in anti-bullying intervention: A study of adolescents' attitudes and initiatives. *Research in Drama Education*, 27(4), 524–538. DOI: 10.1080/13569783.2021.2011715

Mahatme, N., Kakunje, A., Nafisa, D., rinivasan, J., & Puthran, S. (2020). Knowledge and attitude of mental health professionals towards psychodrama as a psychotherapeutic tool. *Telangana Journal of Psychiatry*, 4(2), 92–95. DOI: 10.18231/2455-8559.2018.0010

Mastrothanasis, K., & Grammatas, T. (2022). Reception of the values of the Aeschylus drama and mnemonic imprints by ancient tragedy spectators. *Open Research Europe*, 2, 124. Advance online publication. DOI: 10.12688/openreseurope.15179.1 PMID: 37645271

Mastrothanasis, K., & Kladaki, M. (2020). The Involvement of Children in the Arts during Their Leisure Time. *Asian Journal of Language. Literature and Culture Studies*, 3(2), 10–19.

Mastrothanasis, K., Kladaki, M., & Andreou, A. (2023). A systematic review and meta-analysis of the Readers' Theatre impact on the development of reading skills. *International Journal of Educational Research Open*, 4, 100243. DOI: 10.1016/j.ijedro.2023.100243

Mastrothanasis, K., Zervoudakis, K., & Kladaki, M. (2024). An application of computational intelligence in group formation for digital drama education. *Iran Journal of Computer Science*, 7(3), 551–563. Advance online publication. DOI: 10.1007/s42044-024-00186-9

Mastrothanasis, K., Zervoudakis, K., Kladaki, M., & Tsafarakis, S. (2023). A bio-inspired computational classifier system for the evaluation of children's theatrical anxiety at school. *Education and Information Technologies*, 28(9), 11027–11050. DOI: 10.1007/s10639-023-11645-4

Mavroudis, N., & Bournelli, P. (2016). The role of drama in education in counteracting bullying in schools. *Cogent Education*, 3(1), 1233843. DOI: 10.1080/2331186X.2016.1233843

Maya, J., & Maraver, J. (2020). Teaching-Learning Processes: Application of educational Psychodrama in the university setting. *International Journal of Environmental Research and Public Health*, 17(11), 3922. DOI: 10.3390/ijerph17113922 PMID: 32492890

McDonald, B., Goldstein, T. R., & Kanske, P. (2020). Could Acting Training Improve Social Cognition and Emotional Control? *Frontiers in Human Neuroscience*, 14, 348. Advance online publication. DOI: 10.3389/fnhum.2020.00348 PMID: 33173473

Mertler, C. (2018). *Introduction to Educational Research* (2nd ed.). SAGE Publications, Inc.

Mishler, E. (1991). *Research interviewing: Context and narrative*. Harvard University Press. DOI: 10.2307/j.ctv26070x9

Moreno, M. A., & Vaillancourt, T. (2017). The role of health care providers in cyberbullying. *Canadian Journal of Psychiatry*, 62(6), 364–367. DOI: 10.1177/0706743716684792 PMID: 28562092

Orkibi, H., & Feniger-Schaal, R. (2019). Integrative systematic review of psychodrama psychotherapy research: Trends and methodological implications. *PLoS One*, 14(2), e0212575. DOI: 10.1371/journal.pone.0212575 PMID: 30779787

Orkibi, H., Keisari, S., Sajnani, N. L., & de Witte, M. (2023). Effectiveness of drama-based therapies on mental health outcomes: A systematic review and meta-analysis of controlled studies. *Psychology of Aesthetics, Creativity, and the Arts*. Advance online publication. DOI: 10.1037/aca0000582

O'Toole, J., & Burton, B. (2005). Acting against conflict and bullying. The Brisbane DRACON project 1996–2004—Emergent findings and outcomes. *Research in Drama Education*, 10(3), 269–283. DOI: 10.1080/13569780500275873

Papakosta, A., Mastrothanasis, K., Andreou, A., & Blouti, I. (2020). Psychometric evaluation of recall and recognition tasks for the measurement of young spectators' theatrical memory. *Journal of Literary Education*, 3(3), 177–199. DOI: 10.7203/JLE.3.14835

Park, G. R., Jung, H. O., & Kim, H. S. (2019). Effects of a suicide prevention applied psychodrama in female middle school students. *Journal of Digital Contents Society*, 20(5), 1001–1010. DOI: 10.9728/dcs.2019.20.5.1001

Park, G. R., & Kim, H. S. (2022). The Effects of a suicide prevention program applied on psychodrama among female high school students. *Journal of Korean Academy of Psychiatric and Mental Health Nursing*, 31(3), 269–278. DOI: 10.12934/jkpmhn.2022.31.3.269

Permana, H., & Suwarjo, S. (2022). Psychodrama techniques to improve academic self-efficacy In Madrasah Aliyah students. *AL-ISHLAH: Jurnal Pendidikan*, 14(4), 6773–6782. DOI: 10.35445/alishlah.v14i4.2288

Qiao, X., Wang, Y., & Zhao, J. (2023). Anti-school bullying Forum Theatre in rural boarding middle school in China – Empirical analysis based on programme practice. *The Journal of Drama and Theatre Education in Asia*, 12(1), 43–64.

Roberts, M., Lobo, R., & Sorenson, A. (2017). Evaluating the sharing stories youth theatre program: An interactive theatre and drama-based strategy for sexual health promotion among multicultural youth. *Health Promotion Journal of Australia*, 28(1), 30–36. DOI: 10.1071/HE15096 PMID: 27346537

Ron, Y. (2018). Psychodrama's Role in Alleviating Acute Distress: A Case Study of an Open Therapy Group in a Psychiatric Inpatient Ward. *Frontiers in Psychology*, 9, 2075. Advance online publication. DOI: 10.3389/fpsyg.2018.02075 PMID: 30425674

Shapiro, G. L. (2022). Cyberbullying: Introduction, definition, and impact on mental health in youth. *Journal of the American Academy of Child and Adolescent Psychiatry*, 61(10), S71. DOI: 10.1016/j.jaac.2022.07.299

Shiakou, M., & Piki, L. (2020). Assessing the role of drama on children's understanding of bullying. *International Journal of School & Educational Psychology*, 8(1), 11–20. DOI: 10.1080/21683603.2018.1499574

Shutenko, E. N., Derevyanko, J. P., Kanishcheva, M. A., Kovtun, J. J., & Lokteva, A. V. (2020). Development of students' constructive self-consciousness experience in psychodrama process. *Perspectives of Science and Education*, 47(5), 304–318. DOI: 10.32744/pse.2020.5.21

Şimşek, Ç., Küçük, L., & Akgün Yıldırım, E. (2019). Psychodrama practices in adolescents. *Journal of Academic Research in Nursing*. DOI: 10.5222/jaren.2019.48030

Sourander, A., Brunstein Klomek, A., Ikonen, M., Lindroos, J., Luntamo, T., Koskelainen, M., Ristkari, T., & Helenius, H. (2010). Psychosocial risk factors associated with cyberbullying among adolescents. *Archives of General Psychiatry*, 67(7), 720–728. DOI: 10.1001/archgenpsychiatry.2010.79 PMID: 20603453

Stives, K. L., May, D. C., Mack, M., & Bethel, C. L. (2021). Understanding responses to bullying from the parent perspective. *Frontiers in Education*, 6, 642367. Advance online publication. DOI: 10.3389/feduc.2021.642367

Teng, T. H., Varathan, K. D., & Crestani, F. (2024). A comprehensive review of cyberbullying-related content classification in online social media. *Expert Systems with Applications*, 244, 122644. DOI: 10.1016/j.eswa.2023.122644

Testoni, I., Sblano, V. F., Palazzo, L., Pompele, S., & Wieser, M. A. (2020). The Hospice as a Learning Environment: A Follow-Up Study with a Palliative Care Team. *International Journal of Environmental Research and Public Health*, 17(20), 7460. DOI: 10.3390/ijerph17207460 PMID: 33066375

Touloupis, T. (2024). Facebook Use and cyberbullying by students with learning disabilities: The role of self-rsteem and loneliness. *Psychological Reports*, 127(3), 1237–1270. DOI: 10.1177/00332941221138471 PMID: 36367133

Touloupis, T., Armaou, A., & Vasiou, A. (2023). Internet addiction and self-esteem amid the COVID-19 pandemic: A preliminary study in junior high school students. In R. S. Nazlı & G. Sari (Eds.), *Handbook of research on perspectives on society and technology addiction* (pp. 265–282). IGI Global. DOI: 10.4018/978-1-6684-8397-8.ch017

Touloupis, T., & Athanasiades, C. (2022a). Cyberbullying and empathy among elementary school students: Do special educational needs make a difference? *Scandinavian Journal of Psychology*, 63(6), 609–623. DOI: 10.1111/sjop.12838 PMID: 35698831

Touloupis, T., & Athanasiades, C. (2022b). Evaluation of a cyberbullying prevention program in elementary schools: The role of self-esteem enhancement. *Frontiers in Psychology*, 13, 980091. DOI: 10.3389/fpsyg.2022.980091 PMID: 36211905

Touloupis, T., & Campbell, M. (2024). The role of academic context-related factors and problematic social media use in academic procrastination: A cross-sectional study of students in elementary, secondary, and tertiary education. *Social Psychology of Education*, 27(1), 175–214. DOI: 10.1007/s11218-023-09817-8

Touloupis, T., Campbell, M. A., & Pnevmatikos, D. (2024). Stand by me or not? Academic context-related and individual contributors to university students' intended reaction to cyberbullying. *Psychology of Violence*, 14(4), 270–279. Advance online publication. DOI: 10.1037/vio0000511

Ulusoy, Y., Sumbas, E., & Sertkaya, B. (2023). Psychodrama as an intervention management instrument for internal/external adolescent problems: A systematic literature review. *The Arts in Psychotherapy*, 83, 102000. DOI: 10.1016/j.aip.2023.102000

Vasiou, A., Danou, S., & Sideris, A. (2023). Music listening as an emotion regulation strategy of students during COVID-19 lockdown. *Θέματα Επιστημών Αγωγής, 2*(1), 56–66. DOI: 10.12681/thea.30467

Vassou, V., Vassiou, A., Stavropoulos, V., & Chaintouti, V. (2017). The relationship between boredom, interpersonal closeness / Bullying and victimization in the school environment. *Psychology and Behavioral Science International Journal*, 6(3), 1–8. DOI: 10.19080/PBSIJ.2017.06.555686

Wan, Y. (2023). Is Psychodrama an effective method to intervene high school students social anxiety? *Lecture Notes in Education Psychology and Public Media*, 6(1), 38–46. DOI: 10.54254/2753-7048/6/20220138

Yan, H., Chen, J., & Huang, J. (2019). School Bullying Among Left-Behind Children: The Efficacy of Art Therapy on Reducing Bullying Victimization. *Frontiers in Psychiatry*, 10, 40. Advance online publication. DOI: 10.3389/fpsyt.2019.00040 PMID: 30792670

Yosep, I., Hikmat, R., & Mardhiyah, A. (2023). School-based nursing interventions for preventing bullying and reducing its incidence on students: A Scoping review. *International Journal of Environmental Research and Public Health*, 20(2), 1577. DOI: 10.3390/ijerph20021577 PMID: 36674330

Zaragas, C. K. (2021). The psychodrama and its contribution to the children's competitive confrontation. Case Study. *Cultural-historical Psychology*, 17(3), 143–151. DOI: 10.17759/chp.2021170318

ADDITIONAL READING

Chicote-Beato, M., González-Víllora, S., Bodoque-Osma, A. R., & Navarro, R. (2024). Cyberbullying intervention and prevention programmes in Primary Education (6 to 12 years): A systematic review. *Aggression and Violent Behavior*, 77, 101938. https://doi.org/10.1016/J.AVB.2024.101938

Diamanduros, T., Downs, E., & Jenkins, S. J. (2008). The role of school psychologists in the assessment, prevention, and intervention of cyberbullying. *Psychology in the Schools*, 45(8), 693–704. https://doi.org/10.1002/PITS.20335

Donohoe, P., & O'Sullivan, C. (2015). The Bullying Prevention Pack: Fostering vocabulary and knowledge on the topic of bullying and prevention using role-play and discussion to reduce primary school bullying. *Scenario: A Journal of Performative Teaching, Learning. Research*, 9(1), 97–113. https://doi.org/10.33178/scenario.9.1.6

Froeschle Hicks, J., Le Clair, B., & Berry, S. (2016). Using solution-focused dramatic empathy training to eliminate cyber-bullying. *Journal of Creativity in Mental Health*, 11(3–4), 378–390. https://doi.org/10.1080/15401383.2016.1172533

Goodwin, J., Bradley, S. K., Donohoe, P., Queen, K., O'Shea, M., & Horgan, A. (2019). Bullying in schools: An evaluation of the use of drama in bullying prevention. *Journal of Creativity in Mental Health*, 14(3), 329–342. https://doi.org/10.1080/15401383.2019.1623147

Joronen, K., Konu, A., Rankin, H. S., & Astedt-Kurki, P. (2012). An evaluation of a drama program to enhance social relationships and anti-bullying at elementary school: A controlled study. *Health Promotion International*, 27(1), 5–14. https://doi.org/10.1093/heapro/dar012

Karaosmanoğlu, G. (2024). Looking at cyberbullying from different perspectives and roles: An online process drama research with Turkish participants. *Research in Drama Education*, •••, 1–20. https://doi.org/10.1080/13569783.2024.2360087

Kende, H. (2017). *Psychodrama with Children: Healing Children Through Their Own Creativity*. Routledge.

Orkibi, H., Keisari, S., Sajnani, N. L., & de Witte, M. (2023). Effectiveness of drama-based therapies on mental health outcomes: A systematic review and meta-analysis of controlled studies. *Psychology of Aesthetics, Creativity, and the Arts*. Advance online publication. DOI: 10.1037/aca0000582

KEY TERMS AND DEFINITIONS

Cyberbullying: The repeated infliction of harm on an individual or a group through digital means, including insults and threats via the internet or electronic devices.

Drama: A form of art that involves the enactment of stories through performance. It is used in educational and therapeutic contexts to help individuals explore and express their emotions and experiences.

Emotion Management: The process of understanding, controlling, and expressing one's emotions in a healthy manner.

Empathy: The ability to understand and share the feelings of another person, which is crucial for developing social connections and reducing aggressive behaviors.

Mirroring: A psychodramatic technique where participants observe their own behavior reflected back to them by others.

Psychodrama: A form of group psychotherapy developed by Jacob Levy Moreno, where participants enact events from their lives to gain a deeper understanding of their emotions, thoughts, and behaviors.

Role Reversal: A psychodramatic technique where participants switch roles with others to understand their perspectives and emotions better, fostering empathy and conflict resolution.

Theatre: A collaborative form of performing arts that uses live performers to present a real or imagined event before an audience.

APPENDIX: GUIDE TO SEMI-STRUCTURED INTERVIEWS

1. How do you understand the importance of preventing cyberbullying in the school environment?
2. What techniques/methods would you use if you wanted to carry out an activity related to the prevention of cyberbullying among students?
3. Are you familiar with the psychodrama approach as a method of psychotherapy?
4. Based on your experience, how important do you consider psychodrama as an approach to preventing cyberbullying among students? Why do you believe this?
5. Which techniques of psychodrama do you consider most suitable for the prevention of cyberbullying?
6. Can you describe a psychodrama activity that you have used or could imagine yourself using to prevent cyberbullying?
7. Do you think any other approach would be more effective in preventing cyberbullying? If so, which one?
8. What obstacles or difficulties have you experienced or foresee in using psychodrama to prevent cyberbullying among students?
9. How do you deal with any difficulties that arise in applying new approaches such as psychodrama?
10. Do you think there is a training need among school psychologists regarding the application of psychodramatic approaches to the prevention of cyberbullying?
11. Can you suggest some innovative practices that would help incorporate psychodrama in cyberbullying prevention in schools?
12. How could cooperation between school psychologists, teachers, parents and other professionals be strengthened to promote cyberbullying prevention?

Compilation of References

Abaido, G. (2020). Cyberbullying on social media platforms among university students in the United Arab Emirates. *International Journal of Adolescence and Youth*, 25(1), 407–420. DOI: 10.1080/02673843.2019.1669059

Abilock, R., & Abilock, D. (2016). I agree, but do I know? Privacy and student data. *Knowledge Quest*, 44(4), 10–21.

Aboujaoude, E., Savage, M., Starcevic, V., & Salame, W. (2015). Cyberbullying: Review of an Old Problem Gone Viral. *The Journal of Adolescent Health*, 57(1), 10–18. DOI: 10.1016/j.jadohealth.2015.04.011 PMID: 26095405

Abreu, R. L., & Kenny, M. C. (2018). Cyberbullying and LGBTQ youth: A systematic literature review and recommendations for prevention and intervention. *Journal of Child & Adolescent Trauma*, 11(1), 81–97. DOI: 10.1007/s40653-017-0175-7 PMID: 32318140

Academy of Child and Adolescent Psychiatry. (2015). *Video games and children: playing withviolence*. https://www.aacap.org/AACAP/Families_and_Youth/Facts_for_Families/FFF-Guide/Children-and-Video-Games-Playing-with-Violence-091.aspx

Adhia, A., Bair-Merritt, M., Broder-Fingert, S., Pepen, R. A. N., Suarez-Rocha, A. C., & Rothman, E. F. (2020). The critical lack of data on alcohol and marijuana use by adolescents on the autism spectrum. *Autism in Adulthood: Challenges and Management*, 2(4), 282–288. DOI: 10.1089/aut.2019.0051 PMID: 36600961

Adorjan, M., & Ricciardelli, R. (2023). Educators and synoptic prudentialism: Educator reflections on educator training, student surveillance and using technology for student outreach. *Canadian Review of Sociology*, 60(3), 367–384. DOI: 10.1111/cars.12441 PMID: 37278202

Afriwilda, M. T., & Mulawarman, M. (2021). The effectiveness of motivational interviewing counseling to improve psychological well-being on students with online game addiction tendency. *Islamic Guidance and Counseling Journal*, 4(1), 106–115. DOI: 10.25217/igcj.v4i1.1235

Agustina, J. R., & Gómez-Durán, E. L. (2012). Sexting: Research criteria of a globalized social phenomenon. *Archives of Sexual Behavior*, 41(6), 1325–1328. DOI: 10.1007/s10508-012-0038-0 PMID: 23080397

Agustini, W., & Marleni, M. (2023). The impact of online game addiction on learning enthusiasm to promote the students' motivation to learn. *Esteem Journal of English Education Study Programme*, 6(2), 370–382. DOI: 10.31851/esteem.v6i2.12328

Ahlström, B. H., & Wentz, E. (2014). Difficulties in everyday life: Young persons with attention-deficit/hyperactivity disorder and autism spectrum disorders perspectives. A chat-log analysis. *International Journal of Qualitative Studies on Health and Well-being*, 9(1), 23376. Advance online publication. DOI: 10.3402/qhw.v9.23376 PMID: 24875238

Ahmadu, T. S., & Kontagora, H. L. (2021). How Nigerian junior secondary school students perceive internet child exploitation. In Elshenraki, H. (Ed.), *Combating the exploitation of children in cyberspace: Emerging research and opportunities* (pp. 95–116). IGI Global. DOI: 10.4018/978-1-7998-2360-5.ch005

Aizenkot, D., & Kashy-Rosenbaum, G. (2020). The effectiveness of Safe Surfing, an anti-cyberbullying intervention program in reducing online and offline bullying and improving perceived popularity and self-esteem. *Cyberpsychology (Brno)*, 14(3), 6. DOI: 10.5817/CP2020-3-6

Ajzen, I. (1991). The theory of planned behaviour. *Organizational Behavior and Human Decision Processes*, 50(2), 179–211. DOI: 10.1016/0749-5978(91)90020-T

Ajzen, I. (2011). The theory of planned behaviour: Reactions and reflections. *Psychology & Health*, 26(9), 1113–1127. DOI: 10.1080/08870446.2011.613995

Akin, A., & Iskender, M. (2011). Internet addiction and depression, anxiety and stress. *International Online Journal of Educational Sciences*, 3(1), 138–148.

Alareeki, A., Shipton, L., & Lashewicz, B. (2022). "They're either afraid or ignorant": Experiences of stigma and blame among fathers raising autistic children. *Research in Autism Spectrum Disorders*, 96, 101999. Advance online publication. DOI: 10.1016/j.rasd.2022.101999

Alavi, S. S., Alaghemandan, H., Maracy, M. R., Jannatifard, F., Eslami, M., & Ferdosi, M. (2012). Impact of addiction to internet on a number of psychiatric symptoms in students of Isfahan universities, Iran, 2010. *International Journal of Preventive Medicine*, 3(2), 122–127. PMID: 22347609

Albury, K., & Crawford, K. (2012). Sexting, consent and young people's ethics: Beyond Megan's story. *Continuum (Perth)*, 26(3), 463–473. DOI: 10.1080/10304312.2012.665840

Al-Faham, H., Davis, A. M., & Ernst, R. (2019). Intersectionality: From theory to practice. *Annual Review of Law and Social Science*, 15(1), 247–265. DOI: 10.1146/annurev-lawsocsci-101518-042942

Al-Hariri, M. T., & Al-Hattami, A. A. (2017). Impact of students' use of technology on their learning achievements in physiology courses at the University of Dammam. *Journal of Taibah University Medical Sciences*, 12(1), 82–85. DOI: 10.1016/j.jtumed.2016.07.004 PMID: 31435218

Alhujaili, N., Platt, E., Khalid-Khan, S., & Groll, D. (2022). Comparison of social media use among adolescents with autism spectrum disorder and non-ASD adolescents. *Adolescent Health, Medicine and Therapeutics*, 13, 15–21. DOI: 10.2147/AHMT.S344591 PMID: 35136359

Alhujailli, A., Karwowski, W., Wan, T. T. H., & Hancock, P. (2020). Affective and stress consequences of cyberbullying. *Symmetry*, 12(9), 1536. Advance online publication. DOI: 10.3390/sym12091536

Alismaiel, O. (2023). Digital Media Used in Education: The Influence on Cyberbullying Behaviors among Youth Students. *International Journal of Environmental Research and Public Health*, 20(2), 1370. DOI: 10.3390/ijerph20021370 PMID: 36674128

Alkhayat, L. S. (2023). The effects of cyberbullying on primary-stage students. *Pastoral Care in Education*, 1–15. DOI: 10.1080/02643944.2023.2292139

Allely, C. S., & Creaby-Attwood, A. (2016). Sexual offending and autism spectrum disorders. *Journal of Intellectual Disabilities and Offending Behaviour*, 7(1), 35–51. DOI: 10.1108/JIDOB-09-2015-0029

Allely, C. S., Kennedy, S., & Warren, I. (2019). A legal analysis of Australian criminal cases involving defendants with autism spectrum disorder charged with online sexual offending. *International Journal of Law and Psychiatry*, 66, 101456. Advance online publication. DOI: 10.1016/j.ijlp.2019.101456 PMID: 31706389

Aloraini, S. (2012). The impact of using multimedia on students' academic achievement in the College of Education at King Saud University. *Journal of King Saud University-Languages and Translation*, 24(2), 75–82. DOI: 10.1016/j.jksult.2012.05.002

Alotaibi, N. (2019). Cyber bullying and the expected consequences on the students' academic achievement. *IEEE Access : Practical Innovations, Open Solutions*, 7, 153417–153431. DOI: 10.1109/ACCESS.2019.2947163

Alqahtani, A. M. (2016). Keeping safe online: Perceptions of Gulf adolescents. *Journal of Education and e-learning Research*, 3(4), 150–155. DOI: 10.20448/journal.509/2016.3.4/509.4.150.155

Alsawalqa, R. O. (2021). Cyberbullying, social stigma, and self-esteem: The impact of COVID-19 on students from East and Southeast Asia at the University of Jordan. *Heliyon*, 7(4), e06711. DOI: 10.1016/j.heliyon.2021.e06711 PMID: 33869877

Alwin, D. F., & Felson, J. L. (2010). Religion and child-rearing. In Ellison, C. G., & Hummer, R. A. (Eds.), *Religion, families, and health: Population-based research in the United States* (pp. 40–60). Rutgers University Press.

American Counseling Association. (2014). *2014 ACA code of ethics*. https://www.counseling.org/docs/default-source/default-document-library/ethics/2014-aca-code-of-ethics.pdf

American Psychiatric Association, DSM-5 Task Force. (2013). *Diagnostic and statistical manual of mental disorders: DSM-5* (5th ed.). American Psychiatric Publishing, Inc., DOI: 10.1176/appi.books.9780890425596

American Psychological Association. (2017). *Ethical principles of psychologists and code of conduct* (2002, amended effective June 1, 2010, and January 1, 2017). https://www.apa.org/ethics/code/

American Psychological Association. (n.d.). Bullying. https://www.apa.org/topics/bullying

Andaya, A. M., Andea, J. M. G., & Gallego, E. J. B. (2024). The Experience of the Love for Children in Teaching. *Psychology and Education: A Multidisciplinary Journal, 21*(1), 28-32. DOI: 10.5281/zenodo.12168019

Anderson, M., & Jiang, J. (2018). *Teens, social media and technology 2018*. Pew Research Center. https://www.pewresearch.org/internet/2018/05/31/teens-social-media-technology-2018/

Anderson, C. A., Shibuya, A., Ihori, N., Swing, E. L., Bushman, B. J., Sakamoto, A., Rothstein, H. R., & Saleem, M. (2010). Violent video play effects on aggression, empathy, and prosocial behavior in eastern and western countries: A meta-analytic review. *Psychological Bulletin*, 136(2), 151–173. DOI: 10.1037/a0018251 PMID: 20192553

Anderson, K. E. (2018). Getting acquainted with social networks and apps: Streaming video games on Twitch.tv. *Library Hi Tech News*, 35(9), 7–10. DOI: 10.1108/LHTN-08-2018-0054

Andreassen, C. S., Billieux, J., Griffiths, M. D., Kuss, D. J., Demetrovics, Z., Mazzoni, E., & Pallesen, S. (2016). The relationship between addictive use of social media and video games and symptoms of psychiatric disorders: A large-scale cross-sectional study. *Psychology of Addictive Behaviors*, 30(2), 252–262. DOI: 10.1037/adb0000160 PMID: 26999354

Andreou, E., Vasiou, A., Xafakos, E., & Korona, A. (2022). Animal abuse and bullying/victimization in a community sample of school-age children. *Society & Animals*, 32(4), 1–18. DOI: 10.1163/15685306-bja10104

Ang, R. P. (2015). Adolescent cyberbullying: A review of characteristics, prevention and intervention strategies. *Aggression and Violent Behavior, 25*(A), 35-42. DOI: 10.1016/j.avb.2015.07.011

Annansingh, F., & Veli, T. (2016). An investigation into risks awareness and e-safety needs of children on the internet: A study of Devon, UK. *Interactive Technology and Smart Education*, 13(2), 147–165. DOI: 10.1108/ITSE-09-2015-0029

Antoniou, V., Ragia, L., Nomikou, P., Bardouli, P., Lampridou, D., Ioannou, T., Kalisperakis, I., & Stentoumis, C. (2018). Creating a story map using geographic information systems to explore geomorphology and history of Methana Peninsula. *ISPRS International Journal of Geo-Information*, 7(12), 1–15. DOI: 10.3390/ijgi7120484

Archibald, M. M., Ambagtsheer, R. C., Casey, M. G., & Lawless, M. (2019). Using Zoom videoconferencing for qualitative data collection: Perceptions and experiences of researchers and participants. *International Journal of Qualitative Methods*, 18, 1609406919874596. Advance online publication. DOI: 10.1177/1609406919874596

Armstrong, L., Phillips, J. G., & Saling, L. L. (2000). Potential determinants of heavier internet usage. *International Journal of Human-Computer Studies*, 53(4), 537–550. DOI: 10.1006/ijhc.2000.0400

Arnarsson, Á., Nygren, J., Nyholm, M., Torsheim, T., Augustine, L., Bjereld, Y., Markkanen, I., Schnohr, C., Rasmussen, M., Nielsen, L., & Bendtsen, P. (2020). Cyberbullying and traditional bullying among Nordic adolescents and their impact on life satisfaction. *Scandinavian Journal of Public Health*, 48(5), 502–510. DOI: 10.1177/1403494818817411 PMID: 30672390

Asimidou, A., Lenakakis, A., & Tsiaras, A. (2021). The contribution of drama pedagogy in developing adolescents' self-confidence: A case study. *NJ Drama Australia Journal*, 45(1), 45–58. DOI: 10.1080/14452294.2021.1978145

Associated Press-MTV. (2011, September 2). *Digital Abuse Survey*. Retrieved April 3, 2024, from http://surveys.associatedpress.com/data/KnowledgeNetworks/AP_DigitalAbuseSurvey_ToplineTREND_2nd%20story%20WITHOUT%20hacking.pdf

Atadoga, A., Farayola, O. A., Ayinla, B. S., Amoo, O. O., Abrahams, T. O., & Osasona, F. (2024). A comparative review of data encryption methods in the USA and Europe. *Computer Science & IT Research Journal*, 5(2), 447–460. DOI: 10.51594/csitrj.v5i2.815

Athanasiou, K., Melegkovits, E., Andrie, E., Magoulas, C., Tzavara, C., Richardson, C., Greydanus, D., Tsolia, M., & Tsitsika, A. (2018). Cross-national aspects of cyberbullying victimization among 14–17-year-old adolescents across seven European countries. *BMC Public Health*, 18(1), 800. DOI: 10.1186/s12889-018-5682-4 PMID: 29986687

Atkin, A. J., Sharp, S. J., Corder, K., & van Sluijs, E. M.International Children's Accelerometry Database (ICAD) Collaborators. (2014). Prevalence and correlates of screen time in youth: An international perspective. *American Journal of Preventive Medicine*, 47(6), 803–807. DOI: 10.1016/j.amepre.2014.07.043 PMID: 25241193

Auger, N., Daniel, M., Knäuper, B., Dourian, T., & Raynault, M.-F. (2015). Unintended messages in online advertising to youth: Illicit drug imagery in a Canadian sports marketing campaign. *The Journal of Adolescent Health*, 56(4), 429–432. DOI: 10.1016/j.jadohealth.2014.12.006 PMID: 25650109

Aulia, N., Syamsuddin, H., Irawansah, D., Tiara, Ramadhan, S., & Syahrudin, I. (May 27, 2024). *Protection of ITE Law Against Sexting By Teenagers* [Conference paper]. ICORHESTECH 2024, Situbondo, East Java, Indonesia. https://journal.ibrahimy.ac.id/index.php/icorhestech/article/view/5665/2408

Autism Spectrum Australia. (2023). *Learn more about Aspect's participation in Mardi Gras over the years*. https://www.autismspectrum.org.au/about-aspect/diversity-inclusion/lgbtqia/aspect-at-mardi-gras

Axelsson, C. A. W., Guath, M., & Nygren, T. (2021). Learning how to separate fake from real news: Scalable digital tutorials promoting students' civic online reasoning. *Future Internet*, 13(3), 1–18. DOI: 10.3390/fi13030060

Aznar-Díaz, I., Romero-Rodríguez, J.-M., García-González, A., & Ramírez-Montoya, M.-S. (2020). Mexican and Spanish university students' Internet addiction and academic procrastination: Correlation and potential factors. *PLoS One*, 15(5), e0233655. DOI: 10.1371/journal.pone.0233655 PMID: 32442238

Bacaksiz, F. E., Eskici, G. T., & Seren, A. K. H. (2020). "From my Facebook profile": What do nursing students share on Timeline, Photos, Friends, and About sections? *Nurse Education Today*, 86, 104326. DOI: 10.1016/j.nedt.2019.104326 PMID: 31945672

Bago, B., Rand, D. G., & Pennycook, G. (2020). Fake news, fast and slow: Deliberation reduces belief in false (but not true) news headlines. *Journal of Experimental Psychology. General*, 149(8), 1608–1613. DOI: 10.1037/xge0000729 PMID: 31916834

Bahiss, K., Cunningham, S. J., & Smith, T. (2010). Investigating the usability of social networking sites for teenagers with autism. In *Proceedings of the 11th International Conference of the NZ Chapter of the ACM Special Interest Group on Human-Computer Interaction* (pp. 5-8). ACM. DOI: 10.1145/1832838.1832840

Bahrainian, S. A., Alizadeh, K. H., Raeisoon, M. R., Gorji, O. H., & Khazaee, A. (2014). Relationship of Internet addiction with self-esteem and depression in university students. *Journal of Preventive Medicine and Hygiene*, 55(3), 86–89. PMID: 25902574

Baiden, F., Amankwah, J., & Owusu, A. (2020). Sexting among high school students in a metropolis in Ghana: An exploratory and descriptive study. *Journal of Children and Media*, 14(3), 1–15. DOI: 10.1080/17482798.2020.1719854

Baldry, A. C., Blaya, C., & Farrington, D. P. (Eds.). (2018). *International perspectives on cyberbullying prevalence, risk factors and interventions* (1st ed.). Springer International., DOI: 10.1007/978-3-319-73263-3

Bali, D., Pastore, M., Indrio, F., Giardino, I., Vural, M., Pettoello-Mantovani, C., Pop, T. L., & Pettoello-Mantovani, M. (2023). Bullying and cyberbullying increasing in preadolescent children. *The Journal of Pediatrics*, 261, 113565. DOI: 10.1016/j.jpeds.2023.113565 PMID: 37329977

Ballard, M. E., & Welch, K. M. (2015). Virtual Warfare: Cyberbullying and Cyber-Victimization in MMOG Play. *Games and Culture*, 12(5), 466–491. DOI: 10.1177/1555412015592473

Bandura. (2005). The Primacy of Self-Regulation in Health Promotion. Applied Psychology. *An International Review, 54*(2), 245-254.

Bandura, A. (1977). *Social Learning Theory*. Prentice-Hall.

Bandura, A. (1985). Model of causality in social learning theory. In *Cognition and psychotherapy* (pp. 81–99). Springer US. DOI: 10.1007/978-1-4684-7562-3_3

Bandura, A., & Hall, P. (2018). Social learning theory. In MacBlain, S. (Ed.), *Learning theories for early years* (p. 78). SAGE Publications.

Banerjee, A. (2023). Internet use and autism spectrum disorders. *Journal of Autism and Developmental Disorders*, 53(8), 3307–3308. DOI: 10.1007/s10803-023-05904-z PMID: 36710297

Bankov, K. (2022). *The digital mind: semiotic explorations in digital culture* (Vol. 22). Springer Nature. DOI: 10.1007/978-3-030-92555-0

Bányai, F., Griffiths, M. D., Demetrovics, D., & Király, O. (2019). The mediating effect of motivations between psychiatric distress and gaming disorder among esport gamers and recreational gamers. *Comprehensive Psychiatry*, 94, 152117. Advance online publication. DOI: 10.1016/j.comppsych.2019.152117 PMID: 31422185

Barak, A. (2005). Sexual harassment on the internet. *Social Science Computer Review*, 23(1), 77–92. DOI: 10.1177/0894439304271540

Barkoukis, V., Lazuras, L., Ourda, D., & Tsorbatzoudis, H. (2016). Tackling psychosocial risk factors for adolescent cyberbullying: Evidence from a school-based intervention. *Aggressive Behavior*, 42(2), 114–122. DOI: 10.1002/ab.21625 PMID: 26350445

Barlett, C. P. (2015). Anonymously hurting others online: The effect of anonymity on cyberbullying frequency. *Psychology of Popular Media Culture*, 4(2), 70–79. DOI: 10.1037/a0034335

Baron-Cohen, S., Tager-Flusberg, H., & Lombardo, M. (2013). *Understanding other minds: Perspectives from developmental social neuroscience* (3rd ed.). Oxford University Press. DOI: 10.1093/acprof:oso/9780199692972.001.0001

Barrense-Dias, Y., Akre, C., Auderset, D., Leeners, B., Morselli, D., & Surís, J. C. (2020). Non-consensual sexting: Characteristics and motives of youths who share received-intimate content without consent. *Sexual Health*, 17(3), 270–278. DOI: 10.1071/SH19201 PMID: 32594970

Barrense-Dias, Y., Berchtold, A., Surís, J. C., & Akre, C. (2017). Sexting and the definition issue. *The Journal of Adolescent Health*, 61(5), 544–554. DOI: 10.1016/j.jadohealth.2017.05.009 PMID: 28734631

Barroso, R., Marinho, A. R., Figueiredo, P., Ramião, E., & Silva, A. S. (2023). Consensual and non-consensual sexting behaviors in adolescence: A systematic review. *Adolescent Research Review*, 8(1), 1–20. DOI: 10.1007/s40894-022-00199-0

Barzegar, N., Farjad, S., & Hosseini, N. (2012). The effect of teaching model based on multimedia and network on the student learning (case study: Guidance schools in Iran). *Procedia: Social and Behavioral Sciences*, 47, 1263–1267. DOI: 10.1016/j.sbspro.2012.06.809

Bates, S. (2015). *"Stripped": an analysis of revenge porn victims' lives after victimization* [MA Thesis]. Simon Fraser University. Retrieved from: https://summit.sfu.ca/item/15668

Bates, S. (2017). Revenge Porn and Mental Health: A Qualitative Analysis of the Mental Health Effects of Revenge Porn on Female Survivors. *Feminist Criminology*, 12(1), 22–42. DOI: 10.1177/1557085116654565

Bauer, J., & Kenton, J. (2005). Toward technology integration in the schools: Why it isn't happening. *Journal of Technology and Teacher Education*, 13(4), 519–546. https://www.learntechlib.org/primary/p/4728/

Baugh, C., & Paradis, G. (2016, April). *The relationship between sexting and religiosity* [Poster presentation]. *96th Annual Convention of the Western Psychological Association*, Long Beach, CA, United States.

Baumgartner, S. E., Sumter, S. R., Peter, J., Valkenburg, P. M., & Livingstone, S. (2014). Does country context matter? Investigating the predictors of teen sexting across Europe. *Computers in Human Behavior*, 34, 157–164. DOI: 10.1016/j.chb.2014.01.041

Baumgartner, S. E., Valkenburg, P. M., & Peter, J. (2010). Assessing causality in the relationship between adolescents' risky sexual online behavior and their perceptions of this behavior. *Journal of Youth and Adolescence*, 39(10), 1226–1239. DOI: 10.1007/s10964-010-9512-y PMID: 20177962

Beaulieu, N., Bergeron, S., Brassard, A., Byers, E. S., & Péloquin, K. (2023). Toward an integrative model of intimacy, sexual satisfaction, and relationship satisfaction: A prospective study in long-term couples. *Journal of Sex Research*, 60(8), 1100–1112. DOI: 10.1080/00224499.2022.2129557 PMID: 36205506

Beck, A. T. (1967). *Depression: Clinical, Experimental, and Theoretical Aspects*. University of Pennsylvania Press.

Beck, A. T. (2011). *Cognitive Therapy: Basics and Beyond*. Guilford Press.

Becker, L. B., Welter, V. D. E., Aschermann, E., & Großschedl, J. (2021). Comprehension-Oriented Learning of Cell Biology: Do Different Training Conditions Affect Students' Learning Success Differentially? *Education Sciences*, 11(8), 1–31. DOI: 10.3390/educsci11080438

Beckmeyer, J. J. (2024). Sexting and the Dynamics of Emerging Adults' Romantic Partnerships. *Sexuality & Culture*, 28(2), 447–463. DOI: 10.1007/s12119-023-10125-8

Beckmeyer, J. J., Herbenick, D., & Eastman-Mueller, H. (2022). Sexting with romantic partners during college: Who does it, who doesn't and who wants to. *Sexuality & Culture*, 26(1), 48–66. DOI: 10.1007/s12119-021-09878-x

Beddows, N., & Brooks, R. (2015). Inappropriate sexual behaviour in adolescents with autism spectrum disorder: What education is recommended and why. *Early Intervention in Psychiatry*, 10(4), 282–289. DOI: 10.1111/eip.12265 PMID: 26265030

Bedford, R., Saez de Urabain, I. R., Cheung, C. H. M., Karmiloff-Smith, A., & Smith, T. J. (2016). Toddlers' fine motor milestone achievement is associated with early touchscreen scrolling. *Frontiers in Psychology*, 7, 1108. DOI: 10.3389/fpsyg.2016.01108 PMID: 27531985

Bendou, K., Megder, E., & Cherkaoui, C. (2017). Animated Pedagogical Agents to Assist Learners and keep them motivated in Online Learning Environments (LMS or MOOC). *International Journal of Computer Applications*, 168(6), 46–53. DOI: 10.5120/ijca2017914477

Benedetto, L., & Ingrassia, M. (2021). Digital parenting: Raising and protecting children in media world. *Parenting: Studies By an Ecocultural and Transactional Perspective*, 127-148. https://doi.org/ DOI: 10.5772/intechopen.92579

Benford, P., & Standen, P. (2009). The Internet: A comfortable communication medium for people with Asperger syndrome (AS) and high functioning autism (HFA)? *Journal of Assistive Technologies*, 3(2), 44–53. DOI: 10.1108/17549450200900015

Benham, J. (2015). *Proud to be autistic metaphorical construction and salience of cultural and personal identity in #StopCombatingMe* [Unpublished master's thesis]. Minnesota State University. https://cornerstone.lib.mnsu.edu/etds/420/

Bennett, M., & Goodall, E. (2016). A meta-analysis of DSM-5 autism diagnoses in relation to DSM-IV and DSM-IV-TR. *Review Journal of Autism and Developmental Disorders*, 3(2), 119–124. DOI: 10.1007/s40489-016-0070-4

Benotsch, E. G., Snipes, D. J., Martin, A. M., & Bull, S. S. (2013). Sexting, substance use, and sexual risk behavior in young adults. *The Journal of Adolescent Health*, 52(3), 307–313. DOI: 10.1016/j.jadohealth.2012.06.011 PMID: 23299017

Beran, T. N., Rinaldi, C., Bickham, D. S., & Rich, M. (2012). Evidence for the need to support adolescents dealing with harassment and cyber-harassment: Prevalence, progression, and impact. *School Psychology International*, 33(5), 562–576. DOI: 10.1177/0143034312446976

Beran, T., & Tutty, L. (2002). *An evaluation of the Dare to Care: Bully proofing your school program*. Resolve.

Berceanu, A. I., Matu, S., & Macavei, B. I. (2020). Emotional and cognitive responses to theatrical representations of aggressive behavior. *Frontiers in Psychology*, 11, 1785. Advance online publication. DOI: 10.3389/fpsyg.2020.01785 PMID: 32922328

Berceanu, A. I., Papasteri, C., Sofonea, A., Boldasu, R., Nita, D., Poalelungi, C., Froemke, R., & Carcea, I. (2024). Oxytocin predicts positive affect gains in a role-play interaction. *Frontiers in Psychology*, 15, 1258254. Advance online publication. DOI: 10.3389/fpsyg.2024.1258254 PMID: 38873527

Bergen, N., & Labonté, R. (2020). "Everything is perfect, and we have no problems": Detecting and limiting social desirability bias in qualitative research. *Qualitative Health Research*, 30(5), 783–792. DOI: 10.1177/1049732319889354 PMID: 31830860

Bergmann, C., Dimitrova, N., Alaslani, K., Almohammadi, A., Alroqi, H., Aussems, S., Barokova, M., Davies, C., Gonzalez-Gomez, N., Gibson, S. P., Havron, N., Horowitz-Kraus, T., Kanero, J., Kartushina, N., Keller, C., Mayor, J., Mundry, R., Shinskey, J., & Mani, N. (2022). Young children's screen time during the first COVID-19 lockdown in 12 countries. *Scientific Reports*, 12(1), 2015. DOI: 10.1038/s41598-022-05840-5 PMID: 35132065

Berk, L. E. (2018). *Development Through the Lifespan*. Pearson Education.

Berson, I. R., & Berson, M. J. (2005). Challenging online behaviors of youth: Findings from a comparative analysis of young people in the United States and New Zealand. *Social Science Computer Review*, 23(1), 29–38. DOI: 10.1177/0894439304271532

Bertilsdotter Rosqvist, H., Kourti, H., Jackson-Perry, D., Brownlow, C., Fletcher, K., Bendelman, D., & O'Dell, L. (2019). Doing it differently: Emancipatory autism studies within a neurodiverse academic space. *Disability & Society*, 34(7-8), 1082–1101. DOI: 10.1080/09687599.2019.1603102

Beyens, I., Vandenbosch, L., & Eggermont, S. (2015). Early adolescent boys' exposure to internet pornography: Relationships to pubertal timing, sensation seeking, and academic performance. *The Journal of Early Adolescence*, 35(8), 1045–1068. DOI: 10.1177/0272431614548069

Bianchi, D., Morelli, M., Baiocco, R., Cattelino, E., Laghi, F., & Chirumbolo, A. (2019). Family functioning patterns predict teenage girls' sexting. *International Journal of Behavioral Development*, 43(6), 507–514. DOI: 10.1177/0165025419873037

Bianchi, D., Morelli, M., Nappa, M. R., Baiocco, R., & Chirumbolo, A. (2018). A bad romance: Sexting motivations and teen dating violence. *Journal of Interpersonal Violence*, 1–21. DOI: 10.1177/0886260518817037 PMID: 30537886

Birds, J., & Edwards, S. (2015). Children learning to use technologies through play: A digital play framework. *British Journal of Educational Technology*, 46(6), 1149–1160. DOI: 10.1111/bjet.12191

Black, R., Walsh, L., Waite, C., Collin, P., Third, A., & Idriss, S. (2022). In their own words: 41 stories of young people's digital citizenship. *Learning, Media and Technology*, 47(4), 524–536. DOI: 10.1080/17439884.2022.2044848

Blasco-Fontecilla, H., Menéndez-García, Á., Sanchez-Sanchez, F., & Bella-Fernández, M. (2023). Lack of educational impact of video game addiction in children and adolescents diagnosed with ADHD: A cross-sectional study. *Frontiers in Psychiatry*, 14, 1136671. DOI: 10.3389/fpsyt.2023.1136671 PMID: 37151982

Blatner, A. (1996). *Acting-in: Practical applications of psychodramatic methods* (3rd ed.). Springer Publishing Co.

Blaya, C. (2019). Cyberhate: A review and content analysis of intervention strategies. *Aggression and Violent Behavior*, 45, 163–172. DOI: 10.1016/j.avb.2018.05.006

Bleszynski, J., Rumińska, A., Hamerlińska, A., Stefańska-Klar, R., & Warszawa, A. (2022). The experience of the COVID-19 pandemic by persons with ASD: Social aspects. *PLoS One*, 17(6), e0267123. Advance online publication. DOI: 10.1371/journal.pone.0267123 PMID: 35709250

Blevins, B. (2018). Teaching digital literacy composing concepts: Focusing on the layers of augmented reality in an era of changing technology. *Computers and Composition*, 50, 21–38. DOI: 10.1016/j.compcom.2018.07.003

Bo, A., Hai, A., Chen, D., & Hammock, K. (2021). Risk of bias assessments in systematic reviews and meta-analyses of behavioral interventions for substance use outcomes. *Journal of Clinical Epidemiology*, 139, 20–27. DOI: 10.1016/j.jclinepi.2021.06.012 PMID: 34166755

Boehnke, M. (2011). Gender role attitudes around the globe: Egalitarian vs. traditional views. *Asian Journal of Social Science*, 39(1), 57–74. DOI: 10.1163/156853111X554438

Boislard, M. A., Van de Bongardt, D., & Blais, M. (2016). Sexuality (and lack thereof) in adolescence and early adulthood: A review of the literature. *Behavioral Sciences (Basel, Switzerland)*, 6(1), 8. Advance online publication. DOI: 10.3390/bs6010008 PMID: 26999225

Bolognesi, S., & Bukhalovskaya, A. (2022). Acoso escolar en la red: ciberacoso datos, prevención e intervención [School bullying online: cyberbullying data, prevention and intervention]. *Etic@net, 22*(2), 216-240. DOI: 10.30827/eticanet.v22i2.23791

Bone, K. M. (2017). Trapped behind the glass: Crip theory and disability identity. *Disability & Society*, 32(9), 1297–1314. DOI: 10.1080/09687599.2017.1313722

Bonilla, S., McGinley, M., & Lamb, S. (2021). Sexting, power, and patriarchy: Narratives of sexting from a college population. *New Media & Society*, 23(5), 1099–1116. DOI: 10.1177/1461444820909517

Bonwell, C. C., & Eison, J. A. (1991). Active Learning: Creating Excitement in the Classroom. *ASHE-ERIC Higher Education Report.*

Boonmongkon, P., Ojanen, T. T., Samakkeekarom, R., Samoh, N., Iamsilpa, R., Topananan, S., Cholratana, M., & Guadamuz, T. E. (2013). 'She met her (boy)friend online': Negotiating gender identity and sexuality among young Thai women in online space. *Culture, Health & Sexuality*, 15(10), 1162–1174. DOI: 10.1080/13691058.2013.809609 PMID: 23885969

Bottema-Beutel, K., Cuda, J., Kim, S. Y., Crowley, S., & Scanlon, D. (2020). High school experiences and support recommendations of autistic youth. *Journal of Autism and Developmental Disorders*, 50(9), 3397–3412. DOI: 10.1007/s10803-019-04261-0 PMID: 31630296

Boud, D., Keogh, R., & Walker, D. (Eds.). (1985). *Reflection: Turning Experience into Learning*. Routledge.

Boudi, F. B., Patel, S., Boudi, A., & Chan, C. (2019). Vitamin E acetate as a plausible cause of acute vaping-related illness. *Cureus*, 11(12), e6350. Advance online publication. DOI: 10.7759/cureus.6350 PMID: 31938636

Boyle, A., & O'Sullivan, L. (2010). General and sexual communication in established relationships: An exploration of possible links to condom use among young adults. *The Canadian Journal of Human Sexuality*, 19, 53–64. https://link.gale.com/apps/doc/A229542650/AONE?u=anon~627c2c01&sid=googleScholar&xid=ee5becb0

Bozza, T. C. L., & Vinha, T. P. (2023). Cyberbullying, cyber agressão e riscos on-line: Como a escola pode atuar diante dos problemas da (cyber)convivência. *Revista Ibero-Americana De Estudos Em Educação*, 18(00), e023059. DOI: 10.21723/riaee.v18i00.18444

Bradley, N., Gilea, B., Overton, S., & O'Neill, R. (2020). Sexting between minors: Ethical, legal, and clinical considerations. *Journal of Counselor Practice*, 11(2), 1–20. DOI: 10.22229/sbm1122020

Branch, K., Hilinski-Rosick, C. M., Johnson, E., & Solano, G. (2017). Revenge porn victimization of college students in the United States: An exploratory analysis. *International Journal of Cyber Criminology*, 11(1), 128–142. DOI: 10.5281/zenodo.495777

Brand, M., Wegmann, E., Stark, R., Müller, A., Wölfling, K., Robbins, T. W., & Potenza, M. N. (2019). The interaction of person-affect-cognition-execution (I-PACE) model for addictive behaviors: Update, generalization to addictive behaviors beyond internet-use disorders, and specification of the process character of addictive behaviors. *Neuroscience and Biobehavioral Reviews*, 104, 1–10. DOI: 10.1016/j.neubiorev.2019.06.032 PMID: 31247240

Brauchli, V., Sticca, F., Edelsbrunner, P., Von Wyl, A., & Lannen, P. (2024). Are screen media the new pacifiers? The role of parenting stress and parental attitudes for children's screen time in early childhood. *Computers in Human Behavior*, 152, 108057. DOI: 10.1016/j.chb.2023.108057

Braun, V., & Clarke, V. (2021). Thematic analysis: A practical guide to understanding and doing. *Sage (Atlanta, Ga.)*.

Brevik, L. M. (2019). Explicit reading strategy instruction or daily use of strategies? Studying the teaching of reading comprehension through naturalistic classroom observation in English L2. *Reading and Writing*, 32(9), 2281–2310. DOI: 10.1007/s11145-019-09951-w

Bright, M. A., Sayedul Huq, M., Patel, S., Miller, M. D., & Finkelhor, D. (2022). Child Safety Matters: Randomized Control Trial of a School-Based, Child Victimization Prevention Curriculum. *Journal of Interpersonal Violence*, 37(1-2), 538–556. DOI: 10.1177/0886260520909185 PMID: 32249651

Brinkmann, S. (2013). *Qualitative interviewing*. Oxford University Press., DOI: 10.1093/acprof:osobl/9780199861392.001.0001

British Psychological Society. (2021). *Code of Ethics and Conduct* (amended effective December 12, 2021). DOI: 10.53841/bpsrep.2021.inf94

Brito, R. (2016). "Who taught you how to play?", "I did!" Digital practices and skills of children under 6. *Medical Education*, 7(2), 281–302. DOI: 10.14605/MED721607

Brito, R., Francisco, R., Dias, P., & Chaudron, S. (2017). Family dynamics in digital homes: The role played by parental mediation in young children's digital practices around 14 european countries. *Contemporary Family Therapy*, 39(4), 271–280. DOI: 10.1007/s10591-017-9431-0

Britt, M. A., Rouet, J. F., Blaum, D., & Millis, K. (2019). A reasoned approach to dealing with fake news. *Policy Insights from the Behavioral and Brain Sciences*, 6(1), 94–101. DOI: 10.1177/2372732218814855

Bronfenbrenner, U. (1979). *The ecology of human development: Experiments by nature and design*. Harvard University Press. DOI: 10.4159/9780674028845

Bronfenbrenner, U. (1995). Developmental ecology through space and time: A future perspective. In Moen, P., Elder, G. H.Jr, & Lüscher, K. (Eds.), *Examining lives in context: Perspectives on the ecology of human development* (pp. 619–647). American Psychological Association. DOI: 10.1037/10176-018

Brosnan, M., Holt, S., Yuill, N., Good, J., & Parsons, S. (2017). Beyond autism and technology: Lessons from neurodiverse populations. *Journal of Enabling Technologies*, 11(2), 43–48. DOI: 10.1108/JET-02-2017-0007

Brown, J. S. (2008). *Growing Up Digital: How the Web Changes Work, Education, and Ways People Learn*. Change Magazine.

Brown, S. J. (2024). Assessing the risk of users of child sexual exploitation material committing further offences: A scoping review. *Journal of Sexual Aggression*, 30(1), 1–24. DOI: 10.1080/13552600.2022.2104394

Buchanan, N., & Mahoney, A. (2022). Development of a scale measuring online sexual harassment: Examining gender differences and the emotional impact of sexual harassment victimization online. *Legal and Criminological Psychology*, 27(1), 63–81. DOI: 10.1111/lcrp.12197

Bucharová, M., Malá, A., Kantor, J., & Svobodová, Z. (2020). Arts therapies interventions and their outcomes in the treatment of eating disorders: Scoping review protocol. *Behavioral Sciences (Basel, Switzerland)*, 10(12), 188. DOI: 10.3390/bs10120188 PMID: 33316926

Bucuţă, M. D., Dima, G., & Testoni, I. (2018). "When you thought that there is no one and nothing": The value of psychodrama in working with abused women. *Frontiers in Psychology*, 9, 1518. Advance online publication. DOI: 10.3389/fpsyg.2018.01518 PMID: 30190692

Budak, K. S., & Işıkoğlu, N. (2022). Dijital oyun bağımlılık eğilimi ve ebeveyn rehberlik stratejileri ölçeklerinin geliştirilmesi [Development of children's digital play addiction tendency and parental mediation scales]. *Ankara University Journal of Faculty of Educational Sciences*, 55(3), 693–740. DOI: 10.30964/auebfd.939653

Budak, K. S., & Işıkoğlu, N. (2023). Erken çocuklukta dijital oyun bağımlılık eğilimi: Çocuk ve ebeveyn özelliklerinin etkileri. *Mehmet Akif Ersoy Üniversitesi Eğitim Fakültesi Dergisi*, 66(66), 1–25. DOI: 10.21764/maeuefd.1081497

Buelga-Vázquez, S., Cava-Caballero, M. J., Moreno-Ruiz, D., & Ortega-Barón, J. (2022). Cyberbullying y conducta suicida en alumnado adolescente: Una revisión sistemática. *Review of Education*, 397, 43–67. DOI: 10.4438/1988-592X-RE-2022-397-539

Buglass, S., Binder, J., Betts, L., & Underwood, J. (2021). Asymmetrical third-person effects on the perceptions of online risk and harm among adolescents and adults. *Behaviour & Information Technology*, 40(11), 1090–1100. DOI: 10.1080/0144929X.2020.1742380

Buijs, P. C. M., Boot, E., Shugar, A., Fung, W. L. A., & Bassett, A. S. (2017). Internet safety issues for adolescents and adults with intellectual disabilities. *Journal of Applied Research in Intellectual Disabilities*, 30(2), 416–418. DOI: 10.1111/jar.12250 PMID: 26914835

Burén, J., & Lunde, C. (2018). Sexting among adolescents: A nuanced and gendered online challenge for young people. *Computers in Human Behavior*, 85, 210–217. DOI: 10.1016/j.chb.2018.02.003

Burić, J., Garcia, J. R., & Štulhofer, A. (2020). Is sexting bad for adolescent girls' psychological well-being? A longitudinal assessment in middle to late adolescence. *New Media & Society*, 1–20. DOI: 10.1177/1461444820931091

Burke, G., & Norvilitis, J. M. (2022). The relationships between cyberbullying, sexting, and college student well-being. In *Research Anthology on Combating Cyber-Aggression and Online Negativity* (pp. 789–802). IGI Global. DOI: 10.4018/978-1-6684-5594-4.ch043

Burke, M., Kraut, R., & Williams, D. (2010). Social use of computer-mediated communication by adults on the autism spectrum. In *Proceedings of the 2010 ACM Conference on Computer Supported Cooperative Work* (pp. 425-434). ACM. DOI: 10.1145/1718918.1718991

Burkett, M. (2015). Sex(t) talk: A qualitative analysis of young adults' negotiations of the pleasures and perils of sexting. *Sexuality & Culture*, 19(4), 835–863. DOI: 10.1007/s12119-015-9295-0

Burlet, R. E., & Panahon, C. J. (2022). Cyberbullying prevention and intervention: Current practices in schools. *Journal of Prevention and Health Promotion*, 3(2), 258–267. DOI: 10.1177/26320770221087454

Burton, B., & O'Toole, J. (2009). Power in their hands: The outcomes of the acting against bullying research project. *Applied Theatre Research*, 2009, 1–15.

Butwicka, A., Långström, N., Larsson, H., Lundström, S., Serlachius, E., Almqvist, C., Frisén, L., & Lichtenstein, P. (2017). Increased risk for substance use-related problems in autism spectrum disorders: A population-based cohort study. *Journal of Autism and Developmental Disorders*, 47(1), 80–89. DOI: 10.1007/s10803-016-2914-2 PMID: 27734228

Cabrera, M. C., Larrañaga Rubio, E., & Yubero, S. (2024). Variables sociofamiliares en adolescentes ciberacosadores: prevención e intervención desde el Trabajo Social [Socio-family variables in adolescent cyberbullies: prevention and intervention from Social Work]. *Alternativas. Cuadernos de Trabajo Social*, 31(2), 378–408. DOI: 10.14198/ALTERN.24774

Cagirkan, B., & Bilek, G. (2021). Cyberbullying among Turkish high school students. *Scandinavian Journal of Psychology*, 62(4), 608–616. DOI: 10.1111/sjop.12720 PMID: 33719100

Çalhan, C., & Göksu, İ. (2024). An effort to understand parents' media mediation roles and early childhood children's digital play addiction tendency: A descriptive correlational survey study. *Education and Information Technologies*, 29(14), 17825–17865. Advance online publication. DOI: 10.1007/s10639-024-12544-y

Call, C. (2023). Public perceptions and legal dimensions of juvenile sexting. *Journal of Social, Behavioral and Health Sciences*, 17(1), 196–216. DOI: 10.5590/JSBHS.2023.17.1.14

Camacho, M., Minelli, J., & Grosseck, G. (2-5 February 2012). *Self and Identity: Raising Undergraduate Students' Awareness on Their Digital Footprints. 4th World Conference on Educational Sciences (WCES-2012)*, Barcelona, Spain. DOI: 10.1016/j.sbspro.2012.06.032

Campbell, M., & Bauman, S. (2017). Cyberbullying: Definition, consequences, prevalence. In M. Campbell & S. Bauman (Eds.), *Reducing cyberbullying in schools* (pp. 3–16). Elsevier. DOI: 10.1016/B978-0-12-811423-0.00001-8

Campbell, M., Spears, B., Slee, P., Butler, D., & Kift, S. (2012). Victims' perceptions of traditional and cyberbullying, and the psychosocial correlates of their victimisation. *Emotional & Behavioural Difficulties*, 17(3-4), 389–401. DOI: 10.1080/13632752.2012.704316

Cantone, E., Piras, A. P., Vellante, M., Preti, A., Daníelsdóttir, S., D'Aloja, E., ... Bhugra, D. (2015). Interventions on bullying and cyberbullying in schools: A systematic review. *Clinical Practice and Epidemiology in Mental Health, 11*(Suppl 1), 58-76. DOI: 10.2174/1745017901511010058

Cao, X., Wu, Y., Cheng, B., & Ali, A. (2024). An investigation of the social media overload and academic performance. *Education and Information Technologies*, 29(5), 10303–10328. DOI: 10.1007/s10639-023-12213-6

Cardy, R., Smith, C., Suganthan, H., Jiang, Z., Wang, B., Malihi, M., Anagnostou, E., & Kushki, A. (2023). Patterns and impact of technology use in autistic children. *Research in Autism Spectrum Disorders*, 108, 102253. Advance online publication. DOI: 10.1016/j.rasd.2023.102253

Carrington, S., Campbell, M., Saggers, B., Ashburner, J., Vicig, F., Dillon-Wallace, J., & Hwang, Y. S. (2017). Recommendations of school students with autism spectrum disorder and their parents in regard to bullying and cyberbullying prevention and intervention. *International Journal of Inclusive Education*, 21(10), 1045–1064. DOI: 10.1080/13603116.2017.1331381

Casas, J. A., Ojeda, M., Elipe, P., & Del Rey, R. (2019). Exploring which factors contribute to teens' participation in sexting. *Computers in Human Behavior*, 100, 60–69. DOI: 10.1016/j.chb.2019.06.010

Castellanos, M., Wettstein, A., Wachs, S., Kansok-Dusche, J., Ballaschk, C., Krause, N., & Bilz, L. (2023). Hate speech in adolescents: A binational study on prevalence and demographic differences. *Frontiers in Education*, 8, 1076249. DOI: 10.3389/feduc.2023.1076249

Castro, Á., & Barrada, J. R. (2020). Dating apps and their sociodemographic and psychosocial correlates: A systematic review. *International Journal of Environmental Research and Public Health*, 17(18), 6500. Advance online publication. DOI: 10.3390/ijerph17186500 PMID: 32906632

Çelik, E., Özer, Y., & Özcan, S. (2021). Okul öncesi dönem çocuklarının ekran süresinin ebeveynlerin ekran kullanım alışkanlıkları ve aile işlevleri ile ilişkisi. *Çukurova Tıp Dergisi, 46*(4), 343-351. DOI: 10.17826/cumj.780582

Cernikova, M., Dedkova, L., & Smahel, D. (2018). Youth interaction with online strangers: Experiences and reactions to unknown people on the Internet. *Information Communication and Society*, 21(1), 94–110. DOI: 10.1080/1369118X.2016.1261169

Chadwick, D. D. (2019). Online risk for people with intellectual disabilities. *Tizard Learning Disability Review*, 24(4), 180–187. DOI: 10.1108/TLDR-03-2019-0008

Chadwick, D. D., Chapman, M., & Caton, S. (2019). Digital inclusion for people with an intellectual disability. In Attrill-Smith, A., Fullwood, C., Keep, M., & Kuss, D. J. (Eds.), *The Oxford handbook of cyberpsychology*. Oxford University Press., DOI: 10.1093/oxfordhb/9780198812746.013.17

Chadwick, D. D., Quinn, S., & Fullwood, C. (2017). Perceptions of the risks and benefits of Internet access and use by people with intellectual disabilities. *British Journal of Learning Disabilities*, 45(1), 21–31. DOI: 10.1111/bld.12170

Chalmers, C., Campbell, M. A., Spears, B. A., Butler, D., Cross, D., Slee, P., & Kift, S. (2016). School policies on bullying and cyberbullying: Perspectives across three Australian states. *Educational Research*, 58(1), 91–109. DOI: 10.1080/00131881.2015.1129114

Chamizo-Nieto, M. T., Wallace, A., & Rey, L. (2024). Anti-cyberbullying interventions at school: Comparing the effectiveness of gratitude and psychoeducational programmes. *The Journal of Positive Psychology*, 19(2), 291–300. DOI: 10.1080/17439760.2023.2170821

Champion, A. R., Oswald, F., Khera, D., & Pedersen, C. L. (2022). Examining the Gendered Impacts of Technology-Facilitated Sexual Violence: A Mixed Methods Approach. *Archives of Sexual Behavior*, 51(3), 1607–1624. DOI: 10.1007/s10508-021-02226-y PMID: 35182285

Cham, S., Cheng, G., & Lee, R. (2019). Digital addiction: Negative life experiences and potential for technology-assisted solutions. In Rocha, Á., Adeli, H., Reis, L., & Costanzo, S. (Eds.), *New knowledge in information systems and technologies* (Vol. 931, pp. 921–931). Springer., DOI: 10.1007/978-3-030-16184-2_87

Chang, M. L. Y., & Lee, I. O. (2024). Functional connectivity changes in the brain of adolescents with internet addiction: A systematic literature review of imaging studies. *PLOS Mental Health*, 1(1), e0000022. DOI: 10.1371/journal.pmen.0000022

Chang, W.-L., Wang, E., Chang, W.-H., Hu, H., Chang, T.-Y., Wu, Y., Wang, Y., Liang, Y., Wang, Y., & Kues, S. (2022). Study on the effect of psychodrama therapy on the emotional regulation of college teachers during the epidemic of Covid-19 coronavirus disease. *The International Journal of Neuropsychopharmacology*, 25(Supplement_1), A5–A6. DOI: 10.1093/ijnp/pyac032.006

Chan, H. C., & Wong, D. S. W. (2020). The overlap between cyberbullying perpetration and victimisation: Exploring the psychosocial characteristics of Hong Kong adolescents. *Asia Pacific Journal of Social Work*, 30(3), 164–180. DOI: 10.1080/02185385.2020.1761436

Chapman, S., McPhee, P., & Proudman, B. (1995). What is experiential education? *Journal of Experiential Education*, 18(1), 15–23. https://catalog.csupueblo.edu/academic-policies/experiential-education/experiential-education.pdf

Chatterjee, S. (2021). Impact of addiction to online platforms on quality of life. *AJIS. Australasian Journal of Information Systems*, 25(1), 1–25. DOI: 10.3127/ajis.v25i0.2761

Chaudron, S., Di Gioia, R., & Gemo, M. (2018). Young Children (0-8) and digital technology - A qualitative study across Europe. Jrc Science for Policy Report. DOI: 10.2760/294383

Chaux, E., & León, M. (2016). Homophobic Attitudes and Associated Factors Among Adolescents: A Comparison of Six Latin American Countries. *Journal of Homosexuality*, 63(9), 1253–1276. DOI: 10.1080/00918369.2016.1151697 PMID: 26861958

Chen, R., & MacCallum, K. (2023). Parental perceptions on children's use of digital technology: A systematic review. *ASCILITE Publications*, 334-339. DOI: 10.14742/apubs.2023.715

Cheng, M. M., & Udry, R. (2005). Sexual experience of adolescents with low cognitive abilities in the U.S. *Journal of Developmental and Physical Disabilities*, 17(2), 155–172. DOI: 10.1007/s10882-005-3686-3

Chen, I. H., Lee, Z. H., Dong, X. Y., Gamble, J. H., & Feng, H. W. (2020). The influence of parenting style and time management tendency on internet gaming disorder among adolescents. *International Journal of Environmental Research and Public Health*, 17(23), 9120. DOI: 10.3390/ijerph17239120 PMID: 33291336

Chen, P.-C., & Chen, Y.-H. (2023). Social media addiction and academic engagement as serial mediators between social anxiety and academic performance among college students. *BMC Psychology*, 11, 144. DOI: 10.1186/s40359-023-01110-2

Chen, Q., Chan, K. L., Guo, S., Chen, M., Lo, C. K. M., & Ip, P. (2023). Effectiveness of digital health interventions in reducing bullying and cyberbullying: A meta-analysis. *Trauma, Violence & Abuse*, 24(3), 1986–2002. DOI: 10.1177/15248380221082090 PMID: 35446724

Chen, R., Peng, K., Liu, J., Wilson, A., Wang, Y., Wilkinon, M. R., Wen, S., Cao, X., & Lu, J. (2020). Interpersonal trauma and risk of depression among adolescents: The mediating and moderating effect of interpersonal relationship and physical exercise. *Frontiers in Psychiatry*, 11, 194. DOI: 10.3389/fpsyt.2020.00194 PMID: 32351408

Chen, S. (2023). Modeling the effect of loving pedagogy dispositions and teacher self-efficacy on teacher burnout. *Frontiers in Psychology*, 14, 1157324. DOI: 10.3389/fpsyg.2023.1157324 PMID: 37251022

Chen, S., & Xia, Y. (2012). Research on application of multimedia technology in college physical education. *Procedia Engineering*, 29, 4213–4217. DOI: 10.1016/j.proeng.2012.01.645

Chen, W. W., Yuan, H., Yang, X., & Lai, S. K. (2020). Parenting, self-concept, and attitudes about romantic relationships. *Journal of Adolescence*, 82(1), 41–49. DOI: 10.1016/j.adolescence.2020.06.003 PMID: 32593052

Chen, Y.-L., Chen, S.-H., & Shur-Fen Gau, S. (2015). ADHD and autistic traits, family function, parenting style, and social adjustment for Internet addiction among children and adolescents in Taiwan: A longitudinal study. *Research in Developmental Disabilities*, 39, 20–31. DOI: 10.1016/j.ridd.2014.12.025 PMID: 25617844

Chicote-Beato, M., González-Víllora, S., Bodoque-Osma, A. R., & Navarro, R. (2024). Cyberbullying intervention and prevention programmes in Primary Education (6 to 12 years): A systematic review. *Aggression and Violent Behavior*, 77, 101938. DOI: 10.1016/j.avb.2024.101938

Children's Online Privacy Protection Rule. 16 C.F.R. § 312 (2013). Retrieved from https://www.ecfr.gov/current/title-16/chapter-I/subchapter-C/part-312

Chindamo, S., Buja, A., DeBattisti, E., Terraneo, A., Marini, E., Gomez Perez, L. J., Marconi, L., Baldo, V., Chiamenti, G., Doria, M., Ceschin, F., Malorgio, E., Tommasi, M., Sperotto, M., Buzzetti, R., & Gallimberti, L. (2019). Sleep and new media usage in toddlers. *European Journal of Pediatrics*, 178(4), 483–490. DOI: 10.1007/s00431-019-03318-7 PMID: 30652219

Chiza-Lozano, D., Vásquez-Mendoza, D., & Ramírez-Vega, C. (2021). Adicción a redes sociales y ciberbullying en los adolescentes. *Revista Muro de la Investigación*, 6(1), 34–44. DOI: 10.17162/rmi.v6i1.1437

Choi, S., & Clark, R.E. (2006). Cognitive and affective benefits of an animated pedagogical agent for learning English as a second language. *Journal of Educational Computing Research, 34*(4), 441-466. DOI: 10.2190/A064-U776-4208-N145

Choi, D., & DeLong, M. (2019). Defining Female Self Sexualization for the Twenty-First Century. *Sexuality & Culture*, 23(4), 1350–1371. DOI: 10.1007/s12119-019-09617-3

Choi, N. Y. (2020). The Correlations on Coping with Cyberviolence, Attribution Method and Social Support among Middle School Students. *Asia-Pacific Journal of Convergent Research Interchange*, 6(8), 31–39. DOI: 10.47116/apjcri.2020.08.04

Cho, K. S., & Lee, J. M. (2017). Influence of smartphone addiction proneness of young children on problematic behaviors and emotional intelligence: Mediating self- assessment effects of parents using smartphones. *Computers in Human Behavior*, 66, 303–311. DOI: 10.1016/j.chb.2016.09.063

Choo, H., Sim, T., Liau, A. K. F., Gentile, D. A., & Khoo, A. (2015). Parental influences on pathological symptoms of video-gaming among children and adolescents: A prospective study. *Journal of Child and Family Studies*, 24(5), 1429–1441. DOI: 10.1007/s10826-014-9949-9

Chou, S. W., & Liu, C. H. (2005). Learning effectiveness in a Web-based virtual learning environment: A learner control perspective. *Journal of Computer Assisted Learning*, 21(1), 65–76. DOI: 10.1111/j.1365-2729.2005.00114.x

Chou, W.-J., Huang, M.-F., Chang, Y.-P., Chen, Y.-M., Hu, H.-F., & Yen, C.-F. (2017). Social skills deficits and their association with Internet addiction and activities in adolescents with attention-deficit/hyperactivity disorder. *Journal of Behavioral Addictions*, 6(1), 42–50. DOI: 10.1556/2006.6.2017.005 PMID: 28245666

Chown, N., Robinson, J., Beardon, L., Downing, J., Hughes, L., Leatherland, J., Fox, K., Hickman, L., & MacGregor, D. (2017). Improving research about us, with us: A draft framework for inclusive autism research. *Disability & Society*, 32(5), 720–734. DOI: 10.1080/09687599.2017.1320273

Cho, Y. J., Thrasher, J. F., Reid, J. L., Hitchman, S., & Hammond, D. (2019). Youth self-reported exposure to and perceptions of vaping advertisements: Findings from the 2017 International Tobacco Control Youth Tobacco and Vaping Survey. *Preventive Medicine*, 126, 105775. Advance online publication. DOI: 10.1016/j.ypmed.2019.105775 PMID: 31323286

Chrienová, M., Majerová Kropáčová, K., Oster, J., & Osterová, I. (2019). Výskyt nežiadúcich javov v základných školách v okrese Lučenec. Retrieved from https://preventista.sk/info/prieskum-lucenec.

Christensen, C. M., Horn, M. B., & Johnson, C. W. (2008). *Disrupting class. How disruptive innovation will change the way the world learns.* McGraw-Hill companies.

Christ, S. E., Holt, D. D., White, D. A., & Green, L. (2007). Inhibitory control in children with autism spectrum disorder. *Journal of Autism and Developmental Disorders*, 37(6), 1155–1165. DOI: 10.1007/s10803-006-0259-y PMID: 17066307

Chu, K.-H., Allem, J.-P., Cruz, T. B., & Unger, J. B. (2017). Vaping on Instagram: Cloud chasing, hand checks and product placement. *Tobacco Control*, 26(5), 575–578. DOI: 10.1136/tobaccocontrol-2016-053052 PMID: 27660111

Cingel, D. P., & Krcmar, M. (2013). Predicting media use in very young children: The role of demographics and parent attitudes. *Communication Studies*, 64(4), 374–394. DOI: 10.1080/10510974.2013.770408

Cioppa, V., O'Neil, A., & Craig, W. (2015). Learning from traditional bullying interventions: A review of research on cyberbullying and best practice. *Aggression and Violent Behavior*, 23, 61–68. DOI: 10.1016/j.avb.2015.05.009

Clancy, E. M., Hallford, D., March, E., Howard, D., Toumbourou, J. W., & Klettke, B. (2023). The role of consent and motivations in sext dissemination. *Journal of Interpersonal Violence*, 38(15-16), 9315–9342. DOI: 10.1177/08862605231163886 PMID: 37067003

Clancy, E. M., Howard, D., Chong, S., & Klettke, B. (2021). Dream it, do it? Associations between pornography use, risky sexual behaviour, sexual preoccupation and sexting behaviours among young Australian adults. *Sexes*, 2(4), 433–444. DOI: 10.3390/sexes2040034

Clancy, E. M., Klettke, B., Crossman, A. M., Hallford, D. J., Howard, D., & Toumbourou, J. W. (2021). Sext dissemination: Differences across nations in motivations and associations. *International Journal of Environmental Research and Public Health*, 18(5), 2429. Advance online publication. DOI: 10.3390/ijerph18052429 PMID: 33801431

Clancy, E. M., Klettke, B., Hallford, D. J., Crossman, A. M., Maas, M. K., & Toumbourou, J. W. (2020). Sharing is not always caring: Understanding motivations and behavioural associations with sext dissemination. *Computers in Human Behavior*, 112, 106460. Advance online publication. DOI: 10.1016/j.chb.2020.106460

Clark, J. M., & Paivio, A. (1991). Dual coding theory and education. *Educational Psychology Review*, 3(3), 149–210. DOI: 10.1007/BF01320076

Clark, L. S. (2011). Parental mediation theory for the digital age. *Communication Theory*, 21(4), 323–343. DOI: 10.1111/j.1468-2885.2011.01391.x

Clark, R. C., & Mayer, R. E. (2016). *E-Learning and the Science of Instruction: Proven Guidelines for Consumers and Designers of Multimedia Learning* (4th ed.). Wiley. DOI: 10.1002/9781119239086

Coduto, K. D. (2024). Channel affordances for sexting: Social presence relates to improved self-esteem, sexual gratification, and sexting certainty. *Sexuality & Culture*, 28(1), 228–242. DOI: 10.1007/s12119-023-10112-z

Cole, A. G., Lienemann, B. A., Sun, J., Chang, J., & Zhu, S.-H. (2022). California school staff reports of seeing students vaping at school and disciplinary actions. *The Journal of School Nursing: the Official Publication of the National Association of School Nurses*. Advance online publication. DOI: 10.1177/10598405221127694 PMID: 36168212

Concerto, C., Rodolico, A., Avanzato, C., Fusar-Poli, L., Signorelli, M. S., Battaglia, F., & Aguglia, E. (2021). Autistic traits and attention-deficit hyperactivity disorder symptoms predict the severity of internet gaming disorder in an Italian adult population. *Brain Sciences*, 11(6), 774. Advance online publication. DOI: 10.3390/brainsci11060774 PMID: 34207989

Confalonieri, E., Cuccì, G., Olivari, M. G., Parise, M., Borroni, E., & Villani, D. (2020). What are you sexting? Parental practices, sexting attitudes and behaviors among Italian adolescents. *BMC Psychology, 8*(1), 63 1-11. https://doi.org/DOI: 10.1186/s40359-020-00425-1

Connelly, C. (2023). Hypnosis based treatments for internet addiction disorder: systematic review. *Journal of Addiction Research, 7*(1), 1-6.

Cooper, A., Delmonico, D. L., & Burg, R. (2000). Cybersex users, abusers, and compulsives: New findings and implications. *Sexual Addiction & Compulsivity*, 7(1-2), 5–29. DOI: 10.1080/10720160008400205

Copeland, W. E., Keeler, G., Angold, A., & Costello, E. J. (2007). Traumatic events and posttraumatic stress in childhood. *Archives of General Psychiatry*, 64(5), 577–584. DOI: 10.1001/archpsyc.64.5.577 PMID: 17485609

Copp, J. E., Mumford, E. A., & Taylor, B. G. (2021). Online sexual harassment and cyberbullying in a nationally representative sample of teens: Prevalence, predictors, and consequences. *Journal of Adolescence*, 93(1), 202–211. DOI: 10.1016/j.adolescence.2021.10.003 PMID: 34801812

Corcoran, L., Guckin, C. M., & Prentice, G. (2015). Cyberbullying or Cyber Aggression?: A Review of Existing Definitions of Cyber-Based Peer-to-Peer Aggression. *Societies (Basel, Switzerland)*, 5(2), 245–255. DOI: 10.3390/soc5020245

Cornelius, T. L., Bell, K. M., Kistler, T., & Drouin, M. (2020). Consensual sexting among college students: The interplay of coercion and intimate partner aggression in perceived consequences of sexting. *International Journal of Environmental Research and Public Health*, 17(19), 7141. Advance online publication. DOI: 10.3390/ijerph17197141 PMID: 33003567

Corp, I. B. M. (2019). *IBM SPSS Statistics for Windows (Version 26.0)* [Computer software]. IBM Corp.

Cortés-Pascual, A., Cano-Escorianza, J., Elboj-Saso, C., & Iñiguez-Berrozpe, T. (2020). Positive relationships for the prevention of bullying and cyberbullying: A study in Aragón (Spain). *International Journal of Adolescence and Youth*, 25(1), 182–199. DOI: 10.1080/02673843.2019.1602064

Courtice, E. L., Czechowski, K., Noorishad, P. G., & Shaughnessy, K. (2021). Unsolicited pics and sexual scripts: Gender and relationship context of compliant and non-consensual technology-mediated sexual interactions. *Frontiers in Psychology*, 12, 673202. Advance online publication. DOI: 10.3389/fpsyg.2021.673202 PMID: 34349699

Coutelle, R., Weiner, L., Paasche, C., Pottelette, J., Bertschy, G., Schröder, C. M., & Lalanne, L. (2021). Autism spectrum disorder and video games: Restricted interests or addiction? *International Journal of Mental Health and Addiction*, 1–22. DOI: 10.1007/s11469-021-00511-4

Craig, F., Margari, F., Legrottaglie, A. R., Palumbi, R., de Giambattista, C., & Margari, L. (2016). A review of executive function deficits in autism spectrum disorder and attention-deficit/hyperactivity disorder. *Neuropsychiatric Disease and Treatment*, 12, 1191–1202. DOI: 10.2147/NDT.S104620 PMID: 27274255

Craig, F., Tenuta, F., De Giacomo, A., Trabacca, A., & Costabile, A. (2021). A systematic review of problematic video-game use in people with autism spectrum disorders. *Research in Autism Spectrum Disorders*, 82, 101726. Advance online publication. DOI: 10.1016/j.rasd.2021.101726

Craig, S. D., & Schroeder, N. L. (2017). Reconsidering the voice effect when learning from a virtual human. *Computers & Education*, 114, 193–205. DOI: 10.1016/j.compedu.2017.07.003

Crane, C., Hotton, M., Shelemy, L., & Knowles-Bevis, R. (2024). The association between individual differences in motivational readiness at entry to treatment and treatment attendance and outcome in cognitive behaviour therapy: A systematic review. *Cognitive Therapy and Research*, 48(4), 10504. DOI: 10.1007/s10608-024-10504-x

Cricenti, C., Pizzo, A., Quaglieri, A., Mari, E., Cordellieri, P., Bonucchi, C., Torretta, P., Giannini, A. M., & Lausi, G. (2022). Did they deserve it? Adolescents' perception of online harassment in a real-case scenario. *International Journal of Environmental Research and Public Health*, 19(24), 17040. Advance online publication. DOI: 10.3390/ijerph192417040 PMID: 36554921

Crimmins, D. M., & Seigfried-Spellar, K. C. (2014). Peer attachment, sexual experiences, and risky online behaviors as predictors of sexting behaviors among undergraduate students. *Computers in Human Behavior*, 32, 268–275. DOI: 10.1016/j.chb.2013.12.012

Crofts, T., & Lievens, E. (2018). Sexting and the Law. In M. Walgrave, J. Van Oytsel, K., Ponnet, & J. R. Temple (Eds.), *Sexting. Motives and risk in online sexual self*-representation (pp.119–136). Palgrave Macmillan Cham. *https://doi.org/*DOI: 10.1007/978-3-319-71882-8_8

Cross, D. (2015). School-based strategies to prevent bullying and cyberbullying. *The International Journal of Emotional Education*, 7(1), 78–93.

Cross, D., Monks, H., Hall, M., Shaw, T., Pintabona, Y., Erceg, E., Hamilton, G., Roberts, C., Waters, S., & Lester, L. (2011). Three-year results of the Friendly Schools whole-of-school intervention on children's bullying behaviour. *British Educational Research Journal*, 37(1), 105–129. DOI: 10.1080/01411920903420024

Cross, D., Shaw, T., Hadwen, K., Cardoso, P., Slee, P., Roberts, C., Thomas, L., & Barnes, A. (2016). Longitudinal impact of the Cyber Friendly Schools program on adolescents' cyberbullying behavior. *Aggressive Behavior*, 42(2), 166–180. DOI: 10.1002/ab.21609 PMID: 26351263

Currin, J. M., Hubach, R. D., Sanders, C., & Hammer, T. R. (2017). Sexting leads to "risky" sex? An analysis of sexting behaviors in a nonuniversity-based, older adult population. *Journal of Sex & Marital Therapy*, 43(7), 689–702. DOI: 10.1080/0092623X.2016.1246390 PMID: 27732509

Currin, J. M., Jayne, C. N., Hammer, T. R., Brim, T., & Hubach, R. D. (2016). Explicitly pressing send: Impact of sexting on relationship satisfaction. *The American Journal of Family Therapy*, 44(3), 143–154. DOI: 10.1080/01926187.2016.1145086

Currin, J. M., Pascarella, L. A., & Hubach, R. D. (2020). "To feel close when miles apart": Qualitative analysis of motivations to sext in a relationship. *Sexual and Relationship Therapy*, 35(2), 244–257. DOI: 10.1080/14681994.2020.1714024

Curry, A. E., Metzger, K. B., Carey, M. E., Sartin, E. B., Huang, P., & Yerys, B. E. (2021). Comparison of motor vehicle crashes, traffic violations, and license suspensions between autistic and non-autistic adolescent and young adult drivers. *Journal of the American Academy of Child and Adolescent Psychiatry*, 60(7), 913–923. DOI: 10.1016/j.jaac.2021.01.001 PMID: 33453361

Dabbagh, N., & Kitsantas, A. (2012). Personal Learning Environments, Social Media, and Self-Regulated Learning: A Natural Formula for Connecting Formal and Informal Learning. *The Internet and Higher Education*, 15(1), 3–8. DOI: 10.1016/j.iheduc.2011.06.002

Daher, W., Omar, A., Swaity, H., Allan, B., Issa, S. D., Amer, Z., & Halabi, A. (2022). Upper-Basic Schoolteachers' Beliefs about Their Students' Awareness of Digital Citizenship. *Sustainability (Basel)*, 14(19), 12865. DOI: 10.3390/su141912865

Dalacosta, K., Kamariotaki-Paparrigopoulou, M., Palyvos, J. A., & Spyrellis, N. (2009). Multimedia application with animated cartoons for teaching science in elementary education. *Computers & Education*, 52(4), 741–748. DOI: 10.1016/j.compedu.2008.11.018

Daniels, E. A., Dajches, L., Terán, L., Gahler, H., Choi, H. J., Speno, A., & Stevens, J. (2024). The Sexual Landscape of Youth: How Adolescents From the U.S. Make Sense of Sexting. *Journal of Adolescent Research*. Advance online publication. DOI: 10.1177/07435584241231448

Daradoumis, T., & Arguedas, M. (2020). Cultivating Students' Reflective Learning in Metacognitive Activities through an Affective Pedagogical Agent. *Journal of Educational Technology & Society*, 23(2), 19–31. https://www.jstor.org/stable/26921131

Daud, A., Omar, S. Z., Hassan, M. D. S., Bolong, J., & Teimouri, M. (2014). Parental mediation of children's positive use of the Internet. *Life Science Journal*, 11(8), 360–369.

Day, T. (2010). The New Digital Dating Behavior-Sexting: Teens' Explicit Love Letters: Criminal Justice or Civil Liability. *Hastings Communication & Entertainment Law Journal*, 33(1), 69–96.

De Oliveira Collet, G., De Morais Ferreira, F., Ceron, D. F., De Lourdes Calvo Fracasso, M., & Santin, G. C. (2024). Influence of digital health literacy on online health-related behaviors influenced by internet advertising. *BMC Public Health*, 24(1), 1949. DOI: 10.1186/s12889-024-19506-6 PMID: 39033160

De Pasquale, C., Sciacca, F., Martinelli, V., Chiappedi, M., Dinaro, C., & Hichy, Z. (2020). Relationship of internet gaming disorder with psychopathology and social adaptation in Italian young adults. *International Journal of Environmental Research and Public Health*, 17(21), 8201. DOI: 10.3390/ijerph17218201 PMID: 33172015

De Wit, H. (2009). Impulsivity as a determinant and consequence of drug use: A review of underlying processes. *Addiction Biology*, 14(1), 22–31. DOI: 10.1111/j.1369-1600.2008.00129.x PMID: 18855805

Deckman, T., & DeWall, C. N. (2011). Negative urgency and risky sexual behaviors: A clarification of the relationship between impulsivity and risky sexual behavior. *Personality and Individual Differences*, 51(5), 674–678. DOI: 10.1016/j.paid.2011.06.004

DeJonckheere, M., & Vaughn, L. M. (2019). Semistructured interviewing in primary care research: A balance of relationship and rigour. *Family Medicine and Community Health*, 7(2), e000057. Advance online publication. DOI: 10.1136/fmch-2018-000057 PMID: 32148704

Del Rey, R., Ortega-Ruiz, R., & Casas, J. A. (2019). Asegúrate: An intervention program against cyberbullying based on teachers' commitment and on the design of its instructional materials. *International Journal of Environmental Research and Public Health*, 16(3), 434. DOI: 10.3390/ijerph16030434 PMID: 30717335

Demir, Y., & Kutlu, M. (2018). The relationship among internet addiction, academic motivation, academic procrastination and school attachment in adolescents. *International Online Journal of Educational Sciences*, 9(3), 65–78. DOI: 10.15345/iojes.2018.05.020

Dempsey, A. G., Sulkowski, M. L., Nichols, R., & Storch, E. A. (2009). Differences between peer victimization in cyber and physical settings and associated psychosocial adjustment in early adolescence. *Psychology in the Schools*, 46(10), 962–972. DOI: 10.1002/pits.20437

den Houting, J. (2019). Neurodiversity: An insider's perspective. *Autism*, 23(2), 271–273. DOI: 10.1177/1362361318820762 PMID: 30556743

Dennehy, R., Meaney, S., Walsh, K., Sinnott, C., Cronin, M., & Arensman, E. (2020). Young people's conceptualizations of the nature of cyberbullying: A systematic review and synthesis of qualitative research. *Aggression and Violent Behavior*, 51, 101379. DOI: 10.1016/j.avb.2020.101379

Dennen, V. P., Choi, H., & Word, K. (2020). Social media, teenagers, and the school context: A scoping review of research in education and related fields. *Educational Technology Research and Development*, 68(4), 1635–1658. DOI: 10.1007/s11423-020-09796-z

Denvir, C. (2016). Online and in the know? Public legal education, young people and the Internet. *Computers & Education*, 92–93, 204–220. DOI: 10.1016/j.compedu.2015.10.003

Deol, Y., & Lashai, M. (2022). Impact of Cyberbullying on Adolescent Mental Health in the midst of pandemic – Hidden Crisis. *European Psychiatry : the Journal of the Association of European Psychiatrists*, 65(S1), S432. DOI: 10.1192/j.eurpsy.2022.1096

Derevensky, J. L., Hayman, V., & Lynette Gilbeau, . (2019). Behavioral addictions: Excessive gambling, gaming, internet, and smartphone use among children and adolescents. *Pediatric Clinics of North America*, 66(6), 1163–1182. DOI: 10.1016/j.pcl.2019.08.008 PMID: 31679605

Desrosiers, H., Japel, C., Singh, P. R. P., & Tétreault, K. (2012). *Positive Teacher-Student Relationships: Associations with Child Characteristics and Academic Achievement in Elementary School*. Institut de la Statistique Québec. https://www.jesuisjeserai.stat.gouv.qc.ca/publications/ELDEQ_fasc6no2_an.pdf

Devi, R., & Dhall, P. (2017). Procrastination: A behavior need to be changed to have success. *International Education and esearch Journal, 3*(5), 475-476.

Dewinter, J., De Graaf, H., & Begeer, S. (2017). Sexual orientation, gender identity, and romantic relationships in adolescents and adults with autism spectrum disorder. *Journal of Autism and Developmental Disorders*, 47(9), 2927–2934. DOI: 10.1007/s10803-017-3199-9 PMID: 28597143

Diamanduros, T., Downs, E., & Jenkins, S. J. (2008). The role of school psychologists in the assessment, prevention, and intervention of cyberbullying. *Psychology in the Schools*, 45(8), 693–704. DOI: 10.1002/pits.20335

Dias, C. C. V., da Silva, J. V. C., & Maciel, S. C. (2021). Construction and validity evidence of the Autistic Person's Socialization Beliefs Scale (APSBS). *Trends in Psychology*, 29(4), 581–594. DOI: 10.1007/s43076-021-00071-5

DiClemente, C. C., Schlundt, D., & Gemmell, L. (2004). Readiness and stages of change in addiction treatment. *The American Journal on Addictions*, 13(2), 103–119. DOI: 10.1080/10550490490435777 PMID: 15204662

Dieris-Hirche, J., Bottel, L., Pape, M., Te Wildt, B. T., Wölfling, K., Timmesfeld, N., Neumann, A., Neusser, S., Beckers, R., Henningsen, P., & Herpertz, S. (2021). Effects of an online-based motivational intervention to reduce problematic internet use and promote treatment motivation in internet gaming disorder and internet use disorder (OMPRIS): Study protocol for a randomised controlled trial. *BMJ Open*, 11(8), e045840. DOI: 10.1136/bmjopen-2020-045840 PMID: 34344675

Dinçer, S., & Doğanay, A. (2017). The effects of multiple-pedagogical agents on learners' academic success, motivation, and cognitive load. *Computers & Education*, 11, 74–100. DOI: 10.1016/j.compedu.2017.04.005

Dir, A. L., Coskunpinar, A., Steiner, J. L., & Cyders, M. A. (2013). Understanding differences in sexting behaviors across gender, relationship status, and sexual identity, and the role of expectancies in sexting. *Cyberpsychology, Behavior, and Social Networking*, 16(8), 568–574. DOI: 10.1089/cyber.2012.0545 PMID: 23675996

Dir, A. L., Cyders, M. A., & Coskunpinar, A. (2013). From the bar to the bed via mobile phone: A first test of the role of problematic alcohol use, sexting, and impulsivity-related traits in sexual hookups. *Computers in Human Behavior*, 29(4), 1664–1670. DOI: 10.1016/j.chb.2013.01.039

Doane, A., Kelley, M., & Pearson, M. (2016). Reducing cyberbullying: A theory of reasoned action-based video prevention program for college students. *Aggressive Behavior*, 42(2), 136–146. DOI: 10.1002/ab.21610 PMID: 26349445

Dobson, A. S. (2019). 'The Things You Didn't Do': Gender, Slut-Shaming, and the Need to Address Sexual Harassment in Narrative Resources Responding to Sexting and Cyberbullying. In Vandebosch, H., & Green, L. (Eds.), *Narratives in Research and Interventions on Cyberbullying among Young People* (pp. 147–160). Springer. DOI: 10.1007/978-3-030-04960-7_10

Dodaj, A., Prijatelj, K., & Kuterovac Jagodić, G. (2024). Sexting Behavior Among Youths: Nature, Determinants, and Consequences. *Psihologijske Teme*, 33(1), 171–189. DOI: 10.31820/pt.33.1.9

Dodaj, A., & Sesar, K. (2020). Sexting categories. *Mediterranean Journal of Clinical Psychology*, 8(2). Advance online publication. DOI: 10.6092/2282-1619/mjcp-2432

Dodaj, A., & Sesar, K. (2021). Social Ecological Approach to Sexting Behaviour. *Central European Journal of Paediatrics*, 17(2), 145–156. Advance online publication. DOI: 10.5457/p2005-114.303

Dodaj, A., & Sesar, K. (2023). Individual and cross-cultural predictors of sexting among adults from Bosnia and Herzegovina and Croatia. *Sexuality Research & Social Policy*, 20(4), 1537–1551. DOI: 10.1007/s13178-023-00807-1

Dodaj, A., Sesar, K., Bošnjak, L., & Vučić, M. (2024). Theory of planned behaviour and sexting intention of college student. *Emerging Adulthood*, 12(2), 163–174. DOI: 10.1177/21676968231208343

Dodaj, A., Sesar, K., & Novak, T. (2022). A Cross-Cultural Examination of the Sexting Motives and Attitudes: Bosnia and Herzegovina vs. Croatia. *Human Behavior and Emerging Technologies*, 2022(1), 7606949. Advance online publication. DOI: 10.1155/2022/7606949

Dodaj, A., Sesar, K., Pérez, M. O., Del Rey, R., Howard, D., & Speno, A. G. (2023). Using vignettes in qualitative research to assess young adults' perspectives of sexting behaviours. *Human Technology*, 19(1), 103–120. DOI: 10.14254/1795-6889.2023.19-1.7

Doleac, J., Temple, C., Pritchard, D., & Roberts, A. (2020). Which prisoner reentry programs work? Replicating and extending analyses of three RCTs. *International Review of Law and Economics*, 62, 105902. DOI: 10.1016/j.irle.2020.105902

Dolev-Cohen, M., Nezer, I., & Abu Zumt, A. (2023). A Qualitative Examination of School Counselors' Experiences of Sextortion Cases of Female Students in Israel. *Sexual Abuse*, 35(8), 903–926. DOI: 10.1177/10790632221145925 PMID: 36510813

Dolly, S. K., & Samantaray, N. N. (2024). Navigating the digital landscape: Relationship between type of internet use and well-being among students—A mediation and moderation analysis. *Indian Journal of Psychiatry*, 66(3), 263–271. DOI: 10.4103/indianjpsychiatry.indianjpsychiatry_718_23 PMID: 39100120

Doney, H. (1970). The theory and practice of hypnosis. *Canadian Family Physician Médecin de Famille Canadien*, 16(2), 52. PMID: 20468477

Donohew, L., Zimmerman, R., Cupp, P. S., Novak, S., Colon, S., & Abell, R. (2000). Sensation seeking, impulsive decision-making, and risky sex: Implications for risk-taking and design of interventions. *Personality and Individual Differences*, 28(6), 1079–1091. DOI: 10.1016/S0191-8869(99)00158-0

Donohoe, P. (2016). *Teacher utilisation of role-play to reduce bullying in a primary school setting*. Trinity.

Donohoe, P., & O'Sullivan, C. (2015). The Bullying Prevention Pack: Fostering vocabulary and knowledge on the topic of bullying and prevention using role-play and discussion to reduce primary school bullying. *Scenario: A Journal of Performative Teaching, Learning. Research*, 9(1), 97–113. DOI: 10.33178/scenario.9.1.6

Döring, N. (2014). Consensual sexting among adolescents: Risk prevention through abstinence education or safer sexting? *Cyberpsychology (Brno)*, 8(1), 1–18. DOI: 10.5817/CP2014-1-9

Dotson, E. (2021). *Behold the man: The hype and selling of male beauty in media and culture*. Routledge. DOI: 10.4324/9781315865362

Doty, J. L., Girón, K., Mehari, K. R., Sharma, D., Smith, S. J., Su, Y. W., Ma, X., Rijo, D., & Rousso, B. (2021). The dosage, context, and modality of interventions to prevent cyberbullying perpetration and victimization: A systematic review. *Prevention Science*, 23(4), 523–537. DOI: 10.1007/s11121-021-01314-8 PMID: 34714506

Douglass, B., Solecki, S., & Fay-Hillier, T. (2020). The harmful consequences of vaping: A public health threat. *Journal of Addictions Nursing*, 31(2), 79–84. DOI: 10.1097/JAN.0000000000000332 PMID: 32487933

Douglass, C. H., Wright, C. J. C., Davis, A. C., & Lim, M. S. C. (2020). Non-consensual sharing of personal sexually explicit imagery among young people in Australia: Results from an online survey. *Sexual Health*, 17(2), 182–186. DOI: 10.1071/SH19147 PMID: 32135074

Draucker, C. B., Martsolf, D. S., & Poole, C. (2009). Developing distress protocols for research on sensitive topics. *Archives of Psychiatric Nursing*, 23(5), 343–350. DOI: 10.1016/j.apnu.2008.10.008 PMID: 19766925

Drouin, M. (2015). Sexual communication in the digital age. In L. D. Rosen, C. Nancy & L. M. Carrier (Eds.), *The Wiley handbook of psychology, technology, and society*, (pp. 176–191). John Wiley & Sons. DOI: 10.1002/9781118771952.ch10

Drouin, M., Coupe, M., & Temple, J. R. (2017). Is sexting good for your relationship? It depends.... *Computers in Human Behavior*, 75, 749–756. DOI: 10.1016/j.chb.2017.06.018

Drouin, M., & Landgraff, C. (2012). Texting, sexting, and attachment in college students' romantic relationships. *Computers in Human Behavior*, 28(2), 444–449. DOI: 10.1016/j.chb.2011.10.015

Drouin, M., Ross, J., & Tobin, E. (2015). Sexting: A new, digital vehicle for intimate partner aggression? *Computers in Human Behavior*, 50, 197–204. DOI: 10.1016/j.chb.2015.04.001

Drouin, M., & Tobin, E. (2014). Unwanted but consensual sexting among young adults: Relations with attachment and sexual motivations. *Computers in Human Behavior*, 31, 412–418. DOI: 10.1016/j.chb.2013.11.001

Drouin, M., Tobin, E., & Wygant, K. (2014). "Love the way you lie": Sexting deception in romantic relationships. *Computers in Human Behavior*, 35, 542–547. DOI: 10.1016/j.chb.2014.02.047

Drouin, M., Vogel, K. N., Surbey, A., & Stills, J. R. (2013). Let's talk about sexting, baby: Computer-mediated sexual behaviors among young adults. *Computers in Human Behavior*, 29(5), 25–30. DOI: 10.1016/j.chb.2012.12.030

Duell, N., Steinberg, L., Chein, J., Al-Hassan, S. M., Bacchini, D., Lei, C., Chaudhary, N., Di Giunta, L., Dodge, K. A., Fanti, K. A., Lansford, J. E., Malone, P. S., Oburu, P., Pastorelli, C., Skinner, A. T., Sorbring, E., Tapanya, S., Uribe Tirado, L. M., & Alampay, L. P. (2016). Interaction of reward seeking and self-regulation in the prediction of risk taking: A cross-national test of the dual systems model. *Developmental Psychology*, 52(10), 1593–1605. DOI: 10.1037/dev0000152 PMID: 27598251

Dully, J., Walsh, K., Doyle, C., & O'Reilly, G. (2023). Adolescent experiences of sexting: A systematic review of the qualitative literature, and recommendations for practice. *Journal of Adolescence*, 95(6), 1077–1105. DOI: 10.1002/jad.12181 PMID: 37157169

Dunn, L. W., & Graig, J. G. (2021). *Understanding Human Development* [in Greek]. Papazisi.

Durlak, J. A., Weissberg, R. P., Dymnicki, B. A., Taylor, D. R., & Schellinger, B. K. (2011). The impact of enhancing students' social and emotional learning: A meta-analysis of school-based universal interventions. *Child Development*, 82(1), 405–432. DOI: 10.1111/j.1467-8624.2010.01564.x PMID: 21291449

Durwin, C. C., & Reese-Weber, M. (2024). *Educational Psychology: Theory and Practice* [in Greek]. Tziola.

Dwyer, P. (2022). The neurodiversity approach(es): What are they and what do they mean for researchers? *Human Development*, 66(2), 73–92. DOI: 10.1159/000523723 PMID: 36158596

Eaton, A. A., Jacobs, H. E., & Ruvacalba, Y. (2017). *2017 Nationwide Online Study of Nonconsensual Porn Victimization and Perpetration.* Cyber Civil Rights Initiative. Retrieved from: https://www.cybercivilrights.org/wp-content/uploads/2017/06/CCRI-2017-Research-Report.pdf

Efstratopoulou, M., Delligianidou, S., & Sofologi, M. (2021). Exploring parents' experience on distance learning for students with ASD. *European Journal of Special Education Research*, 7(1), 14–23. DOI: 10.46827/ejse.v7i1.3525

Eirich, R., McArthur, B. A., Anhorn, C., McGuinness, C., Christakis, D. A., & Madigan, S. (2022). Association of screen time with internalizing and externalizing behavior problems in children 12 years or younger: A systematic review and meta-analysis. *JAMA Psychiatry*, 79(5), 393–405. DOI: 10.1001/jamapsychiatry.2022.0155 PMID: 35293954

El Asam, A., & Katz, A. (2018). Vulnerable young people and their experience of online risks. *Human-Computer Interaction*, 33(4), 281–304. DOI: 10.1080/07370024.2018.1437544

Elbedour, S., Alqahtani, S., El Sheikh Rihan, I., Bawalsah, J. A., Booker-Ammah, B., & Turner, J. F.Jr. (2020). Cyberbullying: Roles of school psychologists and school counselors in addressing a pervasive social justice issue. *Children and Youth Services Review*, 109, 104720. DOI: 10.1016/j.childyouth.2019.104720

Elliott, J.. (2013). Teaching and learning digital citizenship in schools: The learning needs of teachers. *Computers & Education*, 69, 46–55.

El-Mazahy, H. (2023). Psychodrama games: A framework for heterogenous psychodrama groups with children from Egypt. *Zeitschrift für Psychodrama und Soziometrie*, 22(2), 365–376. DOI: 10.1007/s11620-023-00736-6

Elpus, K., & Carter, B. A. (2016). Bullying victimization among music ensemble and theatre students in the United States. *Journal of Research in Music Education*, 64(3), 322–343. DOI: 10.1177/0022429416658642

El-Sabagh, H. A. (2021). Adaptive e-learning environment based on learning styles and its impact on development students' engagement. *International Journal of Educational Technology in Higher Education*, 18(1), 53. DOI: 10.1186/s41239-021-00289-4

Emiroğlu İlvan, T., & Ceylan, R. (2023). Predicting preschool children's digital play addiction tendency during Covid-19 pandemic: Regarding the mother-child relationship, and child-and family-related factors. *Education and Information Technologies*, 28(12), 15687–15716. DOI: 10.1007/s10639-023-11802-9 PMID: 37361780

Endendijk, J. J., van Baar, A. L., & Deković, M. (2020). He is a stud, she is a slut! A meta-analysis on the continued existence of sexual double standards. *Personality and Social Psychology Review*, 24(2), 163–190. DOI: 10.1177/1088868319891310 PMID: 31880971

Englander, E. (2012). *Low risk associated with most teenage sexting: A study of 617 18-year-olds*. https://vc.bridgew.edu/marc_reports/6

Englander, E. (2015). Coerced Sexting and Revenge Porn Among Teens. *Bullying, Teen Aggression & Social Media, 1*(2), 19–21. https://vc.bridgew.edu/psychology_fac/69

Englander, E. (2015). Coerced sexting and revenge porn among teens. *Bullying. Teen Aggression & Social Media*, 1(2), 19–21.

Englander, E. (2019). What do we know about sexting, and when did we know it? *The Journal of Adolescent Health*, 65(5), 577–578. DOI: 10.1016/j.jadohealth.2019.08.004 PMID: 31648755

Englander, E. K., & McCoy, M. (2017). Pressured sexting and revenge porn in a sample of Massachusetts adolescents. *International Journal of Technoethics*, 8(2), 16–25. DOI: 10.4018/IJT.2017070102

Englander, E., Donnerstein, E., Kowalski, R., Lin, C., & Parti, K. (2017). Defining Cyberbullying. *Pediatrics*, 140(Supplement_2), 148–151. DOI: 10.1542/peds.2016-1758U PMID: 29093051

Ennis-Cole, D. (2019). *Seeing autism through parents' feedback, sketchnotes, technology, and evidence-based practices*. Springer., DOI: 10.1007/978-3-030-15374-8

eSafety Commissioner (2022). *Mind the gap: Parental awareness of children's exposure to risks online*. Aussie Kids Online, Melbourne; eSafety Commissioner. https://www.esafety.gov.au/research/mind-gap

eSafety Commissioner (2023). *Online hate and discrimination*. https://www.esafety.gov.au/lgbtiq/learning-lounge/dealing-with-online-abuse/online-hate-discrimination eSafety Commissioner. (2024a). *Police and Legal Help*. https://www.esafety.gov.au/key-topics/image-based-abuse/police-and-legal-help

eSafety Commissioner. (2024b). *Receiving Unwanted Nudes*. https://www.esafety.gov.au/young-people/receivingunwanted-nudes

eSafety Commissioner. (2024c). *What Is Illegal and Restricted Online Content?*https://www.esafety.gov.au/report/what-is-illegal-restricted-content

Espelage, D., & Hong, J. (2017). Cyberbullying Prevention and Intervention Efforts: Current Knowledge and Future Directions. *Canadian Journal of Psychiatry*, 62(6), 374–380. DOI: 10.1177/0706743716684793 PMID: 28562094

Esposito, C., De Masi, F., Dragone, M., & Bacchini, D. (2024). Technology-Based Interventions for Preventing Youth Violence: A Systematic Review of Programs, Tools, and Evidence. *Adolescent Research Review*, 9(2), 165–192. DOI: 10.1007/s40894-023-00222-y

Ethier, K. A., Kershaw, T. S., Lewis, J. B., Milan, S., Niccolai, L. M., & Ickovics, J. R. (2006). Self-esteem, emotional distress and sexual behaviour among adolescent females: Inter-relationships and temporal effects. *The Journal of Adolescent Health*, 38(3), 268–274. DOI: 10.1016/j.jadohealth.2004.12.010 PMID: 16488825

Evangelio, C., Rodriguez-Gonzalez, P., Fernandez-Rio, J., & Gonzalez-Villora, S. (2022). Cyberbullying in elementary and middle school students: A systematic review. *Computers & Education*, 176, 104356. DOI: 10.1016/j.compedu.2021.104356

Evans, A. E., Currin, J. M., Garos, S., Stokes, A., Cox, K., & Meyer, C. L. (2022). 'Wasn't this already considered sexual harassment?': Exploring the confusion around the law mandating consent to receive a nude sext message. *American Journal of Sexuality Education*, 17(3), 343–367. DOI: 10.1080/15546128.2021.2025181

Evelyn, S., Clancy, E. M., Klettke, B., & Tatnell, R. (2022). A phenomenological investigation into cyberbullying as experienced by people identifying as transgender or gender diverse. *International Journal of Environmental Research and Public Health*, 19(11), 6560. Advance online publication. DOI: 10.3390/ijerph19116560 PMID: 35682144

Eyuboglu, M., Eyuboglu, D., Pala, S. C., Oktar, D., Demirtas, Z., Arslantas, D., & Unsal, A. (2021). Traditional school bullying and cyberbullying: Prevalence, the effect on mental health problems and self-harm behavior. *Psychiatry Research*, 297, 113730. DOI: 10.1016/j.psychres.2021.113730 PMID: 33486274

Faccio, E., Iudici, A., Costa, N., & Belloni, E. (2014). Cyberbullying and Interventions Programs in School and Clinical Setting. *Procedia: Social and Behavioral Sciences*, 122, 500–505. DOI: 10.1016/j.sbspro.2014.01.1382

Fajardo-Caldera, M. I., Gordillo-Hernández, M., & Regalado-Cuenca, A. B. (2013). Sexting: Nuevos usos de la tecnología y la sexualidad en adolescentes. *International Journal of Developmental and Educational Psychology*, 1(1), 521–533.

Falconer, T. A., Humphreys, T. P., O'Hagan, F. T., & Johnson, J. R. (2023). Influences on sexting in an intimate relationship: Motivations, risks, communication, personality traits, and relationship variables. *The Canadian Journal of Human Sexuality*, 32(3), 275–288. DOI: 10.3138/cjhs.2022-0052

Fang, K. M. M., Liu, K., & He, Y. (2019). Screen time and childhood overweight/obesity: A systematic review and meta-analysis. *Child: Care, Health and Development*, 45(5), 744–753. DOI: 10.1111/cch.12701 PMID: 31270831

Fannin, H. (2020). Sexting among adolescents: examining the association between sexting and self-esteem. *Physician Assistant Studies | Student Articles,* 11. https://doi.org/DOI: 10.33015/dominican.edu/2020.PAS.11

Farchakh, Y., Haddad, C., Sacre, H., Obeid, S., Salameh, P., & Hallit, S. (2020). Video gaming addiction and its association with memory, attention and learning skills in Lebanese children. *Child and Adolescent Psychiatry and Mental Health*, 14(1), 1–11. DOI: 10.1186/s13034-020-00353-3 PMID: 33308272

Farley, F. (1986). The big T in personality. *Psychology Today*, 20(5), 44–52.

Farrington, D. P., Zych, I., Ttofi, M. M., & Gaffney, H. (2023). Cyberbullying research in Canada: A systematic review of the first 100 empirical studies. *Aggression and Violent Behavior*, 69(2), 101811. DOI: 10.1016/j.avb.2022.101811

Fasoli, F., Durante, F., Mari, S., Zogmaister, C., & Volpato, C. (2018). Shades of sexualization: When sexualization becomes sexual objectification. *Sex Roles*, 78(5-6), 338–351. DOI: 10.1007/s11199-017-0808-1

Fazil, A. W., Hakimi, M., Sajid, S., Quchi, M. M., & Khaliqyar, K. Q. (2023). Enhancing Internet Safety and Cybersecurity Awareness among Secondary and High School Students in Afghanistan: A Case Study of Badakhshan Province. *American Journal of Education and Technology*, 2(4), 50–61. DOI: 10.54536/ajet.v2i4.2248

Feher, G., Tibold, A., & Esgalhado, G. (2023). Editorial: New addictions in the era of digitalization. *Frontiers in Human Neuroscience*, 17, 1302635. DOI: 10.3389/fnhum.2023.1302635 PMID: 37905242

Fenty, N. S., & Anderson, E. M. (2014). Examining educators' knowledge, beliefs, and practices about using technology with young children. *Journal of Early Childhood Teacher Education*, 35(2), 114–134. DOI: 10.1080/10901027.2014.905808

Ferguson, C. J. (2011). Sexting behaviors among young Hispanic women: Incidence and association with other high-risk sexual behaviors. *The Psychiatric Quarterly*, 82(3), 239–243. DOI: 10.1007/s11126-010-9165-8 PMID: 21153441

Fernandes, B., Maia, B. R., & Pontes, H. M. (2019). Internet addiction or problematic internet use? Which term should be used? *Psicologia USP, 30,* 1-8(e190020). DOI: 10.1590/0103-6564e190020

Ferraro, I. K., & Taylor, A. M. (2021). Adult attachment styles and emotional regulation: The role of interoceptive awareness and alexithymia. *Personality and Individual Differences*, 173, 110641. Advance online publication. DOI: 10.1016/j.paid.2021.110641

Ferreira, P. C., Simão, A. M. V., Paiva, A., Martinho, C., Prada, R., & Rocha, J. (2022). Serious Game-based Psychosocial Intervention to Foster Prosociality in Cyberbullying Bystanders. *Psychosocial Intervention*, 31(2), 83–96. DOI: 10.5093/pi2022a5 PMID: 37360059

Ferrer-Cascales, R., Albaladejo-Blázquez, N., Sánchez-SanSegundo, M., Portilla-Tamarit, I., Lordan, O., & Ruiz-Robledillo, N. (2019). Effectiveness of the TEI Program for bullying and cyberbullying reduction and school climate improvement. *International Journal of Environmental Research and Public Health*, 16(4), 580. DOI: 10.3390/ijerph16040580 PMID: 30781543

Ferrer-Pérez, C., Montagud-Romero, S., & Blanco-Gandía, M. C. (2024). Neurobiological Theories of Addiction: A Comprehensive Review. *Psychoactives*, 3(1), 35–47. DOI: 10.3390/psychoactives3010003

Ferrer, R., Ali, K., & Hughes, C. (2024). Using AI-Based Virtual Companions to Assist Adolescents with Autism in Recognizing and Addressing Cyberbullying. *Sensors (Basel)*, 24(12), 3875. DOI: 10.3390/s24123875 PMID: 38931659

Finch, H. (2005). Comparison of Distance Measures in Cluster Analysis with Dichotomous Data. *Journal of Data Science : JDS*, 3(1), 85–100. DOI: 10.6339/JDS.2005.03(1).192

Finkelhor, D., Walsh, K., Jones, L., Mitchell, K., & Collier, A. (2021). Youth internet safety education: Aligning programs with the evidence base. *Trauma, Violence & Abuse*, 22(5), 1233–1247. DOI: 10.1177/1524838020916257 PMID: 32242503

Fischer-Grote, L., Fössing, V., Aigner, M., Fehrmann, E., & Boeckle, M. (2024). Effectiveness of online and remote interventions for mental health in children, adolescents, and young adults after the onset of the COVID-19 pandemic: Systematic Review and Meta-Analysis. *JMIR Mental Health*, 11, e46637. DOI: 10.2196/46637 PMID: 38315524

Fleiss, J. L. (1971). Measuring nominal scale agreement among many raters. *Psychological Bulletin*, 76(5), 378–382. DOI: 10.1037/h0031619

Flower, R. L., Richdale, A. L., & Lawson, L. P. (2021). Brief report: What happens after school? Exploring post-school outcomes for a group of autistic and non-autistic Australian youth. *Journal of Autism and Developmental Disorders*, 51(4), 1385–1391. DOI: 10.1007/s10803-020-04600-6 PMID: 32662053

Flowers, A. (2010). *The fantasy factory: An insider's view of the phone sex industry*. University of Pennsylvania Press.

Folkman, S., & Moskowitz, J. T. (2004). Coping: Pitfalls and promise. *Annual Review of Psychology*, 55(1), 745–774. DOI: 10.1146/annurev.psych.55.090902.141456 PMID: 14744233

Folostina, R., Tudorache, L., Michel, T., Erzsebet, B., Agheana, V., & Hocaoglu, H. (2015). Using Play and Drama in Developing Resilience in Children at Risk. *Procedia: Social and Behavioral Sciences*, 197, 2362–2368. DOI: 10.1016/j.sbspro.2015.07.283

Folta, S. C., Bandini, L. G., Must, A., Pelletier, J., Ryan, K., & Curtin, C. (2022). Exploring leisure time use and impact on well-being among transition-age autistic youth. *Research in Autism Spectrum Disorders*, 96, 101996. Advance online publication. DOI: 10.1016/j.rasd.2022.101996

Fongkaew, W., & Fongkaew, K. (2016). My space, my body, my sexual subjectivity: Social media, sexual practice and parental control among teenage girls in urban Chiang Mai. *Culture, Health & Sexuality*, 18(5), 597–607. DOI: 10.1080/13691058.2015.1091948 PMID: 26489939

Foody, M., Samara, M., & Carlbring, P. (2015). A review of cyberbullying and suggestions for online psychological therapy. *Internet Interventions : the Application of Information Technology in Mental and Behavioural Health*, 2(3), 235–242. DOI: 10.1016/j.invent.2015.05.002

Foody, M., Samara, M., El Asam, A., Morsi, H., & Khattab, A. A. (2017). Review of cyberbullying legislation in Qatar: Considerations for policy makers and educators. *International Journal of Law and Psychiatry*, 50, 45–51. DOI: 10.1016/j.ijlp.2016.10.013 PMID: 27837914

Foody, M., Samara, M., & O'Higgins-Norman, J. (2017). Bullying and cyberbullying studies in the school-aged population on the island of Ireland: A meta-analysis. *The British Journal of Educational Psychology*, 87(4), 535–557. DOI: 10.1111/bjep.12163 PMID: 28555753

Fordham, B., Sugavanam, T., Edwards, K., Stallard, P., Howard, R., Nair, R. D., Copsey, B., Lee, H., Howick, J., Hemming, K., & Lamb, S. E. (2021). The evidence for cognitive behavioural therapy in any condition, population or context: A meta-review of systematic reviews and panoramic meta-analysis. *Psychological Medicine*, 51(1), 21–29. DOI: 10.1017/S0033291720005292 PMID: 33455594

Fortin, F., Paquette, S., & Leclerc, C. (2019). The effect of child sexual exploitation images collection size on offender sentencing. *International Review of Law Computers & Technology*, 33(3), 330–348. DOI: 10.1080/13600869.2018.1560553

Fox, J., & Tang, W. Y. (2017). Women's experiences with general and sexual harassment in online video games: Rumination, organizational responsiveness, withdrawal, and coping strategies. *New Media & Society*, 19(8), 1290–1307. DOI: 10.1177/1461444816635778

Franceschi, A. (2024, December). Rodríguez-deArriba María-Luisa, Annalaura Nocentini, & Ersilia Menesini. (2023). Online Sexual Harassment in Adolescence: A Scoping Review. *Sexuality Research & Social Policy*, 21(4), 1480–1499. Advance online publication. DOI: 10.1007/s13178-023-00869-1

Franco, M., Gaggi, O., & Palazzi, C. E. (2023). Can messaging applications prevent sexting abuse? A technology analysis. *IEEE Transactions on Mobile Computing*, 23(2), 1613–1626. DOI: 10.1109/TMC.2023.3238189

Frankel, A. S., Bass, S. B., Patterson, F., Dai, T., & Brown, D. (2018). Sexting, Risk Behavior, and Mental Health in Adolescents: An Examination of 2015 Pennsylvania Youth Risk Behavior Survey Data. *The Journal of School Health*, 88(3), 190–199. DOI: 10.1111/josh.12596 PMID: 29399839

Franzen, A., & Mader, S. (2023). The power of social influence: A replication and extension of the Asch experiment. *PLoS One*, 18(11), e0294325. DOI: 10.1371/journal.pone.0294325 PMID: 38019779

Fraser, B. J., Treagust, D. F., & Dennis, N. C. (1986). Development of an instrument for assessing classroom psychosocial environment at universities and colleges. *Studies in Higher Education*, 11(1), 43–54. DOI: 10.1080/03075078612331378451

Fratti, M. (2018, April 4). *Why sexting is something you should definitely do in a relationship.* https://hellogiggles.com/why-sexting-is-something-you-should-definitely-do-in-a-relationship/

Freeman, J. L., Caldwell, P. H. Y., Bennett, P. A., & Scott, K. M. (2018). How adolescents search for and appraise online health information: A systematic review. *The Journal of Pediatrics*, 195, 244–255. DOI: 10.1016/j.jpeds.2017.11.031 PMID: 29398062

Froeschle Hicks, J., Le Clair, B., & Berry, S. (2016). Using solution-focused dramatic empathy training to eliminate cyber-bullying. *Journal of Creativity in Mental Health*, 11(3–4), 378–390. DOI: 10.1080/15401383.2016.1172533

Fuadah, D. Z. (2021). Intervensi Mindfulness Attention Awareness untuk Mencegah Kecanduan Gadget pada Remaja Setingkat SMA. *Darmabakti: Jurnal Pengabdian dan Pemberdayaan Masyarakat, 2*(1), 38-45. DOI: 10.31102/darmabakti.2021.2.1.38-45

Fullerton, S., Taylor, A. W., Grande, E. D., & Berry, N. (2014). Measuring physical inactivity: Do current measures provide an accurate view of "sedentary" video game time? *Journal of Obesity*, 1-5, 1–5. Advance online publication. DOI: 10.1155/2014/287013 PMID: 25002974

Fung, L. K., Ulrich, T. L., Fujimoto, K. T., & Taheri, M. (2022). Neurodiversity: An invisible strength? *Journal of the Minerals Metals & Materials Society*, 74(9), 3200–3202. DOI: 10.1007/s11837-022-05454-2

Gabrielli, S., Rizzi, S., Carbone, S., & Piras, E. M. (2021). School interventions for bullying–cyberbullying prevention in adolescents: Insights from the UPRIGHT and CREEP Projects. *International Journal of Environmental Research and Public Health*, 18(21), 11697. DOI: 10.3390/ijerph182111697 PMID: 34770212

Gaffney, H., Farrington, D. P., Espelage, D. L., & Ttofi, M. M. (2019). Are cyberbullying intervention and prevention programs effective? A systematic and meta-analytical review. *Aggression and Violent Behavior*, 45, 134–153. DOI: 10.1016/j.avb.2018.07.002

Gaffney, H., Ttofi, M. M., & Farrington, D. P. (2021). Effectiveness of school-based programs to reduce bullying perpetration and victimization: An updated systematic review and meta-analysis. *Campbell Systematic Reviews*, 17(2), e1143. Advance online publication. DOI: 10.1002/cl2.1143 PMID: 37131921

Galovan, A. M., Drouin, M., & McDaniel, B. T. (2018). Sexting profiles in the United States and Canada: Implications for individual and relationship well-being. *Computers in Human Behavior*, 79, 19–29. DOI: 10.1016/j.chb.2017.10.017

Gámez-Guadix, M., & Martínez-Bacaicoa, J. (2023). Technology-Facilitated Sexual Violence: Typologies, Prevalence, and Associated Variables. *Handbook of Anger, Aggression, and Violence*, 375–389. DOI: 10.1007/978-3-031-31547-3_20

Gamez-Guadix, M., & de Santisteban, P. (2018). "Sex Pics?": Longitudinal Predictors of Sexting Among Adolescents. *The Journal of Adolescent Health*, 63(5), 608–614. DOI: 10.1016/j.jadohealth.2018.05.032 PMID: 30170939

Gámez-Guadix, M., & Incera, D. (2021). Homophobia is online: Sexual victimization and risks on the internet and mental health among bisexual, homosexual, pansexual, asexual, and queer adolescents. *Computers in Human Behavior*, 119, 106728. DOI: 10.1016/j.chb.2021.106728

Gámez-Guadix, M., Mateos-Pérez, E., Wachs, S., Wright, M., Martínez, J., & Íncera, D. (2022). Assessing image-based sexual abuse: Measurement, prevalence, and temporal stability of sextortion and nonconsensual sexting ("revenge porn") among adolescents. *Journal of Adolescence*, 94(5), 789–799. DOI: 10.1002/jad.12064 PMID: 35719041

Gámez-Guadix, M., Straus, M. A., & Hershberger, S. L. (2011). Childhood and adolescent victimization and perpetration of sexual coercion by male and female university students. *Deviant Behavior*, 32(8), 712–742. DOI: 10.1080/01639625.2010.514213

Ganca, S.-S., & Kyobe, M. (2023). The Effectiveness of school anti-cyberbullying policies and their compliance with South African laws: A conceptual framework. In Mytton, O., & Thom, L. (Eds.), *School cyberbullying policies and practices* (pp. 234–248). Springer. DOI: 10.1007/978-3-031-28472-4_15

Garaigordobil, M., & Martínez-Valderrey, V. (2015). The effectiveness of Cyberprogram 2.0 on conflict resolution strategies and self-esteem. *The Journal of Adolescent Health*, 57(2), 229–234. DOI: 10.1016/j.jadohealth.2015.04.007 PMID: 26206445

Garaigordobil, M., & Martínez-Valderrey, V. (2016). Impact of Cyberprogram 2.0 on different types of school violence and aggressiveness. *Frontiers in Psychology*, 7, 428. DOI: 10.3389/fpsyg.2016.00428 PMID: 27064802

Garaigordobil, M., & Martínez-Valderrey, V. (2018). Technological resources to prevent cyberbullying during adolescence: The Cyberprogram 2.0 program and the cooperative Cybereduca 2.0 videogame. *Frontiers in Psychology*, 9, 745. DOI: 10.3389/fpsyg.2018.00745 PMID: 29867695

García, G. G., Jiménez, C. R., & Marín, J. A. M. (2020). The transcendence of Augmented Reality in student motivation. A systematic review and meta-analysis. *Alteridad*, 15(1), 36–46. DOI: 10.17163/alt.v15n1.2020.03

García-González, A., Romero-Rodríguez, J. M., Ramírez-Montoya, M. S., & Aznar-Díaz, I. (2021). The Phenomenon of Sexting Among Mexican and Spanish University Students: A Multigroup Model. *Sexuality & Culture*, 25(3), 939–959. DOI: 10.1007/s12119-020-09802-9

Garcia, J. R., Gesselman, A. N., Siliman, S. A., Perry, B. L., Coe, K., & Fisher, H. E. (2016). Sexting among singles in the USA: Prevalence of sending, receiving, and sharing sexual messages and images. *Sexual Health*, 13(5), 428–435. DOI: 10.1071/SH15240 PMID: 27470210

Garcia, J. R., Reiber, C., Massey, S. G., & Merriwether, A. M. (2012). Sexual hookup culture: A review. *Review of General Psychology*, 16(2), 161–176. DOI: 10.1037/a0027911 PMID: 23559846

García-Martínez, S., & García-Zabaleta, E. (2024). El acoso escolar en España: Revisión y análisis de los protocolos de actuación por comunidades autónomas [Bullying in Spain: review and analysis of action protocols by autonomous communities]. *Contextos Educativos: Revista De Educación*, 33(33), 193–217. DOI: 10.18172/con.5765

Garner, A. R., Brem, M. J., Shorey, R. C., Hamlin, J., & Stuart, G. L. (2022). Negative urgency moderates the association between compulsive sexual behaviors and sending unsolicited sexts among men in residential treatment for substance use disorders. *Computers in Human Behavior*, 136, 107385. DOI: 10.1016/j.chb.2022.107385

Garrido-Macías, M., Herrera, A., Alonso-Ferres, M., & Herrera, C. M. (2023). Sexting is not always wanted: Consequences on satisfaction and the role of sexual coercion and online sexual victimization. *Anales de Psicología*, 39(3), 354–363. DOI: 10.6018/analesps.514431

Gaspard, L. (2020). Australian high school students and their internet use: Perceptions of opportunities versus 'problematic situations.'. *Children Australia*, 45(1), 54–63. DOI: 10.1017/cha.2020.2

Gassó, A. M., Agustina, J. R., & Goméz-Durán, E. (2021). Cross-cultural differences in sexting practices between American and Spanish university students. *International Journal of Environmental Research and Public Health*, 18(4), 2058. Advance online publication. DOI: 10.3390/ijerph18042058 PMID: 33672448

Gassó, A. M., & Gómez-Durán, E. (2021). Psychopathological profile of sexting coercion perpetrators. *Spanish Journal of Legal Medicine*, 47(4), 157–163. DOI: 10.1016/j.remle.2021.02.003

Gassó, A. M., Klettke, B., Agustina, J. R., & Montiel, I. (2019). Sexting, mental health, and victimization among adolescents: A literature review. *International Journal of Environmental Research and Public Health*, 16(13), 2364. DOI: 10.3390/ijerph16132364 PMID: 31277335

Gassó, A. M., Mueller-Johnson, K., & Gómez-Durán, E. L. (2021). Victimization as a result of non-consensual dissemination of sexting and psychopathology correlates: An exploratory analysis. *International Journal of Environmental Research and Public Health*, 18(12), 6564. Advance online publication. DOI: 10.3390/ijerph18126564 PMID: 34207211

Gassó, A. M., Mueller-Johnson, K., & Montiel, I. (2020). Sexting, online sexual victimization, and psychopathology correlates by sex: Depression, anxiety, and global psychopathology. *International Journal of Environmental Research and Public Health*, 17(3), 1018. Advance online publication. DOI: 10.3390/ijerph17031018 PMID: 32041115

Gee, J. P. (2003). *What Video Games Have to Teach Us About Learning and Literacy*. Palgrave Macmillan. DOI: 10.1145/950566.950595

Gee, J. P. (2004). *Situated language and learning: A critique of traditional schooling*. Routledge.

Gee, J. P. (2015). *Unified discourse analysis: Language, reality, virtual worlds, and video games*. Routledge.

Gee, J. P., & Handford, M. (2012). *The Routledge handbook of discourse analysis*. Routledge.

Geeng, C., Jevan, H., & Franziska, R. (2020, August 10–11). *Usable Sexurity: Studying People's Concerns and Strategies When Sexting* [Symposium presentation]. Sixteenth Symposium on Usable Privacy and Security, Virtual Conference. https://www.usenix.org/system/files/soups2020-geeng.pdf

Gen, O. I. & žahin, O. (2016). Effect of the use of multimedia on students' performance: A case study of social studies class. *Educational Research Review*, 11(8), 877–882. DOI: 10.5897/ERR2016.2741

Gentile, D. (2009). Pathological video-play use among youth ages 8 to 18: A national study. *Psychological Science*, 20(5), 594–602. DOI: 10.1111/j.1467-9280.2009.02340.x PMID: 19476590

Gentile, D. A., Choo, H., Liau, A., Sim, T., Li, D., Fung, D., & Khoo, A. (2011). Pathological Video Game Use Among Youths: A Two-Year Longitudinal Study. *Pediatrics*, 127(2), 319–329. DOI: 10.1542/peds.2010-1353 PMID: 21242221

Gernsbacher, M. A., Geye, H. M., & Ellis Weismer, S. (2005). The role of language and communication impairments within autism. In Fletcher, P., & Miller, J. F. (Eds.), *Language disorders and developmental theory* (pp. 73–93). John Benjamins Publishing Company. DOI: 10.1075/tilar.4.06ger

Gewirtz-Meydan, A., Mitchell, K. J., & Rothman, E. F. (2018). What do kids think about sexting? *Computers in Human Behavior*, 86, 256–265. DOI: 10.1016/j.chb.2018.04.007

Ghorashi, Z. (2019). Teenage sexting and sexual behaviors in an Iranian setting. *Sexuality & Culture*, 23(4), 1274–1282. DOI: 10.1007/s12119-019-09622-6

Ghorashi, Z., Loripoor, M., & Lotfipur-Rafsanjani, S. M. (2019). Mobile Access and Sexting Prevalence in High School Students in Rafsanjan City, Iran in 2015. *Majallah-i Ravanpizishki va Ravanshinasi-i Balini-i Iran*, 24(4), 416–425. DOI: 10.32598/ijpcp.24.4.416

Ghosh, A. K., Badillo-Urquiola, K., Guha, S., LaViola, J. J.Jr, & Wisniewski, P. J. (2018). Safety vs. surveillance: What children have to say about mobile apps for parental control. In *Proceedings of the 2018 CHI Conference on Human Factors in Computing Systems* (pp. 1-14). ACM. https://doi.org/DOI: 10.1145/3173574.3173698

Gilbert, M., Fernet, M., & Hébert, M. (2023). Diversity of Profiles and Coping Among Adolescent Girl Victims of Sexual Dating Violence. *Article in Journal of Child Sexual Abuse*. DOI: 10.1080/10538712.2023.2195856

Gil-Llario, M. D., Gil-Juliá, B., Morell-Mengual, V., Cárdenas-López, G., & Ballester-Arnal, R. (2021). Analysis of demographic, psychological and cultural aspects associated with the practice of sexting in Mexican and Spanish adolescents. *International Journal of Intercultural Relations*, 82, 197–206. DOI: 10.1016/j.ijintrel.2021.03.013

Gil-Llario, M. D., Giménez, G., Ballester-Arnal, R., Cárdenas-López, G., & Durán-Baca, X. (2017). Gender, Sexuality, and Relationships in Young Hispanic People. *Journal of Sex & Marital Therapy*, 43(5), 456–462. DOI: 10.1080/0092623X.2016.1207732 PMID: 27366863

Gil-Llario, M. D., Morell-Mengual, V., Jiménez-Martínez, M. C., Iglesias-Campos, P., Gil-Julia, B., & Ballester-Arnal, R. (2020). Culture as an influence on sexting attitudes and behaviors: A differential analysis comparing adolescents from Spain and Colombia. *International Journal of Intercultural Relations*, 79, 145–154. DOI: 10.1016/j.ijintrel.2020.08.010

Gill, R. (2007). Post-Feminist Media Culture: Elements of a Sensibility. *European Journal of Cultural Studies*, 10(2), 147–166. DOI: 10.1177/1367549407075898

Gill, R. (2008). Culture and Subjectivity in Neoliberal and Post-Feminist Times. *Subjectivity*, 25(1), 432–445. DOI: 10.1057/sub.2008.28

Giménez-Gualdo, A. M., Sánchez-Romero, E. I., & Torregrosa Díez, M. (2022). El lado oscuro de internet.¿ Predice el cyberbullying la participación en sexting? *Revista Latinoamericana de Psicología*, 54, 112–119. DOI: 10.14349/rlp.2022.v54.13

Ginsburg, K. (2007). The importance of play in promoting healthy child development and maintaining strong parent-child bonds. *Pediatrics*, 119(1), 182–191. DOI: 10.1542/peds.2006-2697 PMID: 17200287

Giordano, A. L., Morey, A. W., Kim, I. K., Song, J., & Kim, O. (2023). School counselors' experiences with student vaping and internet gaming: A report from the field. *International Journal for the Advancement of Counseling*, 45(3), 441–457. DOI: 10.1007/s10447-023-09518-z

Giroux, A. M. (2011). *Sexting: Connections to sexual and social development*. [Unpublished honors thesis]. The University of Arizona.

Giumetti, G. W., & Kowalski, R. M. (2022). Cyberbullying via social media and well-being. *Current Opinion in Psychology, 45*(101314), 1-8. https://doi.org/DOI: 10.1016/j.copsyc.2022.101314

Gkantona, G., Arbyrou, K., Giannopoulou, M. D., Zapantis, R., Karakoula, P., Kitsiou, A., Kogka, G., Nikolakopoulos, S., Ntagkas, F., Patrinou, S., & Rekka, E. (2024). *Cyber Violence against Women & Girls in Greece*. Kentro Ereunon gia Themata Isotitas (K.E.T.H.I.). Ioannina, Greece. Retrieved from: https://www.kethi.gr/ereunes-meletes/diadiktyaki-bia-kata-ton-gynaikon-synoptiki-ekthesi

Global Kids Online. (2016). *Global kids online research toolkit: Qualitative guide*. http://globalkidsonline.net/wp-content/uploads/2016/04/Qualitative-toolkit-guide-final-26-Oct-16.pdf

Goel, D., Subramanyam, A., & Kamath, R. (2013). A study on the prevalence of internet addiction and its association with psychopathology in Indian adolescents. *Indian Journal of Psychiatry*, 55(2), 140–143. DOI: 10.4103/0019-5545.111451 PMID: 23825847

Gohal, G., Alqassim, A., Eltyeb, E., Rayyani, A., Hakami, B., Al Faqih, A., Hakami, A., Qadri, A., & Mahfouz, M. (2023). Prevalence and related risks of cyberbullying and its effects on adolescent. *BMC Psychiatry*, 23(1), 39. DOI: 10.1186/s12888-023-04542-0 PMID: 36641459

Gökçearslan, Ş., & Seferoğlu, S. S. (2016). The use of the Internet among middle school students: Risky behaviors and opportunities. *Kastamonu Education Journal*, 24(1), 383–404.

Goldfarb, E. S., & Lieberman, L. D. (2021). Three decades of research: The case for comprehensive sex education. *The Journal of Adolescent Health*, 68(1), 13–27. DOI: 10.1016/j.jadohealth.2020.07.036 PMID: 33059958

Goldstein, T. R. (2009). Psychological perspectives on acting. *Psychology of Aesthetics, Creativity, and the Arts*, 3(1), 6–9. DOI: 10.1037/a0014644

Goldstein, T. R., & Bloom, P. (2011). The mind on stage: Why cognitive scientists should study acting. *Trends in Cognitive Sciences*, 15(4), 141–142. DOI: 10.1016/j.tics.2011.02.003 PMID: 21398168

Goleman, D. (1995). *Emotional Intelligence: Why It Can Matter More Than IQ*. Bantam Books.

Gomes, M., Vasconcelos-Raposo, J., & Teixeira, C. M. (2021). The impact of technology usage on love and intimacy satisfaction among Portuguese adults. *Computers in Human Behavior Reports*, 4, 100084. Advance online publication. DOI: 10.1016/j.chbr.2021.100084

Gonzalez, R. M., Quinn, P., Gardiner, J., & Sutcliffe, A. (2023). 47 Problematic online gambling and predictors of participation in adolescents. *Archives of Disease in Childhood, 108*, Article A101–A101. https://doi.org/DOI: 10.1136/archdischild-2023-rcpch.170

Gonzalez, A.-J. (2023). Psychodrama in Portugal. *Zeitschrift für Psychodrama und Soziometrie*, 22(1), 67–75. DOI: 10.1007/s11620-023-00717-9

Gonzalez, S.-J., & Holdgate, H. (2023). Is there a place for love in early childhood education and care in England? Early years educators' beliefs. *Research in Teacher Education*, 13(1), 44–48. DOI: 10.1016/j.compedu.2020.103877v

Goodman-Deane, J., Mieczakowski, A., Johnson, D., Goldhaber, T., & Clarkson, P. J. (2016). The impact of communication technologies on life and relationship satisfaction. *Computers in Human Behavior*, 57, 219–229. DOI: 10.1016/j.chb.2015.11.053

Goodwin, J., Bradley, S. K., Donohoe, P., Queen, K., O'Shea, M., & Horgan, A. (2019). Bullying in schools: An evaluation of the use of drama in bullying prevention. *Journal of Creativity in Mental Health*, 14(3), 329–342. DOI: 10.1080/15401383.2019.1623147

Gordon-Messer, D., Bauermeister, J. A., Grodzinski, A., & Zimmerman, M. (2013). Sexting among young adults. *The Journal of Adolescent Health*, 52(3), 301–306. DOI: 10.1016/j.jadohealth.2012.05.013 PMID: 23299018

Gottfredson, M. R., & Hirschi, T. (2017). Self-control and opportunity. In Britt, C. L., & Gottfredson, M. R. (Eds.), *Control Theories of Crime and Delinquency* (1st ed., pp. 5–20). Routledge. DOI: 10.4324/9781351323727-1

Gourd, K. M., & Gourd, T. Y. (2011). Enacting democracy: Using Forum Theatre to confront bullying. *Equity & Excellence in Education*, 44(3), 403–419. DOI: 10.1080/10665684.2011.589275

Gov.uk. (2024, January 31). *Cyberflashing, Epilepsy Trolling and Fake News to Put Online Abusers Behind Bars from Today* [Press release]. https://www.gov.uk/government/news/cyberflashing-epilepsy-trolling-and-fake-news-to-put-online-abusers-behindbars-from-today

Grădinariu, T., & Diac, G. (2023). New perspectives in developing teachers' social-emotional skills to prevent bullying: The role of Forum Theatre. *Review of Artistic Education*, 25(1), 137–147. DOI: 10.2478/rae-2023-0020

Gradinger, P., Yanagida, T., Strohmeier, D., & Spiel, C. (2015). Prevention of cyberbullying and cyber victimization: Evaluation of the ViSC Social Competence Program. *Journal of School Violence*, 14(1), 87–110. DOI: 10.1080/15388220.2014.963231

Graf, W. D., Miller, G., Epstein, L. G., & Rapin, I. (2017). The autism "epidemic": Ethical, legal, and social issues in a developmental spectrum disorder. *Neurology*, 88(14), 1371–1380. DOI: 10.1212/WNL.0000000000003791 PMID: 28275086

Grammatas, T., Mastrothanasis, K., & Papakosta, A. (2023). *The values of Ancient Greek Drama and Theatre in Space and Time: The Presence of the values* (Andreou, A., Trans.). National and Kapodistrian University of Athens Press.

Gray, L. M., Wong-Wylie, G., Rempel, G. R., & Cook, K. (2020). Expanding qualitative research interviewing strategies: Zoom video communications. *The Qualitative Report*, 25(5), 1292–1301. DOI: 10.46743/2160-3715/2020.4212

Greenhow, C. (2011). Youth, learning, and social media. *Journal of Educational Computing Research*, 40(4), 129–130. DOI: 10.2190/EC.45.2.a

Gregg, D., Somers, C. L., Pernice, F. M., Hillman, S. B., & Kernsmith, P. (2018). Sexting rates and predictors from an urban midwest high school. *The Journal of School Health*, 88(6), 423–433. DOI: 10.1111/josh.12628 PMID: 29749003

Griffin, K. A., Cunningham, E. L., & George Mwangi, C. A. (2016). Defining diversity: Ethnic differences in black students' perceptions of racial climate. *Journal of Diversity in Higher Education*, 9(1), 34–49. DOI: 10.1037/a0039255

Griffiths, M. (2010). Excessive online computer use and learning disabilities. *Australian Journal of Dyslexia and Other Learning Disabilities*, 5, 31–34.

Griffiths, M. D. (2009). Online computer gaming: Advice for parents and teachers. *Education for Health*, 27(1), 3–6. https://irep.ntu.ac.uk/id/eprint/20885/1/200593_6996%20Griffiths%20Publisher.pdf

Griffiths, M. D., & Davies, M. N. O. (2005). Videogame addiction: Does it exist? In Goldstein, J., & Raessens, J. (Eds.), *Handbook of computer game studies* (pp. 359–368). MIT Press.

Griswold, M. G., Fullman, N., Hawley, C., Arian, N., Zimsen, S. R. M., Tymeson, H. D., Venkateswaran, V., Tapp, A. D., Forouzanfar, M. H., Salama, J. S., Abate, K. H., Abate, D., Abay, S. M., Abbafati, C., Abdulkader, R. S., Abebe, Z., Aboyans, V., Abrar, M. M., Acharya, P., & Gakidou, E. (2018). Alcohol use and burden for 195 countries and territories, 1990–2016: A systematic analysis for the Global Burden of Disease Study 2016. *Lancet*, 392(10152), 1015–1035. DOI: 10.1016/S0140-6736(18)31310-2 PMID: 30146330

Groshans, G., Mikhailova, E., Post, C., Schlautman, M., Carbajales-Dale, P., & Payne, K. (2019). Digital story map learning for STEM disciplines. *Education Sciences*, 9(2), 75. DOI: 10.3390/educsci9020075

Grove, R., Hoekstra, R. A., Wierda, M., & Begeer, S. (2018). Special interests and subjective wellbeing in autistic adults. *Autism Research*, 11(5), 766–775. DOI: 10.1002/aur.1931 PMID: 29427546

Grove, R., Roth, I., & Hoekstra, R. A. (2016). The motivation for special interests in individuals with autism and controls: Development and validation of the special interest motivation scale. *Autism Research*, 9(6), 677–688. DOI: 10.1002/aur.1560 PMID: 26496939

Grunewald, J. R. (2009). *Increasing Science, Technology, Engineering, and Mathematics Skills Using Project Lead the Way: A Grant Proposal*. Unpublished Doctoral dissertation, University of Wisconsin-Stout.

Gudmundsdottir, G. B., Gassó, H. H., Colomer, J. C., & Hatlevik, O. E. (2020). Student teachers' responsible use of ICT: Examining two samples in Spain and Norway. *Computers & Education*, 152, 103877. DOI: 10.1016/j.compedu.2020.103877

Guerra, C., Montiel, I., Molina, N., Escalona, Y., Riquelme, J., & Rojas, L. (2019). Analysis of a brief scale of Internet risk behaviors in Chilean youth. *Anuario de psicología (Barcelona, Spain)*, 49(1), 32–39. DOI: 10.1344/ANPSIC2019.49.4

Guerra, C., Pinto-Cortez, C., Toro, E., Efthymiadou, E., & Quayle, E. (2021). Online sexual harassment and depression in Chilean adolescents: Variations based on gender and age of the offenders. *Child Abuse & Neglect*, 120, 105219. DOI: 10.1016/j.chiabu.2021.105219 PMID: 34315004

Guest, C., & Denes, A. (2022). Too much too soon?: Perceived appropriateness of sexting across stages of relationship development and attachment tendencies among emerging adults. *Computers in Human Behavior*, 137, 107429. Advance online publication. DOI: 10.1016/j.chb.2022.107429

Guo, L., Shi, G., Du, X., Wang, W., Guo, Y., & Lu, C. (2021). Associations of emotional and behavioral problems with Internet use among Chinese young adults: The role of academic performance. *Journal of Affective Disorders*, 287, 214–221. DOI: 10.1016/j.jad.2021.03.050 PMID: 33799040

Guo, P. J., Kim, J., & Rubin, R. (2014). How video production affects student engagement: An empirical study of MOOC videos. In *Proceedings of the first ACM conference on Learning@ Scale conference*, L@S'14, 41-50. DOI: 10.1145/2556325.2566239

Guo, Y. R., & Goh, D. H. L. (2016). Evaluation of affective embodied agents in an information literacy game. *Computers & Education*, 103, 59–75. DOI: 10.1016/j.compedu.2016.09.013

Haasbroek, H., & Morojele, N. (2022). A systematic literature review on the relationship between autism spectrum disorder and substance use among adults and adolescents. *Review Journal of Autism and Developmental Disorders*, 9(1), 1–20. DOI: 10.1007/s40489-021-00242-1

Hadley, W., Houck, C., Brown, L. K., Spitalnick, J. S., Ferrer, M., & Barker, D. (2019). Moving beyond Role-Play: Evaluating the use of virtual reality to teach emotion regulation for the prevention of adolescent risk behavior within a randomized pilot trial. *Journal of Pediatric Psychology*, 44(4), 425–435. DOI: 10.1093/jpepsy/jsy092 PMID: 30551157

Hagen, R., Havnen, A., Hjemdal, O., Kennair, L. E. O., Ryum, T., & Solem, S. (2020). Protective and vulnerability factors in self-esteem: The role of metacognitions, brooding, and resilience. *Frontiers in Psychology*, 11, 01447. DOI: 10.3389/fpsyg.2020.01447 PMID: 32719640

Hale, L., & Guan, S. (2015). Screen time and sleep among school-aged children and adolescents: A systematic literature review. *Sleep Medicine Reviews*, 21, 50–58. DOI: 10.1016/j.smrv.2014.07.007 PMID: 25193149

Hall, M., Williams, R. D., Ford, M. A., Cromeans, E. M., & Bergman, R. J. (2020). Hooking-up, religiosity, and sexting among college students. *Journal of Religion and Health*, 59(1), 484–496. DOI: 10.1007/s10943-016-0291-y PMID: 27468909

Hally, C., & Pollack, R. (1993). The effects of self-esteem, variety of sexual experience, and erotophilia on sexual satisfaction in sexually active heterosexuals. *Journal of Sex Education and Therapy*, 19(3), 183–192. DOI: 10.1080/01614576.1993.11074081

Hamidi, F., & Sobhani Tabar, S. (2021). Effect of psychodrama on post-traumatic stress disorder symptoms in primary school students living in earthquake-stricken areas. *Majallah-i Ravanpizishki va Ravanshinasi-i Balini-i Iran*, 26(4), 400–417. DOI: 10.32598/ijpcp.26.3.3190.2

Hamid, S., Waycott, J., Kurnia, S., & Chang, S. (2015). Understanding students' perceptions of the benefits of online social networking use for teaching and learning. *The Internet and Higher Education*, 26, 1–9. DOI: 10.1016/j.iheduc.2015.02.004

Hamm, M., Newton, A., Chisholm, A., Shulhan, J., Milne, A., Sundar, P., Ennis, H., Scott, S., & Hartling, L. (2015). Prevalence and Effect of Cyberbullying on Children and Young People: A Scoping Review of Social Media Studies. *JAMA Pediatrics*, 169(8), 770–777. DOI: 10.1001/jamapediatrics.2015.0944 PMID: 26098362

Hammond, C. J., Allick, A., Rahman, N., & Nanavati, J. (2019). Structural and functional neural targets of addiction treatment in adolescents and young adults: A systematic review and meta-analysis. *Journal of Child and Adolescent Psychopharmacology*, 29(7), 498–507. DOI: 10.1089/cap.2019.0007 PMID: 31313938

Hannafin, M., Land, S. M., & Oliver, K. (1999). Open learning environments: foundations, methods, and models. In Reigeluth, C. M. (Ed.), *Instructional design theories and models* (pp. 115–140). Lawrence Erlbaum Associates.

Hare, R. D., & Neumann, C. S. (2008). Psychopathy as a clinical and empirical construct. *Annual Review of Clinical Psychology*, 4(1), 217–246. DOI: 10.1146/annurev.clinpsy.3.022806.091452 PMID: 18370617

Harrington, C., Foster, M., Rodger, S., & Ashburner, J. (2014). Engaging young people with autism spectrum disorder in research interviews. *British Journal of Learning Disabilities*, 42(2), 153–161. DOI: 10.1111/bld.12037

Hartikainen, H., Razi, A., & Wisniewski, P. (2021, October). 'If You Care About Me, You'll Send Me a Pic'-Examining the Role of Peer Pressure in Adolescent Sexting. In *Companion Publication of the 2021 Conference on Computer Supported Cooperative Work and Social Computing* (pp. 67-71). DOI: 10.1145/3462204.3481739

Hartman, D., & Zimberoff, D. (2013). Jung and hypnotherapy. *Journal of Heart-Centered Therapies*, 16(1), 3–52.

Harvey, C. A., Harvey, T. A., & Thompson, A. E. (2020). The "sextual" double standard: An experimental examination of variations in judgments of men and women who engage in computer-mediated sexual communication. *Sexuality & Culture*, 24(3), 712–732. DOI: 10.1007/s12119-019-09658-8

Harwood, J. (2020). Social identity theory. In Bulck, J. (Ed.), *The International Encyclopedia of Media Psychology* (pp. 1–7). John Wiley & Sons., DOI: 10.1002/9781119011071.iemp0153

Hasinoff, A. A. (2013). Sexting as media production: Rethinking social media and sexuality. *New Media & Society*, 15(4), 449–465. DOI: 10.1177/1461444812459171

Hassan, H., Tariq, K., Nasir, M., & Ayub, S. (2023). Personality Traits, Self-Control, and Sexting Attitudes Among Young Adults. *Pakistan Journal of Psychological Research*, 38(1), 147–164. DOI: 10.33824/PJPR.2023.38.1.10

Hastings, E. C., Karas, T. L., Winsler, A., Way, E., Madigan, A., Tyler, S. (2009). Young children's video/computer game use: Relations with school performance and behavior. *Issues in Mental Health Nursing, 30*, 638–649. DOI: 10.1080/01612840903050414

Hatchel, T., Espelage, D. L., & Huang, Y. (2018). Sexual harassment victimization, school belonging, and depressive symptoms among LGBTQ adolescents: Temporal insights. *The American Journal of Orthopsychiatry*, 88(4), 422–430. DOI: 10.1037/ort0000279 PMID: 28617003

Hatton, E., & Trautner, M. N. (2011). Equal Opportunity Objectification? The Sexualization of Men and Women on the Cover of Rolling Stone. *Sexuality & Culture*, 15(3), 256–278. DOI: 10.1007/s12119-011-9093-2

Hatzenbuehler, M., Schwab-Reese, L., Ranapurwala, S., Hertz, M., & Ramirez, M. (2015). Associations Between Antibullying Policies and Bullying in 25 States. *JAMA Pediatrics*, 169(10), e152411. DOI: 10.1001/jamapediatrics.2015.2411 PMID: 26437015

Hawkes, G., & Dune, T. (2013). Introduction: Narratives of the sexual child: Shared themes and shared challenges. *Sexualities*, 16(5-6), 622–634. DOI: 10.1177/1363460713497459

Hayes, A., Herlinger, K., Paterson, L., & Lingford-Hughes, A. (2020c). The neurobiology of substance use and addiction: Evidence from neuroimaging and relevance to treatment. *BJPsych Advances*, 26(6), 367–378. DOI: 10.1192/bja.2020.68

Heinz, A., Beck, A., Halil, M. G., Pilhatsch, M., Smolka, M. N., & Liu, S. (2019). Addiction as learned Behavior patterns. *Journal of Clinical Medicine*, 8(8), 1086. DOI: 10.3390/jcm8081086 PMID: 31344831

Helsper, E. J., Veltri, G. A., & Livingstone, S. (2024). Parental mediation of children's online risks: The role of parental risk perception, digital skills and risk experiences. *New Media & Society*, 26(1), 1–20. DOI: 10.1177/14614448241261945

Helverschou, S. B., Bakken, T. L., & Martinsen, H. (2011). Psychiatric disorders in people with autism spectrum disorders: Phenomenology and recognition. In Matson, J. L., & Sturmey, P. (Eds.), *International handbook of autism and pervasive developmental disorders* (pp. 53–74). Springer. DOI: 10.1007/978-1-4419-8065-6_5

Hemdan, A., Khalil, G., Amin, K., & Elwahab, M. A. (2023). A comprehensive review of autism spectrum disorder detection using the Internet of Things. *Sensors (Basel)*, 23(3), 1649. Advance online publication. DOI: 10.3390/s23031649 PMID: 36772688

Henares-Montiel, J., Pastor-Moreno, G., Ramírez-Saiz, A., Rodríguez-Gómez, M., & Ruiz-Pérez, I. (2023). Characteristics and effectiveness of interventions to reduce cyberbullying: A systematic review. *Frontiers in Public Health*, 11, 1219727. DOI: 10.3389/fpubh.2023.1219727 PMID: 37711240

Henderson, L., & Morgan, E. (2011). Sexting and sexual relationships among teens and young adults. *McNair Scholars Research Journal*, 7, 31–39.

Hendricks, K., Tsibolane, P., & van Belle, J. P. (2020). Cyber-Harassment Victimization Among South African LGBTQIA+ Youth. *Responsible Design, Implementation and Use of Information and Communication Technology: 19th IFIP WG 6.11 Conference on e-Business, e-Services, and e-Society, I3E 2020, Skukuza, South Africa, April 6–8, 2020Proceedings*, 12067(Part II), 135–146. DOI: 10.1007/978-3-030-45002-1_12

Hendry, B. P., Hellsten, L.-A. M., McIntyre, L. J., & Smith, B. R. R. (2023). Recommendations for cyberbullying prevention and intervention: A Western Canadian perspective from key stakeholders. *Frontiers in Psychology, 14*. DOI: 10.3389/fpsyg.2023.1067484

Henneberger, A. K., Mushonga, D. R., & Preston, A. M. (2020). Peer Influence and Adolescent Substance Use: A Systematic Review of Dynamic Social Network Research. *Adolescent Research Review*, 6(1), 57–73. DOI: 10.1007/s40894-019-00130-0

Henningsen, D. D. (2004). Flirting with meaning: An examination of miscommunication in flirting interactions. *Sex Roles*, 50(7-8), 481–489. DOI: 10.1023/B:SERS.0000023068.49352.4b

Henry, N., & Beard, G. (2024). Image-based sexual abuse perpetration: A scoping review. *Trauma, Violence, & Abuse. Trauma, Violence & Abuse*, 15248380241266137(5), 3981–3998. Advance online publication. DOI: 10.1177/15248380241266137 PMID: 39078000

Henry, N., & Powell, A. (2015). Beyond the "sext": Technology-facilitated sexual violence and harassment against adult women. *Australian and New Zealand Journal of Criminology*, 48(1), 104–118. DOI: 10.1177/0004865814524218

Henry, N., & Powell, A. (2016). Technology-Facilitated Sexual Violence: A Literature Review of Empirical Research. *Trauma, Violence & Abuse*, 19(2), 195–208. DOI: 10.1177/1524838016650189 PMID: 27311818

Hernández, L., Hernández, V., Neyra, F., & Carrillo, J. (2022). The use of massive online games in game-based learning activities. *Revista Innova Educación, 4*(3), 7–30. https://dialnet.unirioja.es/descarga/articulo/8510469.pdf

Hernández-León, M. L., Rodríguez-Fernández, M. C., & Cruz-Martínez, I. (2022). Consecuencias psicológicas del sexting y relación con el estrés académico. *Medisan (Santiago de Cuba)*, 26(4), e4093.

Hertlein, K. M., & Twist, M. L. C. (2017). Sexting Behavior Among College Students: Implications for College Clinicians. *Journal of College Student Psychotherapy*, 31(3), 215–230. DOI: 10.1080/87568225.2016.1277814

Hessler, D. M., & Katz, L. F. (2010). Brief report: Associations between emotional competence and adolescent risky behavior. *Journal of Adolescence*, 33(1), 241–246. DOI: 10.1016/j.adolescence.2009.04.007 PMID: 19481247

Higgins, N. R. (2019). *Tobacco and E-cigarette use in youth with autism spectrum disorders*. [Doctoral Dissertation, Florida Institute of Technology]. Florida Tech Scholarship Repository. https://repository.fit.edu/etd/285

Higham, L., Girardi, A., & Edwards, H. V. (2021). Clinical and criminal profile of internet offenders with ASD. *Journal of Intellectual Disabilities and Offending Behaviour*, 12(2), 61–74. DOI: 10.1108/JIDOB-09-2020-0016

Hilinski-Rosick, C. M., & Freiburger, T. L. (2012). An Exploratory Analysis of the Prevalence of Teen Sexting. *Journal of Social Deviance*, 4, 120–149. DOI: 10.1080/10511253.2014.922593

Hill, D., Ameenuddin, N., Reid Chassiakos, Y. L., Cross, C., Hutchinson, J., Levine, A., Boyd, R., Mendelson, R., Moreno, M., & Swanson, W. S.American Academy of Pediatrics. (2016). Media and young minds. *Pediatrics*, 138(5), e20162591. DOI: 10.1542/peds.2016-2591 PMID: 27940793

Hillier, A., Gallop, N., Mendes, E., Tellez, D., Buckingham, A., Nizami, A., & OToole, D. (2020). LGBTQ + and autism spectrum disorder: Experiences and challenges. *International Journal of Transgender Health*, 21(1), 98–110. DOI: 10.1080/15532739.2019.1594484 PMID: 33005905

Hirota, T., McElroy, E., & So, R. (2020). Network analysis of internet addiction symptoms among a clinical sample of Japanese adolescents with autism spectrum disorder. *Journal of Autism and Developmental Disorders*, 51(8), 2764–2772. DOI: 10.1007/s10803-020-04714-x PMID: 33040268

Hirsh-Pasek, K., Zosh, J. M., Golinkoff, R. M., Gray, J. H., Robb, M. B., & Kaufman, J. (2015). Putting education in "educational" apps: Lessons from the science of learning. *Psychological Science in the Public Interest*, 16(1), 3–34. DOI: 10.1177/1529100615569721 PMID: 25985468

Hoff, C. C., Chakravarty, D., Beougher, S. C., Neilands, T. B., & Darbes, L. A. (2012). Relationship characteristics associated with sexual risk behavior among MSM in committed relationships. *AIDS Patient Care and STDs*, 26(12), 738–745. DOI: 10.1089/apc.2012.0198 PMID: 23199191

Holfeld, B., & Mishna, F. (2018). Longitudinal associations in youth involvement as victimized, bullying, or witnessing cyberbullying. *Cyberpsychology, Behavior, and Social Networking*, 21(4), 234–239. DOI: 10.1089/cyber.2017.0369 PMID: 29624446

Holfeld, B., Stoesz, B., & Montgomery, J. (2019). Traditional and cyber bullying and victimization among youth with autism spectrum disorder: An investigation of the frequency, characteristics, and psychosocial correlates. *Journal on Developmental Disabilities*, 24(2), 61–76.

Hollá, K., Jedlickova, P., & Seidler, P. (2020). Sexting types and motives detected among Slovak adolescents. *European Journal of Mental Health*, 15(2), 75–92. DOI: 10.5708/EJMH.15.2020.2.1

Holmes, L. G., Nilssen, A. R., Cann, D., & Strassberg, D. S. (2021). A sex-positive mixed methods approach to sexting experiences among college students. *Computers in Human Behavior*, 115, 106619. Advance online publication. DOI: 10.1016/j.chb.2020.106619

Holt, M. K., Vivolo-Kantor, A. M., Polanin, J. R., Holland, K. M., DeGue, S., Matjasko, J. L., Wolfe, M., & Reid, G. (2015). Bullying and suicidal ideation and behaviors: A meta-analysis. *Pediatrics*, 135(2), e496–e509. DOI: 10.1542/peds.2014-1864 PMID: 25560447

Hongladarom, S. (2011). Personal identity and the self in the online and offline world. *Minds and Machines*, 21(4), 533–548. DOI: 10.1007/s11023-011-9255-x

Ho, T. T. Q., & Gu, C. (2021). Cyberbullying victimization and depression: Self-esteem as a mediator and approach coping strategies as moderators. *Journal of American College Health*, 71(1), 94–101. DOI: 10.1080/07448481.2021.1877718 PMID: 33650940

Houck, C. D., Barker, D., Rizzo, C., Hancock, E., Norton, A., & Brown, L. K. (2014). Sexting and sexual behavior in at-risk adolescents. *Pediatrics*, 133(2), 276–282. DOI: 10.1542/peds.2013-1157 PMID: 24394678

Hou, D. (2023). The factors, impact, and interventions of cyberbullying in schools. *Journal of Education. Humanities and Social Sciences*, 8, 345–353. DOI: 10.54097/ehss.v8i.4272

Howard, T. (2019). Sextortion: Psychological Effects Experienced and Seeking Help and Reporting Among Emerging Adults. *Walden Dissertations and Doctoral Studies*. Retrieved from: https://scholarworks.waldenu.edu/dissertations/6584

Howard, D., Ryter, S., Hu, Y., Clancy, E. M., Klettke, B., & Klas, A. (2024). Unsolicited Sexting and Help-Seeking Behaviours among Australian Adults: A Mixed-Methods Study. *Social Sciences (Basel, Switzerland)*, 13(6), 289. Advance online publication. DOI: 10.3390/socsci13060289

Howie, P. C., & Bagnall, R. (2015). The transmogrification of warm-up: From drama to psychodrama. *The Arts in Psychotherapy*, 44, 35–44. DOI: 10.1016/j.aip.2014.11.004

Howie, P. C., & Bagnall, R. G. (2020). A criterial framework for concept evaluation in social practice and scholarship. *Sociological Methods & Research*, 49(3), 719–741. DOI: 10.1177/0049124118769104

Hoyle, R. H., Fejfar, M. C., & Miller, J. D. (2000). Personality and sexual risk taking: A quantitative review. *Journal of Personality*, 68(6), 1203–1231. DOI: 10.1111/1467-6494.00132 PMID: 11130738

https://www.pewinternet.org/2009/12/15/teens-and-sexting/

Huang, C. L., Alimu, Y., Yang, S. C., & Kang, S. (2023). What you think is a joke is actually cyberbullying: The effects of ethical dissonance, event judgment and humor style on cyberbullying behavior. *Computers in Human Behavior*, 142(4), 107670. DOI: 10.1016/j.chb.2023.107670

Huang, J., Duan, Z., Kwok, J., Binns, S., Vera, L. E., Kim, Y., Szczypka, G., & Emery, S. L. (2018). Vaping versus JUULing: How the extraordinary growth and marketing of JUUL transformed the US retail e-cigarette market. *Tobacco Control*, 28(2), 146–151. DOI: 10.1136/tobaccocontrol-2018-054382 PMID: 29853561

Huang, J.-S., Yang, F.-C., Chien, W.-C., Yeh, T.-C., Chung, C.-H., Tsai, C.-K., Tsai, S.-J., Yang, S.-S., Tzeng, N.-S., Chen, M.-H., & Liang, C.-S. (2021). Risk of substance use disorder and its associations with comorbidities and psychotropic agents in patients with autism. *JAMA Pediatrics*, 175(2), e205371. Advance online publication. DOI: 10.1001/jamapediatrics.2020.5371 PMID: 33394019

Huang, J., Zhong, Z., Zhang, H., & Li, L. (2021). Cyberbullying in Social Media and Online Games among Chinese College Students and Its Associated Factors. *International Journal of Environmental Research and Public Health*, 18(9), 4819. DOI: 10.3390/ijerph18094819 PMID: 33946441

Huang, L., Cao, Y., Liu, Y., Zhu, W., & Zhou, M. (2024). Peer effects on rural children's depression: Do online games matter? *European Child & Adolescent Psychiatry*, 33(6), 1707–1720. DOI: 10.1007/s00787-023-02271-z PMID: 37553541

Huang, T. C., Chen, M. Y., & Lin, C. Y. (2019). Exploring the behavioral patterns transformation of learners in different 3D modeling teaching strategies. *Computers in Human Behavior*, 92, 670–678. DOI: 10.1016/j.chb.2017.08.028

Hudson, H. K. (2011). *Factors affecting sexting behaviors among selected undergraduate students*. [Unpublished doctoral dissertation]. Southern Illinois University at Carbondale.

Hudson, H. K., & Marshall, S. A. (2018). Consequences and predictors of sexting among selected southern undergraduates. *International Journal of Sexual Health, 30*(1), 20–27. . 2017. 14045 40DOI: <ALIGNMENT.qj></ALIGNMENT>10.1080/ 19317 611

Hudson, H. K., Fetro, J. V., & Ogletree, R. (2014). Behavioral indicators and behaviors related to sexting among undergraduate students. *American Journal of Health Education*, 45(3), 183–195. DOI: 10.1080/19325037.2014.901113

Hudson, H. K., & Marshall, S. A. (2018). Consequences and Predictors of Sexting Among Selected Southern Undergraduates. *International Journal of Sexual Health : Official Journal of the World Association for Sexual Health*, 30(1), 20–27. DOI: 10.1080/19317611.2017.1404540

Humayya, A., Windarwati, H. D., & Winarni, I. (2022). Behavior therapy in those who are addicted to online games. *Journal of Nursing Science Update*, 10(1), 76–83. DOI: 10.21776/ub.jik.2022.010.01.10

Hunehäll Berndtsson, K. (2022). "Something you just don't talk about": An analysis of teenage boys' experiences of non-consensual sexting in lower secondary school. *Journal of Men's Studies*, 30(2), 155–173. DOI: 10.1177/10608265211042794

Hunehäll Berndtsson, K., & Odenbring, Y. (2021). They don't even think about what the girl might think about it': Students' views on sexting, gender inequalities and power relations in school. *Journal of Gender Studies*, 30(1), 91–101. DOI: 10.1080/09589236.2020.1825217

Hunter, S. C., Russell, K., & Knifton, L. (2018). *Individual, Family, and School Factors Relating to Sexting and Bullying*. Retrieved July 15, 2019, from https://strathprints.strath.ac.uk/65064/

Hunter, S. C., Russell, K., & Knifton, L. (2018*).Individual, family, and school factors relating to sexting and bullying*. University of Strathclyde. DOI: 10.17605/OSF.IO/2EVG4

Hunter, S. C., Russell, K., Pagani, S., Munro, L., Pimenta, S. M., Marín-López, I., Hong, J. S., & Knifton, L. (2021). A social-ecological approach to understanding adolescent sexting behavior. *Archives of Sexual Behavior*, 50(6), 2347–2357. DOI: 10.1007/s10508-021-01988-9 PMID: 33982213

Hutson, E., Kelly, S., & Militello, L. (2017). Systematic Review of Cyberbullying Interventions for Youth and Parents With Implications for Evidence-Based Practice. *Worldviews on Evidence-Based Nursing*, 15(1), 72–79. DOI: 10.1111/wvn.12257 PMID: 28859246

Hu, Y., Bai, Y., Pan, Y., & Li, S. (2021). Cyberbullying victimization and depression among adolescents: A meta-analysis. *Psychiatry Research*, 305, 114198. DOI: 10.1016/j.psychres.2021.114198 PMID: 34537540

Hu, Y., Clancy, E. M., & Klettke, B. (2023). Longitudinal Sexting Research: A Systematic Review. *Psych*, 5(2), 526–544. DOI: 10.3390/psych5020035

Iorga, M., Pop, L. M., Croitoru, I., Hanganu, E., & Anton-Păduraru, D. T. (2022). Exploring the Importance of Gender, Family Affluence, Parenting Style and Loneliness in Cyberbullying Victimization and Aggression among Romanian Adolescents. *Behavioral Sciences (Basel, Switzerland)*, 12(11), 457. DOI: 10.3390/bs12110457 PMID: 36421753

Irani, E. (2019). The use of videoconferencing for qualitative interviewing: Opportunities, challenges, and considerations. *Clinical Nursing Research*, 28(1), 3–8. DOI: 10.1177/1054773818803170 PMID: 30470151

Işıkoğlu Erdoğan, N., & Ergenekon, E. (2021). Bebeklerin teknolojik araçları kullanmalarıyla ilgili anne görüşleri. *Ankara University Journal of Faculty of Educational Sciences*, 54(1), 117–140. DOI: 10.30964/auebfd.767338

Işıkoğlu, N., Budak, K. S., & Guzen, M. (2024). Longitudinal Study of Children's Digital Play Addiction Tendencies and Parental Guidance Strategies. *Early Childhood Education Journal*. Advance online publication. DOI: 10.1007/s10643-024-01633-9

Isler, A., Beytut, D., Tas, F., & Conk, Z. (2009). A study on sexuality with the parents of adolescents with intellectual disability. *Sexuality and Disability*, 27(4), 229–237. DOI: 10.1007/s11195-009-9130-3

Jahan, N., & Kim, S. W. (2020). Understanding online community participation behaviour and perceived benefits: A social exchange theory perspective. *PSU Research Review*, 5(2), 85–100. DOI: 10.1108/PRR-12-2019-0036

Jaiswal, A., Manchanda, S., Gautam, V., Goel, A. D., Aneja, J., & Raghav, P. R. (2020). Burden of internet addiction, social anxiety and social phobia among University students, India. *Journal of Family Medicine and Primary Care*, 9(7), 3607–3612. DOI: 10.4103/jfmpc.jfmpc_360_20 PMID: 33102337

Jang, Y., & Ko, B. (2023). Online safety for children and youth under the 4Cs framework—A focus on digital policies in Australia, Canada, and the UK. *Children (Basel, Switzerland)*, 10(8), 1415. Advance online publication. DOI: 10.3390/children10081415 PMID: 37628414

Jeanfreau, M. M., Wright, L., & Noguchi, K. (2019). Marital satisfaction and sexting behavior among individuals in relationships. *The Family Journal (Alexandria, Va.)*, 27(1), 17–21. DOI: 10.1177/1066480718819868

Jiang, C., Li, C., Zhou, H., & Zhou, Z. (2020). Individuals with internet gaming disorder have similar neurocognitive impairments and social cognitive dysfunctions as methamphetamine-dependent patients. *Adicciones, 1342*(10.20882). https://doi.org/DOI: 10.20882/adicciones.1342

Jian-Hua, S., & hong, L. (2012). Explore the effective use of multimedia technology in college physics teaching. *Energy Procedia*, 17, 1897–1900. DOI: 10.1016/j.egypro.2012.02.329

Jiménez, T. R., & Orozco, M. (2021). Prompts, not questions: Four techniques for crafting better interview protocols. *Qualitative Sociology*, 44(4), 507–528. DOI: 10.1007/s11133-021-09483-2

Jin, X., Zhang, K., Twayigira, M., Gao, X., Xu, H., Huang, C., Luo, X., & Shen, Y. (2023). Cyberbullying among college students in a Chinese population: Prevalence and associated clinical correlates. *Frontiers in Public Health*, 11, 110006. DOI: 10.3389/fpubh.2023.1100069 PMID: 36908470

Jiujias, M., Kelley, E., & Hall, L. (2017). Restricted, repetitive behaviors in autism spectrum disorder and obsessive–compulsive disorder: A comparative review. *Child Psychiatry and Human Development*, 48(6), 944–959. DOI: 10.1007/s10578-017-0717-0 PMID: 28281020

Johnson, A. M., DiDonato, M. D., & Reisslein, M. (2013). Animated agents in K-12 engineering outreach: Preferred agent characteristics across age levels. *Computers in Human Behavior*, 29(4), 1807–1815. DOI: 10.1016/j.chb.2013.02.023

Johnson, D. W., & Johnson, R. T. (1999). *Learning Together and Alone: Cooperative, Competitive, and Individualistic Learning*. Allyn & Bacon.

Johnson, G. M., & Puplampu, K. P. (2008). Internet use during childhood and the ecological techno-subsystem. *Canadian Journal of Learning and Technology*, 34(1). Advance online publication. DOI: 10.21432/T2CP4T

Johnson, M., & Lee, K. (2023). *Experiential Learning in the Digital Age: Enhancing Psychoeducational Programs*. XYZ Press.

Jones, L. M., & Mitchell, K. J. (2016). Defining and Measuring Youth Digital Citizenship. *New Media & Society*, 18(9), 2066–2083. DOI: 10.1177/1461444815577797

Jonsson, L. S., Priebe, G., Bladh, M., & Svedin, C. G. (2014). Voluntary sexual exposure online among Swedish youth–social background, Internet behavior and psychosocial health. *Computers in Human Behavior*, 30, 181–190. DOI: 10.1016/j.chb.2013.08.005

Jørgensen, C. R., Weckesser, A., Turner, J., & Wade, A. (2019). Young people's views on sexting education and support needs: Findings and recommendations from a UK-based study. *Sex Education*, 19(1), 25–40. DOI: 10.1080/14681811.2018.1475283

Joronen, K., Häkämies, A., & Åstedt-Kurki, P. (2011). Children's experiences of a drama programme in social and emotional learning. *Scandinavian Journal of Caring Sciences*, 25(4), 671–678. DOI: 10.1111/j.1471-6712.2011.00877.x PMID: 21362006

Joronen, K., Konu, A., Rankin, H. S., & Astedt-Kurki, P. (2012). An evaluation of a drama program to enhance social relationships and anti-bullying at elementary school: A controlled study. *Health Promotion International*, 27(1), 5–14. DOI: 10.1093/heapro/dar012 PMID: 21385761

Jozsa, K., Kraus, A., Korpak, A. K., Birnholtz, J., Moskowitz, D. A., & Macapagal, K. (2021). 'Safe behind my screen': Adolescent sexual minority males' perceptions of safety and trustworthiness on geosocial and social networking apps. *Archives of Sexual Behavior*, 50(7), 2965–2980. DOI: 10.1007/s10508-021-01962-5 PMID: 34581948

Just, M., & Berg, T. (2017). Keeping children safe online: Understanding the concerns of carers of children with autism. In Bernhaupt, R., Dalvi, G., Joshi, A., Balkrishan, D. K., O'Neill, J., & Winckler, M. (Eds.), *Human-Computer Interaction – INTERACT 2017* (pp. 34–53). Springer., DOI: 10.1007/978-3-319-67687-6_3

Justus, A. N., Finn, P. R., & Steinmetz, J. E. (2000). The influence of traits of disinhibition on the association between alcohol use and risky sexual behavior. *Alcohol, Clinical and Experimental Research*, 24(7), 1028–1035. DOI: 10.1111/j.1530-0277.2000.tb04646.x PMID: 10924006

Kabali, H. K., Irigoyen, M. M., Nunez-Davis, R., Budacki, J. G., Mohanty, S. H., Leister, K. P., & Bonner, R. L.Jr. (2015). Exposure and use of mobile media devices by young children. *Pediatrics*, 136(6), 1044–1050. DOI: 10.1542/peds.2015-2151 PMID: 26527548

Kahn, J. A., Kaplowitz, R. A., Goodman, E., & Emans, S. J. (2002). The association between impulsiveness and sexual risk behaviors in adolescent and young adult women. *The Journal of Adolescent Health*, 30(4), 229–232. DOI: 10.1016/S1054-139X(01)00391-3 PMID: 11927234

Kalish, R. (2023). Sexting in a post-feminist society: Balancing agentic empowerment and the sexual double standard. *Women's Studies International Forum*, 98, 1–8. DOI: 10.1016/j.wsif.2023.102726

Kallitsounaki, A., & Williams, D. M. (2023). Autism spectrum disorder and gender dysphoria/incongruence. A systematic literature review and meta-analysis. *Journal of Autism and Developmental Disorders*, 53(8), 3103–3117. DOI: 10.1007/s10803-022-05517-y PMID: 35596023

Kamariotis, T. (2021). *The phenomenon of sexting among adolescents and young adults: protective and risk factors [in Greek].* Unpublished Doctoral thesis, Department of Psychology, Aristotle University of Thessaloniki.

Kamaruddin, I. K., Ma'rof, A. M., Mohd Nazan, A. I., & Ab Jalil, H. (2023). A systematic review and meta-analysis of interventions to decrease cyberbullying perpetration and victimization: An in-depth analysis within the Asia Pacific region. *Frontiers in Psychiatry*, 14, 1014258. DOI: 10.3389/fpsyt.2023.1014258 PMID: 36778634

Kandasamy, S., Buhari, A. M., & Janaki, S. (2019). A study on anxiety disorder among college students with internet addiction. *International Journal of Community Medicine and Public Health*, 6(4), 1695–1700. DOI: 10.18203/2394-6040.ijcmph20191407

Kandell, J. J. (1998). Internet addiction on campus: The vulnerability of college students. *Cyberpsychology & Behavior*, 1(1), 11–17. DOI: 10.1089/cpb.1998.1.11

Kansok-Dusche, J., Ballaschk, C., Krause, N., Zeißig, A., Seemann-Herz, L., Wachs, S., & Bilz, L. (2023). A Systematic Review on Hate Speech among Children and Adolescents: Definitions, Prevalence, and Overlap with Related Phenomena. *Trauma, Violence & Abuse*, 24(4), 2598–2615. DOI: 10.1177/15248380221108070 PMID: 35731198

Kapi, A. Y., Osman, N., Ramli, R. Z., & Taib, J. M. (2017). Multimedia education tools for effective teaching and learning. *Journal of Telecommunication, Electronic and Computer Engineering (JTEC)*, *9*(2-8), 143-146.

Karacic, S., & Oreskovic, S. (2017). Internet addiction through the phase of adolescence: A questionnaire study. *JMIR Mental Health*, 4(2), e11. DOI: 10.2196/mental.5537 PMID: 28373154

Karasavva, V., Brunet, L., Smodis, A., Swanek, J., & Forth, A. (2023). Putting the Y in cyberflashing: Exploring the prevalence and predictors of the reasons for sending unsolicited nude or sexual images. *Computers in Human Behavior*, 140, 107593. Advance online publication. DOI: 10.1016/j.chb.2022.107593

Karasavva, V., & Forth, A. (2022). Personality, attitudinal, and demographic predictors of non-consensual dissemination of intimate images. *Journal of Interpersonal Violence*, 37(21–22), NP19265–NP19289. DOI: 10.1177/08862605211043586 PMID: 34507500

Karasavva, V., & Noorbhai, A. (2021). The Real Threat of Deepfake Pornography: A Review of Canadian Policy. *Cyberpsychology, Behavior, and Social Networking*, 24(3), 203–209. DOI: 10.1089/cyber.2020.0272 PMID: 33760666

Karasavva, V., Swanek, J., Smodis, A., & Forth, A. (2022). Expectations VS reality: Expected and actual affective reactions to unsolicited sexual images. *Computers in Human Behavior*, 130, 107181. Advance online publication. DOI: 10.1016/j.chb.2022.107181

Kassis, W., Vasiou, A., Govaris, C., Favre, C., Aksoy, D., & Graf, U. (2023). Social and individual factors predicting students' resilience: A multigroup structural equation model. *Education Sciences*, 14(1), 15. DOI: 10.3390/educsci14010015

Katzman, D. K. (2010). Sexting: Keeping teens safe and responsible in a technologically savvy world. *Paediatrics & Child Health*, 15(1), 41–42. DOI: 10.1093/pch/15.1.41 PMID: 21197169

Kaval, A., & Siyez, D. M. (2024). An internet addiction model based on cognitive-behavioral approach among adolescents: Maladaptive cognitions, psychopathology, and situational cues. *Journal of Rational-Emotive & Cognitive-Behavior Therapy*, 42(2), 194–213. DOI: 10.1007/s10942-023-00502-5

Kawabe, K., Horiuchi, F., Miyama, T., Jogamoto, T., Aibara, K., Ishii, E., & Ueno, S. I. (2019). Internet addiction and attention-deficit/hyperactivity disorder symptoms in adolescents with autism spectrum disorder. *Research in Developmental Disabilities*, 89, 22–28. DOI: 10.1016/j.ridd.2019.03.002 PMID: 30877993

Kawabe, K., Horiuchi, F., Ochi, M., Oka, Y., & Ueno, S. I. (2016). Internet addiction: Prevalence and relation with mental states in adolescents. *Psychiatry and Clinical Neurosciences*, 70(9), 405–412. DOI: 10.1111/pcn.12402 PMID: 27178110

Kaye, L. K., Orben, A., Ellis, D. A., Hunter, S. C., & Houghton, S. (2020). The conceptual and methodological mayhem of "screen time". *International Journal of Environmental Research and Public Health*, 17(10), 3661. DOI: 10.3390/ijerph17103661 PMID: 32456054

Kazerooni, F., Taylor, S., Bazarova, N., & Whitlock, J. (2018). Cyberbullying Bystander Intervention: The Number of Offenders and Retweeting Predict Likelihood of Helping a Cyberbullying Victim. *Journal of Computer-Mediated Communication*, 23(3), 146–162. DOI: 10.1093/jcmc/zmy005

Kebir, C., & Özkaya, H. (2023). 16-36 ay arası çocuklarda ekran maruziyetinin dil gelişimi üzerindeki etkisinin araştırılması. *Türkiye Aile Hekimligi Dergisi*, 27(2), 21–28. DOI: 10.54308/tahd.2023.21033

Kee, D. M. H., Al-Anesi, M. A. L., & Al-Anesi, S. A. L. (2022). Cyberbullying on social media under the influence of COVID-19. *Global Business and Organizational Excellence*, 41(6), 11–22. DOI: 10.1002/joe.22175

Keeley, B., & Little, C. (2017). *The State of the Worlds Children 2017: Children in a Digital World. UNICEF. 3.* Retrieved from https://eric.ed.gov/?id=ED590013

Keengwe, J., Onchwari, G., & Wachira, P. (2008). The use of computer tools to support meaningful learning. *AACE Review (formerly AACE Journal), 16*(1), 77-92. Retrieved from https://www.learntechlib.org/primary/p/23647/

Kelly, R., O'Malley, M.-P., & Antonijevic, S. (2018). "Just trying to talk to people … It's the hardest": Perspectives of adolescents with high-functioning autism spectrum disorder on their social communication skills. *Child Language Teaching and Therapy*, 34(3), 319–334. DOI: 10.1177/0265659018806754

Kende, H. (2017). *Psychodrama with Children: Healing Children Through Their Own Creativity*. Routledge.

Kerman, N. T., Banihashem, S. K., Karami, M., Er, E., Van Ginkel, S., & Noroozi, O. (2023). Online peer feedback in higher education: A synthesis of the literature. *Education and Information Technologies*, 29(1), 763–813. DOI: 10.1007/s10639-023-12273-8

Kerstens, J., & Stol, W. (2014). Receiving online sexual requests and producing online sexual images: The multifaceted and dialogic nature of adolescents' online sexual interactions. *Cyberpsychology (Brno)*, 8(1), 1–12. DOI: 10.5817/CP2014-1-8

Khan, A. N. (2023). Are students at risk? Elucidating the impact of health risks of COVID-19 on emotional exhaustion and academic performance: Role of mindfulness and online interaction quality. *Current Psychology (New Brunswick, N.J.)*, 43(13), 12285–12298. DOI: 10.1007/s12144-023-04355-0 PMID: 36820197

Khurana, A., Bleakley, A., Jordan, A. B., & Romer, D. (2015). The protective effects of parental monitoring and internet restriction on adolescents' risk of online harassment. *Journal of Youth and Adolescence*, 44(5), 1039–1047. DOI: 10.1007/s10964-014-0242-4 PMID: 25504217

Khurana, A., Romer, D., Betancourt, L. M., Brodsky, N. L., Giannetta, J. M., & Hurt, H. (2012). Early Adolescent Sexual Debut: The mediating role of working memory ability, sensation seeking, and impulsivity. *Developmental Psychology*, 48(5), 1416–1428. DOI: 10.1037/a0027491 PMID: 22369334

Kibbe, K., & Thomas, S. S. (2024, May 24). *The 10 best sexting apps that should already be on your phone*. https://www.cosmopolitan.com/sex-love/a28137017/sexting-apps/

Kids Online Safety Act, S. 1409, 118th Cong. (2023). Retrieved from https://www.congress.gov/118/bills/s1409/BILLS-118s1409rs.pdf

Kim, S. (2011). *Effects of internet use on academic achievement and behavioral adjustment among South Korean adolescents: Mediating and moderating roles of parental factors* (Doctoral dissertation, Syracuse University).

Kim, J. U., Kim, Y. J., & Choi, S. H. (2016). The effect of internet addiction on college students' empathy: The mediating effects of social support. *Journal of the Korean Data Analysis Society*, 18(4), 1995–2007. DOI: 10.30773/pi.2018.08.07.2

Kim, S., & Lim, Y. (2020). Peer Pressure and SNS Addiction in Adolescents: The Mediating Role of SNS-Use Motives. *Canadian Journal of School Psychology*, 36(1), 23–33. DOI: 10.1177/0829573520963277

Kim, Y., & Baylor, A. L. (2016). Research-based design of pedagogical agent roles: A review, progress, and recommendations. *International Journal of Artificial Intelligence in Education*, 26(1), 160–169. DOI: 10.1007/s40593-015-0055-y

King, D. L., Delfabbro, P. H., & Griffiths, M. D. (2010). Cognitive behavioral therapy for problematic video game players: Conceptual considerations and practice issues. *Journal of Cyber Therapy and Rehabilitation*, 3(3).

Kingsley, K. V., & Boone, R. (2008). Effects of multimedia software on achievement of middle school students in an American history class. *Journal of Research on Technology in Education*, 41(2), 203–221. DOI: 10.1080/15391523.2008.10782529

Kintonova, A., Vasyaev, A., & Shestak, V. (2021). Cyberbullying and cyber-mobbing in developing countries. *Information and Computer Security*, 29(3), 435–456. DOI: 10.1108/ICS-02-2020-0031

Király, O., & Demetrovics, Z. (2017). Inclusion of gaming disorder in ICD has more advantages than disadvantages: Commentary on: Scholars' open debate paper on the World Health Organization ICD-11 Gaming Disorder proposal (Aarseth et al.). *Journal of Behavioral Addictions*, 6(3), 280–284. DOI: 10.1556/2006.6.2017.046 PMID: 28816495

Kirkpatrick, L. A., & Davis, K. E. (1994). Attachment style, gender, and relationship stability: A longitudinal analysis. *Journal of Personality and Social Psychology*, 66(3), 502–512. Advance online publication. DOI: 10.1037/0022-3514.66.3.502 PMID: 8169762

Kiss, H., Fitzpatrick, K. M., & Piko, B. F. (2020). The digital divide: Risk and protective factors and the differences in problematic use of digital devices among Hungarian youth. *Children and Youth Services Review*, 108, 104612. DOI: 10.1016/j.childyouth.2019.104612

Klettke, B., Hallford, D. J., Clancy, E., Mellor, D. J., & Toumbourou, J. W. (2019). Sexting and Psychological Distress: The Role of Unwanted and Coerced Sexts. *Cyberpsychology, Behavior, and Social Networking*, 22(4), 237–242. DOI: 10.1089/cyber.2018.0291 PMID: 30855187

Klettke, B., Hallford, D. J., & Mellor, D. J. (2014). Sexting prevalence and correlates: A systematic literature review. *Clinical Psychology Review*, 34(1), 44–53. DOI: 10.1016/j.cpr.2013.10.007 PMID: 24370714

Klettke, B., Mellor, D., Silva-Myles, L., Clancy, E., & Sharma, M. K. (2018). Sexting and mental health: A study of Indian and Australian young adults. *Cyberpsychology (Brno)*, 12(2), 2. Advance online publication. DOI: 10.5817/CP2018-2-2

Kline, R. B. (2004). *Principles and practice of structural equation modeling*. The Guilford Press.

Knott, E., Rao, A. H., Summers, K., & Teeger, C. (2022). Interviews in the social sciences. *Nature Reviews. Methods Primers*, 2(1), 1–15. DOI: 10.1038/s43586-022-00150-6

Kocturk, N., & Yuksel, F. (2018). A modern danger for adolescents: From online flirtation to sexual abuse. *Dusunen Adam : Bakirkoy Ruh Ve Sinir Hastaliklari Hastanesi Yayin Organi*, 31(3), 294–300. DOI: 10.5350/DAJPN2018310307

Kolb, A. Y., & Kolb, D. A. (2005). Learning styles and learning spaces: Enhancing experiential learning in higher education. *Academy of Management Learning & Education*, 4(2), 193–212. DOI: 10.5465/amle.2005.17268566

Kolb, D. A. (1984). *Experiential Learning: Experience as the Source of Learning and Development*. Prentice-Hall.

Konca, A. S. (2022). Digital technology usage of young children: Screen time and families. *Early Childhood Education Journal*, 50(7), 1097–1108. DOI: 10.1007/s10643-021-01245-7

Kopecký, K., Szotkowski, R., Krejčí, V., & Gómez-García, G. (2022). Digital safety and its importance in teacher education. Analysis of children's online behaviour in the Czech and Polish context. *Revista Interuniversitaria de Formación del Profesorado, 98*(36.2), 79-92. DOI: 10.47553/rifop.v98i36.2.94062

Kopecký, K. (2012). Sexting among Czech preadolescents and adolescents. *The New Educational Review*, 28(2), 39–48. DOI: 10.1016/j.sbspro.2015.08.289

Kopecký, K., Fernández-Martín, F. D., Szotkowski, R., Gómez-García, G., & Mikulcová, K. (2021). Behaviour of children and adolescents and the use of mobile phones in primary schools in the Czech Republic. *International Journal of Environmental Research and Public Health*, 18(16), 8352. Advance online publication. DOI: 10.3390/ijerph18168352 PMID: 34444102

Kormas, G., Critselis, E., Janikian, M., Kafetzis, D., & Tsitsika, A. (2011). Risk factors and psychosocial characteristics of potential problematic and problematic internet use among adolescents: A cross-sectional study. *BMC Public Health*, 11(1), 595. DOI: 10.1186/1471-2458-11-595 PMID: 21794167

Kostaridou-Eukleidi, A. (2011). *Cognitive Psychology. From the representation of cognition to memory and action*. Pedio.

Kostin, I. A. (2022). Internet safety for schoolchildren and adults with autism spectrum disorders: Vulnerability and areas of assistance. In Arinushkina, A. A., & Korobeynikov, I. A. (Eds.), *Education of Children with Special Needs* (pp. 11–18). Springer., DOI: 10.1007/978-3-031-13646-7_2

Koulianou, M., Mastrothanasis, K., Roussos, P., & Samartzi, S. (2020). Greek adaptation and psychometric validation of the Jr. MAI scale for the assessment of metacognitive learning strategies in adolescent students with and without specific learning difficulties. *Education Sciences*, SI-1, 20–29.

Koulianou, M., Roussos, P., & Samartzi, S. (2019). Metacognitive reading strategies: A Greek adaptation of the MARSI tool and a comparative study in adolescent students with and without specific learning difficulties. *Psychology (Irvine, Calif.)*, 24(1), 138–156. DOI: 10.12681/psy_hps.22391

Kovess-Masfety, V., Keyes, K., Hamilton, A., Hanson, G., Bitfoi, A., Golitz, D., Koç, C., Kuijpers, R., Lesinskiene, S., Mihova, Z., Otten, R., Fremanian, C., & Pez, O. (2016). Is time spent playing video games associated with mental health, cognitive and social skills in young children? *Social Psychiatry and Psychiatric Epidemioly 51*, 349–357. https://link.springer.com/article/10.1007/s00127-016-1179-6?source=post_page5d49aeb02811&fbclid=IwAR0XGN_roQZCbXWDxArrTx52ocPN8QWWUslH3s5QktahdyL3amiodZ49D2c

Kowalski, R. M., & Fedina, C. (2011). Cyber bullying in ADHD and Asperger Syndrome populations. *Research in Autism Spectrum Disorders*, 5(3), 1201–1208. DOI: 10.1016/j.rasd.2011.01.007

Kowalski, R. M., Giumetti, G. W., Schroeder, A. N., & Lattanner, M. R. (2014). Bullying in the digital age: A critical review and meta-analysis of cyberbullying research among youth. *Psychological Bulletin*, 140(4), 1073–1137. DOI: 10.1037/a0035618 PMID: 24512111

Kraut, R., Patterson, M., Lundmark, V., Kiesler, S., Mukopadhyay, T., & Scherlis, W. (1998). Internet paradox: A social technology that reduces social involvement and psychological well-being? *The American Psychologist*, 53(9), 1017–1031. DOI: 10.1037/0003-066X.53.9.1017 PMID: 9841579

Krieger, M. A. (2017). Unpacking "sexting": A systematic review of non-consensual sexting in legal, educational, and psychological literatures. *Trauma, Violence & Abuse*, 18(5), 593–601. DOI: 10.1177/1524838016659486 PMID: 27436858

Kuo, H. J., Yeomans, M., Ruiz, D., & Lin, C. C. (2024). Video games and disability—A risk and benefit analysis. *Frontiers in Rehabilitation Sciences*, 5, 1343057. DOI: 10.3389/fresc.2024.1343057 PMID: 38496777

Kuo, M. H., Orsmond, G. I., Coster, W. J., & Cohn, E. S. (2014). Media use among adolescents with autism spectrum disorder. *Autism*, 18(8), 914–923. DOI: 10.1177/1362361313497832 PMID: 24142797

Kurniawan, E. (2019). *Pengaruh Adiksi Bermain Game Online terhadap Pelaksanaan Ibadah Shalat Siswa Sekolah Menengah Atas Negeri 1 Siak kecamatan Siak kabupaten Siak* [Unpublished Doctoral dissertation, Universitas Islam Negeri Sultan Syarif Kasim Riau] https://repository.uin-suska.ac.id/22682/

Kuss, D. J., & Griffiths, M. D. (2011). Online Social Networking and Addiction—A review of the Psychological literature. *International Journal of Environmental Research and Public Health. International Journal of Environmental Research and Public Health*, 8(9), 3528–3552. DOI: 10.3390/ijerph8093528 PMID: 22016701

Kwak, Y., Kim, H., & Ahn, J.-W. (2022). Impact of internet usage time on mental health in adolescents: Using the 14th Korea Youth Risk Behavior Web-Based Survey 2018. *PLoS One*, 17(3), e0264948. DOI: 10.1371/journal.pone.0264948 PMID: 35320295

Lacina, J., & Griffith, R. (2018). Diverse learners, diverse backgrounds. *The Reading Teacher*, 72(2), 141–142. DOI: 10.1002/trtr.1738

Laird, J., Klettke, B., Clancy, E., & Fuelscher, I. (2021). Relationships between coerced sexting and differentiation of self: An exploration of protective factors. *Sexes*, 2(4), 468–482. DOI: 10.3390/sexes2040037

Lambert, L., Joshanloo, M., Warren, M. A., Christiani, K., Lomas, T., Cody, B., Al Sabah, I., El Chalabi, A., & Kruchlik, G. (2023). Promoting Kindness Through the Positive Theatrical Arts: Assessing Kuwait's Boomerang Programme. *Psychological Studies*, 68(1), 101–113. DOI: 10.1007/s12646-022-00706-2

Lameiras-Fernández, M., Martínez-Román, R., Carrera-Fernández, M. V., & Rodríguez-Castro, Y. (2021). Sex education in the spotlight: What is working? Systematic review. *International Journal of Environmental Research and Public Health*, 18(5), 2555. Advance online publication. DOI: 10.3390/ijerph18052555 PMID: 33806507

Lam, L. T., & Peng, Z. W. (2010). Effect of pathological use of the internet on adolescent mental health: A prospective study. *Archives of Pediatrics & Adolescent Medicine*, 164(10), 901–906. DOI: 10.1001/archpediatrics.2010.159 PMID: 20679157

Lam, L. T., & Wong, E. M. Y. (2015). Stress Moderates the Relationship Between Problematic Internet Use by Parents and Problematic Internet Use by Adolescents. *The Journal of Adolescent Health*, 56(3), 300–306. DOI: 10.1016/j.jadohealth.2014.10.263 PMID: 25703319

Lampri, S., Peristeri, E., Marinis, T., & Andreou, M. (2024). Figurative language processing in autism spectrum disorders: A review. *Autism Research*, 17(4), 674–689. DOI: 10.1002/aur.3069 PMID: 38071498

Lancaster, M. (2018). A Systematic Research Synthesis on Cyberbullying Interventions in the United States. *Cyberpsychology, Behavior, and Social Networking*, 21(10), 593–602. DOI: 10.1089/cyber.2018.0307 PMID: 30334647

Lange, B. P., Blaut, A., Becker, R., & Krämer, N. C. (2021). Digital literacy in children: The role of socio-demographic variables, cognitive abilities, and family characteristics. *Computers & Education*, 160, 104028. DOI: 10.1016/j.compedu.2020.104028

Langos, C. (2012). Cyberbullying: The Challenge to Define. *Cyberpsychology, Behavior, and Social Networking*, 15(6), 285–289. DOI: 10.1089/cyber.2011.0588 PMID: 22703033

Lan, M., Law, N., & Pan, Q. (2022). Effectiveness of anti-cyberbullying educational programs: A socio-ecologically grounded systematic review and meta-analysis. *Computers in Human Behavior*, 130, 107200. DOI: 10.1016/j.chb.2022.107200

Lapierre, M. A., & Custer, B. E. (2021). Testing relationships between smartphone engagement, romantic partner communication, and relationship satisfaction. *Mobile Media & Communication*, 9(2), 155–176. DOI: 10.1177/2050157920935163

Larson, J., Anderson, S., Holman, T., & Niemann, B. (1998). A longitudinal study of the effects of premarital communication, relationship stability, and self-esteem on sexual satisfaction in the first year of marriage. *Journal of Sex & Marital Therapy*, 24(3), 193–206. DOI: 10.1080/00926239808404933 PMID: 9670124

Laurence, P. G., de Melo Rodrigues, M., Tannus, M. C. B. L., Dekaney, E. M., & Macedo, E. C. (2024). Parental executive functions and motivations unveil variations in young children's screen media use. *Psicologia: Reflexão e Crítica : Revista Semestral do Departamento de Psicologia da UFRGS*, 37(1), 20. DOI: 10.1186/s41155-024-00289-z PMID: 38847965

Lauricella, A. R., Wartella, E., & Rideout, V. (2015). Young children's screen time: The complex role of parent and child factors. *Journal of Applied Developmental Psychology*, 36, 11–17. DOI: 10.1016/j.appdev.2014.12.001

Lau-Zhu, A., Anderson, C., & Lister, M. (2023). Assessment of digital risks in child and adolescent mental health services: A mixed-method, theory-driven study of clinicians' experiences and perspectives. *Clinical Child Psychology and Psychiatry*, 28(1), 255–269. DOI: 10.1177/13591045221098896 PMID: 35522928

Lay, A. R. S., Wijaya, R. P. C., & Keraf, M. A. (2021). A Study of Self-Regulation on Online Game Addiction in Kupang City. *Journal of Health and Behavioral Science*, 3(4), 524–535. DOI: 10.35508/jhbs.v3i4.4542

Le, L. (2016). *What's your sext drive: Examining female emerging adults' experiences of sharing visual sexual content through communication technologies.* Unpublished Master's thesis, University of Alberta, Alberta Canada. DOI: 10.7939/R3R785X28

Leadbitter, K., Buckle, K., Ellis, C., & Dekker, M. (2021). Autistic self-advocacy and the neurodiversity movement: Implications for autism early intervention research and practice. *Frontiers in Psychology*, 12, 635690. DOI: 10.3389/fpsyg.2021.635690 PMID: 33912110

Leatham, H. (2017). *Digital privacy in the classroom: an analysis of the intent and realization of Ontario policy in context.* Unpublished Master's thesis, Ontario Tech University. Ontario Tech University - eScholar. https://hdl.handle.net/10155/816

Lebenhagen, C. (2020). Including speaking and nonspeaking autistic voice in research. *Autism in Adulthood: Challenges and Management*, 2(2), 128–131. DOI: 10.1089/aut.2019.0002 PMID: 36601567

Lee, C. H., Moak, S., & Walker, J. T. (2016). Effects of self-control, social control, and social learning on sexting behavior among South Korean youths. *Youth & Society*, 48(2), 242–264. DOI: 10.1177/0044118X13490762

Lee, C., & Shin, N. (2017). Prevalence of cyberbullying and predictors of cyberbullying perpetration among Korean adolescents. *Computers in Human Behavior*, 68, 352–358. DOI: 10.1016/j.chb.2016.11.047

Lee, E. Y., Song, Y. K., Hunter, S., Jeon, J., Kuzik, N., Predy, M., & Carson, V. (2021). Levels and correlates of physical activity and screen time among early years children (2–5 years): Cross-cultural comparisons between Canadian and South Korean data. *Child: Care, Health and Development*, 47(3), 377–386. DOI: 10.1111/cch.12850 PMID: 33463740

Lei, J., Leigh, E., Charman, T., Russell, A., & Hollocks, M. J. (2024). Understanding the relationship between social camouflaging in autism and safety behaviours in social anxiety in autistic and non-autistic adolescents. *Journal of Child Psychology and Psychiatry, and Allied Disciplines*, 65(3), 285–297. DOI: 10.1111/jcpp.13884 PMID: 37632264

Le, L., Goegan, L. D., & Daniels, L. M. (2023). The impact of autonomous and controlled sexting motivations on subjective well-being and relationship quality. *Archives of Sexual Behavior*, 52(1), 243–254. DOI: 10.1007/s10508-022-02361-0 PMID: 35881253

Lemmens, J. S., Valkenburg, P. M., & Peter, J. (2009). Development and validation of a play addiction scale for adolescents. *Media Psychology*, 12(1), 77–95. DOI: 10.1080/15213260802669458

Lenakakis, A., & Koltsida, M. (2017). Disabled and non-disabled actors working in partnership for a theatrical performance: A research on theatrical partnerships as enablers of social and behavioural skills for persons with disabilities. *Research in Drama Education*, 22(2), 251–269. DOI: 10.1080/13569783.2017.1286975

Lenhart, A. (2009, December 15). *Teens and sexting: How and why minor teens are sending sexually suggestive nude or nearly nude images via text messaging*. Pew Internet & American Life Project.

Lenhart, A. (2009c). *Overview: Teens and sexting: How and why minor teens are sending sexually suggestive nude or nearly nude images via text messaging. Pew Internet and American Life Project.* Retrieved July 15, 2013, from https://img.ksl.com/slc/1897/189789/18978984.pdf

Lenhart, A. (2009). *Teens and sexting* (Vol. 15). Pew Internet & American Life Project.

Leung, A., Wong, N., & Farver, J. (2019). Testing the Effectiveness of an E-Course to Combat Cyberbullying. *Cyberpsychology, Behavior, and Social Networking*, 22(9), 569–577. DOI: 10.1089/cyber.2018.0609 PMID: 31526296

Levounis, P. (2015). Bench to Bedside: From the science to the practice of addiction medicine. *Journal of Medical Toxicology; Official Journal of the American College of Medical Toxicology*, 12(1), 50–53. DOI: 10.1007/s13181-015-0515-7 PMID: 26553278

Levy, S. (2022). *Autistic traits, substance use, and social anxiety* (Publication No. 29062026) [Master's thesis, The University of Alabama]. ProQuest Dissertations and Theses.

Lewison, M., Flint, A. S., & Sluys, K. V. (2002). Taking on critical literacy: The journey of newcomers and novices. *Language Arts*, 79(5), 382–392. DOI: 10.58680/la2002255

Ley Orgánica 8/2021, de 4 de junio, de protección integral a la infancia y la adolescencia frente a la violencia [Organic Law 8/2021, of the 4th of June, of integral protection of infancy and adolescence towards violence]. *Boletín Oficial del Estado, 134*, of the 5th of June 2021, 68657-68730. https://www.boe.es/boe/dias/2021/06/05/pdfs/BOE-A-2021-9347.pdf

Liao, H., Lei, L., Wang, Y., & Huang, X. (2022). Exploring the relationship between internet addiction, social isolation, and academic achievement in adolescents: A study in China. *International Journal of Environmental Research and Public Health*, 19(3), 1243. DOI: 10.3390/ijerph19031243 PMID: 35162266

Liau, A. K., Neo, E. C., Gentile, D. A., Choo, H., Sim, T., Li, D., & Khoo, A. (2011). Impulsivity, self-regulation, and pathological video gaming among youth: Testing a mediation model. *Asia-Pacific Journal of Public Health*, 27(2), NP2188–NP2196. DOI: 10.1177/1010539511429369 PMID: 22199156

Licata, N. (2024). The Digital Era Will Prompt Revolutions - as Did the Print Era. *CounterPunch*, 1–5.

Lieberman, D. A., Fisk, M. C., & Biely, E. (2009). Digital games for young children ages three tosix: From research to design. *Computers in the Schools*, 26(3), 299–313. DOI: 10.1080/07380560903360178

Liew, T. W., Mat Zin, N. A., & Sahari, N. (2017). Exploring the affective, motivational and cognitive effects of pedagogical agent enthusiasm in a multimedia learning environment. *Human-centric Computing and Information Sciences*, 7(1), 1–21. DOI: 10.1186/s13673-017-0089-2

Lightfoot, C., Cole, M., & Cole, S. R. (2022). *Children's Development* [in Greek]. Gutenberg.

Lin, C. Y., Potenza, M. N., Broström, A., & Pakpour, A. H. (2021). Internet gaming disorder, psychological distress, and insomnia in adolescent students and their siblings: An actor-partner interdependence model approach. *Addictive Behaviors Reports*, 13, 100332. DOI: 10.1016/j.abrep.2020.100332 PMID: 33437860

Lindenberg, K., Halasy, K., & Schoenmaekers, S. (2017). A randomized efficacy trial of a cognitive-behavioral group intervention to prevent Internet Use Disorder onset in adolescents: The PROTECT study protocol. *Contemporary Clinical Trials Communications*, 6, 64–71. DOI: 10.1016/j.conctc.2017.02.011 PMID: 29740637

Lin, L., Atkinson, R., Christopherson, R., Joseph, S., & Harrison, C. (2013). Animated agents and learning: Does the type of verbal feedback they provide matter? *Computers & Education*, 67, 239–249. DOI: 10.1016/j.compedu.2013.04.017

Lippman, J. R., & Campbell, S. W. (2014). Damned if you do, damned if you don't… if you're a girl: Relational and normative contexts of adolescent sexting in the United States. *Journal of Children and Media*, 8(4), 371–386. DOI: 10.1080/17482798.2014.923009

Li, S., Hong, Y., & Craig, S. D. (2023). A Systematic Literature review of social learning Theory in Online Learning Environments. *Educational Psychology Review*, 35(4), 108. Advance online publication. DOI: 10.1007/s10648-023-09827-0

Liu, H., Zhou, X., Yu, G., & Sun, X. (2019). The effects of the PRISMA statement to improve the conduct and reporting of systematic reviews and meta-analyses of nursing interventions for patients with heart failure. *International Journal of Nursing Practice*, 25(3), e12729. DOI: 10.1111/ijn.12729 PMID: 30790391

Liu, J., Wu, L., Sun, X., Bai, X., & Duan, C. (2023). Active parental mediation and adolescent problematic internet use: The mediating role of Parent–Child relationships and hiding online behavior. *Behavioral Sciences (Basel, Switzerland)*, 13(8), 679. DOI: 10.3390/bs13080679 PMID: 37622819

Liu, Y.-L. (2020). Maternal mediation as an act of privacy invasion: The association with internet addiction. *Computers in Human Behavior*, 112, 106474. DOI: 10.1016/j.chb.2020.106474

Livingstone, S., & Görzig, A. (2011) Sexting. In S., Livingstone, L., Haddon, & A., Gorzig (Eds.), *Children, Risk and Safety on the Internet: Kids online in comparative perspective* (pp.1-10), The Policy Press. DOI: 10.1332/policypress/9781847428837.003.0012

Livingstone, S., & Gorzig, A. (2011). Sexting. In S., Livingstone, L., Haddon, & A., Gorzig (Eds.), *Children, Risk and Safety on the Internet: Kids online in comparative perspective* (pp. 1-10). The Policy Press.

Livingstone, S., Kalmus, V., & Talves, K. (2013). Girls' and boys' experiences of online risk and safety. In *The Routledge Companion to Media & Gender* (pp. 190-200). Routledge.

Livingstone, S., Mascheroni, G., Dreier, M., Chaudron, S., & Lagae, K. (2015). *How parents of young children manage digital devices at home: The role of income, education and parental style*. EU Kids Online, LSE. Retrieved from https://eprints.lse.ac.uk/63378/1/__lse.ac.uk_storage_LIBRARY_Secondary_libfile_shared_repository_Content_EU%20Kids%20Online_EU_Kids_Online_How%20parents%20manage%20digital%20devices_2016.pdf

Livingstone, S. (2012). Children and the internet: Great expectations and challenges. *Polity*.

Livingstone, S. (2014). Developing social media literacy: How children learn to interpret risky opportunities on social network sites. *Communications*, 39(3), 283–303. DOI: 10.1515/commun-2014-0113

Livingstone, S., & Görzig, A. (2014). When adolescents receive sexual messages on the internet: Explaining experiences of risk and harm. *Computers in Human Behavior*, 33, 8–15. DOI: 10.1016/j.chb.2013.12.021

Livingstone, S., & Haddon, L. (Eds.). (2009). *Kids online: Opportunities and risks for children* (1st ed.). Bristol University Press., DOI: 10.2307/j.ctt9qgvdsig

Livingstone, S., & Helsper, E. (2008). Parental mediation of children's internet use. *Journal of Broadcasting & Electronic Media*, 52(4), 581–599. DOI: 10.1080/08838150802437396

Livingstone, S., Mascheroni, G., & Staksrud, E. (2017). European Research on Children's Internet Use: Assessing the Past and Anticipating the Future. *New Media & Society*, 20(3), 1103–1122. DOI: 10.1177/1461444816685930

Livingstone, S., Ólafsson, K., Helsper, E. J., Lupiáñez-Villanueva, F., Veltri, G. A., & Folkvord, F. (2017). Maximizing opportunities and minimizing risks for children online: The role of digital skills in emerging strategies of parental mediation. *Journal of Communication*, 67(1), 82–105. DOI: 10.1111/jcom.12277

Livingstone, S., & Smith, P. K. (2014). Annual research review: Harms experienced by child users of online and mobile technologies: The nature, prevalence and management of sexual and aggressive risks in the digital age. *Journal of Child Psychology and Psychiatry, and Allied Disciplines*, 55(6), 635–654. DOI: 10.1111/jcpp.12197 PMID: 24438579

Livingstone, S., & Stoilova, M. (2021). *The 4Cs: classifying online risk to children* (CO:RE Short Report Series on Key Topics). Hamburg: Leibniz-Institut für Medienforschung | Hans-Bredow-Institut (HBI). https://doi.org/DOI: 10.21241/ssoar.71817

Lloyd, J. (2020). Abuse through sexual image sharing in schools: Response and responsibility. *Gender and Education*, 32(6), 784–802. DOI: 10.1080/09540253.2018.1513456

Löfgren-Mårtenson, L. (2008). Love in cyberspace: Swedish young people with intellectual disabilities and the Internet. *Scandinavian Journal of Disability Research*, 10(2), 125–138. DOI: 10.1080/15017410701758005

Lorang, M. R., McNiel, D. E., & Binder, R. L. (2016). Minors and sexting: Legal implications. *The Journal of the American Academy of Psychiatry and the Law*, 44(1), 73–81. PMID: 26944746

Lowe, R. K., & Schnotz, W. (2014). Animation principles in multimedia learning. *The Cambridge handbook of multimedia learning, 2*, 513-546.

Lubis, H., Rivai, M., Yushar, Y., & Nasution, M. (2019, December). Interactive Map of Historical Sites: The Media of History Learning on the 21st Century in North Sumatra. In *Proceedings of the 2nd International Conference on Social Sciences and Interdisciplinary Studies (formerly ICCSSIS), ICCSIS 2019*. DOI: 10.4108/eai.24-10-2019.2290580

Luchs, C. (2021). Considering neurodiversity in learning design and technology. *TechTrends*, 65(6), 923–924. DOI: 10.1007/s11528-021-00667-9

Lu, H., & Wang, S. (2008). The role of Internet addiction in online game loyalty: An exploratory study. *Internet Research*, 18(5), 499–519. DOI: 10.1108/10662240810912756

Lunde, C., & Joleby, M. (2023). Being Under Pressure to Sext: Adolescents' Experiences, Reactions, and Counter-Strategies. *Journal of Research on Adolescence*, 33(1), 188–201. DOI: 10.1111/jora.12797 PMID: 36059189

Luo, Y. F., Yang, S. C., Chou, K. Y., & Lee, H. T. (2023). Taiwanese parents' perspectives on young children's use of information communication technology. *Frontiers in Psychology*, 14, 1248863. DOI: 10.3389/fpsyg.2023.1248863 PMID: 37799529

Lyngstad, M. B., Baraldsnes, D., & Gjærum, R. G. (2022). Process drama in anti-bullying intervention: A study of adolescents' attitudes and initiatives. *Research in Drama Education*, 27(4), 524–538. DOI: 10.1080/13569783.2021.2011715

MacKenzie, D. L., & Farrington, D. P. (2015). Preventing future offending of delinquents and offenders: What have we learned from experiments and meta-analyses? *Journal of Experimental Criminology*, 11(4), 565–595. DOI: 10.1007/s11292-015-9244-9

Macmillan, K., Berg, T., Just, M., & Stewart, M. E. (2020). Are autistic children more vulnerable online? Relating autism to online safety, child wellbeing and parental risk management. In *Proceedings of the 11th Nordic Conference on Human-Computer Interaction: Shaping Experiences,* Shaping Society (pp. 1-11). ACM. https://doi.org/DOI: 10.1145/3419249.3420160

Macmillan, K., Berg, T., Just, M., & Stewart, M. E. (2022). Online safety experiences of autistic young people: An interpretative phenomenological analysis. *Research in Autism Spectrum Disorders*, 96, 101995. Advance online publication. DOI: 10.1016/j.rasd.2022.101995

Madigan, S., Browne, D., Racine, N., Mori, C., & Tough, S. (2019). Association Between Screen Time and Children's Performance on a Developmental Screening Test. *JAMA Pediatrics*, 173(3), 244–250. DOI: 10.1001/jamapediatrics.2018.5056 PMID: 30688984

Madigan, S., Ly, A., Rash, C. L., Van Ouytsel, J., & Temple, J. R. (2018). Prevalence of Multiple Forms of Sexting Behavior Among Youth: A Systematic Review and Meta-analysis. *JAMA Pediatrics*, 172(4), 327–335. DOI: 10.1001/jamapediatrics.2017.5314 PMID: 29482215

Magis-Weinberg, L., Gys, C., Berger, E., Domoff, S., & Dahl, R. (2021). Positive and negative online experiences and loneliness in Peruvian adolescents during the COVID-19 lockdown. *Journal of Research on Adolescence*, 31(3), 717–733. DOI: 10.1111/jora.12666 PMID: 34448303

Mahatme, N., Kakunje, A., Nafisa, D., rinivasan, J., & Puthran, S. (2020). Knowledge and attitude of mental health professionals towards psychodrama as a psychotherapeutic tool. *Telangana Journal of Psychiatry*, 4(2), 92–95. DOI: 10.18231/2455-8559.2018.0010

Maheux, A. J., Evans, R., Widman, L., Nesi, J., Prinstein, M. J., & Choukas-Bradley, S. (2020). Popular peer norms and adolescent sexting behavior. *Journal of Adolescence*, 78(1), 62–66. DOI: 10.1016/j.adolescence.2019.12.002 PMID: 31841872

Mai, A., Guelmino, L., Pfeffer, K., Weippl, E., & Krombholz, K. (2022). Mental models of the Internet and its online risks: Children and their parent(s). In Moallem, A. (Ed.), Lecture Notes in Computer Science: Vol. 13333. *HCI for Cybersecurity, Privacy and Trust. HCII 2022* (pp. 42–61). Springer., DOI: 10.1007/978-3-031-05563-8_4

Mainwaring, C., Scott, A. J., & Gabbert, F. (2023). Behavioural Intentions of Bystanders to Image-Based Sexual Abuse: A Preliminary Focus Group Study with a University Student Sample. *Journal of Child Sexual Abuse*, 32(3), 318–339. DOI: 10.1080/10538712.2023.2190734 PMID: 36921125

Malanga, D. (2020). *Tackling Gender-Based Cyber Violence against Women and Girls in Malawi Amidst the COVID-19 Pandemic.* African Internet Rights. Retrieved from: https://africaninternetrights.org/sites/default/files/Donald_ Flywell.pdf

Mallick, D., Chakraborty, P., & Ghosh, S. (2023). Visual representation for patterned proliferation of social media addiction: Quantitative model and network analysis. *SN Computer Science*, 4(6), 712. DOI: 10.1007/s42979-023-02164-7

Manago, A. M., Taylor, T., & Greenfield, P. M. (2012). Me and my 400 friends: The anatomy of college students' Facebook networks, their communication patterns, and well-being. *Developmental Psychology*, 48(2), 369–380. DOI: 10.1037/a0026338 PMID: 22288367

Mandau, M. B. H. (2020). 'Directly in your face': A qualitative study on the sending and receiving of unsolicited 'dick pics' among young adults. *Sexuality & Culture*, 24(1), 72–93. DOI: 10.1007/s12119-019-09626-2

Mandau, M. B. H. (2021). "Snaps", "screenshots", and self-blame: A qualitative study of image-based sexual abuse victimization among adolescent Danish girls. *Journal of Children and Media*, 15(3), 431–447. DOI: 10.1080/17482798.2020.1848892

Mansor, N., Ahmad, N., & Zulkefli, N. A. M. (2023). Intrinsic and Extrinsic Factors Associated with Sexting Behavior Among Young People: A Systematic Review. *Malaysian Journal of Public Health Medicine*, 23(1), 42–56. DOI: 10.37268/mjphm/vol.23/no.1/art.1485

Marazziti, D., Presta, S., Picchetti, M., & Dell'Osso, L. (2015). Behavioral addiction: Clinical and therapeutic aspects. *Official Journal of the Italian Society of Psychopathology*, 21, 72–84. DOI: 10.1017/S1092852913001041 PMID: 24589040

March, E., & Wagstaff, D. L. (2017). Sending nudes: Sex, self-rated mate value, and trait Machiavellianism predict sending unsolicited explicit images. *Frontiers in Psychology*, 8, 2210. Advance online publication. DOI: 10.3389/fpsyg.2017.02210 PMID: 29326632

Marco-Fondevila, M., Rueda-Tomás, M., & Latorre-Martínez, M. P. (2022). Active participation and interaction are key performance factors of Face-to-Face learning. *Education Sciences*, 12(7), 429. DOI: 10.3390/educsci12070429

Marcum, C. D., Zaitzow, B. H., & Higgins, G. E. (2002). The role of sexting and related behaviors to victimization via nonconsensual pornography: An exploratory analysis of university students. *Journal of Aggression, Conflict and Peace Research*, 14(1), 43–60. DOI: 10.1108/JACPR-02-2021-0578

Marées, N., & Petermann, F. (2012). Cyberbullying: An increasing challenge for schools. *School Psychology International*, 33(5), 467–476. DOI: 10.1177/0143034312445241

Marganski, A. (2017). Sexting in Poland and the United States: A comparative study of personal and social-situational factors. *International Journal of Cyber Criminology*, 11(2), 183–201. DOI: 10.5281/zenodo.1037385

Marganski, A., & Fauth, K. (2013). Socially Interactive Technology and Contemporary Dating: A Cross-Cultural Exploration of Deviant Behaviors Among Young Adults in the Modern, Evolving Technological World. *International Criminal Justice Review*, 23(4), 357–377. DOI: 10.1177/1057567713513797

Marín, V. I., Carpenter, J. P., & Tur, G. (2021). Pre-service teachers' perceptions of social media data privacy policies. *British Journal of Educational Technology*, 52(2), 519–535. DOI: 10.1111/bjet.13035

Martha, A. S. D., & Santoso, H. B. (2019). The Design and Impact of the Pedagogical Agent: A Systematic Literature Review. *The Journal of Educators Online*, 16(1). Advance online publication. DOI: 10.9743/jeo.2019.16.1.8

Martínez, S. R. (2015). Disability in young people, increases the risk of excessive internet use? *Health and Addictions, 15*(1), 15-24. http://hdl.handle.net/10045/44528

Martinez-Prather, K., & Vandiver, D. M. (2014). Sexting among Teenagers in the United States: A Retrospective Analysis of Identifying Motivating Factors, Potential Targets, and the Role of a Capable Guardian. *International Journal of Cyber Criminology*, 8(1), 21–35.

Martin, F. (2018). Digital literacy and student attitudes to learning: The case of the web-based learning platform. *Education and Information Technologies*, 23(5), 1913–1925.

Martin, F., Bacak, J., Polly, D., Wang, W., & Ahlgrim-Delzell, L. (2023). Teacher and school concerns and actions on elementary school children digital safety. *TechTrends*, 67(3), 561–571. DOI: 10.1007/s11528-022-00803-z PMID: 36249671

Martins, N., King, A., & Beights, R. (2020). Audiovisual media content preferences of children with autism spectrum disorders: Insights from parental interviews. *Journal of Autism and Developmental Disorders*, 50(9), 3092–3100. DOI: 10.1007/s10803-019-03987-1 PMID: 30905049

Marume, A., Maradzika, J., & January, J. (2018). Adolescent Sexting and Risky Sexual Behaviours in Zimbabwe: A Cross-Sectional Study. *Sexuality & Culture*, 22(3), 931–941. DOI: 10.1007/s12119-018-9508-4

Masters, N. T., Norris, J., Stoner, S. A., & George, W. H. (2006). How does it end? Women project the outcome of a sexual assault scenario. *Psychology of Women Quarterly*, 30(3), 291–302. DOI: 10.1111/j.1471-6402.2006.00297.x

Mastrothanasis, K. (2019). Development and psychometric validation of self-reflection of reading comprehension strategies for bilingual students. *Preschool & School Education*, 7(2), 116–138. DOI: 10.12681/ppej.20212

Mastrothanasis, K., & Grammatas, T. (2022). Reception of the values of the Aeschylus drama and mnemonic imprints by ancient tragedy spectators. *Open Research Europe*, 2, 124. Advance online publication. DOI: 10.12688/openreseurope.15179.1 PMID: 37645271

Mastrothanasis, K., & Kladaki, M. (2020). The Involvement of Children in the Arts during Their Leisure Time. *Asian Journal of Language. Literature and Culture Studies*, 3(2), 10–19.

Mastrothanasis, K., Kladaki, M., & Andreou, A. (2023). A systematic review and meta-analysis of the Readers' Theatre impact on the development of reading skills. *International Journal of Educational Research Open*, 4, 100243. DOI: 10.1016/j.ijedro.2023.100243

Mastrothanasis, K., Koulianou, M., Katsifi, S., & Zouganeli, A. (2018). The use of Metacognitive knowledge and regulation strategies' of students with and without special learning difficulties. *International Journal of Special Education*, 33(1), 191–207.

Mastrothanasis, K., Zervoudakis, K., & Kladaki, M. (2024). An application of computational intelligence in group formation for digital drama education. *Iran Journal of Computer Science*, 7(3), 551–563. Advance online publication. DOI: 10.1007/s42044-024-00186-9

Mastrothanasis, K., Zervoudakis, K., Kladaki, M., & Tsafarakis, S. (2023). A bio-inspired computational classifier system for the evaluation of children's theatrical anxiety at school. *Education and Information Technologies*, 28(9), 11027–11050. DOI: 10.1007/s10639-023-11645-4

Mâ ă, L. (2022). Ethical Rules of Online Communication Between University Teachers and Students. In Mâ ă, L. (Ed.), *Ethical Use of Information Technology in Higher Education* (pp. 99–112). Springer. DOI: 10.1007/978-981-16-1951-9_7

Matotek, L., Howard, D., Clancy, E. M., Fuelscher, I., & Klettke, B. (2021). Sexting and relationship satisfaction among emerging adults: Dispelling the myth. *Sexuality & Culture*, 25(4), 1192–1203. DOI: 10.1007/s12119-021-09832-x

Matsui, S. (2015). The criminalization of revenge porn in Japan. *Washington International Law Journal*, 24, 289–317.

Matthews, S. J., Giuliano, T. A., Thomas, K. H., Straup, M. L., & Martinez, M. A. (2018). Not cool, dude: Perceptions of solicited vs. unsolicited sext messages from men and women. *Computers in Human Behavior*, 88, 1–4. DOI: 10.1016/j.chb.2018.06.014

Maurya, C., Muhammad, T., Dhillon, P., & Maurya, P. (2022). The effects of cyberbullying victimization on depression and suicidal ideation among adolescents and young adults: A three-year cohort study from India. *BMC Psychiatry*, 22(1), 599. DOI: 10.1186/s12888-022-04238-x PMID: 36085004

Mavrogianni, A. (2023). *Development of Metacognitive Strategies and Interactive Learning Systems: Designing, Implementing and Evaluating an Interactive Learning Environment for Teaching Expository Texts*. [Doctoral Thesis, University of Crete, Greece]. EKT.

Mavrogianni, A., Vasilaki, E., Spantidakis, I., Papadaki-Michailidi, E., & Linardakis, M. (2018, May). Adaptation to the Greek population of the Metacognitive Awareness of Reading Strategies Inventory (MARSI) version 1.0. *Poster session presented at the 5th Hellenic Cognitive Science Society Conference*, Leukes, Paros.

Mavrogianni, A., Vasilaki, E., Spantidakis, I., Sarris, A., Papadaki Michaelides, E., & Yahnakis, E. (2019). Narrative pedagogical agents to enhance reading strategies in the multimedia learning environment Geo-Histor. *In Proceedings of the 10th International Conference on Open and Distance Education, ICODL* 2019, 22-24 November, Athens, Greece.

Mavrogianni, A., Vassilaki, E., Spantidakis, G., Sarris, A., Papadaki-Michailidi, E., & Yachnakis, E. (2020). An alternative factorization of the metacognitive awareness of reading strategies inventory associated with the Greek national curriculum and its psychometric properties. *Creative Education*, 11(8), 1299–1323. DOI: 10.4236/ce.2020.118096

Mavrogianni, A., Vassilaki, E., & Spantidakis, I. (2023). Pedagogical Agents as Facilitators of Instructional Guidance for the Development of Metacognitive Strategies. Dialogues. *Theory and Practice in Education Sciences*, 9, 90–114. DOI: 10.12681/dial.36288

Mavroudis, N., & Bournelli, P. (2016). The role of drama in education in counteracting bullying in schools. *Cogent Education*, 3(1), 1233843. DOI: 10.1080/2331186X.2016.1233843

Maya, J., & Maraver, J. (2020). Teaching-Learning Processes: Application of educational Psychodrama in the university setting. *International Journal of Environmental Research and Public Health*, 17(11), 3922. DOI: 10.3390/ijerph17113922 PMID: 32492890

Mayer, R. E. (2009). *Multimedia Learning* (2nd ed.). Cambridge University Press. DOI: 10.1017/CBO9780511811678

Mayer, R. E. (2014). *The Cambridge Handbook of Multimedia Learning* (2nd ed.). Cambridge University Press. DOI: 10.1017/CBO9781139547369

Mayer, R. E., & DaPra, C. S. (2012). An Embodiment Effect in Computer-Based Learning with Animated Pedagogical Agents. *Journal of Experimental Psychology*, 18(3), 239–252. DOI: 10.1037/a0028616 PMID: 22642688

Mayer, R. E., & Moreno, R. (2002). Aids to computer-based multimedia learning. *Learning and Instruction*, 12(1), 107–119. DOI: 10.1016/S0959-4752(01)00018-4

Mazurek, M. O., Shattuck, P. T., Wagner, M., & Cooper, B. P. (2012). Prevalence and correlates of screen-based media use among youths with autism spectrum disorders. *Journal of Autism and Developmental Disorders*, 42(8), 1757–1767. DOI: 10.1007/s10803-011-1413-8 PMID: 22160370

Mazurek, M. O., & Wenstrup, C. (2013). Television, video game and social media use among children with ASD and typically developing siblings. *Journal of Autism and Developmental Disorders*, 43(6), 1258–1271. DOI: 10.1007/s10803-012-1659-9 PMID: 23001767

McAloon, J., & Armstrong, S. M. (2024). The effects of online behavioral parenting interventions on child outcomes, parenting ability, and parent outcomes: A systematic review and meta-analysis. *Clinical Child and Family Psychology Review*, 27(2), 523–549. DOI: 10.1007/s10567-024-00477-4 PMID: 38613631

McArthur, B. A., Volkova, V., Tomopoulos, S., & Madigan, S. (2022). Global prevalence of meeting screen time guidelines among children 5 years and younger: A systematic review and meta-analysis. *JAMA Pediatrics*, 176(4), 373–383. DOI: 10.1001/jamapediatrics.2021.6386 PMID: 35157028

McDaniel, B. T., & Drouin, M. (2015). Sexting among married couples: Who is doing it, and are they more satisfied? *Cyberpsychology, Behavior, and Social Networking*, 18(11), 628–634. DOI: 10.1089/cyber.2015.0334 PMID: 26484980

McDaniel, B. T., Drouin, M., & Cravens, J. D. (2017). Do You Have Anything to Hide? Infidelity-Related Behaviors on Social Media Sites and Marital Satisfaction. *Computers in Human Behavior*, 66, 88–95. DOI: 10.1016/j.chb.2016.09.031 PMID: 28439148

McDonald, B., Goldstein, T. R., & Kanske, P. (2020). Could Acting Training Improve Social Cognition and Emotional Control? *Frontiers in Human Neuroscience*, 14, 348. Advance online publication. DOI: 10.3389/fnhum.2020.00348 PMID: 33173473

McLaughlin, J. H. (2012). Exploring the first amendment rights of teens in relationship to sexting and censorship. *University of Michigan Journal of Law Reform. University of Michigan. Law School*, 45(2), 315–350. DOI: 10.36646/mjlr.45.2.exploring

Mclocklin, G., Kellezi, B., Stevenson, C., & Mackay, J. (2024). Disclosure Decisions and Help-Seeking Experiences Amongst Victim-Survivors of Non-Consensual Intimate Image Distribution. *Victims & Offenders*, 1–27. DOI: 10.1080/15564886.2024.2329107

Medrano, J. L. J., Lopez Rosales, F., & Gámez-Guadix, M. (2018). Assessing the links of sexting, cybervictimization, depression, and suicidal ideation among university students. *Archives of Suicide Research*, 22(1), 153–164. DOI: 10.1080/13811118.2017.1304304 PMID: 28287925

Meehan, Z. M., Hubbard, J. A., Moore, C. C., & Mlawer, F. (2022). Susceptibility to peer influence in adolescents: Associations between psychophysiology and behaviour. *Development and Psychopathology*, 36(1), 69–81. DOI: 10.1017/S0954579422000967 PMID: 36148857

Megarry, J. (2014). Online incivility or sexual harassment? Conceptualising women's experiences in the digital age. *Women's Studies International Forum, 47*(PA), 46–55. DOI: 10.1016/j.wsif.2014.07.012

Meherali, S., & Louie-Poon, S. (2021). Challenges in conducting online videoconferencing qualitative interviews with adolescents on sensitive topics. *The Qualitative Report*, 26(9), 2851–2856. DOI: 10.46743/2160-3715/2021.4906

Mehroof, M., & Griffiths, M. D. (2010). Online gaming addiction: The role of sensation seeking, self-control, neuroticism, aggression, state anxiety, and trait anxiety. *Cyberpsychology, Behavior, and Social Networking*, 13(3), 313–316. DOI: 10.1089/cyber.2009.0229 PMID: 20557251

Merrin, G. J., Hong, J. S., & Espelage, D. L. (2015). Are the risk and protective factors similar for gang-involved, pressured-to-join, and non-gang-involved youth? A social-ecological analysis. *The American Journal of Orthopsychiatry*, 85(6), 522–535. DOI: 10.1037/ort0000094 PMID: 26594921

Mertler, C. (2018). *Introduction to Educational Research* (2nd ed.). SAGE Publications, Inc.

Michalopoulou, V., Sarantiti, M., Chatzimbey, C., & Drigas, A. (2023). The effects of augmented reality and video games on mental skills of students with learning disabilities. *World Journal of Advanced Engineering Technology and Sciences*, 9(2), 324–337. DOI: 10.30574/wjaets.2023.9.2.0240

Michikyan, M., Lozada, F. T., Weidenbenner, J. V., & Tynes, B. M. (2014). Adolescent coping strategies in the face of their "worst online experience.". *International Journal of Gaming and Computer-Mediated Simulations*, 6(4), 1–16. DOI: 10.4018/ijgcms.2014100101

Mikulincer, M., Gillath, O., & Shaver, P. R. (2002). Activation of the attachment system in adulthood: Threat-related primes increase the accessibility of mental representations of attachment figures. *Journal of Personality and Social Psychology*, 83(4), 881–895. Advance online publication. DOI: 10.1037/0022-3514.83.4.881 PMID: 12374442

Miller, C., Smith, S., & Pugatch, M. (2020). Experimental and quasi-experimental designs in implementation research. *Psychiatry Research*, 283, 112452. DOI: 10.1016/j.psychres.2019.06.027 PMID: 31255320

Mills, C., Sharp, N. L., Triandafilidis, Z., & Tracey, D. K. (2022). *'Thrown out into the world': Transition to post schooling for autistic young people*. Western Sydney University. https://doi.org/DOI: 10.26183/3gsv-mv41

Milton, A. C., Gill, B. A., Davenport, T. A., Dowling, M., Burns, J. M., & Hickie, I. B. (2019). Sexting, Web-Based Risks, and Safety in Two Representative National Samples of Young Australians: Prevalence, Perspectives, and Predictors. *JMIR Mental Health*, 6(6), 1–16. DOI: 10.2196/13338 PMID: 31210139

Ministry of Education. (n.d.). *Junior High School* [in Greek]. Retrieved from https://www.minedu.gov.gr/gymnasio-m-2/to-thema-gumnasio

Mirick, R. G., & Wladkowski, S. P. (2019). Skype in qualitative interviews: Participant and researcher perspectives. *The Qualitative Report*, 24(12), 3061–3072. DOI: 10.46743/2160-3715/2019.3632

Mishler, E. (1991). *Research interviewing: Context and narrative*. Harvard University Press. DOI: 10.2307/j.ctv26070x9

Mitchell, K. J., Finkelhor, D., Jones, L. M., & Wolak, J. (2012). Prevalence and characteristics of youth sexting: A national study. *Pediatrics*, 129(1), 13–20. DOI: 10.1542/peds.2011-1730 PMID: 22144706

Mitchell, K. J., Finkelhor, D., & Wolak, J. (2001). Risk factors for and impact of online sexual solicitation of youth. *Journal of the American Medical Association*, 285(23), 3011–3014. DOI: 10.1001/jama.285.23.3011 PMID: 11410100

Mitchell, K. J., Ybarra, M. L., & Korchmaros, J. D. (2014). Sexual harassment among adolescents of different sexual orientations and gender identities. *Child Abuse & Neglect*, 38(2), 280–295. DOI: 10.1016/j.chiabu.2013.09.008 PMID: 24148274

Mitchell, K., & Štulhofer, A. (2021). Online sexual harassment and negative mood in Croatian female adolescents. *European Child & Adolescent Psychiatry*, 30(2), 225–231. DOI: 10.1007/s00787-020-01506-7 PMID: 32162054

Mitchell, S. H., Schoel, C., & Stevens, A. A. (2008). Mechanisms underlying heightened risk taking in adolescents as compared with adults. *Psychonomic Bulletin & Review*, 15(2), 272–277. DOI: 10.3758/PBR.15.2.272 PMID: 18488639

Mitsea, E., & Drigas, A. (2019). A journey into the metacognitive learning strategies. *International Journal of Online & Biomedical Engineering*, 15(14), 4–19. DOI: 10.3991/ijoe.v15i14.11379

Mladenović, M., Ošmjanski, V., & Stanković, S. V. (2021). Cyber-aggression, cyberbullying, and cyber-grooming: A survey and research challenges. *ACM Computing Surveys*, 54(1), 1–42. DOI: 10.1145/3424246

Modecki, K. L., Minchin, J., Harbaugh, A. G., Guerra, N. G., & Runions, K. C. (2014). Bullying prevalence across contexts: A meta-analysis measuring cyber and traditional bullying. *The Journal of Adolescent Health*, 55(5), 602–611. DOI: 10.1016/j.jadohealth.2014.06.007 PMID: 25168105

Mokhtari, K., Dimitrov, D. M., & Reichard, C. A. (2018). Revising the Metacognitive Awareness of Reading Strategies Inventory (MARSI) and testing for factorial invariance. *Studies in Second Language Learning and Teaching*, 8(2), 219–246. DOI: 10.14746/ssllt.2018.8.2.3

Mokhtari, K., & Reichard, C. A. (2002). Assessing Students' Metacognitive Awareness of Reading Strategies. *Journal of Educational Psychology*, 94(2), 249–259. DOI: 10.1037/0022-0663.94.2.249

Molin, M., Sorbring, E., & Löfgren-Mårtenson, L. (2015). Teachers' and parents' views on the Internet and social media usage by pupils with intellectual disabilities. *Journal of Intellectual Disabilities*, 19(1), 22–33. DOI: 10.1177/1744629514563558 PMID: 25524596

Molla-Esparza, C., Losilla, J.-M., & López-González, E. (2020). Prevalence of sending, receiving and forwarding sexts among youths: A three-level meta-analysis. *PLoS One*, 15(12), e0243653. DOI: 10.1371/journal.pone.0243653 PMID: 33284862

Moller, V. (2023). Leading for Love, Life, Wisdom, and Voice in Steiner Schools: Constraints and Conditions of Possibility. In K. E. Reimer, S. Windsor, & S. Kemmis (Eds.), *Living Well in a World Worth Living in for All: Volume I. Current Practices of Social Justice, Sustainability and Wellbeing* (pp. 69-86). Springer.

Moody, L., Marsden, L., Nguyen, B., & Third, A. (2021). *Consultations with young people to inform the eSafety Commissioner's engagement strategy for young people*. Young and Resilient Research Centre, Western Sydney University.

Moon, J. W. (2021). Why are world religions so concerned with sexual behavior? *Current Opinion in Psychology*, 40, 15–19. DOI: 10.1016/j.copsyc.2020.07.030 PMID: 32877834

Moore, K. D. (2014). *Effective instructional strategies: From theory to practice*. Sage Publications.

Morelli, M., Bianchi, D., Baiocco, R., Pezzuti, L., & Chirumbolo, A. (2016). Not-allowed sharing of sexts and dating violence from the perpetrator's perspective: The moderation role of sexism. *Computers in Human Behavior*, 56, 163–169. DOI: 10.1016/j.chb.2015.11.047

Morelli, M., Chirumbolo, A., Bianchi, D., Baiocco, R., Cattelino, E., Laghi, F., Sorokowski, P., Misiak, M., Dziekan, M., Hudson, H., Marshall, A., Nguyen, T. T. T., Mark, L., Kopecky, K., Szotkowski, R., Demirtaş, E. T., Van Ouytsel, J., Ponnet, K., Walrave, M., & Drouin, M. (2020). The role of HEXACO personality traits in different kinds of sexting: A cross-cultural study in 10 countries. *Computers in Human Behavior*, 113, 106502. Advance online publication. DOI: 10.1016/j.chb.2020.106502

Morelli, M., Plata, M. G., Isolani, S., Zabala, M. E. Z., Hoyos, K. P. C., Tirado, L. M. U., Gracia, M. S. R., Barbosa, C. P., Pistella, J., Zuffianò, A., Gerbino, M., Laghi, F., Pastorelli, C., & Baiocco, R. (2023). Sexting behaviors before and during COVID-19 in Italian and Colombian young adults. *Sexuality Research & Social Policy*, 20(4), 1515–1527. DOI: 10.1007/s13178-023-00798-z PMID: 37363349

Moreno, M. A., & Vaillancourt, T. (2017). The role of health care providers in cyberbullying. *Canadian Journal of Psychiatry*, 62(6), 364–367. DOI: 10.1177/0706743716684792 PMID: 28562092

Moreno, R. (2010). Cognitive load theory: More food for thought. *Instructional Science*, 38(2), 135–141. DOI: 10.1007/s11251-009-9122-9

Moreno, R., Mayer, R. E., Spires, H. A., & Lester, J. C. (2001). The case for social agency in computer-based teaching: Do students learn more deeply when they interact with animated pedagogical agents? *Cognition and Instruction*, 19(2), 177–213. DOI: 10.1207/S1532690XCI1902_02

Mori, C., Cooke, J. E., Temple, J. R., Ly, A., Lu, Y., Anderson, N., Rash, C., & Madigan, S. (2020). The prevalence of sexting behaviors among emerging adults: A meta-analysis. *Archives of Sexual Behavior*, 49(4), 1103–1119. DOI: 10.1007/s10508-020-01656-4 PMID: 32072397

Mori, C., Park, J., Temple, J. R., & Madigan, S. (2022). Are youth sexting rates still on the rise? A meta-analytic update. *The Journal of Adolescent Health*, 70(4), 531–539. DOI: 10.1016/j.jadohealth.2021.10.026 PMID: 34916123

Morrison, C. M., & Gore, H. (2010). The relationship between excessive internet use and depression: A questionnaire-based study of 1,319 young people and adults. *Psychopathology*, 43(2), 121–126. DOI: 10.1159/000277001 PMID: 20110764

Muhid, A., Amalia, E. R., Hilaliyah, H., Budiana, N., & Wajdi, M. B. N. (2020). The Effect of Metacognitive Strategies Implementation on Students' Reading Comprehension Achievement. *International Journal of Instruction*, 13(2), 847–862. DOI: 10.29333/iji.2020.13257a

Mukhopadhyay, J., & Bhattacharjee, A. (2023). A comprehensive analysis of affective health and sex differences in adolescents as a function of peer pressure and internet addiction. *Journal of Psychosexual Health*, 5(3), 159–166. DOI: 10.1177/26318318231206711

Murali, V., & George, S. (2007). Lost online: An overview of internet addiction. *Advances in Psychiatric Treatment*, 13(1), 24–30. DOI: 10.1192/apt.bp.106.002907

Murphy, G. H., & O'Callaghan, A. (2004). Capacity of adults with intellectual disabilities to consent to sexual relationships. *Psychological Medicine*, 34(7), 1347–1357. DOI: 10.1017/S0033291704001941 PMID: 15697061

Murray, A., Koronczai, B., Király, O., Griffiths, M. D., Mannion, A., Leader, G., & Demetrovics, Z. (2021). Autism, problematic internet use and gaming disorder: A systematic review. *Review Journal of Autism and Developmental Disorders*, 1–21. DOI: 10.1007/s40489-021-00243-0

Murray, C. E., & Campbell, E. C. (2015). The pleasures and perils of technology in intimate relationships. *Journal of Couple & Relationship Therapy*, 14(2), 116–140. DOI: 10.1080/15332691.2014.953651

Muscari, M. E. (2009). *Sexting: New technology, old problem? Medscape Public Health and Prevention.* Retrieved December 7, 2012 https://www.episcopalcollegiate.org/uploaded/Academics/documents/Middle_School/Sexting_article_from_Medscape.pdf

Mustafaoğlu, R., & Yasacı, Z. (2018). Dijital oyun oynamanın çocukların ruhsal ve fiziksel sağlığı üzerine olumsuz etkileri. *Bağımlılık Dergisi, 19*(3), 51-53. Retrieved from https://dergipark.org.tr/tr/pub/bagimli/issue/38282/447021#article_cite

Nadeem, M., Oroszlanyova, M., & Farag, W. (2023). Effect of digital game-based learning on student engagement and motivation. *Computers*, 12(9), 177. DOI: 10.3390/computers12090177

National Institute on Alcohol Abuse and Alcoholism. (2021). *Underage drinking*. https://www.niaaa.nih.gov/publications/brochures-and-fact-sheets/underage-drinking

National Institute on Drug Abuse. (2014). *Drugs, brains, and behavior: The science of addiction*. National Institute on Drug Abuse. https://nida.nih.gov/sites/default/files/soa_2014.pdf

Nazarov, V. L., & Averbuch, N. V. (2023). Traditional bullying and cyberbullying: Bystander strategies. *The Education and Science Journal*, 25(9), 80–117. DOI: 10.17853/1994-5639-2023-9-80-117

Ndlovu, M., & Khupe, N. A. (2023). *Online Harassment of Journalists in Zimbabwe: Experiences, Coping Strategies and Implications*. 95–111. DOI: 10.1007/978-3-031-23625-9_6

Nee, C., Samsudin, N., Chuan, H., Ridzuan, M., Boon, O., Mohamad, A., & Scheithauer, H. (2023). The digital defence against cyberbullying: A systematic review of tech-based approaches. *Cogent Education*, 10(2), 2288492. DOI: 10.1080/2331186X.2023.2288492

Negi, C. (2023). An Overview of Worldwide Cyberbullying and Cyberviolence Against Women, Teenagers, LGBTQ on Social Media: Facebook, Instagram, Telegram, WhatsApp, Snapchat, YouTube, LinkedIn and Twitter. *SSRN*. Advance online publication. DOI: 10.2139/ssrn.4529613

Neumann, M. M., Merchant, G., & Burnett, C. (2018). Young children and tablets: The views of parents and teachers. *Early Child Development and Care*, 1–12. DOI: 10.1080/03004430.2018.1550083

Neupane, A., Satvat, K., Saxena, N., Stavrinos, D., & Bishop, H. J. (2018). Do social disorders facilitate social engineering?: A case study of autism and phishing attacks. In *Proceedings of the 34th Annual Computer Security Applications Conference* (pp. 467-477). Association for Computing Machinery. https://doi.org/DOI: 10.1145/3274694.3274730

Neverkovich, S. D., Bubnova, I. S., Kosarenko, N. N., Sakhieva, R. G., Sizova, Z. M., Zakharova, V. L., & Sergeeva, M. G. (2018). Students' internet addiction: Study and prevention. *Eurasia Journal of Mathematics, Science and Technology Education*, 14(4), 1483–1495. DOI: 10.29333/ejmste/83723

Neyra, O. (2021). Ciberbullying: El acoso escolar en el ciberespacio e implicancias psicológicas. *Hamut'ay*, 8(1), 67–74. DOI: 10.21503/hamu.v8i1.2238

Ng, E. D., Chua, J. Y. X., & Shorey, S. (2022). The effectiveness of educational interventions on traditional bullying and cyberbullying among adolescents: A systematic review and meta-analysis. *Trauma, Violence & Abuse*, 23(1), 132–151. DOI: 10.1177/1524838020933867 PMID: 32588769

Nicklin, L. L., Swain, E., & Lloyd, J. (2020). Reactions to unsolicited violent, and sexual, explicit media content shared over social media: Gender differences and links with prior exposure. *International Journal of Environmental Research and Public Health*, 17(12), 4296. Advance online publication. DOI: 10.3390/ijerph17124296 PMID: 32560142

Nie, N. H., & Erbring, L. (2002). Internet and society: A preliminary report. *ITandSociety*, 1(1), 275–283.

Nikken, P., & Schols, M. (2015). How and why parents guide the media use of young children. *Journal of Child and Family Studies*, 24(11), 3423–3435. DOI: 10.1007/s10826-015-0144-4 PMID: 26472932

Niklová, M. (2020). Prevention of online risk behavior in schools with regard to the socioeducational activity of the school social pedagogue. *Pedagogická Orientace*, 30(4), 542–554. DOI: 10.5817/PedOr2020-4-542

Nilsson, M. G., Pepelasi, K. T., Ioannou, M., & Lester, D. (2019). Understanding the link between Sextortion and Suicide. *International Journal of Cyber Criminology*, 13(1), 55–69. https://pure.hud.ac.uk/en/publications/understanding-the-link-between-sextortion-and-suicide

Niu, G., Chai, H., Li, Z., Wu, L., Sun, X., & Zhou, Z. (2019). Online Parent-Child Communication and Left-Behind Children's Subjective Well-Being: The Effects of Parent-Child Relationship and Gratitude. *Child Indicators Research*, 13(3), 967–980. DOI: 10.1007/s12187-019-09657-z

Nocentini, A., Calmaestra, J., Schultze-Krumbholz, A., Scheithauer, H., Ortega, R., & Menesini, E. (2010). Cyberbullying: Labels, Behaviours and Definition in Three European Countries. *Australian Journal of Guidance & Counselling*, 20(2), 129–142. DOI: 10.1375/ajgc.20.2.129

Noll, J. G., Shenk, C. E., Barnes, J. E., & Haralson, K. J. (2013). Association of maltreatment with high-risk internet behaviors and offline encounters. *Pediatrics*, 131(2), e510–e517. DOI: 10.1542/peds.2012-1281 PMID: 23319522

Noorishad, P.-G., & Trottier, D. (2022). Investigating the relationships between sexting and sexual coercion. *Sexologies*, 31(1), e8–e15. DOI: 10.1016/j.sexol.2021.11.004

Norbekova, G., Safarova, D., Bazarov, B., & Yakubov, F. (2019). Interactive Learning Environment in the English Language Teaching with the help of Computer Technology. *Mental Enlightenment Scientific-Methodological Journal*, 2019(1), 5.

Normand, C. L., & Sallafranque-St-Louis, F. (2016). Cybervictimization of young people with an intellectual or developmental disability: Risks specific to sexual solicitation. *Journal of Applied Research in Intellectual Disabilities*, 29(2), 99–110. DOI: 10.1111/jar.12163 PMID: 25871891

Notten, N., & Nikken, P. (2016). Boys and girls taking risks online: A gendered perspective on social context and adolescents' risky online behavior. *New Media & Society*, 18(6), 966–988. https://psycnet.apa.org/doi/10.1177/1461444814552379. DOI: 10.1177/1461444814552379

Notté, R. J. (2024). Exploring the impact of sextortion on adult males: A narrative approach. *Technology in Society*, 78, 102167. Advance online publication. DOI: 10.1016/j.techsoc.2024.102617

Novak, J. R., Sandberg, J. G., Jeffrey, A. J., & Young-Davis, S. (2016). The impact of texting on perceptions of face-to-face communication in couples in different relationship stages. *Journal of Couple & Relationship Therapy*, 15(4), 274–294. DOI: 10.1080/15332691.2015.1062452

Nowell, K. P., Bernardin, C. J., Brown, C., & Kanne, S. (2021). Characterization of special interests in autism spectrum disorder: A brief review and pilot study using the special interests survey. *Journal of Autism and Developmental Disorders*, 51(8), 2711–2724. DOI: 10.1007/s10803-020-04743-6 PMID: 33034785

Nugraha, Y. P., & Khasanah, F. U. (2023). Can motivational interviewing reduce video game addiction? Viewed from: Regulatory focus theory and interpersonal competence. *Jurnal Integrasi Sains dan Qur'an (JISQu), 2*(1), 141-155.

Nuske, H. J., Pellecchia, M., Kane, C., Seidman, M., Maddox, B. B., Freeman, L. M., Rump, K., Reisinger, E. M., Xie, M., & Mandell, D. S. (2020). Self-regulation is bi-directionally associated with cognitive development in children with autism. *Journal of Applied Developmental Psychology*, 68, 101139. Advance online publication. DOI: 10.1016/j.appdev.2020.101139 PMID: 34177028

Nuzulawati, M. T. N., & Astuti, K. (2022). Behavioral cognitive therapy to reduce cyberbullying behavior in adolescents during the Covid-19 pandemic. *International Journal for Educational and Vocational Studies*, 4(1), 42–45. DOI: 10.29103/ijevs.v4i1.6818

O'Brien, J. E., & Li, W. (2020). The role of the internet in the grooming, exploitation, and exit of United States domestic minor sex trafficking victims. *Journal of Children and Media*, 14(2), 187–203. DOI: 10.1080/17482798.2019.1688668

O'Connor, K., & Drouin, M. (2020). Sexting and social concerns. *The Palgrave Handbook of International Cybercrime and Cyberdeviance*, 1087–1108. DOI: 10.1007/978-3-319-78440-3_50

O'Connor, K., Drouin, M., Yergens, N., & Newsham, G. (2017). Sexting legislation in the United States and abroad: A call for uniformity. *International Journal of Cyber Criminology*, 11(2), 218–245. DOI: 10.5281/zenodo.1037397

O'Toole, J., & Burton, B. (2005). Acting against conflict and bullying. The Brisbane DRACON project 1996–2004—Emergent findings and outcomes. *Research in Drama Education*, 10(3), 269–283. DOI: 10.1080/13569780500275873

Oattes, M., & Offman, A. (2007). Global self-esteem and sexual self-esteem as predictors of sexual communication in intimate relationships. *The Canadian Journal of Human Sexuality*, 16(3-4), 89–100. DOI: 10.1177/01461672241257355

Obegi, J. H., & Berant, E. (Eds.). (2010). *Attachment theory and research in clinical work with adults.* Guilford press.

Obisesan, O. H., Mirbolouk, M., Osei, A. D., Orimoloye, S. M., Uddin, I., Dzaye, O., El Shahawy, O., Al Rifai, M., Bhatnagar, A., Stokes, A., Benjamin, E. J., DeFilippis, A. P., & Blaha, M. J. (2019). Association between e-cigarette use and depression in the behavioral risk factor surveillance system, 2016–2017. *JAMA Network Open*, 2(12), e1916800. Advance online publication. DOI: 10.1001/jamanetworkopen.2019.16800 PMID: 31800073

Odacı, H., & Kalkan, M. (2010). Problematic Internet use, loneliness and dating anxiety among young adult university students. *Computers & Education*, 55(3), 1091–1097. DOI: 10.1016/j.compedu.2010.05.006

Odgers, C. L., & Jensen, M. R. (2020). Annual research review: Adolescent mental health in the digital age: Facts, fears, and future directions. *Journal of Child Psychology and Psychiatry, and Allied Disciplines*, 61(3), 336–348. DOI: 10.1111/jcpp.13190 PMID: 31951670

Ofcom (2023). *Children and parents: media use and attitudes report 2023.* Retrieved from https://www.ofcom.org.uk/media-use-and-attitudes/media-habits-children/children-and-parents-media-use-and-attitudes-report-2023/

Øien, R. A., Nordahl-Hansen, A., & Schjølberg, S. (2018). Mental health and ASD. In Volkmar, F. R. (Ed.), *Encyclopedia of Autism Spectrum Disorders* (2nd ed., pp. 2868–2872). Springer., DOI: 10.1007/978-3-319-91280-6_102050

Ojeda, M., & Del Rey, R. (2022). Lines of action for sexting prevention and intervention: A systematic review. *Archives of Sexual Behavior*, 51(3), 1659–1687. DOI: 10.1007/s10508-021-02089-3 PMID: 34791584

Olenik Shemesh, D., Heiman, T., & Wright, M. F. (2023). Problematic Use of the Internet and Well-Being among Youth from a Global Perspective: A Mediated-Moderated Model of Socio-Emotional Factors. *The Journal of Genetic Psychology*, 1–23. DOI: 10.1080/00221325.2023.2277319 PMID: 37933515

Olson, K. E., O'Brien, M. A., Rogers, W. A., & Charness, N. (2011). Diffusion of Technology: Frequency of Use for Younger and Older Adults. *Ageing International*, 36(1), 123–145. DOI: 10.1007/s12126-010-9077-9 PMID: 22685360

Opsal, A., Kristensen, Ø., & Clausen, T. (2019). Readiness to change among involuntarily and voluntarily admitted patients with substance use disorders. *Substance Abuse Treatment, Prevention, and Policy*, 14(1), 47. DOI: 10.1186/s13011-019-0237-y PMID: 31694664

Oriza, I. I. D., & Hanipraja, M. A. (2020). Sexting and Sexual Satisfaction on Young Adults in Romantic Relationship. *Psychological Research on Urban Society*, 3(1), 30–39. DOI: 10.7454/proust.v3i1.61

Orkibi, H., & Feniger-Schaal, R. (2019). Integrative systematic review of psychodrama psychotherapy research: Trends and methodological implications. *PLoS One*, 14(2), e0212575. DOI: 10.1371/journal.pone.0212575 PMID: 30779787

Orkibi, H., Keisari, S., Sajnani, N. L., & de Witte, M. (2023). Effectiveness of drama-based therapies on mental health outcomes: A systematic review and meta-analysis of controlled studies. *Psychology of Aesthetics, Creativity, and the Arts*. Advance online publication. DOI: 10.1037/aca0000582

Orosco, J. R., Huaytalla, R. P., Rosales, A. M., & Alania, N. R. (2022). Ciberbullying en estudiantes del nivel secundario de la Sierra Central de Perú [Cyberbullying in Secondary Education learners in Sierra Central, Perú]. *Ciencias Pedagógicas e Innovación*, 10(1), 11–20. DOI: 10.26423/rcpi.v10i1.439

Ortega-Barón, J., Buelga, S., Cava, M.-J., & Iranzo, B. (2022). Eficacia del programa Prev@cib 2.0 en cyberbullying, conductas de ayuda y percepción de ayuda del professor [Effectiveness of the Prev@cib 2.0 program in cyberbullying, helping behaviors and perception of teacher help]. *Electronic Journal of Research in Educational Psychology*, 20(2), 427–448. DOI: 10.25115/ejrep.v20i57.6684

Ortega-Barón, J., González-Cabrera, J., Machimbarrena, J. M., & Montiel, I. (2021). Safety.Net: A pilot study on a multi-risk internet prevention program. *International Journal of Environmental Research and Public Health*, 18(8), 4249. DOI: 10.3390/ijerph18084249 PMID: 33923779

Ortega-Ruiz, R., Del Rey, R., & Casas, J. A. (2012). Knowing, building and living together on internet and social networks: The ConRed cyberbullying prevention program. *International Journal of Conflict and Violence*, 6(2), 302–312. DOI: 10.4119/ijcv-2012-030

Ostrager, B. (2010). SMS. OMG! LOL! TTYL: Translating the law to accommodate today's teens and the evolution from texting to sexting. *Family Court Review*, 48(4), 712–726. DOI: 10.1111/j.1744-1617.2010.01345.x

Oswald, F., Lopes, A., Skoda, K., Hesse, C. L., & Pedersen, C. L. (2020). I'll show you mine so you'll show me yours: Motivations and personality variables in photographic exhibitionism. *Journal of Sex Research*, 57(5), 597–609. DOI: 10.1080/00224499.2019.1639036 PMID: 31318606

Özgür, H. (2020). A Systematic Review on Cyberbullying Interventions and Preventions. *Shanlax International Journal of Education*, 9(1), 11–26. DOI: 10.34293/education.v9i1.3373

Paas, F., & Sweller, J., (2011). An Evolutionary Upgrade of Cognitive Load Theory: Using the Human Motor System and Collaboration to Support the Learning of Complex Cognitive Tasks. *Educational Psychology Review, 24*(1), 27–45. DOI: 10.1007/s10648-011-9179-2

Paas, F., & Sweller, J. (2014). Implications of cognitive load theory for multimedia learning. In Mayer, R. E. (Ed.), *The Cambridge handbook of multimedia learning* (2nd ed., pp. 27–42). Cambridge University Press. DOI: 10.1017/CBO9781139547369.004

Page, M. J., McKenzie, J. E., Bossuyt, P. M., Boutron, I., Hoffmann, T. C., Mulrow, C. D., Shamseer, L., Tetzlaff, J. M., Akl, E. A., Brennan, S. E., Chou, R., Glanville, J., Grimshaw, J. M., Hróbjartsson, A., Lalu, M. M., Li, T., Loder, E. W., Mayo-Wilson, E., McDonald, S., & Moher, D. (2021). The PRISMA 2020 statement: An updated guideline for reporting systematic reviews. *International Journal of Surgery*, 88, 105906. DOI: 10.1016/j.ijsu.2021.105906 PMID: 33789826

Paivio, A. (1991). Dual Coding Theory: Retrospect and Current Status. *Canadian Journal of Psychology*, 45(3), 255–287. DOI: 10.1037/h0084295

Palaiologou, I. (2016). Children under five and digital technologies: Implications for early years pedagogy. *European Early Childhood Education Research Journal*, 24(1), 5–24. DOI: 10.1080/1350293X.2014.929876

Palfrey, J., & Gasser, U. (2008). *Born digital: Understanding the first generation of digital natives*. Basic Books.

Palladino, B. E., Nocentini, A., & Menesini, E. (2019). How to stop victims' suffering? Indirect effects of an anti-bullying program on internalizing symptoms. *International Journal of Environmental Research and Public Health*, 16(14), 2631. DOI: 10.3390/ijerph16142631 PMID: 31340598

Pallarés-Piquer, M., Salvador-García, C., Maravé-Vivas, M., Esteve-Sancho, M., & Cabero-Fayos, I. (2022). Acción pedagógica como prevención de ciberagresiones [Pedagogical action to prevent cyberaggressions]. *Espiral: Cuadernos del Profesorado*, 15(31), 22–31. DOI: 10.25115/ecp.v15i31.7125

Paluckaitė, U., & Žardeckaitė-Matulaitienė, K. (2017). Adolescents' perception of risky behavior on the internet. *European Proceedings of Social and Behavioral Sciences*, 30, 284–292. DOI: 10.15405/epsbs.2017.09.27

Pampati, S., Lowry, R., Moreno, M. A., Rasberry, C. N., & Steiner, R. J. (2020). Having a Sexual Photo Shared Without Permission and Associated Health Risks: A Snapshot of Nonconsensual Sexting. *JAMA Pediatrics*, 174(6), 618–619. DOI: 10.1001/jamapediatrics.2020.0028 PMID: 32202601

Pan, G., Sen, S., Starrett, D. A., Bonk, C. J., Rodgers, M. L., Tikoo, M., & Powell, D. V. (2012). Instructor-Made Videos as a learner scaffolding tool. *Journal of Online Learning and Teaching*, 8(1), 298–311. https://citeseerx.ist.psu.edu/viewdoc/summary?doi=10.1.1.297.4017

Papakosta, A., Mastrothanasis, K., Andreou, A., & Blouti, I. (2020). Psychometric evaluation of recall and recognition tasks for the measurement of young spectators' theatrical memory. *Journal of Literary Education*, 3(3), 177–199. DOI: 10.7203/JLE.3.14835

Parker, T. S., Blackburn, K. M., Perry, M. S., & Hawks, J. M. (2013). Sexting as an intervention: Relationship satisfaction and motivation considerations. *The American Journal of Family Therapy*, 41(1), 1–12. DOI: 10.1080/01926187.2011.635134

Park, G. R., Jung, H. O., & Kim, H. S. (2019). Effects of a suicide prevention applied psychodrama in female middle school students. *Journal of Digital Contents Society*, 20(5), 1001–1010. DOI: 10.9728/dcs.2019.20.5.1001

Park, G. R., & Kim, H. S. (2022). The Effects of a suicide prevention program applied on psychodrama among female high school students. *Journal of Korean Academy of Psychiatric and Mental Health Nursing*, 31(3), 269–278. DOI: 10.12934/jkpmhn.2022.31.3.269

Parliament, U. K. (2019). *Being disabled online*. https://publications.parliament.uk/pa/cm201719/cmselect/cmpetitions/759/75905.htm

Parmar, S., & Dutt, S. (2024). Impact of Cyberbullying and Cyber Victimisation on Adolescents Well-being. *International Journal of Interdisciplinary Approaches in Psychology, 2*(5), 823-852. https://www.psychopediajournals.com/index.php/ijiap/article/view/366

Parti, K., Sanders, C. E., & Englander, E. K. (2023). Sexting at an Early Age: Patterns and Poor Health-Related Consequences of Pressured Sexting in Middle and High School. *The Journal of School Health*, 93(1), 73–81. DOI: 10.1111/josh.13258 PMID: 36251455

Patchin, J. W., & Hinduja, S. (2010). Cyberbullying and Self-Esteem. *The Journal of School Health*, 80(12), 614–621. DOI: 10.1111/j.1746-1561.2010.00548.x PMID: 21087257

Patchin, J. W., & Hinduja, S. (2012). *Cyberbullying prevention and response: Expert perspectives.* Routledge. DOI: 10.4324/9780203818312

Patchin, J. W., & Hinduja, S. (2018). Sextortion Among Adolescents: Results From a National Survey of U.S. *Youth*, 32(1), 30–54. DOI: 10.1177/1079063218800469 PMID: 30264657

Patchin, J. W., & Hinduja, S. (2019). The Nature and Extent of Sexting Among a National Sample of Middle and High School Students in the US. *Archives of Sexual Behavior*, 48(8), 1–11. DOI: 10.1007/s10508-019-1449-y PMID: 31309428

Patchin, J. W., & Hinduja, S. (2020). It is time to teach safe sexting. *The Journal of Adolescent Health*, 66(2), 140–143. DOI: 10.1016/j.jadohealth.2019.10.010 PMID: 31831321

Patchin, J. W., & Hinduja, S. (2023). Cyberbullying Among Asian American Youth Before and During the COVID-19 Pandemic. *The Journal of School Health*, 93(1), 82–87. DOI: 10.1111/josh.13249 PMID: 36221854

Patel, U., & Roesch, R. (2020). The Prevalence of Technology-Facilitated Sexual Violence: A Meta-Analysis and Systematic Review, *23*(2), 428–443. DOI: 10.1177/1524838020958057

Paul, F. A., Dangroo, A. A., Saikia, P., Ganie, A. U. R., Zaid, M., Das, M., & Gogoi, R. (2024). Societal and individual impacts of substance abuse. In R. Baikady, S. M., Sajid, J. Przeperski, V. Nadesan, M., Rezaul Islam, & J. Gao (Eds.), *The Palgrave Handbook of Global Social Problems* (Vol. 1, pp. 1–24). Palgrave Macmillan. DOI: 10.1007/978-3-030-68127-2_430-1

Paul, E. L., McManus, B., & Hayes, A. (2000). "Hookups": Characteristics and correlates of college students' spontaneous and anonymous sexual experiences. *Journal of Sex Research*, 37(1), 76–88. DOI: 10.1080/00224490009552023

Pearce, N., Cross, D., Monks, H., Waters, S., & Falconer, S. (2011). Current evidence of best practice in whole-school bullying intervention and its potential to inform cyberbullying interventions. *Australian Journal of Guidance & Counselling*, 21(1), 1–21. DOI: 10.1375/ajgc.21.1.1

Pedersen, W., Bakken, A., Stefansen, K., & von Soest, T. (2023). Sexual Victimization in the Digital Age: A Population-Based Study of Physical and Image-Based Sexual Abuse Among Adolescents. *Archives of Sexual Behavior*, 52(1), 399–410. DOI: 10.1007/s10508-021-02200-8 PMID: 35059946

Pellicano, E., & Houting, J. (2022). Annual research review: Shifting from 'normal science' to neurodiversity in autism science. *Journal of Child Psychology and Psychiatry, and Allied Disciplines*, 63(4), 381–396. DOI: 10.1111/jcpp.13534 PMID: 34730840

Pelligra, V., Isoni, A., Fadda, R., & Doneddu, G. (2015). Theory of mind, perceived intentions and reciprocal behaviour: Evidence from individuals with autism spectrum disorder. *Journal of Economic Psychology*, 49(8), 95–107. DOI: 10.1016/j.joep.2015.05.001

Penal Code. 1871, Section 377BF, Singapore. Sexual exposure. https://sso.agc.gov.sg/Act/PC1871?ProvIds=pr377BF-

Permana, H., & Suwarjo, S. (2022). Psychodrama techniques to improve academic self-efficacy In Madrasah Aliyah students. *AL-ISHLAH: Jurnal Pendidikan*, 14(4), 6773–6782. DOI: 10.35445/alishlah.v14i4.2288

Petersen, J. L., & Hyde, J. S. (2010). A meta-analytic review of research on gender differences in sexuality, 1993–2007. *Psychological Bulletin*, 136(1), 21–38. Advance online publication. DOI: 10.1037/a0017504 PMID: 20063924

Pew Research Center. (2014). *Online Harassment*. Retrieved from: https://www.pewresearch.org/internet/2014/10/22/online-harassment/

Pew Research Center. (2019). *Mobile Technology and Home Broadband 2019*. Retrieved from: https://www.pewresearch.org/internet/wp-content/uploads/sites/9/2019/06/PI_2019.06.13_Mobile-Technology-and-Home-Broadband_FINAL2.pdf

Phippen, A. D., & Kennedy, C. (2018). *Sexting and sexting behaviour- "Oh you're all children, children do silly things. You'll be fine. Get over it!"*. Retrieved July 15, 2019, from https://pearl.plymouth.ac.uk/cgi/viewcontent.cgi?article=1008&context=sc-research

Phippen, A., & Bond, E. (2023). *Policing teen sexting: Supporting children's rights while applying the law*. Springer Nature., DOI: 10.1007/978-3-031-31455-1

Piaget, J. (1952). *The Origins of Intelligence in Children*. International Universities Press. DOI: 10.1037/11494-000

Piccoli, G., Ahmad, R., & Ives, B. (2001). Web-based virtual learning environments: A research framework and a preliminary assessment of effectiveness in basic IT skills training. *Management Information Systems Quarterly*, 25(4), 401–426. DOI: 10.2307/3250989

Pieschl, S., Kuhlmann, C., & Porsch, T. (2015). Beware of Publicity! Perceived Distress of Negative Cyber Incidents and Implications for Defining Cyberbullying. *Journal of School Violence*, 14(1), 111–132. DOI: 10.1080/15388220.2014.971363

Pifarré, M., Cobos, R., & Argelagós, E. (2014). Incidence of group awareness information on students' collaborative learning processes. *Journal of Computer Assisted Learning*, 30(4), 300–317. DOI: 10.1111/jcal.12043

Pina, A., Bell, A., Griffin, K., & Vasquez, E. (2021). Image Based Sexual Abuse proclivity and victim blaming: The role of dark personality traits and moral disengagement. *Oñati Socio-Legal Series*, 11(5), 1179–1197. DOI: 10.35295/osls.iisl/0000-0000-0000-1213

Piotrowski, C. (2012). Cyber-bullying in school settings: A research citation analysis. ERIC, ED525783. https://files.eric.ed.gov/fulltext/ED525783.pdf

Plowman, L., & McPake, J. (2013). Seven myths about young children and technology. *Childhood Education*, 89(1), 27–33. DOI: 10.1080/00094056.2013.757490

Plowman, L., Stevenson, O., Stephen, C., & McPake, J. (2010). Supporting young children's learning with technology at home and in preschool. *Research Papers in Education*, 25(1), 93–113. DOI: 10.1080/02671520802584061

Polanin, J. R., Espelage, D. L., Grotpeter, J. K., Ingram, K., Michaelson, L., Spinney, E., Valido, A., El Sheikh, A., Torgal, C., & Robinson, L. (2021). A systematic review and meta-analysis of interventions to decrease cyberbullying perpetration and victimization. *Prevention Science*, 23(3), 439–454. DOI: 10.1007/s11121-021-01259-y PMID: 34159506

Ponti, M. (2023). Screen time and preschool children: Promoting health and development in a digital world. *Paediatrics & Child Health*, 28(3), 184–202. DOI: 10.1093/pch/pxac125 PMID: 37205134

Pouwels, J. L., Valkenburg, P. M., Beyens, I., van Driel, I. I., & Keijsers, L. (2021). Social media use and friendship closeness in adolescents' daily Llves: An experience sampling study. *Developmental Psychology*, 57(2), 309–323. DOI: 10.1037/dev0001148 PMID: 33539132

Powell, A., Scott, A. J., Flynn, A., & Henry, N. (2020). *Image-Based Sexual Abuse: An International Study of Victims and Perpetrators*. Summary Report. Melbourne: RMIT University. https://doi:DOI: 10.13140/RG.2.2.35166.59209

Powell, A., & Henry, N. (2016). Technology-Facilitated Sexual Violence Victimization: Results From an Online Survey of Australian Adults. *Journal of Interpersonal Violence*, 34(17), 3637–3665. DOI: 10.1177/0886260516672055 PMID: 27697966

Powell, A., Henry, N., Flynn, A., & Scott, A. J. (2019). Image-based sexual abuse: The extent, nature, and predictors of perpetration in a community sample of Australian residents. *Computers in Human Behavior*, 92, 393–402. DOI: 10.1016/j.chb.2018.11.009

Powell, A., Scott, A. J., Flynn, A., & McCook, S. (2022). Perpetration of Image-Based Sexual Abuse: Extent, Nature and Correlates in a Multi-Country Sample. *Journal of Interpersonal Violence*, 37(23-24), NP22864–NP22889. DOI: 10.1177/08862605211072266 PMID: 35184577

Prensky, M. (2010). *Teaching Digital Natives: Partnering for Real Learning*. Corwin Press.

Priya, N., & Maheswari, P. U. (2024). Influence of different parental mediation strategies on adolescents' hedonistic smartphone use: Parent-adolescent reports. *Mobile Media & Communication*, 12(1), 1–22. DOI: 10.1177/20501579241260649

Prot, S., Anderson, C. A., Gentile, D. A., & Swing, E. L. (2014). The positive and negative effects of video play. In A. Jordan & D. Romer (Eds.), *Children and media* (pp. 109-128). Oxford University Press.

Protecting Canadians from Online Crime Act. (2014). S.C., c, 31. https://laws-lois.justice.gc.ca/

Purwaningsih, E., & Nurmala, I. (2021). The impact of online game addiction on adolescent mental health: A systematic review and meta-analysis. *Open Access Macedonian Journal of Medical Sciences (OAMJMS), 9*(F), 260-274. DOI: 10.3889/oamjms.2021.6234

Putnick, D. L., Trinh, M. H., Sundaram, R., Bell, E. M., Ghassabian, A., Robinson, S. L., & Yeung, E. (2023). Displacement of peer play by screen time: Associations with toddler development. *Pediatric Research*, 93(5), 1425–1431. DOI: 10.1038/s41390-022-02261-y PMID: 35986149

Puzio, D., Makowska, I., & Rymarczyk, K. (2022). Raising the child—Do screen media help or hinder? The quality over quantity hypothesis. *International Journal of Environmental Research and Public Health*, 19(16), 9880. DOI: 10.3390/ijerph19169880 PMID: 36011514

Qiao, X., Wang, Y., & Zhao, J. (2023). Anti-school bullying Forum Theatre in rural boarding middle school in China – Empirical analysis based on programme practice. *The Journal of Drama and Theatre Education in Asia*, 12(1), 43–64.

Qu, J., Shen, S., Sun, I. Y., Farmer, A. K., & Xue, J. (2022). Sexting victimization among dating app users: A comparison of US and Chinese college students. *Journal of Interpersonal Violence*, 37(19-20), NP17109–NP17132. DOI: 10.1177/08862605211028281 PMID: 34182820

Radesky, J. S., & Christakis, D. A. (2016). Increased screen time: Implications for early childhood development and behavior. *Pediatric Clinics of North America*, 63(5), 827–839. DOI: 10.1016/j.pcl.2016.06.006 PMID: 27565361

Radesky, J. S., Kaciroti, N., Weeks, H. M., Schaller, A., & Miller, A. L. (2023). Longitudinal associations between use of mobile devices for calming and emotional reactivity and executive functioning in children aged 3 to 5 years. *JAMA Pediatrics*, 177(1), 62–70. DOI: 10.1001/jamapediatrics.2022.4793 PMID: 36508199

Rai, A. (2020). Explainable AI: From black box to glass box. *Journal of the Academy of Marketing Science*, 48(1), 137–141. DOI: 10.1007/s11747-019-00710-5

Ranjan, L. K., Gupta, P. R., Srivastava, M., & Gujar, N. M. (2021). Problematic internet use and its association with anxiety among undergraduate students. *Asian Journal of Social Health and Behavior*, 4(4), 137–141. DOI: 10.4103/shb.shb_30_21

Ravn, S., Coffey, J., & Roberts, S. (2021). The currency of images: Risk, value and gendered power dynamics in young men's accounts of sexting. *Feminist Media Studies*, 21(2), 315–331. DOI: 10.1080/14680777.2019.1642229

Redmond, P., Lock, J. V., & Smart, V. (2020). Developing a cyberbullying conceptual framework for educators. *Technology in Society*, 60, 101223. DOI: 10.1016/j.techsoc.2019.101223

Reed, E., Salazar, M., Behar, A. I., Agah, N., Silverman, J. G., Minnis, A. M., Rusch, M. L. A., & Raj, A. (2019). Cyber Sexual Harassment: Prevalence and association with substance use, poor mental health, and STI history among sexually active adolescent girls. *Journal of Adolescence, 75*, 53. DOI: 10.1016/j.adolescence.2019.07.005

Regulation (EU) 2016/679 of the European Parliament and of the Council of 27 April 2016 on the protection of natural persons with regard to the processing of personal data and on the free movement of such data, and repealing Directive 95/46/EC. *Official Journal of the European Union, L119*, of the 4th of May 2010, 119/1-119/88. https://eur-lex.europa.eu/legal-content/EN/TXT/PDF/?uri=CELEX:32016R0679

Renfrow, D. G., & Rollo, E. A. (2014). Sexting on campus: Minimizing perceived risks and neutralizing behaviors. *Deviant Behavior*, 35(11), 903–920. DOI: 10.1080/01639625.2014.897122

Resett, S., González Caino, P., & Mesurado, B. (2022). Problemas emocionales, personalidad oscura, sexting y grooming en adolescentes: El rol del género y la edad. *CES Psicología*, 15(2), 23–43. DOI: 10.21615/cesp.6132

Restrepo, A., Scheininger, T., Clucas, J., Alexander, L., Salum, G. A., Georgiades, K., Paksarian, D., Merikangas, K. R., & Milham, M. P. (2020). Problematic internet use in children and adolescents: Associations with psychiatric disorders and impairment. *BMC Psychiatry*, 20(1), 252. DOI: 10.1186/s12888-020-02640-x PMID: 32456610

Reyna, V. F., Wilhelms, E. A., McCormick, M. J., & Weldon, R. B. (2015). Development of risky decision making: Fuzzy-trace theory and neurobiological perspectives. *Child Development Perspectives*, 9(2), 122–127. DOI: 10.1111/cdep.12117 PMID: 25983859

Reyns, B. W., Burek, M. W., Henson, B., & Fisher, B. S. (2011). The unintended consequences of digital technology: Exploring the relationship between sexting and cybervictimization. *Journal of Crime and Justice*, 36(1), 1–17. DOI: 10.1080/0735648X.2011.641816

Reyns, B. W., Henson, B., & Fisher, B. S. (2014). Digital deviance: Low self-control and opportunity as explanations of sexting among college students. *Sociological Spectrum*, 34(3), 273–292. DOI: 10.1080/02732173.2014.895642

Rhoades, G. K., Stanley, S. M., & Markman, H. J. (2009). Couples' reasons for cohabitation: Associations with individual well-being and relationship quality: Associations with individual well-being and relationship quality. *Journal of Family Issues*, 30(2), 233–258. DOI: 10.1177/0192513X08324388 PMID: 19756225

Ribble, M. (2015). *Digital Citizenship in Schools: Nine Elements All Students Should Know* (3rd ed.). ISTE.

Ricciardelli, R., & Adorjan, M. (2019). 'If a girl's photo gets sent around, that'sa way bigger deal than if a guy's photo gets sent around': Gender, sexting, and the teenage years. *Journal of Gender Studies*, 28(5), 563–577. DOI: 10.1080/09589236.2018.1560245

Rice, E., Gibbs, J., Winetrobe, H., Rhoades, H., Plant, A., Montoya, J., & Kordic, T. (2014). Sexting and Sexual Behavior Among Middle School Students. *Pediatrics*, 134(1), 21–28. DOI: 10.1542/peds.2013-2991 PMID: 24982103

Rice, E., Rhoades, H., Winetrobe, H., Sanchez, M., Montoya, J., Plant, A., & Kordic, T. (2012). Sexually explicit cell phone messaging associated with sexual risk among adolescents. *Pediatrics*, 130(4), 667–673. DOI: 10.1542/peds.2012-0021 PMID: 22987882

Rice, M. F. (2024). Diffractive perspectives on parents' role in inclusive online, distance, and digital education. *Computers in the Schools*, 41(2), 145–163. DOI: 10.1080/07380569.2024.2325433

Rice, M. F., Cantergiani, K., & Macias, D. (2023). A research-based conceptual framework for inclusive K-12 online, distance, and digital education. *Journal of Research on Technology in Education*, 1–17. Advance online publication. DOI: 10.1080/15391523.2023.2264982

Richards, R. D., & Calvert, C. (2009). When sex and cell phones collide: Inside the prosecution of a teen sexting case. *Hastings Communication & Entertainment LJ, 32*, Article 1.

Ricketts, M. L., Maloney, C., Marcum, C. D., & Higgins, G. E. (2015). The effect of internet related problems on the sexting behaviors of juveniles. *American Journal of Criminal Justice*, 40(2), 270–284. DOI: 10.1007/s12103-014-9247-5

Ricon, T., & Dolev-Cohen, M. (2024). Sexting behavior by young adults: The correlation between emotion regulation and moral judgment. *American Journal of Sexuality Education*, 19(2), 211–229. DOI: 10.1080/15546128.2023.2212189

Rideout, V. J., Foehr, U. G., & Roberts, D. F. (2010). *Generation M2: Media in the Lives of 8- to 18-Year-Olds*. Henry J. Kaiser Family Foundation. Retrieved from https://files.eric.ed.gov/fulltext/ED527859.pdf

Rideout, V., & Katz, V. S. (2016). *Opportunity for all? Technology and learning in lower-income families. A report of the Families and Media Project*. The Joan Ganz Cooney Center at Sesame Workshop. Retrieved from https://www.joanganzcooneycenter.org/wp-content/uploads/2016/01/jgcc_opportunityforall.pdf

Rideout, V., & Robb, M. B. (2020). *The common sense census: Media use by kids age zero to eight*. Retrieved from https://www.commonsensemedia.org/sites/default/files/research/report/2020_zero_to_eight_census_final_web.pdf

Rideout, V. (2011). *Zero to eight: children's media use in America 2011*. Common Sense Media. Retrieved from https://www.commonsensemedia.org/sites/default/files/research/report/zero-to-eight-2013.pdf

Ringrose, J. (2010). Sluts, whores, fat slags and Playboy bunnies: Teen girls' negotiations of "sexy" on social networking sites and at school. In C. Jackson, C. Paechter, & E. Renold (Eds.), *Girls and education 3–16: Continuing concerns, new agendas* (pp. 170-182). Open University Press. DOI: 10.1080/00071005.2011.611290

Ringrose, J., Betsy, M., Tanya, H., & Kaitlynn, M. (2024). Postdigital Bodies: Young People's Experiences of Algorithmic, Tech-Facilitated Body Shaming and Image-Based Sexual Abuse during and after the COVID-19 Pandemic in England. *Youth*, 4(3), 1058–1075. DOI: 10.3390/youth4030066

Ringrose, J., Gill, R., Livingstone, S., & Harvey, L. (2012). *A qualitative study of children, young people and 'sexting': a report prepared for the NSPCC*. National Society for the Prevention of Cruelty to Children.

Ringrose, J., Gill, R., Livingstone, S., & Harvey, L. (2012). *A qualitative study of children, young people and 'sexting': A report prepared for the NSPCC*. National Society for the Prevention of Cruelty to Children. https://eprints.lse.ac.uk/44216/1/__Libfile_repository_Content_Livingstone%2C%20S_A%20qualitative%20study%20of%20children%2C%20young%20people%20and%20%27sexting%27%20%28LSE%20RO%29.pdf

Ringrose, J., Gill, R., Livingstone, S., & Harvey, L. (2012). *A qualitative study of children, young people and "sexting": a report prepared for the NSPCC*. National Society for the Prevention of Cruelty to Children. Retrieved from http://eprints.lse.ac.uk/id/eprint/44216

Ringrose, J., Harvey, L., Gill, R., & Livingstone, S. (2013). Teen girls, sexual double standards and 'sexting': Gendered value in digital image exchange. *Feminist Theory*, 14(3), 305–323. DOI: 10.1177/1464700113499853

Rismark, M., & Sølvberg, A. M. (2019). Video as a Learner Scaffolding Tool. *International Journal of Learning. Teaching and Educational Research*, 18(1), 62–75. DOI: 10.26803/ijlter.18.1.5

Roberts, A. L., Koenen, K. C., Lyall, K., Robinson, E. B., & Weisskopf, M. G. (2015). Association of autistic traits in adulthood with childhood abuse, interpersonal victimization, and posttraumatic stress. *Child Abuse & Neglect*, 45, 135–142. DOI: 10.1016/j.chiabu.2015.04.010 PMID: 25957197

Roberts, M., Lobo, R., & Sorenson, A. (2017). Evaluating the sharing stories youth theatre program: An interactive theatre and drama-based strategy for sexual health promotion among multicultural youth. *Health Promotion Journal of Australia*, 28(1), 30–36. DOI: 10.1071/HE15096 PMID: 27346537

Roberts, R. C. (1985). Carl Rogers and the Christian virtues. *Journal of Psychology and Theology*, 13(4), 263–273. DOI: 10.1177/009164718501300403

Roberts, S., Ravn, S., Maloney, M., & Ralph, B. (2021). Navigating the tensions of normative masculinity: Homosocial dynamics in Australian young men's discussions of sexting practices. *Cultural Sociology*, 15(1), 22–43. DOI: 10.1177/1749975520925358

Rocheleau, J. N., & Chiasson, S. (2022). Privacy and safety on social networking sites: Autistic and non-autistic teenagers' attitudes and behaviors. *ACM Transactions on Computer-Human Interaction*, 29(1), 1–39. DOI: 10.1145/3469859

Rodríguez-Álvarez, J. M., Navarro, R., Yubero, S., & Larrañaga, E. (2022). Apoyo social, competencias socioemocionales y cibervictimización: Estudio longitudinal en estudiantes de Educación Primaria [Social support, socio-emotional skills and cybervictimization: longitudinal study in students of Primary Education]. *Review of Education*, 397, 125–152. DOI: 10.4438/1988-592X-RE-2022-397-542

Rodríguez-Castro, Y., Martínez-Román, R., Alonso-Ruido, P., Adá-Lameiras, A., & Carrera-Fernández, M. V. (2021). Intimate partner cyberstalking, sexism, pornography, and sexting in adolescents: New challenges for sex education. *International Journal of Environmental Research and Public Health*, 18(4), 1–14. DOI: 10.3390/ijerph18042181 PMID: 33672240

Romano, M., & Porto, M. D. (2016). Discourse, cognition and society. In Romano, M., & Porto, M. D. (Eds.), *Exploring discourse strategies in social and cognitive interaction* (Vol. 4, pp. 1–20). John Benjamins Publishing Company. DOI: 10.1075/pbns.262.01rom

Ron, Y. (2018). Psychodrama's Role in Alleviating Acute Distress: A Case Study of an Open Therapy Group in a Psychiatric Inpatient Ward. *Frontiers in Psychology*, 9, 2075. Advance online publication. DOI: 10.3389/fpsyg.2018.02075 PMID: 30425674

Rosenberg, M. (1965). *Society and the adolescent self-image*. Princeton University Press. DOI: 10.1515/9781400876136

Rosendo-Rios, V., Trott, S., & Shukla, P. (2022). Systematic literature review online gaming addiction among children and young adults: A framework and research agenda. *Addictive Behaviors*, 129, 107238. DOI: 10.1016/j.addbeh.2022.107238 PMID: 35104738

Roser, M., & Ortiz-Ospina, E. (2024, March). *Literacy*.https://ourworldindata.org/literacy

Rose, S. W., Mayo, A., Ganz, O., Perreras, L., D'Silva, J., & Cohn, A. (2019). Perceived racial/ethnic discrimination, marketing, and substance use among young adults. *Journal of Ethnicity in Substance Abuse*, 18(4), 558–577. DOI: 10.1080/15332640.2018.1425949 PMID: 29424638

Ross, J. M., Drouin, M., & Coupe, A. (2019). Sexting coercion as a component of intimate partner polyvictimization. *Journal of Interpersonal Violence*, 34(11), 2269–2291. DOI: 10.1177/0886260516660300 PMID: 27443412

Rostam-Abadi, Y., Stefanovics, E. A., & Potenza, M. N. (2024). An exploratory study of the prevalence and adverse associations of in-school traditional bullying and cyberbullying among adolescents in Connecticut. *Journal of Psychiatric Research*, 173, 372–380. DOI: 10.1016/j.jpsychires.2024.03.033 PMID: 38593696

Roth, M. (2015). *Here's Why Sexting May Be Good For Your Relationship – MTV*. http://www.mtv.com/news/2238267/sexting-relationship-study/

Rothman, E. F., Graham Holmes, L., Brooks, D., Krauss, S., & Caplan, R. (2023). Reasons for alcohol use and non-use by underage U.S. autistic youth: A qualitative study. *Autism*, 27(1), 213–225. DOI: 10.1177/13623613221091319 PMID: 35499489

Rotunda, R. J., Kass, S. J., Sutton, M. A., & Leon, D. T. (2003). Internet use and misuse: Preliminary findings from a new assessment instrument. *Behavior Modification*, 27(4), 484–504. DOI: 10.1177/0145445503255600 PMID: 12971124

Rumjaun, A., & Narod, F. (2020). Social learning theory—Albert Bandura. In B. Akpan, & T. J. Kennedy (Eds.), *Science Education in Theory and practice* (Vol. 1, pp. 85–99). Springer Texts in Education. Springer, Cham. DOI: 10.1007/978-3-030-43620-9_7

Runions, K. C., Salmivalli, C., Shaw, T., Burns, S., & Cross, D. (2018). Beyond the reactive-proactive dichotomy: Rage, revenge, reward, and recreational aggression predict early high school bully and bully/victim status. *Aggressive Behavior*, 44(5), 501–511. DOI: 10.1002/ab.21770 PMID: 29956340

Runions, K., & Bak, M. (2015). Online Moral Disengagement, Cyberbullying, and Cyber-Aggression. *Cyberpsychology, Behavior, and Social Networking*, 18(7), 400–405. DOI: 10.1089/cyber.2014.0670 PMID: 26167839

Ruvalcaba, Y., & Eaton, A. A. (2020). Nonconsensual pornography among U.S. adults: A sexual scripts framework on victimization, perpetration, and health correlates for women and men. *Psychology of Violence*, 10(1), 68–78. DOI: 10.1037/vio0000233

Ruvalcaba, Y., Mercer Kollar, L. M., Everett Jones, S., Mercado, M. C., Leemis, R. W., & Ma, Z.-Q. (2023). Adolescent sexting, violence, and sexual behaviors: An analysis of 2014 and 2016 Pennsylvania Youth Risk Behavior survey data. *The Journal of School Health*, 93(8), 690–697. DOI: 10.1111/josh.13290 PMID: 36544265

Saad, M. A. E. (2020). Self-regulated learning and academic procrastination as predictors of smartphone addiction among second year-middle school learning disabled students. *Amazonia Investiga*, 9(26), 236–243. DOI: 10.34069/AI/2020.26.02.27

Saavedra, D. (2022). Responding to technological disruptions during online video interviews conducted via Zoom. *The Qualitative Report*, 27(6), 1479–1484. DOI: 10.46743/2160-3715/2022.5524

Saggers, B. (2015). Student perceptions: Improving the educational experiences of high school students on the autism spectrum. *Improving Schools*, 18(1), 35–45. DOI: 10.1177/1365480214566213

Şahin, D., & Gözün Kahraman, Ö. (2021). Okul dönemi çocuklarının bilgisayar oyun bağımlılığı ile davranış problemleri arasındaki ilişkinin incelenmesi. *Milli Eğitim Dergisi*, 50(230), 13–28. DOI: 10.37669/milliegitim.682086

Şahin, S. S., & Ayaz-Alkaya, S. (2023). Prevalence and predisposing factors of peer bullying and cyberbullying among adolescents: A cross-sectional study. *Children and Youth Services Review*, 155, 107216. DOI: 10.1016/j.childyouth.2023.107216

Saikia, A. M., Das, J., Barman, P., & Bharali, M. D. (2019). Internet addiction and its relationships with depression, anxiety, and stress in urban adolescents of Kamrup District, Assam. *Journal of Family & Community Medicine*, 26(2), 108–112. DOI: 10.4103/jfcm.JFCM_93_18 PMID: 31143082

Saleem, S., Khan, N., & Zafar, S. (2021). Prevalence of cyberbullying victimization among Pakistani Youth. *Technology in Society*, 65, 101577. DOI: 10.1016/j.techsoc.2021.101577

Salerno-Ferraro, A. C., Erentzen, C., & Schuller, R. A. (2022). Young Women's Experiences With Technology-Facilitated Sexual Violence From Male Strangers. *Journal of Interpersonal Violence*, 37(19–20), NP17860–NP17885. DOI: 10.1177/08862605211030018 PMID: 34271829

Salmivalli, C. (2010). Bullying and the Peer Group: A Review. *Aggression and Violent Behavior*, 15(2), 112–120. DOI: 10.1016/j.avb.2009.08.007

Salmon, S., Turner, S., Taillieu, T., Fortier, J., & Afifi, T. O. (2018). Bullying victimization experiences among middle and high school adolescents: Traditional bullying, discriminatory harassment, and cybervictimization. *Journal of Adolescence*, 63(1), 29–40. DOI: 10.1016/j.adolescence.2017.12.005 PMID: 29268108

Samee, N. A., Khan, U., Khan, S., Jamjoom, M. M., Sharif, M., & Kim, D. H. (2023). Safeguarding Online Spaces: A Powerful Fusion of Federated Learning, Word Embeddings, and Emotional Features for Cyberbullying Detection. *IEEE Access : Practical Innovations, Open Solutions*, 11, 124524–124541. DOI: 10.1109/ACCESS.2023.3329347

Samimi, P., & Alderson, K. G. (2014). Sexting among undergraduate students. *Computers in Human Behavior*, 31, 230–241. DOI: 10.1016/j.chb.2013.10.027

Santhanam, S. (2023). An interactive and neurodiversity-affirming approach to communication supports for autistic students through videogaming. *Language, Speech, and Hearing Services in Schools*, 54(1), 120–139. DOI: 10.1044/2022_LSHSS-22-00027 PMID: 36626352

Sari, G. C., Krutka, D. G., & Smits, R. M. (2024). Why is There a Picture of Me on Snapchat?: Educational Approaches to Overposting. *TechTrends*, 68(4), 682–692. DOI: 10.1007/s11528-024-00970-1

Sarshar, M., Farley, F., Fiorello, C. A., & DuCette, J. (2019). T behavior: Psychological implications of thrill-seeking/risk-taking. *Current Psychology (New Brunswick, N.J.)*, 1–8. DOI: 10.1007/s12144-019-00557-7

Sasson, H., & Mesch, G. (2014). Parental mediation, peer norms and risky online behavior among adolescents. *Computers in Human Behavior*, 33, 32–38. DOI: 10.1016/j.chb.2013.12.025

Savoia, E., Harriman, N. W., Su, M., Cote, T., & Shortland, N. (2021). Adolescents' exposure to online risks: Gender disparities and vulnerabilities related to online behaviors. *International Journal of Environmental Research and Public Health*, 18(11), 5786. Advance online publication. DOI: 10.3390/ijerph18115786 PMID: 34072253

Savolainen, I., Kaakinen, M., Sirola, A., & Oksanen, A. (2018). Addictive behaviors and psychological distress among adolescents and emerging adults: A mediating role of peer group identification. *Addictive Behaviors Reports*, 7, 75–81. DOI: 10.1016/j.abrep.2018.03.002 PMID: 29892700

Schade, H. M., Hülür, G., Infurna, F. J., Hoppmann, C. A., & Gerstorf, D. (2016). Partner dissimilarity in life satisfaction: Stability and change, correlates, and outcomes. *Psychology and Aging*, 31(4), 327–339. Advance online publication. DOI: 10.1037/pag0000096 PMID: 27294715

Schmitt, D. P., & Fuller, R. C. (2015). On the varieties of sexual experience: Cross-cultural links between religiosity and human mating strategies. *Psychology of Religion and Spirituality*, 7(4), 314–326. DOI: 10.1037/rel0000036

Schoeps, K., Villanueva, L., Prado-Gascó, V. J., & Montoya-Castilla, I. (2018). Development of emotional skills in adolescents to prevent cyberbullying and improve subjective well-being. *Frontiers in Psychology*, 9, 2050. DOI: 10.3389/fpsyg.2018.02050 PMID: 30416471

Scholes-Balog, K., Francke, N., & Hemphill, S. (2016). Relationships between sexting, self-esteem, and sensation seeking among Australian young adults. *Sexualization. Medicine and Society*, 2(2), 2374623815627790. Advance online publication. DOI: 10.1177/2374623815627790

Schroeder, N. L., Romine, W. L., & Craig, S. D. (2017). Measuring pedagogical agent persona and the influence of agent persona on learning. *Computers & Education*, 109, 176–186. DOI: 10.1016/j.compedu.2017.02.015

Schultze-Krumbholz, A., Schultze, M., Zagorscak, P., Wölfer, R., & Scheithauer, H. (2016). Feeling cybervictims' pain—The effect of empathy training on cyberbullying. *Aggressive Behavior*, 42(2), 147–156. DOI: 10.1002/ab.21613 PMID: 26349848

Schultz, S. M., Jacobs, G., & Schultz, J. (2013). A promising practice: Using Facebook as a communication and social networking tool. *Rural Special Education Quarterly*, 32(4), 38–44. DOI: 10.1177/875687051303200405

Schulz van Endert, T. (2021). Addictive use of digital devices in young children: Associations with delay discounting, self-control and academic performance. *PLoS One*, 16(6), e0253058. DOI: 10.1371/journal.pone.0253058 PMID: 34157026

Schunk, D. H. (2012). *Learning Theories. An Educational Perspective* (6th ed.). Pearson.

Schwartz, S. H., & Boehnke, K. (2004). Evaluating the structure of human values with confirmatory factor analysis. *Journal of Research in Personality*, 38(3), 230–255. DOI: 10.1016/S0092-6566(03)00069-2

Schwarzer, C., Grafe, N., Hiemisch, A., Kiess, W., & Poulain, T. (2021). Associations of media use and early childhood development: Cross-sectional findings from the LIFE Child study. *Pediatric Research*, 91(1), 247–253. DOI: 10.1038/s41390-021-01433-6 PMID: 33658656

Sciacca, B., Mazzone, A., Loftsson, M., O'Higgins Norman, J., & Foody, M. (2023). Nonconsensual Dissemination of Sexual Images Among Adolescents: Associations With Depression and Self-Esteem. *Journal of Interpersonal Violence*, 38(15-16), 9438–9464. DOI: 10.1177/08862605231165777 PMID: 37073923

Sciacca, B., Mazzone, A., Norman, J. O., & Foody, M. (2021). Blame and responsibility in the context of youth produced sexual imagery: The role of teacher empathy and rape myth acceptance. *Teaching and Teacher Education*, 103, 103354. DOI: 10.1016/j.tate.2021.103354

Scott-Barrett, J., Cebula, K., & Florian, L. (2018). Listening to young people with autism: Learning from researcher experiences. *International Journal of Research & Method in Education*, 42(2), 163–184. DOI: 10.1080/1743727X.2018.1462791

Seema, R., & Varik-Maasik, E. (2023, July). Students' digital addiction and learning difficulties: shortcomings of surveys in inclusion. *Frontiers in Education, 8*, 1191817. Frontiers Media SA. DOI: 10.3389/feduc.2023.1191817

Seewald, L., Walsh, T. B., Tolman, R. M., Lee, S. J., Reed, L. A., Ngo, Q., & Singh, V. (2022). Technology-facilitated abuse prevalence and associations among a nationally representative sample of young men. *Annals of Family Medicine*, 20(1), 12–17. DOI: 10.1370/afm.2758 PMID: 35074762

Segovia, A. N., Maxwell, J. A., DiLorenzo, M. G., & MacDonald, G. (2019). No strings attached? How attachment orientation relates to the varieties of casual sexual relationships. *Personality and Individual Differences*, 151, 109455. Advance online publication. DOI: 10.1016/j.paid.2019.05.061

Seidman, I. (2019). *Interviewing as qualitative research: A guide for researchers in education and the social sciences*. Teachers College Press.

Selkie, E. M., Fales, J. L., & Moreno, M. A. (2016). Cyberbullying Prevalence Among US Middle and High School-Aged Adolescents: A Systematic Review and Quality Assessment. *The Journal of Adolescent Health*, 58(2), 125–133. DOI: 10.1016/j.jadohealth.2015.09.026 PMID: 26576821

Senemoğlu, N. (2011). *Gelişim, öğrenme ve öğretim; kuramdan uygulamaya*. Pegem Akademi Yayıncılık.

Şenol, Y., Şenol, F. B., & Can Yaşar, M. (2024). Digital play addiction of preschool children in the Covid-19 pandemic: Social emotional development and parental guidance. *Current Psychology (New Brunswick, N.J.)*, 43(1), 839–847. DOI: 10.1007/s12144-023-04323-8 PMID: 36819754

Servidio, R., Bartolo, M. G., Palermiti, A. L., Casas, J. A., Ruiz, R. O., & Costabile, A. (2019). Internet addiction, self-esteem and the validation of the Italian version of the Internet Related Experiences Questionnaire. *European Review of Applied Psychology*, 69(2), 51–58. DOI: 10.1016/j.erap.2019.03.003

Sesar, K., Dodaj, A., & Jandrić, T. (2021). Young People Who Sext: The Role of Self-Esteem and Body-Esteem. *Central European Journal of Paediatrics*, 17(1), 52–65. DOI: 10.5457/p2005-114.288

Sesar, K., Dodaj, A., & Šimić, N. (2019). Motivational determinants of sexting: Towards a model integrating the research. *Psihologijske Teme*, 28(3), 461–482. DOI: 10.31820/pt.28.3.1

Setty, E. (2019). Meanings of bodily and sexual expression in youth sexting culture: Young women's negotiation of gendered risks and harms. *Sex Roles*, 80(9-10), 586–606. DOI: 10.1007/s11199-018-0957-x

Sexual Offences (Scotland) Act 2009. https://www.legislation.gov.uk/asp/2009/9/section/6

Shah, I., & Khan, M. (2015). Impact of multimedia-aided teaching on students' academic achievement and attitude at elementary level. *US-China Education Review A*, 5(5), 349–360. DOI: 10.17265/2161-623X/2015.05A.006

Shakes, P., & Cashin, A. (2019). Identifying language for people on the autism spectrum: A scoping review. *Issues in Mental Health Nursing*, 40(4), 317–325. DOI: 10.1080/01612840.2018.1522400 PMID: 30633618

Shapiro, G. L. (2022). Cyberbullying: Introduction, definition, and impact on mental health in youth. *Journal of the American Academy of Child and Adolescent Psychiatry*, 61(10), S71. DOI: 10.1016/j.jaac.2022.07.299

Sharabany, R., Eshel, Y., & Hakim, C. (2008). Boyfriend, girlfriend in a traditional society: Parenting styles and development of intimate friendships among Arabs in school. *International Journal of Behavioral Development*, 32(1), 66–75. DOI: 10.1177/0165025407084053

Sharma, R., Sharma, M., & Joshi, S. (2024). Social media mirage-the two actual selves of an individual: Conceptualization and scale development. *Technological Forecasting and Social Change*, 206, 123502. DOI: 10.1016/j.techfore.2024.123502

Shek, D. T. L., Zhu, X., & Ma, C. M. S. (2018). The influence of parental control and parent-child relational qualities on adolescent internet addiction: A 3-year longitudinal study in Hong Kong. *Frontiers in Psychology*, 9, 642. DOI: 10.3389/fpsyg.2018.00642 PMID: 29765349

Shi, C., Hu, P., Fan, W., & Qiu, L. (2023). Competitive peer influence on knowledge contribution behaviors in online Q&A communities: A social comparison perspective. *Internet Research*, Vol. ahead-of-print No. ahead-of-print. DOI: 10.1108/INTR-07-2022-0510

Shiakou, M., & Piki, L. (2020). Assessing the role of drama on children's understanding of bullying. *International Journal of School & Educational Psychology*, 8(1), 11–20. DOI: 10.1080/21683603.2018.1499574

Shin, W., & Ismail, N. (2014). Exploring the role of parents and peers in young adolescents' risk taking on social networking sites. *Cyberpsychology, Behavior, and Social Networking*, 17(9), 578–583. DOI: 10.1089/cyber.2014.0095 PMID: 25126969

Shin, W., & Lwin, M. O. (2017). How does "talking about the internet with others" affect teenagers' experience of online risks? The role of active mediation by parents, peers, and school teachers. *New Media & Society*, 19(7), 1109–1126. DOI: 10.1177/1461444815626612

Shneyderman, Y., & Kiely, M. (2013). Intimate partner violence during pregnancy: Victim or perpetrator? Does it make a difference? *BJOG*, 120(11), 1375–1385. DOI: 10.1111/1471-0528.12357 PMID: 23786367

Shulman, E. P., Smith, A. R., Silva, K., Icenogle, G., Duell, N., Chein, J., & Steinberg, L. (2016). The dual systems model: Review, reappraisal, and reaffirmation. *Developmental Cognitive Neuroscience*, 17, 103–117. DOI: 10.1016/j.dcn.2015.12.010 PMID: 26774291

Shumer, D. E., Reisner, S. L., Edwards-Leeper, L., & Tishelman, A. (2016). Evaluation of asperger syndrome in youth presenting to a gender dysphoria clinic. *LGBT Health*, 3(5), 387–390. DOI: 10.1089/lgbt.2015.0070 PMID: 26651183

Shutenko, E. N., Derevyanko, J. P., Kanishcheva, M. A., Kovtun, J. J., & Lokteva, A. V. (2020). Development of students' constructive self-consciousness experience in psychodrama process. *Perspectives of Science and Education*, 47(5), 304–318. DOI: 10.32744/pse.2020.5.21

Siddiqui, S., & Schultze-Krumbholz, A. (2023). Successful and emerging cyberbullying prevention programs: A narrative review of seventeen interventions applied worldwide. *Societies (Basel, Switzerland)*, 13(9), 212. DOI: 10.3390/soc13090212

Silva, R. B., Teixeira, C. M., Vasconcelos-Raposo, J., & Bessa, M. (2016). Sexting: Adaptation of sexual behavior to modern technologies. *Computers in Human Behavior*, 64, 747–753. DOI: 10.1016/j.chb.2016.07.036

Simons, K. D., & Klein, J. D. (2007). The impact of scaffolding and student achievement levels in a problem-based learning environment. *Instructional Science*, 35(1), 41–72. DOI: 10.1007/s11251-006-9002-5

Simpson, B. (2013). Challenging childhood, challenging children: Children's rights and sexting. *Sexualities*, 16(5/6), 690–709. DOI: 10.1177/1363460713487467

Şimşek, Ç., Küçük, L., & Akgün Yıldırım, E. (2019). Psychodrama practices in adolescents. *Journal of Academic Research in Nursing*. DOI: 10.5222/jaren.2019.48030

Şimşek, Z. C., Canbeldek, M., & Işıkoğlu, N. (2023). Ebeveynlerin pandemi sürecinde dijital ebeveynliğe yönelik deneyimleri. *Dokuz Eylül Üniversitesi Buca Eğitim Fakültesi Dergisi*, 55(55), 250–271. DOI: 10.53444/deubefd.1221315

Singh, A., Khess, C. R. J., Kj, M., Ali, A., & Gujar, N. M. (2020). Loneliness, social anxiety, social support, and internet addiction among postgraduate college students. *Open Journal of Psychiatry & Allied Sciences*, 11(1), 10–13. DOI: 10.5958/2394-2061.2020.00002.6

Sinha, R. (2011). New findings on biological factors predicting addiction relapse vulnerability. *Current Psychiatry Reports*, 13(5), 398–405. DOI: 10.1007/s11920-011-0224-0 PMID: 21792580

Skagerberg, E., Di Ceglie, D., & Carmichael, P. (2015). Brief report: Autistic features in children and adolescents with gender dysphoria. *Journal of Autism and Developmental Disorders*, 45(8), 2628–2632. DOI: 10.1007/s10803-015-2413-x PMID: 25772537

Slonje, R., & Smith, P. (2008). Cyberbullying: Another main type of bullying? *Scandinavian Journal of Psychology*, 49(2), 147–154. DOI: 10.1111/j.1467-9450.2007.00611.x PMID: 18352984

Šmahel, D., & Subrahmanyam, K. (2014). Adolescent sexuality on the internet: A developmental perspective. In Saleh, F. M., Grudzinskas, A., & Judge, A. M. (Eds.), *Adolescent sexual behavior in the digital age* (pp. 62–85). Oxford University Press.

Smith, A., Jones, B., & Roe, T. (2015). *Cyberbullying Prevention and Intervention: Strategies for Teachers and Administrators*. Routledge.

Smith, C. H., & Borden, K. A. (2020). Introduction to the special issue on substance use disorders and addictions. *Professional Psychology, Research and Practice*, 51(1), 1–4. DOI: 10.1037/pro0000299

Smith, J., & Doe, A. (2024). Empowering Students through Psychoeducational Programs: The Role of Experiential Learning. In *Teaching Digital Responsibility: Strategies and Methods*. ABC Publishers.

Smith, L. J. (2015). Minors' Right to Confidentiality: Addressing the Issue of Bullying and the Ethical Obligation to Prevent Harm. *Journal of Human Behavior in the Social Environment*, 25(7), 746–755. DOI: 10.1080/10911359.2015.1032649

Smith, P. K., Mahdavi, J., Carvalho, M., Fisher, S., Russell, S., & Tippett, N. (2008). Cyberbullying: Its nature and impact in secondary school pupils. *Journal of Child Psychology and Psychiatry, and Allied Disciplines*, 49(4), 376–385. DOI: 10.1111/j.1469-7610.2007.01846.x PMID: 18363945

Smusz, M., Birkbeck, C., Bidgood, A., & Allely, C. S. (2024). Exploring the experience of romantic relationships and sexuality education in neurodivergent and neurotypical young individuals. *Sexuality and Disability*, 42(3), 735–764. Advance online publication. DOI: 10.1007/s11195-024-09857-8

Snell, W. E.Jr. (1998). The multidimensional sexual self-concept questionnaire. In Davis, C. M., Yarber, W. L., Bausenman, R., Schreer, G., & Davis, S. L. (Eds.), *Handbook of sexuality-related measures* (pp. 521–524). Sage.

Sorbring, E., Skoog, T., & Bohlin, M. (2014). Adolescent girls' and boys' well-being in relation to online and offline sexual and romantic activity. *Cyberpsychology (Brno)*, 8(1), 7. Advance online publication. DOI: 10.5817/CP2014-1-7

Soror, A. A., Steelman, Z. R., & Limayem, M. (2012, January 04-07). *Discipline yourself before life disciplines you: Deficient self-regulation and mobile phone unregulated use*. [Paper Presentation] 45th Hawaii International Conference on System Sciences, IEEE. https://ieeexplore.ieee.org/document/6148997

Sorrentino, A., Baldry, A. C., & Farrington, D. P. (2018). The efficacy of the Tabby Improved Prevention and Intervention Program in reducing cyberbullying and cybervictimization among students. *International Journal of Environmental Research and Public Health*, 15(11), 2536. DOI: 10.3390/ijerph15112536 PMID: 30428513

Sourander, A., Brunstein Klomek, A., Ikonen, M., Lindroos, J., Luntamo, T., Koskelainen, M., Ristkari, T., & Helenius, H. (2010). Psychosocial risk factors associated with cyberbullying among adolescents. *Archives of General Psychiatry*, 67(7), 720–728. DOI: 10.1001/archgenpsychiatry.2010.79 PMID: 20603453

Sovacool, B. K., & Del Rio, D. D. F. (2020). Smart home technologies in Europe: A critical review of concepts, benefits, risks and policies. *Renewable & Sustainable Energy Reviews*, 120, 1–22. DOI: 10.1016/j.rser.2019.109663

Sparks, B., Stephens, S., & Trendell, S. (2023). Image-based sexual abuse: Victim-perpetrator overlap and risk-related correlates of coerced sexting, non-consensual dissemination of intimate images, and cyberflashing. *Computers in Human Behavior*, 148, 107879. Advance online publication. DOI: 10.1016/j.chb.2023.107879

Speer, S. A. (2017). Flirting: A designedly ambiguous action? *Research on Language and Social Interaction*, 50(2), 128–150. DOI: 10.1080/08351813.2017.1301297

Sprecher, S. (2013). Attachment style and sexual permissiveness: The moderating role of gender. *Personality and Individual Differences*, 55(4), 428–432. DOI: 10.1016/j.paid.2013.04.005

Sprecher, S., & Cate, R. M. (2004). Sexual Satisfaction and Sexual Expression as Predictors of Relationship Satisfaction and Stability. In Harvey, J. H., Wenzel, A., & Sprecher, S. (Eds.), *The handbook of sexuality in close relationships* (pp. 235–256). Lawrence Erlbaum Associates Publishers.

Springston, K. M. (2017). Gender differences in participation in and motivations for sexting: The effects of gender role attitudes, masculinity, and femininity. *Butler Journal of Undergraduate Research, 3*(1), Article 9.

Ståhl, S., & Dennhag, I. (2021). Online and offline sexual harassment associations of anxiety and depression in an adolescent sample. *Nordic Journal of Psychiatry*, 75(5), 330–335. DOI: 10.1080/08039488.2020.1856924 PMID: 33347341

Staksrud, E. (2013). *Children in the online world: Risk, regulation, rights*. Routledge.

Stamates, A. L., Lau-Barraco, C., & Linden-Carmichael, A. N. (2016). Alcohol expectancies mediate the relationship between age of first intoxication and drinking outcomes in college binge drinkers. *Substance Use & Misuse*, 51(5), 598–607. DOI: 10.3109/10826084.2015.1126745 PMID: 27007814

Stasko, E. C., & Geller, P. A. (2015, August 6-9). *Reframing sexting as a positive relationship behavior* [Conference presentation]. In 123rd American Psychological Association Annual Convention, Toronto, Ontario, Canada.

Steinberg, L., Albert, D., Cauffman, E., Banich, M., Graham, S., & Woolard, J. (2008). Age differences in sensation seeking and impulsivity as indexed by behavior and self-report: Evidence for a dual systems model. *Developmental Psychology*, 44(6), 1764–1778. DOI: 10.1037/a0012955 PMID: 18999337

Steinberg, L., & Chein, J. M. (2015). Multiple accounts of adolescent impulsivity. *Proceedings of the National Academy of Sciences of the United States of America*, 112(29), 8807–8808. DOI: 10.1073/pnas.1509732112 PMID: 26150513

Steinfeld, N. (2021). Parental mediation of adolescent Internet use: Combining strategies to promote awareness, autonomy and self-regulation in preparing youth for life on the web. *Education and Information Technologies*, 26(2), 1897–1920. DOI: 10.1007/s10639-020-10342-w

Sternberg, R. J. (1986). A triangular theory of love. *Psychological Review*, 93(2), 119–135. Advance online publication. DOI: 10.1037/0033-295X.93.2.119

Stevens, M., King, D., Dorstyn, D., & Delfabbro, P. (2018). Cognitive–behavioral therapy for internet gaming disorder: A systematic review and meta-analysis. *Clinical Psychology & Psychotherapy*, 26(2), 191203. DOI: 10.1002/cpp.2341 PMID: 30341981

Sticca, F., & Perren, S. (2012). Is Cyberbullying Worse than Traditional Bullying? Examining the Differential Roles of Medium, Publicity, and Anonymity for the Perceived Severity of Bullying. *Journal of Youth and Adolescence*, 42(5), 739–750. DOI: 10.1007/s10964-012-9867-3 PMID: 23184483

Stives, K. L., May, D. C., Mack, M., & Bethel, C. L. (2021). Understanding responses to bullying from the parent perspective. *Frontiers in Education*, 6, 642367. Advance online publication. DOI: 10.3389/feduc.2021.642367

Stone, B. (2018). *The affordances of online multiplayer games for the social interactions of middle-primary school-aged students with ASD* [Doctoral dissertation, Australian Catholic University]. ACU Research Bank. https://acuresearchbank.acu.edu.au/download/f4cd5a0358eeade34196f4ed94bfdb85f780eb4108a9034804b99186e2536199/3529400/STONE_2018_The_affordances_of_online_mulitplayer_games.pdf

Stone, B., Mills, K. A., & Saggers, B. (2018). Online multiplayer games for the social interactions of children with autism spectrum disorder: A resource for inclusive education. *International Journal of Inclusive Education*, 23(2), 209–228. https://doi.org/10.1080/13603116.2018.1426051

Stone, B., Mills, K. A., & Saggers, B. (2019). Multiplayer games: Multimodal features that support friendships of students with autism spectrum disorder. *Australasian Journal of Special and Inclusive Education*, 43(2), 69–82. https://doi.org/10.1017/jsi.2019.6

Stone, B., & Saggers, B. (2023). Autism, literacies, and social communication: A framework of inclusive new literacies. In Tierney, R. J., Rizvi, F., & Ercikan, K. (Eds.), *International encyclopedia of education* (4th ed., pp. 434–447). Elsevier.

Strang, J. F., Janssen, A., Tishelman, A., Leibowitz, S. F., Kenworthy, L., McGuire, J. K., Edwards-Leeper, L., Mazefsky, C. A., Rofey, D., Bascom, J., Caplan, R., Gomez-Lobo, V., Berg, D., Zaks, Z., Wallace, G. L., Wimms, H., Pine-Twaddell, E., Shumer, D., Register-Brown, K., & Anthony, L. G. (2018). Revisiting the link: Evidence of the rates of autism in studies of gender diverse individuals. *Journal of the American Academy of Child and Adolescent Psychiatry*, 57(11), 885–887. DOI: 10.1016/j.jaac.2018.04.023 PMID: 30392631

Strassberg, D. S., Cann, D., & Velarde, V. (2017). Sexting by high school students. *Archives of Sexual Behavior*, 46(6), 1667–1672. DOI: 10.1007/s10508-016-0926-9 PMID: 28050742

Strassberg, D. S., McKinnon, R. K., Sustaita, M. A., & Rullo, J. (2013). Sexting by high school students: An exploratory and descriptive study. *Archives of Sexual Behavior*, 42(1), 15–21. DOI: 10.1007/s10508-012-9969-8 PMID: 22674035

Street, B., Phal, K., & Rowsell, J. (2017). Multimodality and New Literacy Studies. In Jewitt, C. (Ed.), *The Routledge handbook of multimodal analysis* (pp. 227–237). Routledge.

Strohmaier, H., Murphy, M., & Dematteo, D. (2014). Youth sexting: Prevalence rates, driving motivations, and the deterrent effect of legal consequences. *Sexuality Research & Social Policy*, 11(3), 245–255. DOI: 10.1007/s13178-014-0162-9

Strohmeier, D., & Gradinger, P. (2022). Cyberbullying and cyber victimization as online risks for children and adolescents. *European Psychologist*, 27(2), 141–150. DOI: 10.1027/1016-9040/a000479

Sturm, A., & Kasari, C. (2019). Academic and psychosocial characteristics of incoming college freshmen with autism spectrum disorder: The role of comorbidity and gender. *Autism Research*, 12(6), 931–940. DOI: 10.1002/aur.2099 PMID: 30969478

Suargani, G. (2021). Peer Conformity, Time Management and Online Game Addiction to High Schoolers. *Proceedings in6th International Conference on Science, Education and Technology (ISET 2020)*. Atlantis Press.

Sung, Y. T., Chang, K. E., & Liu, T. C. (2017). The Effects of Integrating Mobile Devices with Teaching and Learning on Students' Learning Performance: A Meta-Analysis and Research Synthesis. *Computers & Education*, 94, 252–275. DOI: 10.1016/j.compedu.2015.11.008

Sweller, J. (2011). Cognitive load theory. *Psychology of Learning and Motivation*, 55, 37–76. DOI: 10.1016/B978-0-12-387691-1.00002-8

Syari, W. R., Gusdiansyah, E., & Welly, . (2023). Hypnotherapy is Needed to Reduce Online Gaming Addiction in Adolescence. *Journal of Health Sciences and Epidemiology*, 1(1), 33–39. DOI: 10.62404/jhse.v1i1.7

Tackie, H. N. (2022). (Dis)Connected: Establishing Social Presence and Intimacy in Teacher–Student Relationships During Emergency Remote Learning. *AERA Open*, 8(1), 1–14. DOI: 10.1177/23328584211069525

Tanrikulu, I. (2018). Cyberbullying prevention and intervention programs in schools: A systematic review. *School Psychology International*, 39(1), 74–91. DOI: 10.1177/0143034317745721

Tanrikulu, I., & Erdur-Baker, Ö. (2021). Motives behind cyberbullying perpetration: A test of uses and gratifications theory. *Journal of Interpersonal Violence*, 36(13-14), NP6699–NP6724. DOI: 10.1177/0886260518819882 PMID: 30608015

Tao, S., Reichert, F., Law, N., & Rao, N. (2022). Digital technology use and cyberbullying among primary school children: Digital literacy and parental mediation as moderators. *Cyberpsychology, Behavior, and Social Networking*, 25(9), 571–579. DOI: 10.1089/cyber.2022.0012 PMID: 35877811

Temple, J. R., & Choi, H. (2014). Longitudinal association between teen sexting and sexual behavior. *Pediatrics*, 134(5), 1287–1292. DOI: 10.1542/peds.2014-1974 PMID: 25287459

Temple, J. R., Le, V. D., van den Berg, P., Ling, Y., Paul, J. A., & Temple, B. W. (2014). Brief report: Teen sexting and psychosocial health. *Journal of Adolescence*, 37(1), 33–36. DOI: 10.1016/j.adolescence.2013.10.008 PMID: 24331302

Teng, T. H., Varathan, K. D., & Crestani, F. (2024). A comprehensive review of cyberbullying-related content classification in online social media. *Expert Systems with Applications*, 244, 122644. DOI: 10.1016/j.eswa.2023.122644

ter Beek, M., Brummer, L., Donker, A. S., & Opdenakker, M.-C. J. L. (2018). Supporting secondary school students' reading comprehension in computer environments: A systematic review. *Journal of Computer Assisted Learning*, 34(5), 557–566. DOI: 10.1111/jcal.12260

ter Beek, M., Opdenakker, M.-C., Spijkerboer, A. W., Brummer, L., Ozinga, H. W., & Strijbos, J.-W. (2019). Scaffolding expository history text reading: Effects on adolescents' comprehension, self regulation, and motivation. *Learning and Individual Differences*, 74, 101749. DOI: 10.1016/j.lindif.2019.06.003

Testoni, I., Sblano, V. F., Palazzo, L., Pompele, S., & Wieser, M. A. (2020). The Hospice as a Learning Environment: A Follow-Up Study with a Palliative Care Team. *International Journal of Environmental Research and Public Health*, 17(20), 7460. DOI: 10.3390/ijerph17207460 PMID: 33066375

Thapa, A., Cohen, J., Guffey, S., & Higgins-D'Alessandro, A. (2013). A Review of School Climate Research. *Review of Educational Research*, 83(3), 357–385. DOI: 10.3102/0034654313483907

The National Campaign to Prevent Teen and Unplanned Pregnancy. (2008). *Sex and Tech: Results from a Survey of Teens and Young Adults*. Author.

Third, A. (2016). *Method guide 6: Researching the benefits and opportunities for children online*. Global Kids Online. http://globalkidsonline.net/wp-content/uploads/2016/06/Guide-6-Global-opportunities-for-children-Third.pdf

Thomas, G., Bennie, J., Cocker, K., Ireland, M., & Biddle, S. (2020). Screen-based behaviors in Australian adolescents: Longitudinal trends from a 4-year follow-up study. *Preventive Medicine*, 106258, 106258. Advance online publication. DOI: 10.1016/j.ypmed.2020.106258 PMID: 33022322

Thorne, E., Babchishin, K. M., Fisico, R., & Healey, L. (2024). Sexting in Young Adults: A Normative Sexual Behavior. *Archives of Sexual Behavior*, 53(2), 593–609. DOI: 10.1007/s10508-023-02728-x PMID: 38082175

Throuvala, M. A., Janikian, M., Griffiths, M. D., Rennoldson, M., & Kuss, D. J. (2019). The role of family and personality traits in Internet gaming disorder: A mediation model combining cognitive and attachment perspectives. *Journal of Behavioral Addictions*, 8(1), 48–62. DOI: 10.1556/2006.8.2019.05 PMID: 30739463

Tiego, J., Testa, R., Bellgrove, M. A., Pantelis, C., & Whittle, S. (2018). A hierarchical model of inhibitory control. *Frontiers in Psychology*, 9, 1339. Advance online publication. DOI: 10.3389/fpsyg.2018.01339 PMID: 30123154

Tintori, A., Ciancimino, G., Bombelli, I., De Rocchi, D., & Cerbara, L. (2023). Children's online safety: Predictive factors of cyberbullying and online grooming involvement. *Societies (Basel, Switzerland)*, 13(2), 47. Advance online publication. DOI: 10.3390/soc13020047

Todd, R. J., & Medina, V. G. (2019). Young people's conceptions and practices of safety in online environments: An examination of challenges, theoretical perspectives, current research, findings, and potential instructional interventions. *Proceedings of the 48th Annual Conference of the International Association of School Librarianship and the 23rd International Forum on Research in School Librarianship,* 1–22. https://journals.library.ualberta.ca/slw/index.php/iasl/article/view/7377/4289

Tokunaga, R. S. (2010). Following you home from school: A critical review and synthesis of research on cyberbullying victimization. *Computers in Human Behavior*, 26(3), 277–287. DOI: 10.1016/j.chb.2009.11.014

Torices-Colpisa, A. (2023, mayo 21). *Nueve de cada diez universitarios que sufren "sexting" dejan la carrera. Heraldo de Aragón.* Retrieved from https://www.heraldo.es/noticias/sociedad/2023/05/21/nueve-de-cada-diez-universitarios-que-sufren-sexting-dejan-la-carrera-1653084.html

Torrijos-Fincias, P., Serrate-González, S., Martín-Lucas, J., & Muñoz-Rodríguez, J. M. (2021). Perception of risk in the use of technologies and social media. Implications for identity building during adolescence. *Education Sciences*, 11(9), 523. Advance online publication. DOI: 10.3390/educsci11090523

Touloupis, T. (2024). School Prevention of Non-consensual Sexting among Middle Adolescents: Does Sexual Preoccupation Awareness Matter? *Frontiers in Psychology (section: Media Psychology), 15,* 1384620._DOI: 10.3389/fpsyg.2024.1384620

Touloupis, T., Armaou, A., & Vasiou, A. (2023). Internet addiction and self-esteem amid the COVID-19 pandemic: A preliminary study in junior high school students. In R. S. Nazlı & G. Sari (Eds.), *Handbook of research on perspectives on society and technology addiction* (pp. 265–282). IGI Global. DOI: 10.4018/978-1-6684-8397-8.ch017

Touloupis, T. (2024). Facebook Use and cyberbullying by students with learning disabilities: The role of self-rsteem and loneliness. *Psychological Reports*, 127(3), 1237–1270. DOI: 10.1177/00332941221138471 PMID: 36367133

Touloupis, T., & Athanasiades, C. (2022). Cyberbullying and Empathy among Elementary School Students: Do Special Educational Needs Make a Difference? *Scandinavian Journal of Psychology*, 63(6), 609–623. DOI: 10.1111/sjop.12838 PMID: 35698831

Touloupis, T., & Athanasiades, C. (2022). Evaluation of a cyberbullying prevention program in elementary schools: The role of self-esteem enhancement. *Frontiers in Psychology*, 13, 980091. DOI: 10.3389/fpsyg.2022.980091 PMID: 36211905

Touloupis, T., & Campbell, M. (2024). The role of academic context-related factors and problematic social media use in academic procrastination: A cross-sectional study of students in elementary, secondary, and tertiary education. *Social Psychology of Education*, 27(1), 175–214. DOI: 10.1007/s11218-023-09817-8

Touloupis, T., Campbell, M. A., & Pnevmatikos, D. (2024). Stand by me or not? Academic context-related and individual contributors to university students' intended reaction to cyberbullying. *Psychology of Violence*, 14(4), 270–279. Advance online publication. DOI: 10.1037/vio0000511

Tozzo, P., Cuman, O., Moratto, E., & Caenazzo, L. (2022). Family and educational strategies for cyberbullying prevention: A systematic review. *International Journal of Environmental Research and Public Health*, 19(16), 10452. DOI: 10.3390/ijerph191610452 PMID: 36012084

Traş, Z., & Gökçen, G. (2020). Academic Procrastination and Social Anxiety as Predictive Variables Internet Addiction of Adolescents. *International Education Studies*, 13(9), 23–35. DOI: 10.5539/ies.v13n9p23

Tremblay, M. S., Chaput, J. P., Adamo, K. B., Aubert, S., Barnes, J. D., Choquette, L., Duggan, M., Faulkner, G., Goldfield, G. S., Gray, C. E., Gruber, R., Janson, K., Janssen, I., Janssen, X., Jaramillo Garcia, A., Kuzik, N., LeBlanc, C., MacLean, J., Okely, A. D., & Carson, V. (2017). Canadian 24-hour movement guidelines for the early years (0–4 years): An integration of physical activity, sedentary behaviour, and sleep. *BMC Public Health*, 17(S5, Suppl 5), 874. DOI: 10.1186/s12889-017-4859-6 PMID: 29219102

Trub, L., & Starks, T. J. (2017). Insecure attachments: Attachment, emotional regulation, sexting and condomless sex among women in relationships. *Computers in Human Behavior*, 71, 140–147. DOI: 10.1016/j.chb.2017.01.052

Tsitsika, A., Janikian, M., Schoenmakers, T. M., Tzavela, E. C., Ólafsson, K., Wójcik, S., Macarie, G. F., Tzavara, C., & Richardson, C. (2014). Internet addictive behavior in adolescence: A cross-sectional study in seven European countries. *Cyberpsychology, Behavior, and Social Networking*, 17(8), 528–535. DOI: 10.1089/cyber.2013.0382 PMID: 24853789

Tsitsika, A., Janikian, M., Wójcik, S., Makaruk, K., Tzavela, E., Tzavara, C., Greydanus, D., Merrick, J., & Richardson, C. (2015). Cyberbullying victimization prevalence and associations with internalizing and externalizing problems among adolescents in six European countries. *Computers in Human Behavior*, 51, 1–7. DOI: 10.1016/j.chb.2015.04.048

Turzák, T., Kurincová, B., Hollá, C., & Zelená, D. (2020). Sexting and family environment of children and adolescents. *Ad Alta*, 10(2), 326–330.

Ulusoy, Y., Sumbas, E., & Sertkaya, B. (2023). Psychodrama as an intervention management instrument for internal/external adolescent problems: A systematic literature review. *The Arts in Psychotherapy*, 83, 102000. DOI: 10.1016/j.aip.2023.102000

United Nations. (1989). *Convention on the Rights of the Child*. Retrieved from https://treaties.un.org/doc/Treaties/1990/09/19900902%2003-14%20AM/Ch_IV_11p.pdf

Upenieks, L., Chakraborty, R., & Hill, T. D. (2024). Sin in the Digital Flesh? Religiosity and the Sexting Behavior of Women and Men in the United States. *Journal of Religion and Health*, 63(4), 1–29. DOI: 10.1007/s10943-024-02059-8 PMID: 38753133

Urman, A., & Makhortykh, M. (2024). "Foreign beauties want to meet you": The sexualization of women in Google's organic and sponsored text search results. *New Media & Society*, 26(5), 2932–2953. DOI: 10.1177/14614448221099536

Uslu, M. (2013). Relationship between degrees of self-esteem and peer pressure in high school adolescents. *International Journal of Academic Research*, 5(3), 117–122. DOI: 10.7813/2075-4124.2013/5-3/B.19

Uttarapong, J., Cai, J., & Wohn, D. Y. Y. (2021). Harassment experiences of women and LGBTQ live streamers and how they handled negativity. *IMX 2021 - Proceedings of the 2021 ACM International Conference on Interactive Media Experiences*, 7–19. DOI: 10.1145/3452918.3458794

Valcke, M., Bonte, S., De Wever, B., & Rots, I. (2011). Internet parenting styles and the impact on Internet use of primary school children. *Computers & Education*, 55(2), 454–464. DOI: 10.1016/j.compedu.2010.02.009

Valkenburg, P. M., Krcmar, M., Peeters, A. L., & Marseille, N. M. (1999). Developing a scale to assess three styles of television mediation: "Instructive mediation," "restrictive mediation," and "social coviewing.". *Journal of Broadcasting & Electronic Media*, 43(1), 52–66. DOI: 10.1080/08838159909364474

Valkenburg, P. M., & Peter, J. (2007). Preadolescents' and adolescents' online communication and their closeness to friends. *Developmental Psychology*, 43(2), 267–277. DOI: 10.1037/0012-1649.43.2.267 PMID: 17352538

Valkenburg, P. M., & Peter, J. (2009). The effects of instant messaging on the quality of adolescents' existing friendships: A longitudinal study. *Journal of Communication*, 59(1), 79–97. DOI: 10.1111/j.1460-2466.2008.01405.x

Valkenburg, P. M., & Peter, J. (2011). Online communication among adolescents: An integrated model of its attraction, opportunities, and risks. *The Journal of Adolescent Health*, 48(2), 121–127. DOI: 10.1016/j.jadohealth.2010.08.020 PMID: 21257109

van der Hof, S., Lievens, E., Milkaite, I., Verdoodt, V., Hannema, T., & Liefaard, T. (2020). The child's right to protection against economic exploitation in the digital world. *International Journal of Children's Rights*, 28(4), 833–859. DOI: 10.1163/15718182-28040003

Van Ouytsel, J., Punyanunt-Carter, N. M., Walrave, M., & Ponnet, K. (2020). Sexting within young adults' dating and romantic relationships. *Current Opinion in Psychology*, 36, 55–59. DOI: 10.1016/j.copsyc.2020.04.007 PMID: 32480021

Van Ouytsel, J., Van Gool, E., Walrave, M., Ponnet, K., & Peeters, E. (2017). Sexting: Adolescents' perceptions of the applications used for, motives for, and consequences of sexting. *Journal of Youth Studies*, 20(4), 446–470. DOI: 10.1080/13676261.2016.1241865

Van Ouytsel, J., Walrave, M., & Ponnet, K. (2019). An Exploratory Study of Sexting Behaviors Among Heterosexual and Sexual Minority Early Adolescents. *The Journal of Adolescent Health*, 65(5), 621–626. DOI: 10.1016/j.jadohealth.2019.06.003 PMID: 31473082

Van Ouytsel, J., Walrave, M., & Ponnet, K. (2019). Sexting within adolescents' romantic relationships: How is it related to perceptions of love and verbal conflict? *Computers in Human Behavior*, 97, 216–221. DOI: 10.1016/j.chb.2019.03.029

Van Ouytsel, J., Walrave, M., & Van Gool, E. (2014). Sexting: Between Thrill and Fear—How Schools Can Respond. *The Clearing House: A Journal of Educational Strategies, Issues and Ideas*, 87(5), 204–212. DOI: 10.1080/00098655.2014.918532

Van Rooij, A. J., Kuss, D. J., Griffiths, M. D., Shorter, G. W., Schoenmakers, T. M., & Van de Mheen, D. (2014). The (co-) occurrence of problematic video gaming, substance use, and psychosocial problems in adolescents. *Journal of Behavioral Addictions*, 3(3), 157–165. DOI: 10.1556/JBA.3.2014.013 PMID: 25317339

Van Vleet, M., & Feeney, B. C. (2015). Young at heart: A perspective for advancing research on play in adulthood. *Perspectives on Psychological Science*, 10(5), 639–645. DOI: 10.1177/1745691615596789 PMID: 26386001

Vanden Abeele, M. V., Roe, K., & Eggermont, S. (2012). An exploration of adolescents' sexual contact and conduct risks through mobile phone use. *Communications*, 37(1), 55–77. DOI: 10.1515/commun-2012-0003

VandenAbeele, M., Campbell, S. W., Eggermont, S., & Roe, K. (2014). Sexting, Mobile Porn Use, and Peer Group Dynamics: Boys' and Girls' Self-Perceived Popularity, Need for Popularity, and Perceived Peer Pressure. *Media Psychology*, 17(1), 6–33. DOI: 10.1080/15213269.2013.801725

Vandoninck, S., d'Haenens, L., & Smahel, D. (2014). *Preventive measures: How youngsters avoid online risks*. EU Kids Online. https://eprints.lse.ac.uk/55797/1/EU_Kids_Online_Report_Preventivemeasures.pdf

Vanwesenbeeck, I., Ponnet, K., Walrave, M., & Van Ouytsel, J. (2018). Parents' Role in Adolescents' Sexting Behaviour. In Walrave, M., Van Ouytsel, J., Ponnet, K., & Temple, J. (Eds.), *Sexting. Palgrave Studies in Cyberpsychology*. Palgrave Macmillan. DOI: 10.1007/978-3-319-71882-8_5

Vasilescu, M. D., Serban, A. C., Dimian, G. C., Aceleanu, M. I., & Picatoste, X. (2020). Digital divide, skills and perceptions on digitalisation in the European union-towards a smart labour market. *PLoS One*, 15(4), e0232032. Advance online publication. DOI: 10.1371/journal.pone.0232032 PMID: 32324786

Vasiou, A., Danou, S., & Sideris, A. (2023). Music listening as an emotion regulation strategy of students during COVID-19 lockdown. *Θέματα Επιστημών Αγωγής, 2*(1), 56–66. DOI: 10.12681/thea.30467

Vásquez-Idrovo, J. H., García-Herrera, D. G., Ochoa-Encalada, S. C., & Erazo-Álvarez, J. C. (2020). Ciberbullying y sus factores de riesgo. *Episteme Koinonia*, 3(1), 577. DOI: 10.35381/e.k.v3i1.1028

Vassou, V., Vassiou, A., Stavropoulos, V., & Chaintouti, V. (2017). The relationship between boredom, interpersonal closeness / Bullying and victimization in the school environment. *Psychology and Behavioral Science International Journal*, 6(3), 1–8. DOI: 10.19080/PBSIJ.2017.06.555686

Vauclair, C.-M., Rudnev, M., Hofhuis, J., & Liu, J. H. (2023). Instant messaging and relationship satisfaction across different ages and cultures. *Cyberpsychology (Brno)*, 17(3), 8. Advance online publication. DOI: 10.5817/CP2023-3-8

Vazsonyi, A. T., & Huang, L. (2010). Where self-control comes from: On the development of self-control and its relationship to deviance over time. *Developmental Psychology*, 46(1), 245–257. DOI: 10.1037/a0016538 PMID: 20053021

Vejmelka, L., & Matković, R. (2021). Online interactions and problematic internet use of Croatian students during the COVID-19 pandemic. *Information (Basel)*, 12(10), 399. Advance online publication. DOI: 10.3390/info12100399

Velez-Blasini, C. J. (2008). Evidence against alcohol as a proximal cause of sexual risk taking among college students. *Journal of Sex Research*, 45(2), 118–128. DOI: 10.1080/00224490801987408 PMID: 18569533

Velki, T. & Ivanković, M. (2020). Benefits and dangers of the internet from the perspective of parents of primary school students. *Život i škola. 66*(1), 43–53. https://doi.org/DOI: 10.32903/zs.66.1.4

Verheijen, G. P., Stoltz, S. E., Van de Berg, Y. H., & Cillessen, A. H. (2019). The influence of competitive and cooperative video games on behavior during play and friendship quality in adolescence. *Computers in Human Behavior*, 91, 297–304. DOI: 10.1016/j.chb.2018.10.023

Verma, T. (2019). Managing online video gaming-related addictive behaviors through motivational interviewing. *Indian Journal of Social Psychiatry*, 35(3), 217–219. DOI: 10.4103/ijsp.ijsp_113_18

Verrastro, V., Albanese, C. A., Ritella, G., Gugliandolo, M. C., & Cuzzocrea, F. (2021). Empathy, Social Self-Efficacy, Problematic Internet Use, and Problematic Online Gaming Between Early and Late Adolescence. *Cyberpsychology, Behavior, and Social Networking*, 24(12), 806–814. DOI: 10.1089/cyber.2021.0042 PMID: 34515543

Verrastro, V., Saladino, V., Eleuteri, S., Barberis, N., & Cuzzocrea, F. (2023). Sexting, Self-esteem, and Social Media: A Comparison among Frequent, Occasional, and Non-sexting Italian Adolescent Girls. *Psychology in Russia : State of the Art*, 16(4), 3–20. DOI: 10.11621/PIR.2023.0401 PMID: 38162809

Vijayarani, M., Balamurugan, G., Sevak, S., Gurung, K., Bhuvaneswari, G., Sangeetha, X., Thenmozhi, P., & Tamilselvi, S. (2024). Silent Screams: A Narrative Review of Cyberbullying Among Indian Adolescents. *Cureus*, 16(8), e66292. DOI: 10.7759/cureus.66292 PMID: 39238690

Villacampa, C. (2017). Teen sexting: Prevalence, characteristics and legal treatment. *International Journal of Law, Crime and Justice*, 49, 10–21. DOI: 10.1016/j.ijlcj.2017.01.002

Vincent-Ruz, P., & Schunn, C. D. (2018). The nature of science identity and its role as the driver of student choices. *International Journal of STEM Education*, 5(1), 48. DOI: 10.1186/s40594-018-0140-5 PMID: 30631738

Volkova, I. P., Koroleva, N. N., Bogdanovskaya, I. M., Ikonnikova, G. Y., & Mashkova, A. V. (2019). Problematic internet usage by adolescents with disabilities. *Образование и наука, 21*(9), 98-121.

Vouglanis, T., & Drigas, A. (2022). The internet addiction and the impact on the cognitive, psychological and social side of people's personality with disabilities. *Technium Social Sciences Journal*, 35, 93–110. DOI: 10.47577/tssj.v35i1.7274

Vygotsky, L. S. (1978). *Mind in society: The development of higher psychological processes*. Harvard University Press.

Waasdorp, T., & Bradshaw, C. (2015). The overlap between cyberbullying and traditional bullying. *The Journal of Adolescent Health*, 56(5), 483–488. DOI: 10.1016/j.jadohealth.2014.12.002 PMID: 25631040

Wachs, S., Castellanos, M., Wettstein, A., Bilz, L., & Gámez-Guadix, M. (2023). Associations Between Classroom Climate, Empathy, Self-Efficacy, and Countering Hate Speech Among Adolescents: A Multilevel Mediation Analysis. *Journal of Interpersonal Violence*, 38(5-6), 5067–5091. DOI: 10.1177/08862605221120905 PMID: 36148972

Wachs, S., Gámez-Guadix, M., & Wright, M. F. (2022). Online Hate Speech Victimization and Depressive Symptoms Among Adolescents: The Protective Role of Resilience. *Cyberpsychology, Behavior, and Social Networking*, 25(7), 416–423. DOI: 10.1089/cyber.2022.0009 PMID: 35639126

Wachs, S., & Wright, M. F. (2019). The moderation of online disinhibition and sex on the relationship between online hate victimization and perpetration. *Cyberpsychology, Behavior, and Social Networking*, 22(5), 300–306. DOI: 10.1089/cyber.2018.0551 PMID: 30945942

Wagaman, M. A., Watts, K. J., Lamneck, V., D'Souza, S. A., McInroy, L. B., Eaton, A. D., & Craig, S. (2020). Managing stressors online and offline: LGBTQ+ Youth in the Southern United States. *Children and Youth Services Review*, 110, 104799. Advance online publication. DOI: 10.1016/j.childyouth.2020.104799

Wahl-Jorgensen, K. (2021). The affordances of interview research on Zoom: New intimacies and active listening. *Communication, Culture & Critique*, 14(2), 373–376. DOI: 10.1093/ccc/tcab015

Walker, S., Sanci, L., & Temple-Smith, M. (2013). Sexting: Young women's and men's views on its nature and origins. *The Journal of Adolescent Health*, 52(6), 697–701. DOI: 10.1016/j.jadohealth.2013.01.026 PMID: 23587784

Walrave, M., Heirman, W., & Hallam, L. (2014). Under pressure to sext? Applying the theory of planned behaviour to adolescent sexting. *Behaviour & Information Technology*, 33(1), 86–98. DOI: 10.1080/0144929X.2013.837099

Walrave, M., Ponnet, K., Van Ouytsel, J., Van Gool, E., Heirman, W., & Verbeek, A. (2015). Whether or not to engage in sexting: Explaining adolescent sexting behavior by applying the prototype willingness model. *Telematics and Informatics*, 32(4), 796–808. DOI: 10.1016/j.tele.2015.03.008

Walsh, R. J., Krabbendam, L., Dewinter, J., & Begeer, S. (2018). Brief report: Gender identity differences in autistic adults: Associations with perceptual and socio-cognitive profiles. *Journal of Autism and Developmental Disorders*, 48(12), 4070–4078. DOI: 10.1007/s10803-018-3702-y PMID: 30062396

Walsh, W. A., & Tener, D. (2022). "If you don't send me five other pictures I am going to post the photo online": A qualitative analysis of experiences of survivors of sextortion. *Journal of Child Sexual Abuse*, 31(4), 447–465. DOI: 10.1080/10538712.2022.2067093 PMID: 35445638

Wang, C., Fang, T., & Gu, Y. (2020). Learning performance and behavioral patterns of online collaborative learning: Impact of cognitive load and affordances of different multimedia. *Computers & Education*, 143, 103683. DOI: 10.1016/j.compedu.2019.103683

Wang, F. (2024). Breaking the silence: Examining process of cyber sextortion and victims' coping strategies. *International Review of Victimology*. Advance online publication. DOI: 10.1177/02697580241234331

Wang, J., Iannotti, R. J., & Nansel, T. R. (2009). School bullying among adolescents in the United States: Physical, verbal, relational, and cyber. *The Journal of Adolescent Health*, 45(4), 368–375. DOI: 10.1016/j.jadohealth.2009.03.021 PMID: 19766941

Wang, L., & Jiang, S. (2023). Effectiveness of parent-related interventions on cyberbullying among adolescents: A systematic review and meta-analysis. *Trauma, Violence & Abuse*, 24(5), 3678–3696. DOI: 10.1177/15248380221137065 PMID: 36458864

Wang, L., & Ngai, S. S.-y. (2020). The effects of anonymity, invisibility, asynchrony, and moral disengagement on cyberbullying perpetration among school-aged children in China. *Children and Youth Services Review*, 119, 105613. DOI: 10.1016/j.childyouth.2020.105613

Wang, W., Liu, J., Liu, Y., Wang, P., Guo, Z., Hong, D., & Jiang, S. (2022). Peer relationship and adolescents' smartphone addiction: The mediating role of alienation and the moderating role of sex. *Current Psychology (New Brunswick, N.J.)*, 42(26), 22976–22988. DOI: 10.1007/s12144-022-03309-2

Wang, Y., & Zeng, Y. (2024). Relationship between loneliness and internet addiction: A meta-analysis. *BMC Public Health*, 24(1), 858. DOI: 10.1186/s12889-024-18366-4 PMID: 38504216

Wan, Y. (2023). Is Psychodrama an effective method to intervene high school students social anxiety? *Lecture Notes in Education Psychology and Public Media*, 6(1), 38–46. DOI: 10.54254/2753-7048/6/20220138

Ward, L. M. (2016). Media and sexualization: State of empirical research, 1995–2015. *Journal of Sex Research*, 53(4-5), 560–577. DOI: 10.1080/00224499.2016.1142496 PMID: 26979592

Wardrip, P. S. (2020). Educators enacting online learning support roles in remote educational experiences. *Educational Technology Research and Development*, 69(1), 213–216. DOI: 10.1007/s11423-020-09883-1 PMID: 33250611

Warrier, V., Greenberg, D. M., Weir, E., Buckingham, C., Smith, P., Lai, M.-C., Allison, C., & Baron-Cohen, S. (2020). Elevated rates of autism, other neurodevelopmental and psychiatric diagnoses, and autistic traits in transgender and gender-diverse individuals. *Nature Communications*, 11(1), 3959–3959. DOI: 10.1038/s41467-020-17794-1 PMID: 32770077

Wasserman, D. (2019). A case for greater risk tolerance in Internet use by adults with intellectual disabilities: A comment on Chalghoumi et al. *Ethics & Behavior*, 29(3), 223–226. DOI: 10.1080/10508422.2018.1522256

Watson, E., Milhausen, R., Smoliak, O., & Breen, A. (2018). *How Young Canadian Women Make Sense of their Experiences of Sexting*. Unpublished Doctoral dissertation, The University of Guelph, Guelph, Ontario, Canada. Retrieved July, 15, 2019, from https://atrium.lib.uoguelph.ca/server/api/core/bitstreams/ff78a7e2-8f12-4baa-8e88-f2c773b414d3/content

Watts, L. L., Hamza, E. A., Bedewy, D. A., & Moustafa, A. A. (2023). A meta-analysis study on peer influence and adolescent substance use. *Current Psychology (New Brunswick, N.J.)*, 43(5), 3866–3881. DOI: 10.1007/s12144-023-04944-z

We Are Social. (2023). *Global digital report 2023*. Retrieved from https://datareportal.com/reports/digital-2023-global-overview-report

Weber, R., Eggenberger, L., Stosch, C., & Walther, A. (2022). Gender Differences in Attachment Anxiety and Avoidance and Their Association with Psychotherapy Use-Examining Students from a German University. *Behavioral Sciences (Basel, Switzerland)*, 12(7), 204. Advance online publication. DOI: 10.3390/bs12070204 PMID: 35877274

Wei, H.-S., Hsieh, Y.-P., Chen, Y.-F., Ma, J. K.-H., & Lin, Y.-S. (2024). (in press). Prevalence and associated factors of sexting among Taiwanese adolescents. *Behavioral Sciences & the Law*. Advance online publication. DOI: 10.1002/bsl.2697 PMID: 39267296

Weinstein, E., & James, C. (2022). School-based initiatives promoting digital citizenship and healthy digital media use. In Nesi, J., Telzer, E. H., & Prinstein, M. J. (Eds.), *Handbook of adolescent digital media use and mental health* (Vol. 1, pp. 365–388). Cambridge University Press., DOI: 10.1017/9781108976237.020

Weir, E., Allison, C., & Baron-Cohen, S. (2021a). The sexual health, orientation, and activity of autistic adolescents and adults. *Autism Research*, 14(11), 2342–2354. DOI: 10.1002/aur.2604 PMID: 34536071

Weir, E., Allison, C., & Baron-Cohen, S. (2021b). Understanding the substance use of autistic adolescents and adults: A mixed-methods approach. *The Lancet. Psychiatry*, 8(8), 673–685. DOI: 10.1016/S2215-0366(21)00160-7 PMID: 34217427

Weisskirch, R. S., & Delevi, R. (2011). "Sexting" and adult romantic attachment. *Computers in Human Behavior*, 27(5), 1697–1701. DOI: 10.1016/j.chb.2011.02.008

Weisskirch, R. S., Drouin, M., & Delevi, R. (2017). Relational anxiety and sexting. *Journal of Sex Research*, 54(6), 685–693. DOI: 10.1080/00224499.2016.1181147 PMID: 27247026

Weiss, N. H., Sullivan, T. P., & Tull, M. T. (2015). Explicating the role of emotion dysregulation in risky behaviors: A review and synthesis of the literature with directions for future research and clinical practice. *Current Opinion in Psychology*, 3, 22–29. DOI: 10.1016/j.copsyc.2015.01.013 PMID: 25705711

Weiss, R., & Samenow, C. P. (2010). Smart Phones, Social Networking, Sexting and Problematic Sexual Behaviors—A Call for Research. *Sexual Addiction & Compulsivity*, 17(4), 241–246. DOI: 10.1080/10720162.2010.532079

Wenger, E. (1998). *Communities of Practice: Learning, Meaning, and Identity*. Cambridge University Press. DOI: 10.1017/CBO9780511803932

Wernicke, J., & Montag, C. (2022). Linking gaming disorder tendencies in children to their personality and parental gaming behavior. *Frontiers in Psychiatry*, 12, 748195. DOI: 10.3389/fpsyt.2021.748195 PMID: 35250648

Whiteside, S. P., & Lynam, D. R. (2001). The five factor model and impulsivity: Using a structural model of personality to understand impulsivity. *Personality and Individual Differences*, 30(4), 669–689. DOI: 10.1016/S0191-8869(00)00064-7

Whitney, J., Maslyanskaya, S., & Hultgren, M. (2020). Technology/Sexting/Social Media. In Titchen, K., & Miller, E. (Eds.), *Medical Perspectives on Human Trafficking in Adolescents* (pp. 113–125). Springer., DOI: 10.1007/978-3-030-43367-3_6

Whitty, M. T. (2003). Cyber-flirting: Playing at love on the Internet. *Theory & Psychology*, 13(3), 339–357. DOI: 10.1177/0959354303013003003

Widmer, E. D., Treas, J., & Newcomb, R. (1998). Attitudes toward nonmarital sex in 24 countries. *Journal of Sex Research*, 35(4), 349–358. DOI: 10.1080/00224499809551953

Willard, N. (2007). *Cyberbullying and Cyberthreats: Responding to the Challenge of Online Social Aggression, Threats, and Distress*. Research Press.

Williams, K. R., & Guerra, N. G. (2007). Prevalence and Predictors of Internet Bullying. *The Journal of Adolescent Health*, 41(6), S14–S21. DOI: 10.1016/j.jadohealth.2007.08.018 PMID: 18047941

Williams, L. R., & Anthony, E. K. (2015). A model of positive family and peer relationships on adolescent functioning. *Journal of Child and Family Studies*, 24(3), 658–667. DOI: 10.1007/s10826-013-9876-1

Williams, R. S., & Schmidt, A. (2014). The sales and marketing practices of English-language internet alcohol vendors. *Addiction (Abingdon, England)*, 109(3), 432–439. DOI: 10.1111/add.12411 PMID: 24219065

Williford, A., Elledge, L. C., Boulton, A. J., DePaolis, K. J., Little, T. D., & Salmivalli, C. (2013). Effects of the KiVa Antibullying Program on cyberbullying and cybervictimization frequency among Finnish youth. *Journal of Clinical Child and Adolescent Psychology*, 42(6), 1–14. DOI: 10.1080/15374416.2013.787623 PMID: 23659182

Windle, M. (1994). Substance use, risky behaviors, and victimization among a US national adolescent sample. *Addiction (Abingdon, England)*, 89(2), 175–182. DOI: 10.1111/j.1360-0443.1994.tb00876.x PMID: 8173483

Winkelman, S. B., Smith, K. V., Brinkley, J., & Knox, D. (2014). Sexting on the College Campus. *The Electronic Journal of Human Sexuality*, 17.

Winston, R. B., Vahala, M. E., Nichols, E. C., & Gillis, M. E. (1994). A measure of college classroom climate: The College Classroom Environment Scales. *Journal of College Student Development*, 35(1), 11–18.

Wisniewski, P., Ghosh, A. K., Rosson, M. B., Xu, H., & Carroll, J. M. (2017). Parental control vs. teen self-regulation: Is there a middle ground for mobile online safety? In *Proceedings of the 2017 ACM Conference on Computer Supported Cooperative Work and Social Computing* (pp. 51-69). ACM. https://doi.org/DOI: 10.1145/2998181.2998352

Wisniewski, P., Xu, H., Rosson, M. B., & Carroll, J. M. (2017). Parents just don't understand: Why teens don't talk to parents about their online risk experiences. In *Proceedings of the 2017 ACM Conference on Computer Supported Cooperative Work and Social Computing* (pp. 523-540). ACM. https://doi.org/ DOI: 10.1145/2998181.2998236

Wolak, J. & Finkelhor, D. (2011). *Sexting: A typology*. Crimes against Children Research Center.

Wolak, J., & Finkelhor, D. (2011). 'Sexting: A typology'. *Research Bulletin, University of New Hampshire: Crimes Against Children Research Center*. Retrieved July, 15, 2013, from https://scholars.unh.edu/ccrc/48/

Wolak, J., Finkelhor, D., & Mitchell, K. (2012). How often are teens arrested for sexting? Data from a national sample of police cases. *Pediatrics*, 129(1), 4–12. DOI: 10.1542/peds.2011-2242 PMID: 22144707

Wolak, J., Finkelhor, D., Walsh, W., & Treitman, L. (2018). Sextortion of Minors: Characteristics and Dynamics. *The Journal of Adolescent Health*, 62(1), 72–79. DOI: 10.1016/j.jadohealth.2017.08.014 PMID: 29055647

Wölfer, R., Schultze-Krumbholz, A., Zagorscak, P., Jäkel, A., Göbel, K., & Scheithauer, H. (2014). Prevention 2.0: Targeting Cyberbullying @ School. *Prevention Science*, 15(6), 879–887. DOI: 10.1007/s11121-013-0438-y PMID: 24122481

Wolters, C. A., Won, S., & Hussain, M. (2017). Examining the relations of time management and procrastination within a model of self-regulated learning. *Metacognition and Learning*, 12(3), 381–399. DOI: 10.1007/s11409-017-9174-1

Wood, R. T. A. (2008). Problems with the concept of video game "addiction": Some case study examples. *International Journal of Mental Health and Addiction*, 6(2), 169–178. DOI: 10.1007/s11469-007-9118-0

Wood, W., & Eagly, A. H. (2012). Biosocial construction of sex differences and similarities in behavior. *Advances in Experimental Social Psychology*, 46, 55–123. DOI: 10.1016/B978-0-12-394281-4.00002-7

Woo, H. L. (2009). Designing multimedia learning environments using animated pedagogical agents: Factors and issues. *Journal of Computer Assisted Learning*, 25(3), 203–218. DOI: 10.1111/j.1365-2729.2008.00299.x

Woolard, A. (2011). *The frequency, attitudes, and beliefs of sexting among college students*. Unpublished Master's thesis, Eastern Illinois University. Retrieved July, 15, 2013, from https://thekeep.eiu.edu/cgi/viewcontent.cgi?article=1837&context=theses

World Congress: Child Dignity in the Digital World. (2017, October 6). *The Declaration of Rome*. Retrieved from https://www.childdignity.com/declaration-of-rome

World Health Organization. (2019). *Guidelines on physical activity, sedentary behaviour and sleep for children under 5 years of age*. Retrieved from https://www.who.int/publications/i/item/9789241550536

World Health Organization. (2024) Retrived from https://icd.who.int/browse/2024-01/mms/en#338347362

World Health Organization. (2024, May 13). *Autism*. https://www.who.int/news-room/fact-sheets/detail/autism-spectrum-disorders

Wright, M., & Wachs, S. (2023). Cyberbullying Involvement and Depression among Elementary School, Middle School, High School, and University Students: The Role of Social Support and Gender. *International Journal of Environmental Research and Public Health*, 20(4), 2835. DOI: 10.3390/ijerph20042835 PMID: 36833529

Wrzesińska, M. A., Tabała, K., & Stecz, P. (2021). Gaming Behaviors among Polish Students with Visual Impairment. *International Journal of Environmental Research and Public Health*, 18(4), 1545. DOI: 10.3390/ijerph18041545 PMID: 33561942

Wysocki, D. K., & Childers, C. D. (2011). "Let my fingers do the talking": Sexting and infidelity in cyberspace. *Sexuality & Culture*, 15(3), 217–239. DOI: 10.1007/s12119-011-9091-4

Xefteris, S., Palaigeorgiou, G., & Tsorbari, A. (2019). A Learning Environment for Geography and History Using Mixed Reality, Tangible Interfaces and Educational Robotics. In Auer, M., & Tsiatsos, T. (Eds.), *The Challenges of the Digital Transformation in Education. ICL 2018. Advances in Intelligent Systems and Computing* (Vol. 917). Springer. DOI: 10.1007/978-3-030-11935-5_11

Xia, X. (2020). Learning behavior mining and decision recommendation based on association rules in interactive learning environment. *Interactive Learning Environments*, 1–16. DOI: 10.1080/10494820.2020.1799028

Xiuqin, H., Huimin, Z., Mengchen, L., Jinan, W., Ying, Z., & Ran, T. (2010). Mental health, personality, and parental rearing styles of adolescents with Internet addiction disorder. *Cyberpsychology, Behavior, and Social Networking*, 13(4), 401–406. DOI: 10.1089/cyber.2009.0222 PMID: 20712498

Yalcin, H., Guvener, E., & Kasal, D. (2020). Relationship between gifted children's internet gaming addiction and quality of life. *European Journal of Special Education Research*, 6(4), 1–21.

Yalçın-Irmak, A. & Erdoğan, S. (2016). Ergen ve genç erişkinlerde dijital oyun bağımlılığı: güncel bir bakış. *Türk Psikiyatri Dergisi, 27*(2), 128-37. Retrieved from https://www.turkpsikiyatri.com/PDF/C27S2/07.pdf

Yamada, M., Sekine, M., & Tatsuse, T. (2018). Parental internet use and lifestyle factors as correlates of prolonged screen time of children in Japan: Results from the super Shokuiku school project. *Journal of Epidemiology*, 28(10), 407–413. DOI: 10.2188/jea.JE20170100 PMID: 29576604

Yamamoto, M., Mezawa, H., Sakurai, K., Mori, C., Kamijima, M., Yamazaki, S., Ohya, Y., Kishi, R., Yaegashi, N., Hashimoto, K., Mori, C., Ito, S., Yamagata, Z., Inadera, H., Nakayama, T., Sobue, T., Shima, M., Kageyama, S., Suganuma, N., & Katoh, T.Japan Environment and Children's Study Group. (2023). Screen time and developmental performance among children at 1-3 years of age in the Japan Environment and Children's Study. *JAMA Pediatrics*, 177(11), 1168–1175. DOI: 10.1001/jamapediatrics.2023.3643 PMID: 37721733

Yang, B., Wang, B., Sun, N., Xu, F., Wang, L., Chen, J., Yu, S., Zhang, Y., Zhu, Y., Dai, T., Zhang, Q., & Sun, C. (2021). The consequences of cyberbullying and traditional bullying victimization among adolescents: Gender differences in psychological symptoms, self-harm and suicidality. *Psychiatry Research*, 306, 114219. Advance online publication. DOI: 10.1016/j.psychres.2021.114219 PMID: 34614443

Yan, H., Chen, J., & Huang, J. (2019). School Bullying Among Left-Behind Children: The Efficacy of Art Therapy on Reducing Bullying Victimization. *Frontiers in Psychiatry*, 10, 40. Advance online publication. DOI: 10.3389/fpsyt.2019.00040 PMID: 30792670

Yao, Y. W., Chen, P. R., Chen, C., Wang, L. J., Zhang, J. T., Xue, G., Deng, L.-Y., Liu, Q.-X., Yip, S. W., & Fang, X.-Y. (2014). Failure to utilize feedback causes decision-making deficits among excessive Internet gamers. *Psychiatry Research*, 219(3), 583–588. DOI: 10.1016/j.psychres.2014.06.033 PMID: 25024056

Ybarra, M. L., & Mitchell, K. J. (2004). Online aggressor/targets, aggressors, and targets: A comparison of associated youth characteristics. *Journal of Child Psychology and Psychiatry, and Allied Disciplines*, 45(7), 1308–1316. DOI: 10.1111/j.1469-7610.2004.00328.x PMID: 15335350

Ybarra, M. L., & Mitchell, K. J. (2014). "Sexting" and its relation to sexual activity and sexual risk behavior in a national survey of adolescents. *The Journal of Adolescent Health*, 55(6), 757–764. DOI: 10.1016/j.jadohealth.2014.07.012 PMID: 25266148

Ybarra, M. L., Mitchell, K. J., Palmer, N. A., & Reisner, S. L. (2015a). Online social support as a buffer against online and offline peer and sexual victimization among U.S. LGBT and non-LGBT youth. *Child Abuse & Neglect*, 39, 123–136. DOI: 10.1016/j.chiabu.2014.08.006 PMID: 25192961

Yen, J. Y., Ko, C. H., Yen, C. F., Wu, H. Y., & Yang, M. J. (2007). The comorbid psychiatric symptoms of internet addiction: Attention deficit and hyperactivity disorder (ADHD), depression, social phobia, and hostility. *The Journal of Adolescent Health*, 41(1), 93–98. DOI: 10.1016/j.jadohealth.2007.02.002 PMID: 17577539

Yépez-Tito, P., Ferragut, M., & Blanca, M. J. (2020). Sexting in adolescence: The use of technology and parental supervision. *Revista Latinoamericana de Psicología*, 52, 115–130. DOI: 10.14349/rlp.2020.v52.12

Yeşilay. (2023). Teknoloji bağımlılığı. Retrieved from https://www.yesilay.org.tr/tr/bagimlilik/teknoloji-bagimliligi

Yeung, T. H., Horyniak, D. R., Vella, A. M., Hellard, M. E., & Lim, M. S. (2014). Prevalence, correlates and attitudes towards sexting among young people in Melbourne, Australia. *Sexual Health*, 11(4), 332–339. DOI: 10.1071/SH14032 PMID: 25087581

Yilmaz, E., Yel, S., & Griffiths, M. D. (2018). The Impact of Heavy(Excessive) Video Gaming Students on Peers and Teachers in the School Environment: A Qualitative Study, *5*(2), 147–161. https://core.ac.uk/download/pdf/161338199.pdf

Yilmaz, R., & Kilic-Cakmak, E. (2012). Educational interface agents as social models to influence learner achievement, attitude and retention of learning. *Computers & Education*, 59(2), 828–838. DOI: 10.1016/j.compedu.2012.03.020

Yisa, V., & Orji, R. (2024). Hidden desires, echoed distress: Dissecting Nigeria's sexting landscape and its ties to depression. *Computers in Human Behavior*, 161, 108420. DOI: 10.1016/j.chb.2024.108420

Yoder, J., Hansen, J., & Precht, M. (2018). Correlates and outcomes associated with sexting among justice involved youth: The role of developmental adversity, emotional disinhibitions, relationship context, and dating violence. *Children and Youth Services Review*, 94, 493–499. DOI: 10.1016/j.childyouth.2018.08.020

Yogman, M., Garner, A., Hutchinson, J., Hirsh-Pasek, K., & Golinkoff, R. (2018). The power of play: A pediatric role in enhancing development in young children. *Pediatrics*, 142(3), e20182058. DOI: 10.1542/peds.2018-2058 PMID: 30126932

Yoo, H. J., Cho, S. C., Ha, J., Yune, S. K., Kim, S. J., Hwang, J., Chung, A., Sung, Y. H., & Lyoo, I. K. (2004). Attention deficit hyperactivity symptoms and internet addiction. *Psychiatry and Clinical Neurosciences*, 58(5), 487–494. DOI: 10.1111/j.1440-1819.2004.01290.x PMID: 15482579

York, L., MacKenzie, A., & Purdy, N. (2021). Sexting and institutional discourses of child protection: The views of young people and providers of relationship and sex education. *British Educational Research Journal*, 47(6), 1717–1734. DOI: 10.1002/berj.3751

Yosep, I., Hikmat, R., & Mardhiyah, A. (2023). School-based nursing interventions for preventing bullying and reducing its incidence on students: A Scoping review. *International Journal of Environmental Research and Public Health*, 20(2), 1577. DOI: 10.3390/ijerph20021577 PMID: 36674330

Younes, F., Halawi, G., Jabbour, H., El Osta, N., Karam, L., Hajj, A., & Rabbaa Khabbaz, L. (2016). Internet addiction and relationships with insomnia, anxiety, depression, stress and self-esteem in university students: A cross-sectional designed study. *PLoS One*, 11(9), e0161126. DOI: 10.1371/journal.pone.0161126 PMID: 27618306

Young, K. S. (1998). Internet addiction: The emergence of a new clinical disorder. *Cyberpsychology & Behavior*, 1(3), 237–244. DOI: 10.1089/cpb.1998.1.237

Young, K. S. (1999). Internet addiction: Evaluation and treatment. *BMJ (Clinical Research Ed.)*, 319(Suppl S4), 9910351. Advance online publication. DOI: 10.1136/sbmj.9910351

Yount, K. M., Gram, L., & Peterman, A. (2024). Is intimate partner violence declining? It's still an open question. *The Lancet. Global Health*, 12(4), e559. DOI: 10.1016/S2214-109X(23)00599-5 PMID: 38485422

Yurdakul, Y., & Ayhan, A. B. (2023). The effect of the cyberbullying awareness program on adolescents' awareness of cyberbullying and their coping skills. *Current Psychology (New Brunswick, N.J.)*, 42(28), 24208–24222. DOI: 10.1007/s12144-022-03483-3 PMID: 35935748

Yu, S., & Liu, H. (2023). Longitudinal detection of directed motivational currents in L2 learning: Motivated behaviours and emotional responses. *Current Psychology (New Brunswick, N.J.)*, 43(8), 7497–7510. DOI: 10.1007/s12144-023-04945-y

Zaeske, L. M., Harris, T. P., Williams, A., Long, H., Kerr, B. A., & Birdnow, M. (2022). Adolescent technology-use and creative activities during COVID-19: A qualitative study. *Thinking Skills and Creativity*, 46, e101190. Advance online publication. DOI: 10.1016/j.tsc.2022.101190 PMID: 36405976

Zagloul, N. M., Farghaly, R. M., ELKhatib, H., Issa, S. Y., & El-Zoghby, S. M. (2022). Technology facilitated sexual violence: A comparative study between working and non-working females in Egypt before and during the COVID-19 pandemic. *Egyptian Journal of Forensic Sciences*, 12(1), 1–11. DOI: 10.1186/s41935-022-00278-2 PMID: 35433051

Zagorscak, P., Schultze-Krumbholz, A., Heinrich, M., Wölfer, R., & Scheithauer, H. (2018). Efficacy of cyberbullying prevention on somatic symptoms—Randomized controlled trial applying a reasoned action approach. *Journal of Research on Adolescence*, 28(4), 1232–1249. DOI: 10.1111/jora.12429 PMID: 29974545

Zajac, K., Ginley, M. K., Chang, R., & Petry, N. M. (2017). Treatments for Internet gaming disorder and Internet addiction: A systematic review. *Psychology of Addictive Behaviors*, 31(8), 979–994. DOI: 10.1037/adb0000315 PMID: 28921996

Zaragas, C. K. (2021). The psychodrama and its contribution to the children's competitive confrontation. Case Study. *Cultural-historical Psychology*, 17(3), 143–151. DOI: 10.17759/chp.2021170318

Zatrahadi, M. F., Darmawati, D., & Yusra, N. N. (2021). The Effect of Online Game Addiction on Adjustment Social in Adolescents. *Indonesian Journal of Creative Counseling*, 1(1), 15–19. https://doi.org/http://doi.org/10.47679/ijcc.v1i1.93

Zengin, H., Çaka, Y. S., & Çınar, N. (2017). AMES is a reliable and valid measurement tool of empathy and sympathy for Turkish adolescents. It provides a significant advantage compared to existing measurement tools by distinguishing affective empathy, cognitive empathy and sympathy. *Anatolian Journal of Psychiatry*, 19(2), 184–192. DOI: 10.5455/apd.262004

Zhang, J., & Zeng, Y. (2024). Effect of college students' smartphone addiction on academic achievement: The mediating role of academic anxiety and moderating role of sense of academic control. *Psychology Research and Behavior Management*, 17, 933–944. DOI: 10.2147/PRBM.S442924 PMID: 38464809

Zhang, X., Abbas, J., Shahzad, M. F., Shankar, A., Ercisli, S., & Dobhal, D. C. (2024). Association between social media use and students' academic performance through family bonding and collective learning: The moderating role of mental well-being. *Education and Information Technologies*, 29(11), 14059–14089. DOI: 10.1007/s10639-023-12407-y

Zhang, Y., Qin, X., & Ren, P. (2018). Adolescents' academic engagement mediates the association between Internet addiction and academic achievement: The moderating effect of classroom achievement norm. *Computers in Human Behavior*, 89, 299–307. DOI: 10.1016/j.chb.2018.08.018

Zhao, H., Weng, H., Weng, Q., Huang, Z., & Soon, K. C. (2022). Teachers' management of cyberbullying on China's social media sites: A case study in Shandong Province, China. *Cogent Education, 9*(1), 2127502. https://doi.org/mw5p

Zhao, L. (2021). Social media addiction and its impact on college student's academic performance: The Mediating role of stress. *The Asia-Pacific Education Researcher*, 32(1), 81–90. DOI: 10.1007/s40299-021-00635-0

Zhao, L., & Yu, J. (2021). A Meta-Analytic Review of Moral Disengagement and Cyberbullying. *Frontiers in Psychology*, 12, 681299. DOI: 10.3389/fpsyg.2021.681299 PMID: 34916984

Zheng, L. (2016). The effectiveness of self-regulated learning scaffolds on academic performance in computer-based learning environments: A meta-analysis. *Asia Pacific Education Review*, 17(2), 187–202. DOI: 10.1007/s12564-016-9426-9

Zhou, N., & Fang, X.-Y. (2015). Beyond peer contagion: Unique and interactive effects of multiple peer influences on internet addiction among Chinese adolescents. *Computers in Human Behavior*, 50, 231–238. DOI: 10.1016/j.chb.2015.03.083

Zhu, C., Huang, S., Evans, R., & Zhang, W. (2021). Cyberbullying among adolescents and children: A comprehensive review of the global situation, risk factors, and preventive measures. *Frontiers in Public Health*, 9, 634909. DOI: 10.3389/fpubh.2021.634909 PMID: 33791270

Zuckerman, M. (1990). The psychophysiology of sensation seeking. *Journal of Personality*, 58(1), 313–345. DOI: 10.1111/j.1467-6494.1990.tb00918.x PMID: 2198341

Zych, I., Ortega-Ruiz, R., & Rey, R. (2015). Systematic review of theoretical studies on bullying and cyberbullying: Facts, knowledge, prevention, and intervention. *Aggression and Violent Behavior*, 23, 1–21. DOI: 10.1016/j.avb.2015.10.001

About the Contributors

Thanos Touloupis is an Assistant Professor of "Educational Psychology" at the Department of Primary Education of the University of the Aegean (Greece). He graduated from the Department of Primary Education of the University of Thessaly, while he followed Master's, Doctoral and Postdoctoral studies at the Department of Psychology of the Aristotle University of Thessaloniki (Section of Developmental and School Psychology). He has worked as a Laboratory Teaching Staff (E.D.I.P.) of "Educational Psychology" at the Department of Psychology of the University of Western Macedonia (Greece), and as a contractual Lecturer/Academic Scholar at Higher Educational Institutions in both Greece and Cyprus. Furthermore, he has many years of teaching experience in Primary Schools of Mainstream and Special Education. His research interests focus on problematic online behavior of school and university student populations with and without special educational needs, as well as on socio-emotional and academic factors associated with this behavior. Additionally, he is interested in the interdisciplinary implementation of related prevention programs in the school community. His scientific work has been published and presented in international and Greek scientific journals and conferences respectively. More details about his research work can be found on https://scholar.google.com/citations?user=OED8_W4AAAAJ&hl=el.

Alivisos (Loisos) Sofos is Professor of "Pedagogy, Media Education and Didactics" at the Department of Primary Education, University of the Aegean, Greece (Short presentation in English https://www.lsofos.com/info/). His teaching subjects involve pedagogy, media education, distance education, eLearning, digital literacy and digital video in education, at the Department of Primary Education, University of the Aegean as well as "distance education" in several postgraduate programs in Greece (Aegean University, National and Kapodistrian University of Athens, Open University in Greece). He is director of the experimental schools in Rhodes and the e-Learning team for the development of Lifelong learning programs at the University of the Aegean. Lastly, he is the director of the "Psychology, Pedagogical Research and Media in Education" laboratory and along with his research team (Media Pedagogy Research Group, https://www.mediapedagogy.gr) participates in several European programs. From 1996 to 2003 he has served as a teaching staff member at the Pedagogical Department of the Johannes Gutenberg-Universität in Germany, a research associate at the Jugendschutz net (Central agency for Safer Internet) of the 16 Federal Lands of Germany, as well as a contract lecturer at several university departments in Germany (Mainz, Wiesbaden, Frankfurt, Landau-Koblenz). His relevant publications have appeared in German, Greek, Polish and English https://www.lsofos.com/bivlia/.

Aikaterini Vasiou is an Assistant Professor of "Methodological approaches in Educational Psychology" at the Department of Primary Education of University of Crete (Greece). She holds a PhD in Educational Psychology from the Department of Primary Education of the University of Thessaly, while as part of an

Excellence scholarship she conducted a post-doctoral research in School Psychology and Counseling at the Department of Primary Education of the University of Western Macedonia (Greece). She has participated in an Experimental Study research program of the Kapodistrian University of Athens (Greece) and in Mental Health research programs of University of the Aegean (Greece). She has worked as a Laboratory Teaching Staff (E.D.I.P.) at the Department of Primary Education of the University of Western Macedonia (Greece), and as a contractual Lecturer/Academic Scholar of Higher Educational Institutions in both Greece and Cyprus. She has also many years of teaching experience in Secondary Schools. Her research interests include social and emotional learning, social and individual predictors of students' outcomes, as well as students' well-being. More details about her research work can be found on: https://scholar.google.com/citationshl=el&user=U02mUZMAAAAJ&view_op=list_works &sortby=pubdate.

* * *

Layan Abdullah has a bachelor's degree in Language and a master's degree in Teaching English to Speakers of other Languages (TESOL). She has15 years of teaching experience in Lebanon, Saudi Arabia, and the United Arab Emirates and a career trajectory that included the areas of teacher development, school improvement, curriculum design, and school evaluation. Her research interests were initially second language acquisition, contrastive analysis, and language interference. However, raising a son with autism has sparked a new interest in special education and is currently working on her PhD in Special Education at the United Arab Emirates University. her research interests expanded to include communication and language skills in children with autism hoping to continue to provide support for children and educators in the field.

Servet Altan joined MEF University, Faculty of Education in July 2022. He has been serving as IBEC Coordinator since 2022 and Vice Dean since September 2023. Having completed his Master's and Doctorate studies at Bilkent University, Dr. Altan served in various roles in K12 schools implementing international programs between 2007-2022. He has been continuing teacher training in national and international schools as an International Baccalaureate Lead Educator since 2016. He has published his research in leading journals in his field such as Journal of Teacher Education, Teaching and Teacher Education and Journal of Experimental Education. He continues to serve in various roles and present conferences in AERA and EARLI organizations.

Alexia Andreopoulou is a psychologist specializing in social and clinical psychology. She holds a degree from the University of Ulster and a PhD from the University of Kent. She has worked in psychiatric hospital departments, mental health centers, and supported employment programs. She has served as a researcher at the University of Kent and as a lecturer in academic institutions. Additionally, she has published research and participated in international scientific journals and conferences.

Blanca Berral-Ortiz graduated in Early Childhood Education from the University of Granada, obtaining an average grade of 9,161. She got the paid award for "best records" for the 2019-2020 academic year. She obtained the University Master's Degree in Research and Innovation in Curriculum and Training (University of Granada). She received a Collaboration Grant from the Ministry of Education in the Department of Didactics and School Organization. Likewise, she was granted a scholarship for

Initiation to Research in Master's degree in the same department at the University of Granada. Linked to both scholarships, she has carried out various publications such as articles, book chapters (Dykinson and Octaedro) focused mainly on active methodologies, ICT, social networks, appropriate or abusive use of technologies, among others. In the same way, she has participated in congresses both as an assistant, collaborator and scientific committee and as a communications director. Also, she has collaborated in several innovation projects at the University of Granada. ORCID ID: https://orcid.org/0000-0001-8139-8468.

Marilyn Campbell is a professor in the school of Early Childhood and Inclusive Education in the Faculty of Education. Her main teaching area is in the Masters of School Guidance and Counselling and in the Masters of Educational and Developmental Psychology. Prior to this appointment Marilyn worked as a teacher for 20 years in early childhood, primary and secondary schools. Subsequently she became a registered psychologist and worked as a school counsellor, mainly with young children in early childhood and primary school settings, assessing children and providing counselling and intervention strategies to both parents and teachers. She then supervised both school counsellors and psychologists working in educational settings. Marilyn Campbell's research expertise is in anxiety disorders in children and adolescents and in bullying, especially cyberbullying. She also researches in mental health issues for young people involving web based counselling and promoting resilience in intellectually disabled children and adults. Marilyn has also published papers on international pre-service teachers. She is a registered psychologist and teacher. Marilyn has expertise in quantitative design methodology. She has authored over 200 publications, is the recipient of a number of professional awards, as well as over a million dollars in grants. Dr Campbell was team leader on a consultancy project with adults with an intellectual disability and challenging behaviours, was chief investigator on two ARC linkage grants, one on cyberbullying and the other on online school counselling and an investigator on an ARC Discovery grant on resilience in intellectually impaired children. She is currently a chief investigator on an NHMRC grant investigating the prevention of bullying using motivational interviewing. She is also an Australian Research Council assessor and NHMRC assessor, as well as assessing for AHRC in the United Kingdom; the Israel Science Foundation Social Sciences and Humanities; the Research Council of Canada; the Romanian Executive Agency.

Maria Efstratopoulou is the Head of the Department of Special and Gifted Education, College of Education, United Arab Emirates University. Her research interests are on Autism and Assessment and Diagnosis for children with Emotional, Behavioral and Developmental disorders and Intervention Strategies for professionals and families. She is an Active researcher in the field of Autism, ADHD, Eating Disorders and Psychological Support to Families. She is a Core member of The European Framework on Psychomotor Assessment for Children (EFP) – Research Unit. She is the author of 5 books and several research articles on Children's behaviour, education and health.

Georgia Gkantona is a psychologist, Assistant Professor of Counseling Psychology at the Department of Psychology of the University of Ioannina. Her research interests are centred on the investigation of the individuals internal dialogicality, the development, implementation and evaluation of intervention methods and techniques based on the Systems Approach or the Dialogical Self Theory and the study of counseling or therapeutic processes based on dialogical approaches. At the same time, she deals with research that adopts a gender perspective, such as gender-based online violence. She has published her work in scientific journals and presented it at conferences.

Maria Kladaki is an Associate Professor at the Department of Primary Education at the University of the Aegean, specializing in "Drama Education in Primary Education." She has studied pedagogical and social sciences in Greece, and her teaching focuses on the pedagogy of theater, theater for young audiences, the convergence of applied theater and digital media in education, and gender relations in drama education, among other topics. Her scholarly work includes books and edited volumes, publications in scientific journals, contributions to collective volumes and conference proceedings, as well as participation in research projects and artistic works centered on theater and culture.

Alejandro Martínez Menéndez was granted a Research Initiation Scholarship from the University of Granada during 2023, developing his first approaches to educational research focusing on the relevance and potential of videogames as an educational resource. During the following year, 2024, he received a Collaboration Scholarship from the Spanish Ministry of Education and Professional Training, associated with the Department of Didactics and School Organization at the University of Granada, institution in which he attended the bachelor's degree in Primary Education program between the years of 2020 and 2024. During that time, he has participated in various scientific meetings and congresses both as a collaborating author as well as part of the organizational committee. Additionally, he has co-authored numerous works related to educational technology, active methodologies, school organization and attention to diversity, edited by the Dykinson publishing house.

Konstantinos Mastrothanasis holds a PhD from the Department of Primary Education at the University of the Aegean and is a postdoctoral researcher at the Medical School of the National and Kapodistrian University of Athens. He is an adjunct professor at the University of the Aegean and at the School of Pedagogical and Technological Education. Dr. Mastrothanasis has participated in European research projects and teacher training programs. His studies have been published in reputable journals, monographs, conference proceedings, and edited volumes. He has been awarded by the Institute of Humanities and Social Sciences and the Scientific Association for the Promotion of Educational Innovation for his research contributions.

Aristea Mavrogianni is a postdoctoral researcher at the Department of Primary Education, University of Crete, Greece, specializing in cognitive load, interactive learning environments and pedagogical agents in mobile learning. She obtained her PhD from the University of Crete, receiving the Excellent PhD Dissertation Award in 2023 for her research on metacognitive strategy development through interactive learning systems. As part of her doctoral studies, she designed, implemented and evaluated Geo-Histor, an interactive learning environment for teaching expository texts. She has also validated two psychometric instruments in Greek: the MARSI-2fR (Metacognitive Awareness Reading Strategies Inventory) and the EDIS scale for assessing students' attitudes towards History. She has a degree in History and Archaeology from the Aristotle University of Thessaloniki and completed Postgraduate Studies in Prehistoric Archaeology, graduating with distinction. She has been an adjunct lecturer at the Department of Philosophy of the University of Crete since 2023. She has presented numerous papers at national and international conferences, contributed book chapters and published in peer-reviewed journals. She has also served on organizing committees for international conferences, edited proceedings, and reviewed for international journals.

Fotis Ntagkas studied Psychology (BSc) in the University of Crete and continued his studies in Child and Adolescent Psychology (MSc) in Leiden, Holland. Currently he is trained in systemic/family psychotherapy and he works as a psychologist at the Center of Systemic Therapy & Counselling (KE.Sy.T.H.E.S.) in Ioannina, Greece, where he conducts therapeutic sessions with children, adolescents, couples, and families. He has also participated in European and Greek research projects focused on the socioemotional development of children and gender-based violence.

Anna Papadimitriou is a psychologist and a PhD candidate in Psychology at Panteion University of Social and Political Sciences. She holds a master's degree in Positive Psychology and Business Psychology. She works as psychotherapist with adolescents and adults, practicing CBT, ACT, CFT, and LGBTQ consulting, while also supervising undergraduate and postgraduate theses in Psychology and teaching seminars and training intercultural mediators. She has participated in Panhellenic and European research programs and has publications in research articles, book chapters and conferences.

Panagiotis Parpottas is an Assistant Professor of Counselling Psychology at the European University Cyprus, currently the Head of the University's Counselling Service and the Chair of the Committee of Students with Special Needs. He completed his undergraduate studies in Psychology at National & Kapodistrian University of Athens in 2007 and obtained his Doctorate in Psychotherapeutic & Counselling Psychology from the University of Surrey in 2011. Dr Parpottas is trained in three different models of therapy, the Person-Centred, the Psychodynamic and the Cognitive Behavioural. His clinical work is Integrative and underpinned by Attachment theory. He is a registered and licenced Counselling Psychologist in Cyprus and Greece, and a Chartered Psychologist with the British Psychological Society. His research interests lie in the areas of Attachment theory, interpersonal and therapeutic relationships, psychological distress, critique of psychopathology, supervision, resilience, adaptation and disability.

José-María Romero-Rodríguez is a PhD in Education Sciences from the University of Granada. Master's Degree in Research and Innovation in Curriculum and Training, at the same University. He is currently a Permanent Lecturer attached to the Department of Didactics and School Organisation at the University of Granada (Spain). He carries out his research work within the AREA research group. Author of more than 100 scientific articles of impact (JCR and Scopus) on the use of Information and Communication Technologies (ICT) for the improvement of teaching and learning and on the risks associated with the problematic use of the Internet.

Beth Saggers' research focuses on maximizing the success of schooling experiences for diverse learners, their families and school communities. Her research focuses on the use of qualitative and mixed methods methodologies to strengthen our understanding from a range of perspectives of inclusive practices for learners on the autism spectrum and learners with complex needs. Her research focuses on strengthening student voice in research. Beth has been the research lead for a range of different research projects as part of the Autism CRC that have local, state, national and international impact in the field. Beth's position as an academic was born from her strong belief and passion for lifelong learning as well as a hunger for knowledge for the "real world" to inform her professional practice and research. Her research has a strong transdisciplinary and translational focus which is end-user driven with end-user outcomes. Beth's career has focused on the development of knowledge and expertise in inclusive education principles and practices, specifically in the field of autism. Her effective leadership in hey teaching and learning, research activities work to meet current priorities of end-users within the field of education and allied fields. Beth's academic leadership and authority in the field of autism is driven by the need for end-user driven research to develop evidence based inclusive educational practices to cater to the diversity on 21st century classrooms and support some of the more complex needs learners may experience in school environments.

Yogesh Kanna Sathyamoorthy is an Assistant Professor at Christ University, specializing in neuropsychology. His research interests focus on neuroinflammation-mediated neural damage, functional deficits in focal cerebral ischemia, and traumatic brain injury. He is committed to advancing knowledge and practice in his field through both teaching and research, with a particular emphasis on neuropsychology and blood-brain barrier disruption.

Ranjit Singha is a Doctorate Research Fellow at Christ (Deemed to be University) and holds the prestigious American Psychological Association (APA) membership. With a strong background in Research and Development, he has significantly contributed to various fields such as Mindfulness, Addiction Psychology, Women Empowerment, UN Sustainable Development Goals, and Data Science. With over 15 years of experience in Administration, Teaching, and Research, both in Industry and Higher Education Institutions (HEI), Mr Ranjit has established himself as a seasoned professional. Mr Ranjit is dedicatedly involved in research and teaching endeavours, primarily focusing on mindfulness and compassion-based interventions. His work in these areas aims to promote well-being and foster positive change in individuals and communities. ORCID iD: https://orcid.org/0000-0002-3541-8752.

Iliada Spyrou obtained her MSc in 2018 in Counselling Psychology from European University Cyprus. Prior to obtaining her MSc, she graduated from European University Cyprus with a BA in Psychology, in 2011. She is a licensed Counselling Psychologist in Cyprus. Her greatest passion is in the field of Online Safety, people's intimate relationships and clinically work with people who have been through a stressful experience. For nearly a decade now, she has had the privilege and joy of helping children, teenagers and adults, work through difficult situations, such as cyberbullying, sexting, sextortion, and other online issues. The last 6 years, she has helped adults and teenagers overcome anxiety, recover from trauma and emotional abuse. She is currently working with Asylum Seeker at Cyprus Social Welfare Services.

Bessie Stone is a lecturer in the Faculty of Creative Industries, Education, and Social Justice, Queensland University of Technology. Her research interest lies in the fields of inclusive education, diversity, neurodiversity, autism, digital literacies and media practices, digital literacy pedagogy, multimodality, internet safety, and teacher education. Her experiences in the education industry span over 20 years and range from early childhood to tertiary level in Australia and the Caribbean. Bessie's thesis investigated the affordances of online multiplayer games for social interactions of students with autism. A significant outcome of her research was the development of an innovative conceptual framework—Inclusive New Literacies—which integrated key concepts from inclusive education and New Literacy Studies fields. Bessie continues to develop this conceptual framework to make innovative contributions to research across areas including inclusive pedagogical development, teacher professional experience, and diverse students' literacy practices.

Assimina Tsibidaki is an Associate Professor of Special Education in the Department of Primary Education at the University of the Aegean (Greece). Her research interests focus on the following areas: Students with special educational needs and disabilities (SEND), families raising a child with SEND, home-school collaboration, social support networks, technology and inclusive education, disability in children's literature and cinema. Her published work includes two books, editing and articles in Greece and abroad, as well as various participations in Greek and international conferences.

Malamati Veloni completed her undergraduate studies at the University of Western Macedonia, earning a Bachelor's degree from the Pedagogical Department of Primary Education in 2020. Pursuing further specialization, she graduated with an "Excellent" grade from the Master's programme "Educational Sciences program in New Technologies: Pedagogy with New Technologies" at the University of Western Macedonia in 2023. Currently, she is a PhD Candidate at the University of Crete, further advancing her research and expertise in the field.

Juan José Victoria Maldonado is research teaching staff attached to the SEJ-655 group: Laboratory for Innovation in Education (LabinED) and Analysis of Educational Reality (AREA, HUM-672) at the University of Granada. Graduated in Early Childhood Education and subsequently the Master in Research and Innovation in Curriculum and Training at the University of Granada. His curriculum vitae includes a large number of publications of book chapters in high impact publishers such as Dykinson or Octaedro and articles for different journals (Frontiers in Education, Education Sciences, Journal of Technology and Science Education...). The main line of research is digital competence in the training of future teachers with the aim of improving curricula within initial teacher training.

Christine Yates is an experienced qualitative researcher with expertise in qualitative methodologies such as case studies, field research, narrative inquiry, and phenomenography. She has significant experience working in research positions at several universities in Australia and specialises in undertaking research in the disciplines of Education, Inclusive Education, Humanities, and the Social Sciences. Her qualifications include a Doctor of Philosophy, Master of Information Technology (Information Science) and Bachelor of Business (International Business) from Queensland University of Technology (QUT). Outside of the university sector, Christine has extensive experience working in the community services sector with vulnerable population groups in housing and information service roles.

Index

V

Y